Sources for
America's History

Volume 2: Since 1865

Kevin B. Sheets
State University of New York, College at Cortland

BEDFORD/ST. MARTIN'S   Boston ◆ New York

For Bedford/St. Martin's

Publisher for History: Mary V. Dougherty
Senior Executive Editor for History and Technology: William J. Lombardo
Director of Development for History: Jane Knetzger
Developmental Editor: Robin Soule
Publishing Services Manager: Andrea Cava
Production Supervisor: Steven Dowling
Executive Marketing Manager: Sandra McGuire
Editorial Assistant: Victoria Royal
Project Management: Books By Design, Inc.
Text Design: Lily Yamamoto, LMY Studios
Cover Design: Marine Miller
Cover Photo: Mexican American Parade. Chicago, Illinois, 1963. The Granger Collection, NYC.
 All Rights Reserved.
Composition: Jouve
Printing and Binding: RR Donnelley and Sons

President, Bedford/St. Martin's: Denise B. Wydra
Director of Marketing: Karen R. Soeltz
Production Director: Susan W. Brown
Director of Rights and Permissions: Hilary Newman

For information, write: Bedford/St. Martin's, 75 Arlington Street, Boston, MA 02116
 (617-399-4000)

ISBN 978-1-4576-2891-7

Acknowledgments
Acknowledgments and copyrights are continued at the back of the book on pages 813–815, which constitute an extension of the copyright page. It is a violation of the law to reproduce these selections by any means whatsoever without the written permission of the copyright holder.

PREFACE

Historians are fond of quoting L. P. Hartley's famous line: "The past is a foreign country; they do things differently there." It is a helpful image that emphasizes the distance, remoteness, and inscrutability of the past. Visiting a country whose language you do not speak can be disorienting until you start deciphering the gestures, unlocking the meaning behind facial expressions, and picking apart the cultural practices natives take for granted. For many students, the past is equally disorienting, and to seek safe harbor they ignore differences to emphasize commonalities. "Those people in the past are just like me, except they wear funny clothes." Stripped down, they do resemble us, but more often they encountered their world in radically different ways. Understanding these differences is what makes the study of history so compelling.

My goal in compiling *Sources for America's History* is to help students encounter this different past in its most raw and visceral form. Designed to accompany *America's History, America: A Concise History*, and the Value Edition of *America's History*, the sources collected here put students in unmediated contact with those whose experiences shaped our past. Each chapter includes a variety of both obscure and well-known voices, whose testimony highlights key themes of the period. The sources in each chapter give competing perspectives on leading events and ideas. This purposeful tension between sources is not intended to frustrate the reader. Instead, the differing viewpoints introduce students to the challenge that historians face in sifting through the evidence left to us. How do we make sense of the large body of primary sources that we have related to America's half millennium of lived experience?

Textbook authors present an argument about the past, something historians refer to as a "narrative." Those arguments, of course, are based on historians' interpretation and assessment of primary sources. This document collection makes its own argument based on the specific sources selected for inclusion, but invites debate by encouraging the reader to interpret sources in different ways. *Sources for America's History* is designed to encourage a productive intellectual give-and-take, enabling students of history to offer their own perspective on the past. In this way, students join the ongoing discussion among the community of scholars seeking to understand the long and complex history of what became the United States.

To facilitate this effort, *Sources for America's History* includes a number of key features. Each chapter in the collection includes five or six documents that support the periodization and themes of the corresponding parent text chapter. Every chapter begins with an introduction that situates the documents within their wider historical context. Individual documents follow, each accompanied by its own headnote and a set of Reading and Discussion Questions designed to help students practice historical thinking skills. The variety of readings, ranging from speeches and political cartoons by celebrated historical figures to personal letters and diary entries by ordinary people, offers students the opportunity to compare and contrast different types of documents. Each chapter concludes with Comparative Questions designed to encourage students to recognize connections between documents and relate the sources to larger historical themes. To further support the structure of the parent text, unique Part Document Sets at the end of every part section present five or six sources chosen specifically to illustrate the major themes and developments covered in each of the parent text's nine thematic parts, allowing students to make even broader comparisons and connections across time and place.

Acknowledgments

As with any big undertaking, many hands helped craft the book you are holding. Thanks go to Rebecca Edwards from Vassar College, one of the lead authors of *America's History*, for her confidence in me. Several instructors at the college, community college, and high school levels offered insightful suggestions based on their teaching experiences. They will see here many of the suggestions they recommended, though I could not accommodate all of the excellent ideas they shared. Particular thanks go to Matthew Babcock, University of North Texas at Dallas; Edwin Benson, North Harford High School; Christine Bond-Curtright, Edmond Memorial High School; Kyle T. Bulthuis, Utah State University; Jennifer Castillo, Denver School of the Arts; William Decker, Anderson Preparatory Academy; Angela Dormiani, ASTEC Charter High School; Donald W. Maxwell, Indiana State University; Neil Prendergast, University of Washington–Stevens Point; Erica Ryan, Rider University; Paul Rykken, Black River Falls High School; Sheila L. Skemp, University of Mississippi; Michael Smith, San Gorgonio High School; Geoffrey Stewart, University of Western Ontario; John Struck, Floyd Central High School; and Felicia Viator, San Francisco State University.

My editor, Robin Soule, kept me focused while tutoring me through my first experience of textbook publishing. Her improvements on the text make me sound smarter than I really am. The following colleagues at Bedford/St. Martin's helped in innumerable ways, most of which occurred silently and behind the scenes: Bill Lombardo, Sandi McGuire, Laura Arcari, Jen Jovin, and Victoria Royal. Thanks also to Andrea Cava, and especially to Nancy Benjamin, who oversaw the copyediting and saved countless embarrassments. Her contribution reminds me to practice a bit of humility next time I am grading my own students' papers.

My colleagues in the history department at the State University of New York, College at Cortland, have always provided an intellectually enriching environment in which to work and live. Special thanks go to my wife, Laura Gathagan, a medieval historian who resisted the temptation to smirk at the efforts of a nineteenth-century U.S. historian to write intelligibly about the fifteenth and sixteenth centuries. In the middle of this long process, she began calling herself the "Bedford widow" for the many evenings she spent alone while I toiled away. Finally, to my boys, William and Alexander: Daddy's done. Let's go play ball.

INTRODUCTION FOR STUDENTS

I was this close to wearing Eisenhower's pajamas. During my junior year in college, I interned at the Smithsonian's National Museum of American History in Washington, D.C. Every now and again, when I had a few minutes of free time, I poked around the collection of artifacts in storage. There was Lincoln's top hat. On a high shelf was the table where Lee surrendered to Grant. A pullout metal rack filled with paintings also housed a disturbing framed collection of hair from the first sixteen presidents. One day I spied a box containing President Dwight D. Eisenhower's pajamas. These were the PJs Ike wore while recovering in Denver from his 1955 heart attack. Oh, the temptation to slip them on, but reason and self-preservation prevailed. Back on the shelf they went.

Those whom the past enchants were often first beguiled by the stuff of history. Touching those objects helps collapse time, putting us in the immediate presence of someone else at some other time. I once held John Brown's gun and while peering down the long barrel wondered who or what he was aiming at. His trigger finger and mine overlapped and briefly spirited me back to 1850s Pottawatomie, Kansas, where Brown waged his own civil war against slavery. The past is contained in those leavings, the letters and diaries, the political cartoons and music, the paintings and the guns and pajamas. Primary sources bring alive the past and help us to understand its significance and meaning.

This collection of primary sources aims to engage you in a conversation with the past. There will be times when you burst out laughing. Some sources will make you so mad you'll want to throw the book across the room. (Please don't. I spent a lot of time writing it, but I share your frustration.) Other times, you'll shake your head in disbelief. (Yes, they really thought that back then!) You are about to enter an amazing world of difference populated with people some of whom you will admire, many of whom you won't like, and others whom you will despair of ever really knowing or understanding. Good. I hope you laugh. I hope you get mad. I even hope you get confused at times and scratch your head wondering what on earth these people were talking about. Out of your responses to these texts comes insight.

My advice? Read these texts with a fist full of questions. Historians do something called "sourcing" when they first encounter a primary text, and it is a good practice for you, too. Start with the author. *Who wrote or created the source?* What do you know about this person? Was he rich, poor, or middling? Was she educated? Where was he or she born and to what sort of family? You might know the answers to some of these questions, but even if you do not, keeping the questions in mind might help you understand where the author is coming from. *When was this source created?* While it is important to know the date, it can also be revealing to know when in the person's life he or she created the source. Was she a young girl or an older woman raising children? Was he at the beginning of his career or already famous? *What was happening when the source was created?* We call this "context," and it is an important element in making sense of the source you are reading. (You will encounter the word *context* often in the Reading and Discussion Questions and Comparative Questions following the sources and at the end of each chapter.) In addition to author and context, consider audience and purpose. *Who was this source for, and why was it created?* Was the source intended for a public or private audience? Was the source created to persuade or to inform? Was the author talking to allies or foes? What did he or she assume about their audience? A final and related point touches upon the format of the source. *What type of source is it?* Historians think about and interpret sources differently. You might be more honest in a private letter to your spouse than you would be in a letter to a political opponent, for example. Similarly, a campaign poster for a particular candidate has a different purpose than a portrait of a politician commissioned for a private residence. As these examples show, the format of a source is often linked to audience and purpose.

What a source tells a historian is not always self-evident. Very few of the sources that historians use were created *for* historians. (No one writes letters that begin: "Dear Historian of a hundred years from now, here is what I am thinking about the Obama presidency.") Historians need to "read between the lines" to derive meaning. As you read the documents in this book, you can unearth the meaning in these sources by asking questions, thinking about context, paying attention to vocabulary and cultural references, and comparing them to other sources related to the same topic or event.

This form of active reading takes a bit more time than it would if you were to simply read starting at the first word and running through to the end. To truly think like a historian, be an active reader. Engage the texts. Ask them questions. Write in the book. Draw circles around important words or phrases. Write "key point" in the margins where you think the author is hitting his mark. Don't be afraid to throw in a few question marks where you get confused. If you have a furrowed brow, chances are someone else in class is confused, too. Bring it up in discussion and you'll be the class superhero. Take advantage of the questions I pose at the end of each source and chapter. I wrote them to inspire you to go back to the texts and think about what you read. The end-of-chapter Comparative Questions encourage you to see connections between and among multiple texts.

Remember, the past is about having a conversation. These texts speak to one another. It is OK to eavesdrop on their discussions. In fact (here's me being bold), I think you have an obligation to listen in on their chatter. Many of the issues these sources address, though sometimes distant to us in time, remain relevant: What is just? What kind of society do we want to live in? How should we treat

CONTENTS

15

Reconstruction
1865–1877

The Civil War sparked more questions than it settled. While the Thirteenth Amendment to the Constitution unambiguously decided the question of slavery, practical issues concerning freedmen's rights persisted. In the face of white southern resistance and northern fatigue, the national government created federal agencies to help freedmen transition from slavery to freedom, a journey that was burdened by persistent racism. Opposition came from those who continued to believe African Americans were either incapable of self-government—much less governing the state—or were susceptible to the political manipulation of northern opportunists. Policymakers faced other perplexing questions regarding the relationship of the former Confederate states to the Union and the social, economic, and political challenges facing a defeated South. Though this political turmoil led to a presidential impeachment, exacerbated strained relationships between the North and South, and gave birth to white-hooded violence, one undeniable truth stood out: African Americans were free.

15-1 | President Focuses on Work of Reconstruction

ABRAHAM LINCOLN, *Last Public Address* (1865)

On the night of April 11, 1865, Abraham Lincoln spoke to a joy-filled crowd gathered at the White House to celebrate the surrender of Robert E. Lee's Confederate army, a sign of the war's imminent end. Lincoln took the occasion to address the work ahead. In this speech, Lincoln discussed Louisiana's recent legislative efforts and, by doing so, signaled his approach to Reconstruction. John Wilkes Booth was in the audience that night and heard Lincoln speak. Three days later, at Ford's Theatre, he aimed a pistol at the back of Lincoln's head and pulled the trigger.

We meet this evening, not in sorrow, but in gladness of heart. The evacuation of Petersburg and Richmond, and the surrender of the principal insurgent army, give hope of a righteous and speedy peace whose joyous expression can not be restrained. In the midst of this, however, He from whom all blessings flow, must not be forgotten. A call for a national thanksgiving is being prepared, and will be duly promulgated. Nor must those whose harder part gives us the cause of rejoicing, be overlooked. Their honors must not be parcelled out with others. I myself was near the front, and had the high pleasure of transmitting much of the good news to you; but no part of the honor, for plan or execution, is mine. To Gen. Grant, his skilful officers, and brave men, all belongs. The gallant Navy stood ready, but was not in reach to take active part.

By these recent successes the re-inauguration of the national authority—reconstruction—which has had a large share of thought from the first, is pressed much more closely upon our attention. It is fraught with great difficulty. Unlike a case of a war between independent nations, there is no authorized organ for us to treat with. No one man has authority to give up the rebellion for any other man. We simply must begin with, and mould from, disorganized and discordant elements. Nor is it a small additional embarrassment that we, the loyal people, differ among ourselves as to the mode, manner, and means of reconstruction.

As a general rule, I abstain from reading the reports of attacks upon myself, wishing not to be provoked by that to which I can not properly offer an answer. In spite of this precaution, however, it comes to my knowledge that I am much censured for some supposed agency in setting up, and seeking to sustain, the new State government of Louisiana. In this I have done just so much as, and no more than, the public knows. In the Annual Message of Dec. 1863 and accompanying Proclamation, I presented a plan of re-construction (as the phrase goes) which, I promised, if adopted by any State, should be acceptable to, and sustained by, the Executive government of the nation. I distinctly stated that this was not the only plan which might possibly be acceptable; and I also distinctly protested that the Executive claimed no right to say when, or whether members should be admitted to seats in Congress from such States. This plan was, in

www.abrahamlincolnonline.org/lincoln/speeches/last.htm.

advance, submitted to the then Cabinet, and distinctly approved by every member of it. One of them suggested that I should then, and in that connection, apply the Emancipation Proclamation to the theretofore excepted parts of Virginia and Louisiana; that I should drop the suggestion about apprenticeship for freedpeople, and that I should omit the protest against my own power, in regard to the admission of members to Congress; but even he approved every part and parcel of the plan which has since been employed or touched by the action of Louisiana. The new constitution of Louisiana, declaring emancipation for the whole State, practically applies the Proclamation to the part previously excepted. It does not adopt apprenticeship for freed-people; and it is silent, as it could not well be otherwise, about the admission of members to Congress. So that, as it applies to Louisiana, every member of the Cabinet fully approved the plan. The message went to Congress, and I received many commendations of the plan, written and verbal; and not a single objection to it, from any professed emancipationist, came to my knowledge, until after the news reached Washington that the people of Louisiana had begun to move in accordance with it. From about July 1862, I had corresponded with different persons, supposed to be interested, seeking a reconstruction of a State government for Louisiana. When the message of 1863, with the plan before mentioned, reached New-Orleans, Gen. Banks wrote me that he was confident the people, with his military co-operation, would reconstruct, substantially on that plan. I wrote him, and some of them to try it; they tried it, and the result is known. Such only has been my agency in getting up the Louisiana government. As to sustaining it, my promise is out, as before stated. But, as bad promises are better broken than kept, I shall treat this as a bad promise, and break it, whenever I shall be convinced that keeping it is adverse to the public interest. But I have not yet been so convinced.

I have been shown a letter on this subject, supposed to be an able one, in which the writer expresses regret that my mind has not seemed to be definitely fixed on the question whether the seceding States, so called, are in the Union or out of it. It would perhaps, add astonishment to his regret, were he to learn that since I have found professed Union men endeavoring to make that question, I have purposely forborne any public expression upon it. As appears to me that question has not been, nor yet is, a practically material one, and that any discussion of it, while it thus remains practically immaterial, could have no effect other than the mischievous one of dividing our friends. As yet, whatever it may hereafter become, that question is bad, as the basis of a controversy, and good for nothing at all—a merely pernicious abstraction.

We all agree that the seceded States, so called, are out of their proper relation with the Union; and that the sole object of the government, civil and military, in regard to those States is to again get them into that proper practical relation. I believe it is not only possible, but in fact, easier to do this, without deciding, or even considering, whether these States have ever been out of the Union, than with it. Finding themselves safely at home, it would be utterly immaterial whether they had ever been abroad. Let us all join in doing the acts necessary to restoring the proper practical relations between these States and the Union; and each forever after, innocently indulge his own opinion whether, in doing the acts, he brought the States from without, into the Union, or only gave them proper assistance, they never having been out of it.

The amount of constituency, so to speak, on which the new Louisiana government rests, would be more satisfactory to all, if it contained fifty, thirty, or even twenty thousand, instead of only about twelve thousand, as it does. It is also unsatisfactory to some that the elective franchise is not given to the colored man. I would myself prefer that it were now conferred on the very intelligent, and on those who serve our cause as soldiers. Still the question is not whether the Louisiana government, as it stands, is quite all that is desirable. The question is, "Will it be wiser to take it as it is, and help to improve it; or to reject, and disperse it?" "Can Louisiana be brought into proper practical relation with the Union sooner by sustaining, or by discarding her new State government?"

Some twelve thousand voters in the heretofore slave-state of Louisiana have sworn allegiance to the Union, assumed to be the rightful political power of the State, held elections, organized a State government, adopted a free-state constitution, giving the benefit of public schools equally to black and white, and empowering the Legislature to confer the elective franchise upon the colored man. Their Legislature has already voted to ratify the constitutional amendment recently passed by Congress, abolishing slavery throughout the nation. These twelve thousand persons are thus fully committed to the Union, and to perpetual freedom in the state—committed to the very things, and nearly all the things the nation wants—and they ask the nation[']s recognition and it's [sic] assistance to make good their committal. Now, if we reject, and spurn them, we do our utmost to disorganize and disperse them. We in effect say to the white men "You are worthless, or worse—we will neither help you, nor be helped by you." To the blacks we say "This cup of liberty which these, your old masters, hold to your lips, we will dash from you, and leave you to the chances of gathering the spilled and scattered contents in some vague and undefined when, where, and how." If this course, discouraging and paralyzing both white and black, has any tendency to bring Louisiana into proper practical relations with the Union, I have, so far, been unable to perceive it. If, on the contrary, we recognize, and sustain the new government of Louisiana the converse of all this is made true. We encourage the hearts, and nerve the arms of the twelve thousand to adhere to their work, and argue for it, and proselyte for it, and fight for it, and feed it, and grow it, and ripen it to a complete success. The colored man too, in seeing all united for him, is inspired with vigilance, and energy, and daring, to the same end. Grant that he desires the elective franchise, will he not attain it sooner by saving the already advanced steps toward it, than by running backward over them? Concede that the new government of Louisiana is only to what it should be as the egg is to the fowl, we shall sooner have the fowl by hatching the egg than by smashing it? Again, if we reject Louisiana, we also reject one vote in favor of the proposed amendment to the national Constitution. To meet this proposition, it has been argued that no more than three fourths of those States which have not attempted secession are necessary to validly ratify the amendment. I do not commit myself against this, further than to say that such a ratification would be questionable, and sure to be persistently questioned; while a ratification by three-fourths of all the States would be unquestioned and unquestionable.

I repeat the question, "Can Louisiana be brought into proper practical relation with the Union *sooner* by *sustaining* or by *discarding* her new State Government?"

What has been said of Louisiana will apply generally to other States. And yet so great peculiarities pertain to each state, and such important and sudden changes occur in the same state; and withal, so new and unprecedented is the whole case, that no exclusive, and inflexible plan can be safely prescribed as to details and colatterals [sic]. Such exclusive, and inflexible plan, would surely become a new entanglement. Important principles may, and must, be inflexible.

In the present "*situation*" as the phrase goes, it may be my duty to make some new announcement to the people of the South. I am considering, and shall not fail to act, when satisfied that action will be proper.

READING AND DISCUSSION QUESTIONS

1. How would you characterize Lincoln's policy toward Reconstruction? Does Lincoln come across as an idealist, like Radical Republicans, or a pragmatist who accepted compromise for the sake of progress?

2. What can you infer about Louisiana's recent experience that angered some, encouraged others, and led to Lincoln's support and approval?

3. What about his speech do you think provoked John Wilkes Booth, a southerner and Confederate sympathizer, to murder Lincoln?

15-2 | A Freed Family's Dream of Landownership

BETTY POWERS, *Federal Writers' Project Interview* (c. 1936)

Betty Powers was eight or nine years old when the Civil War ended. She was born a slave on a Texas plantation and shared in her family's jubilation when slavery ended. Seventy years later, she was interviewed by the New Deal's Federal Writers' Project, which conducted oral histories with former slaves. Despite her "head mis'ry," which she claimed impaired her memory, she recalled poignant details of her family's life in slavery and their transition to freedom with a farm of their own.

What for you wants dis old nigger's story 'bout de old slavery days? 'Tain't worth anythin'. I's jus' a hard workin' person all my life and raised de family and done right by 'em as best I knowed. To tell the truf 'bout my age, I don't know

Library of Congress, *Born in Slavery: Slave Narratives from the Federal Writers' Project, 1936–1938*, Texas Narratives, vol. XVI, Part 3, 190–192.

'zactly. I 'members de war time and de surrender time. O's old 'nough to fan flies off de white folks and de tables when surrender come. If you come 'bout five year ago, I could telt you lots more, but I's had de head mis'ry.

I's born in Harrison County, 'bout twenty-five miles from Marshall. Mass's name am Dr. Howard Perry and next he house am a li'l buildin' for he office. De plantation an awful big one, and miles long, and more'n two hundred slaves was dere. Each cabin have one family and dere am three rows of cabins 'bout half a mile long.

Mammy and pappy and us twelve chillen live in one cabin, so mammy has to cook for fourteen people, 'sides her field work. She am up way befo' daylight fixin' breakfast and supper after dark, with de pine knot torch to make de light. She cook on de fireplace in winter and in de yard in summer. All de rations measure out Sunday mornin' and it have to do for de week. It am not 'nough for heavy eaters and we has to be real careful or we goes hungry. We has meat and cornmeal and 'lasses and 'taters and peas and beans and milk. Dem short rations causes plenty trouble, 'cause de niggers has to steal food and it am de whippin' if dey gets cotched. Dey am in a fix if dey can't work for bein' hungry, 'cause it am de whippin' den, sho', so dey has to steal, and most of 'em did and takes de whippin'. Dey has de full stomach, anyway.

De babies has plenty food, so dey grow up into strong, portly men and women. Dey stays in de nursery whilst dey mammies works in de fields, and has plenty milk with cornbread crumble up in it, and potlicker, too, and honey and 'lasses on bread.

De massa and he wife am fine, but de overseer am tough, and he wife, too. Dat woman have no mercy. You see dem long ears I has? Dat's from de pullin' dey gits from her. De field hands works early and late and often all night. Pappy makes de shoes and mammy weaves, and you could hear de bump, bump of dat loom at night, when she done work in de field all day.

Missy know everything what go on, 'cause she have de spies 'mongst de slaves. She purty good, though. Sometimes de overseer tie de nigger to a log and lash him with de whip. If de lash cut de skin, dey puts salt on it. We ain't 'low to go to church and has 'bout two parties a year, so dere ain't much fun. Lawd, Lawd, most dem slaves too tired to have fun noway. When all dat work am finish, dey's glad to git in de bed and sleep.

Did we'uns have weddin's? White man, you knows better'n dat. Dem times, cullud folks am jus' put together. De massa say, "Jim and Nancy, you go live together," and when dat order give, it better be done. Dey thinks nothin' on de plantation 'bout de feelin's of de women and dere ain't no 'spect for dem. De overseer and white mens took 'vantage of de women like dey wants to. De woman better not make no fuss 'bout sich. If she do, it am de whippin' for her. I sho' thanks the Lawd surrender done come befo' I's old 'nough to have to stand for sich. Yes, sar, surrender saves dis nigger from sich.

When de war am over, thousands of sojers passes our place. Some camps nearby, and massa doctors dem. When massa call us to say we's free, dere am a yardful of niggers. He give every nigger de age statement and say dey could work on halves or for wages. He 'vises dem to stay till dey git de foothold and larn how to do. Lots stays and lots goes. My folks stays 'bout four years and works on shares. Den pappy buys de piece of land 'bout five miles from dere.

De land ain't clear, so we'uns al pitches in and clears it and builds de cabin. Was we'uns proud? There 'twas, our place to do as we pleases, after bein' slaves. Dat sho' am de good feelin'. We works live beavers puttin' de crop in, and my folks stays dere till dey dies. I leaves to git married de next year and I's only thirteen years old, and marries Boss Powers.

We'uns lives on rent land nearby for six years and has three chillen and den he dies. After two years I marries Henry Ruffins and has three more chillen, and he dies in 1911. I's livin' with two of dem now. I never took de name of Ruffins, 'cause I's dearly love Powers and can't stand to give up he name. Powers done make de will and wrote on de paper, "To my beloved wife, I gives all I has." Wasn't dat sweet of him?

I comes to Fort Worth after Ruffin dies and does housework till I's too old. Now I gits de $12.00 pension every month and dat help me git by.

READING AND DISCUSSION QUESTIONS

1. How does Powers's account help historians understand the period of Reconstruction from the perspective of social history, or the history of ordinary people?

2. Analyze and evaluate the details Powers recalls about her fellow slaves' experiences to understand the contrast she draws with her life in the era after slavery. How do those details help you understand the meaning of freedom as former slaves experienced it?

3. How does the context of this historical source, an oral history recorded decades after the events it describes, impact your assessment of its utility as evidence for the Civil War and Reconstruction eras?

15-3 | A Former Slave Owner Complains of "Negro Problem"

FRANCES BUTLER LEIGH, *Letter to a Friend in England* (1867)

While Betty Powers experienced the era of Reconstruction with the optimism of the newly freed, Frances Butler Leigh wrote defiant and discouraging letters from her father's Sea Island plantation on St. Simon's Island, Georgia. She and her father, divorced years earlier from Leigh's mother, the British actress and antislavery advocate Frances Kemble, moved from Philadelphia to the plantation just after the war ended in a failed effort to keep the family's estate afloat. Within a few years, she sold the plantation and moved to England, where she wrote *Ten Years on a Georgia Plantation Since the War* in 1883, a memoir defending the Old South.

Frances Butler Leigh, *Ten Years on a Georgia Plantation Since the War* (London: Richard Bentley & Son, Publishers in Ordinary to her Majesty the Queen, 1883), 66–71.

S. Simon's Island: June 23, 1867

Dearest S——, We are, I am afraid, going to have terrible trouble by-and-by with the Negroes, and I see nothing but gloomy prospects for us ahead. The unlimited power that the war has put into the hands of the present government at Washington seems to have turned the heads of the party now in office, and they don't know where to stop. The whole South is settled and quiet, and the people too ruined and crushed to do anything against the government, even if they felt so inclined, and all are returning to their former pursuits, trying to rebuild their fortunes and thinking of nothing else. Yet the treatment we receive from the government becomes more and more severe every day, the last act being to divide the whole South into five military districts, putting each under the command of a United States general, doing away with all civil courts and law. Even D——who you know is a Northern republican, says it is most unjustifiable, not being in any way authorised by the existing state of things, which he confesses he finds very different from what he expected before he came. If they would frankly say they intend to keep us down, it would be fairer than making a pretence of readmitting us to equal rights, and then trumping up stories of violence to give a show of justice to treating us as the conquered foes of the most despotic Government on earth, and by exciting the negroes to every kind of insolent lawlessness, to goad the people into acts of rebellion and resistance.

The other day in Charleston, which is under the command of that respectable creature General S——, they had a firemen's parade, and took the occasion to hoist a United States flag, to which this modern Gesler[1] insisted on everyone raising his cap as he passed underneath. And by a hundred other such petty tyrannies are the people, bruised and sore, being roused to desperation; and had this been done directly after the war it would have been bad enough, but it was done the other day, three years after the close of the war.

The true reason is the desire and intention of the Government to control the elections of the South, which under the constitution of the country they could not legally do. So they have determined to make an excuse for setting aside the laws, and in order to accomplish this more fully, each commander in his separate district has issued an order declaring that unless a man can take an oath that he had not voluntarily borne arms against the United States Government, nor in any way aided or abetted the rebellion, he cannot vote. This simply disqualifies every white man at the South from voting, disfranchising the whole white population, while the negroes are allowed to vote *en masse*.

This is particularly unjust, as the question of negro voting was introduced and passed in Congress as an amendment to the constitution, but in order to become a law a majority of two-thirds of the State Legislatures must ratify it, and so to them it was submitted, and rejected by all the Northern States with two exceptions, where the number of negro voters would be so small as to be

---

[1]Gesler, or Gessler, was the tyrant in the folktale *William Tell* who abused the people and forced the title character to shoot an arrow through an apple resting atop the head of Tell's son.

harmless. Our Legislatures are not allowed to meet, but this law, which the North has rejected, is to be forced upon us, whose very heart it pierces and prosperity it kills. Meanwhile, in order to prepare the negroes to vote properly, stump speakers from the North are going all through the South, holding political meetings for the negroes, saying things like this to them: "My friends, you will have your rights, won't you?" ("Yes," from the negroes.) "Shall I not go back to Massachusetts and tell your brothers there that you are going to ride in the street cars with white ladies if you please?" ("Yes, yes," from the crowd.) "That if you pay your money to go to the theatre you will sit where you please, in the best boxes if you like?" ("Yes," and applause.) This I copy verbatim from a speech made at Richmond the other day, since which there have been two serious negro riots there, and the General commanding had to call out the military to suppress them.

These men are making a tour through the South, speaking in the same way to the negroes everywhere. Do you wonder we are frightened? I have been so forcibly struck lately while reading Baker's "Travels in Africa," and some of Du Chaillu's lectures,[2] at finding how exactly the same characteristics show themselves among the negroes there, in their own native country, where no outside influences have ever affected them, as with ours here. Forced to work, they improve and are useful; left to themselves they become idle and useless, and never improve. Hard ethnological facts for the abolitionists to swallow, but facts nevertheless.

It seems foolish to fill my letter to you with such matters, but all this comes home to us with such vital force that it is hard to write, or speak, or think of anything else, and the one subject that Southerners discuss whenever they meet is, "What is to become of us?"

Affectionately yours,

F——

READING AND DISCUSSION QUESTIONS

1. Compare Leigh's point of view concerning slaves and slavery with the perspective of Susan Dabney Smedes (Document 12-5). How might you account for the differences you see in their assessments of the Old South? What factors might have shaped each viewpoint?

2. From Leigh's letter, what conclusions can you draw regarding the challenges facing the national government in mending the political divisions between northern and southern states and between the federal and state or local governments in the South?

---

[2]Leigh may be referring to Samuel White Baker's 1855 book *Eight Years' Wandering in Ceylon* and to Paul du Chaillu's 1861 *Explorations and Adventures in Equatorial Africa*.

15-4 | A Liberal Republican Opposes Universal Suffrage

CHARLES FRANCIS ADAMS JR., *The Protection of the Ballot in National Elections* (1869)

Southerners like Frances Leigh were not the only ones who doubted the wisdom of granting former slaves the right to vote. Charles Francis Adams Jr., the grandson and great-grandson of presidents, penned an article in the 1869 issue of the *Journal of Social Science* advocating restrictions on voting rights, a timely issue as the Fifteenth Amendment was wending its way toward ratification in February 1870. Adams was sympathetic to the Republican Party's liberal wing, a faction opposed to the continued federal presence in the South and to President Grant's administration for its apparent corruption. Their ideal was government by the "best men," which they hoped to achieve through civil service reforms and a more scientific approach to government administration. Restricting the vote to those with the education to understand its meaning, Adams assumed, ensured enlightened government.

If the study of social problems teaches any one lesson more distinctly than another, it is that political virtue and political corruption are never the peculiar property of any particular party in the State. Only the partisan believes that all virtue is to be found in one organization, and all vice in another. The observer soon discovers that an almost imperceptible line separates, in these respects, contemporary political organizations, and that the charges made against one faction existing in the State, with slight changes of form and detail, may, with equal justice, be made against every other. Fraud in one party begets fraud in another, and corruption begets corruption, if only under the plausible argument that the devil must be fought with the weapons of darkness. . . .

Government, through representation and suffrage, as at present developed into a system, is but one way, and a very imperfect and unsatisfactory one, of arriving at a given result. The object of every political system is to bring the loftiest development of moral and intellectual education which any given community affords to the direction of its affairs. Just at present it is the fashion to consider an extension of the suffrage,—a more elaborate and careful enumeration of noses as it were,—as the grand and effectual panacea for all political evils. This idea will certainly last out the present, and probably several succeeding generations. Without at all conceding that this system is the best that can, or, in process of time, will be devised, it is yet the system under which we and our children have perforce got to live, and the student of Social Science can devote himself to no better task than to the purifying and protecting of the system, however crude and unsatisfactory it at best may appear to him. . . .

An exciting and important national election has just been passed through, and the usual good fortune of the American people has presided over the result, in that it has not proved to be in result a disputed election. The popular verdict has been sufficiently decisive to cover any margin of fraud, on the one side or the other, and all parties concede that the new occupant will not be cheated into the Presidential Chair. This may not always be the case. The election was preceded by loud charges of wholesale fraud, made indiscriminately by each of the parties which divided the country, against the other,—the election day was marked by many scandalous incidents which well might have vitiated the results in important localities, and, finally, it has been succeeded by a general desire that something should be done, resulting in the usual unlimited suggestions of crude legislation. Two things seem likely to result from the agitation now dying away,—first, an extension of the suffrage, and, secondly, a renewed discussion of the long vexed question of the naturalization laws.

Both are important questions; in fact, without exaggeration, they might be spoken of as vital questions; and both are deserving of a calmer and more philosophical discussion, and of a decision more exempt from party exigencies, than they seem likely to receive. Yet it may possibly be that the immediate evil which presses upon the country does not lie in either of these directions; it may well be found more on the surface, a mere matter of detail or of defective organic law. The first question necessarily is,—what is the difficulty? That found, the remedy may not be far to seek. What is it that the popular instinct has been apprehensive of? What dangerous elements have developed, themselves,—what weak points in our system, which create this manifest uneasiness for the future, and the desire for change? It probably would be generally conceded that the real trouble has been that the mass of the people of all parties has been apprehensive that the purity of the ballot was not sufficiently protected; that somehow the election both could and would be carried by fraud; that the will of the people was to be corruptly set aside through some perversion of the forms of law. If this brief statement of the case is accepted as correct, it only remains to consider the manner in which, and the machinery through which the election was held, and the result arrived at, and then to suggest, if possible, some remedy for the evil experienced. . . .

Under the existing system . . . a premium is placed upon fraud. The violation of the ballot-box by one party, makes its violation by the other what is called, in the parlance of the day, a political necessity. This, indeed, is the saddest and most alarming feature of the whole system. The community not only becomes accustomed to political fraud, but it learns to excuse it as in some way a necessity. We are losing the moral sense, and censure failure alone. While the moral perceptions thus become blunted, the opportunity for fraud is more and more, in each successive election, localized and designated. The least astute politician knows just where votes are necessary and just where they are useless. The more astute know also just how many are wanted and how they are to be had, as well as where they are wanted. Fraud,—energetic, well-directed fraud, will probably soon decide every closely contested Presidential election, unless the system of Electoral Colleges is reformed out of existence. . . .

Hitherto the discussion has looked solely to the removal from our system of the great fictitious incentive to fraud at the polls,—that which unconsciously makes the whole community approach this question with an instinctive sense of its importance. It now remains to say a few words of the fraud itself, as we see and feel it, and to consider if anything can be done to insure to the ballot exemption from it. . . .

As society develops itself, and wealth, population and ignorance increase, — as the struggle for existence becomes more and more severe, the inherent difficulties of a broadly extended suffrage will make themselves felt. Starving men and women care very little for abstract questions of the general good. Political power becomes one means simply of private subsistence. In any case there are, however, but two ways of perverting the expression of the popular will, — one by the corruption of the individual voter, the other by the falsification of votes. The first of these methods is easily disposed of. It is useless and almost silly to try to prevent bribery and corruption by law. There is, in fact, no sound distinction between the citizen who sells his vote for cash, and the citizen who makes his political course subserve his personal ambition, or lends himself to some demagogue who bribes by an agrarian law. . . . No real protection to the ballot lies in that direction.

Though the law, however, cannot well prevent a man from selling his own single vote, and no penalty can reach him who does, the law can prevent a man from multiplying ballots at his own will, and selling himself for a day's steady voting, from early dawn to dewy eve, unlimited by any eight-hour law, and for every recurring election. Men cannot by law be made to respect their own rights, but they can be made not to violate those of other people. In this point of view again, the suffrage question is a national one. Under the present system, a single fraudulent vote in New York or Philadelphia is of infinitely greater public interest than a score of such votes in Boston or Chicago. Yet the control of the citizen over this question, upon which more than upon any other, his rights as a citizen depend, is limited to his own immediate neighborhood, and just beyond that, neighborhood, within his sight almost, he is conscious that he is defrauded to an unlimited extent, and yet has no power for reform. Such a condition of affairs is not a healthy one. It is one thing as regards local and State, and another as regards National elections. If certain local communities are willing to live under a lax and unregulated system of suffrage, if they do not object to seeing the franchise rendered valueless by fraud within their own limits, of course they have a right to gratify their inclinations; but they have not a right to extend that system beyond their own limits to the grave prejudice of their neighbors.

The only real protection of the purity of the ballot, under an extended system of suffrage, must, of necessity, be found in some arrangement for the careful registration of voters. . . . In view of our vastly, increasing emigration, and of the direct bearing of the naturalization laws upon every National election, it may become a serious question whether the United States will not ultimately be obliged to take the whole management of National elections into the hands of National officers. One uniform law and day for such elections, once in two years, conducted by officers of the United States for the time being, under a well digested system of registration, and with an effective law for the detection and punishment of fraud, would, while in itself open to grave objections, yet strike at the root of many of the most crying evils of the present system. . . .

For the first time in the history of mankind, America seems now approaching a practical trial of universal suffrage. It is not manhood suffrage, as at present; nor white suffrage, as formerly; nor impartial suffrage, as sometimes proposed; nor educational suffrage;—but universal suffrage in the largest sense of the term. All signs point that way. One day we hear of a Womans Rights Convention, and some Legislature barely fails to concede the principle of female suffrage; the next day some Senator proposes the total repeal of the naturalization laws, while the adopted citizen demands that he shall no longer be legally excluded from the chair of Washington. It is then proposed to extend the ballot to children, as it has already been given to freedmen. Presently impartial suffrage is suggested, and party organs at once declare it to be a dogma of American faith, that the ballot is the *inherent* right of all *white* men, "be they rich or poor, learned or unlearned." Finally the Senate of the United States, that body to which all the political wisdom of the country is supposed to gravitate, has recently, after long discussion, proposed to submit to the Legislatures an amendment to the Constitution, prohibiting all discrimination for the future among the citizens of the United States, in the right to hold office or in the exercise of the elective franchise, because "of race, color, nativity, property, education or creed." Had the single word "sex" but been included in this amendment, the bars would have been wholly thrown down, and the experiment of universal suffrage, incorporated into the organic law, would have been tried in its full simplicity.

It may well be questioned whether the American people fully appreciate the logical conclusions of the present tendency to make the suffrage a free gift to all comers. The new experiment will indeed eradicate the last vestige of caste from our institutions, and in so far is consistent with reason and experience. The future has nothing to fear from that quarter. In avoiding one danger, however, there is no absolute necessity of running into another. Caste will have been eradicated at a fearful price, if the elements leading directly to a proletariat are introduced in its place. Now universal suffrage necessarily introduces three new and untried influences into the action of the body politic. Of these the female is the first; for, though in order of time she must be enfranchised after the African and the alien, yet only those who believe in that strange political science which is evolved from party exigencies, can bow to a logic, which, while pretending to eradicate caste, refuses to grant to the Anglo-Saxon female what has been thrust on the African male. Opinions differ more as to the expediency of female suffrage than as to its logic. Experience has seemed to indicate that a certain vigorous, masculine, common-sense and self-control,—a faculty of restraint under excitement—a certain persistence and belief in the wisdom of biding his time, which characteristics have hitherto more especially developed themselves in the Anglo-Saxon race, have everywhere proved the only real safe-guards of popular liberty. Excitable natures rarely strengthen free institutions. How far a large infusion of the more voluble, demonstrative and impulsive female element into the arena of politics will tend to affect what little of calmness and reason is still found therein, remains to be seen. The white female, however, is at least of the same blood and education as the white male. This cannot be said of the African, the second of the untried influences now to be introduced. Whatever may be his latent faculty of development, however high he now should or ultimately may stand in the scale of created beings, it is safe to say that the sudden and indiscriminate elevation of his whole race to the ballot is a portentous experiment. The Anglo-Saxon was not educated to his efforts at self-government, at best but partially successful, by two centuries of Slavery superimposed on unnumbered centuries of barbarism.

The third influence about to be infused by wholesale into our system, is that of the aliens. Of the workings and tendency of this influence we have already enjoyed some experience. We now appreciate to a degree how much the purity and the significance of the suffrage have deteriorated with us through the irruption of those swarms of foreigners, who have within forty years landed on our shores. While the experience of the past throws some light on the future in this respect, it, in all probability, very inadequately foreshadows it. We have as yet witnessed only the day of small things in the way of emigration. Take the Irish exodus as an example. It has been no easy thing for us to deplete the Celtic race from one small island, and to absorb it into our body politic: still it has been done, and has resulted only in deterioration, not in catastrophe. But how is it for the future, as regards China and the East? . . .

Working upon such a mass as must result from the blending of all these incongruous elements, Universal Suffrage can only mean in plain English the government of ignorance and vice:—it means a European, and especially Celtic, proletariat on the Atlantic coast; an African proletariat on the shores of the Gulf, and a Chinese proletariat on the Pacific. One only of these has developed itself as yet and acquired firm political power,—the Celtic proletariat has possessed itself of the New York City Government and will soon be in control of that of the State;—those who wish to study the early development of the system will find ample food for reflection in the daily columns of the New York press. Those who choose may then strive to extend it.

If then the proletariat,—the organization of ignorance and vice to obtain political control,—is destructive both to the purity and significance of the ballot;—if Universal Suffrage inevitably tends with an advancing civilization to bring about such a vicious combination, then no one who believes in a Social Science as applied to the study of permanence in free institutions, can place any faith in that form of suffrage. The tendency of the day is clearly in a wrong direction. . . .

Education then only remains. A knowledge of the language of our laws and the faculty of informing oneself without aid of their provisions, would in itself constitute a test, if rigorously enforced, incompatible with the existence of a proletariat. Our efforts should be devoted to the practical development of these two principles of intelligence and impartiality in the suffrage, and of the kindred theory of the just representation of minorities. In the ideal Government, founded on the popular consent, every voice will be audible through a system of perfect representation. No barrier to a purified suffrage will be recognized which cannot be surmounted by the moderate efforts of average humanity, and the highest privilege of the citizen, at once a right and a reward, will be given or refused on the principles of even justice and stern regard for the common good.

CHARLES FRANCIS ADAMS JR.

READING AND DISCUSSION QUESTIONS

1. Analyze and evaluate Adams's argument for evidence of a historical pattern of continuity or change in America's commitment to expanded democratic rights. Are there truths within his claims?

2. How does the historical context of the Reconstruction era help you to understand the point of view held by Adams?

15-5 | Nast Lampoons Freedmen's Government

THOMAS NAST, *Colored Rule in a Reconstructed State* (1874)

Political cartoons developed sophistication in the years after the Civil War largely through the talents of the influential artist Thomas Nast, whose compositions effectively captured a frustrated electorate's disgust. In this image, Nast plays on then-common stereotypes and foregrounds the pervasive assumption northern and southern whites held about black political incompetence and corruption. Many white South Carolinians popularized these beliefs in their effort to redeem state government from the African American majority that controlled the legislature.

Harper's Weekly XVIII, no. 898 (March 14, 1874): 229.

VOL. XVIII.—No. 898.]   NEW YORK, SATURDAY, MARCH 14, 1874.   [WITH A SUPPLEMENT. PRICE TEN CENTS.

Entered according to Act of Congress, in the Year 1874, by Harper & Brothers, in the Office of the Librarian of Congress, at Washington.

COLORED RULE IN A RECONSTRUCTED (?) STATE.—[SEE PAGE 242.]

(THE MEMBERS CALL EACH OTHER THIEVES, LIARS, RASCALS, AND COWARDS.)

COLUMBIA. "You are Aping the lowest Whites. If you disgrace your Race in this way you had better take Back Seats."

READING AND DISCUSSION QUESTIONS

1. Analyze and evaluate Nast's image to identify the racial stereotypes it conveys. Whose view of black political abilities does it express?

2. What is the significance of the Columbia figure standing at the speaker's platform, and what is she trying to accomplish?

3. To what extent do the stereotypes Nast employed reflect the historical context of race relations during the Reconstruction period?

15-6 | African American Congressman Urges Support of Civil Rights Bill

ROBERT BROWNE ELLIOTT, *Speech to Congress* (1874)

While planters and their former slaves negotiated a new relationship in the wake of slavery's abolition, Congress was abuzz with legislative activity to secure the rights of citizenship freedmen had so recently won. The Civil Rights Act of 1875, which the African American member of Congress Robert Elliott supported in a speech to Congress, guaranteed to African Americans equal treatment in public accommodations. In 1873, the U.S. Supreme Court decided in the *Slaughterhouse Cases* to construe the Fourteenth Amendment protections narrowly, arguing that states properly retained the exercise of power over domestic and civil rights. Here Elliott is attempting to counter anti–civil rights efforts to use these cases to frustrate federal legislative action on behalf of freedmen.

Mr. Speaker: While I am sincerely grateful for this high mark of courtesy that has been accorded to me by this House, it is a matter of regret to me that it is necessary at this day that I should rise in the presence of an American Congress to advocate a bill which simply asserts equal rights and equal public privileges for all classes of American citizens. I regret, sir, that the dark hue of my skin may lend a color to the imputation that I am controlled by motives personal to myself in my advocacy of this great measure of national justice. Sir, the motive that impels me is restricted by no such narrow boundary, but is as broad as your Constitution. I advocate it, sir, because it is right. The bill, however, not only appeals to your justice, but it demands a response from your gratitude. . . .

[S]ir, we are told by the distinguished gentleman from Georgia (Mr. Stephens) that Congress has no power under the Constitution to pass such a law, and that the passage of such an act is in direct contravention of the rights of the states. I cannot assent to any such proposition. The Constitution of a free government ought always to be construed in favor of human rights. Indeed, the thirteenth, fourteenth, and fifteenth amendments, in positive words, invest Congress with the power to protect the citizen in his civil and political rights. Now, sir, what are

Lift Every Voice: African American Oratory, 1787–1900, ed. Philip S. Foner and Robert James Branham (Tuscaloosa and London: The University of Alabama Press, 1998), 521–525, 527–528, 532–536.

civil rights? Rights natural, modified by civil society. Mr. Lieber says: "By civil liberty is meant, not only the absence of individual restraint, but liberty within the social system and political organism—a combination of principles and laws which acknowledge, protect and favor the dignity of man . . . civil liberty is the result of man's twofold character as an individual and social being, so soon as both are equally respected." . . .

Are we then, sir, with the amendments to our Constitution staring us in the face; with these grand truths of history before our eyes; with innumerable wrongs daily inflicted upon five million citizens demanding redress, to commit this question to the diversity of legislation? In the words of Hamilton, "Is it the interest of the government to sacrifice individual rights to the preservation of the rights of an artificial being called the states? There can be no truer principle than this, that every individual of the community at large has an equal right to the protection of government. Can this be a free government if partial distinctions are tolerated or maintained?"

The rights contended for in this bill are among "the sacred rights of mankind, which are not to be rummaged for among old parchments or musty records; they are written as with a sunbeam in the whole volume of human nature, by the hand of the divinity itself, and can never be erased or obscured by mortal power."

But the Slaughterhouse cases!—The Slaughterhouse cases!

The honorable gentleman from Kentucky, always swift to sustain the failing and dishonored cause of proscription, rushes forward and flaunts in our faces the decision of the Supreme Court of the United States in the Slaughterhouse cases, and in that act he has been willingly aided by the gentleman from Georgia. Hitherto, in the contests which have marked the progress of the cause of equal civil rights, our opponents have appealed sometimes to custom, sometimes to prejudice, more often to pride of race, but they have never sought to shield themselves behind the Supreme Court. But now, for the first time, we are told that we are barred by a decision of that court, from which there is no appeal. If this be true we must stay our hands. The cause of equal civil rights must pause at the command of a power whose edicts must be obeyed till the fundamental law of our country is changed.

Has the honorable gentleman from Kentucky considered well the claim he now advances? If it were not disrespectful I would ask, has he ever read the decision which he now tells us is an insuperable barrier to the adoption of this great measure of justice?

In the consideration of this subject, has not the judgment of the gentleman from Georgia been warped by the ghost of the dead doctrines of states' rights? Has he been altogether free from prejudices engendered by long training in that school of politics that well-nigh destroyed this government?

Mr. Speaker, I venture to say here in the presence of the gentleman from Kentucky and the gentleman from Georgia, and in the presence of the whole country, that there is not a line or word, not a thought or dictum even, in the decision of the Supreme Court in the great Slaughterhouse cases, which casts a shadow of doubt on the right of Congress to pass the pending bill, or to adopt such other legislation as it may judge proper and necessary to secure perfect equality before the law to every citizen of the Republic. Sir, I protest against the dishonor now cast upon our Supreme Court by both the gentleman from Kentucky and the gentleman from Georgia. In other days, when the whole country was bowing beneath the yoke of slavery, when press, pulpit, platform, Congress and courts felt the fatal power of the slave oligarchy, I remember a decision of that court which no American now reads without shame and humiliation. But those days are past; the Supreme Court of today is a tribunal as true to freedom as any department of this government, and I am honored with the opportunity of repelling a deep disgrace which the gentleman from Kentucky, backed and sustained as he is by the gentleman from Georgia, seeks to put upon it. . . .

Before we proceed to examine more critically the provisions of this amendment, on which the plaintiffs in error rely, let us complete and discuss the history of the recent amendments, as that history related to the general purpose which pervades them all. A few years' experience satisfied the thoughtful men who had been the authors of the other two amendments that, notwithstanding the restraints of those articles on the States and the laws passed under the additional powers granted to Congress, these were inadequate for the protection of life, liberty, and property, without which freedom to the slave was no boon. They were in all those States denied the right of suffrage. The laws were administered by the white man alone. It was urged that a race of men distinctively marked as was the negro, living in the midst of another and dominant race, could never be fully secured in their person and their property without the right of suffrage.

Hence the fifteenth amendment, which declares that "the right of a citizen of the United States to vote shall not be denied or abridged by any State on account of race, color, or previous condition of servitude." The negro having, by the fourteenth amendment, been declared to be a citizen of the United States, is thus made a voter in every State of the Union.

We repeat, then, in the light of this recapitulation of events almost too recent to be called history, but which are familiar to us all, and on the most casual examination of the language of these amendments, no one can fail to be impressed with the one pervading purpose found in them all, lying at the foundation of each, and without which none of them would have been even suggested: we mean, the freedom of the slave race, the security and firm establishment of that freedom, and the protection of the newly made freeman and citizen from the oppressions of those who had formerly exercised unlimited dominion over him. It is true that only the fifteenth amendment in terms mentions the negro by speaking of his color and his slavery. But it is just as true that each of the other articles was addressed to the grievances of that race, and designed to remedy them, as the fifteenth.

These amendments, one and all, are thus declared to have as their all-pervading design and ends the security of the recently enslaved race, not only their nominal freedom, but their complete protection from those who had formerly exercised unlimited dominion over them. It is in this broad light that all these amendments must be read, the purpose to secure the perfect equality before the law of all citizens of the United States. What you give to one class you must give to all, what you deny to one class you shall deny to all, unless in the exercise of the common and universal police power of the state, you find it needful to confer exclusive privileges on certain citizens, to be held and exercised still for the common good of all. . . .

Now, sir, recurring to the venerable and distinguished gentleman from Georgia (Mr. Stephens) who has added his remonstrance against the passage of this bill, permit me to say that I share in the feeling of high personal regard for that gentleman which pervades this House. His years, his ability, and his long experience in public affairs entitle him to the measure of consideration which has been accorded to him on this floor. But in this discussion I cannot and will not forget that the welfare and rights of my whole race in this country are involved. When, therefore, the honorable gentleman from Georgia lends his voice and influence to defeat this measure, I do not shrink from saying that it is not from him that the American House of Representatives should take lessons in matters touching human rights or the joint relations of the state and national governments. While the honorable gentleman contented himself with harmless speculations in his study, or in the columns of a newspaper, we might well smile at the impotence of his efforts to turn back the advancing tide of opinion and progress, but, when he comes again upon this national arena, and throws himself with all his power and influence across the path which leads to the full enfranchisement of my race, I meet him only as an adversary; nor shall age or any other consideration restrain me from saying that he now offers this government, which he has done his utmost to destroy, a very poor return for its magnanimous treatment, to come here and seek to continue, by the assertion of doctrines obnoxious to the true principles of our government, the burdens and oppressions which rest upon five millions of his countrymen who never failed to lift their earnest prayers for the success of this government when the gentleman was seeking to break up the union of these states and to blot the American Republic from the galaxy of nations. [Loud applause.]

Sir, it is scarcely twelve years since that gentleman shocked the civilized world by announcing the birth of a government which rested on human slavery as its cornerstone. The progress of events has swept away that pseudo government which rested on greed, pride and tyranny, and the race whom he then ruthlessly spurned and trampled on is here to meet him in debate, and to demand that the rights which are enjoyed by its former oppressors—who vainly sought to overthrow a government which they could not prostitute to the base uses of slavery—shall be accorded to those who even in the darkness of slavery kept their allegiance true to freedom and the Union. Sir, the gentleman from Georgia has learned much since 1861, but he is still a laggard. Let him put away entirely the false and fatal theories which have so greatly marred an otherwise enviable record. Let him accept, in its fullness and beneficence, the great doctrine that American citizenship carries with it every civil and political right which manhood can confer. Let him lend his influence with all his masterly ability, to complete the proud structure of legislation which makes this nation worthy of the great declaration which heralded its birth, and he will have done that which will most nearly redeem his reputation in the eyes of the world and best vindicate the wisdom of that policy which has permitted him to regain his seat upon this floor. . . .

Sir, equality before the law is now the broad, universal, glorious rule and mandate of the Republic. No state can violate that. Kentucky and Georgia may crowd their statute books with retrograde and barbarous legislation; they may rejoice in the odious eminence of their consistent hostility to all the great steps of human progress which have marked our national history since slavery tore down the Stars and Stripes on Fort Sumter; but, if Congress shall do its duty, if Congress shall enforce the great guarantees which the Supreme Court has declared to be the one pervading purpose of all the recent amendments, then their unwise and unenlightened conduct will fall with the same weight upon the gentlemen from those states who now lend their influence to defeat this bill, as upon the poorest slave who once had no rights which the honorable gentlemen were bound to respect. . . .

Sir, I have replied to the extent of my ability to the arguments which have been presented by the opponents of this measure. I have replied also to some of the legal propositions advanced by gentlemen on the other side; and now that I am about to conclude, I am deeply sensible of the imperfect manner in which I have performed the task. Technically, this bill is to decide upon the civil status of the colored American citizen; a point disputed at the very formation of our present form of government, when by a short-sighted policy repugnant to true republican government, one Negro counted as three fifths of a man. The logical result of this mistake of the framers of the Constitution strengthened the cancer of slavery, which finally spread its poisonous tentacles over the Southern portion of the body politic. To arrest its growth and save the nation we have passed through the harrowing operation of intestine war, dreaded at all times, resorted to at the last extremity, like the surgeon's knife, but absolutely necessary to extirpate the disease which threatened with the life of the nation the overthrow of civil and political liberty on this continent. In that dire extremity the members of the race which I have the honor in part to represent—the race which pleads for justice at your hands to-day—forgetful of their inhuman and brutalizing servitude at the South, their degradation and ostracism at the North, flew willingly and gallantly to the support of the national government. Their sufferings, assistance, privations and trials in the swamps and in the rice fields, their valor on the land and on the sea, form a part of the ever-glorious record which makes up the history of a nation preserved, and might, should I urge the claim, incline you to respect and guarantee their rights and privileges as citizens of our common Republic. But I remember that valor, devotion and loyalty are not always rewarded according to their just deserts, and that after the battle some who have borne the brunt of the fray may, through neglect or contempt, be assigned to a subordinate place, while the enemies in war may be preferred to the sufferers.

The results of the war, as seen in reconstruction, have settled forever the political status of my race. The passage of this bill will determine the civil status, not only of the Negro, but of any other class of citizens who may feel themselves discriminated against. It will form the capstone of that temple of liberty, begun on this continent under discouraging circumstances, carried on in spite of the sneers of monarchists and the cavils of pretended friends of freedom, until at last it stands, in all its beautiful symmetry and proportions, a building the grandest which the world has ever seen, realizing the most sanguine expectations and the highest hopes of those who, in the name of equal, impartial and universal liberty, laid the foundation stone.

The Holy Scriptures tell us of an humble handmaiden who long, faithfully and patiently gleaned in the rich fields of her wealthy kinsman, and we are told further that at last, in spite of her humble antecedents she found favor in his sight. For over two centuries our race has "reaped down your fields," the cries and woes which we have uttered have "entered into the ears of the Lord of Sabaoth" and we are at last politically free. The last vestiture only is needed—civil rights. Having gained this, we may, with hearts overflowing with gratitude and thankful that our prayer has been answered, repeat the prayer of Ruth: "Entreat me not to leave thee, or to return from following after thee, for whither thou goest, I will go; and where thou lodgest, I will lodge; thy people shall be my people, and thy God my God; where thou diest I will die, and there will I be buried; the Lord do so to me, and more also, if ought but death part thee and me." [Great applause.]

READING AND DISCUSSION QUESTIONS

1. Summarize and evaluate the argument Elliott makes in support of the civil rights bill. What can you infer about the opposition from his argument?

2. What does it suggest to you about the nature of politics in the Reconstruction-era South that an African American member of Congress from South Carolina was able to speak in support of a civil rights bill on the floor of the House of Representatives in 1874? How does this document help you to understand the historical context of the period?

▪ COMPARATIVE QUESTIONS ▪

1. Explain whether you see the era of Reconstruction as the end or the beginning of a distinctive period in American history. What evidence from the documents in this chapter can you provide to prove your thesis?

2. Compare Reconstruction and the early national period as historical moments when issues of federal-state power and citizenship were debated. What similarities and differences do you note in the eligibility requirements for citizenship as referenced by Adams?

3. To what extent was the Jeffersonian regard for land as a source of one's independence an enduring ideal in the era of Reconstruction?

4. Historians have debated whether Reconstruction was a success, a failure, or an incomplete fulfillment of the American promise. How do the multiple perspectives represented by these sources help you develop your own argument about the historical significance of Reconstruction?

16

Conquering a Continent
1854–1890

The Civil War is a pivot point in American history, but the focused attention it receives sometimes obscures significant continuities. Such is the case with Americans' drive to expand the bounds of their country. The earlier period of Manifest Destiny in the 1840s led to the Mexican War and the political crises over the extension of slavery that precipitated the Civil War. In the postwar years, however, the itch to move was no less powerful a motive than it had been decades earlier. This continuing historical pattern of expansion shaped the latter decades of the nineteenth century. Railroads became the means of realizing continental dreams. The political muscle required to push them west both reflected the economic goals of the Republican Party and jeopardized the lives of Native Americans whose territorial claims became obstacles to industrialists' expansionist efforts. Western boosters convinced others that the cost to American Indians served the broader aims of integrating the West into the national economy, tapping the vast mineral, timber, and animal resources the continent offered. The costs were indeed high, and not only to Native Americans. Chinese laborers were hired to lay the tracks for railroads that hauled away the West's natural resources and changed its geography forever.

16-1 | Promoting the Transcontinental Railroad
The Pacific Railway Act (1862)

A year into the Civil War, President Lincoln signed the Pacific Railway Act, a bill that harvested old Whig Party ideas supporting internal improvements, to encourage the building of a transcontinental railway. This bill and the 1862 Homestead Act, which granted title to parcels of

Pacific Railway Act, July 1, 1862; Enrolled Acts and Resolutions of Congress, 1789–1996; Record Group 11; General Records of the United States Government; National Archives.

federal territory to adult citizens who resided on and improved the land for five years, were part of Republicans' efforts to encourage national economic development. The Union Pacific Railroad Company received grants of federal land to survey and build a line connecting the Missouri River and the Pacific Ocean. It raised funds by selling land along rail lines, a pull factor for those seeking new opportunities.

Be it enacted by the Senate and House of Representatives of the United States of America in Congress assembled, That [the commissioners] together with commissioners to be appointed by the Secretary of the Interior, and all persons who shall or may be associated with them, and their successors, are hereby created and erected into a body corporate and politic in deed and in law, by the name, style, and title of "The Union Pacific Railroad Company"; and by that name shall have perpetual succession, and shall be able to sue and to be sued, plead and be impleaded, defend and be defended, in all courts of law and equity within the United States, and may make and have a common seal; and the said corporation is hereby authorized and empowered to layout, locate, construct, furnish, maintain, and enjoy a continuous railroad and telegraph, with the appurtenances, from a point on the one hundredth meridian of longitude west from Greenwich, between the south margin of the valley of the Republican River and the north margin of the valley of the Platte River, in the Territory of Nebraska, to the western boundary of Nevada Territory, upon the route and terms hereinafter provided, and is hereby vested with all the powers, privileges, and immunities necessary to carry into effect the purposes of this act as herein set forth. The capital stock of said company shall consist of one hundred thousand shares of one thousand dollars each, which shall be subscribed for and held in not more than two hundred shares by anyone person, and shall be transferable in such manner as the by-laws of said corporation shall provide.

SEC. 2. And be it further enacted, That the right of way through the public lands be, and the same is hereby, granted to said company for the construction of said railroad and telegraph line; and the right, power, and authority is hereby given to said company to take from the public lands adjacent to the line of said road, earth, stone, timber, and other materials for the construction thereof; said right of way is granted to said railroad to the extent of two hundred feet in width on each side of said railroad where it may pass over the public lands, including all necessary grounds for stations, buildings, workshops, and depots, machine shops, switches, side tracks, turntables, and, water stations. The United States shall extinguish as rapidly as may be the Indian titles to all lands falling under the operation of this act and required for the said right of way and; grants hereinafter made.

SEC 3. And be it further enacted, That there be, and is hereby, granted to the said company, for the purpose of aiding in the construction, of said railroad and telegraph line, and to secure the safe and speedy transportation of the mails, troops, munitions of war, and public stores thereon, every alternate section of public land, designated by odd numbers, to the amount of five alternate sections per mile on each side of said railroad, on the line thereof, and within the limits of ten miles on each side of said road, not sold, reserved, or otherwise disposed of by the United States, and to which a preemption or homestead claim may not have attached, at the time the line of said road is definitely fixed: Provided, That all mineral lands shall be excepted from the operation of this act; but where the same shall contain timber, the timber thereon is hereby granted to said company. And all such lands, so granted by this section, which shall not be sold or disposed of by said company within three years after the entire road shall have been completed, shall be subject to settlement and preemption, like other lands, at a price not exceeding one dollar and twenty-five cents per acre, to be paid to said company.

SEC. 4. And be it further enacted, That whenever said company shall have completed forty consecutive miles of any portion of said railroad and telegraph line, ready for the service contemplated by this act, and supplied with all necessary . . . appurtenances of a first class railroad . . . the President of the United States shall appoint three commissioners to examine the same and report to him in relation thereto; and if it shall appear to him that forty consecutive miles of said railroad and telegraph line have been completed and equipped in all respects as required by this act, then, upon certificate of said commissioners to that effect, patents shall issue conveying the right and title to said lands to said company, on each side of the road as far as the same is completed, to the amount aforesaid; and patents shall in like manner issue as each forty miles of said railroad and telegraph line are completed, upon certificate of said commissioners.

SEC. 5. And be it further enacted, That for the purposes herein mentioned the Secretary of the Treasury shall, upon the certificate in writing of said commissioners of the completion and equipment of forty consecutive miles of said railroad and telegraph, in accordance with the provisions of this act, issue to said company bonds of the United States of one thousand dollars each, payable in thirty years after date, bearing six per centum per annum interest (said interest payable semi-annually), which interest may be paid in United States treasury notes or any other money or currency which the United States have or shall declare lawful money and a legal tender, to the amount of sixteen of said bonds per mile for such section of forty miles. . . .

SEC. 7. And be it further enacted, That said company shall file their assent to this act, under the seal of said company, in the Department of the Interior, within one year after the passage of this act, and shall complete said railroad and telegraph from the point of beginning, as herein provided, to the western boundary of Nevada Territory before the first day of July, one thousand eight hundred and seventy-four: Provided, That within two years after the passage of this act said company shall designate the general route of said road, as near as may be, and shall file a map of the same in the Department of the Interior, whereupon the Secretary of the Interior shall cause the lands within fifteen miles of said designated route or routes to be withdrawn from preemption, private entry, and sale; and when any portion of said route shall be finally located, the Secretary of the Interior shall cause the said lands herein before granted to be surveyed and set off as fast as may be necessary for the purposes herein named: Provided, That in fixing the point of connection of the main trunk with the eastern connections, it shall be fixed at the most practicable point for the construction of the Iowa and Missouri branches, as hereinafter provided.

SEC. 8. And be it further enacted, That the line of said railroad and telegraph shall commence at a point on the one hundredth meridian of a longitude west from Greenwich, between the south margin of the valley of the Republican River and the north margin of the valley of the Platte River, in the Territory of Nebraska, at a point to be fixed by the President of the United States, after actual surveys; thence running westerly upon the most direct, central, and practicable route, through the territories of the United States, the western boundary of the Territory of Nevada, there to meet and connect with the line of the Central Pacific Railroad Company of California. . . .

SEC. 11. And be it further enacted, That for three hundred miles of said road most mountainous and difficult of construction, to wit: one hundred and fifty miles westwardly from the eastern base of the Rocky Mountains, and one hundred and fifty miles eastwardly from the western base of the Sierra Nevada mountains, said points to be fixed by the President of the United States, the bonds to be issued to aid in the construction thereof shall be treble the number per mile hereinbefore provided, and the same shall be issued, and the lands herein granted be set apart, upon the construction of every twenty miles thereof, upon the certificate of the commissioners as aforesaid that twenty consecutive miles of the same are completed, and between the sections last named of one hundred and fifty miles each, the bonds to be issued to aid in the construction thereof shall be double the number per mile first mentioned, and the same shall be issued, and the lands herein granted be set apart, upon the construction of every twenty miles thereof, upon the certificate of the commissioners as aforesaid that twenty consecutive miles of the same are completed: Provided, That no more than fifty thousand of said bonds shall be issued under this act to aid in constructing the main line of said railroad and telegraph.

SEC. 12. And be it further enacted, That whenever the route of said railroad shall cross the boundary of any State or Territory, or said meridian of longitude, the two companies meeting or uniting there shall agree upon its location at that point, with reference to the most direct and practicable through route, and in case of difference between them as to said location the President of the United States shall determine the said location; the companies named in each State and Territory to locate the road across the same between the points so agreed upon, except as herein provided. The track upon the entire line of railroad and branches shall be of uniform width, to be determined by the President of the United States, so that, when completed, cars can be run from the Missouri River to the Pacific coast; the grades and curves shall not exceed the maximum grades and curves of the Baltimore and Ohio railroad; the whole line of said railroad and branches and telegraph shall be operated and used for all purposes of communication, travel, and transportation, so far as the public and government are concerned, as one connected, continuous line; and the companies herein named in Missouri, Kansas, and California, filing their assent to the provisions of this act, shall receive and transport . . . all materials required for constructing and furnishing said first-mentioned line between the aforesaid point, on the one hundredth meridian of longitude and western boundary of Nevada Territory, whenever the same is required by said first-named company, at cost, over that portion of the roads of said companies constructed under the provisions of this act.

SEC. 15. And be it further enacted, That any other railroad company now incorporated, or hereafter to be incorporated, shall have the right to connect their road with the road and branches provided for by this act, at such places and upon such just and equitable terms as the President of the United States may prescribe. Wherever the word company is used in this act it shall be construed to embrace the words their associates, successors, and assigns, the same as if the words had been properly added thereto.

SEC. 16. And be it further enacted, That at any time after the passage of this act all of the railroad companies named herein, and assenting hereto, or any two or more of them, are authorized to form themselves into one consolidated company; notice of such consolidation, in writing, shall be filed in the Department of the Interior, and such consolidated company shall thereafter proceed to construct said railroad and branches and telegraph line upon the terms and conditions provided in this act.

SEC. 17. And be it further enacted, That in case said company or companies shall fail to comply with the terms and conditions of this act, by not completing said road and telegraph and branches within a reasonable time, or by not keeping the same in repair and use, but shall permit the same, for an unreasonable time, to remain unfinished, or out of repair, and unfit for use, Congress may pass any act to insure the speedy completion of said road and branches, or put the same in repair and use, and may direct the income of said railroad and telegraph line to be thereafter devoted to the use of the United States, to repay all such expenditures caused by the default and neglect of such company or companies: Provided, That if said roads are not completed, so as to form a continuous line of railroad, ready for use, from the Missouri River to the navigable waters of the Sacramento River, in California, by the first day of July, eighteen hundred and seventy-six, the whole of all of said railroads before mentioned and to be constructed under the provisions of this act, and property of every kind and character, shall be forfeited to and be taken possession of by the United States.

SEC. 18. And be it further enacted, That whenever it appears that the net earnings of the entire road and telegraph, including the amount allowed for services rendered for the United States, after deducting all, expenditures, including repairs, and the furnishing, running, and managing of said road, shall exceed ten per centum upon its cost, exclusive of the five per centum to be paid to the United States, Congress may reduce the rates of fare thereon, if unreasonable in amount, and may fix and establish the same by law. And the better to accomplish the object of this act, namely, to promote the public interest and welfare by the construction of said railroad and telegraph line, and keeping the same in working order, and to secure to the government at all times (but particularly in time of war) the use and benefits of the same for postal, military and other purposes,

Congress may, at any time, having due regard for the rights of said companies named herein, add to, alter, amend, or repeal this act.

SEC. 19. And be it further enacted, That the several railroad companies herein named are authorized to enter into an arrangement with the Pacific Telegraph Company, the Overland Telegraph Company, and the California State Telegraph Company, so that the present line of telegraph between the Missouri River and San Francisco may be moved upon or along the line of said railroad and branches as fast as said roads and branches are built; and if said arrangement be entered into and the transfer of said telegraph line be made in accordance therewith to the line of said railroad and branches, such transfer shall, for all purposes of this act, be held and considered a fulfillment on the part of said railroad companies of the provisions of this act in regard to the construction of said line of telegraph. And, in case of disagreement, said telegraph companies are authorized to remove their line of telegraph along and upon the line of railroad herein contemplated without prejudice to the rights of said railroad companies named herein.

SEC. 20. And be it further enacted, That the corporation hereby created and the roads connected therewith, under the provisions of this act, shall make to the Secretary of the Treasury an annual report wherein shall be set forth—

First. The names of the stockholders and their places of residence, so far as the same can be ascertained;

Second. The names and residences of the directors, and all other officers of the company;

Third. The amount of stock subscribed, and the amount thereof actually paid in;

Fourth. A description of the lines of road surveyed, of the lines thereof fixed upon for the construction of the road, and the cost of such surveys;

Fifth. The amount received from passengers on the road;

Sixth. The amount received for freight thereon;

Seventh. A statement of the expense of said road and its fixtures;

Eighth. A statement of the indebtedness of said company, setting forth the various kinds thereof. Which report shall be sworn to by the president of the said company, and shall be presented to the Secretary of the Treasury on or before the first day of July in each year.

APPROVED, July 1, 1862.

READING AND DISCUSSION QUESTIONS

1. The latter half of the nineteenth century is often depicted as a laissez-faire era when the federal government embraced a "hands-off" approach to the national economy. What evidence can you find in the Pacific Railway Act that supports or challenges this traditional interpretation?

2. What can you infer from the act regarding its sponsors' expectations of the railroad's importance to the nation's economic, political, and social growth and development?

3. Considering this source from multiple perspectives, which aspects of the legislation would have encouraged supporters and angered opponents?

16-2 | Railroad Transforms the Nation

CURRIER & IVES, *Across the Continent* (1868)

For better or worse, the railroad altered the geography of America and ushered in economic, social, and political changes that touched the lives of nearly all Americans. Like the canal era before it, the period of rapid railroad development promised market revolutions as goods and resources crossed the continent and local economies integrated with national and global trade networks. Once-isolated communities found themselves connected to consumer and communication webs hardly imagined in the horse and wagon days. The Currier & Ives print "Across the Continent, Westward the Course of Empire Takes Its Way" captures the revolution at its beginning, with the anticipation and foreboding it inspired.

Across the Continent, Westward the Course of Empire Takes Its Way, 1868 (litho), Currier, N. (1813–1888), and Ives, J. M. (1824–1895) / Private Collection / The Bridgeman Art Library.

READING AND DISCUSSION QUESTIONS

1. Analyze and evaluate the elements of this print for evidence of the artist's point of view with respect to the railroad and western development. What does the artist suggest about the effect the railroad had on Americans and their communities?

2. How might you explain the popularity of this Currier & Ives print? Why do you think this image resonated with those who purchased it to decorate their homes?

16-3 | Harvesting the Bison Herds
J. WRIGHT MOOAR, *Buffalo Days* (1933)

Railroads helped integrate the West into the national and global economy. The Great Plains, in particular, developed as a key region for America's economic growth, a development that would have surprised an earlier generation accustomed to thinking of the vast interior as a worthless desert. Commercialized buffalo hunting drove the economic transformation while also working to eliminate American Indians as obstacles to westward expansion. J. Wright Mooar, whose stories of his buffalo-hunting days were first published in 1933, claimed to have killed twenty thousand buffalo, selling meat to feed the proliferating numbers of railroad workers and the hides to East Coast tanneries. The destruction of the herds opened the plains to cattle ranching and sealed the fate of Plains Indians whose lives were organized around the buffalo.

Curing Buffalo Meat

It was in October, 1877, while I was killing buffalo on Deep Creek, that John returned from a trip to Fort Griffin after the mail, and reported that a large herd of cattle was coming into the country, and that the John Hum outfit was then only twenty miles east of our hunting grounds.

It was immediately determined to move camp seventy miles north, to Double Lake in Lynn County. Here headquarters were maintained and the meat was hauled to the old Deep Creek camp, where the smokehouse for curing the meat was located.

As soon as the hide was stripped from the fallen bison, the meat was cut from the hams in four large pieces, the bone being cut out. When from one thousand to twelve hundred pounds of meat was thus collected, it was piled in a vat constructed by driving four stakes into the ground in a square four by four feet, the stakes standing four feet high. To these four corner stakes, a hide, hair side out, was tied by its corners, and let sag in the middle to form a sack or sort of vat. Into this the meat was thrown, and salted as it was thrown in. A brine was then

---

J. Wright Mooar, "The Killing of the White Buffalo," *Buffalo Days: Stories from J. Wright Mooar as Told to James Winford Hunt*, ed. Robert F. Pace (Abilene, TX: State House Press, McMurry University, 2005), 76–81.

poured over this until the meat was covered. A hide was stretched over the whole for a lid, thus keeping out sun and dirt. Four days later, sugar and saltpeter were added in precise measure to the brine. This was left for two weeks. The thoroughly medicated meat was then taken out and placed in the smokehouse for final seasoning.

The smokehouse was constructed by stretching buffalo hides over a framework of hackberry poles, put together with eightpenny nails, one hundred pounds of which had been hauled from Fort Worth. The house thus constructed was one hundred and ten feet long and twenty feet wide. Along the center of the floor space were ten square pits for the fire. For wood, hackberry and chinaberry logs were used, and the smoking process required ten or twelve days. This prepared meat was hauled to Fort Griffin and sold.

During this winter of '77, we took three thousand seven hundred hides, which were hauled to Fort Worth, and twenty-five thousand pounds of meat, which were sold locally.

Cattle were now being driven into the country very rapidly, and the Mooar Brothers bought the John Goff cattle in Fisher County and changed the brand from XTS to SXT. This brand was kept up in Fisher County for ten years, and then moved to the old buffalo camp on Deep Creek, where my ranch is today.

Passing of the Buffalo

By the arrival of 1879, the hunters were leaving for the mining states, or seeking other lines of business, as they realized the great hunting days were over. Mooar Brothers, however, continued pursuit of the dwindling herds to the great plains country, and during the year of 1878 secured two thousand eight hundred hides and twenty thousand pounds of meat. The last of the buffalo, save a few scattered bands of young animals too young for the hunters to bother with, fell to my big guns in March, 1879. Loading seven thousand pounds of cured meat on two wagons drawn by six good mules, and accompanied by a seventeen-year-old boy, [we] headed west on a fifty-two day trip to Prescott and Phoenix, Arizona, where the meat was sold to the miners. I did not return to Texas until October, 1880.

In the meantime, John had moved the Deep Creek camp to the Fisher County cattle camp. The last of the buffalo hides were sold to Charley Rath, who had bought all interest in the Reynolds store in Stonewall County. As the buffalo days ended, he moved the goods remaining in this store to Camp Supply, in Indian Territory. John did the hauling for Rath on this move, making the long journey with his ox teams. From Camp Supply, he made one trip for Rath to Dodge City, and returned to Texas in December, 1879, loaded with corn from the Red River Country. This he sold to the Texas Ranger camp at Big Spring, Texas. R.C. Ware was in charge of the Ranger camp. He became a noted citizen of the changing Southwest.

Thus ended eight full years of continuous and eventful hunting of the great American bison.

The Indians realized very keenly that the work of the buffalo hunters was the real menace to the wild, free life they wished to lead, and never lost an opportunity to wreak vengeance. This made the life of the hunter one of constant peril. He was always under observation, wild eyes from some covert watching his every move. It is past comprehension to people of today how, under such circumstances, a lone hunter could wander at will and escape ambush or sudden assault in overwhelming numbers. Two things alone protected him: his rifle and his marksmanship. Perhaps one might also add that, while seemingly wandering at will, be was as alert as an Indian and seldom caught off his guard.

The Half-Inch Rifle

His rifle was one made at the request of his guild at the very outset, and was manufactured by the Sharps Rifle Manufacturing Company to meet the requirements for the biggest game on the North American continent—the buffalo. The weapon was a gun weighing from twelve to sixteen pounds, and the caliber was .50-110. One hundred and ten grains of powder, in a long brass shell, hurled from the beautifully rifled muzzle of the great gun a heavy leaden missle that in its impact and its tearing, shattering qualities would instantly bring down the biggest bison, if properly aimed, and that reached out to incredible distances for rifles of that period.

In the account of our trek to Deep Creek, a strip of country like the plains country is mentioned. This plain was evidently once a part of the great Central Plain, but this was at some distant period cut off to itself by upheavals in the general level. In extent it is thirty or forty miles long and from five to fifteen miles wide. Deep Creek marks its western boundary.

Riding eastward across this level, open stretch, and with a wagon and mule team following, I came one afternoon to the broken country east of the tableland. A sunken country rolled away to the east, and the terrain was marked by deep draws, mesquite flats, and small knolls and mesas called the Sugar Loaf Hills. The country looked to be a good place for hunting, with plenty of wood and water at hand, but somewhat dangerous because furnishing plenty of covert for Indian ambuscades. No Indians had been seen in that part, however, and I was about to select a place for a camp and indicate it to my wagoner, when a slight movement at the head of a brushy draw caught my attention. Watching closely I was rewarded in a moment by seeing an Indian rush his pony down into the draw, and in a few moments another stealthily followed him. I had been just alert enough to see the last two Indians of what turned out to be a large band.

Concealing myself, I became the eyewitness of Indian travel tactics. When the band reappeared it had reached the mouth of the draw, and dashed one at a time across to the mouth of another draw breaking down from the plain. They traveled back up this, concealed from all observers, until they would be forced to rush across to the head of another draw and so down it, approaching in this stealthy and devious manner the objective sought.

We drove quickly back to the camp on Deep Creek, content to hunt in more open country.

READING AND DISCUSSION QUESTIONS

1. What evidence do Mooar's stories provide for understanding the historical patterns of change transforming the Great Plains into a commercialized region of economic activity?

2. What can you infer about the historical interpretation, or meaning, Mooar gave to his 1870s Great Plains adventures? Do you think he saw himself participating in a historically significant moment?

16-4 | Addressing the Indian Question

FRANCIS A. WALKER, *Annual Report of the Commissioner of Indian Affairs* (1872)

Another war raged during the 1860s, but unlike the Civil War, the war with the Plains Indians persisted for decades. Following policies established by Andrew Jackson in the 1830s, the federal government in the 1860s and 1870s attempted to open western settlement by corralling American Indians onto reservations. Native resistance to these efforts inevitably resulted in a military response from the federal government, leading to notorious conflicts at such places as Sand Creek, Colorado; Fort Phil Kearny, Wyoming; Little Big Horn in the Montana Territory; and Wounded Knee, South Dakota. These clashes stirred debate about the long-term effectiveness of U.S. policy, which Francis Walker, commissioner of Indian affairs in the early 1870s, attempts to describe and justify.

The Indian policy, so called, of the Government, is a policy, and it is not a policy, or rather it consists of two policies, entirely distinct, seeming, indeed, to be mutually inconsistent and to reflect each upon the other: the one regulating the treatment of the tribes which are potentially hostile, that is, whose hostility is only repressed just so long as, and so far as, they are supported in idleness by the Government; the other regulating the treatment of those tribes which, from traditional friendship, from numerical weakness, or by the force of their location, are either indisposed toward, or incapable of, resistance to the demands of the Government. . . . This want of completeness and consistency in the treatment of the Indian tribes by the Government has been made the occasion of much ridicule and partisan abuse; and it is indeed calculated to provoke criticism and to afford scope for satire; but it is none the less compatible with the highest expediency of the situation. . . . And yet, for all this, the Government is right and its

Francis A. Walker, *Annual Report of the Commissioner of Indian Affairs*, November 1, 1872. *Documents of United States Indian Policy*, 3rd ed., ed. Francis Paul Prucha (Lincoln: University of Nebraska Press, 2000), 135–140.

critics wrong; and the "Indian policy" is sound, sensible, and beneficent, because it reduces to the minimum the loss of life and property upon our frontier, and allows the freest development of our settlements and railways possible under the circumstances. . . .

The Use of the Military Arm

The system now pursued in dealing with the roving tribes dangerous to our frontier population and obstructing our industrial progress, is entirely consistent with, and, indeed, requires the occasional use of the military arm, in restraining or chastising refractory individuals and bands. Such a use of the military constitutes no abandonment of the "peace policy," and involves no disparagement of it. It was not to be expected — it was not in the nature of things — that the entire body of wild Indians should submit to be restrained in their Ishmaelitish proclivities without a struggle on the part of the more audacious to maintain their traditional freedom. In the first announcement made of the reservation system, it was expressly declared that the Indians should be made as comfortable on, and as uncomfortable off, their reservations as it was in the power of the Government to make them; that such of them as went right should be protected and fed, and such as went wrong should be harassed and scourged without intermission. It was not anticipated that the first proclamation of this policy to the tribes concerned would effect the entire cessation of existing evils; but it was believed that persistence in the course marked out would steadily reduce the number of the refractory, both by the losses sustained in actual conflict and by the desertion of individuals as they should become weary of a profitless and hopeless struggle, until, in the near result, the system adopted should apply without exception to all the then roving and hostile tribes. Such a use of the strong arm of the Government is not war, but discipline. . . .

The Forbearance of the Government

It is unquestionably true that the Government has seemed somewhat tardy in proceeding under the second half of the reservation policy, and in applying the scourge to individuals and bands leaving their prescribed limits without authority, or for hostile purposes. This has been partly from a legitimate deference to the conviction of the great body of citizens that the Indians have been in the past unjustly and cruelly treated, and that great patience and long forbearance ought to be exercised in bringing them around to submission to the present reasonable requirements of the Government, and partly from the knowledge on the part of the officers of the Government charged with administering Indian affairs, that, from the natural jealously [*sic*] of these people, their sense of wrongs suffered in the past, and their suspiciousness arising from repeated acts of treachery on the part of the whites; from the great distance of many bands and individuals from points of personal communication with the agents of the Government, and the absence of all means of written communication with them; from the efforts of abandoned and degraded whites, living among the Indians and exerting much influence over them, to misrepresent the policy of the Government, and to keep alive the hostility and suspicion of the savages; and, lastly, from the extreme untrustworthiness of many of the interpreters on whom the Government is obliged to rely for bringing its intentions to the knowledge of the Indians: that by the joint effect of all these obstacles, many tribes and bands could come very slowly to hear, comprehend, and trust the professions and promises of the Government. . . .

The patience and forbearance exercised have been fully justified in their fruits. The main body of the roving Indians have, with good grace or with ill grace, submitted to the reservation system. Of those who still remain away from the assigned limits, by far the greater part are careful to do so with as little offense as possible; and when their range is such as for the present not to bring them into annoying or dangerous contact with the whites, this Office, has, from the motive of economy, generally been disposed to allow them to pick up their own living still by hunting and fishing, in preference to tying them up at agencies where they would require to be fed mainly or wholly at the expense of the Government. . . .

The Beginning of the End

It belongs not to a sanguine, but to a sober view of the situation, that three years will see the alternative of war eliminated from the Indian question, and the most powerful and hostile bands of to-day thrown in entire helplessness on the mercy of the Government. Indeed, the progress of two years more, if not of another summer, on the Northern Pacific Railroad will of itself completely solve the great Sioux problem, and leave the ninety thousand Indians ranging between the two trans-continental lines as incapable of resisting the Government as are the Indians of New York or Massachusetts. Columns moving north from the Union Pacific, and south from the Northern Pacific, would crush the Sioux and their confederates as between the upper and the nether millstone; while the rapid movement of troops along the northern line would prevent the escape of the savages, when hard pressed, into the British Possessions, which have heretofore afforded a convenient refuge on the approach of a military expedition.

Toward the south the day of deliverance from the fear of Indian hostility is more distant, yet it is not too much to expect that three summers of peaceful progress will forever put it out of the power of the tribes and bands which at present disturb Colorado, Utah, Arizona, and New Mexico to claim consideration of the country in any other attitude than as pensioners upon the national bounty. The railroads now under construction, or projected with a reasonable assurance of early completion, will multiply fourfold the striking force of the Army in that section; the little rifts of mining settlement, now found all through the mountains of the southern Territories will have become self-protecting communities; the feeble, wavering line of agricultural occupation, now sensitive to the faintest breath of Indian hostility, will then have grown to be the powerful "reserve" to lines still more closely advanced upon the last range of the intractable tribes.

Submission the Only Hope of the Indians

No one certainly will rejoice more heartily than the present Commissioner when the Indians of this county cease to be in a position to dictate, in any form or degree, to the Government; when, in fact, the last hostile tribe becomes reduced to the condition of suppliants for charity. This is, indeed, the only hope of salvation for the aborigines of the continent. If they stand up against the progress of civilization and industry, they must be relentlessly crushed. The westward course of population is neither to be denied nor delayed for the sake of all the Indians that ever called this country their home. They must yield or perish; and there is something that savors of providential mercy in the rapidity with which their fate advances upon them, leaving them scarcely the chance to resist before they shall be surrounded and disarmed. It is not feebly and futilely to attempt to stay this tide, whose depth and strength can hardly be measured, but to snatch the remnants of the Indian race from destruction from before it, that the friends of humanity should exert themselves in this juncture, and lose no time. And it is because the present system allows the freest extension of settlement and industry possible under the circumstances, while affording space and time for humane endeavors to rescue the Indian tribes from a position altogether barbarous and incompatible with civilization and social progress, that this system must be approved by all enlightened citizens. . . .

The Claims of the Indian

The people of the United States can never without dishonor refuse to respect these two considerations: 1st. That this continent was originally owned and occupied by the Indians, who have on this account a claim somewhat larger than the privilege of one hundred and sixty acres of land, and "find himself" in tools and stock, which is granted as a matter of course to any newly-arrived foreigner who declares his intention to become a citizen; that something in the nature of an endowment, either capitalized or in the form of annual expenditures for a series of years for the benefit of the Indians, though at the discretion of the Government as to the specific objects, should be provided for every tribe or band which is deprived of its roaming privilege and confined to a diminished reservation: such an endowment being not in the nature of a gratuity, but in common honesty the right of the Indian on account of his original interest in the soil. 2d. That inasmuch as the progress of our industrial enterprise has cut these people off from modes of livelihood entirely sufficient for their wants, and for which they were qualified, in a degree which has been the wonder of more civilized races, by inherited aptitudes and by long pursuit, and has left them utterly without resource, they have a claim on this account again to temporary support and to such assistance as may be necessary to place them in a position to obtain a livelihood by means which shall be compatible with civilization.

　　Had the settlements of the United States not been extended beyond the frontier of 1867, all the Indians of the continent would to the end of time have found upon the plains an inexhaustible supply of food and clothing. Were the westward course of population to be stayed at the barriers of to-day, notwithstanding the tremendous inroads made upon their hunting-grounds since 1867, the Indians would still have hope of life. But another such five years will see the Indians of Dakota and Montana as poor as the Indians of Nevada and Southern California; that is, reduced to an habitual condition of suffering from want of food.

The freedom of expansion which is working these results is to us of incalculable value. To the Indian it is of incalculable cost. Every year's advance of our frontier takes in a territory as large as some of the kingdoms of Europe. We are richer by hundreds of millions; the Indian is poorer by a large part of the little that he has. This growth is bringing imperial greatness to the nation; to the Indian it brings wretchedness, destitution, beggary. Surely there is obligation found in considerations like these, requiring us in some way, and in the best way, to make good to these original owners of the soil the loss by which we so greatly gain.

Can any principle of national morality be clearer than that, when the expansion and development of a civilized race involve the rapid destruction of the only means of subsistence possessed by the members of a less fortunate race, the higher is bound as a simple right to provide for the lower some substitute for the means of subsistence which it has destroyed? That substitute is, of course, best realized, not by systematic gratuities of food and clothing continued beyond a present emergency, but by directing these people to new pursuits which shall be consistent with the progress of civilization upon the continent; helping them over the first rough places on "the white man's road," and, meanwhile, supplying such subsistence as is absolutely necessary during the period of initiation and experiment. . . .

READING AND DISCUSSION QUESTIONS

1. Analyze and evaluate the policy recommendations Walker endorses with respect to Native American tribes facing the expansion of white commerce and settlement. To what extent is he sympathetic to their plight?

2. What does Walker see as the ultimate fate of American Indians?

3. What conclusions about the political culture of the 1870s can you draw from Walker's annual report as commissioner of Indian affairs?

16-5 | Remembering Indian Boarding School Days

MOURNING DOVE, *A Salishan Autobiography* (1990)

Okanogan Indian Christine Quintasket, or Mourning Dove, experienced the effects of America's Native American policies in the late nineteenth century, a period she writes about in her autobiography, published half a century after her death. By the time of her birth in the mid-1880s, those policies rejected earlier efforts to concentrate Native Americans onto

Mourning Dove, *Mourning Dove: A Salishan Autobiography*, ed. Jay Miller (Lincoln: University of Nebraska Press, 1990), 24–31.

reservations. With the passage of the Dawes Severalty Act in 1887, the federal government's new aim was to eradicate "the Indian" within Native Americans. By discouraging reservations, where tribes had been able to maintain native languages and customs, the new policy hoped to "Americanize" them. Part of that effort led to an Indian boarding school movement where Native Americans were taught English, forced to adopt non-native clothes and customs, and made to live apart from their extended families.

Although Mother continued persistently to give me my ancient education with the help of my native teacher, she was also a fanatically religious Catholic. We never missed mass or church unless it was absolutely necessary. If church was not scheduled at the little mission below our cabin, then we "pilgrimed" to Goodwin Mission to attend church. Winter and summer, she never failed to make her confession and communion on the first Friday of every month. To her mind, and that of many of the early converts, the word of the priest was law. She strictly observed anything that the pioneer Father De Rouge so much as hinted at. On the other hand, my father was considered a "slacker" or a black sheep of the flock. He attended church only occasionally and without the devotion of my mother. . . .

During one of our monthly trips to Goodwin for the first Friday service, we met Father De Rouge on the big steps of the church, where he had come outside to mingle with his beloved Indian congregation.

The good [Jesuit] priest came forward and shook hands with Mother, spying me behind her wide skirts. He looked right at me and asked if I had made my first communion. He had a way of jumbling up words from several Indian languages he had learned so that his words sounded childish, but I dared not chuckle at his comment. Instead, I shook my head in answer to his question. He looked at mother reproachfully and, shaking his head, said, "Tut, Tut, Lucy. You must let your child go to school with the good sisters to learn her religion so that she can make her first communion like other children of her age." Mother tried to make a protest, saying she needed me at home to care for the babies. But Father De Rouge could seldom be enticed to change his mind. He always had a very strict, ruling hand with the Indians. His word was much respected by the natives of the Colville Reservation.

He shook his finger at Mother and said, "Tut, Tut, Lucy. I command you." Then, pointing at the cross atop the bell tower of the church, he continued, "Your church commands that your child must go to school to learn her religion and the laws of the church." In obedience, Mother promised to send me to the mission for the fall term of 1898.

I had known Father De Rouge all my life. He had been a stationary superior at the Goodwin Mission until the arrival of Father Carnia [Caruana], whom the Indians called T-quit-na-wiss (Large Stomach), since the new priest had plenty of abdominal carriage. After that De Rouge became a traveling priest, covering all the territory of the Colville Reservation and beyond. He taught the Indians their prayers and erected the first little cabins that served as chapels until they were later remodeled into larger frame churches. These early church locations included Ellisford, St. Mary's Mission on Omak Creek, Nespelem, Keller, and Inchelium. These last four compose the modern districts of the Colville Reservation. Earlier these districts all had their share of the faithful work of the self-sacrificing Father Etienne (Stephen) De Rouge.

He was the descendant of a rich and influential French count, but he rejected his claim to this title to fulfill his mission among his beloved Colville. Many times he would stop by our cabin home at Pia to visit with the family. He traveled astride his cayuse leading a pack animal loaded with the sacred belongings needed to say mass. This gave him the convenience of holding services in any Indian tipi or cabin where night would overtake him. He was never too busy to answer a call for help, rushing in the night to visit the sick or administer the last sacraments to poor, dying natives. His life was thoroughly wrapped up in his chosen work. He spent every penny he could get from his rich family and from small Indian contributions to aid the needy.

It was through his influence and encouragement that the Indians gradually discontinued their ancient customs and were more willing to send their children to school at Goodwin. He later erected a fine and roomy school at St. Mary's Mission, after he had permanently established other churches that were maintained either by traveling priests or by one permanently settled in the location to teach the Indians and provide an example. This boarding school, built with his own money and contributions from Catholic whites in the East, remains a successful monument to his life's work. . . .

When my father told me I had better start at school, I was scared. It took much coaxing, and buying me candy and nuts along with other luxuries at the log store at Marcus, before I consented to go.

Father was holding my hand when we went through the big white gates into the clean yard of the school. A high whitewashed fence enclosed all the huge buildings, which looked so uninviting. I hated to stay but promised Father I would not get lonesome. I walked at his side as he briskly entered a building to meet a woman in a long black skirt, with a roll of stiff white, oval cloth around her pale face. I looked away from her lovely, tapered fingers. I loved my mother's careworn hands better.

Since I could not understand English, I could not comprehend the conversation between Father and the kind woman in black. Later I learned she was the superior at the school. When my father was ready to leave, I screamed, kicked, and clung to him, begging to go home. This had always worked before, but now his eyes grew dim and he gently handed me to the sister and shamelessly ran out the door. When the sister tried to calm me, I screamed all the louder and kicked her. She picked me up off the floor and marched me into a dark closet under the long stairway to scream as loud as I could. She left me to sob myself to sleep. This cured my temper.

I was too young to understand. I did not know English, and the other girls were forbidden to speak any native language. I was very much alone. Most of the time I played with wooden blocks and the youngest girls. I did not attend much school.

Each morning the children got up and dressed to attend church before breakfast. We walked in a double row along the path that climbed the slope to the large church, where my parents came for feast days. We entered the church from the west side door as the boys entered from the east one. The few adults came through the front double doors. There was also a small school chapel that we used when the weather was too bad to march outside.

Our dormitory had three rows of single iron beds, covered every day with white spreads and stiff-starched pillow shams that we folded each night and laid on a small stand beside the bed. Every Sunday night we were issued spotlessly clean nighties. This was the first nightgown I ever wore. Previously, I had slept in all my clothes.

Our dining hall, called the refectory, looked big to me, perhaps because I was used to eating in a cramped space. I was afraid of falling off the chair and always waited for others to sit first. The tables were lined up close to the walls, and the sister in charge had her table in the center, where she served our food on white enamel plates. We brought them up to her empty and carried them back full. Then we all waited until she rang the bell to begin eating.

The school ran strictly. We never talked during meals without permission, given only on Sunday or special holidays. Otherwise there was silence—a terrible silent silence. I was used to the freedom of the forest, and it was hard to learn this strict discipline. I was punished many times before I learned.

I stayed at the mission for less than a year because I took ill and father had to come and take me to the family camp at Kettle Falls. People were catching late salmon and eel. I returned to the mission again until my mother died in 1902 and I went home to care for my siblings. . . .

My second stay at the school was less traumatic. I was anxious to learn more English and read. The school had been enlarged, with much larger buildings adjoining the old ones. The old chicken yard was moved farther away from the hospital windows. There was a fine white modern building, with a full veranda along the front, for the white students who paid fifteen dollars a month to board there. Although they were next door, we never met them; it was as if we lived in different worlds. They had their own playroom, refectory, classrooms, and dormitory. We only saw them in church, when they filed in ahead of us and sat in front of the guardian sisters. Our own teachers sat on long benches behind our rows. The only white girls we got to know were the charity orphans who boarded with us.

The paying boarders got school tuition, books, meals, and free music lessons for their money. This price was so low that many white families around Marcus, Meyers Falls, Colville, and Chewelah sent their children to Goodwin. Native children only went as far as the lower grades, but some had the privilege of attending more academic grades in the classroom of the white girls. Only two girls ever did this, and they were both white charity cases. Some Indian children studied music free, learning piano and organ. We all learned to sing church hymns. Eva, the chunky little daughter of Bridgett Lemere, became a fine organist and choir leader at the Pia Mission. She had a beautiful voice, and her fingers flew over the keys so lightly that the sacred music would ring through the building. Her sister Annie was a few years older than I and became my chum. I stayed away from the girls my own age because my whole life was spent around older people, except for my sisters. . . .

I was very interested in my work. With the knowledge Jimmy Ryan[1] had taught me from his yellowback novels, I passed first grade during the first semester. After my promotion the sisters had no second reader, so I had to study out of the third-year one. My marks were so good in all classes but grammar, which I never could understand, that I graduated at third level. I worked hard on catechism, which Mother had taught me in the native language. When I passed, I made my first communion in the big church, with many younger girls, including Eva and Annie Lemere. Our white dresses and shoes were supplied by the sisters. We wore flowing veils with flowered wreaths to hold them in place. It was Easter morning of 1899. We filed back to the convent, and the sisters gave us a big banquet with many goodies. It was a memorable day, and I thoroughly believed in the Catholic creed. I honored it as much as my native tutor had taught me to revere the ancient traditions of my forebears. I saw no difference between them and never questioned the priest.

I was so enthusiastic that I promised the sisters and girls I would come back in the fall. We were dismissed in June on the feast of Corpus Christi, always a big event in our year.

I never got back to Goodwin, however. Mother had a son, christened Johnny, whom I had to take care of because the duties of the ranch took much of her time. I began secretly to read Jimmy's books. My parents scolded and rebuked me many times because they thought reading was an excuse for being idle. There was much work to be done around the cabin and in the fields.

One day I heard about the Tonasket Indian School, where the Pierre children went to school. I begged Mother to go, but she replied in agitated tones, "Do you want to know too much, and be like the other schoolgirls around here? They come home from school and have no shame for their good character. That is all girls learn in government schools—running around and exposing their bodies." I ran outside into the rosebushes and cried in bitter humiliation. I wanted to go to school and learn the Mysteries of books. My meager education was just enough to make out the simplest words. Jimmy Ryan was only a little better, but he could speak English well.

READING AND DISCUSSION QUESTIONS

1. Describe Mourning Dove's experiences at school. What can you infer about the school's educational goals, practices, and policies with respect to Native American children?

2. What conclusions can you draw about Mourning Dove's attitude toward the education she received at the boarding school? To what extent did her native traditions exist alongside the culture of whites she was expected to embrace?

---

[1]**Jimmy Ryan**: A young Irish boy adopted by Mourning Dove's parents. He shared his collection of cheap dime novels, from which she learned to read.

▪ COMPARATIVE QUESTIONS ▪

1. How do the decades following the Civil War compare to the 1840s as two periods of expansionism? Were the motivations similar or different?

2. Compare the history of white–American Indian relations during the 1870s to the point of view expressed by Thomas Hariot (Document 1-1) and the Reverend Father Louis Cellot (Document 2-6). How do these documents show continuity or change in attitudes toward Native Americans?

3. To what extent do the multiple perspectives in this chapter support or challenge the argument that railroads and western expansion represented positive developments in the history of the United States?

4. Compare the image of "the west" that emerges from these sources with earlier sources such as *The Panoplist and Missionary Herald* (Document 7-4) and Lansford Hastings's *Emigrant's Guide* (Document 13-1). Explain how these documents reveal a diversity of perspective about the region as a land of opportunity, a hazard to life and limb, or a bit of both depending on one's experience.

5. Compare the artist's perspective in *Across the Continent* with the point of view expressed by the artist depicting the Erie Canal (Document 8-1). What historical patterns of continuity and change are suggested by these two images?

Americans Debate the Meaning of the Constitution

1844–1877

The Civil War era was driven by themes of politics and power. The political crisis over slavery and territorial expansion that surfaced in the wake of the war with Mexico engaged reformers, politicians, and ordinary Americans in heated debates over the true meaning of the Constitution, the relationship between federal and state government, and the definition of citizenship. The outbreak of war in 1861 was evidence of the failure of those debates to reach agreement. While many no doubt harbored a hope that the Union victory had settled accounts, fundamental disagreements persisted into the Reconstruction era and linger even today. Different political and social groups during these years competed for influence, shaping political institutions and values, and contested the meaning of citizenship. The status of enslaved African Americans was, of course, central to these debates, but so too were the rights of women and Native Americans and the participation of immigrant groups who diversified the nation's growing population. In the boisterous democracy of the mid-nineteenth century, all those who called America home were caught up in the deafening argument over the values shaping the political system and the part they were to play in strengthening the political process.

P5-1 | Women Reformers Demand Citizenship Rights

ELIZABETH CADY STANTON, *Declaration of Rights and Sentiments* (1848)

In 1848, the basic rights of citizenship guaranteed in the Constitution were denied to half of the population on account of their sex. Women could not exercise the right to vote, and they enjoyed limited legal rights to property. They were excluded by custom and barred by law from certain professions and suffered discrimination in wages. Elizabeth Cady Stanton and other reformers convened a meeting in Seneca Falls, New York, in 1848 to organize a protest of society's narrow interpretation of female citizenship under the Constitution. Using the model of Jefferson's Declaration of Independence, Stanton and ninety-nine others signed the Declaration of Rights and Sentiments, thereby focusing the debate on the meaning of citizenship for women.

When, in the course of human events, it becomes necessary for one portion of the family of man to assume among the people of the earth a position different from that which they have hitherto occupied, but one to which the laws of nature and of nature's God entitle them, a decent respect to the opinions of mankind requires that they should declare the causes that impel them to such a course.

We hold these truths to be self-evident: that all men and women are created equal; that they are endowed by their Creator with certain inalienable rights; that among these are life, liberty, and the pursuit of happiness; that to secure these rights governments are instituted, deriving their just powers from the consent of the governed. Whenever any form of government becomes destructive of these ends, it is the right of those who suffer from it to refuse allegiance to it, and to insist upon the institution of a new government, laying its foundation on such principles, and organizing its powers in such form, as to them shall seem most likely to effect their safety and happiness. Prudence, indeed, will dictate that governments long established should not be changed for light and transient causes; and accordingly all experience hath shown that mankind are more disposed to suffer while evils are sufferable, than to right themselves by abolishing the forms to which they are accustomed. But when a long train of abuses and usurpations, pursuing invariably the same object, evinces a design to reduce them under absolute despotism, it is their duty to throw off such government, and to provide new guards for their future security. Such has been the patient sufferance of the women under this government, and such is now the necessity which constrains them to demand the equal station to which they are entitled. The history of mankind is a history of repeated injuries and usurpations on the part of man toward woman, having in direct object the establishment of an absolute tyranny over her. To prove this, let facts be submitted to a candid world.

He has never permitted her to exercise her inalienable right to the elective franchise.

Elizabeth Cady Stanton, *A History of Woman Suffrage*, vol. 1 (Rochester, NY: Fowler and Wells, 1889), 70–71.

He has compelled her to submit to laws, in the formation of which she had no voice.

He has withheld from her rights which are given to the most ignorant and degraded men—both natives and foreigners.

Having deprived her of this first right of a citizen, the elective franchise, thereby leaving her without representation in the halls of legislation, he has oppressed her on all sides.

He has made her, if married, in the eye of the law, civilly dead.

He has taken from her all right in property, even to the wages she earns.

He has made her, morally, an irresponsible being, as she can commit many crimes with impunity, provided they be done in the presence of her husband. In the covenant of marriage, she is compelled to promise obedience to her husband, he becoming, to all intents and purposes, her master—the law giving him power to deprive her of her liberty, and to administer chastisement.

He has so framed the laws of divorce, as to what shall be the proper causes of divorce; in case of separation, to whom the guardianship of the children shall be given; as to be wholly regardless of the happiness of women—the law, in all cases, going upon a false supposition of the supremacy of man, and giving all power into his hands.

After depriving her of all rights as a married woman, if single, and the owner of property, he has taxed her to support a government which recognizes her only when her property can be made profitable to it.

He has monopolized nearly all the profitable employments, and from those she is permitted to follow, she receives but a scanty remuneration.

He closes against her all the avenues to wealth and distinction which he considers most honorable to himself. As a teacher of theology, medicine, or law, she is not known.

He has denied her the facilities for obtaining a thorough education—all colleges being closed against her.

He allows her in Church, as well as State, but a subordinate position, claiming Apostolic authority for her exclusion from the ministry, and, with some exceptions, from any public participation in the affairs of the Church.

He has created a false public sentiment, by giving to the world a different code of morals for men and women, by which moral delinquencies which exclude women from society, are not only tolerated, but deemed of little account in man.

He has usurped the prerogative of Jehovah himself, claiming it as his right to assign for her a sphere of action, when that belongs to her conscience and to her God.

He has endeavored, in every way that he could, to destroy her confidence in her own powers, to lessen her self-respect, and to make her willing to lead a dependent and abject life.

Now, in view of this entire disfranchisement of one-half the people of this country, their social and religious degradation,—in view of the unjust laws above mentioned, and because women do feel themselves aggrieved, oppressed, and fraudulently deprived of their most sacred rights, we insist that they have immediate admission to all the rights and privileges which belong to them as citizens of the United States.

In entering upon the great work before us, we anticipate no small amount of misconception, misrepresentation, and ridicule; but we shall use every instrumentality within our power to effect our object. We shall employ agents, circulate tracts, petition the state and national legislatures, and endeavor to enlist the pulpit and the press in our behalf. We hope this Convention will be followed by a series of Conventions, embracing every part of the country. . . .

Resolutions

Whereas the great precept of nature is conceded to be, "that man shall pursue his own true and substantial happiness." Blackstone,[1] in his Commentaries, remarks, that this law of Nature being coeval with mankind, and dictated by God himself, is of course superior in obligation to any other. It is binding over all the globe, in all countries, and at all times; no human laws are of any validity if contrary to this, and such of them as are valid, derive all their force, and all their validity, and all their authority, mediately and immediately, from this original; therefore,

Resolved, That such laws as conflict, in any way, with the true and substantial happiness of woman, are contrary to the great precept of nature, and of no validity; for this is "superior in obligation to any other."

Resolved, That all laws which prevent woman from occupying such a station in society as her conscience shall dictate, or which place her in a position inferior to that of man, are contrary to the great precept of nature, and therefore of no force or authority.

Resolved, That woman is man's equal—was intended to be so by the Creator—and the highest good of the race demands that she should be recognized as such.

Resolved, That the women of this country ought to be enlightened in regard to the laws under which they live, that they may no longer publish their degradation, by declaring themselves satisfied with their present position, nor their ignorance, by asserting that they have all the rights they want.

Resolved, That inasmuch as man, while claiming for himself intellectual superiority, does accord to woman moral superiority, it is pre-eminently his duty to encourage her to speak, and teach, as she has an opportunity, in all religious assemblies.

Resolved, That the same amount of virtue, delicacy, and refinement of behavior, that is required of woman in the social state, should also be required of man, and the same transgressions should be visited with equal severity on both man and woman.

---

[1]Sir William Blackstone, English jurist, published volume 1 of his *Commentaries on the Laws of England* in 1766, which became the most authoritative scholarly overview of English common law, influencing American legal thinkers through the nineteenth century.

Resolved, That the objection of indelicacy and impropriety, which is so often brought against woman when she addresses a public audience, comes with a very ill-grace from those who encourage, by their attendance, her appearance on the stage, in the concert, or in the feats of the circus.

Resolved, That woman has too long rested satisfied in the circumscribed limits which corrupt customs and a perverted application of the Scriptures have marked out for her, and that it is time she should move in the enlarged sphere which her great Creator has assigned her.

Resolved, That it is the duty of the women of this country to secure to themselves their sacred right to the elective franchise.

Resolved, That the equality of human rights results necessarily from the fact of the identity of the race in capabilities and responsibilities.

Resolved, therefore, That, being invested by the Creator with the same capabilities, and the same consciousness of responsibility for their exercise, it is demonstrably the right and duty of woman, equally with man, to promote every righteous cause, by every righteous means; and especially in regard to the great subjects of morals and religion, it is self-evidently her right to participate with her brother in teaching them, both in private and in public, by writing and by speaking, by any instrumentalities proper to be used, and in any assemblies proper to be held; and this being a self-evident truth, growing out of the divinely implanted principles of human nature, any custom or authority adverse to it, whether modern or wearing the hoary sanction of antiquity, is to be regarded as self-evident falsehood, and at war with the interests of mankind.

READING AND DISCUSSION QUESTIONS

1. Analyze the efforts of the Seneca Falls delegates to define and gain access to individual rights and citizenship for women. What definition of citizenship did they embrace for women?

2. What impact on the interpretation of constitutional rights do you think these women expected their reforms to provoke?

P5-2 | Defining Native American Rights and Limits

STATUTES OF CALIFORNIA, *An Act for the Government and Protection of Indians* (1850)

California entered the Union on September 9, 1850, having ratified its state constitution the year before forbidding slavery and declaring that "all men are by nature free and independent." Thus it embraced the rhetoric of the U.S. Constitution. However, on April 22, 1850,

---

Compiled Laws of the State of California: Containing all the Acts of the Legislature of a Public and General Nature, Now in Force, Passed at the Sessions of 1850–51–52–53, comp. S. Garfielde and F. A. Snyder (Boston: Press of the Franklin Printing House, 1853), 822–825.

more than four months before officially entering the Union, the state Senate and Assembly passed legislation ostensibly for the protection of Native Americans that in reality restricted them, evidence of the state's narrow and exclusive interpretation of Bill of Rights protections.

The People of the State of California, represented in Senate and Assembly, do enact as follows:

SECTION 1. Justices of the Peace shall have jurisdiction in all cases of complaints by, for or against Indians, in their respective townships in this State.

SEC. 2. Persons and proprietors of land on which Indians are residing, shall permit such Indians peaceably to reside on such lands, unmolested in the pursuit of their usual avocations for the maintenance of themselves and families: Provided; the white person or proprietor in possession of lands may apply to a justice of the peace in the township where the Indians reside, to set off to such Indians a certain amount of land, and, on such application, the justice shall set off a sufficient amount of land for the necessary wants of such Indians, including the site of their village or residence, if they so prefer it; and in no case shall such selection be made to the prejudice of such Indians, nor shall they be forced to abandon their homes or villages where they have resided for a number of years; and either party feeling themselves aggrieved, can appeal to the county court from the decision of the justice: and then divided, a record shall be made of the lands so set off in the court so dividing them, and the Indians shall be permitted to remain thereon until otherwise provided for.

SEC. 3. Any person having or hereafter obtaining a minor Indian, male or female, from the parents or relations of such Indian minor, and wishing to keep it, such person shall go before a justice of the peace in his township, with the parents or friends of the child, and if the justice of the peace becomes satisfied that no compulsory means have been used to obtain the child from its parents or friends, shall enter on record, in a book kept for that purpose, the sex and probable age of the child, and shall give to such person a certificate, authorizing him or her to have the care, custody, control, and earnings of such minor, until he or she attain the age of majority. Every male Indian shall be deemed to have attained his majority at eighteen, and the female at fifteen years.

SEC. 4. Any person having a minor Indian in his care, as described in the foregoing section of this act, who shall neglect to clothe and suitably feed such minor Indian, or shall inhumanely treat him or her, on conviction thereof shall be subject to a fine not less than ten dollars, at the discretion of a court or jury; and the justice of the peace, in his own discretion, may place the minor Indian in the care of some other person, giving him the same rights and liabilities that the former master of said minor was entitled and subject to.

SEC. 5. Any person wishing to hire an Indian, shall go before a justice of the peace with the Indian, and make such contract as the justice may approve, and the justice shall file such contract in writing in his office, and all contracts so made shall be binding between the parties; but no contract between a white man and an Indian, for labor shall otherwise be obligatory on the part of the Indian.

SEC. 6. Complaints may be made before a justice of the peace, by white persons or Indians; but in no case shall a white man be convicted on any offence upon the testimony of an Indian, or Indians. And in all cases it shall be discretionary with the court or jury after hearing the complaint of an Indian.

SEC. 7. If any person forcibly conveys any Indian from his home, or compels him to work, or perform any service against his will, in this state, except as provided in this act, he or they shall, on conviction, be fined in any sum not less than fifty dollars, at the discretion of the court or jury.

SEC. 8. It shall be the duty of the justices of the peace, once in six months in every year, to make a full and correct statement to the court of sessions of their county, of all moneys received for fines imposed on Indians . . . and the treasurer shall keep a correct statement of all money so received, which shall be termed the "Indian fund" of the county. The treasurer shall pay out any money of said funds in his hands . . . for fees and expenditures incurred in carrying out the provisions of this law.

SEC. 9. It shall be the duty of the justices of the peace, in their respective townships, as well as all other peace officers in this state, to instruct the Indians in their neighborhood in the laws which relate to them, giving them such advice as they may deem necessary and proper; and if any tribe or village of Indians refuse or neglect to obey the laws, the justice of the peace may punish the guilty chiefs or principal men by reprimand or fine, or otherwise reasonably chastise them.

SEC. 10. If any person or persons shall set the prairie on fire, or refuse to use proper exertions to extinguish the fire when the prairies are burning, such persons shall be subject to fine or punishment, as court may adjudge proper.

SEC. 11. If any Indian shall commit an unlawful offence against a white person, such person shall not inflict punishment for such offence, but may, without process, take the Indian before a justice of the peace, and, on conviction, the Indian shall be punished according to the provisions of this act.

SEC. 12. In all cases of trial between a white man and an Indian, either party may require a jury.

SEC. 13. Justices may require the chiefs and influential men of any village to apprehend and bring before them or him any Indian charged or suspected of an offence.

SEC. 14. When an Indian is convicted of an offence before a justice of the peace punishable by fine, any white person may, by consent of the justice, give bond for said Indian, conditioned for the payment of said fine and costs, and in such case the Indian shall be compelled to work for the person so bailing, until he has discharged or cancelled the fine assessed against him: Provided; the person bailing shall treat the Indian humanely, and feed and clothe him properly; the allowance given for such labor shall be fixed by the Court, when the bond is taken.

SEC. 15. If any person in this State shall sell, give, or furnish to any Indian, male or female, any intoxicating liquors (except when administered for sickness), for good cause shown, he, she, or they so offending shall, on conviction thereof, be fined not less than twenty dollars for each offence, or be imprisoned not less than five days, or fined and imprisoned as the court may determine.

SEC. 16. An Indian convicted of stealing horses, mules, cattle, or any valuable thing, shall be subject to receive any number of lashes not exceeding twenty-five, or shall be subject to a fine not exceeding two hundred dollars, at the discretion of the court or jury.

SEC. 17. When an Indian is sentenced to be whipped, the justice may appoint a white man, or an Indian at his discretion, to execute the sentence in his presence, and shall not permit unnecessary cruelty in the execution of the sentence.

SEC. 18. All fines, forfeitures, penalties recovered under or by this act, shall be paid into the treasury of the county, to the credit of the Indian fund as provided in section eight.

SEC. 19. All white persons making application to a justice of the peace, for confirmation of a contract with or in relation to an Indian, shall pay the fee, which shall not exceed two dollars for each contract determined and filed as provided in this act, and for all other services, such fees are allowed for similar services under other laws of this state: Provided, the application fee for hiring Indians, or keeping minors, and fees and expenses for setting off lands to Indians, shall be paid by the white person applying.

SEC. 20. Any Indian able to work and support himself in some honest calling, not having wherewithal to maintain himself, who shall be found loitering and strolling about, or frequenting public places where liquors are sold, begging, or leading an immoral or profligate course of life, shall be liable to be arrested on the complaint of any resident citizen of the county, and brought before the justice of the peace of the proper county, mayor or recorder of any incorporated town or city, who shall examine said accused Indian, and hear the testimony in relation thereto, and if said justice, mayor, or recorder shall be satisfied that he is a vagrant . . . he shall make out a warrant under his hand and seal, authorizing and requiring the officer having him in charge or custody, to hire out such vagrant within twenty-four hours to the highest bidder.

READING AND DISCUSSION QUESTIONS

1. What can you infer about the values that guided the political system in 1850s California with respect to citizenship rights for whites and Native Americans?

2. What do these provisions directed to Native Americans tell you about the conflicting interpretation and application of rights guaranteed by the U.S. Constitution? How did California legislators interpret those Bill of Rights protections as applied to American Indians in California?

P5-3 | The Catholic Threat to American Politics

SAMUEL F. B. MORSE, *Foreign Conspiracy Against the Liberties of the United States* (1855)

European immigration was on the rise in the 1830s, when Samuel Morse published in book form his editorials first serialized in the *New York Observer*. By the time the seventh edition was published in the mid-1850s, immigration had increased even more, spurred on by the revolutions in Europe in 1848. Morse, who is better known for the telegraphic code he invented, was a nativist who justified his opposition to Catholic immigration as a defense of constitutional liberties and republican government against papal conspiracies directed from Rome. His understanding of the Constitution powered such antebellum political movements as the Nativist or Know-Nothing Party of the 1840s and 1850s.

[S]ome of my readers . . . may be inclined to ask in what manner can the despots of Europe effect, by means of Popish emissaries, any thing in this country to counteract the influence of our liberal institutions? In what way can they operate here?

With the *necessity existing of doing something, from the instinct of self-preservation*, to check the influence of our free institutions on Europe, with the *funds* provided, and *agents* on the spot interested in their plans, one would think it needed but little sagacity to find modes and opportunities of operating; especially, too, when such *vulnerable points* as I have exposed (and there are many more which I have not brought forward) invite attack.

To any such inquirers, let me say there are many ways in which a body organized as are the Catholics, and moving in concert, might *disturb* (to use the mildest term) the good order of the republic, and thus compel us to present to observing Europe the spectacle of republican anarchy. Who is not aware that a great portion of that stuff which composes a mob, ripe for riot or excess of any kind, and of which we have every week or two a fresh example in some part of the country, is a Catholic population? And what makes it turbulent? Ignorance — an ignorance which it is for the interest of its leaders not to enlighten; for, enlighten a man, and he will think for himself, and have some self-respect; he will understand the laws, and know his interest in obeying them. Keep him in ignorance, and he is the slave of the man who will flatter his passions and appetites, or awe him by superstitious fears. Against the outbreakings of such men, society, as it is constituted on our free system, can protect itself only in one of two ways: it must either bring these men under the influence and control of a sound republican and religious education, or it must call in the aid of *the priests* who govern them, and who may *permit* and *direct*, or *restrain* their turbulence, in accordance with what they may judge at any particular time to be the *interest of the church.* Yes, be it well remarked, the same hands that can, whenever it suits

Samuel F. B. Morse, *Foreign Conspiracy Against the Liberties of the United States* (New York: American and Foreign Christian Union, 1855), 89–96, 98–99.

their interest, *restrain*, can also, at the proper time, *"let slip the dogs of war."* In this mode of restraint by a *police of priests*, by substituting the *ecclesiastical* for the *civil* power, the *priest-led* mobs of Portugal and Spain, and South America, are instructive examples. And start not, American reader, *this kind of police is already established in our country!* We have had mobs again and again, which neither the civil nor military power have availed any thing to quell, until the magic *"peace, be still,"* of the *Catholic priest* has hushed the winds, and calmed the waves of popular tumult. . . .

And what now prevents the interference of Catholics, as a sect, directly in the *political elections* of the country? They are organized under their priests: is there any thing in their religious principles to restrain them? Do not Catholics of the present day use the bonds of religious union to effect political objects in other countries? . . .

It is not true that Popery meddles not with the politics of the country. The cloven foot has already shown itself. *Popery is organized at the elections!* For example: in Michigan, the Bishop Richard, a Jesuit (since deceased), was several times chosen delegate to Congress from the territory, the majority of the people being Catholics. As Protestants became more numerous, the contest between the bishop and his Protestant rival was more and more close, until at length, by the increase of Protestant emigration, the latter triumphed. The bishop, in order to detect any delinquency in his flock at the polls, *had his ticket printed on colored paper!* . . . Does it not show that Popery, with all its speciousness, is the same here as elsewhere? It manifests, when it has the opportunity, its genuine disposition to use *spiritual* power for the promotion of its *temporal* ambition. It uses its ecclesiastical weapons to control an election. . . .

It is unnecessary to multiply facts of this nature. . . . Surely American Protestants . . . will see that Popery is now, what it has ever been, a system of the darkest *political* intrigue and despotism, cloaking itself, to avoid attack, under the sacred name of religion. They will be deeply impressed with the truth, that Popery is a political as well as a religious system; that in this respect it differs totally from all other sects, from all other forms of religion in the country. *Popery imbodies in itself* THE CLOSEST UNION OF CHURCH AND STATE. . . .

Can we not discern the *political* character of Popery? Shall the name of *Religion*, artfully connected with it, still blind our eyes? Let us suppose a body of men to combine together, and claim as their right, that *all public and private property, of whatever kind, is held at their disposal; that they alone are to judge of their own right to dispose of it; that they alone are authorized to think or speak on the subject; that they who speak or write in opposition to them are traitors, and must be put to death; that all temporal power is secondary to theirs, and amenable to their superior and infallible judgment;* and the better to hide the presumption of these tyrannical claims, suppose that these men should pretend to *divine right*, and call their system *Religion*, and so claim the protection of our laws, and pleading *conscience*, demand to be tolerated. Would the name of *Religion* be a cloak sufficiently thick to hide such absurdity, and shield it from public indignation? Take, then, from *Popery* its name of *Religion*; strip its *officers* of their pompous titles of *sacredness*, and its *decrees* of the nauseous cant of piety, and what have you remaining? Is it not a *naked, odious Despotism,* depending for its strength on the observance of the strictest military discipline in its ranks, from the Pope, through his Cardinals, Archbishops, Bishops, &c. down to the lowest priest of his dominions? And is not this despotism acting *politically* in this country? . . .

What is the difference between the *real* claims, and efforts, and condition of Popery at this moment in these United States, and the *supposed* claims, and efforts, and condition of the Russian despotism? The one comes disguised under the name of *Religion,* the other, more honest and more harmless, would come in its real *political* name. Give the latter the name of *Religion,* call the *Emperor, Pope,* and his *Viceroys, Bishops,* interlard the *imperial decrees* with *pious cant,* and you have the case of pretension, and intrigue, and success, too, which has actually passed in these United States! Yes, the King of Rome, acting by the promptings of the Austrian Cabinet, and in the plentitude of his usurpation, has already extended his sceptre over our land; he has divided us up into provinces, and appointed his Viceroys, who claim their *jurisdiction* from a higher power than exists in this country, even from his majesty himself, who appoints them, who removes them at will, to whom they owe allegiance; for the extension of whose temporal kingdom they are exerting themselves, and whose success, let it be indelibly impressed on your minds, is the *certain destruction of the free institutions of our country.*

READING AND DISCUSSION QUESTIONS

1. How does Morse's argument about the Catholic threat to America provide evidence for the impact of anti-immigrant ideas on the political system? What social effect might his efforts to limit participation by Catholics have had on antebellum American politics?

2. Why do you think his ideas about the Constitution's vulnerabilities toward Catholic influence found a receptive audience?

P5-4 | Debating the Meaning of the Constitution

ABRAHAM LINCOLN, *Cooper Union Address* (1860)

In 1860, the clear point of contention between Republicans and Democrats was the authority of Congress to regulate slavery within the territories. Illinois senator Stephen Douglas, whom Lincoln had famously debated in 1858, promoted the idea of "popular sovereignty" whereby voters would decide the fate of slavery in a territory, claiming the founding fathers had endorsed such a policy in the Constitution. Lincoln's meticulous rejoinder in his Cooper Union address in New York City argued instead that the founders had acknowledged Congress's duty to regulate slavery in the territories. A minor political figure before the speech, Lincoln's New

www.abrahamlincolnonline.org/lincoln/speeches/cooper.htm.

York triumph propelled him to the front ranks of Republican Party politics, leading later that year to his nomination for president.

The facts with which I shall deal this evening are mainly old and familiar; nor is there anything new in the general use I shall make of them. If there shall be any novelty, it will be in the mode of presenting the facts, and the inferences and observations following that presentation.

In his speech last autumn, at Columbus, Ohio, as reported in "The New-York Times," Senator Douglas said:

"Our fathers, when they framed the Government under which we live, understood this question just as well, and even better, than we do now."

I fully indorse this, and I adopt it as a text for this discourse. I so adopt it because it furnishes a precise and an agreed starting point for a discussion between Republicans and that wing of the Democracy headed by Senator Douglas. It simply leaves the inquiry: "What was the understanding those fathers had of the question mentioned?"

What is the frame of government under which we live?

The answer must be: "The Constitution of the United States." That Constitution consists of the original, framed in 1787 (and under which the present government first went into operation), and twelve subsequently framed amendments, the first ten of which were framed in 1789.

Who were our fathers that framed the Constitution? I suppose the "thirty-nine" who signed the original instrument may be fairly called our fathers who framed that part of the present Government. It is almost exactly true to say they framed it, and it is altogether true to say they fairly represented the opinion and sentiment of the whole nation at that time. Their names, being familiar to nearly all, and accessible to quite all, need not now be repeated.

I take these "thirty-nine," for the present, as being "our fathers who framed the Government under which we live."

What is the question which, according to the text, those fathers understood "just as well, and even better than we do now"?

It is this: Does the proper division of local from federal authority, or anything in the Constitution, forbid our *Federal Government* to control as to slavery in *our Federal Territories*?

Upon this, Senator Douglas holds the affirmative, and Republicans the negative. This affirmation and denial form an issue; and this issue — this question — is precisely what the text declares our fathers understood "better than we."

Let us now inquire whether the "thirty-nine," or any of them, ever acted upon this question; and if they did, how they acted upon it — how they expressed that better understanding?

In 1784, three years before the Constitution — the United States then owning the Northwestern Territory, and no other, the Congress of the Confederation had before them the question of prohibiting slavery in that Territory; and four of the "thirty-nine" who afterward framed the Constitution, were in that Congress, and voted on that question. Of these, Roger Sherman, Thomas Mifflin, and Hugh

Williamson voted for the prohibition, thus showing that, in their understanding, no line dividing local from federal authority, nor anything else, properly forbade the Federal Government to control as to slavery in federal territory. . . .

In 1787, still before the Constitution . . . the same question of prohibiting slavery in the territory again came before the Congress of the Confederation; and two more of the "thirty-nine" who afterward signed the Constitution . . . both voted for the prohibition—thus showing that, in their understanding, no line dividing local from federal authority, nor anything else, properly forbids the Federal Government to control as to slavery in Federal territory. . . .

In 1789, by the first Congress which sat under the Constitution, an act was passed to enforce the Ordinance of '87, including the prohibition of slavery in the Northwestern Territory. The bill . . . passed both branches without yeas and nays, which is equivalent to a unanimous passage. In this Congress there were sixteen of the thirty-nine fathers who framed the original Constitution. . . .

This shows that, in their understanding, no line dividing local from federal authority, nor anything in the Constitution, properly forbade Congress to prohibit slavery in the federal territory; else both their fidelity to correct principle, and their oath to support the Constitution, would have constrained them to oppose the prohibition.

Again, George Washington, another of the "thirty-nine," was then President of the United States, and, as such approved and signed the bill; thus completing its validity as a law, and thus showing that, in his understanding, no line dividing local from federal authority, nor anything in the Constitution, forbade the Federal Government, to control as to slavery in federal territory. . . .

In 1803, the Federal Government purchased the Louisiana country. . . . Congress did not, in the Territorial Act, prohibit slavery; but they did interfere with it—take control of it—in a more marked and extensive way than they did in the case of Mississippi. The substance of the provision therein made, in relation to slaves, was:

First. That no slave should be imported into the territory from foreign parts.

Second. That no slave should be carried into it who had been imported into the United States since the first day of May, 1798.

Third. That no slave should be carried into it, except by the owner, and for his own use as a settler; the penalty in all the cases being a fine upon the violator of the law, and freedom to the slave. . . .

In the Congress which passed it, there were two of the "thirty-nine." . . . They would not have allowed it to pass without recording their opposition to it, if, in their understanding, it violated either the line properly dividing local from federal authority, or any provision of the Constitution. . . .

The cases I have mentioned are the only acts of the "thirty-nine," or of any of them, upon the direct issue, which I have been able to discover. . . .

The sum of the whole is, that of our thirty-nine fathers who framed the original Constitution, twenty-one—a clear majority of the whole—certainly understood that no proper division of local from federal authority, nor any part of the Constitution, forbade the Federal Government to control slavery in the federal territories; while all the rest probably had the same understanding. Such, unquestionably, was the understanding of our fathers who framed the original Constitution; and the text affirms that they understood the question "better than we." . . .

But enough! *Let all who believe that "our fathers, who framed the Government under which we live, understood this question just as well, and even better, than we do now," speak as they spoke, and act as they acted upon it. This is all Republicans ask—all Republicans desire—in relation to slavery. As those fathers marked it, so let it be again marked, as an evil not to be extended, but to be tolerated and protected only because of and so far as its actual presence among us makes that toleration and protection a necessity. Let all the guarantees those fathers gave it, be, not grudgingly, but fully and fairly, main-tained.* For this Republicans contend, and with this, so far as I know or believe, they will be content.

And now, if they would listen—as I suppose they will not—I would address a few words to the Southern people. . . .

You say we are sectional. We deny it. That makes an issue; and the burden of proof is upon you. You produce your proof; and what is it? Why, that our party has no existence in your section—gets no votes in your section. The fact is sub-stantially true; but does it prove the issue? . . . The fact that we get no votes in your section, is a fact of your making, and not of ours. And if there be fault in that fact, that fault is primarily yours, and remains until you show that we repel you by some wrong principle or practice. . . . Do you accept the challenge? No! Then you really believe that the principle which "our fathers who framed the Govern-ment under which we live" thought so clearly right as to adopt it, and indorse it again and again, upon their official oaths, is in fact so clearly wrong as to demand your condemnation without a moment's consideration.

Some of you delight to flaunt in our faces the warning against sectional parties given by Washington in his Farewell Address. Less than eight years before Washington gave that warning, he had, as President of the United States, approved and signed an act of Congress, enforcing the prohibition of slavery in the Northwestern Territory, which act embodied the policy of the Government upon that subject up to and at the very moment he penned that warning; and about one year after he penned it, he wrote LaFayette[1] that he considered that prohibition a wise measure, expressing in the same connection his hope that we should at some time have a confederacy of free States. . . .

Again, you say we have made the slavery question more prominent than it formerly was. We deny it. We admit that it is more prominent, but we deny that we made it so. It was not we, but you, who discarded the old policy of the fathers. We resisted, and still resist, your innovation; and thence comes the greater prom-inence of the question. Would you have that question reduced to its former pro-portions? Go back to that old policy. What has been will be again, under the same

---

[1]**LaFayette**: Marquis de Lafayette was a French aristocrat who served with Washington as a major general in the Continental army during the American Revolution.

conditions. If you would have the peace of the old times, readopt the precepts and policy of the old times.

You charge that we stir up insurrections among your slaves. We deny it; and what is your proof? Harper's Ferry! John Brown!! John Brown was no Republican; and you have failed to implicate a single Republican in his Harper's Ferry enterprise. . . .

Under all these circumstances, do you really feel yourselves justified to break up this Government unless such a court decision as yours is, shall be at once submitted to as a conclusive and final rule of political action? But you will not abide the election of a Republican president! In that supposed event, you say, you will destroy the Union; and then, you say, the great crime of having destroyed it will be upon us! That is cool. A highwayman holds a pistol to my ear, and mutters through his teeth, "Stand and deliver, or I shall kill you, and then you will be a murderer!" . . .

A few words now to Republicans. . . .

Wrong as we think slavery is, we can yet afford to let it alone where it is, because that much is due to the necessity arising from its actual presence in the nation; but can we, while our votes will prevent it, allow it to spread into the National Territories, and to overrun us here in these Free States? If our sense of duty forbids this, then let us stand by our duty, fearlessly and effectively. Let us be diverted by none of those sophistical contrivances wherewith we are so industriously plied and belabored—contrivances such as groping for some middle ground between the right and the wrong, vain as the search for a man who should be neither a living man nor a dead man—such as a policy of "don't care" on a question about which all true men do care—such as Union appeals beseeching true Union men to yield to Disunionists, reversing the divine rule, and calling, not the sinners, but the righteous to repentance—such as invocations to Washington, imploring men to unsay what Washington said, and undo what Washington did.

Neither let us be slandered from our duty by false accusations against us, nor frightened from it by menaces of destruction to the Government nor of dungeons to ourselves. LET US HAVE FAITH THAT RIGHT MAKES MIGHT, AND IN THAT FAITH, LET US, TO THE END, DARE TO DO OUR DUTY AS WE UNDERSTAND IT.

READING AND DISCUSSION QUESTIONS

1. Summarize Lincoln's interpretation of the Constitution with respect to the issue of slavery's expansion within federal territories. What impact do you think his views had on southerners in the historical context of the 1850s and 1860s?

2. What argument does Lincoln make about the role of the federal government and its potential as an agent of political change in the context of the slavery issue?

P5-5 | Southern Leader Contrasts Union and Confederate Constitutions

ALEXANDER STEPHENS, *"Cornerstone" Speech* (1861)

The federal and Confederate constitutions that Alexander Stephens described during the secession crisis in March 1861 were a study in contrasts. Whereas Lincoln at Cooper Union had claimed that the Constitution granted Congress the authority to regulate slavery in the territories, Stephens emphasized instead its guarantee of slavery. Regardless, Stephens declared that the federal Constitution rested on flawed assumptions concerning the equality of the races. He therefore championed the new Confederate Constitution for its attachment to what he called "this great physical, philosophical, and moral truth." This truth, which he labeled the cornerstone of the Confederacy, was the inflexible belief in "the Negro's" inferiority.

This new constitution, or form of government, constitutes the subject to which your attention will be partly invited. In reference to it, I make this first general remark. It amply secures all our ancient rights, franchises, and liberties. All the great principles of Magna Charta are retained in it. No citizen is deprived of life, liberty, or property, but by the judgment of his peers under the laws of the land. The great principle of religious liberty, which was the honor and pride of the old constitution, is still maintained and secured. All the essentials of the old constitution, which have endeared it to the hearts of the American people, have been preserved and perpetuated. [Applause.] Some changes have been made. Of these I shall speak presently. Some of these I should have preferred not to have seen made; but these, perhaps, meet the cordial approbation of a majority of this audience, if not an overwhelming majority of the people of the Confederacy. Of them, therefore, I will not speak. But other important changes do meet my cordial approbation. They form great improvements upon the old constitution. So, taking the whole new constitution, I have no hesitancy in giving it as my judgment that it is decidedly better than the old. [Applause.]

Allow me briefly to allude to some of these improvements. The question of building up class interests, or fostering one branch of industry to the prejudice of another under the exercise of the revenue power, which gave us so much trouble under the old constitution, is put at rest forever under the new. We allow the imposition of no duty with a view of giving advantage to one class of persons, in any trade or business, over those of another. All, under our system, stand upon the same broad principles of perfect equality. Honest labor and enterprise are left free and unrestricted in whatever pursuit they may be engaged. . . .

Again, the subject of internal improvements, under the power of Congress to regulate commerce, is put at rest under our system. The power claimed by construction under the old constitution, was at least a doubtful one—it rested solely upon construction. We of the South, generally apart from considerations of

---

Alexander H. Stephens, in Public and Private. With Letters and Speeches, Before, During, and Since the War, ed. Henry Cleveland (Philadelphia: National Publishing Company, 1866), 718–723.

constitutional principles, opposed its exercise upon grounds of its inexpediency and injustice. Notwithstanding this opposition, millions of money, from the common treasury had been drawn for such purposes. Our opposition sprang from no hostility to commerce, or all necessary aids for facilitating it. With us it was simply a question, upon whom the burden should fall. . . .

The true principle is to subject the commerce of every locality, to whatever burdens may be necessary to facilitate it. If Charleston harbor needs improvement, let the commerce of Charleston bear the burden. If the mouth of the Savannah river has to be cleared out, let the sea-going navigation which is benefitted by it, bear the burden. . . . Just as the products of the interior, our cotton, wheat, corn, and other articles, have to bear the necessary rates of freight over our railroads to reach the seas. This is again the broad principle of perfect equality and justice. [Applause.] And it is especially set forth and established in our new constitution. . . .

But not to be tedious in enumerating the numerous changes for the better, allow me to allude to one other — though last, not least. The new constitution has put at rest, *forever,* all the agitating questions relating to our peculiar institution — African slavery as it exists amongst us — the proper *status* of the negro in our form of civilization. This was the immediate cause of the late rupture and present revolution. Jefferson in his forecast, had anticipated this, as the "rock upon which the old Union would split." He was right. What was conjecture with him, is now a realized fact. But whether he fully comprehended the great truth upon which that rock *stood* and *stands,* may be doubted. The prevailing ideas entertained by him and most of the leading statesmen at the time of the formation of the old constitution, were that the enslavement of the African was in violation of the laws of nature; that it was wrong in *principle*, socially, morally, and politically. It was an evil they knew not well how to deal with, but the general opinion of the men of that day was that, somehow or other in the order of Providence, the institution would be evanescent and pass away. This idea, though not incorporated in the constitution, was the prevailing idea at that time. The constitution, it is true, secured every essential guarantee to the institution while it should last, and hence no argument can be justly urged against the constitutional guarantees thus secured, because of the common sentiment of the day. Those ideas, however, were fundamentally wrong. They rested upon the assumption of the equality of races. This was an error. It was a sandy foundation, and the government built upon it fell when the "storm came and the wind blew."

Our new government is founded upon exactly the opposite idea; its foundations are laid, its corner-stone rests upon the great truth, that the negro is not equal to the white man; that slavery — subordination to the superior race — is his natural and normal condition. [Applause.]

This, our new government, is the first, in the history of the world, based upon this great physical, philosophical, and moral truth. This truth has been slow in the process of its development, like all other truths in the various departments of science. It has been so even amongst us. Many who hear me, perhaps, can recollect well, that this truth was not generally admitted, even within their day. The errors of the past generation still clung to many as late as twenty years ago. Those at the North, who still cling to these errors, with a zeal above knowledge, we justly denominate fanatics. All fanaticism springs from an aberration of the mind — from a defect in reasoning. It is a species of insanity. One of the most striking characteristics of insanity, in many instances, is forming correct conclusions from fancied or erroneous premises; so with the anti-slavery fanatics; their conclusions are right if their premises were. They assume that the negro is equal, and hence conclude that he is entitled to equal privileges and rights with the white man. If their premises were correct, their conclusions would be logical and just — but their premise being wrong, their whole argument fails. . . .

May we not, therefore, look with confidence to the ultimate universal acknowledgment of the truths upon which our system rests? It is the first government ever instituted upon the principles in strict conformity to nature, and the ordination of Providence, in furnishing the materials of human society. Many governments have been founded upon the principle of the subordination and serfdom of certain classes of the same race; such were and are in violation of the laws of nature. Our system commits no such violation of nature's laws. With us, all of the white race, however high or low, rich or poor, are equal in the eye of the law. Not so with the negro. Subordination is his place. He, by nature, or by the curse against Canaan, is fitted for that condition which he occupies in our system. The architect, in the construction of buildings, lays the foundation with the proper material — the granite; then comes the brick or the marble. The substratum of our society is made of the material fitted by nature for it, and by experience we know that it is best, not only for the superior, but for the inferior race, that it should be so. It is, indeed, in conformity with the ordinance of the Creator. It is not for us to inquire into the wisdom of his ordinances, or to question them. For his own purposes, he has made one race to differ from another, as he has made "one star to differ from another star in glory."

The great objects of humanity are best attained when there is conformity to his laws and decrees, in the formation of governments as well as in all things else. Our confederacy is founded upon principles in strict conformity with these laws. This stone which was rejected by the first builders "is become the chief of the corner" — the real "corner-stone" — in our new edifice. [Applause.]

READING AND DISCUSSION QUESTIONS

1. Summarize the differences in interpretation that separated Lincoln and Stephens on the question of the federal Constitution's position on slavery and the slavery extension issue. How did these arguments over the meaning of the Constitution affect American politics in the 1850s and 1860s?

2. To what extent do these interpretive differences represent short- or long-term causes of the Civil War?

3. How did the Confederate interpretation of constitutional values, as reflected in Stephens's speech, help southern politicians distinguish their Constitution from the federal Constitution they rejected?

P5-6 | Freedman Claiming the Rights of Citizenship

REV. HENRY MCNEAL TURNER, *Speech Before the Georgia State Legislature* (1868)

Despite the ratification of the Fourteenth and Fifteenth Amendments to the Constitution in 1868 and 1870 respectively, core questions of citizenship remained in dispute for African Americans, who suffered the withering and persistent racism of the era. Some African American men, like the Reverend Henry Turner, won election to state office in the postwar years, but their triumph dimmed under the ridicule and deceit they faced. In his case, the white majority in the Georgia legislature, in a blatant obstruction of the democratic process, expelled Turner from his elected office. Their vote prompted Turner's impassioned speech where he claimed his rights under the Constitution as he read it.

MR. SPEAKER: Before proceeding to argue this question upon its intrinsic merits, I wish the members of this House to understand the position that I take. I hold that I am a member of this body. Therefore, sir, I shall neither fawn nor cringe before any party, nor stoop to beg them for my rights. Some of my colored fellow members, in the course of their remarks, took occasion to appeal to the sympathies of members on the opposite side, and to eulogize their character for magnanimity. It reminds me very much, sir, of slaves begging under the lash. I am here to demand my rights and to hurl thunderbolts at the men who would dare to cross the threshold of my manhood. There is an old aphorism which says, "fight the devil with fire," and if I should observe the rule in this instance, I wish gentlemen to understand that it is but fighting them with their own weapon.

The scene presented in this House, today, is one unparalleled in the history of the world. From this day, back to the day when God breathed the breath of life into Adam, no analogy for it can be found. Never, in the history of the world, has a man been arraigned before a body clothed with legislative, judicial or executive functions, charged with the offense of being a darker hue than his fellow men. I know that questions have been before the courts of this country, and of other countries, involving topics not altogether dissimilar to that which is being discussed here today. But, sir, never in the history of the great nations of this world never before has a man been arraigned, charged with an offense committed by the God of Heaven Himself. Cases may be found where men have been deprived of their rights for crimes and misdemeanors; but it has remained for the state of Georgia, in the very heart of the nineteenth century, to call a man before the bar, and there charge him with an act for which he is no more responsible than for the head which he carries upon his shoulders. The Anglo-Saxon race, sir, is a most surprising one. No man has ever been more deceived in that race than I have been for the last three weeks. I was not aware that there was in the character of that race so much cowardice or so much pusillanimity. The treachery which has

Lift Every Voice: African American Oratory, 1787–1900 (Tuscaloosa and London: The University of Alabama Press, 1998), 476–483.

been exhibited in it by gentlemen belonging to that race has shaken my confidence in it more than anything that has come under my observation from the day of my birth. . . .

Whose legislature is this? Is it a white man's legislature, or is it a black man's legislature? Who voted for a constitutional convention, in obedience to the mandate of the Congress of the United States? Who first rallied around the standard of Reconstruction? Who set the ball of loyalty rolling in the state of Georgia? And whose voice was heard on the hills and in the valleys of this state? It was the voice of the brawny armed Negro, with the few humanitarian hearted white men who came to our assistance. I claim the honor, sir, of having been the instrument of convincing hundreds—yea, thousands—of white men, that to reconstruct under the measures of the United States Congress was the safest and the best course for the interest of the state. . . .

The great question, sir, is this: Am I a man? If I am such, I claim the rights of a man. Am I not a man because I happen to be of a darker hue than honorable gentlemen around me? Let me see whether I am or not. I want to convince the House today that I am entitled to my seat here. A certain gentleman has argued that the Negro was a mere development similar to the orangoutang or chimpanzee, but it so happens that, when a Negro is examined, physiologically, phrenologically and anatomically, and I may say, physiognomically, he is found to be the same as persons of different color. I would like to ask any gentleman on this floor, where is the analogy? Do you find me a quadruped, or do you find me a man? Do you find three bones less in my back than in that of the white man? Do you find fewer organs in the brain? If you know nothing of this, I do; for I have helped to dissect fifty men, black and white, and I assert that by the time you take off the mucous pigment—the color of the skin—you cannot, to save your life, distinguish between the black man and the white. Am I a man? Have I a soul to save, as you have? Am I susceptible of eternal development, as you are? Can I learn all the arts and sciences that you can? Has it ever been demonstrated in the history of the world? Have black men ever exhibited bravery as white men have done? Have they ever been in the professions? Have they not as good articulative organs as you? . . . God has weaved and tissued variety and versatility throughout the boundless space of His creation. Because God saw fit to make some red, and some white, and some black, and some brown, are we to sit here in judgment upon what God has seen fit to do? As well might one play with the thunderbolts of heaven as with that creature that bears God's image—God's photograph. . . .

It is said that Congress never gave us the right to hold office. I want to know, sir, if the Reconstruction measures did not base their action on the ground that no distinction should be made on account of race, color or previous condition? Was not that the grand fulcrum on which they rested? And did not every reconstructed state have to reconstruct on the idea that no discrimination, in any sense of the term, should be made? There is not a man here who will dare say No. . . .

We are a persecuted people. Luther was persecuted; Galileo was persecuted; good men in all nations have been persecuted; but the persecutors have been handed down to posterity with shame and ignominy. If you pass this bill, you will never get Congress to pardon or enfranchise another rebel in your lives. You are going to fix an everlasting disfranchisement upon Mr. Toombs and the other leading men of Georgia. You may think you are doing yourselves honor by expelling us from this House; but when we go, we will do as Wickliffe and as Latimer did. We will light a torch of truth that will never be extinguished—the impression that will run through the country, as people picture in their mind's eye these poor black men, in all parts of this Southern country, pleading for their rights. When you expel us, you make us forever your political foes, and you will never find a black man to vote a Democratic ticket again; for, so help me God, I will go through all the length and breadth of the land, where a man of my race is to be found, and advise him to beware of the Democratic party. Justice is the great doctrine taught in the Bible. God's Eternal justice is founded upon Truth, and the man who steps from justice steps from Truth, and cannot make his principles to prevail. . . .

I hope that our poor, downtrodden race may act well and wisely through this period of trial, and that they will exercise patience and discretion under all circumstances.

You may expel us, gentlemen, by your votes, today; but, while you do it, remember that there is a just God in Heaven, whose All-Seeing Eye beholds alike the acts of the oppressor and the oppressed, and who, despite the machinations of the wicked, never fails to vindicate the cause of Justice, and the sanctity of His own handiwork.

READING AND DISCUSSION QUESTIONS

1. What can you infer about Turner's interpretation of the Constitution and the contrary meaning his white legislative colleagues drew from the same source?

2. What changes to state institutions and society did African American activists like Turner cause by their rhetoric and actions?

3. What conclusions about the values Turner believed should guide America's political system can you draw from the speech he delivered before the Georgia legislature?

▪ COMPARATIVE QUESTIONS ▪

1. How would you examine and evaluate the multiple perspectives on American politics for evidence of the values guiding the political system during the Civil War era?

2. How did arguments over the meaning and interpretation of the nation's founding documents, such as the Declaration of Independence and the Constitution, affect American politics in the period from the Mexican War through Reconstruction?

17

Industrial America: Corporations and Conflicts
1877–1911

The deafening roar of America's industrial era ushered in epic changes that affected the lives of workers, immigrants, and the entrepreneurs who employed them. In this period, the scope, scale, and meaning of work underwent radical transformations, brought about by innovations in manufacturing, corporate structure, and labor management. These changes resulted in conflict between capital and labor, a theme that drives historical interpretations of the period. The rise of big business was heralded by some as evidence of ingenuity and pluck, leading to efficiencies never before imagined. Those who labored in the shops and factories of this industrializing economy saw the trend of consolidation differently, as a threat to their autonomy and skill and a menace to America's democratic institutions. Immigrants, whose increasing numbers in these years enabled industrial gains, found themselves in the crosshairs, victims of native-born resentments and capitalist manipulations as they tried to catch for themselves a slender piece of America's promise.

17-1 | Industrialist Justifies Fortunes Used for the Common Good

ANDREW CARNEGIE, *Wealth* (1889)

Andrew Carnegie was a Scottish immigrant, whose life reflected the aspect of the American Dream that inspired many poor boys in nineteenth-century America, though few ever came close to matching his phenomenal success. A tenacious self-starter, Carnegie worked hard and took advantage of key opportunities to invest in the telegraphic, railroad, oil, and steel industries, ultimately amassing an enormous fortune as head of Carnegie Steel Company, which he later sold for a staggering profit to J. Pierpont Morgan. In this 1889 essay, Carnegie justifies such colossal capital accumulation, not as an end in itself, but as a means to advance the common good.

The problem of our age is the proper administration of wealth, so that the ties of brotherhood may still bind together the rich and poor in harmonious relationship. The conditions of human life have not only been changed, but revolutionized, within the past few hundred years. In former days there was little difference between the dwelling, dress, food, and environment of the chief and those of his retainers. The Indians are to-day where civilized man then was. When visiting the Sioux, I was led to the wigwam of the chief. It was just like the others in external appearance, and even within the difference was trifling between it and those of the poorest of his braves. The contrast between the palace of the millionaire and the cottage of the laborer with us to-day measures the change which has come with civilization.

This change, however, is not to be deplored, but welcomed as highly beneficial. It is well, nay, essential for the progress of the race, that the houses of some should be homes for all that is highest and best in literature and the arts, and for all the refinements of civilization, rather than that none should be so. Much better this great irregularity than universal squalor. Without wealth there can be no Mæcenas.[1] The "good old times" were not good old times. Neither master nor servant was as well situated then as to-day. A relapse to old conditions would be disastrous to both — not the least so to him who serves — and would sweep away civilization with it. But whether the change be for good or ill, it is upon us, beyond our power to alter, and therefore to be accepted and made the best of. It is a waste of time to criticise the inevitable.

It is easy to see how the change has come. One illustration will serve for almost every phase of the cause. In the manufacture of products we have the whole story. It applies to all combinations of human industry, as stimulated and enlarged by the inventions of this scientific age. Formerly articles were manufactured at the domestic hearth or in small shops which formed part of the household. The master and his apprentices worked side by side, the latter living with

---

Andrew Carnegie, "Wealth," *North American Review*, no. CCCXCI (June 1889): 653–664.

[1]**Mæcenas**: First-century B.C. Roman patron of the arts.

the master, and therefore subject to the same conditions. When these apprentices rose to be masters, there was little or no change in their mode of life, and they, in turn, educated in the same routine succeeding apprentices. There was, substantially social equality, and even political equality, for those engaged in industrial pursuits had then little or no political voice in the State.

But the inevitable result of such a mode of manufacture was crude articles at high prices. To-day the world obtains commodities of excellent quality at prices which even the generation preceding this would have deemed incredible. In the commercial world similar causes have produced similar results, and the race is benefited thereby. The poor enjoy what the rich could not before afford. What were the luxuries have become the necessaries of life. The laborer has now more comforts than the landlord had a few generations ago. The farmer has more luxuries than the landlord had, and is more richly clad and better housed. The landlord has books and pictures rarer, and appointments more artistic, than the King could then obtain.

The price we pay for this salutary change is, no doubt, great. We assemble thousands of operatives in the factory, in the mine, and in the counting-house, of whom the employer can know little or nothing, and to whom the employer is little better than a myth. All intercourse between them is at an end. Rigid Castes are formed, and, as usual, mutual ignorance breeds mutual distrust. Each Caste is without sympathy for the other, and ready to credit anything disparaging in regard to it. Under the law of competition, the employer of thousands is forced into the strictest economies, among which the rates paid to labor figure prominently, and often there is friction between the employer and the employed, between capital and labor, between rich and poor. Human society loses homogeneity.

The price which society pays for the law of competition, like the price it pays for cheap comforts and luxuries, is also great; but the advantages of this law are also greater still, for it is to this law that we owe our wonderful material development, which brings improved conditions in its train. . . .

Objections to the foundations upon which society is based are not in order, because the condition of the race is better with these than it has been with any others which have been tried. Of the effect of any new substitutes proposed we cannot be sure. The Socialist or Anarchist who seeks to overturn present conditions is to be regarded as attacking the foundation upon which civilization itself rests, for civilization took its start from the day that the capable, industrious workman said to his incompetent and lazy fellow, "If thou dost not sow, thou shalt not reap," and thus ended primitive Communism by separating the drones from the bees. . . .

The question then arises,—What is the proper mode of administering wealth after the laws upon which civilization is founded have thrown it into the hands of the few? And it is of this great question that I believe I offer the true solution. . . .

There are but three modes in which surplus wealth can be disposed of. It can be left to the families of the decedents; or it can be bequeathed for public purposes; or, finally, it can be administered during their lives by its possessors. . . .

There are instances of millionaires' sons unspoiled by wealth, who, being rich, still perform great services in the community. Such are the very salt of the earth, as valuable as, unfortunately, they are rare; still it is not the exception, but the rule, that men must regard, and, looking at the usual result of enormous sums conferred upon legatees, the thoughtful man must shortly say, "I would as soon leave to my son a curse as the almighty dollar," and admit to himself that it is not the welfare of the children, but family pride, which inspires these enormous legacies.

As to the second mode, that of leaving wealth at death for public uses, it may be said that this is only a means for the disposal of wealth, provided a man is content to wait until he is dead before it becomes of much good in the world. Knowledge of the results of legacies bequeathed is not calculated to inspire the brightest hopes of much posthumous good being accomplished. The cases are not few in which the real object sought by the testator is not attained, nor are they few in which his real wishes are thwarted. In many cases the bequests are so used as to become only monuments of his folly. It is well to remember that it requires the exercise of not less ability than that which acquired the wealth to use it so as to be really beneficial to the community. . . .

There remains, then, only one mode of using great fortunes; but in this we have the true antidote for the temporary unequal distribution of wealth, the reconciliation of the rich and the poor—a reign of harmony—another ideal, differing, indeed, from that of the Communist in requiring only the further evolution of existing conditions, not the total overthrow of our civilization. It is founded upon the present most intense individualism, and the race is projected to put it in practice by degree whenever it pleases. Under its sway we shall have an ideal state, in which the surplus wealth of the few will become, in the best sense the property of the many, because administered for the common good, and this wealth, passing through the hands of the few, can be made a much more potent force for the elevation of our race than if it had been distributed in small sums to the people themselves. Even the poorest can be made to see this, and to agree that great sums gathered by some of their fellow-citizens and spent for public purposes, from which the masses reap the principal benefit, are more valuable to them than if scattered among them through the course of many years in trifling amounts. . . .

This, then, is held to be the duty of the man of Wealth: First, to set an example of modest, unostentatious living, shunning display or extravagance; to provide moderately for the legitimate wants of those dependent upon him; and after doing so to consider all surplus revenues which come to him simply as trust funds, which he is called upon to administer, and strictly bound as a matter of duty to administer in the manner which, in his judgment, is best calculated to produce the most beneficial results for the community—the man of wealth thus becoming the mere agent and trustee for his poorer brethren, bringing to their service his superior wisdom, experience and ability to administer, doing for them better than they would or could do for themselves. . . .

Thus is the problem of Rich and Poor to be solved. The laws of accumulation will be left free; the laws of distribution free. Individualism will continue, but the millionaire will be but a trustee for the poor; intrusted for a season with a great part of the increased wealth of the community, but administering it for the community far better than it could or would have done for itself. The best minds will thus have reached a stage in the development of the race in which it is clearly seen that there is no mode of disposing of surplus wealth creditable to thoughtful and earnest men into whose hands it flows save by using it year by year for the general good. This day already dawns. But a little while, and although, without incurring the pity of their fellows, men may die sharers in great business enterprises from which their capital cannot be or has not been withdrawn, and is left chiefly at death for public uses, yet the man who dies leaving behind many millions of available wealth, which was his to administer during life, will pass away "unwept, unhonored, and unsung," no matter to what uses he leaves the dross which he cannot take with him. Of such as these the public verdict will then be: "The man who dies thus rich dies disgraced."

Such, in my opinion, is the true Gospel concerning Wealth, obedience to which is destined some day to solve the problem of the Rich and the Poor, and to bring "Peace on earth, among men Good-Will."

READING AND DISCUSSION QUESTIONS

1. What argument does Carnegie make about the uses to which the great fortunes of industrialists should be devoted?

2. What factors might have motivated Carnegie to write his essay on wealth, and for whom do you think he wrote it? What inferences can you draw about the social and political context during which Carnegie wrote, which may have inspired his essay?

3. Why does Carnegie insist that his "gospel of wealth" was founded "upon the present most intense individualism"? What can you conclude about the cultural significance of that term as Carnegie used it?

17-2 | Industrial Brotherhood Counters Excesses of Capitalist Power

TERENCE POWDERLY, *Thirty Years of Labor* (1889)

The Knights of Labor emerged in the 1880s as a major labor organization. Knights were dedicated to the idea of uniting the "producing" classes in cooperative efforts to advance workers' interests and counter the power of capitalists, whose outsized wealth they saw as a threat to America's republican traditions. Terence Powderly was the national leader of the Knights of Labor, who tried to unite skilled and unskilled workers and opened membership to women and African Americans. The group's inclusive vision, expressed here in its platform, was quickly eclipsed by craft-based unionism promoted by the American Federation of Labor.

T. V. Powderly, *Thirty Years of Labor, 1859 to 1889* (Columbus, OH: Excelsior Publishing House, 1889), 116–120.

The recent alarming development and aggression of aggregated wealth, which, unless checked, will inevitably lead to the pauperization and hopeless degradation of the toiling masses, render it imperative, if we desire to enjoy the blessings of the government bequeathed to us by the founders of the republic, that a check should be placed upon its power and unjust accumulation, and a system adopted which will secure to the laborer the fruits of his toil; and as this much desired object can only be accomplished by the thorough unification of labor, and the united efforts of those who obey the divine injunction, that "in the sweat of thy face thou shalt eat bread," we have formed the INDUSTRIAL BROTHERHOOD, with a view of securing the organization and direction, by co-operative effort of the power of the industrial classes, and we submit to the people of the United States the objects sought to be accomplished by our organization, calling upon all who believe in securing "the greatest good to the greatest number," to aid and assist us:

    I.   To bring within the folds of organization every department of productive industry, making knowledge a standpoint for action, and industrial, moral, and social worth—not wealth—the true standard of individual and national greatness.

    II.   To secure to the toilers a proper share of the wealth that they create; more of the leisure that rightfully belongs to them; more societary advantages; more of the benefits, privileges and emoluments of the world; in a word, all those rights and privileges necessary to make them capable of enjoying, appreciating, defending and perpetuating the blessings of republican institutions.

    III.   To arrive at the true condition of the producing masses in their educational, moral, and financial condition, we demand from the several States and from the national government the establishment of bureaus of labor statistics.

    IV.   The establishment of co-operative institutions, productive and distributive.

    V.   The reserving of the public lands, the heritage of the people, for the actual settler—not another acre for railroads or speculators.

    VI.   The abrogation of all laws that do not bear equally upon capital and labor, the removal of unjust technicalities, delays, and discriminations in the administration of justice, and the adoption of measures providing for the health and safety of those engaged in mining, manufacturing or building pursuits.

    VII.   The enactment of a law to compel chartered corporations to pay their employes at least once in every month in full for labor performed during the preceding month in the lawful money of the country.

    VIII.   The enactment of a law giving mechanics and other laborers a first lien on their work.

    IX.   The abolishment of the contract system on national, state, and municipal work.

    X.   To inaugurate a system of public markets, to facilitate the exchange of the productions of farmers and mechanics, tending to do away with middlemen and speculators.

XI. To inaugurate systems of cheap transportation to facilitate the exchange of commodities.

XII. The substitution of arbitration for strikes, whenever and wherever employers and employees are willing to meet on equitable grounds.

XIII. The prohibition of the importation of all servile races, the discontinuance of all subsidies granted to national vessels bringing them to our shores, and the abrogation of the Burlingame treaty.[1]

XIV. To advance the standard of American mechanics by the enactment and enforcement of equitable apprentice laws.

XV. To abolish the system of contracting the labor of convicts in our prisons and reformatory institutions.

XVI. To secure for both sexes equal pay for equal work.

XVII. The reduction of the hours of labor to eight per day, so that laborers may have more time for social enjoyment and intellectual improvement, and be enabled to reap the advantages conferred by labor-saving machinery, which their brains have created.

XVIII. To prevail upon the government to establish a just standard of distribution between capital and labor by providing a purely national circulating medium based upon the faith and resources of the nation, issued directly to the people, without the intervention of any system of banking corporations, which money shall be a legal tender in the payment of all debts, public or private, and interchangeable at the option of the holder for government bonds, bearing a rate of interest not to exceed three and sixty-five hundredths per cent., subject to future legislation of Congress.

READING AND DISCUSSION QUESTIONS

1. Analyze and evaluate the Knights' platform for evidence of the union's point of view toward the federal government. What role does it see for the state in regulating the relationship between workers and employers?

2. Imagine Carnegie's reaction to the reforms advocated by the Knights of Labor in their statement of principles. Which specific statements might have elicited the strongest reaction and why?

3. From the union's platform, what conclusion can you draw about the status of labor in industrial America? What obstacles and challenges do Powderly and his fellow Knights identify as stumbling blocks to the equitable society they sought?

---

[1]**Burlingame treaty**: The Burlingame-Seward Treaty (1868) granted most favored nation trading status to China, but was abrogated by the Chinese Exclusion Act (1882).

17-3 | Worker Finds His Way on the Shop Floor

ANTANAS KAZTAUSKIS, *Life Story of a Lithuanian* (c. 1906)

America's industrial engine ran on the fuel of immigrant labor. Workers hailed from all parts of Europe, Asia, and the Americas, resulting in a diverse workforce with distinctive cultural, linguistic, and religious customs. What united them was the hope that had inspired Antanas Kaztauskis's migration from Lithuania, the prospect of a life better than the one back home. Though the reality dimmed his initial optimism, Kaztauskis found stability in the company of others.

The next morning my friends woke me up at five o'clock and said, "Now, if you want life, liberty and happiness," they laughed, "you must push for yourself. You must get a job. Come with us." And we went to the yards. Men and women were walking in by thousands as far as we could see. We went to the doors of one big slaughter house. There was a crowd of about 200 men waiting there for a job. They looked hungry and kept watching the door. At last a special policeman came out and began pointing to men, one by one. Each one jumped forward. Twenty three were taken. Then they all went inside, and all the others turned their faces away and looked tired. I remember one boy sat down and cried, just next to me, on a pile of boards. Some policemen waved their clubs and we all walked on. I found some Lithuanians to talk with, who told me they had come every morning for three weeks. Soon we met other crowds coming away from other slaughter houses, and we all walked around and felt bad and tired and hungry.

That night I told my friends that I would not do this many days, but would go some place else. "Where?" they asked me, and I began to see then that I was in bad trouble, because I spoke no English. Then one man told me to give him $5 to give the special policeman. I did this and the next morning the policeman pointed me out, so I had a job. I have heard some big talk since then about my American freedom of contract, but I do not think I had much freedom in bargaining for this job with the Meat Trust. My job was in the cattle killing room. I pushed the blood along the gutter. Some people think these jobs make men bad. I do not think so. The men who do the killing are not as bad as the ladies with fine clothes who come every day to look at it, because they have to do it. The cattle do not suffer. They are knocked senseless with a big hammer and are dead before they wake up. This is done not to spare them pain, but because if they got hot and sweating with fear and pain the meat would not be so good. I soon saw that every job in the room was done like this—so as to save everything and make money. One Lithuanian, who worked with me, said, "They get all the blood out of those cattle and all the work out of us men." This was true, for we worked that first day from

The Life Stories of Undistinguished Americans, As Told by Themselves, ed. Hamilton Holt, Intr. Edwin E. Slosson (New York: James Pott & Company, 1906), 24–33.

six in the morning till seven at night. The next day we worked from six in the morning till eight at night. The next day we had no work. So we had no good, regular hours. It was hot in the room that summer, and the hot blood made it worse.

I held this job six weeks and then I was turned off. I think some other man had paid for my job, or perhaps I was too slow. The foreman in that room wanted quick men to make the work rush, because he was paid more if the work was done cheaper and quicker. I saw now that every man was helping himself, always trying to get all the money he could. At that time I believed that all men in Chicago were grafters when they had to be. They only wanted to push themselves. Now, when I was idle I began to look about, and everywhere I saw sharp men beating out slow men like me. Even if we worked hard it did us no good. I had saved $13—$5 a week for six weeks makes $30, and take off $15 for six weeks' board and lodging and $2 for other things. I showed this to a Lithuanian, who had been here two years, and he laughed. "It will be taken from you," he said. He had saved a hundred dollars once and had begun to buy a house on the installment plan, but something had happened that he did not know about and his landlord put him out and kept the hundred dollars. I found that many Lithuanians had been beaten this way. At home we never made a man sign contract papers. We only had him make the sign of a cross and promise he would do what he said. But this was no good in Chicago. So these sharp men were beating us.

I saw this, too, in the newspaper. I was beginning to learn English, and at night in the boarding house the men who did not play cards used to read the paper to us. The biggest word was "Graft" in red letters on the front page. Another word was "Trust." This paper kept putting these two words together. Then I began to see how every American man was trying to get money for himself. . . . I felt very bad and sorrowful in that month. I kept walking around with many other Lithuanians who had no job. Our money was going and we could find nothing to do. At night we got homesick for our fine green mountains. We read all the news about home in our Lithuanian Chicago newspaper, *The Katalikas*. It is a good paper and gives all the news. In the same office we bought this song, which was written in Brooklyn by P. Brandukas. He, too, was homesick. It is sung all over Chicago now and you can hear it in the summer evenings through the open windows. In English it is something like this:

Oh, Lithuania, so dear to me,
Good-by to you, my Fatherland.
Sorrowful in my heart I leave you,
I know not who will stay to guard you.

Is it enough for me to live and enjoy between my neighbors,
In the woods with the flowers and birds?
Is it enough for me to live peaceful between my friends?
No, I must go away from my old father and mother.

The sun shines bright,
The flowers smell sweet,
The birds are singing,
They make the country glad;
But I cannot sing because I must leave you.

Those were bad days and nights. At last I had a chance to help myself. Summer was over and Election Day was coming. The Republican boss in our district, Jonidas, was a saloon keeper. A friend took me there. Jonidas shook hands and treated me fine. He taught me to sign my name, and the next week I went with him to an office and signed some paper, and then I could vote. I voted as I was told, and then they got me back into the yards to work, because one big politician owns stock in one of those houses. Then I felt that I was getting in beside the game. I was in a combine like other sharp men. Even when work was slack I was all right, because they got me a job in the street cleaning department. I felt proud, and I went to the back room in Jonidas's saloon and got him to write a letter to Alexandria to tell her she must come soon and be my wife.

But this was just the trouble. All of us were telling our friends to come soon. Soon they came—even thousands. The employers in the yard liked this, because those sharp foremen are inventing new machines and the work is easier to learn, and so these slow Lithuanians and even green girls can learn to do it, and then the Americans and Germans and Irish are put out and the employer saves money, because the Lithuanians work cheaper. This was why the American labor unions began to organize us all just the same as they had organized the Bohemians and Poles before us.

Well, we were glad to be organized. We had learned that in Chicago every man must push himself always, and Jonidas had taught us how much better we could push ourselves by getting into a combine. Now, we saw that this union was the best combine for us, because it was the only combine that could say, "It is our business to raise your wages."

But that Jonidas—he spoilt our first union. He was sharp. First he got us to hire the room over his saloon. He used to come in at our meetings and sit in the back seat and grin. There was an Irishman there from the union headquarters, and he was trying to teach us to run ourselves. He talked to a Lithuanian, and the Lithuanian said it to us, but we were slow to do things, and we were jealous and were always jumping up to shout and fight. So the Irishman used to wipe his hot red face and call us bad names. He told the Lithuanian not to say these names to us, but Jonidas heard them, and in his saloon, where we all went down after the meeting when the Irishman was gone, Jonidas gave us free drinks and then told us the names. I will not write them here.

One night that Irishman did not come and Jonidas saw his chance and took the chair. He talked very fine and we elected him President. We made him Treasurer, too. Down in the saloon he gave us free drinks and told us we must break away from the Irish grafters. The next week he made us strike, all by himself. We met twice a day in his saloon and spent all of our money on drinks and then the strike was over. I got out of this union after that. I had been working hard in the cattle killing room and I had a better job. I was called a cattle butcher now and I joined the Cattle Butchers' Union. This union is honest and it has done me a great deal of good.

It has raised my wages. The man who worked at my job before the union came was getting through the year an average of $9 a week. I am getting $11. In my first job I got $5 a week. The man who works there now gets $5.75.

It has given me more time to learn to read and speak and enjoy life like an American. I never work now from 6 A.M. to 9 P.M. and then be idle the next day. I work now from 7 A.M. to 5.30 P.M., and there are not so many idle days. The work is evened up.

With more time and more money I live much better and I am very happy. So is Alexandria. She came a year ago and has learned to speak English already. Some of the women go to the big store the day they get here, when they have not enough sense to pick out the clothes that look right, but Alexandria waited three weeks till she knew, and so now she looks the finest of any woman in the district. We have four nice rooms, which she keeps very clean, and she has flowers growing in boxes in the two front windows. We do not go much to church, because the church seems to be too slow. But we belong to a Lithuanian society that gives two picnics in summer and two big balls in winter, where we have a fine time. I go one night a week to the Lithuanian Concertina Club. On Sundays we go on the trolley out into the country.

But we like to stay at home more now because we have a baby. When he grows up I will not send him to the Lithuanian Catholic school. They have only two bad rooms and two priests, who teach only in Lithuanian from prayer books. I will send him to the American school, which is very big and good. The teachers there are Americans and they belong to the Teachers' Labor Union, which has three thousand teachers and belongs to our Chicago Federation of Labor. I am sure that such teachers will give him a good chance.

Our union sent a committee to Springfield last year and they passed a law which prevents boys and girls below sixteen from working in the stockyards.

We are trying to make the employers pay on Saturday night in cash. Now they pay in checks and the men have to get money the same night to buy things for Sunday, and the saloons cash checks by thousands. You have to take one drink to have the check cashed. It is hard to take one drink.

The union is doing another good thing. It is combining all the nationalities. The night I joined the Cattle Butchers' Union I was led into the room by a negro member. With me were Bohemians, Germans and Poles, and Mike Donnelly, the President, is an Irishman. He spoke to us in English and then three interpreters told us what he said. We swore to be loyal to our union above everything else except the country, the city and the State—to be faithful to each other—to protect the women-workers—to do our best to understand the history of the labor movement, and to do all we could to help it on. Since then I have gone there every two weeks and I help the movement by being an interpreter for the other Lithuanians who come in. That is why I have learned to speak and write good

English. The others do not need me long. They soon learn English, too, and when they have done that they are quickly becoming Americans.

But the best thing the union does is to make me feel more independent. I do not have to pay to get a job and I cannot be discharged unless I am no good. For almost the whole 30,000 men and women are organized now in some one of our unions and they all are directed by our central council. No man knows what it means to be sure of his job unless he has been fired like I was once without any reason being given.

So this is why I joined the labor union. There are many better stories than mine, for my story is very common. There are thousands of immigrants like me. Over 300,000 immigrants have been organized in the last three years by the American Federation of Labor. The immigrants are glad to be organized if the leaders are as honest as Mike Donnelly is. You must get money to live well, and to get money you must combine. I cannot bargain alone with the Meat Trust. I tried it and it does not work.

READING AND DISCUSSION QUESTIONS

1. What evidence of unions' effectiveness can you discover in the story Kaztauskis tells of his experiences working in the Chicago stockyards? What advantages does he attribute to his membership in the union?

2. How does Kaztauskis's point of view toward industrialization compare with the views expressed by Carnegie in his essay on wealth?

17-4 | Congress Closes Door to Chinese Laborers
Chinese Exclusion Act (1882)

The cooperative ethos Powderly and the Knights espoused had its limits, and immigration was one of them. Many American-born workers who struggled to find work or survive the job they had blamed the influx of immigrants for their unemployment and depressed wages. On the West Coast, in mining and railroad industries, Chinese immigrants found themselves the targets of nativist resentment from other workers, culminating in this 1882 congressional act, the first of its kind, which excluded immigration from China.

Whereas in the opinion of the Government of the United States the coming of Chinese laborers to this country endangers the good order of certain localities within the territory thereof: Therefore,

---

"An Act to Execute Certain Treaty Stipulations Relating to the Chinese," May 6, 1882; Enrolled Acts and Resolutions of Congress, 1789–1996; General Records of the United States Government; Record Group 11; National Archives.

Be it enacted [that] . . . the coming of Chinese laborers to the United States be, and the same is hereby, suspended; and during such suspension it shall not be lawful for any Chinese laborer to come, or having so come after the expiration of said ninety days to remain within the United States.

SEC. 2. That the master of any vessel who shall knowingly bring within the United States on such vessel, and land or permit to be landed, any Chinese laborer, from any foreign port or place, shall be deemed guilty of a misdemeanor, and on conviction thereof shall be punished by a fine of not more than five hundred dollars for each and every such Chinese laborer so brought, and maybe also imprisoned for a term not exceeding one year.

SEC. 3. That the two foregoing sections shall not apply to Chinese laborers who were in the United States on the seventeenth day of November, eighteen hundred and eighty, or who shall have come into the same before the expiration of ninety days next after the passage of this act, and who shall produce to such master before going on board such vessel, and shall produce to the collector of the port in the United States at which such vessel shall arrive, the evidence hereinafter in this act required of his being one of the laborers in this section mentioned; nor shall the two foregoing sections apply to the case of any master whose vessel, being bound to a port not within the United States, shall come within the jurisdiction of the United States by reason of being in distress or in stress of weather, or touching at any port of the United States on its voyage to any foreign port or place: Provided, That all Chinese laborers brought on such vessel shall depart with the vessel on leaving port.

SEC. 4. That for the purpose of properly identifying Chinese laborers who were in the United States on the seventeenth day of November eighteen hundred and eighty, or who shall have come into the same before the expiration of ninety days next after the passage of this act, and in order to furnish them with the proper evidence of their right to go from and come to the United States of their free will and accord . . . the collector of customs . . . shall . . . go on board each vessel having on board any such Chinese laborers and cleared or about to sail from his district for a foreign port, and on such vessel make a list of all such Chinese laborers, which shall be entered in registry-books to be kept for that purpose, in which shall be stated the name, age, occupation, last place of residence, physical marks [or] peculiarities, and all facts necessary for the identification of each of such Chinese laborers, which books shall be safely kept in the custom-house; and every such Chinese laborer so departing from the United States shall be entitled to . . . a certificate, signed by the collector or his deputy and attested by his seal of office, in such form as the Secretary of the Treasury shall prescribe, which certificate shall contain a statement of the name, age, occupation, last place of residence, persona[l] description, and facts of identification of the Chinese laborer to whom the certificate is issued, corresponding with the said list and registry in all particulars. . . . The certificate herein provided for shall entitle the Chinese laborer to whom the same is issued to return to and re-enter the United States upon producing and delivering the same to the collector of customs of the district at which such Chinese laborer shall seek to re-enter; and upon delivery of such certificate by such Chinese laborer to the collector of customs at the time of re-entry in the United States said collector shall cause the same to be filed in the custom-house [and] duly canceled.

SEC. 5. That any Chinese laborer mentioned in section four of this act being in the United States, and desiring to depart from the United States by land, shall have the right to demand and receive, free of charge or cost, a certificate of identification similar to that provided for in section four of this act to be issued to such Chinese laborers as may desire to leave the United States by water; and it is hereby made the duty of the collector of customs of the district next adjoining the foreign country to which said Chinese laborer desires to go to issue such certificate, free of charge or cost, upon application by such Chinese laborer, and to enter the same upon registry-books to be kept by him for the purpose, as provided for in section four of this act.

SEC. 6. That in order to the faithful execution of articles one and two of the treaty in this act before mentioned, every Chinese person other than a laborer who may be entitled by said treaty and this act to come within the United States, and who shall be about to come to the United States, shall be identified as so entitled by the Chinese Government in each case, such identity to be evidenced by a certificate issued under the authority of said government, which certificate shall be in the English language or (if not in the English language) accompanied by a translation into English, stating such right to come, and which certificate shall state the name, title or official rank, if any, the age, height, and all physical peculiarities, former and present occupation or profession, and place of residence in China of the person to whom the certificate is issued and that such person is entitled, conformably to the treaty in this act mentioned to come within the United States. Such certificate shall be prima-facie evidence of the fact set forth therein, and shall be produced to the collector of customs, or his deputy, of the port in the district in the United States at which the person named therein shall arrive.

SEC. 7. That any person who shall knowingly and falsely alter or substitute any name for the name written in such certificate or forge any such certificate, or knowingly utter any forged or fraudulent certificate, or falsely personate any person named in any such certificate, shall be deemed guilty of a misdemeanor; and upon conviction thereof shall be fined in a sum not exceeding one thousand dollars, and imprisoned in a penitentiary for a term of not more than five years.

SEC. 8. That the master of any vessel arriving in the United States from any foreign port or place shall, at the same time he delivers a manifest of the cargo, and if there be no cargo, then at the time of making a report of the entry of the vessel pursuant to law, in addition to the other matter required to be reported, and before landing, or permitting to land, any Chinese passengers, deliver and report to the collector of customs of the district in which such vessels shall have arrived a separate list of all Chinese passengers taken on board his vessel at any foreign port or place, and all such passengers on board the vessel at that time. . . .

SEC. 9. That before any Chinese passengers are landed from any such line vessel, the collector, or his deputy, shall proceed to examine such passenger, comparing the certificate with the list and with the passengers; and no passenger shall be allowed to land in the United States from such vessel in violation of law.

SEC. 10. That every vessel whose master shall knowingly violate any of the provisions of this act shall be deemed forfeited to the United States, and shall be liable to seizure and condemnation in any district of the United States into which such vessel may enter or in which she may be found.

SEC. 11. That any person who shall knowingly bring into or cause to be brought into the United States by land, or who shall knowingly aid or abet the same, or aid or abet the landing in the United States from any vessel of any Chinese person not lawfully entitled to enter the United States, shall be deemed guilty of a misdemeanor, and shall, on conviction thereof, be fined in a sum not exceeding one thousand dollars, and imprisoned for a term not exceeding one year.

SEC. 12. That no Chinese person shall be permitted to enter the United States by land without producing to the proper officer of customs the certificate in this act required of Chinese persons seeking to land from a vessel. And any Chinese person found unlawfully within the United States shall be caused to be removed therefrom to the country from whence he came, by direction of the President of the United States, and at the cost of the United States, after being brought before some justice, judge, or commissioner of a court of the United States and found to be one not lawfully entitled to be or remain in the United States.

SEC. 13. That this act shall not apply to diplomatic and other officers of the Chinese Government traveling upon the business of that government, whose credentials shall be taken as equivalent to the certificate in this act mentioned, and shall exempt them and their body and house-hold servants from the provisions of this act as to other Chinese persons.

SEC. 14. That hereafter no State court or court of the United States shall admit Chinese to citizenship; and all laws in conflict with this act are hereby repealed.

SEC. 15. That the words "Chinese laborers," wherever used in this act shall be construed to mean both skilled and unskilled laborers and Chinese employed in mining.

READING AND DISCUSSION QUESTIONS

1. What argument about nineteenth-century immigration policy does the Chinese Exclusion Act support?

2. How might a historian interpret the Chinese Exclusion Act within the historical context of nineteenth-century immigration policy, the history of race and ethnicity, and the history of American labor?

17-5 | Pointing Out the Irony of Nativist Policies
JOSEPH KEPPLER, *Looking Backward* (1893)

By the 1890s, America had become a nation of immigrants, and for the next two decades the wave of European immigrants washing ashore drove its industrial development and changed its demographic mix. Many industrialists welcomed the cheap labor immigrants brought, while urban political machines manipulated newcomers for partisan gains. Increasing immigration, however, raised alarms from native-born whites who caricatured many immigrants as radicals and culturally inferior, just the sort who might destroy American customs and institutions. In this cartoon, published in *Puck*, an American magazine of political satire, artist and editor Joseph Keppler comments on America's immigration policies.

READING AND DISCUSSION QUESTIONS

1. Analyze and evaluate the point of view Keppler expresses in his cartoon. What do the shadows behind the elegantly dressed gentlemen represent?

2. How would you compare Keppler's cartoon with the Chinese Exclusion Act for evidence of the diversity of opinion on the immigrant question in the latter nineteenth century?

Joseph Keppler, "Looking Backward." The Ohio State University Billy Ireland Cartoon Library & Museum.

17-6 | Economist Scores the Costs and Benefits of Monopoly

ARTHUR TWINING HADLEY, *The Good and the Evil of Industrial Combination* (1897)

The polarized assessment of big business in America often reflected perceptions of the good or evil of monopolies, as Yale economist and president Arthur Twining Hadley underscored in an 1897 article for *The Atlantic Monthly*, a New England–based journal of culture and ideas. No foe of capitalism, Hadley highlighted the economic benefits of the emerging corporate structure, emphasizing the lower costs of goods and the general trend of rising wages, a view disputed by labor's advocates. Still, Hadley did acknowledge the limitations of monopoly, or what he called combinations, and offered an economist's view of how best to control them without undermining the advantages he identified.

This is a subject on which it is easy to argue, and hard to judge. The apologist for modern corporate methods can show that the good which they have done and are doing is likely to be permanent, while the evil with which they are accompanied tends to correct itself in the long run. His opponent can answer that this self-correcting process is very slow; and that even if we could be sure that it would work itself out right in the end,—which he is not always disposed to admit,—nevertheless the evils and losses attendant upon the intermediate stages of the process make it a terribly expensive one, both materially and morally. In short, he thinks that society is paying too high a price for its industrial education and improvement; and that more stringent methods of state control would enable us to get at the good results of combination by a shorter road, which would avoid most of the dangers and hardships of the longer one. . . .

The tendency of monopoly to retard the introduction of industrial improvements is, in the opinion of the present writer, a more serious thing than its tendency to allow unfair rates. This aspect of the matter has hardly received proper attention. We have been so accustomed to think of competition as a regulator of prices that we have lost sight of its equally important function as a stimulus to efficiency. Wherever competition is absent, there is a disposition to rest content with old methods, not to say slack ones. In spite of notable exceptions this is clearly the rule. Especially is it true of those organizations whose monopoly has legal recognition and protection. It was most marked in the case of mediaeval guilds in their later stages of development. The monopoly which their members enjoyed was so abused as to stand in the way of industrial progress, until the cry for its abolition became too powerful to resist. The same sort of abuse has been seen sometimes in recent monopolies of capital. The French railroads may serve as a noticeable instance. The government of France was so impressed with the evils due to unnecessary duplication of companies in England, and with the gain that might result from a systematic arrangement of lines, that it gave a few great companies a monopoly of railroad construction and operation in their respective

Arthur Twining Hadley, "The Good and the Evil of Industrial Combination," *The Atlantic Monthly* 79, no. 479 (March 1897): 377, 383–385.

districts. The result has been that much-needed railroads have remained for years unbuilt, that salutary reductions in rates have been delayed, and that the evil effects of combination have been more conspicuous than the good ones. Similar instances of over-conservatism might easily be found nearer home, in those industries where a combination has enjoyed patent rights broad enough to protect it against the possibility of outside competition for a term of years; or where the power of an organization to protect itself against home competition has been reinforced by an unduly high tariff against its foreign competitors. And it is in precisely these cases that the danger of political corruption becomes greatest. If a monopoly finds its power and its profit depending upon favorable legislation rather than upon its superior efficiency in serving the consumers, it will tend to devote more attention to politics and less to business. . . .

Enough has been said on both sides to show the difficulty of passing judgment on the absolute merits or demerits of modern industrial monopoly. It is a somewhat easier as well as a much more important task to examine the relative merits of the different methods of control which have been suggested.

These methods may be grouped under five heads: (1) Direct Prohibition, (2) State Ownership, (3) Limitation of Profits, (4) Control of Prices, (5) Enforced Publicity.

Of direct prohibition, it is enough to say that it has been persistently tried, and has had very little success. State laws, and even national laws, against monopoly exist in plenty. The majority of them are dead letters. A few have affected the form of combination adopted; but even these have not made any substantial change in the process or in its results. The Interstate Commerce Law has prohibited railroad pools; in so doing it has simply driven the railroads to adopt other devices for securing the end to which pooling was a means. The legislation of the years 1891 and 1892 led to the dissolution of the Standard Oil Trust; but the Standard Oil Companies have continued to be managed with undiminished unity of aim and centralization of power. . . .

State ownership of industry is urged on such a variety of grounds that it would require a separate article, or series of articles, to discuss them all. But on the ground of industrial efficiency and public service, it has not, on the whole, shown itself equal to private ownership. On the question of relative rates there is perhaps room for a good deal of argument on both sides, but on the question of industrial progress there is no comparison between the two systems. All the great inventions of modern times—the steam-engine, the steamship, the railroad, the telegraph, the telephone—have been developed and introduced by private enterprise. . . .

In short, government ownership seems to intensify those very evils which we have characterized as the most dangerous consequences of private monopoly. Nor would it appear that it lessens the political corruption with which such organized monopoly is attended. Where such corruption exists, state ownership substitutes one ring for two; making it easier to keep the evil secret, and correspondingly harder to do any real work in uprooting it.

Limitation of profits has not proved a successful method of dealing with monopolies. It is easy for a company to reduce its profits to the prescribed minimum by diminishing its efficiency and economy instead of by reducing its rates. We have seen how great is the danger of slack service when the stimulus of competition is removed. . . .

Control of prices has worked better than limitation of profits. In fact, it sometimes seems like a necessity. We cannot allow a monopolist to kill all his neighbors for the sake of proving the unwisdom of such a policy to himself. Where the conduct of monopolies has been short-sighted and extortionate, as in the case of railroad rates at noncompetitive Western points immediately after the war, the public has been apt to resort to this remedy. But it is by no means a satisfactory one. In the first place, such rates are very often made too low; and the reduction of service that follows proves a worse evil than the extortion in charge that preceded. . . .

Where this responsibility for the future can be brought home to the managers of corporate enterprise, it furnishes a better means of control than any of the methods hitherto considered. If, as was indicated at the outset, the permanent interests of the capitalist coincide pretty closely with those of his customers or employers, any agency which shall give force to those permanent interests points the way to a solution desirable for all parties. Where the short-sighted policy is due to corrupt interests within the corporation, which knowingly antagonize the real interests of the investors, it may be restricted by enforced publicity of accounts or by better laws governing responsibility of directors. The former lessens the opportunity for abuse, the latter lessens the motive. Where the short-sighted policy is pursued in good faith, a better understanding may be promoted by commissions like those in whose development Massachusetts has taken the lead, or perhaps still more effectively by the highest class of judicial decisions. Such agencies serve to create an intelligent public sentiment on matters of business, and one that can be developed in no other way.

It is a slow process to educate a community to the point where we can rely on rational egoism to subserve public good; but the community which has attained that result, in any department of life, possesses an inestimable advantage. Thanks to the decisions of the courts, supplemented by the influence of a few great writers like Adam Smith, we have pretty nearly reached this stage of development in competitive business. In monopolized business we have not done so. Our capitalists have learned to look a day or a month ahead, but not always a year or a decade. It is when we take it in this connection that we see the full significance of the problem of industrial combination at the present day. It marks a critical phase in the education which a community must undergo to fit itself for the increasingly difficult problems of industrial freedom. If we resort to systems of prescribed rates, we defer this education to a day when it may be a harder process than it is now. If we resort to state ownership, we abandon the hope of such education altogether, and pass from the traditional lines of development of England and America to those of France or Germany. But if we can meet

the evils of the present crisis by the creation of a more enlightened public sentiment, we shall be handling the problems of our day as our fathers handled those
of their day, and shall leave our children the legacy of a freedom enlarged rather
than impaired by the magnitude of the burdens imposed upon it.

READING AND DISCUSSION QUESTIONS

1. How does Hadley summarize the arguments for and against monopoly?
   Whereas some attributed rising prices to the power of monopolies, what did
   Hadley see as their "more serious" problem? Why do you think he identifies that
   problem as his leading concern?

2. Analyze the methods for controlling monopolies that Hadley describes for evidence of the political conflict between the interests of capital and labor that existed
   during this period. What reformers does he allude to in discussing the popular
   methods of control, which he criticizes as ineffective and counterproductive?

▪ COMPARATIVE QUESTIONS ▪

1. Analyze and evaluate historical patterns of nativist thought over time for evidence of continuity and change by comparing the Chinese Exclusion Act and the
   Looking Backward cartoon with Charles Francis Adams's views on suffrage
   (Document 15-4). What similarities do you see continuing into the twenty-first
   century?

2. How would you evaluate and synthesize the conflicting evidence in this chapter
   to construct a convincing historical argument about immigration during the
   latter nineteenth century?

3. In thinking about the period from 1877 to 1911, what theme or themes emerge
   from the sources that serve to unify these years as a coherent block of time for
   historical analysis and interpretation?

4. Evaluate monopoly as a source of political conflict by considering the multiple
   views in this chapter. What similarities and conflicts do you see?

5. How does this period of industrialization compare with the period of rapid economic development during the early national period? Explain and evaluate the
   similarities and differences that you see across time and place.

18

The Victorians Make the Modern

1880–1917

The turn of the twentieth century witnessed clashing paradigms as Victorian sentimentality based on genteel ideas of refinement and religion bumped uneasily into modern notions of hard-nosed progress and science. These caricatures, of course, belie the complexity of cultural conflict during these years, but aptly summarize what many considered the stakes as an industrializing economy and society transformed before their eyes. Darwinism provided a frame of reference for understanding these changes, justifying as it did the endemic competition and struggle witnessed over these years. This theme was bold-faced in the thinking of some, like Theodore Roosevelt, who praised the effects on self and society of a life "strenuously" lived. For others, it lurked in the recesses, shaping perceptions about society that helped them challenge Victorian domesticity. This was true for women and their advocates whose spirited claims on their behalf opened educational and career possibilities previously closed to them. African Americans continued to face discrimination, now cloaked in scientific interpretation, but they too pushed an agenda for change, though the means to realize in full the freedoms they sought remained a point of dispute within reform circles. As new ideas eclipsed American Victorianism, old certainties passed away, making room for a modern American culture.

18-1 | Pursuing the Manly Sports for Self and Society
THEODORE ROOSEVELT, *Professionalism in Sports* (1890)

Industrialization brought luxury within reach of the managerial classes, providing them with leisure, vacations, and a work life defined by the desk and office, not the machine or plough. This white-collared world alarmed some, including Theodore Roosevelt, who championed physical activity as an antidote to what many termed "over civilization." Roosevelt's advocacy, eleven years before becoming president, reflects a late-nineteenth-century drive to ensure America's emerging position in the world by encouraging what he described as "manly, healthy, vigorous pastimes." This muscular citizenship would benefit the individual and through him the nation.

It is hardly necessary at the present day to enter a plea for athletic exercise and manly out-door sports. During the last twenty-five years there has been a wonderful growth of interest in and appreciation of healthy muscular amusements; and this growth can best be promoted by stimulating, within proper bounds, the spirit of rivalry on which all our games are based. The effect upon the physique of the sedentary classes, especially in the towns and cities, has already been very marked. We are much less liable than we were to reproaches on the score of our national ill health, of the bad constitutions of our men, and of the fragility and early decay of our women.

There are still plenty of people who look down on, as of little moment, the proper development of the body; but the men of good sense sympathize as little with these as they do with the even more noxious extremists who regard physical development as an end instead of a means. As a nation we have many tremendous problems to work out, and we need to bring every ounce of vital power possible to their solution. No people has ever yet done great and lasting work if its physical type was infirm and weak. Goodness and strength must go hand in hand if the Republic is to be preserved. The good man who is ready and able to strike a blow for the right, and to put down evil with the strong arm, is the citizen who deserves our most hearty respect. There is a certain tendency in the civilization of our time to underestimate or overlook the need of the virile, masterful qualities of the heart and mind which have built up and alone can maintain and defend this very civilization, and which generally go hand in hand with good health and the capacity to get the utmost possible use out of the body. There is no better way of counteracting this tendency than by encouraging bodily exercise, and especially the sports which develop such qualities as courage, resolution, and endurance.

The best of all sports for this purpose are those which follow the Macedonian rather than the Greek model: big-game hunting, mountaineering, the chase with

Theodore Roosevelt, "'Professionalism' in Sports," *The North American Review* 151, no. 405 (August 1890): 187–191.

horse and hound, all wilderness life with all its keen, hardy pleasures. The hunter and mountaineer lead healthier lives—in time of need they would make better soldiers—than the trained athlete. Nor need these pleasures be confined to the rich. The trouble with our men of small means is quite as often that they do not know how to enjoy pleasures lying at their doors as that they cannot afford them. From New York to Minneapolis, from Boston to San Francisco, there is no large city from which it is impossible to reach a tract of perfectly wild, wooded or mountainous land within forty-eight hours; and any two young men who can get a month's holiday in August or September cannot use it to better advantage than by tramping on foot, pack on back, over such a tract. Let them go alone; a season or two will teach them much woodcraft, and will enormously increase their stock of health, hardihood, and self-reliance. . . .

However, most of our people, whether from lack of means, time, or inclination, do not take to feats of this kind, and must get their fun and exercise in athletics proper. The years of late boyhood and early manhood—say from twelve or fourteen to twenty-eight or thirty, and often until much later—are those in which athletic sports prove not only most attractive, but also most beneficial to the individual and the race. In college—and in most of the schools which are preparatory for college—rowing, foot-ball, base-ball, running, jumping, sparring, and the like have assumed a constantly increasing prominence. Nor is this in any way a matter for regret. Of course any good is accompanied by some evil; and a small number of college boys, who would probably turn out badly anyhow, neglect everything for their sports, and so become of little use to themselves or any one else. But as a whole college life has been greatly the gainer by the change. Only a small proportion of college boys are going to become real students and do original work in literature, science, or art; and these are certain to study their best in any event. The others are going into business or law or some kindred occupation; and these, of course, can study but little that will be directly of use to them in after-life. The college education of such men should be largely devoted to making them good citizens, and able to hold their own in the world; and character is far more important than intellect in making a man a good citizen or successful in his calling—meaning by character not only such qualities as honesty and truthfulness, but courage, perseverance, and self-reliance.

Now, athletic sports, if followed properly, and not elevated into a fetish, are admirable for developing character, besides bestowing on the participants an invaluable fund of health and strength. . . .

The colleges contain but a small proportion of the men interested in amateur athletics, as can be seen by the immense number of ball clubs, rowing clubs, polo clubs, hunt clubs, bicycle clubs, snow-shoe clubs, lacrosse clubs, and athletic clubs proper which are to be found scattered among our cities and towns. Almost any man of sedentary life who wishes to get exercise enough to keep him in vigorous health can readily do so at one of these clubs; and an increasing proportion of our young men are finding this out and acting accordingly. . . .

Already this awakening of interest in manly sports, this proper care of the body, have had a good effect upon our young men; but there are, of course, accompanying dangers in any such movement. With very few exceptions the man who makes some athletic pursuit his main business, instead of turning to it as a health-giving pastime, ceases to be a particularly useful citizen. Of course I do not refer to the men who act as trainers and instructors at the different colleges and clubs; these perform a most useful and honorable function, and among them several could be named who have rendered as high service as any men in the community.

But the amateur athlete who thinks of nothing but athletics, and makes it the serious business of his life, becomes a bore, if nothing worse. A young man who has broken a running or jumping record, who has stroked a winning club crew, or played on his college nine or eleven, has a distinct claim to our respect; but if, when middle-aged, he has still done nothing more in the world, he forfeits even this claim which he originally had.

It is so in an even more marked degree with the "professional" athlete. In America the difference between amateurs and professionals is in one way almost the reverse of what it is in England, and accords better with the ways of life of our democratic community. In England the average professional is a man who works for his living, and the average amateur is one who does not; whereas with us the amateur usually is, and always ought to be, a man who, like other American citizens, works hard at some regular calling,—it matters not what, so long as it is respectable,—while the professional is very apt to be a gentleman of more or less elegant leisure, aside from his special pursuit.

The mere statement of the difference is enough to show that the amateur, and not the professional, is the desirable citizen, the man who should be encouraged. Our object is to get as many of our people as possible to take part in manly, healthy, vigorous pastimes, which will benefit the whole nation; it is not to produce a limited class of athletes who shall make it the business of their lives to do battle with one another for the popular amusement. Most masterful nations have shown a strong taste for manly sports. In the old days, when we ourselves were still a people of backwoodsmen, at every merrymaking there were sure to be trials of skill and strength, at running, wrestling, and rifle-shooting, among the young men. We should encourage by every method the spirit which makes such trials popular; it is a very excellent revival of old-time American ways. But the existence of a caste of gladiators in the midst of a population which does not itself participate in any manly sports is usually, as it was at Rome, a symptom of national decadence.

The Romans who, when the stern and simple strength of Rome was departing, flocked to the gladiatorial shows, were influenced only by a ferocious craving for bloody excitement; not by any sympathy with men of stout heart and tough sinew. So it is, to a lesser extent, today. In baseball alone, the professional teams, from a number of causes, have preserved a fairly close connection with non-professional players, and have done good work in popularizing a most admirable and characteristic American game; but even here the outlook is now less favorable, and, aside from this one pastime, professionalism is the curse of many an athletic sport, and the chief obstacle to its healthy development.

Professional rowing is under a dark cloud of suspicion because of the crooked practices which have disgraced it. Horse-racing is certainly not in an ideal condition. A prize-fight is simply brutal and degrading. The people who attend it, and make a hero of the prizefighter, are,—excepting boys who go for fun and don't know any better,—to a very great extent, men who hover on the border-line of criminality; and those who are not are speedily brutalized, and are never rendered more manly. They form as ignoble a body as do the kindred frequenters of rat-pit and cock-pit. The prizefighter and his fellow professional athletes of the same ilk are, together with their patrons in every rank of life, the very worst foes with whom the cause of general athletic development has to contend.

READING AND DISCUSSION QUESTIONS

1. What distinction does Roosevelt make between the amateur and the professional in sport? Which does he value more and why?

2. What conclusions about audience can you draw from Roosevelt's essay published in *The North American Review*? How might you describe the sort of individuals who subscribed to the magazine? What can you infer about Roosevelt's perspective on class?

3. How does Roosevelt's argument about sport reflect the broader historical context of late-nineteenth-century culture?

18-2 | Arguing the Merits of College for Women

ELIZABETH SHEPLEY SERGEANT, *Educated for What?* (1916)

The imagined fireside conversation Elizabeth Shepley Sergeant drew for readers of *The New Republic* highlights the ambivalence with which early-twentieth-century Americans considered the subject of women's higher education. By the time Sergeant was writing in 1916, women's and coeducational colleges had welcomed young women to the point that some complained about the "feminization" of the university. Still, doubt lingered as to the purpose of women's education. The Victorian sentimentality describing women as better fitted to the roles of mother and wife came into conflict with the modern, which embraced new opportunities for women's personal and professional fulfillment. Sergeant herself blazed trails: graduating from Bryn Mawr in 1903 and pursuing a career in journalism, including a stint as war correspondent in 1917 Paris, where she sustained a battlefield injury.

"Why are women in the professions so halfhearted?" asked Tom suddenly. The question fell like a bomb into the group of five that sat lazily drinking tea by his farmhouse fire. Both Jane and Mary—one an unmarried social investigator, the

Elizabeth Shepley Sergeant, "Educated for What?" *The New Republic*, vol. V (January 1, 1916): 219–220.

other a doctor as well as a wife—sat up argumentatively in their chairs. But Felicia, the hostess, pointing out that men were in a minority, asked Mary's husband, Dr. Jim, to speak his mind first.

"Of course we are all feminists here," he began. "I have given the best proof of it a man can. My own experience of professional women is limited—the only set I've known well were Mary's fellow students at the medical school. But I'm sorry to say I agree with Tom: the first thing that struck me about them was that nine-tenths of them didn't seem to know why they were there. They weren't single-minded about their work as men are. You felt a sort of hesitation, a sort of sag in them. The difference in the spirit—well, it was startling." He shook his head. "Those poor girls seemed sort of haunted."

"Nagged at," suggested Mary.

"That's it. It was as if they had been so nagged at all their lives by non-essentials that they had lost the faculty of keeping their eye on one goal as we two were doing."

Mary returned his look. Their goal was biological research, and they had been pursuing it together through their young twenties with complete unity and an almost dedicated aloofness.

"These are burning questions to Tom and me," said Felicia. "Here we are with three girls to educate. We passionately believe that they must all do some self-supporting work in the world. In fact, even if we could afford not to, we should turn them out of the house at the age of eighteen on principle. But where are we going to direct them? So far they themselves show no interest in the subject."

"Well, it's up to you," said Dr. Jim. "I believe it comes back to home training. Girls have never had a profession kept before them as boys have. Till they do, we won't get anything but amateur professional women."

"Heaven knows," broke out his wife, "why girls do well even in college. It's in spite of their families. Now most of my friends' parents, like my own, were kind, intelligent people, tolerant of college education for girls. You could go if you wanted, and you could probably go on to something else afterward if you insisted. But nobody cared. What I studied, the marks I got—it was all a matter of course, of indifference. They never asked me or themselves what I was being educated for. It happened by miracle that Jim and my career coincided very early in the game."

"Aha!" exclaimed Tom, "now we are getting to the point. Where does matrimony come into woman's education? That is the real question, isn't it?"

"Rot," retorted the doctor briskly. "Don't you go worrying about the mating instinct, Tom. It's quite strong enough to take care of itself. It comes in anywhere and everywhere, because it has to. What we need to cultivate is the professional instinct. Now take my lovely sisters—can't do a blessed thing but sit around and wait to get married. I was never allowed to forget for a day that I had to earn a living and 'make good.' But nothing was expected of the dear girls but domestic accomplishments."

"Now, Jim," protested Felicia, "domestic accomplishments can't be dismissed so easily. Wait till you have a home and children. You're speaking as an interne. I want my daughters to have occupations but I also frankly want them to have husbands, so I believe they should be educated also for domesticity. Indeed, I go farther—I think they must have the sort of occupation that makes the two compatible. You scorn 'odd jobs,' but who's going to do them if not women? The men simply haven't time in the midst of the economic struggle. Of course there are cases where the woman is more creative or a better wage-earner than the man—then he should fill in. But generally speaking, a woman, I don't care what her profession, has got to be willing and able, well—not only to do the marketing, but to go and see a sick grandmother at the end of a hard day, or sit up with the baby."

"Look here," protested Jane, "I claim the right to speak at last, and I object strenuously to sex distinctions in the matter of patchwork—as I do to Felicia's assumption that the professional woman is not in the economic struggle. She *is* there. That's the crux of the matter, and the odd job has got to be either eliminated or shared. Even now we are so handicapped by the necessity of doing our so-called 'woman's work' as well as the other, that it's no wonder the Mme. Curies are unique. Give us five hundred years of really equal opportunity, and, as Jim says, equal psychological expectancy and see what happens. Give us co-education in the professional school and you won't find the sag he noted. I don't believe the women at Johns Hopkins are half-hearted."

"You are trying to evade the issue, Jane," objected Tom. "The handicap, as I see it, is chiefly nature. Surely you don't deny woman's instinct for service? Even in your case, if there's a choice between your work and a human being the work suffers. I myself have seen you wobble."

"You haven't," protested Jane indignantly. "Or if you have it's only because the odd job is there to do, not because I want to do it. And I assure you that if I had been what Felicia calls educated for domesticity I shouldn't have got anywhere at all. It was my academic training that kept me going and made me cherish my small spark."

"You talk, my dear," objected Felicia, "as if you were being less creative when you help to make beautiful human relations than when you write your sociological treatises."

"Can't you understand why the college graduate of my generation takes it hard when radicals like you and Tom turn on her? We had just barely achieved the right to our opportunity against those who claimed it would injure our chances of matrimony. It had even been conceded that we might be old maids if we chose. And now we are wept over because we wither on the tree, and asked to revert to domestic science. What if I prefer a book to a husband? Jim is right: a little mental discipline, a little objectivity of purpose, *will do more* for us, *married* or single, than any lessons in dusting."

"Dusting, nothing!" said Tom. "We are speaking scientifically, I hope. Go on and marry your old book, though the state needs your children, also, and the real problem before feminists to-day is whether it can or can't have both. It's positively ostrich-like to go on assuming that you are training women to be just doctors and sociologists. The college professor knows it isn't so and is bothered, and the modern father, hang it, does insist on knowing what his daughter is being educated for. Can't he pretty well assume it is half for motherhood?"

"So that's what you're driving at, Tom?" remarked Jim. "But reflect that if the lack of outlet for the maternal instinct were the only difficulty, trained nurses—I forgot to mention them before—would be perfectly happy. They are satisfying their instinctive motherhood every hour of the day, yet it is the very exceptional nurse, as I see her, who gets much out of her job but filthy lucre."

"And who isn't ready to cut it all to hook on to the first available man?" added Tom. "Just so. Having chosen to earn her living by satisfying her strongest need, she follows the need through to its logical conclusion."

"The nurse's case is a little outside of our argument," commented Felicia, "but there must be something significant in the enormous proportion of college graduates who go in for teaching and social work—the so to speak maternal professions."

"Nonsense," said Jane. "Those callings attract many besides the born mothers; first because they are obvious, traditional; second because they are cheap and easy so far as higher training goes—by comparison, I mean, with law or medicine."

"But are social workers whole-hearted?" insisted Tom. "Only the exceptional again. And the Lord knows we all complain of the way school teachers dry up. What America needs is more mixing up of work and matrimony, instead of the present artificial separation."

"What women need," said Mary, "is, I insist, professional training. Now science has given me all the weapons I need for life if I can only use them; clearness of sight, economy and honesty of mind, straightness of emotion. It doesn't allow any side tracks or any falterings. So when I have children I shall not hang broodingly over them as you do, Felicia; I shall firmly engage a competent nurse and firmly send them off to a good school later. They will be expected to get more out of my biological discoveries than from my constant attention. But even if I should give up research to-morrow," she added reflectively, "it *would* be worth the grind and the sacrifice of these last years."

Tom burst into a delighted laugh. "There's where I score," he exclaimed. "Six years of medicine in order to be a good wife!"

"Not at all," said Mary, stiffly. "It is true that my profession helps me to stand behind Jim, prevents me from quarrelling with his inevitable detachment as most scientists' wives do. What I personally get out of medicine is a sense of having a share in the independent world of impersonal truth. Half-hearted? Not if I never have children."

"The answer to that is, wait till you do have them, Mary," said Felicia. "Then we shall really be able to judge whether—excuse my pompous language—you can serve both science and the race."

READING AND DISCUSSION QUESTIONS

1. Consider the multiple perspectives on women's education, which Sergeant highlights in her *New Republic* article. What conclusions can you draw about the reasons why some supported and others questioned the usefulness of women's education?

2. How does Sergeant's article reflect the broader historical context of the period? To what extent does the discussion over women's education echo other debates between traditionalists and those pushing new ways of thinking?

18-3 | A Black Leader's Compromise for Racial Opportunity

BOOKER T. WASHINGTON, *Atlanta Cotton States and International Exposition Speech* (1895)

Few speeches in American history have elicited the same attention and controversy as Booker T. Washington's 1895 address before the mostly white audience at the Cotton States and International Exposition held in Atlanta, Georgia. Born a slave, Washington worked and pursued schooling in the Reconstruction era, ultimately becoming president of Tuskegee Normal and Industrial Institute, the all-black college in Alabama. His speech was well received by many whites but infuriated some blacks, including W. E. B. Du Bois, who labeled Washington's ideas for racial advance a compromise to white prejudice.

One-third of the population of the South is of the Negro race. No enterprise seeking the material, civil, or moral welfare of this section can disregard this element of our population and reach the highest success. I but convey to you, Mr. President and Directors, the sentiment of the masses of my race when I say that in no way have the value and manhood of the American Negro been more fittingly and generously recognized than by the managers of this magnificent Exposition at every stage of its progress. It is a recognition that will do more to cement the friendship of the two races than any occurrence since the dawn of our freedom.

Not only this, but the opportunity here afforded will awaken among us a new era of industrial progress. Ignorant and inexperienced, it is not strange that in the first years of our new life we began at the top instead of at the bottom; that a seat in Congress or the state legislature was more sought than real estate or industrial skill; that the political convention or stump speaking had more attractions than starting a dairy farm or truck garden.

A ship lost at sea for many days suddenly sighted a friendly vessel. From the mast of the unfortunate vessel was seen a signal, "Water, water; we die of thirst!" The answer from the friendly vessel at once came back, "Cast down your bucket where you are." A second time the signal, "Water, water; send us water!" ran up from the distressed vessel, and was answered, "Cast down your bucket where you are." And a third and fourth signal for water was answered, "Cast down your bucket where you are." The captain of the distressed vessel, at last heeding the injunction, cast down his bucket, and it came up full of fresh, sparkling water from the mouth of the Amazon River. To those of my race who depend on

Louis R. Harlan, ed., *The Booker T. Washington Papers*, vol. 3 (Urbana: University of Illinois Press, 1974), 583–587.

bettering their condition in a foreign land or who underestimate the importance of cultivating friendly relations with the Southern white man, who is their next-door neighbor, I would say: "Cast down your bucket where you are"—cast it down in making friends in every manly way of the people of all races by whom we are surrounded.

Cast it down in agriculture, mechanics, in commerce, in domestic service, and in the professions. And in this connection it is well to bear in mind that whatever other sins the South may be called to bear, when it comes to business, pure and simple, it is in the South that the Negro is given a man's chance in the commercial world, and in nothing is this Exposition more eloquent than in emphasizing this chance. Our greatest danger is that in the great leap from slavery to freedom we may overlook the fact that the masses of us are to live by the productions of our hands, and fail to keep in mind that we shall prosper in proportion as we learn to dignify and glorify common labour, and put brains and skill into the common occupations of life; shall prosper in proportion as we learn to draw the line between the superficial and the substantial, the ornamental gewgaws of life and the useful. No race can prosper till it learns that there is as much dignity in tilling a field as in writing a poem. It is at the bottom of life we must begin, and not at the top. Nor should we permit our grievances to overshadow our opportunities.

To those of the white race who look to the incoming of those of foreign birth and strange tongue and habits for the prosperity of the South, were I permitted I would repeat what I say to my own race, "Cast down your bucket where you are." Cast it down among the eight millions of Negroes whose habits you know, whose fidelity and love you have tested in days when to have proved treacherous meant the ruin of your firesides. Cast down your bucket among these people who have, without strikes and labour wars, tilled your fields, cleared your forests, builded [sic] your railroads and cities, and brought forth treasures from the bowels of the earth, and helped make possible this magnificent representation of the progress of the South. Casting down your bucket among my people, helping and encouraging them as you are doing on these grounds, and to education of head, hand, and heart, you will find that they will buy your surplus land, make blossom the waste places in your fields, and run your factories. While doing this, you can be sure in the future, as in the past, that you and your families will be surrounded by the most patient, faithful, law-abiding, and un-resentful people that the world has seen. As we have proved our loyalty to you in the past, in nursing your children, watching by the sick-bed of your mothers and fathers, and often following them with tear-dimmed eyes to their graves, so in the future, in our humble way, we shall stand by you with a devotion that no foreigner can approach, ready to lay down our lives, if need be, in defense of yours, interlacing our industrial, commercial, civil, and religious life with yours in a way that shall make the interests of both races one. In all things that are purely social we can be as separate as the fingers, yet one as the hand in all things essential to mutual progress.

There is no defense or security for any of us except in the highest intelligence and development of all. If anywhere there are efforts tending to curtail the fullest growth of the Negro, let these efforts be turned into stimulating, encouraging, and making him the most useful and intelligent citizen. Effort or means so invested will pay a thousand per cent interest. These efforts will be twice blessed—"blessing him that gives and him that takes."

There is no escape through law of man or God from the inevitable:—

The laws of changeless justice bind
Oppressor with oppressed;
And close as sin and suffering joined
We march to fate abreast.

Nearly sixteen millions of hands will aid you in pulling the load upward, or they will pull against you the load downward. We shall constitute one-third and more of the ignorance and crime of the South, or one-third its intelligence and progress; we shall contribute one-third to the business and industrial prosperity of the South, or we shall prove a veritable body of death, stagnating, depressing, retarding every effort to advance the body politic.

Gentlemen of the Exposition, as we present to you our humble effort at an exhibition of our progress, you must not expect overmuch. Starting thirty years ago with ownership here and there in a few quilts and pumpkins and chickens (gathered from miscellaneous sources), remember the path that has led from these to the inventions and production of agricultural implements, buggies, steam-engines, newspapers, books, statuary, carving, paintings, the management of drug stores and banks, has not been trodden without contact with thorns and thistles. While we take pride in what we exhibit as a result of our independent efforts, we do not for a moment forget that our part in this exhibition would fall far short of your expectations but for the constant help that has come to our educational life, not only from the Southern states, but especially from Northern philanthropists, who have made their gifts a constant stream of blessing and encouragement.

The wisest among my race understand that the agitation of questions of social equality is the extremest folly, and that progress in the enjoyment of all the privileges that will come to us must be the result of severe and constant struggle rather than of artificial forcing. No race that has anything to contribute to the markets of the world is long in any degree ostracized. It is important and right that all privileges of the law be ours, but it is vastly more important that we be prepared for the exercise of these privileges. The opportunity to earn a dollar in a factory just now is worth infinitely more than the opportunity to spend a dollar in an opera-house.

In conclusion, may I repeat that nothing in thirty years has given us more hope and encouragement, and drawn us so near to you of the white race, as this opportunity offered by the Exposition; and here bending, as it were, over the altar that represents the results of the struggles of your race and mine, both starting practically empty-handed three decades ago, I pledge that in your effort to work out the great and intricate problem which God has laid at the doors of the

South, you shall have at all times the patient, sympathetic help of my race; only let this be constantly in mind, that, while from representations in these buildings of the product of field, of forest, of mine, of factory, letters, and art, much good will come, yet far above and beyond material benefits will be that higher good, that, let us pray God, will come, in a blotting out of sectional differences and racial animosities and suspicions, in a determination to administer absolute justice, in a willing obedience among all classes to the mandates of law. This, coupled with our material prosperity, will bring into our beloved South a new heaven and a new earth.

READING AND DISCUSSION QUESTIONS

1. What inferences about Washington's audience can you make from the tone and message of his Atlanta speech? How does his argument reflect the historical context of race relations at the time?

2. To what extent did the context of American industrialization shape the reform program Washington advocated for African Americans?

18-4 | Women's Club Movement Attacks Social and Racial Injustice

MARY WHITE OVINGTON, *Black and White Sat Down Together: The Reminiscences of an NAACP Founder* (1932–1933)

The disruptions and unrest industrialization brought as the price for cheap goods and enormous profits inspired women reformers to unite in clubs to define and study social problems. The women's club movement drew on earlier female reform activities, expanding their maternal roles into the public sphere. Mary White Ovington, cofounder of the National Association for the Advancement of Colored People, was a white woman from New York whose family had long supported progressive social causes including women's rights and civil rights for African Americans. In a series of reminiscences published in the *Baltimore Afro-American* in the early 1930s, Ovington honored the work of African American women in advancing the cause of racial justice and social progress.

I have written of my work at the NAACP as Branch Director. It led to my speaking before a number of branches, but I did not go far afield until 1920. That year I was invited to attend the annual conference of the National Association of Colored Women (NACW) at Denver, Colorado. If I went, my expenses would

Mary White Ovington, *Black and White Sat Down Together: The Reminiscences of an NAACP Founder*, ed. Ralph E. Luker (New York: The Feminist Press at the City University of New York, 1995), 94–98.

have to be paid by our Association, so it was arranged that I should do a considerable amount of Branch work on my way to Denver and on my return.

I felt quite professional starting out, not only with the usual suitcase, but also with a briefcase and a typewriter. . . .

It so happens that I have many friends in the library world and I went to the public library at Omaha to meet one of them. As usual, I found her interested in my work. I think that the Negro does not see the library as a public center as much as he might. Librarians want to please their public and they always welcome the intelligent reader of books. The careful reader would be amazed to know how much careless reading there is, a book taken out, skimmed for a possible thrill, never finished. The demand for fiction in such excess of anything else is disheartening. When, therefore, a colored person comes to the library and asks what recent accessions there have been on the Negro or on race prejudice (two subjects one must be up on), it is a pleasure to the librarian to help him. Many librarians will put the *Crisis* on their shelves. More than the school, the library could be used to put the race problem before the country. For the more the Negroes take out good books, the more they will be bought.

At Kansas City, Missouri, and at Kansas City, Kansas, I found Mrs. Cook and Mrs. Dwiggan among the unforgettable women who have been loyal to the NAACP. They had many engagements for me to fill, and when I reached Denver I was ready to go to a hotel and rest before the National Association of Colored Women opened its session.

Resting, with me, included taking a walk. I thought I would start to find my way about the city and I walked to the Negro section and back. The altitude hit me on the head! The remainder of the day was spent resting, quite literally. I wish someone would explain why the altitude in the Rockies is more difficult to endure than the altitude in Switzerland.

Mrs. Mary Talbert was the president of the National at that time and opened the session with her usual dignity and sincerity. She was then engaged in the prodigious and successful work of saving the Frederick Douglass home. I had the honor of knowing Mrs. Talbert and of visiting her at Buffalo in her old-fashioned home, and I want to pay tribute to one of the most intelligent workers with whom I have ever cooperated. She worked untiringly for the NACW. She worked for the NAACP investigating jim crow[1] conditions in Texas, starting branches, and encouraging those already existing. When James Weldon Johnson became secretary, she organized a woman's auxiliary that made possible his great work against lynching.

The women turned in, not hundreds, but thousands of dollars. They made possible our spectacular page in the *New York Times* headed "The Shame of America." They aroused their public to give us money. Mrs. Talbert worked to her physical limit. But her spirit refused to recognize this limit and she ended her life through zeal for service.

---

[1]**jim crow**: Jim Crow was a system of legal discrimination against African Americans.

My readers know a great deal more about the National Association of Colored Women than I do. Some know it from the inside with its discouragements and jealousies. I saw it at its best, but, making all allowance for the optimism of reports, I was profoundly moved by the character and amount of work done. My impressions, as a white woman conversant with social work, may be of interest.

Two existing women's organizations formed the NACW, one of them, the National Federation of Colored Women's Clubs. Perhaps because this was a New England movement, the National Federation was the name in my mind when I went to Denver and I expected to meet with women's clubs somewhat similar to the clubs among whites with which I was familiar.

My mother joined the Brooklyn Woman's Club when I started, and when only one other woman's club could claim priority, Sorosis, of New York. These clubs were frankly cultural. Women had few opportunities then for education and the club was intended to keep up their reading and study, to give them something beside the daily household round. My generation, that had more opportunity for education, looked down on these clubs and made fun of the papers that discussed Roman history in half an hour or covered the field of painting in one session. Clubs like this, I do not doubt, were in the National Federation of New England and in Washington and other cities. But the National Association of Colored Women, as I met with it, was not working along cultural lines but along social service lines. It was starting kindergartens and day nurseries and looking after old people. And it was raising money, in nickels and dimes and quarters, but to an astonishing amount. I never saw anything like it before, and I have never seen anything like it since.

Their motto was, "Lifting as We Climb." Not kicking down the ladder as soon as a slight social eminence was reached, but helping up the one below. The work was given its first impetus nearly thirty years ago by a white physician who wrote an insulting article in which he made the statement that there was not a chaste colored woman in the United States over sixteen.

Some Negro club women met, drew up a strong statement to the country, and then all came together determined to begin service for those young girls of whom this indictment was true. They met at Washington. Frederick Douglass was there. Among the many prominent women was Mrs. Ruffin of Boston; Mrs. Hunton, then a young bride; and, of course, one who has always fought for colored women, Mary Church Terrell. Mrs. Terrell was elected the first president of the National Association of Colored Women.

I listened at Denver to the reports from all sections of the country. In the North, the National's work supplemented the work of organizing charity and of the city and state. In the South, the Negro had to do pretty much everything. What money the city or county or state appropriated for the poor, the sick, the delinquent, was appropriated for the white. Only the courts were busy with the Negro, sending the young boy to the chain gang, the girl to execution, as in the case already mentioned of Virginia Christian. So, the Negro women went to work and out of their scanty means provided old people's homes, opened day nurseries, started work among delinquents.

As I sat and listened, I was thankful that the NAACP existed, pounding away as it did on the issue of full citizenship. But I was glad that the women were doing what they could before these rights were won. Their accomplishments were many. Their work was not always up to the standard, but they had little money and must do the best with that [*sic*] they had. They were all volunteers, and the desire for position, the only reward that can be given a volunteer, was obvious. The greatest menace, common in all volunteer organizations, was the tendency of some workers to grow inactive after the positions they desired were won. But by and large they were hard workers, generous givers.

I wish their story might be written someday and given to the world. Negro work built up by some individual has been frequently featured. Individual Negroes have been honored, but the white world, and white women especially, have no appreciation of the amount of social service work that colored women, without wealth or leisure, have accomplished.

I made my little speech at Denver and was warmly received. I left, grateful for this opportunity. I went as far north as St. Paul and Minneapolis on my return trip, and, when at length I sat down at my desk, I felt that the *New Yorker* was provincial as well as Sinclair Lewis's hero of *Main Street*. There still is diversity in this country if we want to find it. But who wants diversity, anyway? Many are the Americans who ask for fried eggs and cornbeef hash at a Paris restaurant.

READING AND DISCUSSION QUESTIONS

1. What differences does Ovington see in the work and organization of her mother's generation of club women and her own? What factors at the turn of the century might account for the differences she describes? Do these differences clarify distinctions between "Victorian" and "modern"?

2. To what extent were club women like Ovington a contributing cause in the history of the American civil rights movement? How would you assess the contributions of these activists in pushing reform efforts?

18-5 | Social Darwinist Explanation of Women's Dependence
CHARLOTTE PERKINS GILMAN, *Women and Economics* (1898)

The late nineteenth century was deeply imprinted with an interpretation of Charles Darwin's ideas concerning natural selection, which many American intellectuals embraced and modified to help explain the modern world they were inheriting. The feminist social activist and author Charlotte Perkins Gilman was among these intellectuals who saw in Darwin's theories

Charlotte Perkins Gilman, *Women and Economics: A Study of the Economic Relation Between Men and Women as a Factor in Social Evolution* (Boston: Small, Maynard & Company, 1898), 59–63, 71–75.

the explanation for women's subordinate economic relationship to men. Her book *Women and Economics*, published in 1898, became an immediate success, inspiring women's rights activists to challenge the male-dominated cultural norms that led to women's dependence on men.

It should be clear to any one accustomed to the working of biological laws that all the tendencies of a living organism are progressive in their development, and are held in check by the interaction of their several forces. Each living form, with its dominant characteristics, represents a balance of power, a sort of compromise. The size of earth's primeval monsters was limited by the tensile strength of their material. Sea monsters can be bigger, because the medium in which they move offers more support. Birds must be smaller for the opposite reason. The cow requires many stomachs of a liberal size, because her food is of low nutritive value; and she must eat large quantities to keep her machine going. The size of arboreal animals, such as monkeys or squirrels, is limited by the nature of their habitat: creatures that live in trees cannot be so big as creatures that live on the ground. Every quality of every creature is relative to its condition, and tends to increase or decrease accordingly; and each quality tends to increase in proportion to its use, and to decrease in proportion to its disuse. Primitive man and his female were animals, like other animals. They were strong, fierce, lively beasts; and she was as nimble and ferocious as he, save for the added belligerence of the males in their sex-competition. In this competition, he, like the other male creatures, fought savagely with his hairy rivals; and she, like the other female creatures, complacently viewed their struggles, and mated with the victor. At other times she ran about the forest, and helped herself to what there was to eat as freely as he did.

There seems to have come a time when it occurred to the dawning intelligence of this amiable savage that it was cheaper and easier to fight a little female, and have it done with, than to fight a big male every time. So he instituted the custom of enslaving the female; and she, losing freedom, could no longer get her own food or that of her young. The mother ape, with her maternal function well fulfilled, flees leaping through the forest,—plucks her fruit and nuts, keeps up with the movement of the tribe, her young one on her back or held in one strong arm. But the mother woman, enslaved, could not do this. Then man, the father, found that slavery had its obligations: he must care for what he forbade to care for itself, else it died on his hands. So he slowly and reluctantly shouldered the duties of his new position. He began to feed her, and not only that, but to express in his own person the thwarted uses of maternity: he had to feed the children, too. It seems a simple arrangement. When we have thought of it at all, we have thought of it with admiration. The naturalist defends it on the grounds of advantage to the species through the freeing of the mother from all other cares and confining her unreservedly to the duties of maternity. The poet and novelist, the painter and sculptor, the priest and teacher, have all extolled this lovely relation. It remains for the sociologist, from a biological point of view, to note its effects on the constitution of the human race, both in the individual and in society.

When man began to feed and defend woman, she ceased proportionately to feed and defend herself. When he stood between her and her physical environment, she ceased proportionately to feel the influence of that environment and respond to it. When he became her immediate and all-important environment, she began proportionately to respond to this new influence, and to be modified accordingly. In a free state, speed was of as great advantage to the female as to the male, both in enabling her to catch prey and in preventing her from being caught by enemies; but, in her new condition, speed was a disadvantage. She was not allowed to do the catching, and it profited her to be caught by her new master. Free creatures, getting their own food and maintaining their own lives, develope an active capacity for attaining their ends. Parasitic creatures, whose living is obtained by exertions of others, develope powers of absorption and of tenacity,—the powers by which they profit most. The human female was cut off from the direct action of natural selection, that mighty force which heretofore had acted on male and female alike with inexorable and beneficial effect, developing strength, developing skill, developing endurance, developing courage,—in a word, developing species. She now met the influence of natural selection acting indirectly through the male, and developing, of course, the faculties required to secure and obtain a hold on him. Needless to state that these faculties were those of sex-attraction, the one power that has made him cheerfully maintain, in what luxury he could, the being in whom he delighted. For many, many centuries she had no other hold, no other assurance of being fed. The young girl had a prospective value, and was maintained for what should follow; but the old woman, in more primitive times, had but a poor hold on life. She who could best please her lord was the favorite slave or favorite wife, and she obtained the best economic conditions.

With the growth of civilization, we have gradually crystallized into law the visible necessity for feeding the helpless female; and even old women are maintained by their male relatives with a comfortable assurance. But to this day—save, indeed, for the increasing army of women wage-earners, who are changing the face of the world by their steady advance toward economic independence—the personal profit of women bears but too close a relation to their power to win and hold the other sex. From the odalisque with the most bracelets to the débutante with the most bouquets, the relation still holds good,—woman's economic profit comes through the power of sex-attraction. . . .

To the young man confronting life the world lies wide. Such powers as he has he may use, must use. If he chooses wrong at first, he may choose again, and yet again. Not effective or successful in one channel, he may do better in another. The growing, varied needs of all mankind call on him for the varied service in which he finds his growth. What he wants to be, he may strive to be. What he wants to get, he may strive to get. Wealth, power, social distinction, fame,—what he wants he can try for.

To the young woman confronting life there is the same world beyond, there are the same human energies and human desires and ambition within. But all that she may wish to have, all that she may wish to do, must come through a single channel and a single choice. Wealth, power, social distinction, fame,—not only these, but home and happiness, reputation, ease and pleasure, her bread and butter,—all, must come to her through a small gold ring. This is a heavy pressure. It has accumulated behind her through heredity, and continued about her through environment. It has been subtly trained into her through education, till she herself has come to think it a right condition, and pours its influence upon her daughter with increasing impetus. Is it any wonder that women are over-sexed? But for the constant inheritance from the more human male, we should have been queen bees, indeed, long before this. But the daughter of the soldier and the sailor, of the artist, the inventor, the great merchant, has inherited in body and brain her share of his development in each generation, and so stayed somewhat human for all her femininity. . . .

The inevitable trend of human life is toward higher civilization; but, while that civilization is confined to one sex, it inevitably exaggerates sex-distinction, until the increasing evil of this condition is stronger than all the good of the civilization attained, and the nation falls. Civilization, be it understood, does not consist in the acquisition of luxuries. Social development is an organic development. A civilized State is one in which the citizens live in organic industrial relation. The more full, free, subtle, and easy that relation; the more perfect the differentiation of labor and exchange of product, with their correlative institutions,—the more perfect is that civilization. . . . But to serve each other more and more widely; to live only by such service; to develop special functions, so that we depend for our living on society's return for services that can be of no direct use to ourselves,—this is civilization, our human glory and race-distinction.

All this human progress has been accomplished by men. Women have been left behind, outside, below, having no social relation whatever, merely the sex-relation, whereby they lived. Let us bear in mind that all the tender ties of family are ties of blood, of sex-relationship. A friend, a comrade, a partner,—this is a human relative. Father, mother, son, daughter, sister, brother, husband, wife,—these are sex-relatives. Blood is thicker than water, we say. True. But ties of blood are not those that ring the world with the succeeding waves of progressive religion, art, science, commerce, education, all that makes us human. Man is the human creature. Woman has been checked, starved, aborted in human growth; and the swelling forces of race-development have been driven back in each generation to work in her through sex-functions alone.

This is the way in which the sexuo-economic relation has operated in our species, checking race-development in half of us, and stimulating sex-development in both.

READING AND DISCUSSION QUESTIONS

1. Analyze Gilman's use of Social Darwinism to explain women's dependent economic relationship with men. What does she say has been the effect of the sexual division of labor between men and women?

2. Explain how her ideas drew from contemporary intellectual and cultural debates. How did her ideas connect with late-nineteenth-century feminism, social activism, and social science?

▪ COMPARATIVE QUESTIONS ▪

1. Analyze the role gender played in shaping the cultural meaning of terms like *Victorian* and *modern*. How does gender as a lens for interpreting the world show up in the sources in this chapter?

2. In thinking about the effort by historians to interpret particular periods of time, how would you assess the usefulness of the terms *Victorian* and *modern* as descriptors of cultural norms during the years between 1880 and 1916?

3. Analyze the multiple perspectives from this period to offer a coherent interpretation of turn-of-the-century American culture. What conclusions can you draw from the sources to support your argument?

4. To what extent are the cultural changes of these years a cause or consequence of America's industrialization in the late nineteenth century?

5. Compare Washington's advocacy for African Americans with Robert Elliott's speech to Congress (Document 15-6). How did each define the challenge facing African Americans, and what solutions did they propose?

19

"Civilization's Inferno": The Rise and Reform of Industrial Cities

1880–1917

Urban America was full of Dickensian contrasts. The industrial city made possible the enormous wealth that enriched an elite class, built the infrastructure, and endowed the cultural institutions and entertainments that marked America's urban renaissance. At the same time, many immigrant and working-class families struggled to survive. Factories and sweatshops provided jobs but dangers, too. Few workplace health and safety policies existed until tragedies forced legislators to heed the calls of reformers. Living conditions in the ethnically defined neighborhoods inspired social settlement work and a style of journalism exposing the seedy underbelly of America's urban sprawl. African Americans faced their own challenges including lynching and mob violence for crimes committed and alleged. In the face of mounting urban challenges, labor and reform activists, including many women who pioneered and led these movements, targeted local, state, and national legislatures, pressuring them to institute reforms to make city living a decent and healthy possibility for the millions squeezed into the small spaces within the very large and bruising world of urban America.

19-1 | Escaping the City for a Fantasy World of Pleasure
Luna Park at Night (c. 1913)

This postcard of Coney Island's Luna Park captures the thrill and wonder enchanting city dwellers as they escaped, however briefly, the mundane and hard-knock lives they endured as part of New York's working class. Amusement parks like this one treated their customers to dazzling displays, exhilarating rides, and attractions, including Luna Park's famous "Trip to the Moon." This postcard image shows the incandescent main entrance to the park, radiant from the million electric lights beguiling visitors into the nighttime revelry.

READING AND DISCUSSION QUESTIONS

1. This image was the front of a postcard. What conclusions might the historian draw from this artifact, considering its function as a postcard and its depiction of Luna Park? What might have motivated visitors to Luna Park to purchase and use the postcard? What sorts of comments do you imagine senders of these cards wrote?

2. Examine and analyze the details of the image for evidence of early-twentieth-century ideas about work and leisure. What role did amusements play among the middle and working classes?

"Luna Park at Night." © Lake County Museum/Corbis.

19-2 | Competing Against the Party Machine

JANE ADDAMS, *Why the Ward Boss Rules* (1898)

Pioneering social reformer and founder of Hull House, Jane Addams knew political corruption when she saw it. She also understood its power to seduce the poor who depended on the largesse of party bosses dispensing jobs and food to the hungry and unemployed. She intended for the settlement house she established in a poor immigrant neighborhood in Chicago to counter those seductions through educational programs for mothers, classes for children, and activities to uplift, improve, and better both the poor she served and the middle-class women reformers who sought a useful outlet for their time and talents.

[The unusual struggle in Chicago, described in The Outlook last week, between the boss of the Nineteenth Ward and Hull House, was, in a measure, precipitated by a paper prepared by Miss Jane Addams, the head of Hull House, for the "International Journal of Ethics," but read at a meeting in Chicago, and so reported by the Chicago daily papers as to stir the wrath of the Alderman described. The entire paper has just appeared in the "International Journal of Ethics," to the courtesy of whose editors The Outlook is indebted for permission to reprint. We have selected those passages which show why the Alderman, who is the most obedient servant of the monopolies, holds a thus far impregnable position in a ward composed of the very poor. The situation presented is so far from confirming the conclusions of pessimists that it awakens new faith in the supremacy of human virtue, when that virtue manifests itself in constant neighborly kindness instead of annual political sermons. — THE EDITORS.][1]

Primitive people, such as the South Italian peasants who live in the Nineteenth Ward, deep down in their hearts admire nothing so much as the good man. The successful candidate must be a good man according to the standards of his constituents. He must not attempt to hold up a morality beyond them, nor must he attempt to reform or change the standard. If he believes what they believe, and does what they are all cherishing a secret ambition to do, he will dazzle them by his success and win their confidence. Any one who has lived among poorer people cannot fail to be impressed with their constant kindness to each other: that unfailing response to the needs and distresses of their neighbors, even when in danger of bankruptcy themselves. This is their reward for living in the midst of poverty. They have constant opportunities for self-sacrifice and generosity, to which, as a rule, they respond. A man stands by his friend when he gets too drunk to take care of him self, when he loses his wife or child, when he is evicted for non-payment of rent, when he is arrested for a petty crime. It seems to such a man entirely fitting that his Alderman should do the same thing on a larger

---

Jane Addams, "Why the Ward Boss Rules," *Outlook*, vol. LVII (April 2, 1898): 879–882.

[1]This paragraph written by the editors of *Outlook* magazine accompanied the edited text from Jane Addams included in the original 1898 issue and informed readers of the political context she addressed.

scale—that he should help a constituent out of trouble just because he is in trouble, irrespective of the justice involved.

The Alderman, therefore, bails out his constituents when they are arrested, or says a good word to the police justice when they appear before him for trial; uses his "pull" with the magistrate when they are likely to be fined for a civil misdemeanor, or sees what he can do to "fix up matters" with the State's attorney when the charge is really a serious one.

Because of simple friendliness, the Alderman is expected to pay rent for the hard-pressed tenant when no rent is forthcoming, to find jobs when work is hard to get, to procure and divide among his constituents all the places which he can seize from the City Hall. The Alderman of the Nineteenth Ward at one time made the proud boast that he had two thousand six hundred people in his ward upon the public pay-roll. This, of course, included day laborers, but each one felt under distinct obligations to him for getting the job.

If we recollect, further, that the franchise-seeking companies pay respectful heed to the applicants backed by the Alderman, the question of voting for the successful man becomes as much an industrial as a political one. An Italian laborer wants a job more than anything else, and quite simply votes for the man who promises him one. . . .

The Alderman gives presents at weddings and christenings. He seizes these days of family festivities for making friends. It is easiest to reach people in the holiday mood of expansive good will, but on their side it seems natural and kindly that he should do it. The Alderman procures passes from the railroads when his constituents wish to visit friends or to attend the funerals of distant relatives; he buys tickets galore for benefit entertainments given for a widow or a consumptive in peculiar distress; he contributes to prizes which are awarded to the handsomest lady or the most popular man. At a church bazaar, for instance, the Alderman finds the stage all set for his dramatic performance. When others are spending pennies he is spending dollars. Where anxious relatives are canvassing to secure votes for the two most beautiful children who are being voted upon, he recklessly buys votes from both sides, and laughingly declines to say which one he likes the best, buying off the young lady who is persistently determined to find out, with five dollars for the flower bazaar, the posies, of course, to be sent to the sick of the parish. The moral atmosphere of a bazaar suits him exactly. He murmurs many times, "Never mind: the money all goes to the poor" or, "It is all straight enough if the church gets it."

There is something archaic in a community of simple people in their attitude towards death and burial. Nothing so easy to collect money for as a funeral. If the Alderman seizes upon festivities for expressions of his good will, much more does he seize upon periods of sorrow. At a funeral he has the double advantage of ministering to a genuine craving for comfort and solace and at the same time of assisting at an important social function. . . .

A man who would ask at such a time where all this money comes from would be considered sinister. Many a man at such a time has formulated a lenient judgment of political corruption and has heard kindly speeches which he has remembered on election day. "Ah, well, he has a big Irish heart. He is good to the widow and the fatherless." "He knows the poor better than the big guns who are always about talking civil service and reform."

Indeed, what headway can the notion of civic purity, of honesty of administration, make against this big manifestation of human friendliness, this stalking survival of village kindness? . . .

Such an Alderman will keep a standing account with an undertaker, and telephone every week, and sometimes more than once, the kind of outfit he wishes provided for a bereaved constituent, until the sum may roll up into hundreds a year. Such a man understands what the people want, and ministers just as truly to a great human need as the musician or the artist does. I recall an attempt to substitute what we might call a later standard.

A delicate little child was deserted in the Hull House nursery. An investigation showed that it had been born ten days previously in the Cook County Hospital, but no trace could be found of the unfortunate mother. The little thing lived for several weeks, and then, in spite of every care, died. We decided to have it buried by the county, and the wagon was to arrive by eleven o'clock. About nine o'clock in the morning the rumor of this awful deed reached the neighbors. A half-dozen of them came, in a very excited state of mind, to protest. They took up a collection out of their poverty with which to defray a funeral. We were then comparatively new in the neighborhood. We did not realize that we were really shocking a genuine moral sentiment of the community. In our crudeness, we instanced the care and tenderness which had been expended upon the little creature while it was alive; that it had had every attention from a skilled physician and trained nurse; we even intimated that the excited members of the group had not taken part in this, and that it now lay with us to decide that the child should be buried, as it had been born, at the county's expense. It is doubtful whether Hull House has ever done anything which injured it so deeply in the minds of some of its neighbors. We were only forgiven by the most indulgent on the ground that we were spinsters and could not know a mother's heart. No one born and reared in the community could possibly have made a mistake like that. No one who had studied the ethical standards with any care could have bungled so completely. . . .

The question does, of course, occur to many minds. Where does the money come from with which to dramatize so successfully? The more primitive people accept the truthful statement of its sources without any shock to their moral sense. To their simple minds he gets it "from the rich," and so long as he again gives it out to the poor, as a true Robin Hood, with open hand, they have no objections to offer. Their ethics are quite honestly those of the merry making foresters. The next less primitive people of the vicinage are quite willing to admit that he leads "the gang" in the City Council, and sells out the city franchises; that he makes deals with the franchise-seeking companies; that he guarantees to steer dubious measures through the Council, for which he demands liberal pay: that he is, in short, a successful boodler.[1] But when there is intellect enough to get this point of view, there is also enough to make the contention that this is universally

---

[1]**boodler**: Corrupt politician who gives or accepts bribes.

done: that all the Aldermen do it more or less successfully, but that the Alderman of the Nineteenth Ward is unique in being so generous: that such a state of affairs is to be deplored of course, but that that is the way business is run, and we are fortunate when a kind-hearted man who is close to the people gets a large share of the boodle; that he serves these franchised companies who employ men in the building and construction of their enterprises, and that they are bound in return to give jobs to his constituency. Even when they are intelligent enough to complete the circle, and to see that the money comes, not from the pockets of the companies' agents, but from the street-car fares of people like themselves, it almost seems as if they would rather pay two cents more each time they ride than give up the consciousness that they have a big, warm-hearted friend at court who will stand by them in an emergency. The sense of just dealing comes apparently much later than the desire for protection and kindness. The Alderman is really elected because he is a good friend and neighbor.

During a campaign a year and a half ago, when a reform league put up a candidate against our corrupt Alderman, and when Hull House worked hard to rally the moral sentiment of the ward in favor of the new man, we encountered another and unexpected difficulty. Finding that it was hard to secure enough local speakers of the moral tone which we desired, we imported orators from other parts of the town, from the "better element," so to speak. Suddenly we heard it rumored on all sides that, while the money and speakers for the reform candidate were coming from the swells, the money which was backing our corrupt Alderman also came from a swell source: it was rumored that the president of a street-car combination, for whom he performed constant offices in the City Council, was ready to back him to the extent of fifty thousand dollars; that he, too, was a good man, and sat in high places; that he had recently given a large sum of money to an educational institution, and was, therefore, as philanthropic, not to say good and upright, as any man in town: that our Alderman had the sanction of the highest authorities, and that the lecturers who were talking against corruption, and the selling and buying of franchises, were only the cranks, and not the solid business men who had developed and built up Chicago.

All parts of the community are bound together in ethical development. If the so-called more enlightened members of the community accept public gifts from the man who buys up the Council, and the so-called less enlightened members accept individual gifts from the man who sells out the Council, we surely must take our punishment together.

Another curious experience during that campaign was the difference of standards between the imported speakers and the audience. One man, high in the council of the "better element," one evening used as an example of the philanthropic politician an Alderman of the vicinity, recently dead who was devotedly loved and mourned by his constituents. When the audience caught the familiar name in the midst of the platitudes, they brightened up wonderfully. But, as the speaker went on, they first looked puzzled, then astounded, and gradually their astonishment turned to indignation. The speaker, all unconscious of the situation, went on, imagining, perhaps, that he was addressing his usual audience, and totally unaware that he was perpetrating an outrage upon the finest feelings of the people who were sitting before him. He certainly succeeded in irrevocably injuring the chances of the candidate for whom he was speaking. The speaker's standard of ethics was upright dealing in positions of public trust. The standard of ethics held by his audience was, being good to the poor and speaking gently of the dead. If he considered them corrupt and illiterate voters, they quite honestly held him a blackguard.

If we would hold to our political democracy, some pains must be taken to keep on common ground in our human experiences, and to some solidarity in our ethical conceptions. And if we discover that men of low ideals and corrupt practice are forming popular political standards simply because such men stand by and for and with the people, then nothing remains but to obtain a like sense of identification before we can hope to modify ethical standards.

READING AND DISCUSSION QUESTIONS

1. What challenge does Addams see blocking the efforts of urban reformers trying to improve the lives of the working class in Chicago? How did the reform aid she provided differ from the work of party bosses?

2. To what extent do issues of class and gender help and hinder the work of reform she undertook at Hull House? What conclusions about women's role in reform can you draw from Addams's essay?

19-3 | American Dream Meets Tenement Reality

MARIE GANZ AND NAT J. FERBER, *Rebels: Into Anarchy, and Out Again* (1920)

Five-year-old Marie Ganz emigrated with her mother from the central European region of Galicia to join her father, Lazarus, in New York City in 1896. Like millions of other immigrants, Marie and her family left the world they knew for the unknown, but promising, opportunities in America. Her memoir, published in 1920 when she was thirty, evokes the dreams and disappointments immigrant families faced in their early years. Ganz's early experiences inspired her labor reform efforts and anarchism.

It was a home of two tiny rooms. The room in the rear was not much larger than a good-sized clothes closet, and not the stuffiest of closets could be more lacking in sunlight and air. The walls were as blank as an underground dungeon's. There was neither window nor ventilating shaft. The room in front, almost twice as large, though half a dozen steps would have brought anybody with full-grown legs across its entire length, was a kitchen and living-room by day, a bedroom by

Marie Ganz, in collaboration with Nat J. Ferber, *Rebels: Into Anarchy—and Out Again* (New York: Dodd, Mead and Company, 1920), 1–5.

night. Its two little windows gave a view of a narrow, stone-paved court and, not ten feet away, the rear wall of another tenement. The sunlight never found its way into that little court. By day it was dim and damp, by night a fearsome place, black and sepulchral.

In this little bit of a home lived five persons, my father and mother, myself, my baby brother, and Schmeel, our boarder. What squalid home in New York's crowded ghetto is without its boarder? How can that ever-present bogy, the rent, be met without him? He must be wedged in somehow, no matter how little space there may be.

My father had established this home, our first in the New World, through God knows how much toil and worry and self-sacrifice. It took him two years to do it, and he must have haggled with all the bartering instinct of his race over the price of many a banana in the stock on his pushcart in Hester Street before his little hoard of savings had grown large enough to hire and furnish those two miserable rooms and to send tickets to his family in Galicia.

I was only five years old when in the summer of 1896 we joined him in America, but I remember well the day when he met us at Ellis Island. He was like a stranger to me, for I had been not much more than a baby when he left us on our Galician farm, but no child could be on distant terms with him long. Children took to him at once. He understood them, and was never so happy as when joining in their play. A quiet, unobtrusive man was my father, tall and slender, with a short yellow beard and mild blue eyes, and I have not forgotten the childlike glow of happiness that was in his face as he welcomed us.

I suppose it is the experience of most people that among the little scraps of our past lives that we carry with us the most insignificant things are apt to stand out more clearly than others of greater moment. I have found it so. I like to go groping into the past now and then, stirred by curiosity as to how far memory will carry me. It is a fascinating game, this of peering into the dim vistas of the long ago, where the mists of time are shifting as if blown by the wind. Now against the far horizon one scene stands out clearly, then another, as the mists fall apart and close again. Now the perfume of flowers comes to me, and I see our garden in front of the old Galician home—the bright little spot which is all I remember of the Old World. Now a breath of salt air is in my face, and I see a rolling sea and a distant, low-lying shore—my one memory of our journey to America.

But however disconnected and far apart the few scenes that still come back to me from the first years of my life, I have glimpses of our arrival in New York that are as vivid as if it had been only yesterday. In a quiet hour alone I wave the years away, and I am a child again, trudging along beside my father, who, weighted down with the great rolls of bedding we had brought with us from the old home, is guiding us through strange, noisy streets. I am staring in wonder at the great buildings and the never-ending crowds of people. I am frightened, bewildered, ready to cry. I keep a tiny hand twisted in the tail of my father's coat, fearing to lose him.

At last we turn into a dark, dirty alley, which runs like a tunnel under a tenement house and leads us to our future home in the building in the rear.

Oh, how hot and stuffy were those two little rooms that we entered! The city was scorching under one of the hot waves that bring such untold misery to the tenements. Not a breath of air stirred. The place was an oven. But, flushed with heat and perspiring though he was, my father ushered us in with a great show of joy and enthusiasm. Suddenly his smile gave way to an expression that reflected bitter disappointment and injured pride as he became aware of the disgust which my mother could not conceal.

"So we have crossed half the world for this!" she cried, thinking bitterly of the comfortable farmhouse we had left behind us. I can see her now as she stood that moment facing my father, her eyes full of reproach—a pretty, slender woman with thick, black hair and a face as fresh and smooth as a girl's.

I am sure it had never occurred to poor, dreamy, impractical Lazarus Ganz that his wife might be disappointed with the new home he had provided for her, or that he had ever fully realized how squalid it was. He was one of the most sensitive of men, and the look of pain in his face as he saw the impression the place made on her filled me with pity for him, young as I was. A five-year-old child is not apt to carry many distinct memories from that age through life, but that scene I have never forgotten.

When at last it grows dark we creep up flight after flight of narrow stairs, lighted by only a tiny gas flame at each landing, to the roof. Long rows of men, women and children are lying there under the stars. We look off over miles and miles of housetops to where they disappear in a blue haze. We spread the bedding we have carried from below, and we lie down to sleep. All the stars of heaven are winking roguishly down at me as I slip away into dreamland.

Beginning with that first night our housetop had a wonderful fascination for me—the cool breezes, the far vistas over the city's roofs, the mysteries of the night sky, the magic moonlight—a fairyland, a place of romance after the dreary day in the stuffy little rooms below or in the crowded, noisy streets.

READING AND DISCUSSION QUESTIONS

1. Evaluate Ganz's impressions of the city upon her arrival in New York. What conclusions can you draw that help you understand the impact of the urban environment on the lives of immigrants?

2. Ganz's story was a child's experience filtered through the memory of her older self. How was her point of view different from her mother's, and what evidence of her changing perspective does her memoir provide?

3. How does Ganz's experience connect to the broader national and global history of turn-of-the-century migration? Assess whether her experience was determined by her Eastern European roots or if her experience was more a reflection of the general experiences of the immigrant poor.

19-4 | Persistent and Violent Racism Against African Americans

NEW YORK WORLD, *New York Negroes Stage Silent Parade of Protest* (1916)

African Americans had begun to move away from the rural South into more urban areas, including northern cities, by the second decade of the twentieth century, a migration that would peak during the Great Migration of World War I. They continued to suffer persistent racism, bearing the disdain of many whites who never reconciled with emancipation's legacy. Sometimes this hostility erupted into fatal violence. Lynching became epidemic during the late nineteenth and early twentieth centuries, provoking an antilynching campaign among reformers. A silent parade in New York City in 1916 focused attention on this crisis in the African American community, as described in this article from the *New York World*.

Leaders among the negroes of New York City decided that a silent parade would be the most dramatic and effective way to make felt the protest of their race against injustice and inhumanity growing out of lynch law.

And this silent parade was staged with real impressiveness and dignity and with an indefinable appeal to the heart in Fifth Avenue yesterday afternoon.

From the time that the 3,500 or 4,000 men, women, and children marchers left Fifty-sixth Street shortly after 1 o'clock until they were completing their dispersal in Twenty-fourth Street about 3[,] no note of discord was struck.

Police Inspector Morris, who, with upward of one hundred policemen, was in charge of the arrangement down to Forty-second Street, expressed his warm admiration for those in the silent lines.

"They have done everything just right," he said to a reporter for *The World*. "They have been lovely."

And it might be mentioned that this was the first time that the reporter, who has observed many parades in the past few years in New York, ever heard a police official use the adjective "lovely" to describe those whom it is his task to keep in order.

Of the many printed signs prepared by the marchers, Inspector Morris doubted the good taste of only one. It showed a colored mother crouching protectively over two cowering children with the caption, "East St. Louis." And then it showed a photograph of President Wilson and his assertion that the world must be made safe for democracy.

"I asked them if they did not think it was in bad taste too," the Inspector said. "And they agreed that it was and put it aside. They made every effort to have this parade exactly what it was planned to be."

The only sound as the marchers passed down the avenue was the slow tum, tum, tum-tum-tum. And except for little cries of sympathy and admiration from women when they saw a tiny, bright-eyed, kinky-haired baby peeping solemnly

---

Ralph Ginzburg, *100 Years of Lynchings* (Baltimore: Black Classic Press, 1988), 104–106.

over the moist neck of its marching mother, the silence of the parade spread to and enveloped the watchers on the sidewalk too.

There must have been as many colored men and women and babies on the sidewalk as there were in the parade. Probably there were more. And they too showed the same restraint and sense of decorum that governed the marchers.

The parade was led by a drum corps of boys in khaki. Then there were fourteen lines of young girls. After them were six rows of boys, eight-five rows of women, many of them mothers with babies in their arms, and fifty-five lines of men. The lines appeared to average twenty persons.

In the line of march were doctors, lawyers, ministers, school teachers and trained nurses. Many veterans of the Spanish-American War were there too. The Grand Marshal, Capt. Hubert Jackson, served in Cuba and the Philippines as Captain of Company L of the Sixth Massachusetts. Clifton G. A. French, a lawyer, was in the Twenty-third Kansas. He explained the purpose of the parade this way:

"We love our Government. And we want our Government to love us too."

The banners carried aloft bore the following inscriptions:

"Thou shalt not kill."

"Unto the least of these, my brethren."

"Mother, do lynchers go to heaven?"

"Suffer little children and forbid them not."

"Give me a chance to live."

"Mr. President, why not make America safe for democracy."

"The first blood for American independence was shed by a negro, Crispus Attucks."[1]

"Put the spirit of Christ in the making and the execution of laws."

"Your hands are full of blood."

"We have 30,000 teachers."

"Race prejudice is the offspring of ignorance and the mother of lynching."

"Ten thousand of us fought in the Spanish-American War."

"Three thousand negroes fought for American independence under George Washington."

"No negro has ever betrayed his country or attempted to assassinate a President or any official of the Government."

"Patriotism and loyalty presuppose protection and liberty."

"America has lynched without trial 2,867 negroes in thirty-one years. Not a single murderer has suffered."

"Memphis and Waco, centres of American culture?"

"Twenty thousand black men fought for your liberty in the Civil War."

"The world owes no man a living, but every man an opportunity to earn a living."

"Thirty-four negroes have received Carnegie hero medals."

"Our music is the only American music."

---

[1]**Crispus Attucks**: African American killed during the Boston Massacre in 1770.

"A square deal for every man."

And there was another one to the effect that if there is any fault to be found with color, either white people or God is responsible.

READING AND DISCUSSION QUESTIONS

1. Interpret the tone of this newspaper article. To what extent is the author sympathetic to the plight of African Americans? What residue of racism remains? Consider, for instance, the author's attention to the orderliness of the parade.

2. Analyze the inscriptions on the banners African Americans carried in the parade. What message(s) do you think they intended to send and to whom? Who was the audience for their signs and for the silent parade itself?

19-5 | Garment Workers Stand with Union

MARY BROWN SUMNER, *The Spirit of the Strikers* (1910)

In 1909, women workers in the shirtwaist factories in New York left their machines in a strike protesting sweatshop working conditions in the city. Mary Brown Sumner, journalist and activist in women's suffrage, penned an admiring profile of two of the striking women, Fannie Zinsher and Clara Lemlich, in a 1910 article in *The Survey*, a social reform journal. An example of "advocacy journalism," Sumner's sketch praised their solidarity with the cause of workers' rights and what Lemlich called "decent human living." Many of these shirtwaist workers perished in the Triangle Shirtwaist Factory fire in March 1911.

"I hear them say this strike is historical," said a young working girl who stood watching a group of shirtwaist pickets. She did not follow her words up; probably she did not know exactly what she meant to express, but between the lines of slighting jocularity in the newspaper accounts of the strike and the strikers, she had somehow caught an idea that made a strong appeal to her imagination.

And well it might, for this spontaneous strike of the 20,000 is the greatest single event in the history of woman's work. Most remarkable of all, these girls — few of them are over twenty years old — are under the domination of no strong individuals. Secretary Schindler handles the enormously increased volume of executive work quietly and unobtrusively, aided by the volunteer services of Secretary Goldstein of the Bakers' Union. Committees of the various shops meet nightly, then between midnight and three in the morning report in Clinton Hall to the general executive committee which arranges the next day's campaign. Beside them as an efficient advertising medium stands the Woman's Trade Union League which co-operates with the union in committee work, shop meetings and picket duty. Behind them is the Central Federated Union and their faithful reporter, the New York Call, whose employes even gave extra service to get out the strike edition. But where are the agitators, where are the labor leaders who, the girls in the settled shops say their employers tell them, must be plotting for power and pelf somewhere in the background?

There are none—or rather, "their name is legion." Into the foreground of this great moving picture comes the figure of one girl after another as her services are needed. For the time being she is perfectly regardless of self. With extraordinary simplicity and eloquence she will tell before any kind of audience, without false shame and without self-glorification, the conditions of her work, her wages, and the pinching poverty of her home and the homes of her comrades. Then she withdraws into the background to undertake quietly the danger and humiliation of picket duty or to become a nameless sandwich-girl selling papers on the street; no longer the center of interested attention, but the butt of the most unspeakable abuse. "Streetwalker" is one of the terms that the police and the thugs apply daily to the strikers, in fact it has become in their vocabulary almost synonymous with striker.

Many visits to Clinton Hall during the strike have brought me into contact with numbers of these little soldiers of the common good. Two stand out in my mind, Fanny Zinsher of the Triangle Shop, and Clara Lemlich of Leiserson's.[1] Their stories are typical of many others, their personalities are distinctively their own. Both of them are only twenty years old, both came to this country from Russia five years ago, both are ambitious to rise out of their trade into a profession, and both have sacrificed for the sake of this strike money saved to attain this end. These girls are typical, this same outline of a life history applies equally well to many other young strikers. All have stood as one to improve the conditions in a trade which most of them, all but the weaker,—those that could not have stood up for themselves—will leave for marriage or a higher profession. . . .

I have two pictures of Fanny Zinsher in my mind, one as she came from Russia at fourteen, fleeing from persecution to free America, with round cheeks, smiling, irresponsible lips and clear eyes full of interest and delight in living; the other after five years of American freedom, with sad sweet eyes whose sight was strained by the flashing of the needle and by study late at night, mouth drooping with a weight of sadness and responsibility and an expression of patience and endurance far beyond her twenty years.

She came a little high school girl from Kishineff to San Francisco. She did not know what work for wages was, but she and her brother four years older had to turn to and support a mother and a little brother. Three hundred power-machines in one long room of the garment factory welcomed this little human machine-in-the-making. The roar and flash of the needles terrified her. She tried to work but her nerves went more and more to pieces, her frightened eyes failed to follow her

---

[1]**Leiserson's:** Like the Triangle Shirtwaist Company, Leiserson's was another sweatshop employing large numbers of women whose employees went out on strike.

fingers as they guided her work and the second day she slit a finger open and was laid up for three weeks. When she returned she could adapt herself no better to the nervous strain. At piece work she could earn little over one dollar a week, until a kind forewoman removed her to a smaller room where in time she rose to five dollars.

To the older generation among the Russian Jews the hardest thing of all about America is to find that they can take no part in industry; that it is only their little children, cherished and protected by their patriarchal institutions at home, who are quick and "smart" enough to be used in our industries. For the sixteen years of her widowhood Mrs. Zinsher had supported her family in Russia trying to give them a fair start in life, and now after six months in California she felt that the fear of persecution at home, near relatives and friends, was not so deadly for her children as the machine, with no hope, even, of better things to follow. With what remained of the money she had brought to America she came east to sail, only to learn that a second massacre of her race was going on at Kishineff. So the two children settled down again to the machine and in a year the third boy took up the work. . . .

In the four years preceding the strain was continuous—to adjust oneself to mechanical work at a high tension all day and then turn to mental work at night and all Sunday. And during that time distress and worry of mind were seldom absent. The student frequently lost her place because school prevented her from working the prescribed number of hours a day—that is, from 8 A.m. to 8:30 P.m. for about six months in the year, and Sunday from 8 to 1, or sometimes to 5. For the same reason her pay was small, even when she had work. The end of mingled study and work came a year ago when she went to the position she held when the strike began, making nine dollars a week for the long day—tucking 2,200 yards a day, for which she should have received $13.20 at the piece wage of $2.20 a day—and planning to save for study. . . .

For eighteen weeks Fanny has been out of work and her only fear is that her brother's idleness may force her back into a "settled shop" while her services are still needed by the union. Since the beginning she has been indefatigable, speaking before clubs and trade unions in town and in the suburbs, taking charge at Clinton Hall of the sale of the special strike editions of the newspapers; on hand from early morning till 11 o'clock at night, working harder than she ever worked at a machine. She believes that the strike will be won; she says that if nothing else, the very conditions in the shops which employ strike-breakers will win it in the end for the union. Those that now offer double pay for bad work, short hours and the long lunch hour, the free lunch and waltz music on the gramophone, will be forced to withdraw these privileges and the strike-breakers will be pressed down lower than the strikers were. Then they, too, will recognize, she says, that "the boss wants to get the most out of the workers and that their only hope of decent human living is in sticking together."

Fannie Zinsher is strong and steadfast, but the soul of this young women's revolution is Clara Lemlich, a spirit of fire and tears, devoid of egotism, unable to tolerate the thought of human suffering. The dramatic climax of the strike came when this girl was raised to the platform at Cooper Union and "with the simplicity of genius," as one reporter says, put the motion for the general strike. "I have listened to all the speakers and I have no patience for talk. I am one who feels and suffers for the things pictured. I move that we go on a general strike," she said. Dramatic, too, was the moment two years before when she stood, a solitary little figure, distributing circulars of her union to the girls employed in "the worst shop in New York." For this "disorderly conduct" she was arrested and had her first experience of a prison cell. . . .

At sixteen her real education began—in the shop. Her description of the slow and blundering way she pieced together the relation of the workers to their work and their employer recalls the slow dawning in Judge Lindsey's[2] mind of the outline of the "Beast." What outraged her most from the beginning were the petty persecutions, the meannesses, and the failure to recognize the girls as human beings. She tells of the forewoman following a girl if she left the room and hurrying her back again, of the pay of the new girls kept down because they did not know what the market rate was, of excessive fines, of frequent "mistakes" in pay envelopes hard and embarrassing to rectify; of a system of registering on the time clock that stole more than twenty minutes from the lunch hour, of the office clock covered so that the girls could not waste time looking at it, or put back an hour so that they should not know that they were working overtime. She sat and worked and observed, and her greatest wonder was that the workers endured this constant dragging down of their self-respect.

Very soon she began to say things that made her parents call her a "socialist." She thought more deeply about her industrial experiences in America, and became one. At the same time she joined the International Union of Shirtwaist Makers—one of the handful who fought for years to keep that infant union alive. From that time she became an agitator in a small way. She had no personal grievance. She was a draper, always well paid and in demand. She needed money, furthermore, because she wished to take a course in medicine, but this did not prevent her from trying persistently to organize every shop she worked in. She tells of one time when she felt that she must keep her place and determined to be "a good girl"—from the boss's point of view—but in two days found herself talking unionism again. She found, too, then as almost always, that the girls listened and in a crude sort of way hung together in the shop even when they did not join the union. She gradually learned to look for work in the smaller shops where she could make her influence felt. Two years ago the girls in her shop went out on strike because in one department married men were being turned off to make room for cheap girls. That is Clara Lemlich's idea of solidarity.

In this present strike the girls "walked out to prevent themselves from being starved out," she says. Their employer who is reckoned worth $100,000—the

---

[2]**Judge Lindsey's**: Judge Ben Lindsey of Denver won fame for his reform of juvenile court procedures and for his opposition to the "beast," the political machine running the city's government.

whole of it made in the garment trade in the last three years—decided that his employes were too expensive and, as in Fannie Zinsher's shop, tried to get rid of them gradually on the ground of slack work. Soon the girls found that he was sending his work to a cheap shop he had started downtown, or giving it to the low paid girls in their own shop. Then the battle was joined in good earnest. Clara went on picket duty, was attacked and so badly hurt that she was laid up for several days. This did not deter her; she went back to her post and, being a logical talker, straightforward and well fitted to gain the confidence of her comrades, she was able to add to the number of the strikers. She even gathered a crowd around her on the street corner and enlisted their sympathies in the strikers.

Through the monotonous years when nobody took an interest in the union, when even those who were nominally members would not attend or properly support it, Clara Lemlich's hope lived on the vivid appeal to the imagination of the idea of the brotherhood of labor, and the pitiful plight of the young and light-headed and helpless in her trade kept her fighting spirit up. And now with the general strike her faith had justified itself far beyond her expectation. "We never really expected," she said after the Cooper Union meeting, "that the mass of the workers would be inspired and come out." But they did, and so strongly was she moved by their action that, she tells you with a faint flush, she ended her report on the floor of the Central Federated Union the next day with the words, "I seem to see the realization of the words of Karl Marx: 'Workers of the world, unite. You have nothing to lose but your chains; you have the world to gain.'"

But all is not exhilaration in this struggle. There is much hard work and much discouragement. The hard work she has done bravely. She has refused a paid position in the union but speaks continually in public in its behalf, serves on shop committees and on the general executive committee. She faces with a full realization the long, discouraging task of keeping alive the union spirit and putting it on the basis of a permanent intellectual and moral appeal. She faces the laborious task of adjusting the details of agreements with employers in the various shops and is already looking forward to the next steps, when they shall demand the union label on shirtwaists and set on foot a broad system of training for learners in the shops. She does not believe that the strike can fail for it has a spirit that will carry it through, and she feels that even after "the tumult and the shouting dies," a new understanding of their relation to each other will have dawned on the girls, and from this time on the workers in the garment trades will stand together.

READING AND DISCUSSION QUESTIONS

1. Analyze Sumner's point of view toward what she calls the "spirit" of the striking women workers. How does she describe this spirit and its effects on women and on the labor movement?

2. What evidence of women's power does Sumner's profile of the shirtwaist strike provide historians seeking to understand the early-twentieth-century labor movement?

19-6 | Muckraker Exposes Chicago's Meat-Packing Industry
UPTON SINCLAIR, *The Jungle* (1906)

Social reformers exposed the evils of the industrial economy through a new form of investigative journalism caricatured by some as "muckraking" for the filth they stirred while peering into the unhealthy and dehumanizing conditions then existing in the nation's factories. With a journalist's eye for detail, author Upton Sinclair investigated Chicago's meat-packing industry, expecting to shock readers of his novel *The Jungle* with scenes of a workplace dystopia, where laborers were abused to the point of mental and physical collapse. In the end, the novel's graphic depictions of the "disassembly" line, where pigs were butchered into the nation's packaged meat industry, captured the most attention, resulting in a public outcry and passage of the Meat Inspection Act and the Pure Food and Drug Act.

There is over a square mile of space in the yards, and more than half of it is occupied by cattle-pens; north and south as far as the eye can reach there stretches a sea of pens. And they were all filled—so many cattle no one had ever dreamed existed in the world. Red cattle, black, white, and yellow cattle; old cattle and young cattle; great bellowing bulls and little calves not an hour born; meek-eyed milch cows and fierce, long-horned Texas steers. The sound of them here was as of all the barnyards of the universe; and as for counting them—it would have taken all day simply to count the pens. Here and there ran long alleys, blocked at intervals by gates; and Jokubas told them that the number of these gates was twenty-five thousand. Jokubas had recently been reading a newspaper article which was full of statistics such as that, and he was very proud as he repeated them and made his guests cry out with wonder. Jurgis[1] too had a little of this sense of pride. Had he not just gotten a job, and become a sharer in all this activity, a cog in this marvellous machine?

Here and there about the alleys galloped men upon horseback, booted, and carrying long whips; they were very busy, calling to each other, and to those who were driving the cattle. They were drovers and stock-raisers, who had come from far states, and brokers and commission-merchants, and buyers for all the big packing-houses. Here and there they would stop to inspect a bunch of cattle, and there would be a parley, brief and businesslike. The buyer would nod or drop his whip, and that would mean a bargain; and he would note it in his little book, along with hundreds of others he had made that morning. Then Jokubas pointed out the place where the cattle were driven to be weighed, upon a great scale that would weigh a hundred thousand pounds at once and record it automatically. It was near to the east entrance that they stood, and all along this east side of the yards ran the railroad tracks, into which the cars were run, loaded with cattle. All

Upton Sinclair, *The Jungle* (New York: Doubleday, Page & Company, 1906), 37–41.

[1]Jokubas Szedvilas and Jurgis Rudkus, two characters in the novel, both emigrate from Lithuania and ultimately succumb to what Sinclair describes as the brutalities of capitalism.

night long this had been going on, and now the pens were full; by to-night they would all be empty, and the same thing would be done again.

"And what will become of all these creatures?" cried Teta Elzbieta.

"By to-night," Jokubas answered, "they will all be killed and cut up; and over there on the other side of the packing-houses are more railroad tracks, where the cars come to take them away."

There were two hundred and fifty miles of track within the yards, their guide went on to tell them. They brought about ten thousand head of cattle every day, and as many hogs, and half as many sheep—which meant some eight or ten million live creatures turned into food every year. One stood and watched, and little by little caught the drift of the tide, as it set in the direction of the packing-houses. There were groups of cattle being driven to the chutes, which were roadways about fifteen feet wide, raised high above the pens. In these chutes the stream of animals was continuous; it was quite uncanny to watch them, pressing on to their fate, all unsuspicious—a very river of death. Our friends were not poetical, and the sight suggested to them no metaphors of human destiny; they thought only of the wonderful efficiency of it all. The chutes into which the hogs went climbed high up—to the very top of the distant buildings; and Jokubas explained that the hogs went up by the power of their own legs, and then their weight carried them back through all the processes necessary to make them into pork.

"They don't waste anything here," said the guide, and then he laughed and added a witticism, which he was pleased that his unsophisticated friends should take to be his own: "They use everything about the hog except the squeal." In front of Brown's General Office building there grows a tiny plot of grass, and this, you may learn, is the only bit of green thing in Packingtown; likewise this jest about the hog and his squeal, the stock in trade of all the guides, is the one gleam of humor that you will find there.

After they had seen enough of the pens, the party went up the street, to the mass of buildings which occupy the centre of the yards. These buildings, made of brick and stained with innumerable layers of Packingtown smoke, were painted all over with advertising signs, from which the visitor realized suddenly that he had come to the home of many of the torments of his life. It was here that they made those products with the wonders of which they pestered him so—by placards that defaced the landscape when he travelled, and by staring advertisements in the newspapers and magazines—by silly little jingles that he could not get out of his mind, and gaudy pictures that lurked for him around every street corner. Here was where they made Brown's Imperial Hams and Bacon, Brown's Dressed Beef, Brown's Excelsior Sausages! Here was the headquarters of Durham's Pure Leaf Lard, of Durham's Breakfast Bacon, Durham's Canned Beef, Potted Ham, Devilled Chicken, Peerless Fertilizer!

Entering one of the Durham buildings, they found a number of other visitors waiting; and before long there came a guide, to escort them through the place. They make a great feature of showing strangers through the packing-plants, for it is a good advertisement. But ponas [Mr.] Jokubas whispered maliciously that the visitors did not see any more than the packers wanted them to.

They climbed a long series of stairways outside of the building, to the top of its five or six stories. Here were the chute, with its river of hogs, all patiently toiling upward; there was a place for them to rest to cool off, and then through another passageway they went into a room from which there is no returning for hogs.

It was a long, narrow room, with a gallery along it for visitors. At the head there was a great iron wheel, about twenty feet in circumference, with rings here and there along its edge. Upon both sides of this wheel there was a narrow space, into which came the hogs at the end of their journey; in the midst of them stood a great burly negro, bare-armed and bare-chested. He was resting for the moment, for the wheel had stopped while men were cleaning up. In a minute or two, however, it began slowly to revolve, and then the men upon each side of it sprang to work. They had chains which they fastened about the leg of the nearest hog, and the other end of the chain they hooked into one of the rings upon the wheel. So, as the wheel turned, a hog was suddenly jerked off his feet and borne aloft.

At the same instant the ear was assailed by a most terrifying shriek; the visitors started in alarm, the women turned pale and shrank back. The shriek was followed by another, louder and yet more agonizing — for once started upon that journey, the hog never came back; at the top of the wheel he was shunted off upon a trolley, and went sailing down the room. And meantime another was swung up, and then another, and another, until there was a double line of them, each dangling by a foot and kicking in frenzy — and squealing. The uproar was appalling, perilous to the ear-drums; one feared there was too much sound for the room to hold — that the walls must give way or the ceiling crack. There were high squeals and low squeals, grunts, and wails of agony; there would come a momentary lull, and then a fresh outburst, louder than ever, surging up to a deafening climax. It was too much for some of the visitors — the men would look at each other, laughing nervously, and the women would stand with hands clenched, and the blood rushing to their faces, and the tears starting in their eyes.

Meantime, heedless of all these things, the men upon the floor were going about their work. Neither squeals of hogs nor tears of visitors made any difference to them; one by one they hooked up the hogs, and one by one with a swift stroke they slit their throats. There was a long line of hogs, with squeals and life-blood ebbing away together; until at last each started again, and vanished with a splash into a huge vat of boiling water.

It was all so very businesslike that one watched it fascinated. It was pork-making by machinery, pork-making by applied mathematics. And yet somehow the most matter-of-fact person could not help thinking of the hogs; they were so innocent, they came so very trustingly; and they were so very human in their protests — and so perfectly within their rights! They had done nothing to deserve it; and it was adding insult to injury, as the thing was done here, swinging them up in this cold-blooded, impersonal way, without a pretence at apology, without the homage of a tear. Now and then a visitor wept, to be sure; but this slaughtering-machine ran on, visitors or no visitors. It was like some horrible crime committed in a dungeon, all unseen and unheeded, buried out of sight and of memory.

One could not stand and watch very long without becoming philosophical, without beginning to deal in symbols and similes, and to hear the hog-squeal of the universe. Was it permitted to believe that there was nowhere upon the earth, or above the earth, a heaven for hogs, where they were requited for all this suffering? Each one of these hogs was a separate creature. Some were white hogs, some were black; some were brown, some were spotted; some were old, some were young; some were long and lean, some were monstrous. And each of them had an individuality of his own, a will of his own, a hope and a heart's desire; each was full of self-confidence, of self-importance, and a sense of dignity. And trusting and strong in faith he had gone about his business, the while a black shadow hung over him and a horrid Fate waited in his pathway. Now suddenly it had swooped upon him, and had seized him by the leg. Relentless, remorseless, it was; all his protests, his screams, were nothing to it—it did its cruel will with him, as if his wishes, his feelings, had simply no existence at all; it cut his throat and watched him gasp out his life. And how was one to believe that there was nowhere a god of hogs, to whom this hog-personality was precious, to whom these hog-squeals and agonies had a meaning? Who would take this hog into his arms and comfort him, reward him for his work well done, and show him the meaning of his sacrifice? Perhaps some glimpse of all this was in the thoughts of our humble-minded Jurgis, as he turned to go on with the rest of the party, and muttered: "Dieve [God]—but I'm glad I'm not a hog!"

READING AND DISCUSSION QUESTIONS

1. How do you assess *The Jungle* as a cause of Progressive-Era legislation? Distinguish between short-term or immediate causes, like the publication of Sinclair's novel, and longer-term causes of reform legislation, such as unsanitary working conditions.

2. Analyze and explain Sinclair's point of view toward workplace conditions. To what extent does his depiction of the Chicago meat-packing industry reflect Progressive-Era concerns about social democracy or the ability of individuals to live and participate fully in civil society?

▪ COMPARATIVE QUESTIONS ▪

1. Compare Jane Addams's reform efforts with the women's club activities Mary White Ovington describes in Document 18-4. What similarities do you see in their approach to reform and in the challenges they faced?

2. What response do you think *The Jungle* would have elicited from such different reformers as Jane Addams and Marie Ganz? How might each have interpreted the evidence of workplace abuse Sinclair presented in novel form?

3. Why do you think Progressive-Era reformers adopted the strategies they did? What methods did they believe would achieve the most lasting effect? Were their methods successful? Did they have in mind similar audiences?

4. After having read and analyzed the multiple perspectives presented in this chapter, describe the ways in which working-class Americans responded to the challenges of the industrial city. Which tactics seemed to work best, and which hindered or did not have much effect on their struggle?

20

Whose Government? Politics, Populists, and Progressives
1880–1917

Turn-of-the-century reformers had plenty of targets. The industrial economy and urban development created opportunities and problems. The
problems kept both Populists and progressives busy but in different ways.
Both groups pointed to failures in the laissez-faire capitalist system as it
had matured in the context of industrialization, spawning monopolies and
political manipulation and corruption that threatened the fabric of democratic self-governance. These reform groups, irritated by the indifference of
the two major parties controlled by political bosses and Wall Street manip-
ulators, forged new movements designed to wrest control from vested
interests and return power to the people. Of course, specific issues divided
reformers, rendering any coherence within progressive ranks all but
impossible to achieve. Still, the era accomplished a great deal, mobilizing
efforts to reform civic government, introducing workplace health and
safety regulations, and addressing persistent racism and discrimination
against African Americans. Despite an unfinished agenda, this period of
reform helped create the modern state whose architecture survives into the
twenty-first century.

20-1 | Populist Manifesto for a Reformed America
Omaha Platform (1892)

The People's Party crested then fell in the 1890s, but at the time it was the only viable alternative to the entrenched political interests represented by Republicans and Democrats. Formed largely from local and regional Farmers' Alliances and the Granger movement in the 1880s, populism represented a broad spectrum of disgruntled Americans critical of concentrated wealth and corporate power. Their agenda, clarified in the party's 1892 platform, pushed a series of political reforms. More broadly, they offered an alternative vision for government's role in modern America, one whose details alarmed corporate interests and the more affluent Americans profiting from the status quo.

Assembled upon the 116th anniversary of the Declaration of Independence, the People's Party of America, in their first national convention, invoking upon their action the blessing of Almighty God, put forth in the name and on behalf of the people of this country, the following preamble and declaration of principles:

Preamble

The conditions which surround us best justify our co-operation; we meet in the midst of a nation brought to the verge of moral, political, and material ruin. Corruption dominates the ballot-box, the Legislatures, the Congress, and touches even the ermine of the bench. The people are demoralized; most of the States have been compelled to isolate the voters at the polling places to prevent universal intimidation and bribery. The newspapers are largely subsidized or muzzled, public opinion silenced, business prostrated, homes covered with mortgages, labor impoverished, and the land concentrating in the hands of capitalists. The urban workmen are denied the right to organize for self-protection, imported pauperized labor beats down their wages, a hireling standing army, unrecognized by our laws, is established to shoot them down, and they are rapidly degenerating into European conditions. The fruits of the toil of millions are boldly stolen to build up colossal fortunes for a few, unprecedented in the history of mankind; and the possessors of those, in turn, despise the republic and endanger liberty. From the same prolific womb of governmental injustice we breed the two great classes — tramps and millionaires.

The national power to create money is appropriated to enrich bondholders; a vast public debt payable in legal tender currency has been funded into gold-bearing bonds, thereby adding millions to the burdens of the people.

Silver, which has been accepted as coin since the dawn of history, has been demonetized to add to the purchasing power of gold by decreasing the value of

---

The World Almanac, 1893 (New York: 1893), 83–85. Reprinted in George Brown Tindall, ed., *A Populist Reader, Selections from the Works of American Populist Leaders* (New York: Harper & Row, 1966), 90–96.

all forms of property as well as human labor, and the supply of currency is purposely abridged to fatten usurers, bankrupt enterprise, and enslave industry. . . .

We have witnessed for more than a quarter of a century the struggles of the two great political parties for power and plunder, while grievous wrongs have been inflicted upon the suffering people. We charge that the controlling influences dominating both these parties have permitted the existing dreadful conditions to develop without serious effort to prevent or restrain them. Neither do they now promise us any substantial reform. They have agreed together to ignore, in the coming campaign, every issue but one. They propose to drown the outcries of a plundered people with the uproar of a sham battle over the tariff, so that capitalists, corporations, national banks, rings, trusts, watered stock, the demonetization of silver and the oppressions of the usurers may all be lost sight of. They propose to sacrifice our homes, lives, and children on the altar of mammon;[1] to destroy the multitude in order to secure corruption funds from the millionaires.

Assembled on the anniversary of the birthday of the nation, and filled with the spirit of the grand general and chief who established our independence, we seek to restore the government of the Republic to the hands of "the plain people," with which class it originated. We assert our purposes to be identical with the purposes of the National Constitution; to form a more perfect union and establish justice, insure domestic tranquillity, provide for the common defence, promote the general welfare, and secure the blessings of liberty for ourselves and our posterity.

We declare that this Republic can only endure as a free government while built upon the love of the whole people for each other and for the nation; that it cannot be pinned together by bayonets; that the civil war is over, and that every passion and resentment which grew out of it must die with it, and that we must be in fact, as we are in name, one united brotherhood of free men.

Our country finds itself confronted by conditions for which there is no precedent in the history of the world; our annual agricultural productions amount to billions of dollars in value, which must, within a few weeks or months, be exchanged for billions of dollars' worth of commodities consumed in their production; the existing currency supply is wholly inadequate to make this exchange; the results are falling prices, the formation of combines and rings, the impoverishment of the producing class. We pledge ourselves that if given power we will labor to correct these evils by wise and reasonable legislation, in accordance with the terms of our platform. . . .

Platform

We declare, therefore—

First.—That the union of the labor forces of the United States this day consummated shall be permanent and perpetual; may its spirit enter into all hearts for the salvation of the Republic and the uplifting of mankind.

---

[1]**mammon**: Riches, or material wealth.

Second.—Wealth belongs to him who creates it, and every dollar taken from industry without an equivalent is robbery. "If any will not work, neither shall he eat." The interests of rural and civic labor are the same; their enemies are identical.

Third.—We believe that the time has come when the railroad corporations will either own the people or the people must own the railroads, and should the government enter upon the work of owning and managing all railroads, we should favor an amendment to the Constitution by which all persons engaged in the government service shall be placed under a civil-service regulation of the most rigid character, so as to prevent the increase of the power of the national administration by the use of such additional government employes.

FINANCE.—We demand a national currency, safe, sound, and flexible, issued by the general government only, a full legal tender for all debts, public and private, and that without the use of banking corporations, a just, equitable, and efficient means of distribution direct to the people, at a tax not to exceed 2 per cent. per annum, to be provided as set forth in the sub-treasury plan of the Farmers' Alliance, or a better system; also by payments in discharge of its obligations for public improvements.

1. We demand free and unlimited coinage of silver and gold at the present legal ratio of 16 to 1.
2. We demand that the amount of circulating medium be speedily increased to not less than $50 per capita.
3. We demand a graduated income tax.
4. We believe that the money of the country should be kept as much as possible in the hands of the people, and hence we demand that all State and national revenues shall be limited to the necessary expenses of the government, economically and honestly administered.
5. We demand that postal savings banks be established by the government for the safe deposit of the earnings of the people and to facilitate exchange.

TRANSPORTATION.—Transportation being a means of exchange and a public necessity, the government should own and operate the railroads in the interest of the people. The telegraph, telephone, like the post-office system, being a necessity for the transmission of news, should be owned and operated by the government in the interest of the people.

LAND.—The land, including all the natural sources of wealth, is the heritage of the people, and should not be monopolized for speculative purposes, and alien ownership of land should be prohibited. All land now held by railroads and other corporations in excess of their actual needs, and all lands now owned by aliens should be reclaimed by the government and held for actual settlers only.

Expression of Sentiments

Your Committee on Platform and Resolutions beg leave unanimously to report the following:

Whereas, Other questions have been presented for our consideration, we hereby submit the following, not as a part of the Platform of the People's Party, but as resolutions expressive of the sentiment of this Convention.

1. RESOLVED, That we demand a free ballot and a fair count in all elections and pledge ourselves to secure it to every legal voter without Federal Intervention, through the adoption by the States of the unperverted Australian or secret ballot system.

2. RESOLVED, That the revenue derived from a graduated income tax should be applied to the reduction of the burden of taxation now levied upon the domestic industries of this country.

3. RESOLVED, That we pledge our support to fair and liberal pensions to ex-Union soldiers and sailors.

4. RESOLVED, That we condemn the fallacy of protecting American labor under the present system, which opens our ports to the pauper and criminal classes of the world and crowds out our wage-earners; and we denounce the present ineffective laws against contract labor, and demand the further restriction of undesirable emigration.

5. RESOLVED, That we cordially sympathize with the efforts of organized workingmen to shorten the hours of labor, and demand a rigid enforcement of the existing eight-hour law on Government work, and ask that a penalty clause be added to the said law.

6. RESOLVED, That we regard the maintenance of a large standing army of mercenaries, known as the Pinkerton system, as a menace to our liberties, and we demand its abolition. . . .

7. RESOLVED, That we commend to the favorable consideration of the people and the reform press the legislative system known as the initiative and referendum.

8. RESOLVED, That we favor a constitutional provision limiting the office of President and Vice-President to one term, and providing for the election of Senators of the United States by a direct vote of the people.

9. RESOLVED, That we oppose any subsidy or national aid to any private corporation for any purpose.

10. RESOLVED, That this convention sympathizes with the Knights of Labor and their righteous contest with the tyrannical combine of clothing manufacturers of Rochester, and declare it to be a duty of all who hate tyranny and oppression to refuse to purchase the goods made by the said manufacturers, or to patronize any merchants who sell such goods.

READING AND DISCUSSION QUESTIONS

1. Analyze the party's platform for evidence of Populists' diagnosis of society's ills. What specifically did they see wrong with the national economy, and what measures did they advocate as part of their reform agenda?

2. In reading the party's platform, what conclusions can you draw about the constituencies they hoped to win? Do their proposals appeal to specific demographics? Consider such factors as race, class, gender, region, and occupational types.

20-2 | Progressive Leader Identifies the Problem with Cities
FREDERIC HOWE, *The City: The Hope of Democracy* (1909)

Frederic Howe fit the description of a progressive reformer. Though born in a small town, he spent most of his life in cities (Cleveland and New York), earned a college degree (and a PhD), and became active in local civic reform associations including settlement house work and urban government. Howe was the author of many books, and his text on the city became a classic, defining the progressives' interest in municipal reform and diagnosing the systemic problems facing urban America.

The literature on the city deals almost exclusively with the machinery, the personnel, the charter, the legal limitations and relations. Either this or the corruption of the officials. It is a literature of forms and functions. Its point of view is ethical, personal, political. The economic foundations have been passed by as incidental, as a subject of administrative detail. In like manner, municipal reform has been viewed as a thing of conventional morals, of improving the individual citizen, and stimulating his patriotism.

This volume is a reversal of method. It is an attempt at the Economic Interpretation of the City. It holds that the corruption, the indifference, the incompetence of the official and the apathy of the citizen, the disparity of wealth, the poverty, vice, crime, and disease, are due to causes economic and industrial. They are traceable to our Institutions, rather than to the depravity of human nature. Their correction is not a matter of education or of the penal code. It is a matter of industrial democracy. The incidental conditions are personal and ethical. Whether we adopt the personal or the economic interpretation will determine our attitude towards the problems of modern city life.

The convictions of this volume are the result of several years of actual political experience in the administration of the city of Cleveland, Ohio, as well as of personal study of municipal conditions in the leading cities of America and Great Britain. They represent a drift away from what I have termed the personnel, which is the orthodox view of politics. Instead of the city being controlled by the charter, the suffrage, or by purely political institutions, I have become convinced that it is the economic environment which creates and controls man's activities as well as his attitude of mind. This arouses his civic or his self interest; this underlies the poverty and the social problems with which the city is confronted. This explains contemporary politics. . . .

We do not question this motive in the saloon keeper, who organizes his precinct for a liberal Sunday. His politics are not ethical, they are due to self-interest. The same instinct is reflected, consciously or unconsciously, in the leaders of finance, the franchise-seekers, the banker, and the broker, the lawyer, and the

Frederic C. Howe, *The City: The Hope of Democracy* (New York: Charles Scribner's Sons, 1909), vii–xi.

Press; all are fearful of democracy, when democracy dares to believe in itself. We all know that economic self-interest determines the politics of the saloon. We are beginning to realize that the same self-interest is the politics of big business. This realization explains the awakening of democracy, which is taking place in city and state all over the land.

The same is true of the social problems of city life. The worst of the distressing poverty, as well as the irresponsible wealth, is traceable to economic institutions, to franchise privileges and unwise taxation; to laws which are open to correction as they were to creation. Conditions in the tenement are not ethical, not personal, they are traceable to laws of our own enactment. There is no other possible explanation of the fact that destitution is greatest where wealth is most abundant and industry most highly developed.

Almost without question we have accepted the other, the personal explanation of these things. Our programme has been to improve the individual man by education, by charity; not to improve the city by a change in our industrial policy. We have been bailing water with a sieve. The reformatory sends forth one offender only to find two others at the gate. The big business man may grow disgusted with his traffic in privilege, only to see another man less critical of means take his place. Only by exiling privileges shall we exile corruption. Only by offering opportunity to labor shall we close the doors of our hospitals, almshouses, and prisons. Only by taxing monopoly, will monopoly be forced to let go its hold on the resources of the earth and the means for a livelihood.

My own mind has passed through the evolution here suggested. Starting with the conviction that our evils were traceable to personal causes, to the absence of educational or property qualifications in our suffrage; to the activity of the spoilsman and the saloon keeper in alliance with the foreign voter; to the indifference of our best citizens to politics because it was politics, I have been forced by experience to a changed point of view, to a belief that democracy has not failed by its own inherent weakness so much as by virtue of the privileged interests which have taken possession of our institutions for their own enrichment. From a belief in a business man's government I have come to a belief in a people's government; from a conviction that we had too much democracy I have come to the conviction that we have too little democracy; from a study of history I have been forced to the realization that the progress of civilization has been a constant struggle of liberty against privilege; that wherever privilege has been dominant liberty has passed away and national life has decayed, and that our democratic forms are no more immune from the same dominion than were the nations of antiquity or of modern Europe. It is privilege of an industrial rather than a personal sort that has given birth to the boss, created the machine, and made of the party an agency for the control of our cities, states, and nation, rather than for the advancement of political ideals.

It is the economic motive that makes municipal reform a class struggle; on the one hand are the few who enjoy privileges which they are seeking to retain; on the other hand are millions awakening to the conviction of industrial democracy.

Two facts must be faced. First, the motive of those who control our politics and whose chief interest in the city lies in the direction of their own advantage. Second, the economic environment of those who are compelled to a lifelong struggle for the barest necessities of existence. It is only by facing these facts that the problems of the city may be solved and its possibilities achieved.

READING AND DISCUSSION QUESTIONS

1. Define the transformation Howe says he experienced in his understanding of the problems cities faced. How had reformers been accustomed to thinking about urban problems?

2. How might Howe's argument about the root of urban problems have influenced the reform methods progressives pursued? What connections can you make between Howe's ideology and some of the actions taken by progressive reformers and lawmakers in the first two decades of the twentieth century?

3. Consider the title of his book. What do you think he means by the "hope of democracy"? Is democracy a solution or a problem for urban reformers like Howe?

20-3 | Radical Reformer Appeals to Chicago's Voters

JOSEPHINE CONGER-KANEKO, *What a Socialist Alderman Would Do* (1914)

While progressive reformers like Frederic Howe lamented the economic disparities driving the wealthy and poorer classes apart, he did not go so far as Josephine Conger-Kaneko in calling for the collective ownership of factories, railroads, and utilities. Conger-Kaneko was active in socialist circles in the early twentieth century, emphasizing issues important to working-women, which she promoted in *The Socialist Woman*, a small newspaper she edited based in Chicago. Her 1914 campaign speech for alderman of Chicago's Sixth Ward lays out her vision for an improved America.

I WAS BORN A DEMOCRAT. I was raised a Democrat. I am a Democrat today. I hope I shall die a DEMOCRAT.

And yet, in spite of the fact that I got my first lessons of real life in the office of a country Democratic newspaper, and in spite of the fact that I have followed the Bryan band wagon, and sung in a Bryan glee club, I am today a dues-paying member of the Socialist party.

I am a Socialist because I believe that Socialism is more democratic than the Democratic party.

Soon after I left the little Democratic paper, upon which I had been working, I became associated editorially with the largest Socialist weekly in the world.

Josephine Conger-Kaneko, "What a Socialist Alderman Would Do," *The Coming Nation: A Magazine for the Creators of the New Social Order* 1, no. 5 (March 1914): 10, 13.

Here I learned many things. It was like standing on a high hill and watching the activities of the peoples of a great nation. For we were connected with every nook and corner of this country, and in communication with numerous places outside. Formerly I had not believed in suffrage for women. I, a working woman, was not interested in using the ballot in my own behalf. My family were the dyed-in-the-wool Democrats of the old South, suh. They were of that next to impenetrable combination, Democratic from both principle and prejudice, and they stood right where our present Democratic Congress stands on the woman question.

Therefore, I realized for the first time, while working on this great Socialist journal, that women are a part of our social order, that they help to bear its burdens, and that they should share its privileges with the rest of mankind. I learned that I was not a consistent Socialist unless I was an active advocate of woman suffrage. So I joined a suffrage club. And thus I became, through Socialism, a suffragist.

I found further, that while the Democratic party stands for the welfare of the middle class under the present system, that the Socialist party stands for the welfare of all the people through its advocacy of the abolition of our present insane system of production and distribution of the necessities of life. For instance, our present system is driving the middle class out of existence, and forcing its members into the ranks of the working class, through the monopolization of the industries. The little business man, once respectable in his small line, today sees his business devoured by the great trust, while he is left to seek employment at so much a week wherever he can get it, and his children, instead of inheriting his business as was the process in former years, become employes of some big concern for the rest of their days. Then big business lowers wages to the lowest possible point, and raises the price of its goods to the highest possible point, and thus both the worker and the consumer fare badly.

Socialism would have the big industries owned by the people and controlled by the people for the benefit of the people, instead of the benefit of private owners, and thus would be the ally, or friend, of ALL the people.

These are, briefly, some of the things I found out about Socialism.

When I began to look into the woman movement of this country I found that the women were also looking out for the interests of the people, rather than the interests of the private corporations. The women did not get as far as the Socialists, and yet their demands were almost identical with what we call the immediate demands of the Socialist party.

The annual reports of the women's federated clubs are interesting commentaries on the ideals and outlook of the women. They show committees organized for the abolition of child labor; for the eight-hour day for working women; for the extension of play grounds; for sanitation; for good housing ordinances; for food inspection; pure milk; for mother's pensions; for juvenile courts; for reduction of the cost of living, and for many things that are essential to the welfare of the whole people. That the old political parties did not stand for these things is proven in the fact that women have had to fight for every reform they have gone after. . . .

In the South child labor is a splendid profit-maker for the factory owner, who, by the way, is often a Northerner. For this reason the legislators will not abolish child labor. They are owned body and soul by the big factory interests. The women, however, are not worrying about the interests of the factory owners. I believe the women would be willing to see the government own the factories if this would abolish child labor.

Socialism says the government should own the factories. And that it should pay men and women living wages, and keep the children in the schools where they belong.

The program of the Socialist party calls for the following, among other things:

"The collective ownership and democratic management of railroads, wire and wireless telegraphs and telephones, express services, steamboat lines and all other social means of transportation and communication and of large-scale industries.

"The extension of the public domain to include mines, quarries, oil wells, forests and water power.

"The further conservation and development of natural resources for the use and benefit of all the people.

"The collective ownership of land wherever practicable, and in such cases where such ownership is impracticable, the appropriation by taxation of the annual rental of all land held for speculation or exploitation." . . .

The Socialists would further establish—

"The immediate government relief of the unemployed by the extension of all useful public works. All persons employed on such works to be engaged directly by the government under a workday of not more than eight hours and at not less than the prevailing wages. The government also to establish employment bureaus, to lend money to states and municipalities without interest for the purpose of carrying on public works, and to take such other measures within its power as will lessen the widespread misery of the workers caused by the misrule of the capitalist class."

These are typical of the entire policy of the Socialist party.

What a Socialist woman alderman would do if elected to office in Chicago ought to be clear in your minds. . . . The Socialists stand for progress, the women stand for progress. As a Socialist I could not do one thing that would be against the interests of the masses of the people, as a woman I would not want to do any such thing. As a member of the city council from your ward it would be my duty and my pleasure to see that our streets are kept in good repair; that sanitary conditions exist throughout the ward; that the housing and other existing ordinances are enforced; that all new laws making for the betterment of the general comfort are enacted.

Co-operating with the entire council for the city at large, I would insist upon municipal ownership of public utilities wherever possible, such as telephone, gas and electric light, rail traffic, etc.; upon the inauguration of municipal markets where food and clothing could be sold direct from the producer to the consumer, thus cutting out the cost of middlemen; upon the erection of municipal lodging houses for working women and girls; upon a minimum wage for workers of both sexes; upon relief of the unemployed by the extension of useful public works; upon the extension of the playgrounds system to the public parks, and the opening of the schools for social centers. I would do what I could toward the alleviation and abolition of the white slave traffic by providing employment for working girls, and by paying both men and women a living wage, and opening respectable places of amusement for the city's great army of young people who today resort to the nickel shows without guardianship for their only pleasure. I believe that women in plain clothes, or ordinary dress, should be added to the police force as watchers in the amusement centers, to prevent young girls from being led into wrong paths.

It is impossible to point out in a brief talk like this what might be done for the betterment of a city like Chicago. But there is one fundamental point upon which we can agree—that is, we cannot expect much from a home in which children are hungry and ragged and dirty. Neither can we expect the best results from a city whose workers are underpaid, poorly fed, badly housed. Crime and ignorance and big police costs will inevitably result from such conditions. The wisest and safest plan is first to give our multitudes employment at a living wage; feed and clothe them at the lowest possible cost to themselves, and furnish them with wholesome, satisfying amusements. If, as a city we can do this, every other good thing will be added unto us. For then we shall have the REAL democracy.

I do not believe there is a woman here who can criticise this program, and if you are true to yourselves you will try and see that it is put into effect as soon as possible.

READING AND DISCUSSION QUESTIONS

1. Describe the appeal of socialism, more than the Democratic Party, for someone like Conger-Kaneko. How did she distinguish between the two?

2. What connection did Conger-Kaneko draw between socialism and "the woman movement"? How did they support each other as reform movements?

20-4 | Black Populist Handicaps Texas Election

THE SOUTHERN MERCURY, *The Colored Brother: A Spicy Letter from J. B. Rayner* (1895)

African American support for the Republican Party waned in the late 1870s when many whites in the party wearied of Reconstruction. Led by Redeemers, southern Democrats used legitimate as well as illegal and violent means to destroy black political power. The only alternative for African Americans emerged in the local and regional Farmers' Alliances and Granger movement, which culminated in populism. Many African Americans joined the People's Party, posing a direct threat to Democrats' electoral prospects. Here, *The Southern Mercury* newspaper transcribes a speech by John B. Rayner, a black political activist from Texas and organizer of "colored Populist clubs," promoting the People's Party.

He Briefly Reviews the Five Parties That Will be in the Field Next Year and Pays His Respects to Each One of Them

"I am glad the time has come when the monster breath demagogues will have to quit talking about 'social equality,' 'negro supremacy' and the 'solid south.' 'Social equality' and 'negro supremacy' are slang phrases and were once powerful weapons in the hand of southern democracy to destroy carpetbagism. Since this tenebreous and blighting influence is gone, never to return, let the democrats quit using these slang phrases and take up the wand of southern prosperity and strike the soil until exploitation shall make the valley fruitful and the hills ring with spindles and flying shuttles and the roll of mighty machinery shall bless and make glad the human family.

There will be five distinct parties in the next campaign, viz: Lily White republicans, Cuney republicans,[1] renegade or silver democrats, democrats pure and simple and the people's party.

Let us examine each of these parties and see what their tactics will be to capture negro votes, etc. The Lily White republicans are that class of white republicans who would not endure negro domination in republican conventions. Those men did not quit the old republican organization because they were jealous of or hated my race (the negroes), but they quit because my race sent too many incompetent and ignorant delegates to republican conventions, thus making the deliberation in these conventions ridiculous. The orators in this party will not speak for negro votes, but will strive to capture the business men of Texas, and they

---

Milton Park, ed., *The Southern Mercury* (Dallas, TX), vol. 14, no. 50, ed. 1, Thursday, December 12, 1895, Newspaper, December 12, 1895; digital images (http://texashistory.unt.edu/ark:/67531 /metapth185637/), University of North Texas Libraries, The Portal to Texas History, http:// texashistory.unt.edu; crediting UNT Libraries, Denton, Texas.

[1]**Cuney republicans:** Presumably, Rayner is referring to Norris Wright Cuney, an African American politician who became the Texas national committeeman of the Republican Party in 1886. According to the Texas State Historical Association, the period between 1884 and 1896 is sometimes referred to as the "Cuney era" in Texas Republican politics.

will gloriously succeed, for the business men of the south are sick and tired of democratic legislation.

The orators in this party, to capture white votes, will appeal to complexional prejudices, blue veins, straight hair and business sentiments.

The Cuney republicans are 95 per cent negroes and 5 per cent whites. The negroes in this party are hotel flunkies, barbers, dude school teachers, ignorant preachers, saloon waiters, etc. The whites in this party are the mephitic vaporings from a cadaverous carpetbagism. The men in this party are the sordid mercenaries in politics, and they will make a republican ticket if the renegade or silver democrats will pay them to do so, and this will be done just to keep the negroes from voting the people's party ticket.

Those men nominated a republican ticket in the last campaign, but, for pelf, they elected Culberson for governor and one Pendleton from Bell county to congress.

The silver democrats are the chronic office-seekers, and have no political conscience or principle; they will accept any platform to get a democratic nomination, and then jeer and ignore it to get elected. The leaders in this party are populists in faith, but are too cowardly to confess it.

The sooner the leaders in this party and their individious practice goes to pluto's laboratory for the purpose of studying the science of pyrology tentatively or somatically, the better it will be for the south.

The leaders in this party are only three men, and they would eat the golden calf that Aaron made,[2] and worship the golden image that Nebuchadnezzar set up in the plain of Dura,[3] to get a democratic nomination, and then pick up the thirty pieces of silver that their antetype Judas Iscariot cast away,[4] for the purpose of buying mean whisky and cigars to treat the delegates that gave them the nomination, and then steal the people's party silver plank to get elected.

In their next convention this party will write a boustrophidon[5] platform and fill it with platitudes and ambiguous terms, and, to mislead the people, they will resort to the political sin, esoter[i]cism. This party in their next election will use bribes, deception and shotgun intimidation to capture negro votes.

The democratic party, pure and simple, is headed by Hon. George Clark of Waco, and is made up of men, the sons of southern chivalry, and they belong to the patriarchal order of southern knighthood. . . .

The leaders of this party have the cool, calculating intellect of a Robert E. Lee, the boldness of a Stonewall Jackson and the stubbornness of a Roman

---

[2]**the golden calf that Aaron made**: In Moses's absence, Aaron created a golden calf out of the Israelites' jewelry for the Israelites to worship as a god. (Ex. 32)

[3]**the golden image that Nebuchadnezzar set up in the plain of Dura**: Golden statue that Nebuchadnezzar erected in Babylon and commanded that all of his people worship. (Dan. 3)

[4]**the thirty pieces of silver that . . . Judas Iscariot cast away**: Judas agreed to hand Jesus over to the chief priests in exchange for thirty pieces of silver before the Last Supper. Feeling remorse, Judas ultimately returned the silver to the priests. (Matt. 26)

[5]**boustrophidon**: (Boustrophedon) Writing alternate lines in opposite directions. Some ancient texts were written in this style.

soldier, and behind this party is unlimited wealth and the influence of Cleveland's administration. This party will make a platform that will not antagonize the democratic national platform; in fact, this is true blue democracy, and I admire their boldness and determination, because if they get in office, they expect to do so by standing on their platform.

The protagonist in this party is to President Cleveland as Nicolo Machiavelli was to Lorenzo de Medici, and President Cleveland is to our American financial system as Benedict Arnold was to West Point.

This party will make no effort to capture the negro voters, but will aim to capture the white republicans of the Cuney type.

The next is the people's party, God's viceregent in politics, and this party is made up of the middle class or yeomanry of the country."

Then follows Mr. Rayner's appeal to the negroes to vote with the people's party. He says the republican party in the south is broken down and worn out.

"The only rights we negroes will ever enjoy will be the right the southern white man gives us. Vote the people's party ticket; we will get better wages for our work and we will have better times in the south."

READING AND DISCUSSION QUESTIONS

1. *The Southern Mercury* was a reform newspaper affiliated with the Farmers' Alliance in Texas. What inferences can you draw from the fact that it reported a speech by a black political activist? What light might this shed on the historical context of race relations within Populist circles?

2. Analyze Rayner's perspective on the political prospects for African Americans in the 1890s. Why does he urge support for populism over Republicans, the traditional political home for African Americans in the Reconstruction era?

20-5 | President Calls for Conservation of Natural Resources
THEODORE ROOSEVELT, *Annual Message to Congress* (1907)

Protecting natural resources was one aspect of turn-of-the-century progressive reform, complementing efforts to clean up municipal government, improve health and safety conditions, and restrain monopoly power. Conservation, of the type Theodore Roosevelt recommended to Congress in 1907, differed from preservation, which set aside natural landscapes to protect their unspoiled beauty. Though Roosevelt was inspired by nature's sublime beauty, here he urges Congress to manage and regulate the use of the nation's waterways and timber resources.

Theodore Roosevelt, "Seventh Annual Message," December 3, 1907. Online by Gerhard Peters and John T. Woolley, *The American Presidency Project*. www.presidency.ucsb.edu/ws/?pid=29548.

The conservation of our natural resources and their proper use constitute the fundamental problem which underlies almost every other problem of our National life. We must maintain for our civilization the adequate material basis without which that civilization can not exist. We must show foresight, we must look ahead. As a nation we not only enjoy a wonderful measure of present prosperity but if this prosperity is used aright it is an earnest of future success such as no other nation will have. The reward of foresight for this Nation is great and easily foretold. But there must be the look ahead, there must be a realization of the fact that to waste, to destroy, our natural resources, to skin and exhaust the land instead of using it so as to increase its usefulness, will result in undermining in the days of our children the very prosperity which we ought by right to hand down to them amplified and developed. . . .

Our great river systems should be developed as National water highways, the Mississippi, with its tributaries, standing first in importance, and the Columbia second, although there are many others of importance on the Pacific, the Atlantic and the Gulf slopes. The National Government should undertake this work, and I hope a beginning will be made in the present Congress; and the greatest of all our rivers, the Mississippi, should receive especial attention. From the Great Lakes to the mouth of the Mississippi there should be a deep waterway, with deep waterways leading from it to the East and the West. Such a waterway would practically mean the extension of our coast line into the very heart of our country. It would be of incalculable benefit to our people. If begun at once it can be carried through in time appreciably to relieve the congestion of our great freight-carrying lines of railroads. . . . Moreover, the development of our waterways involves many other important water problems, all of which should be considered as part of the same general scheme. The Government dams should be used to produce hundreds of thousands of horsepower as an incident to improving navigation; for the annual value of the unused water-power of the United States perhaps exceeds the annual value of the products of all our mines. . . .

Irrigation should be far more extensively developed than at present, not only in the States of the Great Plains and the Rocky Mountains, but in many others, as, for instance, in large portions of the South Atlantic and Gulf States, where it should go hand in hand with the reclamation of swamp land. The Federal Government should seriously devote itself to this task, realizing that utilization of waterways and water-power, forestry, irrigation, and the reclamation of lands threatened with overflow, are all interdependent parts of the same problem. The work of the Reclamation Service in developing the larger opportunities of the western half of our country for irrigation is more important than almost any other movement. The constant purpose of the Government in connection with the Reclamation Service has been to use the water resources of the public lands for the ultimate greatest good of the greatest number; in other words, to put upon the land permanent home-makers, to use and develop it for themselves and for their children and children's children. There has been, of course, opposition to this work; opposition from some interested men who desire to exhaust the land for their own immediate profit without regard to the welfare of the next generation, and opposition from honest and well-meaning men who did not fully understand the subject or who did not look far enough ahead. This opposition is, I think, dying away, and our people are understanding that it would be utterly wrong to allow a few individuals to exhaust for their own temporary personal profit the resources which ought to be developed through use so as to be conserved for the permanent common advantage of the people as a whole.

The effort of the Government to deal with the public land has been based upon the same principle as that of the Reclamation Service. The land law system which was designed to meet the needs of the fertile and well-watered regions of the Middle West has largely broken down when applied to the dryer regions of the Great Plains, the mountains, and much of the Pacific slope, where a farm of 160 acres is inadequate for self-support. In these regions the system lent itself to fraud, and much land passed out of the hands of the Government without passing into the hands of the home-maker. The Department of the Interior and the Department of Justice joined in prosecuting the offenders against the law; and they have accomplished much, while where the administration of the law has been defective it has been changed. But the laws themselves are defective. Three years ago a public lands commission was appointed to scrutinize the law, and defects, and recommend a remedy. Their examination specifically showed the existence of great fraud upon the public domain, and their recommendations for changes in the law were made with the design of conserving the natural resources of every part of the public lands by putting it to its best use. . . .

Some such legislation as that proposed is essential in order to preserve the great stretches of public grazing land which are unfit for cultivation under present methods and are valuable only for the forage which they supply. These stretches amount in all to some 300,000,000 acres, and are open to the free grazing of cattle, sheep, horses and goats, without restriction. Such a system, or lack of system, means that the range is not so much used as wasted by abuse. As the West settles the range becomes more and more over-grazed. Much of it can not be used to advantage unless it is fenced, for fencing is the only way by which to keep in check the owners of nomad flocks which roam hither and thither, utterly destroying the pastures and leaving a waste behind so that their presence is incompatible with the presence of home-makers. The existing fences are all illegal. Some of them represent the improper exclusion of actual settlers, actual home-makers, from territory which is usurped by great cattle companies. Some of them represent what is in itself a proper effort to use the range for those upon the land, and to prevent its use by nomadic outsiders. All these fences, those that are hurtful and those that are beneficial, are alike illegal and must come down. But it is an outrage that the law should necessitate such action on the part of the Administration. The unlawful fencing of public lands for private grazing must be stopped, but the necessity which occasioned it must be provided for. The Federal Government should have control of the range, whether by permit or lease, as local necessities may determine. The destruction of the public range will continue until some . . . laws . . . are enacted. . . .

Optimism is a good characteristic, but if carried to an excess it becomes foolishness. We are prone to speak of the resources of this country as inexhaustible; this is not so. The mineral wealth of the country, the coal, iron, oil, gas, and the like, does not reproduce itself, and therefore is certain to be exhausted ultimately; and wastefulness in dealing with it to-day means that our descendants will feel the exhaustion a generation or two before they otherwise would. But there are certain other forms of waste which could be entirely stopped — the waste of soil by washing, for instance, which is among the most dangerous of all wastes now in progress in the United States, is easily preventable, so that this present enormous loss of fertility is entirely unnecessary. The preservation or replacement of the forests is one of the most important means of preventing this loss. We have made a beginning in forest preservation, but it is only a beginning. At present lumbering is the fourth greatest industry in the United States; and yet, so rapid has been the rate of exhaustion of timber in the United States in the past, and so rapidly is the remainder being exhausted, that the country is unquestionably on the verge of a timber famine which will be felt in every household in the land. There has already been a rise in the price of lumber, but there is certain to be a more rapid and heavier rise in the future. The present annual consumption of lumber is certainly three times as great as the annual growth; and if the consumption and growth continue unchanged, practically all our lumber will be exhausted in another generation, while long before the limit to complete exhaustion is reached the growing scarcity will make itself felt in many blighting ways upon our National welfare. About 20 per cent of our forested territory is now reserved in National forests; but these do not include the most valuable timber lands, and in any event the proportion is too small to expect that the reserves can accomplish more than a mitigation of the trouble which is ahead for the nation. Far more drastic action is needed. Forests can be lumbered so as to give to the public the full use of their mercantile timber without the slightest detriment to the forest, any more than it is a detriment to a farm to furnish a harvest; so that there is no parallel between forests and mines, which can only be completely used by exhaustion. But forests, if used as all our forests have been used in the past and as most of them are still used, will be either wholly destroyed, or so damaged that many decades have to pass before effective use can be made of them again. . . . Every business man in the land, every writer in the newspapers, every man or woman of an ordinary school education, ought to be able to see that immense quantities of timber are used in the country, that the forests which supply this timber are rapidly being exhausted, and that, if no change takes place, exhaustion will come comparatively soon, and that the effects of it will be felt severely in the every-day life of our people. Surely, when these facts are so obvious, there should be no delay in taking preventive measures. Yet we seem as a nation to be willing to proceed in this matter with happy-go-lucky indifference even to the immediate future. It is this attitude which permits the self-interest of a very few persons to weigh for more than the ultimate interest of all our people. There are persons who find it to their immense pecuniary benefit to destroy the forests by lumbering. They are to be blamed for thus sacrificing the future of the Nation as a whole to their own self-interest of the moment; but heavier blame attaches to the people at large for permitting such action, whether in the White Mountains, in the southern Alleghenies, or in the Rockies and Sierras. . . . Of course to check the waste of timber means that there must be on the part of the public the acceptance of a temporary restriction in the lavish use of the timber, in order to prevent the total loss of this use in the future. There are plenty of men in public and private life who actually advocate the continuance of the present system of unchecked and wasteful extravagance, using as an argument the fact that to check it will of course mean interference with the ease and comfort of certain people who now get lumber at less cost than they ought to pay, at the expense of the future generations. Some of these persons actually demand that the present forest reserves be thrown open to destruction, because, forsooth, they think that thereby the price of lumber could be put down again for two or three or more years. Their attitude is precisely like that of an agitator protesting against the outlay of money by farmers on manure and in taking care of their farms generally. Undoubtedly, if the average farmer were content absolutely to ruin his farm, he could for two or three years avoid spending any money on it, and yet make a good deal of money out of it. But only a savage would, in his private affairs, show such reckless disregard of the future; yet it is precisely this reckless disregard of the future which the opponents of the forestry system are now endeavoring to get the people of the United States to show. The only trouble with the movement for the preservation of our forests is that it has not gone nearly far enough, and was not begun soon enough. It is a most fortunate thing, however, that we began it when we did. We should acquire in the Appalachian and White Mountain regions all the forest lands that it is possible to acquire for the use of the Nation. These lands, because they form a National asset, are as emphatically national as the rivers which they feed, and which flow through so many States before they reach the ocean.

READING AND DISCUSSION QUESTIONS

1. Compare conservation to other progressive reforms. What can you infer about a common motive uniting conservation with restraints on monopolies or the regulation of workplaces and tenements?

2. Conservationists, of course, believed they were ensuring the long-term use of natural resources, but what impact might these reforms have had on local populations where regulations took effect? Think about Native Americans in the West and white settlers in the Adirondack forest whose uninterrupted use of natural resources became regulated by the federal and state government.

20-6 | Negro Problem Solved Through Education of Leadership Class

W. E. B. DU BOIS, *The Talented Tenth* (1903)

Progressives invested enormous faith in education as a lever for social progress, an idea not lost on the leading black intellectual of the early twentieth century, W. E. B. Du Bois. Born and raised in New England, Du Bois attended Fisk University (a historically black college in Nashville), then Harvard, where in 1895 he became the first African American to earn the PhD degree. As a sociologist, he was active in black civil rights and cofounded the National Association for the Advancement of Colored People (NAACP) in 1909. Du Bois challenged Booker T. Washington's approach to advancing black interests in his "Talented Tenth" essay published in 1903.

The Negro race, like all races, is going to be saved by its exceptional men. The problem of education, then, among Negroes must first of all deal with the Talented Tenth; it is the problem of developing the Best of this race that they may guide the Mass away from the contamination and death of the Worst, in their own and other races. Now the training of men is a difficult and intricate task. Its technique is a matter for educational experts, but its object is for the vision of seers. If we make money the object of man-training, we shall develop money-makers but not necessarily men; if we make technical skill the object of education, we may possess artisans but not, in nature, men. Men we shall have only as we make manhood the object of the work of the schools—intelligence, broad sympathy, knowledge of the world that was and is, and of the relation of men to it—this is the curriculum of that Higher Education which must underlie true life. On this foundation we may build bread winning, skill of hand and quickness of brain, with never a fear lest the child and man mistake the means of living for the object of life. . . .

From the very first it has been the educated and intelligent of the Negro people that have led and elevated the mass, and the sole obstacles that nullified and retarded their efforts were slavery and race prejudice; for what is slavery but the legalized survival of the unfit and the nullification of the work of natural internal leadership? Negro leadership, therefore, sought from the first to rid the race of this awful incubus that it might make way for natural selection and the survival of the fittest. . . .

Who are to-day guiding the work of the Negro people? The "exceptions" of course. And yet so sure as this Talented Tenth is pointed out, the blind worshippers of the Average cry out in alarm: "These are exceptions, look here at death, disease and crime—these are the happy rule." Of course they are the rule, because a silly nation made them the rule: Because for three long centuries this people lynched Negroes who dared to be brave, raped black women who dared

W. E. B. Du Bois, "The Talented Tenth," in *The Negro Problem: A Series of Articles by Representative American Negroes of To-Day*, contributions by Booker T. Washington, Principal of Tuskegee Institute, W. E. Burghardt Du Bois, Paul Laurence Dunbar, Charles W. Chestnutt, and others (New York: James Pott & Company, 1903), 33–35, 43–48, 57–63, 73–75.

to be virtuous, crushed dark-hued youth who dared to be ambitious, and encouraged and made to flourish servility and lewdness and apathy. But not even this was able to crush all manhood and chastity and aspiration from black folk. A saving remnant continually survives and persists, continually aspires, continually shows itself in thrift and ability and character. Exceptional it is to be sure, but this is its chiefest promise; it shows the capability of Negro blood, the promise of black men. Do Americans ever stop to reflect that there are in this land a million men of Negro blood, well-educated, owners of homes, against the honor of whose womanhood no breath was ever raised, whose men occupy positions of trust and usefulness, and who, judged by any standard, have reached the full measure of the best type of modern European culture? Is it fair, is it decent, is it Christian to ignore these facts of the Negro problem, to belittle such aspiration, to nullify such leadership and seek to crush these people back into the mass out of which by toil and travail, they and their fathers have raised themselves?

Can the masses of the Negro people be in any possible way more quickly raised than by the effort and example of this aristocracy of talent and character? Was there ever a nation on God's fair earth civilized from the bottom upward? Never; it is, ever was and ever will be from the top downward that culture filters. The Talented Tenth rises and pulls all that are worth the saving up to their vantage ground. This is the history of human progress; and the two historic mistakes which have hindered that progress were the thinking first that no more could ever rise save the few already risen; or second, that it would better the unrisen to pull the risen down.

How then shall the leaders of a struggling people be trained and the hands of the risen few strengthened? There can be but one answer: The best and most capable of their youth must be schooled in the colleges and universities of the land. . . .

A university is a human invention for the transmission of knowledge and culture from generation to generation, through the training of quick minds and pure hearts, and for this work no other human invention will suffice, not even trade and industrial schools.

All men cannot go to college but some men must; every isolated group or nation must have its yeast, must have for the talented few centers of training where men are not so mystified and befuddled by the hard and necessary toil of earning a living, as to have no aims higher than their bellies, and no God greater than Gold. . . .

Where ought they to have begun to build? At the bottom, of course, quibbles the mole with his eyes in the earth. Aye! truly at the bottom, at the very bottom; at the bottom of knowledge, down in the very depths of knowledge there where the roots of justice strike into the lowest soil of Truth. And so they did begin; they founded colleges, and up from the colleges shot normal schools, and out from the normal schools went teachers, and around the normal teachers clustered other teachers to teach the public schools; the college trained in Greek and Latin and mathematics, 2,000 men; and these men trained full 50,000 others in morals and manners, and they in turn taught thrift and the alphabet to nine millions of men, who to-day hold $300,000,000 of property. It was a miracle—the most wonderful peace-battle of the 19th century, and yet to-day men smile at it, and in fine superiority tell us that it was all a strange mistake; that a proper way to found a system of education is first to gather the children and buy them spelling books and hoes; afterward men may look about for teachers, if haply they may find them; or again they would teach men Work, but as for Life—why, what has Work to do with Life, they ask vacantly. . . .

The main question, so far as the Southern Negro is concerned, is: What under the present circumstance, must a system of education do in order to raise the Negro as quickly as possible in the scale of civilization? The answer to this question seems to me clear: It must strengthen the Negro's character, increase his knowledge and teach him to earn a living. Now it goes without saying, that it is hard to do all these things simultaneously or suddenly, and that at the same time it will not do to give all the attention to one and neglect the others; we could give black boys trades, but that alone will not civilize a race of ex-slaves; we might simply increase their knowledge of the world, but this would not necessarily make them wish to use this knowledge honestly; we might seek to strengthen character and purpose, but to what end if this people have nothing to eat or to wear? A system of education is not one thing, nor does it have a single definite object, nor is it a mere matter of schools. Education is that whole system of human training within and without the school house walls, which molds and develops men. If then we start out to train an ignorant and unskilled people with a heritage of bad habits, our system of training must set before itself two great aims—the one dealing with knowledge and character, the other part seeking to give the child the technical knowledge necessary for him to earn a living under the present circumstances. These objects are accomplished in part by the opening of the common schools on the one, and of the industrial schools on the other. But only in part, for there must also be trained those who are to teach these schools—men and women of knowledge and culture and technical skill who understand modern civilization, and have the training and aptitude to impart it to the children under them. There must be teachers, and teachers of teachers, and to attempt to establish any sort of a system of common and industrial school training, without *first* (and I say *first* advisedly) without *first* providing for the higher training of the very best teachers, is simply throwing your money to the winds. School houses do not teach themselves—piles of brick and mortar and machinery do not send out *men*. It is the trained, living human soul, cultivated and strengthened by long study and thought, that breathes the real breath of life into boys and girls and makes them human, whether they be black or white, Greek, Russian or American. Nothing, in these latter days, has so dampened the faith of thinking Negroes in recent educational movements, as the fact that such movements have been accompanied by ridicule and denouncement and decrying of those very institutions of higher training which made the Negro public school possible, and make Negro industrial schools thinkable. . . .

I would not deny, or for a moment seem to deny, the paramount necessity of teaching the Negro to work, and to work steadily and skillfully; or seem to depreciate in the slightest degree the important part industrial schools must play in the accomplishment of these ends, but I *do* say, and insist upon it, that it is industrialism drunk with its vision of success, to imagine that its own work can be accomplished without providing for the training of broadly cultured men and women to teach its own teachers, and to teach the teachers of the public schools. . . .

I am an earnest advocate of manual training and trade teaching for black boys, and for white boys, too. I believe that next to the founding of Negro colleges the most valuable addition to Negro education since the war, has been industrial training for black boys. Nevertheless, I insist that the object of all true education is not to make men carpenters, it is to make carpenters men. . . .

Thus, again, in the manning of trade schools and manual training schools we are thrown back upon the higher training as its source and chief support. There was a time when any aged and wornout carpenter could teach in a trade school. But not so to-day. Indeed the demand for college-bred men by a school like Tuskegee, ought to make Mr. Booker T. Washington the firmest friend of higher training. Here he has as helpers the son of a Negro senator, trained in Greek and the humanities, and graduated at Harvard; the son of a Negro congressman and lawyer, trained in Latin and mathematics, and graduated at Oberlin; he has as his wife, a woman who read Virgil and Homer in the same class room with me; he has as college chaplain, a classical graduate of Atlanta University; as teacher of science, a graduate of Fisk; as teacher of history, a graduate of Smith,—indeed some thirty of his chief teachers are college graduates, and instead of studying French grammars in the midst of weeds, or buying pianos for dirty cabins, they are at Mr. Washington's right hand helping him in a noble work. And yet one of the effects of Mr. Washington's propaganda has been to throw doubt upon the expediency of such training for Negroes, as these persons have had.

———

Men of America, the problem is plain before you. Here is a race transplanted through the criminal foolishness of your fathers. Whether you like it or not the millions are here, and here they will remain. If you do not lift them up, they will pull you down. Education and work are the levers to uplift a people. Work alone will not do it unless inspired by the right ideals and guided by intelligence. Education must not simply teach work—it must teach Life. The Talented Tenth of the Negro race must be made leaders of thought and missionaries of culture among their people. No others can do this work and Negro colleges must train men for it. The Negro race, like all other races, is going to be saved by its exceptional men.

READING AND DISCUSSION QUESTIONS

1. How radical do you think readers in 1903 considered Du Bois's reform message? What from his own experiences or from the recent history of his time gave him confidence in his solution to the "Negro problem"?

2. Examine Du Bois's argument as a reflection of the historical context of progressivism and race relations in the early twentieth century. Are his ideas relevant to the discussion of race relations today? Explain.

▪ COMPARATIVE QUESTIONS ▪

1. Compare Populists, progressives, and socialists by identifying similarities in the ways they diagnosed society's problems and the reforms they championed. In what ways did their ideologies differ?

2. What change in the form and function of government did reformers in this period advocate? How did their ideas of government's proper role differ from earlier conceptions of government's power and responsibilities?

3. Assess populism by comparing its reforms (Document 20-1) with the views expressed by Terence Powderly and the Knights of Labor (Document 17-2). What common cause do you see between them? Why do you think both failed as reform movements?

4. To what extent did questions of race and ethnicity help or hurt reform movements? Compare the works of Du Bois and Rayner in this chapter with those of Booker T. Washington (Document 18-3), Antanas Kaztauskis (Document 17-3), Marie Ganz (Document 19-3), and the account of the Negro parade (Document 19-4).

5. Compare Du Bois's approach to reform for African Americans to the proposal Booker T. Washington advanced in his Atlanta speech (Document 18-3). How might you explain their different emphases? What role did class and geography play in shaping their divergent ideas?

The Clash of Cultural Values and Ideas in an Industrializing Era

1877–1917

A critic for the *New York Times* warned readers attending the 1913 Armory Show of international modern art that they would be entering "a stark region of abstractions" with paintings "hideous to our unaccustomed eyes" and "revolting in their inhumanity." The bold experimentation that Cubists and postimpressionists showcased in 1913 rejected prevailing cultural norms of the nineteenth century, overturning convention in favor of "modern" cultural values. The clash of realism with modern art symbolized but one cultural revolution witnessed during these years. The conflicting ideas, beliefs, and creative expressions of the period affected not only art and literature, but also broader philosophical, moral, and scientific ideas touching on gender, race, and ethnicity. Shaped by the growing influence of Charles Darwin's theory of natural selection, philosophers and social scientists adapted his insights related to biology and the natural world to promote a sociology that exalted struggle as the means to effect progress. This strict and exacting philosophy rewarded the victor with assurances of his superiority while justifying the fate of those at the bottom. The period's changing cultural values defined the era, as individuals sought to understand the implications both for themselves and for society as a whole.

P6-1 | Social Darwinist Explains Relationship Between Classes

WILLIAM GRAHAM SUMNER, *What Social Classes Owe to Each Other* (1883)

William Graham Sumner, Yale sociologist and devotee of English philosopher Herbert Spencer, embraced Social Darwinism as a philosophy that structured and framed his understanding of society's development and progress over time. Inspired by Charles Darwin's theories of natural selection, Sumner spoke for many latter-nineteenth-century champions of laissez-faire capitalism, who saw the race of life as a struggle that rewarded only those "fittest" to survive. When considering the question of what the social classes owed to one another, the short answer, according to Sumner, was nothing.

"The poor," "the weak," "the laborers," are expressions which are used as if they had exact and well-understood definition. Discussions are made to bear upon the assumed rights, wrongs, and misfortunes of certain social classes; and all public speaking and writing consists, in a large measure, of the discussion of general plans for meeting the wishes of classes of people who have not been able to satisfy their own desires. These classes are sometimes discontented, and sometimes not. Sometimes they do not know that anything is amiss with them until the "friends of humanity" come to them with offers of aid. Sometimes they are discontented and envious. They do not take their achievements as a fair measure of their rights. They do not blame themselves or their parents for their lot, as compared with that of other people. Sometimes they claim that they have a right to everything of which they feel the need for their happiness on earth. To make such a claim against God or Nature would, of course, be only to say that we claim a right to live on earth if we can. But God and Nature have ordained the chances and conditions of life on earth once for all. The case cannot be reopened. We cannot get a revision of the laws of human life. We are absolutely shut up to the need and duty, if we would learn how to live happily, of investigating the laws of Nature, and deducing the rules of right living in the world as it is. These are very wearisome and commonplace tasks. They consist in labor and self-denial repeated over and over again in learning and doing. When the people whose claims we are considering are told to apply themselves to these tasks they become irritated and feel almost insulted. They formulate their claims as rights against society— that is, against some other men. In their view they have a right, not only to pursue happiness, but to get it; and if they fail to get it, they think they have a claim to the aid of other men—that is, to the labor and self-denial of other men—to get it for them. They find orators and poets who tell them that they have grievances, so long as they have unsatisfied desires.

Now, if there are groups of people who have a claim to other people's labor and self-denial, and if there are other people whose labor and self-denial are

William Graham Sumner, *What Social Classes Owe to Each Other* (New York and London: Harper & Brothers Publishers, 1883), 13–16, 21–24.

liable to be claimed by the first groups, then there certainly are "classes," and classes of the oldest and most vicious type. For a man who can command another man's labor and self-denial for the support of his own existence is a privileged person of the highest species conceivable on earth. Princes and paupers meet on this plane, and no other men are on it at all. On the other hand, a man whose labor and self-denial may be diverted from his maintenance to that of some other man is not a free man, and approaches more or less toward the position of a slave. Therefore we shall find that, in all the notions which we are to discuss, this elementary contradiction, that there are classes and that there are not classes, will produce repeated confusion and absurdity. We shall find that, in our efforts to eliminate the old vices of class government, we are impeded and defeated by new products of the worst class theory. We shall find that all the schemes for producing equality and obliterating the organization of society produce a new differentiation based on the worst possible distinction—the right to claim and the duty to give one man's effort for another man's satisfaction. We shall find that every effort to realize equality necessitates a sacrifice of liberty. . . .

The humanitarians, philanthropists, and reformers, looking at the facts of life as they present themselves, find enough which is sad and unpromising in the condition of many members of society. They see wealth and poverty side by side. They note great inequality of social position and social chances. They eagerly set about the attempt to account for what they see, and to devise schemes for remedying what they do not like. In their eagerness to recommend the less fortunate classes to pity and consideration they forget all about the rights of other classes; they gloss over all the faults of the classes in question, and they exaggerate their misfortunes and their virtues. They invent new theories of property, distorting rights and perpetrating injustice, as any one is sure to do who sets about the readjustment of social relations with the interests of one group distinctly before his mind, and the interests of all other groups thrown into the background. When I have read certain of these discussions I have thought that it must be quite disreputable to be respectable, quite dishonest to own property, quite unjust to go one's own way and earn one's own living, and that the only really admirable person was the good-for-nothing. The man who by his own effort raises himself above poverty appears, in these discussions, to be of no account. The man who has done nothing to raise himself above poverty finds that the social doctors flock about him, bringing the capital which they have collected from the other class, and promising him the aid of the State to give him what the other had to work for. In all these schemes and projects the organized intervention of society through the State is either planned or hoped for, and the State is thus made to become the protector and guardian of certain classes. The agents who are to direct the State action are, of course, the reformers and philanthropists. Their schemes, therefore, may always be reduced to this type—that A and B decide what C shall do for D. It will be interesting to inquire, at a later period of our discussion, who C is, and what the effect is upon him of all these arrangements. In all the discussions attention is concentrated on A and B, the noble social reformers, and on D, the "poor man." I call C the Forgotten Man, because I have never seen that any notice was taken of him in any of the discussions. When we have disposed of A, B, and D we can better appreciate the case of C, and I think that we shall find that he deserves our attention, for the worth of his character and the magnitude of his unmerited burdens. Here it may suffice to observe that, on the theories of the social philosophers to whom I have referred, we should get a new maxim of judicious living: Poverty is the best policy. If you get wealth, you will have to support other people; if you do not get wealth, it will be the duty of other people to support you.

READING AND DISCUSSION QUESTIONS

1. How were Sumner's philosophical ideas of Social Darwinism used to defend the dominant economic and social order of the latter nineteenth century?

2. Who is Sumner targeting for criticism as a "school of writers" heralding "the coming duty and the coming woe"? How might these people have responded to Sumner's analysis of the relationship between social classes?

P6-2 | Critic Praises Realism in Novels

WILLIAM DEAN HOWELLS, *Pernicious Fiction: Tests of the Poison* (1887)

While some fiction was undoubtedly poorly written, according to William Dean Howells the product of some novelists' pens was flat-out pernicious. The author of countless novels and the leading literary critic of his day, Howells championed a new school of fiction writers dedicated to realism who rejected the idealism and dewy-eyed romance characteristic of nineteenth-century art and culture. The shock of the Civil War, heightened by graphic photographs, and the urban blight reported by muckraking journalists burst the bubble of American naiveté and led Howells to urge fiction writers to tell the truth.

It must have been a passage from Vernon Lee's *Baldwin,*[1] claiming for the novel an indefinitely vast and subtle influence on modern character, which provoked the following suggestive letter from one of our readers:

> Dear Sir,—With regard to article IV in the Editor's Study in the September *Harper,* allow me to say that I have very grave doubts as to the whole list of magnificent things that you seem to think novels have done for the race, and can witness in myself many evil things which they have done for me. Whatever in my mental make-up is wild and visionary, whatever is untrue,

William Dean Howells, "Pernicious Fiction: Tests of the Poison," *Harper's New Monthly Magazine* 74, no. 443 (April 1887): 824–826.

[1]**Vernon Lee**: The pen name of English author Violet Paget, who wrote a series of essays in the form of conversations about art and literature, published as *Baldwin: Being Dialogues on Views and Aspirations* in 1886.

whatever is injurious, I can trace to the perusal of some work of fiction. Worse than that, they beget such high-strung and supersensitive ideas of life that plain industry and plodding perseverance are despised, and matter-of-fact poverty, or every-day, commonplace distress, meets with no sympathy, if indeed noticed at all, by one who has wept over the impossibly accumulated sufferings of some gaudy hero or heroine. . . .

We are not sure that we have the controversy with the writer which he seems to suppose, and we should perhaps freely grant the mischievous effects which he says novel-reading has wrought upon him, if we were not afraid that he had possibly reviewed his own experience with something of the inaccuracy we find in his report of our opinions. By his confession he is himself proof that Vernon Lee is right in saying, "The modern human being has been largely fashioned by those who have written about him, and most of all by the novelist," and there is nothing in what he urges to conflict with her claim that "the chief use of the novel" is "to make the shrewd and tolerant a little less shrewd and tolerant, and to make the generous and austere a little more skeptical and easy-going." If he will look more closely at these postulates, we think he will see that in the one she deals with the effect of the novel in the past, and in the other with its duty in the future. We still think that there "is sense if not final wisdom" in what she says, and we are quite willing to acknowledge something of each in our correspondent.

But novels are now so fully accepted by everyone pretending to cultivated taste—and they really form the whole intellectual life of such immense numbers of people, without question of their influence, good or bad, upon the mind—that it is refreshing to have them frankly denounced, and to be invited to revise one's ideas and feelings in regard to them. A little honesty, or a great deal of honesty, in this quest will do the novel, as we hope yet to have it, and as we have already begun to have it, no harm; and for our own part we will confess that we believe fiction in the past to have been largely injurious, as we believe the stage play to be still almost wholly injurious, through its falsehood, its folly, its wantonness, and its aimlessness. It may be safely assumed that most of the novel-reading which people fancy as an intellectual pastime is the emptiest dissipation hardly more related to thought or the wholesome exercise of the mental faculties than opium-eating; in either case the brain is drugged, and left weaker and crazier for the debauch. If this may be called the negative result of the fiction habit, the positive injury that most novels work is by no means so easily to be measured in the case of young men whose character they help so much to form or deform, and the women of all ages whom they keep so much in ignorance of the world they misrepresent. Grown men have little harm from them, but in the other cases, which are the vast majority, they hurt because they are not true—not because they are malevolent, but because they are idle lies about human nature and the social fabric, which it behooves us to know and to understand, that we may deal justly with ourselves and with one another. One need not go so far as our correspondent, and trace to the fiction habit "whatever is wild and visionary, whatever is untrue, whatever is injurious," in one's life; bad as the fiction habit is, it is probably not responsible for the whole sum of evil in its victims, and we believe that if the reader will use care in choosing from this fungus-growth with which the fields of literature teem every day, he may nourish himself as with the true mushroom, at no risk from the poisonous species.

The tests are very plain and simple, and they are perfectly infallible. If a novel flatters the passions, and exalts them above the principles, it is poisonous; it may not kill, but it will certainly injure; and this test will alone exclude an entire class of fiction, of which eminent examples will occur to all. Then the whole spawn of so-called un-moral romances, which imagine a world where the sins of sense are unvisited by the penalties following, swift or slow, but inexorably sure, in the real world, are deadly poison: these do kill. The novels that merely tickle our prejudices and lull our judgment, or that coddle our sensibilities, or pamper our gross appetite for the marvellous, are not so fatal, but they are innutritious, and clog the soul with unwholesome vapors of all kinds. No doubt they too help to weaken the mental fibre, and make their readers indifferent to "plodding perseverance and plain industry," and to "matter-of-fact poverty and commonplace distress."

Without taking them too seriously, it still must be owned that the "gaudy hero and heroine" are to blame for a great deal of harm in the world. That heroine long taught by example, if not precept, that Love, or the passion or fancy she mistook for it, was the chief interest of a life which is really concerned with a great many other things; that it was lasting in the way she knew it; that it was worthy of every sacrifice, and was altogether a finer thing than prudence, obedience, reason; that love alone was glorious and beautiful, and these were mean and ugly in comparison with it. More lately she has begun to idolize and illustrate Duty, and she is hardly less mischievous in this new role, opposing duty, as she did love, to prudence, obedience, and reason. The stock hero, whom, if we met him, we could not fail to see was a most deplorable person, has undoubtedly imposed himself upon the victims of the fiction habit as admirable. With him, too, love was and is the great affair, whether in its old romantic phase of chivalrous achievement or manifold suffering for love's sake, or its more recent development of the "virile," the bullying, and the brutal, or its still more recent agonies of self-sacrifice, as idle and useless as the moral experiences of the insane asylums. With his vain posturings and his ridiculous splendor he is really a painted barbarian, the prey of his passions and his delusions, full of obsolete ideals, and the motives and ethics of a savage, which the guilty author of his being does his best—or his worst—in spite of his own light and knowledge, to foist upon the reader as something generous and noble. We are not merely bringing this charge against that sort of fiction which is beneath literature and outside of it, "the shoreless lakes of ditch-water," whose miasms fill the air below the empyrean where the great ones sit; but we are accusing the work of some of the most famous, who have, in this instance or in that, sinned against the truth, which can alone exalt and purify men. We do not say that they have constantly done so, or even commonly done so; but that they have done so at all marks them as of the past, to be read with the due historical allowance for their epoch and their conditions. For we believe that, while inferior writers will and must continue to imitate them in their foibles and their errors, no one hereafter will be able to achieve greatness who is false to humanity, either in its facts or its duties. The light of civilization has already broken even upon the novel, and no conscientious man can now set about painting an image of life without perpetual question of the verity of his work, and without feeling bound to distinguish so clearly that no reader of his may be misled, between what is right and what is wrong, what is noble and what is base, what is health and what is perdition, in the actions and the characters he portrays.

The fiction that aims merely to entertain—the fiction that is to serious fiction as the opera bouffe, the ballet, and the pantomime are to the true drama—need not feel the burden of this obligation so deeply; but even such fiction will not be gay or trivial to any reader's hurt, and criticism will hold it to account if it passes from painting to teaching folly.

More and more not only the criticism which prints its opinions, but the infinitely vaster and powerfuler criticism which thinks and feels them merely, will make this demand. For our own part we confess that we do not care to judge any work of the imagination without first of all applying this test to it. We must ask ourselves before we ask anything else, Is it true?—true to the motives, the impulses, the principles that shape the life of actual men and women? This truth, which necessarily includes the highest morality and the highest artistry—this truth given, the book *cannot* be wicked and cannot be weak; and without it all graces of style and feats of invention and cunning of construction are so many superfluities of naughtiness. It is well for the truth to have all these, and shine in them, but for falsehood they are merely meretricious, the bedizenment of the wanton; they atone for nothing, they count for nothing. But in fact they come naturally of truth, and grace it without solicitation; they are added unto it. In the whole range of fiction we know of no *true* picture of life—that is, of human nature—which is not also a masterpiece of literature, full of divine and natural beauty. It may have no touch or tint of this special civilization or of that; it had *better* have this local color well ascertained; but the truth is deeper and finer than aspects, and if the book is true to what men and women know of one another's souls it will be true enough, and it will be great and beautiful. It is the conception of literature as something apart from life, super-finely aloof, which makes it really unimportant to the great mass of mankind, without a message or a meaning for them; and it is the notion that a novel may be false in its portrayal of causes and effects that makes literary art contemptible even to those whom it amuses, that forbids them to regard the novelist as a serious or right-minded person. If they do not in some moment of indignation cry out against all novels, as our correspondent does, they remain besotted in the fume of the delusions purveyed to them, with no higher feeling for the author than such maudlin affection as the *habitué* of an opium-joint perhaps knows for the attendant who fills his pipe with the drug.

READING AND DISCUSSION QUESTIONS

1. Though Howells does not mention them specifically, how might you interpret his dissatisfaction with idealism as a response to the Civil War and postwar industrialization? To what extent do you think his interest in realism was spurred by his impatience with romance novels whose themes, characters, and plot were irrelevant to the pressing social and economic crisis of industrial America?

2. Analyze Howells's critique of fiction for evidence that Progressive-Era social scientists, reformers, and exposé journalists, whose own investigations surfaced truths about industrializing America, influenced him. To what extent did journalism provide a model for the type of fiction he encouraged?

P6-3 | The New Woman Challenges the Social Order

CAROLINE TICKNOR, *The Steel-Engraving Lady and the Gibson Girl* (1901)

Gender ideals were in flux at the start of the twentieth century. Conventional attitudes had set off a domestic sphere of house and family for middle- and upper-class women to inhabit, which was seen as the correct and natural place for them to exercise their nurturing instincts. As feminists chipped away at these prescriptions, new ideals emerged, including the "Gibson girl," who was modern, educated, and professional, if not as politically radical as the activist "New Woman." Author and literary biographer Caroline Ticknor's satire on the Gibson girl hints at the ambivalence some felt toward feminism, which they saw as a threat to the domestic ideal.

The Steel-Engraving Lady[1] sat by the open casement, upon which rested one slender arm. Her drapery sleeve fell back, revealing the alabaster whiteness of her hand and wrist. Her glossy, abundant hair was smoothly drawn over her ears, and one rose nestled in the coil of her dark locks.

Her eyes were dreamy, and her embroidery frame lay idly upon the little stand beside her. An air of quiet repose pervaded the apartment, which, in its decorations, bespoke the lady's industry. Under a glass, upon a gleaming mirror, floated some waxen pond lilies, modeled by her slim fingers. A large elaborate sampler told of her early efforts with her needle, and gorgeous mottoes on the walls suggested the pleasing combination of household ornamentation with Scriptural advice.

Suddenly a heavy step was heard upon the stair. A slight blush mantled the Steel-Engraving Lady's cheek.

Caroline Ticknor, "The Steel-Engraving Lady and the Gibson Girl," *The Atlantic Monthly* 88 (July 1901): 105–108.

[1]**Steel-Engraving Lady**: Referred to the Victorian ideal of a morally proper woman, so named because of the printing process, using lithography, by which her image was reproduced in magazines.

"Can that be Reginald?" she murmured.

The door flew open, and on the threshold stood the Gibson Girl.

"Excuse me for dropping in upon you," she said, with a slight nod, tossing a golf club down upon the sofa near by. "You see I've been appointed to write a paper on Extinct Types, and I am anxious to scrape acquaintance with you."

The Steel-Engraving Lady bowed a trifle stiffly. "Won't you be seated?" she said, with dignity.

The Gibson Girl dropped into a low chair, and crossed one knee over the other; then she proceeded to inspect the room, whistling meanwhile a snatch from the last comic opera. She wore a short skirt and heavy square-toed shoes, a mannish collar, cravat, and vest, and a broad-brimmed felt hat tipped jauntily upon one side.

She stared quite fixedly at the fair occupant of the apartment, who could with difficulty conceal her annoyance.

"Dear me! you're just as slender and ethereal as any of your pictures," she remarked speculatively. "You need fresh air and exercise; and see the color of my hands and face beside your own."

The Steel-Engraving Lady glanced at her vis-à-vis, and shrugged her shoulders.

"I like a healthy coat of tan upon a woman," the Gibson Girl announced, in a loud voice. "I never wear a hat throughout the hottest summer weather. The day is past when one deplores a sunburned nose and a few freckles."

"And is a browned and sunburned neck admired in the ballroom?" the other queried. "Perhaps your artists of to-day prefer studies in black and white entirely, and scoff at coloring such as that ivory exhibits?" She pointed to a dainty miniature upon the mantel.

"No wonder you can't walk in those slim, tiny slippers!" the Gibson Girl exclaimed.

"And can you walk in those heavy men's shoes?" the Steel-Engraving Lady questioned. "Methinks my slippers would carry me with greater ease. Are they your own, or have you possibly put on your brother's shoes for an experiment? If they were only hidden beneath an ample length of skirt, they might seem less obtrusive. And is it true you walk the streets in such an abridged petticoat? You surely cannot realize it actually displays six inches of your stockings. I blush to think of any lady upon the street in such a guise."

"Blushing is out of style." The Gibson Girl laughed heartily.

"Nor would it show through such a coat of sunburn," the other suggested archly.

"It very likely seems odd to you," the visitor continued, "who are so far behind the times; but we are so imbued with modern thought that we have done away with all the oversensitiveness and overwhelming modesty in which you are enveloped. We have progressed in every way. When a man approaches, we do not tremble and droop our eyelids, or gaze adoringly while he lays down the law. We meet him on a ground of perfect fellowship, and converse freely on every topic."

The Steel-Engraving Lady caught her breath. "And does he like this method?" she queried.

"Whether he *likes* it or not makes little difference; *he* is no longer the one whose pleasure is to be consulted. The question now is, not 'What does man like?' but 'What does woman prefer?' That is the keynote of modern thought. You see, I've had a liberal education. I can do everything my brothers do: and do it rather better, I fancy. I am an athlete and a college graduate, with a wide, universal outlook. My point of view is free from narrow influences, and quite outside of the home boundaries."

"So I should have imagined by your dress and manner," the Steel-Engraving Lady said, under her breath.

"I am prepared to enter a profession," the visitor announced. "I believe thoroughly in every woman's having a distinct vocation."

The Steel-Engraving Lady gasped. "Does not a woman's home furnish her ample employment and occupation?"

"Undoubtedly it keeps her busy," the other said; "but what is she *accomplishing*, shut in, walled up from the world's work and interests? In my profession I shall be brought in contact with universal problems."

"A public character! Perhaps you're going on the stage?"

"Oh no. I'm to become a lawyer."

"Perhaps your home is not a happy one?" the Steel-Engraving Lady said, with much perplexity.

"Indeed it is, but I have little time to stay there."

"Have you no parents?"

"Parents? Why, to be sure; but when a woman is capable of a career, she can't sit down at home just to amuse her parents. Each woman owes a duty to herself, to make the most of her Heaven-given talents. Why, I've a theory for the entire reorganization of our faulty public school system."

"And does it touch upon the influence at home, which is felt in the nursery as well as in the drawing-room?"

"It is outside of all minor considerations," the Gibson Girl went on. "I think we women should do our utmost to purify the world of politics. Could I be content to sit down at home, and be a toy and a mere ornament,"—here she glanced scornfully at her companion,—"when the great public needs my individual aid?"

"And can no woman serve the public at home?" the other said gently. Her voice was very sweet and low. "I have been educated to think that our best service was"—

"To stand and wait," the Gibson Girl broke in. "Ah, but we all know better nowadays. You see the motto 'Heaven helps her who helps herself' suits the 'new woman.' We're not a shy, retiring, uncomplaining generation. We're up to date and up to snuff, and every one of us is self-supporting."

"Dear me!" the Steel-Engraving Lady sighed. "I never realized I had aught to complain of; and why should woman not be ornamental as well as useful? Beauty of person and manner and spirit is surely worthy of our attainment."

"It was all well enough in your day, but this is a utilitarian age. We cannot sit down to be admired; we must be 'up and doing'; we must leave 'footprints on the sands of time.' "

The Steel-Engraving Lady glanced speculatively at her companion's shoes. "Ah, but such great big footprints!" she gasped; "they make me shudder. And do your brothers approve of having you so clever that you compete with them in everything, and are there business places enough for you and them?"

"We don't require their approval. Man has been catered to for ages past, while woman was a patient, subservient slave. Today she assumes her rightful place, and man accepts the lot assigned him. And as for business chances, if there is but one place, and I am smarter than my brother, why, it is fair that I should take it, and let him go without. But tell me," the Gibson Girl said condescendingly, "what did your so-called education consist of?"

"The theory of my education is utterly opposed to yours, I fear," the other answered. "Mine was designed to fit me for my home; yours is calculated to unfit you for yours. You are equipped for contact with the outside world, for competition with your brothers in business; my training merely taught me to make my brother's home a place which he should find a source of pleasure and inspiration. I was taught grace of motion, drilled in a school of manners, made to enter a room properly, and told how to sit gracefully, to modulate my voice, to preside at the table with fitting dignity. In place of your higher education, I had my music and languages and my embroidery frame. I was persuaded there was no worthier ambition than to bring life and joy and beauty into a household, no duty higher than that I owed my parents. Your public aspirations, your independent views, your discontent, are something I cannot understand."

The Steel-Engraving Lady rose from her chair with grace and dignity; she crossed the room, and paused a moment on the threshold, where she bowed with the air of a princess who would dismiss her courtiers; then she was gone.

"She surely is an extinct type!" the Gibson Girl exclaimed. "I realize now what higher education has done toward freeing woman from chains of prejudice. I must be off. I'm due at the golf links at three-fifteen."

When the sun set, the Steel-Engraving Lady might have been seen again seated beside the open casement. Her taper fingers lightly touched the strings of her guitar as she hummed a low lullaby. Once more she heard a step upon the stair, and once again the color mantled her damask cheek, and as she breathed the word "Reginald" a tall and ardent figure came swiftly toward her. He dropped upon one knee, as if to pay due homage to his fair one, and, raising her white hand to his lips, whispered, "My queen, my lady love."

And at this moment the Gibson Girl was seated upon a fence, swinging her heavy boots, while an athletic youth beside her busied himself with filling a corn-cob pipe.

"I say, Joe," he said, with friendly accent, "just you hop down and stand in front of me to keep the wind off, while I light this pipe."

And the sun dropped behind the woods, and the pink afterglow illumined the same old world that it had beautified for countless ages.

Its pink light fell upon the Steel-Engraving Lady as she played gently on her guitar and sang a quaint old ballad, while her fond lover held to his lips the rose that had been twined in her dark looks.

The sunset's glow lighted the Gibson Girl upon her homeward path as she strode on beside the athletic youth, carrying her golf clubs, while he puffed his corn-cob pipe. They stopped at a turn in the road, and he touched his cap, remarking: "I guess I'll leave you here, as I am late to dinner. I'll try to be out at the links to-morrow; but if I don't show up, you'll know I've had a chance to join that hunting trip. Ta-ta!"

And the night breeze sprang up, and murmured: "Hail the new woman,— behold she comes apace! Woman, ONCE MAN'S SUPERIOR, NOW HIS EQUAL!"

CAROLINE TICKNOR.

READING AND DISCUSSION QUESTIONS

1. Examine Ticknor's point of view regarding the Gibson girl for evidence of competing gender ideals that supported and challenged the dominant social structure at the turn of the century. What can you infer about Ticknor's attitude as well as the attitude of readers of *The Atlantic Monthly*, the periodical where Ticknor's article appeared?

2. How does this source relate to the historical context of the early twentieth century, a period when modern ideas about gender shaped cultural values and popular culture?

P6-4 | Anthropologist Undermines Racial Stereotypes
FRANZ BOAS, *The Mind of Primitive Man* (1911)

Through most of the nineteenth century, "culture" was used to denote high-minded art, literature, and music, but with the rise of university-based social sciences, anthropologists like Franz Boas redefined the term to mean the values, beliefs, and attitudes that shaped people's worldview and influenced their behavior and conduct. Boas chaired the Department of Anthropology at Columbia University after stints working at the Field Museum in Chicago and the American Museum of Natural History in New York, where his controversial approach to anthropology challenged existing ideas of racial determinism.

Until the first decade of our century the opinion that race determines culture had been, in Europe at least, rather a subject of speculation of amateur historians and sociologists than a foundation of public policy. Since that time it has spread among the masses. Slogans like "blood is thicker than water," are expressions of its new emotional appeal. The earlier concept of nationality has been given a new

Franz Boas, *The Mind of Primitive Man* (New York: The Macmillan Company, 1911; revised edition, 1938), 253–254, 268–272.

meaning by identifying nationality with racial unity and by assuming that national characteristics are due to racial descent. It is particularly interesting to note that in the anti-Semitic movement in Germany of the time of 1880 it was not the Jew as a member of an alien race who was subject to attack, but the Jew who was not assimilated to German national life. The present policy of Germany is based on an entirely different foundation, for every person is supposed to have a definite, unalterable character according to his racial descent and this determines his political and social status. The conditions are quite analogous to the status assigned to the Negro at an earlier period, when licentiousness, shiftless laziness, lack of initiative were considered as racially determined, unescapable qualities of every Negro. It is a curious spectacle to see that serious scientists, wherever free to express themselves, have on the whole been drifting away from the opinion that race determines mental status, excepting however those biologists who have no appreciation of social factors because they are captivated by the apparent hereditary determinism of morphological forms, while among the uninformed public to which unfortunately a number of powerful European politicians belong, race prejudice has been making and is still making unchecked progress. I believe it would be an error to assume that we are free of this tendency: if nothing else the restrictions imposed upon members of certain "races," abridging their right to own real estate, to tenancy in apartment houses, membership of clubs, to their right to visit hotels and summer resorts, to admission to schools and colleges shows at least that there is no abatement of old prejudices directed against Negroes, Jews, Russians, Armenians or whatever they may be. The excuse that these exclusions are compelled by economic considerations, or by the fear of driving away from schools or colleges other social groups is merely an acknowledgment of a widespread attitude. . . .

The Negro problem as it presents itself in the United States is from a biological viewpoint not essentially different from those just discussed. We have found that no proof of an inferiority of the Negro type could be given, except that it seemed barely possible that perhaps the race would not produce quite so many men of highest genius as other races, while there was nothing at all that could be interpreted as suggesting any material difference in the mental capacity of the bulk of the Negro population as compared with the bulk of the White population. There will undoubtedly be endless numbers of men and women who will be able to outrun their White competitors, and who will do better than the defectives whom we permit to drag down and retard the healthy children of our public schools.

Ethnological observation does not countenance the view that the traits observed among our poorest Negro population are in any sense racially determined. A survey of African tribes exhibits to our view cultural achievements of no mean order. To those unfamiliar with the products of native African art and industry, a walk through one of the large museums of Europe would be a revelation. Few of our American museums have made collections that exhibit this subject in any way worthily. The blacksmith, the wood carver, the weaver, the potter these all produce ware original in form, executed with great care, and exhibiting that love of labor, and interest in the results of work, which are apparently so often lacking among the Negroes in our American surroundings. . . . The power of organization as illustrated in the government of native states is of no mean order, and when wielded by men of great personality has led to the foundation of extended empires. All the different kinds of activities that we consider valuable in the citizens of our country may be found in aboriginal Africa. Neither is the wisdom of the philosopher absent. A perusal of any of the collections of African proverbs that have been published will demonstrate the homely practical philosophy of the Negro, which is often proof of sound feeling and judgment.

It would be out of place to enlarge on this subject, because the essential point that anthropology can contribute to the practical discussion of the adaptability of the Negro is a decision of the question how far the undesirable traits that are at present undoubtedly found in our Negro population are due to racial traits, and how far they are due to social surroundings for which we are responsible. To this question anthropology can give the decided answer that the traits of African culture as observed in the aboriginal home of the Negro are those of a healthy primitive people, with a considerable degree of personal initiative, with a talent for organization, with imaginative power, with technical skill and thrift. Neither is a warlike spirit absent in the race, as is proved by the mighty conquerors who overthrew states and founded new empires, and by the courage of the armies that follow the bidding of their leaders. . . .

There is . . . no evidence whatever that would stigmatize the Negro as of weaker build, or as subject to inclinations and powers that are opposed to our social organization. An unbiased estimate of the anthropological evidence so far brought forward does not permit us to countenance the belief in a racial inferiority which would unfit an individual of the Negro race to take his part in modern civilization. We do not know of any demand made on the human body or mind in modern life that anatomical or ethnological evidence would prove to be beyond his powers.

The traits of the American Negro are adequately explained on the basis of his history and social status. The tearing-away from the African soil and the consequent complete loss of the old standards of life, which were replaced by the dependency of slavery and by all it entailed, followed by a period of disorganization and by a severe economic struggle against heavy odds, are sufficient to explain the inferiority of the status of the race, without falling back upon the theory of hereditary inferiority.

In short, there is every reason to believe that the Negro when given facility and opportunity, will be perfectly able to fulfill the duties of citizenship as well as his White neighbor. . . .

Our tendency to evaluate an individual according to the picture that we form of the class to which we assign him, although he may not feel any inner connection with that class, is a survival of primitive forms of thought. The characteristics of the members of the class are highly variable and the type that we construct from the most frequent characteristics supposed to belong to the class is never more than an abstraction hardly ever realized in a single individual, often not even a result of observation, but an often heard tradition that determines our judgment.

Freedom of judgment can be attained only when we learn to estimate an individual according to his own ability and character. Then we shall find, if we were to select the best of mankind, that all races and all nationalities would be represented. Then we shall treasure and cultivate the variety of forms that human thought and activity has taken, and abhor, as leading to complete stagnation, all attempts to impress one pattern of thought upon whole nations or even upon the whole world.

READING AND DISCUSSION QUESTIONS

1. In what way did Boas's understanding of race and culture challenge prevailing ideas that had defined Anglo-Saxon superiority and "Negro" inferiority? What fundamental assumption about race did his anthropological work overturn?

2. Examine the historical context of turn-of-the-century America to understand anthropology's impact on the politics of race and ethnicity. How do the issues raised in this source relate to American debates over immigration and the "Negro problem" from this period?

P6-5 | A Reaction to Modernism at the New York Armory Show
ROYAL CORTISSOZ, *A Memorable Exhibition* (1913)

The 1913 Armory Show held at the 69th Street Armory building in New York City introduced Americans to modern art, featuring European postimpressionist and Cubist painters like Paul Cézanne, Henri Matisse, and Marcel Duchamp. These canvases challenged the more academic art Americans were accustomed to seeing by eschewing realism for a different aesthetic, one self-consciously abstract. Cubists, for instance, reduced nature to its elemental forms as seen in Duchamp's scandalous painting *Nude Descending a Staircase*. The *New York Herald Tribune*'s art critic, Royal Cortissoz, dismissed much of the avant-garde as amateurish work, but many others caught the significance of the event as a cultural thunderclap.

It is enough to say that these "Independents," keen upon having their own way, have done a good deal to put into the air the idea that "freedom" is not as widespread in the world of American art as it ought to be, and that something should be done clearly to establish a more liberal, more open-minded and sympathetic attitude toward every "new" thing. It was toward the advancement of this principle that the Association of American Painters and Sculptors, itself a new body, directed its efforts when it set out to make what soon came to be known simply as the Armory show. . . .

Royal Cortissoz, *Art and Common Sense* (New York: Charles Scribner's Sons, 1913), 143, 145, 148, 151–152, 155–158.

It was a fine and stirring exhibition. The collection of about a thousand examples of modern art included some of the most stupidly ugly pictures in the world and not a few pieces of sculpture to match them. But while these undoubtedly made the "sensation" of the affair it was plain that the latter was organized with no sensational purpose, and it was not freakish violence that gave the collection as a whole its tone. That tone was determined by nothing more nor less than a healthy independence in most of the types represented. The merely eccentric artists occupied a comparatively subordinate position. If at first this did not seem to be so it was only because things that are bizarre naturally make themselves conspicuous. . . .

Be it said to the credit of our countrymen that their indulgence in egotistical fatuity has as yet been slight. A few of them swagger about, so to say, making portentous use of their new-found "independence," but, frankly, it is not to them that the show owed such fantasticality as it possessed. This was to be ascribed to the French Post-Impressionists and Cubists, with a few of their Spanish, German, Italian and Russian fellows. Those whirling dervishes, seeking, like the Fat Boy in "Pickwick,"[1] to make our flesh creep, succeeded only too easily amongst some observers, though it is hard to see why they should have been taken so seriously. The Cubist agglomerations of line and color possess, sometimes, expressive qualities. It is like the monstrous potato or gourd which the farmer brings to the village store to see if his cronies can make out in certain "bumps" which he indicates the resemblance that he has found to General Grant or the late P. T. Barnum. . . .

[L]et us turn to the paintings of Cezanne. This well-to-do Frenchman . . . had no pot-boilers to paint, but could use his brush for his own amusement, had in him, despite wholesome personal traits, the taint of the amateur. He had some feeling for landscape and the figure. He groped toward an expressive treatment of form, and in his nudes you can dimly make out some rather handsome intentions, just as in his landscapes you can just discern the aims of a colorist and a designer. But Cezanne's dreams didn't "come true" and this not because he was in the throes of some new, abstruse conception of art, but because he simply did not know his trade. There are no esoteric glories about Cezanne, hidden from the vulgar. He was merely a second-rate Impressionist who had now and then fair luck in painting a moderately good picture, but would never have come into fame at all if the dealers had not taken him up and there had not been the usual band of scribes ready to applaud something new. . . . The only mystery we have to reckon with in his case lies in the fuss that has been made about him. . . .

It is not credible that Matisse has not known just what he was about. There is a legend to the effect that the man had some academic ability, and it is easy to believe that once, at all events, he knew how to draw. Vaguely, beneath what is monstrous in the paintings by him in this exhibition, one discerned the grasp upon form and movement which a man has when he has been trained in the

---

[1]**Fat Boy**: A character in Charles Dickens's novel *The Posthumous Papers of the Pickwick Club*.

rudiments and has used his eyes. But first going after some will-o'-the-wisp leading him into ways of wanton ugliness, and then, I infer, persuading himself that he had a "mission," Matisse proceeded to paint his nudes and his studies of still life not with the naivete of a child, but with the forced simplicity of an adult playing a trick. In the process he would appear to have relinquished all respect for technique, all feeling for his medium, to have been content to daub his canvas with linear and tonal coarseness. The bulbous, contorted bodies in his figure pieces are in no wise expressive of any new and rationalized canon of form. They are false to nature, they are ugly as the halting efforts of the veriest amateur are ugly, and, in short, their negation of all that true art implies is significant of just the smug complacency to which I have alluded. Whether through laziness or through ignorance, Matisse has come to the point where he feels that in painting an interior like his "Panneau Rouge," or nudes like "Les Capucines" or "Le Luxe," he is exercising the function of an artist, and, of course, there are crowds of half-baked individuals who are ready to tell him that he is right. As a matter of fact, these things are not works of art; they are feeble impertinences. . . .

When we bid farewell to Matisse, whose nudes, preposterous as they are, yet suggest the forms of men and women, we find ourselves in the company of "revolutionaries" who are not dealing with form as we understand it at all. With them a man begins to look like something else, preferably like some mass of faceted or curved little bodies thrown together in a heap. The Cubist steps in and gives us not pictures but so many square yards of canvas, treated as though they were so many square yards of wall-paper. But the Cubist wants to eat his cake and have it, too. He paints you his riddle of line and color, and then, as in the case of M. Marcel Duchamp, calls it "Nude Descending a Staircase." In other words, he has the effrontery to assert that his "picture" bears some relation to human life. Who shall argue with him? For my part I flatly refuse to offer him the flattery of argument. According to the Spanish proverb it is a waste of lather to shave an ass, and that criticism of the Cubists is thrown away which does not deny at the outset their right to serious consideration. Are we to be at great pains to explain that a chunk of marble is not a statue? Are we elaborately to demonstrate that a battered tin can is not in the same category with a goblet fashioned by Cellini? Are we to accept these Cubists as painters of pictures because they have covered canvas with paint? Are they indeed "forces which cannot be ignored because they have had results"? These "results" have nothing to do with art. Why should they not be ignored?

READING AND DISCUSSION QUESTIONS

1. From Cortissoz's critique of the Armory Show, what conclusions can you draw about the shift in artistic expression in the early twentieth century?

2. What aesthetic value did Cortissoz prize? How does the cultural context of this period help you to understand his reaction to the "modern" work on display?

P6-6 | Solving the Problems Plaguing Native Americans
CARLOS MONTEZUMA, *What Indians Must Do* (1914)

The fate of Native Americans twisted and turned on the changing ideas and attitudes with which whites viewed them. The latter nineteenth century, witness to infamous Indian wars and deliberate efforts to decimate their population, toggled between policies of assimilation and separation on reservations. Carlos Montezuma, an Apache activist and doctor, emerged in the early twentieth century as a national leader for Indian civil rights, attacking the reservation system and the federal bureaucracy that supported it, by drawing on prevailing theories of social philosophy.

We must free ourselves. Our peoples' heritage is freedom. Freedom reigned in their whole make-up. They harmonized with nature and lived accordingly. Preaching freedom to our people on reservations does not make them free any more than you can, by preaching, free those prisoners who are in the penitentiary. Reservations are prisons where our people are kept to live and die, where equal possibilities, equal education and equal responsibilities are unknown.

For our people to know what freedom is they must go outside of the reservation and in order for them to harmonize with it and get used to it, they must live outside of the reservations. . . .

Sons of the aboriginal Indians, do you know we have been driven from the heritage of our fathers from generation to generation until we can not take another step! What are we going to do? We must decide for ourselves very quickly. Are we to disappear as the buffaloes or rise above the horizon of the twentieth century and respond, "We are here!" The sound of your own voice at the roll call will be at the end of the final battle to gain your freedom, be your individual self. The Society of American Indians will not cease until Indians have gained that standard that makes one true and free.

We must do away with the Indian Bureau. The reservation system has debarred us as a race from acquiring that knowledge to appreciate our property. The Government after teaching us how to live without work has come to the conclusion "that the Indians are not commercialists" and, therefore, "we (his guardian) will remove them as we think best and use them as long as our administration lasts and make friends." The Indian Department has drifted into commercialism at the expense of our poor benighted people. So they go on and say: "Let us not allot those Indians on that sweet flowing water because there are others who will profit by damming it up and selling it out to the newcomers; that the Indians do not use or develop their lands; five acres of irrigated land is all that one Indian can manage, but in order to be generous, we will give him ten acres and close up the books and call it square; that their vast forest does them no good, before the Indian can open his eyes let us transfer it to the Forestry Reserve Department.

Carlos Montezuma, "What Indians Must Do," *The Quarterly Journal of The Society of American Indians* II, no. 4 (October–December 1914): 294–299.

Never mind, let the Indian scratch for his wood to cook with and to warm himself in the years to come; that the Indians have no use for rivers, therefore, we will go into damming business and build them on their lands without their consent. Pay? No! Why should we?" They give us "C" class water instead of "A" class. They have got us! Why? Because we do not know the difference. . . .

My Indian friends, it seems that we have no voice in our affairs. It seems that all we can do is to sit there like dummies and see our property fade away and wonder what next. Our woods go to the forestry reserve; our fertile lands to the Irrigation Project; our rich minerals to the miners, and our waters to the interested parties that build dams and reap the profit within our reservations. In all of these it seems that we are counted out. If our Society is going to amount to anything do you not think we ought in some way stand up for our people? If this taking away what belongs to us continues very much longer, where do you suppose we will land?

As the Society of American Indians, it is our duty to protect and aid in some way, to stop these wholesale smuggling away of our people's property. Can you imagine any other race allowing this without their consent?

The sooner the Government abolishes the Indian Bureau, the better it will be for we Indians in every way. The system that has kept alive the Indian Bureau has been instrumental in dominating over our race for fifty years. In that time the Indian's welfare has grown to the secondary and the Indian Bureau the whole thing, and therefore a necessary political appendage of the Government. It sends out exaggerated and wonderful reports to the public in order to suck the blood of our race, so that it may have perpetual life to sap your life, my life and our children's future prospects. There are many good things to say about the Indian Department. It started out right with our people. It fed them, clothed them and protected them from going outside of the reservations. It was truly a place of refuge. Then they were dominated by agents; now they are called superintendents. On the reservation our people did not act without the consent of the Superintendent; they did not express themselves without the approval of the Superintendent, and they did not dare to think, for that would be to rival, to the Superintendent. Yesterday, today, our people are in the same benighted condition. As Indians they are considered non-entities. They are not anything to themselves and not anything to the world.

It would be wrong for me to come here and tell you that the reservation system is good and helpful to our people, and that the Indian Bureau should be perpetuated when I know in my heart that it has been the greatest hindrance on the road from Indian life to civilization. Look at New York and Chicago, and then at the tepees on reservations. Look at Harvard, Yale, Princeton, and Madison, and then at the day schools on Indian reservations; hear the screeching locomotives and the whirr of industry and see the light of electricity; behold the grand panorama of agriculture of green gardens from the Atlantic to the Pacific coasts, from Canada to the Gulf of Mexico; and then behold the lounging Indians around agency buildings and under shady trees. Paradoxical as the statement may sound, it is nevertheless true, that the greatest obstacle that lies along the path toward the solution of our problem is the existence of the "helpful" Indian Bureau at Washington. It is the power plant that supplies life current to the reservations. It is long range, outside life, and does not grow from within.

The Indian Bureau seems to exist for no other purpose than to preserve the reservations. In other words the source from which the Indian ought to find relief from the evils of the reservation system is the very source without which the evil would not exist. . . .

The time has come that we Indians are ready to battle our own way in the world. Justice from the world can be no worse than the reservation system.

After starvation, rubbing up against the world and perchance surviving our reward will be independence. Once upon a time our ancestors were supremely independent. All they surveyed was theirs. There was none to dispute their claim. It was an ideal independence and worthy of imitation, but time has changed and conditions have changed with it. Somehow and for no other reason but that our people were Indians were they enslaved to separate existence and governed under different rules from the general government of the country. It is an appalling thing to think of such a thing and it does not look right and just. As their children's children we ought to be ashamed of ourselves that we tolerate this national abuse any longer without our resentment, without trying to redeem our people.

To a great extent it is our fault because we have taken no interest, no thought and no consideration to change and to look around to be really free. We Indians must let loose from these things that cause us to be separate from the laws and rules that other races enjoy. It is a delusion to think that we are free when we are reservation Indians and governed by the Indian Bureau.

We must be independent. When with my people for a vacation in Arizona I must live outdoors; I must sleep on the ground; I must cook in the fire on the ground; I must sit on the ground, I must eat nature's food and I must be satisfied with inconveniences that I do not enjoy at my Chicago home. Yet those blood relations of mine are independent, happy, because they were born and brought up in that environment, while as a greenhorn I find myself dependent and helpless in such simple life. In order for we Indians to be independent in the whirl of this other life, we must get into it and get used to it and live up to its requirements and take our chances with the rest of our fellow creatures. Being caged up and not permitted to develop our facilities has made us a dependent race. We are looked upon as hopeless to save and as hopeless to do anything for ourselves. The only Christian way, then, is to leave us alone and let us die in that condition. The conclusion is true that we will die that way if we do not hurry up and get out of it and hustle for our salvation. Did you ever notice how other races hustle and bustle in order to achieve independence? Reservation Indians must do the same as the rest of the wide world.

As a full-blooded Apache Indian I have nothing more to say. Figure out your responsibility and the responsibility of every Indian that hears my voice.

READING AND DISCUSSION QUESTIONS

1. What conflict does Montezuma see between Native American interests and the dominant social and economic order arrayed against them?

2. To what extent does Montezuma draw on Social Darwinist ideas and values regarding survival of the fittest in mounting his attack on the federally supported reservation system?

▪ COMPARATIVE QUESTIONS ▪

1. Using the sources in this chapter, construct an argument demonstrating the role that ideas, beliefs, and creative expression played in effecting a cultural transformation in the period from 1877 to 1917.

2. Compare Howells's advocacy of realism with Cortissoz's rejection of the abstract qualities of modern art. Do you think their criticism of fiction and painting, respectively, share common assumptions about what makes great art? Explain.

3. Compare Sumner's views with those of Charlotte Perkins Gilman (Document 18-5) for evidence of Social Darwinism's impact on American intellectuals. How did each use Darwinian ideas to structure a critique of the late nineteenth century?

4. How do the values and attitudes toward gender roles demonstrated in Ticknor's satire compare with those of Theodore Roosevelt (Document 18-1), Elizabeth Shipley Sergeant (Document 18-2), and Charlotte Perkins Gilman (Document 18-5)? To what extent did race and class intersect with gender to shape society's ideals for both sexes?

5. Is the period 1877 to 1917 better defined as the end of Victorianism or the birth of modernism? Which is the more convincing way of interpreting the period? Identify the sources that support your argument.

21

An Emerging World Power
1890–1918

The Protestant minister Josiah Strong defined America's responsibility to "civilize and Christianize" the world by encouraging missionaries to promote the gospel. This evangelical motive was but one among a number of impulses driving late-nineteenth-century supporters of American expansionism, a latter-day expression of Manifest Destiny. Others emphasized the strategic and economic importance of overseas territories as critical to America's Social Darwinist competition with other world powers. The confluence of motives led policymakers to step offshore into the Caribbean, the Pacific, and Asia as well as Europe during World War I, but not without resistance. Opponents marshaled compelling counterarguments to American imperialism, bolstered by native protests and the evidence of domestic unrest inspired by wartime curtailment of civil liberties. This turn-of-the-century debate about the United States's legitimate and necessary role on the world stage splintered the American public into factions and colored the politics of the period. The disillusionment of World War I tempered overseas enthusiasm, but President Woodrow Wilson's lofty rhetoric about "making the world safe for democracy" established a precedent for future interventions framed as the selfless duty of a privileged nation.

21-1 | Senator Defends America's Imperial Ambitions

ALBERT BEVERIDGE, *"The March of the Flag" Speech* (1898)

In his popular speech before Republicans in the fall 1898 campaign season, Albert Beveridge rallied the party faithful in support of an ambitious international role for the United States. Elected to the Senate from Indiana, he served two terms as a member of the more progressive wing of the Republican Party, supporting policies he would later renounce, such as expanded government regulation. By the time he delivered his speech, the War of 1898 was over. Spain had already capitulated to the United States, ending what John Hay called the "splendid little war" and bolstering advocates for American expansion.

It is a noble land that God has given us; a land that can feed and clothe the world; a land whose coastlines would inclose half the countries of Europe; a land set like a sentinel between the two imperial oceans of the globe, a greater England with a nobler destiny.

It is a mighty people that He has planted on this soil; a people sprung from the most masterful blood of history; a people perpetually revitalized by the virile, man-producing working-folk of all the earth; a people imperial by virtue of their power, by right of their institutions, by authority of their Heaven-directed purposes — the propagandists and not the misers of liberty.

It is a glorious history our God has bestowed upon His chosen people; a history heroic with faith in our mission and our future; a history of statesmen who flung the boundaries of the Republic out into unexplored lands and savage wilderness; a history of soldiers who carried the flag across blazing deserts and through the ranks of hostile mountains, even to the gates of sunset; a history of a multiplying people who overran a continent in half a century; a history of prophets who saw the consequences of evils inherited from the past and of martyrs who died to save us from them; a history divinely logical, in the process of whose tremendous reasoning we find ourselves to-day.

Therefore, in this campaign, the question is larger than a party question. It is an American question. It is a world question. Shall the American people continue their march toward the commercial supremacy of the world? Shall free institutions broaden their blessed reign as the children of liberty wax in strength, until the empire of our principles is established over the hearts of all mankind?

Have we no mission to perform, no duty to discharge to our fellow-man? Has God endowed us with gifts beyond our deserts and marked us as the people of His peculiar favor, merely to rot in our own selfishness, as men and nations must, who take cowardice for their companion and self for their deity — as China has, as India has, as Egypt has?

Albert Beveridge, *The Meaning of the Times and Other Speeches* (Indianapolis: The Bobbs-Merrill Company, 1908), 47–57.

Shall we be as the man who had one talent and hid it, or as he who had ten talents and used them until they grew to riches? And shall we reap the reward that waits on our discharge of our high duty; shall we occupy new markets for what our farmers raise, our factories make, our merchants sell—aye, and, please God, new markets for what our ships shall carry?

Hawaii is ours; Porto Rico is to be ours; at the prayer of her people Cuba finally will be ours; in the islands of the East, even to the gates of Asia, coaling stations are to be ours at the very least; the flag of a liberal government is to float over the Philippines, and may it be the banner that Taylor unfurled in Texas and Fremont carried to the coast.

The Opposition tells us that we ought not to govern a people without their consent. I answer, The rule of liberty that all just government derives its authority from the consent of the governed, applies only to those who are capable of self-government. We govern the Indians without their consent, we govern our territories without their consent, we govern our children without their consent. How do they know that our government would be without their consent? Would not the people of the Philippines prefer the just, humane, civilizing government of this Republic to the savage, bloody rule of pillage and extortion from which we have rescued them?

And, regardless of this formula of words made only for enlightened, self-governing people, do we owe no duty to the world? Shall we turn these peoples back to the reeking hands from which we have taken them? Shall we abandon them, with Germany, England, Japan, hungering for them? Shall we save them from those nations, to give them a self-rule of tragedy?

They ask us how we shall govern these new possessions. I answer: Out of local conditions and the necessities of the case methods of government will grow. If England can govern foreign lands, so can America. If Germany can govern foreign lands, so can America. If they can supervise protectorates, so can America. Why is it more difficult to administer Hawaii than New Mexico or California? Both had a savage and an alien population; both were more remote from the seat of government when they came under our dominion than the Philippines are to-day.

Will you say by your vote that American ability to govern has decayed; that a century's experience in self-rule has failed of a result? Will you affirm by your vote that you are an infidel to American power and practical sense? Or will you say that ours is the blood of government; ours the heart of dominion; ours the brain and genius of administration? Will you remember that we do but what our fathers did—we but pitch the tents of liberty farther westward, farther southward—we only continue the march of the flag?

The march of the flag! In 1789 the flag of the Republic waved over 4,000,000 souls in thirteen states, and their savage territory which stretched to the Mississippi, to Canada, to the Floridas. The timid minds of that day said that no new territory was needed, and, for the hour, they were right. But Jefferson, through whose intellect the centuries marched; Jefferson, who dreamed of Cuba as an American state; Jefferson, the first Imperialist of the Republic—Jefferson

acquired that imperial territory which swept from the Mississippi to the mountains, from Texas to the British possessions, and the march of the flag began!

The infidels to the gospel of liberty raved, but the flag swept on! The title to
that noble land out of which Oregon, Washington, Idaho and Montana have been
carved was uncertain; Jefferson, strict constructionist of constitutional power
though he was, obeyed the Anglo-Saxon impulse within him, whose watchword
then and whose watchword throughout the world to-day is, "Forward!": another
empire was added to the Republic, and the march of the flag went on!

Those who deny the power of free institutions to expand urged every argument, and more, that we hear, today; but the people's judgment approved the
command of their blood, and the march of the flag went on!

A screen of land from New Orleans to Florida shut us from the Gulf, and
over this and the Everglade Peninsula waved the saffron flag of Spain; Andrew
Jackson seized both, the American people stood at his back, and, under Monroe,
the Floridas came under the dominion of the Republic, and the march of the flag
went on! The Cassandras prophesied every prophecy of despair we hear, to-day,
but the march of the flag went on!

Then Texas responded to the bugle calls of liberty, and the march of the flag
went on! And, at last, we waged war with Mexico, and the flag swept over the
southwest, over peerless California, past the Gate of Gold to Oregon on the north,
and from ocean to ocean its folds of glory blazed.

And, now, obeying the same voice that Jefferson heard and obeyed, that
Jackson heard and obeyed, that Monroe heard and obeyed, that Seward heard
and obeyed, that Grant heard and obeyed, that Harrison heard and obeyed, our
President to-day plants the flag over the islands of the seas, outposts of commerce, citadels of national security, and the march of the flag goes on! . . .

The ocean does not separate us from lands of our duty and desire—the
oceans join us, rivers never to be dredged, canals never to be repaired. Steam
joins us; electricity joins us—the very elements are in league with our destiny.
Cuba not contiguous! Porto Rico not contiguous! Hawaii and the Philippines not
contiguous! The oceans make them contiguous. And our navy will make them
contiguous.

But the Opposition is right—there is a difference. We did not need the western Mississippi Valley when we acquired it, nor Florida, nor Texas, nor California,
nor the royal provinces of the far northwest. We had no emigrants to people this
imperial wilderness, no money to develop it, even no highways to cover it. No
trade awaited us in its savage fastnesses. Our productions were not greater than
our trade. There was not one reason for the land-lust of our statesmen from
Jefferson to Grant, other than the prophet and the Saxon within them. But, to-day,
we are raising more than we can consume, making more than we can use.
Therefore we must find new markets for our produce.

And so, while we did not need the territory taken during the past century at
the time it was acquired, we do need what we have taken in 1898, and we need it
now. The resources and the commerce of these immensely rich dominions will be
increased as much as American energy is greater than Spanish sloth. In Cuba,

alone, there are 15,000,000 acres of forest unacquainted with the ax, exhaustless mines of iron, priceless deposits of manganese, millions of dollars' worth of which we must buy, to-day, from the Black Sea districts. There are millions of acres yet unexplored.

The resources of Porto Rico have only been trifled with. The riches of the Philippines have hardly been touched by the finger-tips of modern methods. And they produce what we consume, and consume what we produce—the very predestination of reciprocity—a reciprocity "not made with hands, eternal in the heavens." They sell hemp, sugar, cocoanuts, fruits of the tropics, timber of price like mahogany; they buy flour, clothing, tools, implements, machinery and all that we can raise and make. Their trade will be ours in time. Do you indorse that policy with your vote? . . .

Our trade with Porto Rico, Hawaii and the Philippines must be as free as between the states of the Union, because they are American territory, while every other nation on earth must pay our tariff before they can compete with us. Until Cuba shall ask for annexation, our trade with her will, at the very least, be like the preferential trade of Canada with England. That, and the excellence of our goods and products; that, and the convenience of traffic; that, and the kinship of interests and destiny, will give the monopoly of these markets to the American people.

The commercial supremacy of the Republic means that this Nation is to be the sovereign factor in the peace of the world. For the conflicts of the future are to be conflicts of trade—struggles for markets—commercial wars for existence. And the golden rule of peace is impregnability of position and invincibility of preparedness. So, we see England, the greatest strategist of history, plant her flag and her cannon on Gibraltar, at Quebec, in the Bermudas, at Vancouver, everywhere.

So Hawaii furnishes us a naval base in the heart of the Pacific; the Ladrones another, a voyage further on; Manila another, at the gates of Asia—Asia, to the trade of whose hundreds of millions American merchants, manufacturers, farmers, have as good right as those of Germany or France or Russia or England; Asia, whose commerce with the United Kingdom alone amounts to hundreds of millions of dollars every year; Asia, to whom Germany looks to take her surplus products; Asia, whose doors must not be shut against American trade. Within five decades the bulk of Oriental commerce will be ours. . . .

There are so many real things to be done—canals to be dug, railways to be laid, forests to be felled, cities to be builded, fields to be tilled, markets to be won, ships to be launched, peoples to be saved, civilization to be proclaimed and the flag of liberty flung to the eager air of every sea. Is this an hour to waste upon triflers with nature's laws? Is this a season to give our destiny over to word-mongers and prosperity-wreckers? No! It is an hour to remember our duty to our homes. It is a moment to realize the opportunities fate has opened to us. And so it is an hour for us to stand by the Government.

Wonderfully has God guided us. Yonder at Bunker Hill and Yorktown His providence was above us. At New Orleans and on ensanguined seas His hand sustained us. Abraham Lincoln was His minister and His was the altar of freedom the Nation's soldiers set up on a hundred battle-fields. His power directed Dewey in the East and delivered the Spanish fleet into our hands, as He delivered the elder Armada into the hands of our English sires two centuries ago. The American people can not use a dishonest medium of exchange; it is ours to set the world its example of right and honor. We can not fly from our world duties; it is ours to execute the purpose of a fate that has driven us to be greater than our small intentions. We can not retreat from any soil where Providence has unfurled our banner; it is ours to save that soil for liberty and civilization.

READING AND DISCUSSION QUESTIONS

1. Analyze Beveridge's language for evidence of his understanding of race and its role in defining "civilization." How does he define the "mission of our race"?

2. To what extent does Beveridge draw on nineteenth-century notions of Manifest Destiny that had supported antebellum territorial expansion? How did he and other pro-expansionists adapt that language to the geopolitical needs of the turn of the century?

3. How does Beveridge answer critics who opposed American imperialism in the latter nineteenth century?

21-2 | Deposed Queen Pleads for Her Island Kingdom
LILIUOKALANI, *Hawaii's Story by Hawaii's Queen* (1898)

In 1898, when the United States entered a war with Spain over Cuba and the Philippines, Congress passed a resolution annexing the Hawaiian Islands, part of a growing colonization interest among many policymakers to extend the power and influence of the United States around the world. Hawaii was key for its strategic position in the central Pacific and for its trade, promoted by American business interests who in the early 1890s engineered the overthrow of the island's Queen Liliuokalani. Her 1898 memoir, published amidst failed efforts to lobby American politicians to oppose annexation, presented her island's plea for its restored sovereignty.

I have felt much perplexity over the attitude of the American press, that great vehicle of information for the people, in respect of Hawaiian affairs. Shakespeare has said it is excellent to have a giant's strength, but it is tyrannous to use it like a giant. It is not merely that, with few exceptions, the press has seemed to favor the extinction of Hawaiian sovereignty, but that it has often treated me with coarse allusions and flippancy, and almost uniformly has commented upon me

Liliuokalani, *Hawaii's Story by Hawaii's Queen* (Boston: Lothrop, Lee & Shepard Co., 1898), 370–374.

adversely, or has declined to publish letters from myself and friends conveying correct information upon matters which other correspondents had, either wilfully or through being deceived, misrepresented. Perhaps in many cases *libellous* matter was involved. Possibly the press was not conscious of how cruelly it was exerting its strength, and will try, I now trust, to repair the injury.

It has been shown that in Hawaii there is an alien element composed of men of energy and determination, well able to carry through what they undertake, but not scrupulous respecting their methods. They doubtless control all the resources and influence of the present ruling power in Honolulu, and will employ them tirelessly in the future, as they have in the past, to secure their ends. This annexationist party might prove to be a dangerous accession even to American politics, both on account of natural abilities, and because of the training of an autocratic life from earliest youth.

Many of these men are anything but ideal citizens for a democracy. That custom of freely serving each other without stipulation or reward which exists as a very nature among our people has been even exaggerated in our hospitality to our teachers and advisers. Their children, and the associates they have drawn to themselves, are accustomed to it. They have always been treated with distinction. They would hardly know how to submit to the contradictions, disappointments, and discourtesies of a purely emulative society.

It would remain necessary for them to rule in Hawaii, even if the American flag floated over them. And if they found they could be successfully opposed, would they seek no remedy? Where would men, already proved capable of outwitting the conservatism of the United States and defeating its strongest traditions, capable of changing its colonial and foreign policy at a single *coup*, stop in their schemes?

Perhaps I may even venture here upon a final word respecting the American advocates of this annexation of Hawaii. I observe that they have pretty successfully striven to make it a party matter. It is chiefly Republican statesmen and politicians who favor it. But is it really a matter of party interest? Is the American Republic of States to degenerate, and become a colonizer and a land-grabber?

And is this prospect satisfactory to a people who rely upon self-government for their liberties, and whose guaranty of liberty and autonomy to the whole western hemisphere, the grand Monroe doctrine, appealing to the respect and the sense of justice of the masses of every nation on earth, has made any attack upon it practically impossible to the statesmen and rulers of armed empires? There is little question but that the United States could become a successful rival of the European nations in the race for conquest, and could create a vast military and naval power, if such is its ambition. But is such an ambition laudable? Is such a departure from its established principles patriotic or politic?

Here, at least for the present, I rest my pen. During my stay in the capital, I suppose I must have met, by name and by card, at least five thousand callers. From most of these, by word, by grasp of hand, or at least by expression of countenance, I have received a sympathy and encouragement of which I cannot write fully. Let it be understood that I have not failed to notice it, and to be not only flattered by its universality, but further very grateful that I have had the opportunity to know the real American people, quite distinct from those who have assumed this honored name when it suited their selfish ends.

But for the Hawaiian people, for the forty thousand of my own race and blood, descendants of those who welcomed the devoted and pious missionaries of seventy years ago,—for them has this mission of mine accomplished anything?

Oh, honest Americans, as Christians hear me for my down-trodden people! Their form of government is as dear to them as yours is precious to you. Quite as warmly as you love your country, so they love theirs. With all your goodly possessions, covering a territory so immense that there yet remain parts unexplored, possessing islands that, although near at hand, had to be neutral ground in time of war, do not covet the little vineyard of Naboth's, so far from your shores, lest the punishment of Ahab fall upon you, if not in your day, in that of your children, for "be not deceived, God is not mocked." The people to whom your fathers told of the living God, and taught to call "Father," and whom the sons now seek to despoil and destroy, are crying aloud to Him in their time of trouble; and He will keep His promise, and will listen to the voices of His Hawaiian children lamenting for their homes.

It is for them that I would give the last drop of my blood; it is for them that I would spend, nay, am spending, everything belonging to me. Will it be in vain? It is for the American people and their representatives in Congress to answer these questions. As they deal with me and my people, kindly, generously, and justly, so may the Great Ruler of all nations deal with the grand and glorious nation of the United States of America.

READING AND DISCUSSION QUESTIONS

1. What strategy does Liliuokalani use in her memoir to convince Americans to resist annexation? What does she imply will be the consequences for America of its overreach into the Pacific?

2. Whom does she blame for the political crisis in Hawaii? What inferences about American foreign policy can you draw from her assessment of Hawaii's experiences?

21-3 | Filipino Protests America's Foreign Policy
SEMPER VIGILANS, *Aguinaldo's Case Against the United States* (1899)

The War of 1898 toppled Spain's control over the Philippines and encouraged American expansionists like Senator Albert Beveridge to advocate for an overseas empire. Subduing the Philippines was not as easy as many had expected, having assumed its population to be of an "inferior" race. Emilio Aguinaldo, a Filipino independence leader, initially sided with the Americans to oust Spain, but after U.S. policy turned to occupation, not liberation for the

"Aguinaldo's Case Against the United States," *North American Review* 169 (September 1899): 425–432.

Philippines, he led the resistance movement against American imperialism. Published in the *North American Review*, this letter, written anonymously by Semper Vigilans (or "always vigilant"), appeals to the American people.

We Filipinos have all along believed that if the American nation at large knew exactly, as we do, what is daily happening in the Philippine Islands, they would rise *en masse*, and demand that this barbaric war should stop. There are other methods of securing sovereignty—the true and lasting sovereignty that has its foundation in the hearts of the people. . . . And, did America recognize this fact, she would cease to be the laughing stock of other civilized nations, as she became when she abandoned her traditions and set up a double standard of government—government by consent in America, government by force in the Philippine Islands. . . .

You have been deceived all along the line. You have been greatly deceived in the personality of my countrymen. You went to the Philippines under the impression that their inhabitants were ignorant savages, whom Spain had kept in subjection at the bayonet's point. The Filipinos have been described in serious American journals as akin to the hordes of the Khalifa; and the idea has prevailed that it required only some unknown American Kitchener to march triumphantly from north to south to make the military occupation complete. We have been represented by your popular press as if we were Africans or Mohawk Indians. We smile, and deplore the want of ethnological knowledge on the part of our literary friends. We are none of these. We are simply Filipinos. You know us now in part: you will know us better, I hope, by and by.

Some clear-headed men in the United States Senate knew the facts; but, alas, genius and correct thinking are ever in the minority.

I will not deny that there are savages in the Philippine Islands, if you designate by that name those who lead a nomad life, who do not pay tribute or acknowledge sovereignty to any one save their chief. For, let it be remembered, Spain held these islands for three hundred years, but never conquered more than one-quarter of them, and that only superficially and chiefly by means of priestcraft. The Spaniards never professed to derive their just powers from the consent of those whom they attempted to govern. What they took by force, they lost by force at our hands; and you deceived yourselves when you bought a revolution for twenty million dollars, and entangled yourselves in international politics. "*Non decipimur specie recti.*"[1] You imagined you had bought the Philippines and the Filipinos for this mess of pottage. Your imperialism led you, blind-fold, to purchase "sovereignty" from a third party who had no title to give you—a confidence trick, certainly, very transparent; a bad bargain, and one we have had sufficient perspicuity and education to see through.

---

[1] *Non decipimur specie recti* ("we are not deceived by the appearance of right"): A play on a line from the Roman poet Horace, meaning in this context that the Filipinos are not deceived by U.S. government claims that American intervention will bring freedom and liberty to the Philippines.

In the struggle for liberty which we have ever waged, the education of the masses has been slow; but we are not, on that account, an uneducated people, as our records show. Your Senators, even, admit that our political documents are worthy of a place in the archives of any civilized nation. It is the fittest and the best of our race who have survived the vile oppression of the Spanish Government, on the one hand, and of their priests on the other; and, had it not been for their tyrannous "sovereignty" and their execrable colonial methods, we would have been, ere this time, a power in the East, as our neighbors, the Japanese, have become by their industry and their modern educational methods.

You repeat constantly the dictum that we cannot govern ourselves. Macaulay long ago exposed the fallacy of this statement as regards colonies in general. With equal reason, you might have said the same thing some fifty or sixty years ago of Japan; and, little over a hundred years ago, it was extremely questionable, when you, also, were rebels against the English Government, if you could govern yourselves. You obtained the opportunity, thanks to political combinations and generous assistance at the critical moment. You passed with credit through the trying period when you had to make a beginning of governing yourselves, and you eventually succeeded in establishing a government on a republican basis, which, theoretically, is as good a system of government as needs be, as it fulfils the just ideals and aspirations of the human race.

Now, the moral of all this obviously is: Give us the chance; treat us exactly as you demanded to be treated at the hands of England, when you rebelled against her autocratic methods. Deal only with facts in a rational and consistent way. . . .

You declared war with Spain for the sake of Humanity. You announced to the world that your programme was to set Cuba free, in conformity with your constitutional principles. One of your ablest officials gave it as his opinion that the Filipinos were far more competent to govern themselves than the Cuban people were. You entered into an alliance with our chiefs at Hong Kong and at Singapore, and you promised us your aid and protection in our attempt to form a government on the principles and after the model of the government of the United States. . . .

You went to Manila under a distinct understanding with us, fully recognized by Admiral Dewey, that your object and ours was a common one. We were your accepted allies; we assisted you at all points. We besieged Manila, and we prevented the Spaniards from leaving the fortified town. We captured all the provinces of Luzon. We received arms from you. Our chiefs were in constant touch with your naval authorities. Your consuls vied with each other in their efforts to arrange matters according to the promise made to us by your officials. We hailed you as the long-prayed-for Messiah.

Joy abounded in every heart, and all went well, with Admiral George Dewey as our guide and friend, until the arrival of General Merritt. Either on his own responsibility, or by orders from the Government at Washington, this general substituted his policy for that of Admiral Dewey, commencing by ignoring all promises that had been made and ending by ignoring the Philippine people, their personality and rights, and treating them as a common enemy.

Never has a greater mistake been made in the entire history of the nations. Here you had a people who placed themselves at your feet, who welcomed you as their savior, who wished you to govern them and protect them. In combination with the genius of our countrymen and their local knowledge, you would have transformed the Philippine Islands from a land of despotism, of vicious governmental methods and priestcraft, into an enlightened republic, with America as its guide—a happy and contented people—and that in the short space of a few months, without the sacrifice of a single American life. The means were there, and it only required the magic of a master-hand to guide them, as your ships were guided into Manila Bay.

Who is responsible for the contrast between the picture I have just drawn and that which meets the eye at the present moment with all its ghastly horrors? . . .

You have been deceived from the beginning, and deception is the order of the day. You continue to deceive yourselves by the thought that once the military power is established in the Philippines, the rest is a matter for politicians. Verily you are falling into the pit you have dug for yourselves. Your officials and generals have broken their promises with our countrymen over and over again. Your atrocious cruelties are equalled only by those of Spain.

You take into your confidence the odious reptiles of Spanish priestcraft. You have established a reputation for the historical *Punica Fides*. In the face of the world you emblazon Humanity and Liberty upon your standard, while you cast your political constitution to the winds and attempt to trample down and exterminate a brave people whose only crime is that they are fighting for their liberty. You ask my countrymen to believe in you, to trust you, and you assure them that, if they do so, all will be well. But your action is on a plane with the trick which the vulgar charlatan at a country fair plays upon the unwary with three cards and an empty box.

You will never conquer the Philippine Islands by force alone. How many soldiers in excess of the regular army do you mean to leave in every town, in every province? How many will the climate claim as its victims, apart from those who may fall in actual warfare? What do the American people, who have thousands of acres yet untilled, want with the Philippines? Have you figured up the cost?

The conclusion of the whole matter is this: You were duped at the beginning. You took a wrong step, and you had not sufficient moral courage to retrace it. You must begin by conquering the hearts of the Philippine people. Be absolutely just, and you can lead them with a silken cord where chains of steel will not drag them. We excuse your want of knowledge in the past, for you have had no experience in treating with our people; but retrieve your mistake now, while there is time. . . .

But this question of sovereignty—why, such a transparent farce has never before been flouted before an intelligent people and the world in general. Can you wonder our people mistrust you and your empirical methods? They do not even regard you as being serious—a nation which professes to derive its just power of government from the consent of the governed.

"Lay down your arms," you say. Did you lay down your arms when you, too, were rebels, and the English under good King George demanded your submission? How in the name of all that is serious do you demand that we shall do what you, being rebels, refused to do? . . .

Your scheme of military occupation has been a miserable failure. You have gained practically nothing. . . . Our forces are manufacturing thousands of cartridges and other improved means to continue the struggle, and it will continue until you are convinced of your error. . . .

Be convinced, the Philippines are for the Filipinos. We are a virile race. We have never assimilated with our former oppressors, and we are not likely to assimilate with you.

READING AND DISCUSSION QUESTIONS

1. Based on this source, what can you infer about the ordinary American's interest in U.S. foreign policy? What does the author suggest about Americans' knowledge of the Philippines?

2. How does the author use America's own history in his appeal on behalf of the Filipino resistance movement led by Aguinaldo? What reaction do you think he was expecting his letter to have on Americans and their elected representatives?

21-4 | Antiwar Song Stirs Peace Movement

ALFRED BRYAN AND AL PIANTADOSI, *"I Didn't Raise My Boy to Be a Soldier"* (1915)

Despite overseas adventures in the War of 1898 and subsequent interference in Latin American affairs, many Americans embraced the tradition of isolationism. With the outbreak of war in Europe in 1914, peace advocates resisted the interventionists' cry for the beginning of war preparations. A song by Alfred Bryan and Al Piantadosi, published in 1915, captures the spirit of the peace movement.

Ten million soldiers to the war have gone,
Who may never return again.
Ten million mothers' hearts must break
For the ones who died in vain.
Head bowed down in sorrow
In her lonely years,
I heard a mother murmur thro' her tears:

I didn't raise my boy to be a soldier,
I brought him up to be my pride and joy.
Who dares to place a musket on his shoulder,
To shoot some other mother's darling boy?
Let nations arbitrate their future troubles,

"I Didn't Raise My Boy to Be a Soldier," lyrics by Alfred Bryan, music by Al Piantadosi, 1915, Library of Congress, Music Division.

It's time to lay the sword and gun away.
There'd be no war today,
If mothers all would say,
"I didn't raise my boy to be a soldier."

What victory can cheer a mother's heart,
When she looks at her blighted home?
What victory can bring her back
All she cared to call her own?
Let each mother answer
In the years to be,
Remember that my boy belongs to me!

READING AND DISCUSSION QUESTIONS

1. What challenges and opportunities does this sheet music, as a historical artifact, present to a historian using it to understand the domestic politics of the World War I era?

2. What inferences can you draw from the lyrics to support an argument concerning women's political influence in the early twentieth century? To what extent do you think the lyricist was advocating for a woman's right to vote?

21-5 | Workers Protest Wartime Attacks

THE LIBERATOR, *Tulsa, November 9th* (1918)

The Industrial Workers of the World (IWW), the radical labor union organized in 1905, opposed America's entry into the world war, condemning it as a capitalist's war and a laborer's fight. Government propaganda marginalized antiwar activists, and the 1917 Espionage Act criminalized many of their activities. The IWW became an easy target, as members reported in this article published in April 1918 describing their November 1917 run-in with the Tulsa, Oklahoma, police and Ku Klux Klan, who terrorized blacks, Jews, and immigrants, many of whom were IWW members.

Tulsa, November 9th.

[Editor's Note:—In this story of persecution and outrage at Tulsa, Oklahoma, told in the sworn statement of one of the victims, there is direct and detailed evidence of one of the most menacing by-products of the war. Here in Tulsa, as in Bisbee and Butte and Cincinnati, patriotic fervor was used by employers with the connivance or open cooperation of local officials, as a mask for utterly lawless attacks upon workingmen who attempted to organize for better conditions. This false resort to loyalty on the part of certain war profiteers is emphasized in the recent Report of the President's Mediation Commission. These cowardly masked upper-class mobs, calling themselves "Knights of Liberty" and mumbling hypocritical words about "the women and children of Belgium," will not succeed in terrorizing the labor movement of America, nor will they tend to make it more patriotic.]

On November 9, 1917, seventeen men, taken from the custody of the city police of Tulsa, Oklahoma, were whipped, tarred and feathered, and driven out of the city with a warning never to return.

In a letter dated December 21, a resident of Tulsa, writes:

"I think it is only fair to say that the bottom cause of this trouble locally was that a few men, presumably belonging to the I.W.W. came into the oilfields something like a year ago and were meeting with considerable success in getting oilfield workers—especially pipe-line and tank builders—to fight for better wages and shorter hours.

"Not long after the outrage was committed in Butte, Mont., on the crippled I.W.W. leader (Frank Little), the home of J. Edgar Pew in this city was partly destroyed by some kind of explosion and Mr. and Mrs. Pew narrowly escaped being killed. The news agencies at once published it as a dastardly act of the I.W.W.'s. Mr. Pew is the vice-president and active manager of the Carter Oil Co., which by the way, is owned and controlled by Standard Oil and is one of its largest producing subsidiary companies. A few weeks after the Pew home incident, an explosion followed by a fire partially destroyed an oil refinery that is located at Norfolk, Okla. This property was under the Carter Oil Co. management. Two men lost their lives in this accident. The news agencies without exception (so far as I know) exploited this as another I.W.W. outrage."

From this point we take up the story in a sworn statement made by the secretary of the Tulsa local.

"On the night of November 5, 1917, while sitting in the hall at No. 6 W. Brady Street, Tulsa, Okla. (the room leased and occupied by the Industrial Workers of the World, and used as a union meeting room), at about 8:45 P.M., five men entered the hall, to whom I at first paid no attention, as I was busy putting a monthly stamp in a member's union card book. After I had finished with the member, I walked back to where these five men had congregated at the baggage-room at the back of the hall, and spoke to them, asking if there was anything I could do for them.

"One who appeared to be the leader, answered 'No, we're just looking the place over.' Two of them went into the baggage-room flashing an electric flashlight around the room. The other three walked toward the front end of the hall. I stayed at the baggage-room door, and one of the men came out and followed the other three up to the front end of the hall. The one who stayed in the baggage-room asked me if I was 'afraid he would steal something.' I told him we were paying rent for the hall, and I did not think anyone had a right to search this place without a warrant. He replied that he did not give a damn if we were paying rent for four places, they would search them whenever they felt like it.

Presently he came out and walked toward the front end of the hall, and I followed a few steps behind him.

"In the meantime the other men, who proved to be officers, appeared to be asking some of our members questions. Shortly after, the patrol-wagon came and all the members in the hall—10 men—were ordered into the wagon. I turned out the light in the back end of the hall, closed the desk, put the key in the door and told the 'officer' to turn out the one light. We stepped out, and I locked the door, and at the request of the 'leader of the officers,' handed him the keys. He told me to get in the wagon, I being the 11th man taken from the hall, and we were taken to the police station.

"November 6th, after staying that night in jail, I put up $100.00 cash bond so that I could attend to the outside business, and the trial was set for 5 o'clock P.M., November 6th. Our lawyer, Chas. Richardson, asked for a continuance and it was granted. Trial on a charge of vagrancy was set for November 7th at 5 P.M. by Police Court Judge Evans. After some argument by both sides the cases were continued until the next night, November 8th, and the case against Gunnard Johnson, one of our men, was called. After four and a half hours' session the case was again adjourned until November 9th at 5 P.M., when we agreed to let the decision in Johnson's case stand for all of us. . . .

"Johnson said he had come into town Saturday, November 3d, to get his money from the Sinclair Oil & Gas Co. and could not get it until Monday, the 5th, and was shipping out Tuesday, the 6th, and that he had $7.08 when arrested. He was reprimanded by the judge for not having a Liberty Bond, and as near as anyone could judge from the closing remarks of Judge Evans, he was found guilty and fined $100 for not having a Liberty Bond.

"Our lawyer made a motion to appeal the case and the bonds were then fixed at $200 each. I was immediately arrested, *as were also five spectators in the open court-room*, for being I.W.W.'s. One arrested was not a member of ours, but a property-owner and citizen. I was searched and $30.87 taken from me, as also was the receipt for the $100 bond, and we then were all placed back in the cells.

"In about forty minutes, as near as we could judge, about 11 P.M., the turnkey came and called 'Get ready to go out you I.W.W. men.' We dressed as rapidly as possible, were taken out of the cells, and the officer gave us back our possessions, Ingersoll watches, pocketknives and money, with the exception of $3 in silver of mine which they kept, giving me back $27.87. I handed the receipt for the $100 bond I had put up to the desk sergeant, and he told me he did not know anything about it, and handed the receipt back to me, which I put in my trousers pocket with the 87 cents. Twenty-seven dollars in bills was in my coat pocket. We were immediately ordered into automobiles waiting in the alley. Then we proceeded one block north to 1st Street, west one-half block to Boulder Street, north across the Frisco tracks and stopped.

"Then the masked mob came up and ordered everybody to throw up their hands. Just here I wish to state I never thought any man could reach so high as those policemen did. We were then bound, some with hands in front, some with hands behind, and others bound with arms hanging down their sides, the rope being wrapped around the body. Then the police were ordered to 'beat it,' which they did, running, and we started for the place of execution.

"When we arrived there, a company of gowned and masked gunmen were there to meet us standing at 'present arms.' We were ordered out of the autos, told to get in line in front of these gunmen and another bunch of men with automatics and pistols, lined up between us. Our hands were still held up, and those who were bound, in front. Then a masked man walked down the line and slashed the ropes that bound us, and we were ordered to strip to the waist, which we did, threw our clothes in front of us, in individual piles—coats, vests, hats, shirts and undershirts. The boys not having had time to distribute their possessions that were given back to them at the police stations, everything was in the coats, everything we owned in the world.

"Then the whipping began. A double piece of new rope, ⅝ or ¾ hemp, being used. A man, 'the chief' of detectives, stopped the whipping of each man when he thought the victim had enough. After each one was whipped another man applied the tar with a large brush, from the head to the seat. Then a brute smeared feathers over and rubbed them in.

"After they had satisfied themselves that our bodies were well abused, our clothing was thrown into a pile, gasoline poured on it and a match applied. By the light of our earthly possessions, we were ordered to leave Tulsa, and leave running and never come back. The night was dark, the road very rough, and as I was one of the last two that was whipped, tarred and feathered, and in the rear when ordered to run, I decided to be shot rather than stumble over the rough road. After going forty or fifty feet I stopped and went into the weeds. I told the man with me to get in the weeds also, as the shots were coming very close over us, and ordered him to lie down flat. We expected to be killed, but after 150 or 200 shots were fired they got in their autos.

"After the last one had left, we went through a barbed-wire fence, across a field, called to the boys, collected them, counted up, and had all the 16 safe, though sore and nasty with tar. After wandering around the hills for some time—ages it seemed to me—we struck the railroad track. One man, Jack Sneed, remembered then that he knew a farmer in that vicinity, and he and J.F. Ryan volunteered to find the house. I built a fire to keep us from freezing.

"We stood around the fire expecting to be shot, as we did not know but what some tool of the commercial club had followed us. After a long time Sneed returned and called to us, and we went with him to a cabin and found an I.W.W. friend in the shack and 5 gallons of coal oil or kerosene, with which we cleaned the filthy stuff off of each other, and our troubles were over, as friends sent clothing and money to us that day, it being about 3 or 3:30 A.M. when we reached the cabin.

"The men abused, whipped and tarred were: Tom McCaffery, John Myers, John Boyle, Charles Walsh, W.H. Walton, L.R. Mitchell, Jos. French, J.R. Hill, Gunnard Johnson, Robt. McDonald, John Fitzsimmons, Jos. Fischer, Gordon Dimikson, J.F. Ryan, E.M. Boyd, Jack Sneed (not an I.W.W.).

"This is a copy of my sworn statement and every word is truth."

In answer to special inquiry the writer added to his statement as follows:

"It was very evident that the police force knew what was going to happen when they took us from jail, as there were extra gowns and masks provided *which were put on by the Chief of Police and one detective named Blaine, and the number of blows we received were regulated by the Chief of Police himself, who was easily recognizable by six of us at least.*"

The above account is substantiated at every point by a former employee of The Federal Industrial Relations Commission, who at the request of the National Civil Liberties Bureau made a special investigation of the whole affair. His report names directly nine leaders of the mob, including five members of the police force.

The part played by the press in this orgy of "Patriotism" is illustrated by the following excerpts from an editorial which appeared in the Tulsa Daily World on the afternoon of the 9th:

Get Out the Hemp

"Any man who attempts to stop the supply for one-hundredth part of a second is a traitor and ought to be shot! . . .

"In the meantime, if the I.W.W. or its twin brother, the Oil Workers' Union, gets busy in your neighborhood, kindly take occasion to decrease the supply of hemp. A knowledge of how to tie a knot that will stick might come in handy in a few days. It is no time to dally with the enemies of the country. The unrestricted production of petroleum is as necessary to the winning of the war as the unrestricted production of gunpowder. We are either going to whip Germany or Germany is going to whip us. The first step in the whipping of Germany is to strangle the I.W.W.'s. Kill them, just as you would kill any other kind of a snake. Don't scotch 'em: kill 'em. And kill 'em dead. It is no time to waste money on trials and continuances and things like that. All that is necessary is the evidence and a firing squad. Probably the carpenters' union will contribute the timber for the coffins."

READING AND DISCUSSION QUESTIONS

1. Analyze the testimony of IWW members for evidence of the domestic impact of the war, including its effect on civil liberties. What factors combined to make members of the IWW a particular target?

2. What conclusions can you draw regarding the crimes IWW members were alleged to have committed?

3. How do you interpret the editorial from the *Tulsa Daily World*, which the article quotes? What evidence does it provide for your understanding of the wartime relationship between industry, labor, and government? What veiled threat implied by the editorial is directed to members of the IWW?

21-6 | President's Fourteen Points for Postwar Peace
WOODROW WILSON, *War Aims and Peace Terms* (1918)

President Wilson initially avoided intervening in the world war begun in 1914. However, the resumption of German submarine attacks on American ships reversed Wilson's nonintervention policies, leading him to support the Allies in what he once called a "war to end all wars." American troops joined the fight after Congress declared war against Germany on April 6, 1917. Despite German battlefield gains, Wilson was anticipating peace in January 1918 when he addressed Congress, laying out his famous Fourteen Points upon which he hoped the postwar settlement would be based. His hopes were dashed in the Treaty of Versailles that ended the war and established terms very different from what he had envisioned.

It will be our wish and purpose that the processes of peace, when they are begun, shall be absolutely open and that they shall involve and permit henceforth no secret understandings of any kind. The day of conquest and aggrandizement is gone by; so is also the day of secret covenants entered into in the interest of particular governments and likely at some unlooked-for moment to upset the peace of the world. It is this happy fact, now clear to the view of every public man whose thoughts do not still linger in an age that is dead and gone, which makes it possible for every nation whose purposes are consistent with justice and the peace of the world to avow [now] or at any other time the objects it has in view.

We entered this war because violations of right had occurred which touched us to the quick and made the life of our own people impossible unless they were corrected and the world secure once for all against their recurrence. What we demand in this war, therefore, is nothing peculiar to ourselves. It is that the world be made fit and safe to live in; and particularly that it be made safe for every peace-loving nation which, like our own, wishes to live its own life, determine its own institutions, be assured of justice and fair dealing by the other peoples of the world as against force and selfish aggression. All the peoples of the world are in effect partners in this interest, and for our own part we see very clearly that unless justice be done to others it will not be done to us. The programme of the world's peace, therefore, is our programme; and that programme, the only possible programme, as we see it, is this:

   I. Open covenants of peace, openly arrived at, after which there shall be no private international understandings of any kind but diplomacy shall proceed always frankly and in the public view.

   II. Absolute freedom of navigation upon the seas, outside territorial waters, alike in peace and in war, except as the seas may be closed in whole or in part by international action for the enforcement of international covenants.

   III. The removal, so far as possible, of all economic barriers and the establishment of an equality of trade conditions among all the nations consenting to the peace and associating themselves for its maintenance.

Woodrow Wilson, Message to Congress, January 8, 1918, Records of the United States Senate; Record Group 46; National Archives.

IV. Adequate guarantees given and taken that national armaments will be reduced to the lowest point consistent with domestic safety.

V. A free, open-minded, and absolutely impartial adjustment of all colonial claims, based upon a strict observance of the principle that in determining all such questions of sovereignty the interests of the populations concerned must have equal weight with the equitable claims of the government whose title is to be determined.

VI. The evacuation of all Russian territory and such a settlement of all questions affecting Russia as will secure the best and freest cooperation of the other nations of the world in obtaining for her an unhampered and unembarrassed opportunity for the independent determination of her own political development and national policy and assure her of a sincere welcome into the society of free nations under institutions of her own choosing; and, more than a welcome, assistance also of every kind that she may need and may herself desire. The treatment accorded Russia by her sister nations in the months to come will be the acid test of their good will, of their comprehension of her needs as distinguished from their own interests, and of their intelligent and unselfish sympathy.

VII. Belgium, the whole world will agree, must be evacuated and restored, without any attempt to limit the sovereignty which she enjoys in common with all other free nations. No other single act will serve as this will serve to restore confidence among the nations in the laws which they have themselves set and determined for the government of their relations with one another. Without this healing act the whole structure and validity of international law is forever impaired.

VIII. All French territory should be freed and the invaded portions restored, and the wrong done to France by Prussia in 1871 in the matter of Alsace-Lorraine, which has unsettled the peace of the world for nearly fifty years, should be righted, in order that peace may once more be made secure in the interest of all.

IX. A readjustment of the frontiers of Italy should be effected along clearly recognizable lines of nationality.

X. The peoples of Austria-Hungary, whose place among the nations we wish to see safeguarded and assured, should be accorded the freest opportunity to autonomous development.

XI. Rumania, Serbia, and Montenegro should be evacuated; occupied territories restored; Serbia accorded free and secure access to the sea; and the relations of the several Balkan states to one another determined by friendly counsel along historically established lines of allegiance and nationality; and international guarantees of the political and economic independence and territorial integrity of the several Balkan states should be entered into.

XII. The Turkish portion of the present Ottoman Empire should be assured a secure sovereignty, but the other nationalities which are now under Turkish rule should be assured an undoubted security of life and an absolutely unmolested opportunity of autonomous development, and the Dardanelles should be permanently opened as a free passage to the ships and commerce of all nations under international guarantees.

XIII. An independent Polish state should be erected which should include the territories inhabited by indisputably Polish populations, which should be assured a free and secure access to the sea, and whose political and economic independence and territorial integrity should be guaranteed by international covenant.

XIV. A general association of nations must be formed under specific covenants for the purpose of affording mutual guarantees of political independence and territorial integrity to great and small states alike.

In regard to these essential rectifications of wrong and assertions of right we feel ourselves to be intimate partners of all the governments and peoples associated together against the Imperialists. We cannot be separated in interest or divided in purpose. We stand together until the end.

For such arrangements and covenants we are willing to fight and to continue to fight until they are achieved; but only because we wish the right to prevail and desire a just and stable peace such as can be secured only by removing the chief provocations to war, which this programme does remove. We have no jealousy of German greatness, and there is nothing in this programme that impairs it. We grudge her no achievement or distinction of learning or of pacific enterprise such as have made her record very bright and very enviable. We do not wish to injure her or to block in any way her legitimate influence or power. We do not wish to fight her either with arms or with hostile arrangements of trade if she is willing to associate herself with us and the other peace-loving nations of the world in covenants of justice and law and fair dealing. We wish her only to accept a place of equality among the peoples of the world,—the new world in which we now live,—instead of a place of mastery.

READING AND DISCUSSION QUESTIONS

1. Analyze Wilson's Fourteen Points to understand the reasons why he believed the war was fought in the first place. What failures did his plan for peace seek to correct?

2. To what extent were Wilson's Fourteen Points a repudiation of the policies of American expansionists like Beveridge?

▪ COMPARATIVE QUESTIONS ▪

1. Compare Beveridge's assumptions about race with the anthropological ideas about race articulated by Franz Boas (Document P6-4). How do you imagine Boas would have responded to Beveridge's argument that Anglo-Saxons had a special role to play in world affairs?

2. To what extent did President Wilson's rhetoric about national self-determination reflect the policies of the United States during the period from 1890 to 1918? To what extent did the United States's interactions with Hawaii and the Philippines expose gaps between rhetoric and reality?

3. What evidence of Social Darwinist ideas can you identify in the arguments used by those advocating for a more expansive U.S. role in world affairs? Compare the evidence in this chapter with William Graham Sumner's use of Social Darwinism (Document P6-1).

4. What lessons about civil liberties during wartime do you think Americans learned in this period? How relevant are those concerns today?

5. The period from 1890 to 1918 saw the United States assume a more aggressive role in world affairs. To what extent were these years an exception? What were the most significant factors shaping America's interaction with the rest of the world?

22

Cultural Conflict, Bubble, and Bust

1919–1932

The years following World War I were hardly the period of "normalcy" President Warren Harding had hoped for. Instead, the twenties both roared and retreated at the same time. For many, the postwar era opened possibilities for self-expression and a turn to life's pleasures, encouraged by a booming consumer culture promising self-fulfillment and high living. For others, the so-called modern world's hedonism beguiled Americans into abandoning traditional values of God and country for false values and empty promises. This core conflict about American values played itself out in the politics of the period. Suffragists finally won ratification of the Nineteenth Amendment in 1920, and African American culture bloomed into a renaissance that proclaimed blacks' self-confident identity. Yet the era's more conservative leanings sought to purge society's demons, whether they took form in liquor bottles, radical labor ideologies, subversive immigrants, or godless attacks on traditional values. The 1929 stock market crash revealed the economic strains that had fueled the 1920s exuberance and ushered in a new era of austerity.

22-1 | Condemned Radical Protests Political Hysteria

BARTOLOMEO VANZETTI, *Last Statement to the Court of Massachusetts* (1927)

The trial and execution of two Italian immigrants, Nicola Sacco and Bartolomeo Vanzetti, illustrates the crippling nativist fear that seized so many Americans in the 1920s. Arrested for allegedly murdering two men during a robbery in Braintree, Massachusetts, they were convicted in 1920. Unsuccessful appeals resulted in a death sentence by electrocution, carried out in 1927. Vanzetti's defiant final statement failed to move the court, but it did provoke a public outcry as well as national and worldwide demonstrations condemning the verdict.

Yes. What I say is that I am innocent, not only of the Braintree crime, but also of the Bridgewater crime.[1] That I am not only innocent of these two crimes, but in all my life I have never stole and I have never killed and I have never spilled blood. That is what I want to say. And it is not all. Not only am I innocent of these two crimes, not only in all my life I have never stole, never killed, never spilled blood, but I have struggled all my life, since I began to reason, to eliminate crime from the earth.

Everybody that knows these two arms knows very well that I did not need to go in between the street and kill a man to take the money. I can live with my two arms and live well. But besides that, I can live even without work with my arm for other people. I have had plenty of chance to live independently and to live what the world conceives to be a higher life than not to gain our bread with the sweat of our brow. . . .

We were tried during a time that has now passed into history. I mean by that, a time when there was a hysteria of resentment and hate against the people of our principles, against the foreigner, against slackers, and it seems to me — rather, I am positive of it, that both you and Mr. Katzmann[2] has done all what it were in your power in order to work out, in order to agitate still more the passion of the juror, the prejudice of the juror, against us. . . .

But the jury were hating us because we were against the war, and the jury don't know that it makes any difference between a man that is against the war because he believes that the war is unjust, because he hate no country, because he is a cosmopolitan, and a man that is against the war because he is in favor of the other country that fights against the country in which he is, and therefore a spy, and he commits any crime in the country in which he is in behalf of the other

---

The Sacco-Vanzetti Case: Transcript of the Record of the Trial of Nicola Sacco and Bartolomeo Vanzetti in the Courts of Massachusetts and Subsequent Proceedings, 1920–7, vol. 5: Pages 4360–5621, with General Index (New York: Henry Holt & Company, 1929), 4896–4905.

[1]**Bridgewater crime**: Vanzetti was accused of robbery in Bridgewater, Massachusetts, and, with Sacco, another robbery and the murder of two men in Braintree, Massachusetts.

[2]**Mr. Katzmann**: Frederick Katzmann was the district attorney prosecuting the case against Vanzetti.

country in order to serve the other country. We are not men of that kind. Katzmann know very well that. Katzmann know that we were against the war because we did not believe in the purpose for which they say that the war was done. We believe it that the war is wrong, and we believe this more now after ten years that we understood it day by day, — the consequences and the result of the after war. We believe more now than ever that the war was wrong, and we are against war more now than ever, and I am glad to be on the doomed scaffold if I can say to mankind, "Look out; you are in a catacomb of the flower of mankind. For what? All that they say to you, all that they have promised to you — it was a lie, it was an illusion, it was a cheat, it was a fraud, it was a crime. They promised you liberty. Where is liberty? They promised you prosperity. Where is prosperity? They have promised you elevation. Where is the elevation?" . . .

Where is the moral good that the War has given to the world? Where is the spiritual progress that we have achieved from the War? Where are the security of life, the security of the things that we possess for our necessity? Where are the respect for human life? Where are the respect and the admiration for the good characteristics and the good of the human nature? Never as now before the war there have been so many crimes, so many corruptions, so many degeneration as there is now. . . . .

Well, I have already say that I not only am not guilty of these two crimes, but I never commit a crime in my life, — I have never steal and I have never kill and I have never spilt blood, and I have fought against the crime, and I have fought and I have sacrified myself even to eliminate the crimes that the law and the church legitimate and sanctify.

This is what I say: I would not wish to a dog or to a snake, to the most low and misfortunate creature of the earth — I would not wish to any of them what I have had to suffer for things that I am not guilty of. But my conviction is that I have suffered for things that I am guilty of. I am suffering because I am a radical and indeed I am a radical; I have suffered because I was an Italian, and indeed I am an Italian; I have suffered more for my family and for my beloved than for myself; but I am so convinced to be right that if you could execute me two times, and if I could be reborn two other times, I would live again to do what I have done already.

I have finished. Thank you.

READING AND DISCUSSION QUESTIONS

1. Why does Vanzetti believe that he and Sacco were tried and convicted of the murders?

2. What does the Sacco and Vanzetti trial reveal about the anti-immigrant and anti-radical politics of the 1920s? How does this trial help you to understand the passage of the 1924 National Origins Act limiting immigration?

22-2 | Women's Rights Champion Pushes to Finish the Fight

CARRIE CHAPMAN CATT, *Passing the Federal Suffrage Amendment* (1918)

Twice elected president of the National American Woman Suffrage Association (NAWSA), Carrie Chapman Catt led the fight for ratification of the Nineteenth Amendment granting women the right to vote. Her superior skills at organizing were instrumental in national and international efforts to advance women's rights. In this introduction to *The Woman Citizen*, a civics handbook written for women, Catt describes the work remaining and the significance of the vote for women.

To convince the legislatures of thirty-six states that ratification of the Federal Suffrage Amendment is necessary will be the last task of the suffragists of the United States before their organizations disband in victory or, as is more usual, are turned into good government leagues and civic associations.

The twelve equal suffrage states will ratify automatically. In the eight other states whose legislatures have recently bestowed a large degree of suffrage on women, ratification will also be easy.

The end and aim of suffragists is "a vote for every woman of every state by the next presidential election." Forty-two legislatures sit in 1919 and the bulk of the work for ratification will easily be finished before 1920.

This will be the fitting climax of the work of three generations of American women; for the grandmothers of young women now working for the vote began the struggle. . . .

In spite of the handicap of a required two-thirds vote, which allows a small minority to checkmate the will of a large majority, certainty grows that the Amendment will pass.

Great Britain and Canada have extended suffrage to women as a war measure; France and Italy have virtually promised to do so.

President Wilson, himself, has recognized it as a national war measure— a part of the struggle to make the world safe for democracy—and as such has urged it on Congress.

In June, 1918, he said: "The full and sincere democratic reconstruction of the world for which we are striving, and which we are determined to bring about at any cost, will not have been completely or adequately attained until women are admitted to the suffrage, and only by that action can the nations of the world realize for the benefit of future generations the full ideal force of opinion or the full humane force of action." . . .

Prejudice and tradition are breaking down everywhere before the onslaughts of reason. Women have proved that their service to the State is efficient and essential. Arguments against their complete enfranchisement now sound churlish.

Carrie Chapman Catt, "Passing the Federal Suffrage Amendment," introduction to *The Woman Citizen*, by Mary Sumner Boyd (New York: Frederick A. Stokes Company, 1918), 1–9.

And men are in a mood of gratitude and appreciation, and not disposed to be churlish.

Ideas of freedom, locked and padlocked in the back of men's minds, have been breaking jail. Men had not previously shut the door on women deliberately. They had been serenely sure they didn't need them in public life until of late. Now they are getting strangely humble. Doubtless statesmen in the United States are thinking in terms of political freedom as they have not since the Civil War.

Thus the political significance of an issue which now affects many millions of women is not lost upon political leaders.

Leaders of all political parties, major and minor, have begun to demand it, and the national committees of the major parties have endorsed the Federal Amendment. Almost 8,000,000 voters, men and women, demand it in the twelve equal suffrage states and already the legislatures of many of these states, notably New York, the youngest of the group, have virtually ratified the Amendment in advance by sending resolutions to the Senate, urging its passage. Two million organized suffragists, uncounted millions of their unorganized helpers, women who are to-day trying to give themselves in two directions by laboring for suffrage and for the war, clamor to be relieved from their double task and to be allowed to give all their time to war work.

For months past page after page of the *Congressional Record* has been filled with the text or titles of petitions to Congress, and these are, according to the statements of Senators themselves, only a few of those received from organizations which represent millions of men and women.

All these things show that public sentiment is in favor of woman suffrage. When in a case like this one-third of the Senate plus one vote can defeat the will of democracy, there must be some among the "doubtful" senators who will, as the vote approaches, feel the pressure of public opinion and shrink from the odium of being handed down to posterity for voting against democracy during a war for democracy.

Once through Congress, the Amendment will be given over to the state legislatures. The sovereign states will then decide the fate of woman suffrage. Thirty-six legislatures must ratify before the Federal Amendment becomes the law of the land, and every prospect now promises that the states will respond cordially.

It is not conceivable that there will be delay or resistance to the suffrage measure in the smaller units of government when once the federal measure is passed. For the question of enfranchisement of the women of the land has involved a progressive education, starting with resistance to the basic idea that woman is a distinct civic entity, capable of holding and conveying property, of being educated, of being the guardian of her own children.

The last defense of males who protect women from sharing in the common human desire for freedom, is that women do not want to vote. . . .

Overwhelming evidence has shown that it is not true; that women are as ready as are men to share the burdens of democracy. Not only did New York State give a final and effective blow to this reason when it enrolled the names of

1,030,000 women of the State who asked for their enfranchisement, but in every political step since their emancipation have they shown a full conscience ready for full citizenship.

In the same manner women of Texas registered an alert conscience, an incontrovertible patriotism, and a high sense of political honor in their use of the vote at the 1918 primaries, when they relentlessly overthrew politicians proved unworthy of trust.

Always before this, electoral changes have meant extension of the franchise to new groups of voters; loosely speaking they have meant more voters. Votes for women is a movement concerned far less with numbers than with inner meanings. It means informing the whole field of public life with the woman spirit, if it means anything at all. It is this that war has made evident in Europe, and will make evident in America. Woman suffrage is preeminently a war measure.

It is this which has recently aroused women of the South and Middle West to renewed demand for the vote in those states where the alien man has been permitted to vote when he was too little in sympathy with the ideals of this government to fight for them.

Not only a burning patriotism has aroused the women of these states as never before to work for their right to voice their own principles of government, but a real desire to protect the interests of their sons and husbands at the front from possible domination by a hostile spirit at home has inflamed them into a new crusade.

It is the spirit of the mother, the wife, the loyal American which has been injected into the states where this question is acute. And having once been awakened, men and women everywhere see that the woman's point of view cannot be pushed out of the councils which are to make for a better State.

The housewife's own knowledge must enter into food conservation if it is to be an effective conservation. The nurse's own experience must obtain to make the Red Cross do its effective best. The understanding women have of woman must be taken into account to keep the camp zone clean, for this is a problem that touches women and men both. The mother's voice is above all the one which will be wanted for deliberations about an increased birth rate to make up for war's ravages unless the world is to be thrust back into that disrespect for the child's right to be well born out of which it has been slowly emerging.

It is these considerations and not the granting of rewards to ammunition-making women, which has made statesmen declare that the ballot for women is a measure needed by a world at war as a safeguard of civilization and an assurance that the world is safe for democracy.

READING AND DISCUSSION QUESTIONS

1. By the time Carrie Chapman Catt wrote this introduction, she had become convinced that ratification was certain. What do you think encouraged her in this view? How do you differentiate between long- and short-term causes of ratification?

2. What inference can you draw regarding Catt's understanding of women's role in American society? What role does she envision women playing in shaping the modern world?

22-3 | Progressive Party's Call for Greater Democracy

Platform of the Conference for Progressive Political Action (1924)

Progressivism crested in the prewar years but crashed due to the political divisions regarding America's entry into World War I. In 1924, Wisconsin senator Robert M. La Follette organized a revived Progressive Party, embracing usual progressive ideas together with earlier proposals pushed by late-nineteenth-century Populists. La Follette ran unsuccessfully against Republican Calvin Coolidge for president in 1924, losing every state except his native Wisconsin but winning 17 percent of the popular vote nationwide, a remarkable showing for a candidate endorsed by the Socialist Party. The 1924 platform lays out its ambitious agenda for democratic mobilization.

For 148 years the American people have been seeking to establish a government for the service of all and to prevent the establishment of a government for the mastery of the few. Free men of every generation must combat renewed efforts of organized force and greed to destroy liberty. Every generation must wage a new war for freedom against new forces that seek through new devices to enslave mankind.

Under our representative democracy the people protect their liberties through their public agents.

The test of public officials and public polities alike must be: Will they serve or will they exploit the common need?

The reactionary continues to put his faith in mastery for the solution of all problems. He seeks to have what he calls the strong men and best minds rule and impose their decisions upon the masses of their weaker brethren.

The progressive, on the contrary, contends for less autocracy and more democracy in government, for less power of privilege and greater obligations of service.

Under the principle of ruthless individualism and competition, that government is deemed best which offers to the few the greatest chance of individual gain.

Under the progressive principle of co-operation, that government is deemed best which offers to the many the highest level of average happiness and well being.

It is our faith that we all go up or down together—that class gains are temporary delusions and that eternal laws of compensation make every man his brother's keeper.

"Platform of the Conference for Progressive Political Action," *The Socialist World* 5, no. 7 (July 1924): 2–3.

Program of Public Service

In that faith we present our program of public service:

1. The use of the power of the federal government to crush private monopoly, not to foster it.

2. Unqualified enforcement of the constitutional guarantees of freedom of speech, press and assemblage.

3. Public ownership of the nation's water power and creation of a public super-power system. Strict public control and permanent conservation of all natural resources, including coal, iron and other ores, oil and timber lands in the interest of the people. Promotion of public works in times of business depression.

4. Retention of surtax on swollen incomes, restoration of the tax on excess profits, taxation of stock dividends, profits undistributed to evade taxes, rapidly progressive taxes on large estates and inheritances, and repeal of excessive tariff duties, especially on trust-controlled necessities of life and of nuisance taxes on consumption, to relieve the people of the present unjust burden of taxation and compel those who profited by the war to pay their share of the war's costs, and to provide the funds for adjusted compensation solemnly pledged to the veterans of the World War.

5. Reconstruction of the federal reserve and federal farm loan systems to provide for direct public control of the nation's money and credit to make it available on fair terms to all, and national and state legislation to permit and promote co-operative banking.

6. Adequate laws to guarantee to farmers and industrial workers the right to organize and bargain collectively through representatives of their own choosing for the maintenance or improvement of their standard of life.

7. Creation of a government marketing corporation to provide a direct route between farm producer and city consumer and to assure farmers fair prices for their products, and protect consumers from the profiteers in foodstuffs and other necessaries of life. Legislation to control the meat-packing industry.

8. Protection and aid of cooperative enterprises by national and state legislation.

9. Common international action to effect the economic recovery of the world from the effects of the World War.

10. Repeal of the Cummins-Esch law. Public ownership of railroads, with democratic operation, and with definite safeguards against bureaucratic control.

11. Abolition of the tyranny and usurpation of the courts, including the practice of nullifying legislation in conflict with the political, social or economic theories of the judges. Abolition of injunctions in labor disputes and of the power to punish for contempt without trial by jury. Election of all federal judges without party designation for limited terms.

For Child Labor Amendment

12. Prompt ratification of the child labor amendment and subsequent enactment of a federal law to protect children in industry. Removal of legal discriminations against women by measures not prejudicial to legislation necessary for the protection of women and for the advancement of social welfare.

13. A deep waterway from the great lakes to the sea.
14. We denounce the mercenary system of degraded foreign policy under recent administrations in the interests of financial imperialists, oil monopolists and international bankers, which has at times degraded our state department from its high service as a strong and kindly intermediary of defenseless governments to a trading outpost for those interests and concession seekers engaged in the exploitation of weaker nations, as contrary to the will of the American people, destructive of domestic development and provocative of war. We favor an active foreign policy to bring about a revision of the Versailles treaty in accordance with the terms of the armistice, and to promote firm treaty agreements with all nations to outlaw wars, abolish conscription, drastically reduce land, air and naval armaments and guarantee public referendum on peace and war.

In supporting this program we are applying to the needs of today the fundamental principles of American democracy, opposing equally the dictatorship of plutocracy and the dictatorship of the proletariat.

We appeal to all Americans without regard to partisan affiliation and we raise the standards of our faith so that all of like purpose may rally and march in this campaign under the banners of progressive union.

The nation may grow rich in the vision of greed. The nation will grow great in the vision of service.

READING AND DISCUSSION QUESTIONS

1. What were the problems Progressives saw in the existing social, political, and economic conditions in America? What were their solutions to these problems?

2. What examples of "autocracy" do you think Progressives in 1924 were referencing in their platform?

3. How might historians account for the electoral loss Progressives faced in the 1924 election? Were the party's political ideas out of sync with the political culture of the twenties?

22-4 | Evangelist Condemns the Curse of Alcohol
BILLY SUNDAY, *Get on the Water Wagon* (1915)

Evangelist Billy Sunday joined a long line of antialcohol reformers each time he delivered his famous "booze sermon," a version of which he published as "Get on the Water Wagon" in 1915, but preached hundreds of times leading up to prohibition in 1920. A nondenominational

William Ashley Sunday, *Get on the Water Wagon* (Sturgis, MI: The Journal Publishing Company, 1915), 3–29.

fundamentalist preacher, Sunday had a dynamic voice, pulpit choreography, and socially conservative message that resonated with those who despaired of the liberal drift of the era.

I am the sworn, eternal, uncompromising enemy of the Liquor Traffic. I ask no
quarter and I give none. I have drawn the sword in defense of God, home, wife,
children and native land, and I will never sheathe it until the undertaker pumps
me full of embalming fluid[.] . . .

The saloon is the sum of all villainies. It is worse than war, worse than pesti-
lence, worse than famine. It is the crime of crimes. It is the mother of sins. It is the
appalling source of misery, pauperism, and crime. It is the source of three-fourths
of all the crime, thus it is the source of three-fourths of all the taxation necessary to
prosecute the criminals and care for them after they are in prison. To license such
an incarnate fiend of hell is one of the blackest spots on the American Government.

"Why anti-saloon?" asks someone. "Why not anti-grocery store, anti-dry
goods, anti-furniture, anti-bakery, anti-butcher shop, anti-boot and shoe store,
anti-coal yard? Why single out this one business and attack that?"

"Anti-Saloon." Who is against it? The church is against it, the school is
against it, the home is against it, the scientific world is against it, the military
world is against it, the business world is against it, the railroads are against it, and
every world-wide interest on earth, except the underworld, the criminal world,
the immoral world and the world of crime. All cry "away with the saloon. Down
with these licensed distributing centers of crime, misery and drunkeness!" . . .

Who foots the bills? The landlord who loses his rent, the baker, butcher,
grocer, coal man, dry goods merchant, whose goods the drunkard needs for himself and family, but cannot buy — the charitable people, who pity the children of
drunkards, and go down in their pockets to keep them from starving — the tax
payers, who are taxed to support the jails, penitentiaries, hospitals, almshouses,
reformatories that this cursed business keeps filled.

Who makes the money? The brewers, distillers, saloon-keepers, who are
privileged to fill the land with poverty, wretchedness, madness, crime, disease,
damnation, and death, authorized by the sovereign right of the people, who vote
for this infamous business.

For every $800.00 spent in producing useful and necessary commodities, the
working man receives $143.50 in wages. For every $800.00 spent in producing
booze, the working man receives $9.85 in wages.

The saloon comes as near being a rat hole for the working man to dump his
wages in as any thing I know of.

To know what the devil will do, find out what the saloon is doing.

The man who votes for the saloon, helps the devil get his boy. The man who
doesn't believe in a hell, has never seen a drunkard's home. The devil and the
saloon-keeper are always pulling on the same rope. . . .

The saloon is usually found in partnership with the foes of good government. It supports the boodle alderman, corrupt law maker, the political boss and
machine. It only asks to be let alone in its law nullifying, vice and crime producing work. I have never known of a movement for good government that was not

opposed by the saloon. If you believe in better civic conditions, if you believe in a greater and better city, if you believe in men going home sober, if you believe in men going to heaven instead of hell, then down with the saloon.

The liquor interests are still fat—sleek—smug and powerful with many city, state, and national governments at their feet; and they are reaching out with their slimy hands to choke, throttle and assassinate the character of those whom it cannot debauch, and who dare attack their hellish business. But their doom is sealed. If the people are fit for self government, if the people are fit for liberty, the wrath of an outraged public will never be quenched until the putrid corpse of the saloon is hanging from the gibbet of shame; praise God from whom all blessings flow. . . .

I tell you, gentlemen, the American home is the dearest heritage of the people, for the people, and by the people, and when a man can go from home in the morning with the kisses of wife and children on his lips, and come back at night with an empty dinner bucket to a happy home, that man is a better man, whether white or black. Whatever takes away the comforts of home—whatever degrades that man or woman—whatever invades the sanctity of the home, is the deadliest foe to the home, to church, to state and school, and the saloon is the deadliest foe to the home, the church and the state, on top of God Almighty's dirt. And if all the combined forces of Hell should assemble in conclave, and with them all the men on earth that hate and despise God, and purity, and virtue—if all the scum of the earth could mingle with the denizens of Hell to try to think of the deadliest institution to home, to church and state, I tell you, sir, the combined hellish intelligence could not conceive of or bring forth an institution that could touch the hem of the garment of the open licensed saloon to damn the home and manhood, and womanhood and business and every other good thing on God's earth. . . .

I tell you it [the saloon] strikes in the night. It fights under cover of darkness and assassinates the characters that it cannot damn, and it lies about you. It attacks defenseless womanhood and childhood. The saloon is a coward. It is a thief, it is not an ordinary court defender that steals your money, but it robs you of manhood and leaves you in rags and takes away your friends, and it robs your family. It impoverishes your children and it brings insanity and suicide. It will take the shirt off your back and it will steal the coffin from a dead child and yank the last crust of bread out of the hand of the starving child; it will take the last bucket of coal out of your cellar, and the last cent out of your pocket, and will send you home bleary-eyed and staggering to your wife and children. It will steal the milk from the breast of the mother and leave her with nothing with which to feed her infant. It will take the virtue from your daughter. It is the dirtiest, most low-down, damnable business that ever crawled out of the pit of Hell. It is a sneak, and a thief and a coward.

It is an infidel. It has no faith in God; has no religion. It would close every church in the land. It would hang its beer signs on the abandoned altars. It would close every public school. It respects the thief and it esteems the blasphemer. It fills the prisons and the penitentiaries. It despises Heaven, hates love, scorns virtue. It tempts the passions. Its music is the song of a siren. Its sermons are a collection of lewd, vile stories. It wraps a mantle about the hope of this world and that to come. Its tables are full of the vilest literature. It is the moral clearing house for rot, and damnation, and poverty, and insanity, and it wrecks homes and blights lives today.

The saloon is a liar. It promises good cheer and sends sorrow. It promises health and causes disease. It promises prosperity and sends adversity. It promises happiness and sends misery. Yes, it sends the husband home with a lie on his lips to his wife; and the boy home with a lie on his lips to his mother; and it causes the employee to lie to his employer. It degrades. It is God's worst enemy and the devil's best friend. Seventy-five per cent of impurity comes from the grog-shop. It spares neither youth nor old age. It is waiting with a dirty blanket for the baby to crawl into this world. It lies in wait for the unborn.

It cocks the highwayman's pistol. It puts the rope in the hands of the mob. It is the anarchist of the world and its dirty red flag is dyed with the blood of women and children, and it sent the bullet through the body of Lincoln; it nerved the arm that sent the bullet through Garfield and William McKinley. Yes, it is a murderer. Every plot that was ever hatched against our flag and every anarchist plot against the government and law, was born and bred, and crawled out of the grog-shop to damn this country.

I tell you that the curse of God Almighty is on the saloon. Legislatures are legislating against it. Decent society is barring it out. The fraternal brotherhoods are knocking it out. The Masons and the Odd Fellows, and the Knights of Pythias, and the A. O. U. W., are closing their doors to the whiskey sellers. They don't want you wriggling your carcass in their lodges. Yes, sir, I tell you, the curse of God is on it. It is on the down grade. It is headed for Hell, and by the grace of God, I am going to give it push, with a whoop, for all I know how. . . .

I want every man to say: "God, you can count on me to protect my wife, my home, my mother and my children and the manhood of America."

By the mercy of God, which has given to you the unshaken and unshakable confidence of her you love, I beseech you make a fight for the women who wait tonight until the saloons spew out their husbands and their sons, and send them home maudlin, brutish, devilish, vomiting, stinking, blear-eyed, bloated-faced drunkards.

READING AND DISCUSSION QUESTIONS

1. Analyze Sunday's sermon to identify the specific arguments he makes against alcohol. What are the individual and social effects of alcohol consumption that he targets?

2. How might a historian use this source to illustrate the intersection of several themes important to the history of the 1920s, including fundamentalism, prohibition, and social conservatism? How does Sunday's sermon reflect these overlapping topics?

22-5 | Harlem Renaissance Poet Declares Black Is Beautiful
LANGSTON HUGHES, *Negro Artist and the Racial Mountain* (1926)

The Great Migration of African Americans out of the South to northern cities, including New York's Harlem neighborhood, constitutes one of the major demographic transformations of the twentieth century. The development of a black middle class supported the self-conscious cultural flowering known as the Harlem Renaissance, a 1920s outpouring of black artistic expression represented by poet Langston Hughes among many others. Here Hughes affirms the beauty of the black experience as inspiration for the poet, musician, and painter.

One of the most promising of the young Negro poets said to me once, "I want to be a poet—not a Negro poet," meaning, I believe, "I want to write like a white poet"; meaning subconsciously, "I would like to be a white poet"; meaning behind that, "I would like to be white." And I was sorry the young man said that, for no great poet has ever been afraid of being himself. And I doubted then that, with his desire to run away spiritually from his race, this boy would ever be a great poet. But this is the mountain standing in the way of any true Negro art in America—this urge within the race toward whiteness, the desire to pour racial individuality into the mold of American standardization, and to be as little Negro and as much American as possible.

But let us look at the immediate background of this young poet. His family is of what I suppose one would call the Negro middle class: people who are by no means rich yet never uncomfortable nor hungry—smug, contented, respectable folk, members of the Baptist church. The father goes to work every morning. He is a chief steward at a large white club. The mother sometimes does fancy sewing or supervises parties for the rich families of the town. The children go to a mixed school. In the home they read white papers and magazines. And the mother often says "Don't be like niggers" when the children are bad. A frequent phrase from the father is, "Look how well a white man does things." And so the word white comes to be unconsciously a symbol of all virtues. It holds for the children beauty, morality, and money. The whisper of "I want to be white" runs silently through their minds. This young poet's home is, I believe, a fairly typical home of the colored middle class. One sees immediately how difficult it would be for an artist born in such a home to interest himself in interpreting the beauty of his own people. He is never taught to see that beauty. He is taught rather not to see it, or if he does, to be ashamed of it when it is not according to Caucasian patterns.

For racial culture the home of a self-styled "high-class" Negro has nothing better to offer. Instead there will perhaps be more aping of things white than in a less cultured or less wealthy home. The father is perhaps a doctor, lawyer, land-owner, or politician. The mother may be a social worker, or a teacher, or she may do nothing and have a maid. Father is often dark but he has usually married the

---

lightest woman he could find. The family attend a fashionable church where few really colored faces are to be found. And they themselves draw a color line. In the North they go to white theaters and white movies. And in the South they have at least two cars and house "like white folks." Nordic manners, Nordic faces, Nordic hair, Nordic art (if any), and an Episcopal heaven. A very high mountain indeed for the would-be racial artist to climb in order to discover himself and his people.

But then there are the low-down folks, the so-called common element, and they are the majority—may the Lord be praised! The people who have their hip of gin on Saturday nights and are not too important to themselves or the community, or too well fed, or too learned to watch the lazy world go round. They live on Seventh Street in Washington or State Street in Chicago and they do not particularly care whether they are like white folks or anybody else. Their joy runs, bang! into ecstasy. Their religion soars to a shout. Work maybe a little today, rest a little tomorrow. Play awhile. Sing awhile. O, let's dance! These common people are not afraid of spirituals, as for a long time their more intellectual brethren were, and jazz is their child. They furnish a wealth of colorful, distinctive material for any artist because they still hold their own individuality in the face of American standardizations. And perhaps these common people will give to the world its truly great Negro artist, the one who is not afraid to be himself. Whereas the better-class Negro would tell the artist what to do, the people at least let him alone when he does appear. And they are not ashamed of him—if they know he exists at all. And they accept what beauty is their own without question.

Certainly there is, for the American Negro artist who can escape the restrictions the more advanced among his own group would put upon him, a great field of unused material ready for his art. Without going outside his race, and even among the better classes with their "white" culture and conscious American manners, but still Negro enough to be different, there is sufficient matter to furnish a black artist with a lifetime of creative work. And when he chooses to touch on the relations between Negroes and whites in this country, with their innumerable overtones and undertones surely, and especially for literature and the drama, there is an inexhaustible supply of themes at hand. To these the Negro artist can give his racial individuality, his heritage of rhythm and warmth, and his incongruous humor that so often, as in the Blues, becomes ironic laughter mixed with tears. But let us look again at the mountain.

A prominent Negro clubwoman in Philadelphia paid eleven dollars to hear Raquel Meller[1] sing Andalusian popular songs. But she told me a few weeks before she would not think of going to hear "that woman," Clara Smith, a great black artist, sing Negro folksongs. And many an upper-class Negro church, even now, would not dream of employing a spiritual in its services. The drab melodies in white folks' hymnbooks are much to be preferred. "We want to worship the Lord correctly and quietly. We don't believe in 'shouting.' Let's be dull like the Nordics," they say, in effect.

The road for the serious black artist, then, who would produce a racial art is most certainly rocky and the mountain is high. Until recently he received almost

---

[1]**Meller**: Raquel Meller, Spanish singer, dancer, and film star of the 1920s and 1930s.

no encouragement for his work from either white or colored people. The fine novels of Chesnutt go out of print with neither race noticing their passing. The quaint charm and humor of Dunbar's dialect verse brought to him, in his day, largely the same kind of encouragement one would give a sideshow freak (A colored man writing poetry! How odd!) or a clown (How amusing!).

The present vogue in things Negro, although it may do as much harm as good for the budding colored artist, has at least done this: it has brought him forcibly to the attention of his own people among whom for so long, unless the other race had noticed him beforehand, he was a prophet with little honor. . . .

But in spite of the Nordicized Negro intelligentsia and the desires of some white editors we have an honest American Negro literature already with us. Now I await the rise of the Negro theater. Our folk music, having achieved world-wide fame, offers itself to the genius of the great individual American composer who is to come. And within the next decade I expect to see the work of a growing school of colored artists who paint and model the beauty of dark faces and create with new technique the expressions of their own soul-world. And the Negro dancers who will dance like flame and the singers who will continue to carry our songs to all who listen—they will be with us in even greater numbers tomorrow.

Most of my own poems are racial in theme and treatment, derived from the life I know. In many of them I try to grasp and hold some of the meanings and rhythms of jazz. I am as sincere as I know how to be in these poems and yet after every reading I answer questions like these from my own people: Do you think Negroes should always write about Negroes? I wish you wouldn't read some of your poems to white folks. How do you find anything interesting in a place like a cabaret? Why do you write about black people? You aren't black. What makes you do so many jazz poems?

But jazz to me is one of the inherent expressions of Negro life in America: the eternal tom-tom beating in the Negro soul—the tom-tom of revolt against weariness in a white world, a world of subway trains, and work, work, work; the tom-tom of joy and laughter, and pain swallowed in a smile. Yet the Philadelphia clubwoman is ashamed to say that her race created it and she does not like me to write about it. The old subconscious "white is best" runs through her mind. Years of study under white teachers, a lifetime of white books, pictures, and papers, and white manners, morals, and Puritan standards made her dislike the spirituals. And now she turns up her nose at jazz and all its manifestations—likewise almost everything else distinctly racial. She doesn't care for the Winold Reiss' portraits of Negroes because they are "too Negro." She does not want a true picture of herself from anybody. She wants the artist to flatter her, to make the white world believe that all Negroes are as smug and as near white in soul as she wants to be. But, to my mind, it is the duty of the younger Negro artist, if he accepts any duties at all from outsiders, to change through the force of his art that old whispering "I want to be white," hidden in the aspirations of his people, to "Why should I want to be white? I am a Negro—and beautiful!"

So I am ashamed for the black poet who says, "I want to be a poet, not a Negro poet," as though his own racial world were not as interesting as any other world. I am ashamed, too, for the colored artist who runs from the painting of Negro faces to the painting of sunsets after the manner of the academicians because he fears the strange unwhiteness of his own features. An artist must be free to choose what he does, certainly, but he must also never be afraid to do what he might choose.

Let the blare of Negro jazz bands and the bellowing voice of Bessie Smith singing the Blues penetrate the closed ears of the colored near-intellectuals until they listen and perhaps understand. Let Paul Robeson singing Water Boy, and Rudolph Fisher writing about the streets of Harlem, and Jean Toomer holding the heart of Georgia in his hands, and Aaron Douglas's[2] drawing strange black fantasies cause the smug Negro middle class to turn from their white, respectable, ordinary books and papers to catch a glimmer of their own beauty. We younger Negro artists who create now intend to express our individual dark-skinned selves without fear or shame. If white people are pleased we are glad. If they are not, it doesn't matter. We know we are beautiful. And ugly too. The tom-tom cries and the tom-tom laughs. If colored people are pleased we are glad. If they are not, their displeasure doesn't matter either. We build our temples for tomorrow, strong as we know how, and we stand on top of the mountain, free within ourselves.

READING AND DISCUSSION QUESTIONS

1. How does Hughes define the "racial mountain" African Americans must climb? Who created the mountain, and what obstacle does it throw up for the "Negro poet"?

2. From Hughes's essay, what conclusions can you make regarding his perspective of race relations in the early twentieth century? How have those social relations impacted relationships within the black community?

3. Twice Hughes mentions "American standardization" in his essay. What do you think he means by it, and what impact did it have on African American culture?

22-6 | Advertising the American Dream
Westinghouse Advertisement (1924) **and** *Chevrolet Advertisement* (1927)

After an initial postwar recession, many sectors of the American economy rebounded, inducing the middle and upper class to indulge in a consumer culture manufactured by sophisticated marketers and advertisers. Americans bought products to adorn themselves and their homes in the latest and most modern fashions. Not everyone had the means to participate,

---

Westinghouse Advertisement (1924), The Granger Collection, New York.
Chevrolet Advertisement (1927), The Granger Collection, New York.

[2]Paul Robeson, Rudolph Fisher, Jean Toomer, and Aaron Douglas were all prominent African American contributors to the Harlem Renaissance.

and even those who purchased their way to happiness often did so on borrowed money, an overextension that snapped when the stock market crashed. These advertisements show the marketing strategies used to sell goods and an ideal of the good life.

All the distinction, elegance and luxury of marvelous new bodies by Fisher . . . All the smoothness, handling ease and dependability of Chevrolet's proved and modern design, enhanced by scores of important mechanical improvements . . . And, too, amazing new low prices. It is easy to understand why a new vogue is sweeping America—the vogue of the Most Beautiful Chevrolet in Chevrolet History.

Touring or Roadster $525, Coach $595, Coupe $625, Sedan $695, Sport Cabriolet $715, Landau $745, ½-Ton Truck $595 (Chassis only), 1-Ton Truck $595 (Chassis only). Balloon tires standard equipment on all models. All prices f. o. b. Flint, Michigan.

CHEVROLET MOTOR COMPANY, DETROIT, MICHIGAN
Division of General Motors Corporation

Q U A L I T Y   A T   L O W   C O S T

READING AND DISCUSSION QUESTIONS

1. Examine these advertisements from the 1920s for evidence of the consumer culture that had emerged in that decade. What appeal to consumers do these advertisements make?

2. From these advertisements, what inference can you draw about the consumers these marketers targeted with their advertising campaign? Which consumers

were excluded from the appeal in these ads and why? What do these advertisements reveal about 1920s society?

▪ COMPARATIVE QUESTIONS ▪

1. Compare the views of Hughes on African American culture with the perspectives of Booker T. Washington (Document 18-3), J. B. Rayner (Document 20-4), and W. E. B. Du Bois (Document 20-6). To what extent did they agree on the means for surpassing the social, economic, and political limitations imposed by a majority white culture?

2. Examine Sunday's appeal in light of longer-term cultural values of the latter nineteenth and early twentieth centuries. Do you see his antialcohol crusade akin to Victorianism or an expression of progressivism, both, or neither? If you were writing a biography of Sunday, in what context would you place him?

3. What argument about the immigrant experience in America can you make using the evidence from the Sacco and Vanzetti trial together with Kaztauskis's experience (Document 17-3), the Chinese Exclusion Act (Document 17-4), and Ganz's memory of the tenements (Document 19-3)?

4. How do Hughes and Catt use the popular impressions of their respective groups to advocate for their betterment or recognition? What other parallels do you find between the Harlem Renaissance and the women's rights movement?

23

Managing the Great Depression, Forging the New Deal

1929–1939

The stock market crash of 1929 and the resulting depression burst the inflated economic bubble of the 1920s and plunged many Americans into an uncertain future. The thousands of distressed letters that Eleanor Roosevelt received from Americans recounting their tragic circumstances hint at the despair the economic crisis caused. When Franklin Roosevelt entered the White House in 1933, replacing Herbert Hoover's fiscally conservative approach, he launched a "new deal" program of reforms demonstrating the active engagement of the federal government. Critics complained he did not go far enough, while others described him as dictatorial in his control of the economy. To the broad coalition of American voters, however, FDR inspired hope that "happy days" were fast approaching. From his initial efforts to shore up financial institutions, Roosevelt's New Deal broadened in response to labor and working-class concerns to embrace public programs providing basic necessities and creating "safety net" guarantees that came to define a liberal consensus regarding government's role and responsibility in the twentieth century.

23-1 | Defeated President Explains the Cause of the Depression
HERBERT HOOVER, *Letter to Simeon Fess* (1933)

Herbert Hoover's efforts in war-ravaged Belgium as head of the U.S. Food Administration earned him international acclaim as a humanitarian, a reputation that did not survive his presidency. When the stock market crashed, President Hoover's conservative economic principles restrained government action based on the idea that the market was self-correcting and the tide would soon turn. His "too little too late" approach disillusioned many Americans and led to Roosevelt's victory in the election of 1932. In this 1933 letter to Senator Simeon Fess written just weeks before the inauguration, Hoover offers his own history of the great crash.

February 21, 1933

Hon. Simeon D. Fess
United States Senate
Washington, D.C.

My dear Mr. Senator:

I am glad to respond to your request that I put in writing for your records, the statement I made to you yesterday as to the economic situation at the moment, and the causes thereof.

Today we are on the verge of financial panic and chaos. Fear for the policies of the new administration has gripped the country. People do not await events, they act. Hoarding of currency, and of gold, has risen to a point never before known; banks are suspending not only in isolated instances, but in one case an entire state. Prices have fallen since last autumn below the levels which debtors and creditors can meet. Men over large areas are unable or are refusing to pay their debts. Hundreds of millions of orders placed before election have been cancelled. Unemployment is increasing, there are evidences of the flight of capital from the United States to foreign countries, men have abandoned all sense of new enterprise and are striving to put their affairs in defense against disaster.

Some days before election the whole economic machine began to hesitate from the upward movement of last summer and fall. For some time after election it continued to hesitate but hoped for the best. As time has gone on, however, every development has stirred the fear and apprehension of the people. They have begun to realize what the abandonment of a successful program of this administration which was bringing rapid recovery last summer and fall now means and they are alarmed at possible new deal policies indicated by the current events. It is not this fear that now dominates the national situation. It is not lack of resources, currency or credit.

The incidents which have produced this fear are clear. There was a delay by the President-elect of over two months in willingness to cooperate with us to

Herbert Hoover to Simeon D. Fess, February 21, 1933, Simeon D. Fess Papers, National Archives.

bring about order from confusion in our foreign economic relations. There have been a multitude of speeches, bills, and statements of democratic members of Congress and others proposing inflation or tinkering with the currency. My proposals for reduction of expenditures have been ignored to the extent of over $200,000,000 by the Democratic House of Representatives. The differences between Democratic leaders and the President-elect over the basis of taxation with which to balance the budget caused them to reject the balancing of the budget. The publication by Democratic leaders of the House of the Reconstruction Corporation loans has caused runs on hundreds of banks, failures of many of them, and hoarding on a wide scale. There have been proposed in the Congress by Democratic leaders and publicly even by the President-elect, projects involving federal expenditure of tremendous dimensions which would obviously lie beyond the capacity of the federal government to borrow without tremendous depreciation in government securities. Such proposals as the bills to assume Federal responsibility for billions of mortgages, loans to municipalities for public works, the Tennessee improvement and Muscle Shoals, are all of this order. The proposals of Speaker Garner that a constitutional government should be abandoned because the Congress, in which there will be an overwhelming majority, is unable to face reduction of expenses, has started a chatter of dictatorship. The President-elect has done nothing publicly to disavow any of these proposals.

The Democratic House has defeated a measure to increase tariffs so as to prevent invasion of goods from depreciated currency countries, thus stopping increased unemployment from this source. There have been interminable delays and threatened defeat of the Glass Banking Bill, and the Bankruptcy bill.

How much this whole situation is the result of fear of the policies of the new administration is further indicated by a short review of the five distinct periods in recent economic history.

The first period began with the financial and monetary collapse of Europe in the last half of 1931 culminating in October, bringing contraction of credit and reduction of exports, falling prices of both commodities and securities, followed by great fear and apprehension in the people which was promptly represented by hoarding, bank failures, flight of capital, withdrawal of foreign gold balances with final interpretation in decreased employment, demoralization of agriculture and general stagnation.

The second period following the approval by Congress of our measures of reconstruction in early February 1932 was a period of sharp recovery over a period between 60 and 90 days; during this period public confidence was restored, prices of commodities and securities rose, currency began to return from hoarding, gold shipments abroad were greatly lessened, bank failures practically ceased and the whole country moved upward.

The third period began in April and continued through July. This was a period of a sharp debacle which was brought about by the Democratic House by the same character of proposals we now see again, that is by the original failure of the revenue bill, the failure to reduce expenditures recommended by the Executive with consequent fear that the movement toward balancing the budget would not be successful; the passage of a group of inflationary measures including the Patman Bill, the Goldsborough Bill, etc. The passage of a series of projects which would have required greater issues of government securities than the Treasury could support including the Garner Bills for gigantic public works and unlimited loans by the Reconstruction Corporation, etc. Public confidence was destroyed; hoarding, withdrawal of foreign gold, decrease in employment, falling prices and general economic demoralization took place.

The fourth period began about the adjournment of Congress when it was assured that these destructive measures were defeated and that constructive measures would be held. This period extended from July until October and was a period of even more definite march out of the depression. Employment was increasing at the rate of half a million men a month, bank failures ceased, hoarded currency was flowing back steadily and gold was returning from abroad, car loadings, commodity and security prices and all the other proofs of emergence from the depression were visible to every one. Fear and despair had again been replaced by hope and confidence.

The fifth period began shortly before election when the outcome became evident, and has lasted until today. I have already recited its events.

The causes of this terrible retrogression and fear in this *fifth* period have an exact parallel in the *third* period of last spring. The fact that there was no disavowal of the actions of last spring by the Democratic candidates during the campaign lends added color and alarm that the same actions and proposals which are now repeated in this period positively represent the policies of the new administration—and the people are seeking to protect themselves individually but with national damage. The movement forward in recovery of our people is again defeated by precisely the same factors as last spring and again emanating from the Democratic leaders.

In the interest of every man, woman and child, the President-elect has, during the past week, been urged by the saner leaders of his own party such as Senator Glass and others, by myself, and by Democratic bankers and economists whom he has called on for advice, to stop the conflagration before it becomes uncontrollable, by announcing firmly and at once (a) that the budget will be balanced even if it means increased taxation; (b) new projects will be so restricted that government bond issues will not in any way endanger stability of government finances; (c) there will be no inflation or tampering with the currency; to which some have added that as the Democratic party coming in with an overwhelming majority in both houses, there can be no excuse for abandonment of Constitutional processes.

The President-elect is the only man who has the power to give assurances which will stabilize public mind as he alone can execute them. Those assurances should have been given before now but must be given at once if the situation is to be greatly helped. It would allay some fear and panic whereas delay will make the situation more acute.

The present administration is devoting its days and nights to put out the fires or to localize them. I have scrupulously refrained from criticism which is well merited, but have instead been giving repeated assurances to the country of our desire to cooperate and help the new administration.

What is needed, if the country is not to drift into great grief, is the immediate and emphatic restoration of confidence in the future. The resources of the country are incalculable, the available credit is ample but lenders will not lend, and men will not borrow unless they have confidence. Instead they are withdrawing their resources and their energies. The courage and enterprise of the people still exist and only await release from fears and apprehension.

The day will come when the Democratic party will endeavor to place the responsibility for the events of this *Fifth period* on the Republican Party. When that day comes I hope you will invite the attention of the American people to the actual truth.

Yours faithfully,

HERBERT HOOVER

READING AND DISCUSSION QUESTIONS

1. What does the tone of Hoover's letter to Senator Fess suggest about his perspective on the depression and the actions of president-elect Roosevelt? Why do you think he wrote this letter?

2. What conclusions can you draw concerning the policy differences Hoover had with the incoming administration? What can you infer about Hoover's understanding of the causes and remedies of the Great Depression?

23-2 | President Inspires Depressed Nation with Promise of Action

FRANKLIN D. ROOSEVELT, *Inaugural Address* (1933)

During the 1932 election, Roosevelt's campaign had exuded a desperately needed optimism in the face of the worst economic collapse in American history. His inaugural address, where he allayed the fear Americans felt, called for immediate action, a counterpoint to the more conservative approach of his predecessor, who had presided over the first years of the Great Depression. Roosevelt's call for "action, and action now" anticipated the frenzy of his first hundred days, when he launched the programs collectively described as the New Deal.

I am certain that my fellow Americans expect that on my induction into the Presidency I will address them with a candor and a decision which the present situation of our Nation impels. This is preeminently the time to speak the truth, the whole truth, frankly and boldly. Nor need we shrink from honestly facing

Franklin D. Roosevelt, Inaugural Address, March 4, 1933. Online by Gerhard Peters and John T. Woolley, *The American Presidency Project*. www.presidency.ucsb.edu/ws/?pid=14473.

conditions in our country today. This great Nation will endure as it has endured, will revive and will prosper. So, first of all, let me assert my firm belief that the only thing we have to fear is fear itself—nameless, unreasoning, unjustified terror which paralyzes needed efforts to convert retreat into advance. In every dark hour of our national life a leadership of frankness and vigor has met with that understanding and support of the people themselves which is essential to victory. I am convinced that you will again give that support to leadership in these critical days.

In such a spirit on my part and on yours we face our common difficulties. They concern, thank God, only material things. Values have shrunken to fantastic levels; taxes have risen; our ability to pay has fallen; government of all kinds is faced by serious curtailment of income; the means of exchange are frozen in the currents of trade; the withered leaves of industrial enterprise lie on every side; farmers find no markets for their produce; the savings of many years in thousands of families are gone.

More important, a host of unemployed citizens face the grim problem of existence, and an equally great number toil with little return. Only a foolish optimist can deny the dark realities of the moment.

Yet our distress comes from no failure of substance. We are stricken by no plague of locusts. Compared with the perils which our forefathers conquered because they believed and were not afraid, we have still much to be thankful for. Nature still offers her bounty and human efforts have multiplied it. Plenty is at our doorstep, but a generous use of it languishes in the very sight of the supply. Primarily this is because rulers of the exchange of mankind's goods have failed through their own stubbornness and their own incompetence, have admitted their failure, and have abdicated. Practices of the unscrupulous money changers stand indicted in the court of public opinion, rejected by the hearts and minds of men.

True they have tried, but their efforts have been cast in the pattern of an outworn tradition. Faced by failure of credit they have proposed only the lending of more money. Stripped of the lure of profit by which to induce our people to follow their false leadership, they have resorted to exhortations, pleading tearfully for restored confidence. They know only the rules of a generation of self-seekers. They have no vision, and when there is no vision the people perish.

The money changers have fled from their high seats in the temple of our civilization. We may now restore that temple to the ancient truths. The measure of the restoration lies in the extent to which we apply social values more noble than mere monetary profit.

Happiness lies not in the mere possession of money; it lies in the joy of achievement, in the thrill of creative effort. The joy and moral stimulation of work no longer must be forgotten in the mad chase of evanescent profits. These dark days will be worth all they cost us if they teach us that our true destiny is not to be ministered unto but to minister to ourselves and to our fellow men.

Recognition of the falsity of material wealth as the standard of success goes hand in hand with the abandonment of the false belief that public office and high political position are to be valued only by the standards of pride of place and personal profit; and there must be an end to a conduct in banking and in business which too often has given to a sacred trust the likeness of callous and selfish wrongdoing. Small wonder that confidence languishes, for it thrives only on honesty, on honor, on the sacredness of obligations, on faithful protection, on unselfish performance; without them it cannot live. Restoration calls, however, not for changes in ethics alone. This Nation asks for action, and action now.

Our greatest primary task is to put people to work. This is no unsolvable problem if we face it wisely and courageously. It can be accomplished in part by direct recruiting by the Government itself, treating the task as we would treat the emergency of a war, but at the same time, through this employment, accomplishing greatly needed projects to stimulate and reorganize the use of our natural resources.

Hand in hand with this we must frankly recognize the overbalance of population in our industrial centers and, by engaging on a national scale in a redistribution, endeavor to provide a better use of the land for those best fitted for the land. The task can be helped by definite efforts to raise the values of agricultural products and with this the power to purchase the output of our cities. It can be helped by preventing realistically the tragedy of the growing loss through foreclosure of our small homes and our farms. It can be helped by insistence that the Federal, State, and local governments act forthwith on the demand that their cost be drastically reduced. It can be helped by the unifying of relief activities which today are often scattered, uneconomical, and unequal. It can be helped by national planning for and supervision of all forms of transportation and of communications and other utilities which have a definitely public character. There are many ways in which it can be helped, but it can never be helped merely by talking about it. We must act and act quickly.

Finally, in our progress toward a resumption of work we require two safeguards against a return of the evils of the old order: there must be a strict supervision of all banking and credits and investments, so that there will be an end to speculation with other people's money; and there must be provision for an adequate but sound currency.

These are the lines of attack. I shall presently urge upon a new Congress, in special session, detailed measures for their fulfillment, and I shall seek the immediate assistance of the several States.

Through this program of action we address ourselves to putting our own national house in order and making income balance outgo. Our international trade relations, though vastly important, are in point of time and necessity secondary to the establishment of a sound national economy. I favor as a practical policy the putting of first things first. I shall spare no effort to restore world trade by international economic readjustment, but the emergency at home cannot wait on that accomplishment.

The basic thought that guides these specific means of national recovery is not narrowly nationalistic. It is the insistence, as a first consideration, upon the interdependence of the various elements in and parts of the United States—a recognition of the old and permanently important manifestation of the American spirit of the pioneer. It is the way to recovery. It is the immediate way. It is the strongest assurance that the recovery will endure.

In the field of world policy I would dedicate this Nation to the policy of the good neighbor—the neighbor who resolutely respects himself and, because he does so, respects the rights of others—the neighbor who respects his obligations and respects the sanctity of his agreements in and with a world of neighbors.

If I read the temper of our people correctly, we now realize as we have never realized before our interdependence on each other; that we cannot merely take but we must give as well; that if we are to go forward, we must move as a trained and loyal army willing to sacrifice for the good of a common discipline, because without such discipline no progress is made, no leadership becomes effective. We are, I know, ready and willing to submit our lives and property to such discipline, because it makes possible a leadership which aims at a larger good. This I propose to offer, pledging that the larger purposes will bind upon us all as a sacred obligation with a unity of duty hitherto evoked only in time of armed strife.

With this pledge taken, I assume unhesitatingly the leadership of this great army of our people dedicated to a disciplined attack upon our common problems.

Action in this image and to this end is feasible under the form of government which we have inherited from our ancestors. Our Constitution is so simple and practical that it is possible always to meet extraordinary needs by changes in emphasis and arrangement without loss of essential form. That is why our constitutional system has proved itself the most superbly enduring political mechanism the modern world has produced. It has met every stress of vast expansion of territory, of foreign wars, of bitter internal strife, of world relations.

It is to be hoped that the normal balance of Executive and legislative authority may be wholly adequate to meet the unprecedented task before us. But it may be that an unprecedented demand and need for undelayed action may call for temporary departure from that normal balance of public procedure.

I am prepared under my constitutional duty to recommend the measures that a stricken Nation in the midst of a stricken world may require. These measures, or such other measures as the Congress may build out of its experience and wisdom, I shall seek, within my constitutional authority, to bring to speedy adoption.

But in the event that the Congress shall fail to take one of these two courses, and in the event that the national emergency is still critical, I shall not evade the clear course of duty that will then confront me. I shall ask the Congress for the one remaining instrument to meet the crisis—broad Executive power to wage a war against the emergency, as great as the power that would be given to me if we were in fact invaded by a foreign foe.

For the trust reposed in me I will return the courage and the devotion that befit the time. I can do no less.

We face the arduous days that lie before us in the warm courage of national unity; with the clear consciousness of seeking old and precious moral values;

with the clean satisfaction that comes from the stern performance of duty by old and young alike. We aim at the assurance of a rounded and permanent national life.

We do not distrust the future of essential democracy. The people of the United States have not failed. In their need they have registered a mandate that they want direct, vigorous action. They have asked for discipline and direction under leadership. They have made me the present instrument of their wishes. In the spirit of the gift I take it.

In this dedication of a Nation we humbly ask the blessing of God. May He protect each and every one of us. May He guide me in the days to come.

READING AND DISCUSSION QUESTIONS

1. Compare the tone of Roosevelt's address with the tone of Hoover's letter (Document 23-1). How much of the difference between the two can be attributed to the nature of the source (a speech vs. a private letter), the occasion, or the personality of those involved?

2. What might Roosevelt's audience have anticipated about his approach to solving the economic crisis based on his inaugural address? Which lines might have cheered those hit hard by the depression? Which lines might have worried big business?

23-3 | Outflanking Roosevelt with Plan to Share the Nation's Wealth

HUEY LONG, *"Every Man a King"* (1934)

Two years into the New Deal, recovery still seemed distant for many Americans. Their continued despair buoyed the political ambitions of Democratic senator Huey Long from Louisiana. A brilliant orator and political operator, Long took advantage of the new popularity of radio to blast the New Deal's failures and cultivate a national audience for his radical "Share Our Wealth" program. Long's presidential ambitions, which could have compromised Roosevelt's support, were cut short when an assassin's bullet silenced him in 1935.

We have in America today more wealth, more goods, more food, more clothing, more houses than we have ever had. We have everything in abundance here.

We have the farm problem, my friends, because we have too much cotton, because we have too much wheat, and have too much corn, and too much potatoes.

We have a home loan problem, because we have too many houses, and yet nobody can buy them and live in them.

Huey Long, *Share Our Wealth, Every Man a King* (Washington, DC, n.d.), 7–17.

We have trouble, my friends, in the country, because we have too much money owing, the greatest indebtedness that has ever been given to civilization, where it has been shown that we are incapable of distributing the actual things that are here, because the people have not money enough to supply themselves with them, and because the greed of a few men is such that they think it is necessary that they own everything, and their pleasure consists in the starvation of the masses, and in their possessing things they cannot use, and their children cannot use, but who bask in the splendor of sunlight and wealth, casting darkness and despair and impressing it on everyone else. . . .

We have in America today, ladies and gentlemen, $272,000,000,000 of debt. Two hundred and seventy-two thousand millions of dollars of debts are owed by the various people of this country today. Why, my friends, that cannot be paid. It is not possible for that kind of debt to be paid.

The entire currency of the United States is only $6,000,000,000. That is all of the money that we have got in America today. All the actual money you have got in all of your banks, all that you have got in the Government Treasury, is $6,000,000,000; and if you took all that money and paid it out today you would still owe $266,000,000,000; and if you took all that money and paid again you would still owe $260,000,000,000; and if you took it, my friends, 20 times and paid it you would still owe $150,000,000,000.

You would have to have 45 times the entire money supply of the United States today to pay the debts of the people of America and then they would just have to start out from scratch, without a dime to go on with. . . .

So, we have in America today, my friends, a condition by which about 10 men dominate the means of activity in at least 85 percent of the activities that you own. They either own directly everything or they have got some kind of mortgage on it, with a very small percentage to be excepted. They own the banks, they own the steel mills, they own the railroads, they own the bonds, they own the mortgages, they own the stores, and they have chained the country from one end to the other until there is not any kind of business that a small, independent man could go into today and make a living, and there is not any kind of business that an independent man can go into and make any money to buy an automobile with; and they have finally and gradually and steadily eliminated everybody from the fields in which there is a living to be made, and still they have got little enough sense to think they ought to be able to get more business out of it anyway.

If you reduce a man to the point where he is starving to death and bleeding and dying, how do you expect that man to get hold of any money to spend with you? It is not possible. . . .

Now, we have organized a society, and we call it "Share Our Wealth Society," a society with the motto "Every Man a King."

Every man a king, so there would be no such thing as a man or woman who did not have the necessities of life, who would not be dependent upon the whims and caprices and ipsi dixit of the financial barons for a living. What do we propose by this society? We propose to limit the wealth of big men in the country. There is an average of $15,000 in wealth to every family in America. That is right here today.

We do not propose to divide it up equally. We do not propose a division of wealth, but we propose to limit poverty that we will allow to be inflicted upon any man's family. We will not say we are going to try to guarantee any equality, or $15,000 to a family. No; but we do say that one third of the average is low enough for any one family to hold, that there should be a guarantee of a family wealth of around $5,000; enough for a home, an automobile, a radio, and the ordinary conveniences, and the opportunity to educate their children; a fair share of the income of this land thereafter to that family so there will be no such thing as merely the select to have those things, and so there will be no such thing as a family living in poverty and distress.

We have to limit fortunes. Our present plan is that we will allow no one man to own more tha[n] $50,000,000. We think that with that limit we will be able to carry out the balance of the program. It may be necessary that we limit it to less than $50,000,000. It may be necessary, in working out of the plans that no man's fortune would be more than $10,000,000 or $15,000,000. But be that as it may, it will still be more than any one man, or any one man and his children and their children, will be able to spend in their lifetimes; and it is not necessary or reasonable to have wealth piled up beyond that point where we cannot prevent poverty among the masses.

Another thing we propose is old-age pension of $30 a month for everyone that is 60 years old. Now, we do not give this pension to a man making $1,000 a year, and we do not give it to him if he has $10,000 in property, but outside of that we do.

We will limit hours of work. There is not any necessity of having overproduction. I think all you have got to do, ladies and gentlemen, is just limit the hours of work to such an extent as people will work only so long as it is necessary to produce enough for all of the people to have what they need. Why, ladies and gentlemen, let us say that all of these labor-saving devices reduce hours down to where you do not have to work but 4 hours a day; that is enough for these people, and then praise be the name of the Lord, if it gets that good. Let it be good and not a curse, and then we will have 5 hours a day and 5 days a week, or even less than that, and we might give a man a whole month off during a year, or give him 2 months; and we might do what other countries have seen fit to do, and what I did in Louisiana, by having schools by which adults could go back and learn the things that have been discovered since they went to school.

We will not have any trouble taking care of the agricultural situation. All you have to do is balance your production with your consumption. You simply have to abandon a particular crop that you have too much of, and all you have to do is store the surplus for the next year, and the Government will take it over. When you have good crops in the area in which the crops that have been planted are sufficient for another year, put in your public works in the particular year when you do not need to raise any more, and by that means you get everybody employed. When the Government has enough of any particular crop to take care of all of the people, that will be all that is necessary; and in order to do all of this, our taxation is going to be to take the billion-dollar fortunes and strip them down to frying size, not to exceed $50,000,000, and if it is necessary to come to

$10,000,000, we will come to $10,000,000. We have worked the proposition out to guarantee a limit upon property (and no man will own less than one-third the average), and guarantee a reduction of fortunes and a reduction of hours to spread wealth throughout this country. We would care for the old people above 60 and take them away from this thriving industry and give them a chance to enjoy the necessities and live in ease, and thereby lift from the market the labor which would probably create a surplus of commodities.

Those are the things we propose to do. "Every Man a King." Every man to eat when there is something to eat; all to wear something when there is something to wear. That makes us all a sovereign.

You cannot solve these things through these various and sundry alphabetical codes. You can have the N. R. A. and P. W. A. and C. W. A. and the U. U. G. and G. I. N. and any other kind of dad-gummed lettered code. You can wait until doomsday and see 25 more alphabets, but that is not going to solve this proposition. Why hide? Why quibble? You know what the trouble is. The man that says he does not know what the trouble is is just hiding his face to keep from seeing the sunlight. . . .

Now, my friends, we have got to hit the root with the ax. Centralized power in the hands of a few, with centralized credit in the hands of a few, is the trouble.

Get together in your community tonight or tomorrow and organize one of our Share Our Wealth Societies. If you do not understand it, write me and let me send you the platform; let me give you the proof of it.

This is Huey P. Long talking, United States Senator, Washington, D.C. Write me and let me send you the data on this proposition. Enroll with us. Let us make known to the people what we are going to do. I will send you a button, if I have got enough of them left. We have got a little button that some of our friends designed, with our message around the rim of the button, and in the center "Every Man a King." Many thousands of them are meeting through the United States, and every day we are getting hundreds and hundreds of letters. Share Our Wealth Societies are now being organized, and people have it within their power to relieve themselves from this terrible situation. . . .

I thank you, my friends, for your kind attention, and I hope you will enroll with us, take care of your own work in the work of this Government, and share or help in our Share Our Wealth Societies.

I thank you.

READING AND DISCUSSION QUESTIONS

1. Analyze Long's proposal for evidence of his political solution to the economic crisis of the Great Depression. How does he define the crisis and the solution?

2. What similarities to populism and progressivism can you identify in Long's "Share Our Wealth" program? What audience was he addressing, and what strategies did he use in his appeal?

23-4 | FDR's New Deal Programs in Action

Michigan Artist Alfred Castagne Sketching WPA Construction Workers (1939)

Roosevelt's New Deal embraced several aims as it evolved, but a central focus was finding jobs for the unemployed. The 1933 Public Works Administration (PWA) funded municipal projects including the building of roads, dams, bridges, and schools, funneling federal money to states and localities to hire workers. Two years later, Roosevelt created the Works Progress Administration (WPA), which funded similar projects and programs, such as the Federal Art Project and the Federal Writers' Project, which employed artists, novelists, and actors. This image, by an unknown photographer, depicts both programs at work.

READING AND DISCUSSION QUESTIONS

1. Analyze this photograph for evidence of Roosevelt's goals for his New Deal programs. What do you think Roosevelt was trying to accomplish beyond just providing jobs? Why, for instance, do you think the WPA funded artists like the one shown sketching in this scene?

Michigan Artist Alfred Castagne Sketching WPA Construction Workers, Unknown Photographer (May 19, 1939), National Archives, Records of the Work Projects Administration (69-AG-410).

2. By examining this photograph and evaluating the WPA, what conclusions might you draw about the evolving relationship between the American people and the federal government? To what extent do you think Americans began changing their understanding of government's role and responsibility in supporting those in need?

23-5 | Labor Leader Campaigns for Workers' Rights

JOHN L. LEWIS, *The Battle for Industrial Democracy* (1936)

In 1935, Congress passed the National Labor Relations Act (or Wagner Act), which for the first time recognized a worker's right to collective bargaining. This milestone legal achievement boosted the power (and membership) of unions, though as workers discovered, their victory in Congress did not effortlessly result in workplace gains. In a 1936 national radio address, United Mine Workers union president John Lewis urged workers to join the battle against "economic dictatorship."

I salute the members of my own union as they listen tonight in every mining community on this continent. . . . To them, whose servant I am, I express my pride in their courage and loyalty. They are the household troops of the great movement for industrial democracy and from their collective sentiment and crystallized power I derive my strength. In their daily calling the mine workers toil with the spectre, death, ever at their side and the women of the mining camps share their Spartan fortitude. Enduring hardship, inured to danger, contemptuous of death, breathing the air of freedom, is there anyone who believes that the men of the mines will flinch in the face of the battle for industrial democracy which now impends in America?

The American Iron and Steel Institute last week published a full page advertisement in 375 newspapers, at an estimated cost of one-half million of dollars. Its purpose was to justify the outmoded labor policy of the Institute and to announce the determination of the steel corporations to oppose the campaign now in progress for the organization of the workers in the iron and steel industry. That statement is sinister in its implications; it is designed to be terrifying to the minds of those who fail to accept the theory that the financial interests behind the steel corporations shall be regarded as the omnipresent overlord of industrial America. That statement amounts to a declaration of industrial and civil war. It controvenes the law! It pledges the vast resources of the industry against the right of its workers to engage in self-organization or modern collective bargaining. . . .

John L. Lewis, "The Battle for Industrial Democracy," in *Vital Speeches of the Day*, vol. 2 (August 1, 1936): 675–678.

The American Iron and Steel Institute boasts that it includes ninety-five per cent of the steel production of the country and represents an associate corporate investment of $5,000,000,000. This gigantic financial and industrial combination announces that its members "are ready to employ their resources to the full" to prevent the independent organization of their employees. It controvenes the law! . . .

The Institute says that it favors the right of organization among its employees without coercion from any source. What coercion can the representatives of organized labor exert upon the workers in these plants, and what appeal can they make to them except the appeal that they bring themselves within the organized labor movement for their own protection and for the common good of those who toil. The Institute does not propose to meet that argument; it does not propose to trust in the independent action of the steel workers; it does not intend to grant them the free liberty of organization. Interference and coercion of employees trying to organize, come from the economic advantages held by the employer. In the steel industry it is manifested in an elaborate system of spies, and in a studied discharge of those who advocate any form of organization displeasing to the management. It is shown by confining all yearning for organization to make-believe company unions, controlled and dominated by the management itself. This coercion is finally shown in the implied threat of a black-list which attends the announcement of a joint and common policy for all the steel corporations of this country.

Why shouldn't organized labor throw its influence into this unequal situation? What chance have the steel workers to form a free and independent organization without the aid of organized labor? What opportunity will they have to bargain collectively through representatives of their own choosing except by the formation of an organization free from management control?

These company unions are pious pretexts for denying the steel workers the right of organization. Their constitutions and by-laws are drawn by lawyers for the company. No changes can be made without the company approval. The officials are selected under company supervision. No method of independent wage negotiation is provided. No wage contracts have in fact been made between the companies and their employees under the company union plan.

The statement of The Institute is an open warning to representatives of recognized and firmly established labor unions that if by any legal and peaceful methods—public meetings, personal solicitations, or otherwise—they are so bold as to attempt to persuade steel workers to become members of recognized, standard labor unions, the brutal and ruthless forces of the steel oligarchy will be unloosed against them. From bitter experience we know what this means. It means that meetings of steel employees will be disrupted by thugs and hoodlums employed by the steel corporations; that the organizers themselves will be brutally beaten; that the police and judicial authorities of steel manufacturing communities, who are designated and dominated by the steel companies, will be used to arrest labor union organizers, to imprison them on false charges, to maltreat them cruelly while imprisoned, and in many cases forcibly to drive them from the community. . . .

[W]hen the pronouncement of the Steel Institute states it "fears" industrial strife and dislocations may develop, it really means that as the organizing campaign of our Committee is meeting with success, the steel corporations themselves, through their private legions of armed guards, despicable under-cover spies, and *agents provocateurs* will deliberately provoke strife and bloodshed, and attempt to place the blame for its occurrence upon the representatives of legitimate labor. . . .

The statement of the steel industry calls attention to the fact that under their company union plans no dues are required from employees. The company pays all of the expenses of these miserable subterfuges. They pay these expenses to secure an advantage over their employees. The cost of maintaining a company union is trifling, compared to the savings it affords in pay-rolls. These companies assert a determination to see that their employees belong to no labor union which maintains itself by dues. Smug in their own control over all the labor within their plants, they profess to see nothing but a racket in any independent autonomous self-supported organization of their workers. The stake involved is not the small contribution that may be made by the employees to the union, but in the pay-rolls where, on any basis of fair bargaining, millions would be added to the wage envelopes of the workers. This is the stake, this and the right of labor to have a voice in the fixation of its hours and working conditions, and to enter into a state of economic and civil freedom befitting men who perform the labor in this great industry. . . .

The industry has constantly sought to give the impression that it pays exceptionally high wages, and so far reaching and efficient are its means of publicity that this idea is widely accepted.

Actually, there is no basis for this belief. When comparisons are made between the earnings of workers in the steel industry and the earnings of workers in other industries of a comparable character, the standing of the steel industry is at best no more than mediocre and at worst no less than disgraceful.

Thus, in contrast with hourly earnings of 65.6 cents in the steel industry in March, 1936, bituminous coal mining, in the same month was paying 79.3 cents; anthracite mining, 83.2 cents; petroleum producing, 77.5 cents; and building construction, 79.8 cents. These are all industries which, as regards severity of labor and working conditions, might be compared with the steel industry. . . .

Greater payments have not been made to wage and salary workers because the large monopoly earnings realized have been used to pay dividends on fictitious capital stock, to add physical values in the way of plant extensions, and to multiply the machines that displace human labor.

Under the wildest flight of imagination, what greater injury could be done to steel workers by labor unions or any other legitimate agency than is evidenced by this financial exploitation by private bankers and promoters! . . .

Our Committee would bring to the steel workers economic and political freedom; a living wage to those lowest in the scale of occupations, sufficient for the support of the worker and his family in health and modest comfort, and sufficient to enable him to send his children to school; to own a home and accessories; to provide against sickness, death, and the ordinary contingencies of life. In other words, a wage sufficient for him to live as an independent American citizen with hope and assurance in the future for himself and his family. Above this basic wage, our Committee believes that differentials should be paid to other workers according to skill, training hazard and responsibility. . . .

No greater truth, of present day significance, was ever stated by a President of the United States, than the declaration made by President Roosevelt in his speech at Franklin Field to the effect that America was really ruled by an economic dictatorship which must be eliminated before the democratic and economic welfare of all classes of our people can be fully realized. . . .

In its earlier manifestations—from the beginning of the century to the World War—this financial dictatorship was named by those who vainly but gallantly fought against it—Congressman Lindbergh, the elder LaFollette, President Theodore Roosevelt, Justice Brandeis, President Wilson, Senator Norris, and a score of other crusaders for democracy and humanity—as the "Money Trust," or "The Invisible Government."

Profiteering during the World War greatly augmented the sources and power of this group. Its corporate and political control was also greatly extended by the speculative excesses of the so-called "New Era" of 1923–1929.

In his inaugural address of March 4, 1933 President Roosevelt, in reviewing essential reforms, referred to the fundamental significance of this group by the declaration that "The Money-Changers must be driven from the Temple." The Banking and Currency Committee of the United States Senate after several years of careful investigation later reported, during the summer of 1934, that during the post-war decade this financial oligarchy had usurped "the wealth stream of the nation to its very capillaries."

An economic dictatorship has thus become firmly established in America which at the present time is focusing its efforts upon retaining the old system of finance-capitalism which was in operation before the depression and thus preventing the attainment of political and industrial democracy by the people.

Organized labor in America accepts the challenge of the omnipresent overlords of steel to fight for the prize of economic freedom and industrial democracy. The issue involves the security of every man or woman who works for a living by hand or by brain. The issue cuts across every major economic, social and political problem now pressing with incalculable weight upon the 130 millions of people of this nation. It is an issue of whether the working population of this country shall have a voice in determining their destiny or whether they shall serve as indentured servants for a financial and economic dictatorship which would shamelessly exploit our natural resources and debase the soul and destroy the pride of a free people. On such an issue there can be no compromise for labor or for a thoughtful citizenship. I call upon the workers in the iron and steel industry who are listening to me tonight to throw off their shackles of servitude and join the union of their industry. I call upon the workers in the textile, lumber, rubber, automotive and other unorganized industries to join with their comrades in the steel industry and forge for themselves the modern instruments of labor wherewith to demand and secure participation in the increased wealth and increased productive efficiency of modern industrial America. The more than a million members of the twelve great National and International Unions associated with the Committee for Industrial Organization will counsel you and aid you in your individual and collective efforts to establish yourselves as free men and women in every economic, social and political sense. I unhesitatingly place the values represented by thirty million human beings engaged in industry and their sixty million dependents as being above and superior in every moral consideration to the five billions of inanimate dollars represented by the resources of the American Iron and Steel Institute or to the additional billions of inanimate dollars that perforce may be allied with the empire of steel in the impending struggle which the Institute, in the brutality of its arrogance, seeks to make inevitable.

READING AND DISCUSSION QUESTIONS

1. How does Lewis describe the challenge facing organized labor in its efforts to realize the gains won with the National Labor Relations Act? Why does he single out the American Iron and Steel Institute?

2. What does Lewis mean by "industrial democracy"? What role does he foresee unions playing in helping workers to achieve their goals?

23-6 | Reporting the Plight of Depression Families

MARTHA GELLHORN, *Field Report to Harry Hopkins* (1934)

Journalist and novelist Martha Gellhorn's heart-rending field report describing impoverished Gastonia, North Carolina, families vividly captures the desperate hope of depression-era families. Hired by Harry Hopkins, Franklin Roosevelt's point man for federal relief efforts, Gellhorn detailed the enormous challenge facing the administration. Compounding the epic humanitarian crisis she encountered was the political opposition, which she singled out as one among many obstacles hampering relief efforts.

All during this trip [to North Carolina] I have been thinking to myself about that curious phrase "red menace," and wondering where said menace hid itself. Every house I visited—mill worker or unemployed—had a picture of the President. These ranged from newspaper clippings (in destitute homes) to large colored prints, framed in gilt cardboard. The portrait holds the place of honour over the mantel. . . . He is at once God and their intimate friend; he knows them all by name, knows their little town and mill, their little lives and problems. And, though everything else fails, he is there, and will not let them down.

From Martha Gellhorn to Harry Hopkins, Report, Gaston County, North Carolina, November 11, 1934, Franklin D. Roosevelt Library, Harry Hopkins Papers, Box 66.

I have been seeing people who, according to almost any standard, have practically nothing in life and practically nothing to look forward to or hope for. But there is hope; confidence, something intangible and real: "the president isn't going to forget us."

Let me cite cases: I went to see a woman with five children who was living on relief ($3.40 a week). Her picture of the President was a small one, and she told me her oldest daughter had been married some months ago and had cried for the big, coloured picture as a wedding present. The children have no shoes and that woman is terrified of the coming cold as if it were a definite physical entity. There is practically no furniture left in the home, and you can imagine what and how they eat. But she said, suddenly brightening, "I'd give my heart to see the President. I know he means to do everything he can for us; but they make it hard for him; they won't let him." I note this case as something special; because here the faith was coupled with a feeling (entirely sympathetic) that the President was not entirely omnipotent.

I have been seeing mill workers; and in every mill when possible, the local Union president. There has been widespread discrimination in the south; and many mills haven't re-opened since the strike. Those open often run on such curtailment that workers are getting from 2 to 3 days work a week. The price of food has risen (especially the kind of food they eat: fat-back bacon, flour, meal, sorghum) as high as 100%. It is getting cold; and they have no clothes. The Union presidents are almost all out of work, since the strike. In many mill villages, evictions have been served; more threatened. These men are in a terrible fix. (Lord, how barren the language seems: these men are faced by hunger and cold, by the prospect of becoming dependent beggars—in their own eyes: by the threat of homelessness, and their families dispersed. What more can a man face, I don't know.) You would expect to find them maddened with fear; with hostility. I expected and waited for "lawless" talk; threats; or at least, blank despair. And I didn't find it. I found a kind of contained and quiet misery; fear for their families and fear that their children wouldn't be able to go to school. ("All we want is work and the chance to care for our families like a man should.") But what is keeping them sane, keeping them going on and hoping, is their belief in the President. . . .

These are the things they say to me: "We trust in the Supreme Being and Franklin Roosevelt."—"You heard him talk over the radio, ain't you? He's the only president who ever said anything about the forgotten man. We know he's going to stand by us."—"He's a man of his word and he promised us; we aren't worrying as long as we got him."—"The president won't let these awful conditions go on."—"The president wanted the Code. The president knows why we struck."—"The president said no man was going to go hungry and cold; he'll get us our jobs." . . .

I am going on and on about this because I think it has vast importance. These people will be slow to give up hope; terribly slow to doubt the president. But if they don't get their jobs; then what? If the winter comes on and they find themselves on our below-subsistence relief; then what? I think they might strike again; hopelessly and apathetically. In very few places, there might be some violence speedily crushed. But if they lose this hope, there isn't much left for them as a group. And I feel [if] this class (whatever marvelous stock they are, too) loses its courage or morale or whatever you want to call it, there will be an even worse social problem than there now is. And I think that with time, adding disillusionment and suffering, they might actually go against their own grain and turn into desperate people. As it is, between them and fear, stands the President. But only the President . . . .

What has been constantly before me is the health problem. To write about it is difficult only in that one doesn't know where to begin. Our relief people are definitely on below subsistence living scales. (This is the unanimous verdict of anyone connected with relief; and a brief study of budgets clinches the matter.)

The result is that dietary diseases abound. I know that in this area there has always been pelagra;[1] but that doesn't make matters better. In any case it is increasing; and I have seen it ranging from scaly elbows in children to insanity in a grown man. Here is what doctors say: "It's no use telling mothers what to feed their children; they haven't the food to give." . . . "Conditions are really horrible here; it seems as if the people were degenerating before your eyes: the children are worse mentally and physically than their parents." . . . "All the mill workers I see are definite cases of undernourishment; that's the best breeding ground I know for disease." . . . "There's not much use prescribing medicine; they haven't the money to buy it." . . . "You can't do anything with these people until they're educated to take care of themselves; they don't know what to eat; they haven't the beginning of an idea how to protect themselves against sickness." . . .

The medical set-up, from every point of view, in this area is tragic. In Gaston County there is not one county clinic or hospital; and only one health officer (appointed or elected?). This gentleman has held his job for more than a dozen years; and must have had droll medical training sometime during the last century. He believes oddly that three shots of neo-salvarsan will cure syphilis; and thinks that injecting this into the arm muscle is as good as anything. Result: he cripples and paralyzes his patients who won't go back. He likewise refuses to sign sterilization warrants on imbeciles: grounds "It's a man's prerogative to have children." Another doctor in this area owns a drug store. He was selling bottled tonic (home-made I think) to his mill worker patients as a cure for syphilis. This was discovered by a 21 year old case worker, who wondered why her clients' money was disappearing so fast. When asked why he did this he said that syphilis was partly a "run-down" condition, and that "you ought to build the patients up." Every doctor says that syphilis is spreading unchecked and uncured. One doctor even said that it had assumed the proportions of an epidemic and wouldn't be stopped unless the government stepped in; and treated it like small-pox. . . .

Which brings us to birth control. Every social worker I saw, and every doctor, and the majority of mill owners, talked about birth control as the basic need of this class. I have seen three generations of unemployed (14 in all) living in one room; and both mother and daughter were pregnant. Our relief people have a

---

[1]**pelagra**: A serious vitamin deficiency caused by poor nutrition.

child a year; large families are the despair of the social worker and the doctor. The doctors say that the more children in a family the lower the health rating. These people regard children as something the Lord has seen fit to send them, and you can't question the Lord even if you don't agree with him. There is absolutely no hope for these children; I feel that our relief rolls will double themselves given time. The children are growing up in terrible surroundings; dirt, disease, overcrowding, undernourishment. Often their parents were farm people, who at least had air and enough food. This cannot be said for the children. I know we could do birth control in this area; it would be a slow and trying job beginning with education. (You have to fight superstition, stupidity and lack of hygiene.) But birth control would be worked into prenatal clinics; and the grape vine telegraph is the best propaganda I know. I think if it isn't done that we may as well fold up; these people cannot be bettered under present circumstances. Their health is going to pieces; the present generation of unemployed will be useless human material in no time; their housing is frightful (talk about European slums); they are ignorant and often below-par intelligence. What can we do: feed them—feed them pinto beans and corn bread and sorghum and watch the pelagra spread. And in twenty years, what will there be; how can a decent civilization be based on a decayed substrata, which is incapable physically and mentally to cope with life?

As for their homes: I have seen a village where the latrines drain nicely down a gully to a well from which they get their drinking water. Nobody thinks anything about this; but half the population is both syphilitic and moronic; and why they aren't all dead of typhoid I don't know. (It would probably be a blessing if they were). . . .

[T]here is [also] a problem of education. (Do you know that the highest paid teacher in a school in North Carolina gets $720 a year? This is not criticism of the teachers; it is a downright woe.) But the schooling is such awful nonsense. Teach the kids to recite the Gettysburg address by heart: somehow one is not impressed. And they don't know what to eat or how to cook it; they don't even know that their bodies can be maintained in health by protective measures; they don't know that one needn't have ten children when one can't feed one; they don't know that syphilis is destroying and contagious. And with all this, they are grand people. If there is any meaning in the phrase "American stock" it has some meaning here. They are sound and good humored; kind and loyal. I don't believe they are lazy; I believe they are mostly ill and ignorant. They have a strong family feeling; and one sees this in pitiful ways—for instance: if there is any means of keeping the children properly or prettily clothed, it is done; but the mother will be a prematurely aged, ugly woman who has nothing to put on her back. And the father's first comment will be: could we get shoes for the children so they can go to school (though the father himself may be walking on the ground). . . .

I hope you won't misunderstand this report. It's easy to see what the government is up against. What with a bunch of loathsome ignoramuses talking about "lavish expenditure" and etc. And all right-minded citizens virtuously protesting against anything which makes sense or sounds new. I'm writing this extra report because you did send us out to look; and you ought to get as much as we see. It isn't all there is to see, by any means; and naturally I have been looking at the worst and darkest side. But it is a terribly frightening picture. Is there no way we can get it before the public, no way to make them realize that you cannot build a future on bad basic material? We are so proud of being a new people in a free land. And we have a serf class; a serf class which seems to me to be in as bad a state of degeneration maybe, in this area, worse than the low class European who has learned self-protection through centuries of hardship. It makes me raging mad to hear talk of "red revolution," the talk of cowards who would deserve what they got, having blindly and selfishly fomented revolution themselves. Besides I don't believe it; it takes time for all things including successful rebellion; time and a tradition for revolutions which does not exist in this country. But it's far more terrible to think that the basis of our race is slowly rotting, almost before we have had time to become a race.

READING AND DISCUSSION QUESTIONS

1. What does Gellhorn's discussion of the "red menace" suggest about the opposition Roosevelt faced in administering relief programs as part of the New Deal? What evidence of the "red menace" did she find in her field observations among North Carolina's poor?

2. How would you describe the tone of Gellhorn's reporting? How optimistic is she that these families will survive the Great Depression? What does she describe as the short- and long-term consequences of the depression?

3. Imagine you are Harry Hopkins reading Gellhorn's report. What advice would you give to Roosevelt concerning relief efforts for the nation's poor? How would you advise Roosevelt to navigate the obstacles to relief?

■ COMPARATIVE QUESTIONS ■

1. Compare Roosevelt's first inaugural address with the economic and social philosophy of William Graham Sumner (Document P6-1). What evidence do these documents provide of how the role of government changed over time?

2. What similarities can you identify between Gellhorn's reporting and Upton Sinclair's *The Jungle* (Document 19-6)? To what extent is Gellhorn an heir to a Progressive-Era tradition of muckraking journalism?

3. Assess the New Deal by identifying the arguments for and against Roosevelt's programs. To what extent are those arguments of the 1930s relevant today?

4. How might you interpret the New Deal within the broader narrative of American history? Would you emphasize continuities in the New Deal by linking Roosevelt's ideas to the earlier Populist and progressive reform movements? Or would you see the New Deal as a break with the past and the beginning of something new? Explain.

24

The World at War
1937–1945

Physicist Luis Alvarez was in one of the B-29 bomber planes accompanying the *Enola Gay* when it dropped an atomic bomb on Hiroshima on August 6, 1945. Moments after the blast, Alvarez wrote a letter to his young son, describing the mushroom cloud as "awe-inspiring" and the light flash "many times brighter than the sun." His front-row seat to history marked a beginning and an end. The two bombs dropped on Hiroshima and Nagasaki led to the end of World War II, the second fantastically destructive war of the twentieth century. Those bombs also inaugurated a new era in America's global dominance. The war had significant and immediate effects on the United States, even before the nation formally entered the war following the 1941 attack on Pearl Harbor. As with many wars, this global conflict transformed lives, including those of the American soldiers called to fight and those they left behind. The social and political consequences of war on the home front took many forms, from the mobilization of the wartime economy to constraints on economics and civil liberties. For many, World War II fought to preserve liberty and freedom while at the same time it highlighted the persistent shortcomings plaguing American race relations. Alvarez witnessed the end of the war, but could only imagine the battles yet to come.

24-1 | President Roosevelt Defines the Four Freedoms at Risk

FRANKLIN D. ROOSEVELT, *Annual Message to Congress on the State of the Union* (1941)

Following the disaster of World War I, Americans had little taste for another European war when conflict erupted on the Continent once again in 1939. Eleven months before the attack on Pearl Harbor, President Roosevelt pressed the case against isolationism and for the protection of American security in his January 1941 State of the Union address. Here, Roosevelt articulates a vision for the world defined by guarantees of four essential freedoms.

I address you, the Members of the Seventy-seventh Congress, at a moment unprecedented in the history of the Union. I use the word "unprecedented," because at no previous time has American security been as seriously threatened from without as it is today.

Since the permanent formation of our Government under the Constitution, in 1789, most of the periods of crisis in our history have related to our domestic affairs. Fortunately, only one of these—the four-year War Between the States— ever threatened our national unity. Today, thank God, one hundred and thirty million Americans, in forty-eight States, have forgotten points of the compass in our national unity.

It is true that prior to 1914 the United States often had been disturbed by events in other Continents. We had even engaged in two wars with European nations and in a number of undeclared wars in the West Indies, in the Mediterranean and in the Pacific for the maintenance of American rights and for the principles of peaceful commerce. But in no case had a serious threat been raised against our national safety or our continued independence.

What I seek to convey is the historic truth that the United States as a nation has at all times maintained clear, definite opposition, to any attempt to lock us in behind an ancient Chinese wall while the procession of civilization went past. Today, thinking of our children and of their children, we oppose enforced isolation for ourselves or for any other part of the Americas.

That determination of ours, extending over all these years, was proved, for example, during the quarter century of wars following the French Revolution.

While the Napoleonic struggles did threaten interests of the United States because of the French foothold in the West Indies and in Louisiana, and while we engaged in the War of 1812 to vindicate our right to peaceful trade, it is nevertheless clear that neither France nor Great Britain, nor any other nation, was aiming at domination of the whole world.

In like fashion from 1815 to 1914—ninety-nine years—no single war in Europe or in Asia constituted a real threat against our future or against the future of any other American nation.

Franklin D. Roosevelt, "Annual Message to Congress on the State of the Union," January 6, 1941. Online by Gerhard Peters and John T. Woolley, *The American Presidency Project*. www.presidency .ucsb.edu/ws/?pid=16092.

Except in the Maximilian interlude in Mexico, no foreign power sought to establish itself in this Hemisphere; and the strength of the British fleet in the Atlantic has been a friendly strength. It is still a friendly strength.

Even when the World War broke out in 1914, it seemed to contain only small threat of danger to our own American future. But, as time went on, the American people began to visualize what the downfall of democratic nations might mean to our own democracy.

We need not overemphasize imperfections in the Peace of Versailles. We need not harp on failure of the democracies to deal with problems of world reconstruction. We should remember that the Peace of 1919 was far less unjust than the kind of "pacification" which began even before Munich, and which is being carried on under the new order of tyranny that seeks to spread over every continent today. The American people have unalterably set their faces against that tyranny.

Every realist knows that the democratic way of life is at this moment being directly assailed in every part of the world—assailed either by arms, or by secret spreading of poisonous propaganda by those who seek to destroy unity and promote discord in nations that are still at peace.

During sixteen long months this assault has blotted out the whole pattern of democratic life in an appalling number of independent nations, great and small. The assailants are still on the march, threatening other nations, great and small.

Therefore, as your President, performing my constitutional duty to "give to the Congress information of the state of the Union," I find it, unhappily, necessary to report that the future and the safety of our country and of our democracy are overwhelmingly involved in events far beyond our borders.

Armed defense of democratic existence is now being gallantly waged in four continents. If that defense fails, all the population and all the resources of Europe, Asia, Africa and Australasia will be dominated by the conquerors. Let us remember that the total of those populations and their resources in those four continents greatly exceeds the sum total of the population and the resources of the whole of the Western Hemisphere—many times over.

In times like these it is immature—and incidentally, untrue—for anybody to brag that an unprepared America, single-handed, and with one hand tied behind its back, can hold off the whole world.

No realistic American can expect from a dictator's peace international generosity, or return of true independence, or world disarmament, or freedom of expression, or freedom of religion—or even good business.

Such a peace would bring no security for us or for our neighbors. "Those, who would give up essential liberty to purchase a little temporary safety, deserve neither liberty nor safety."

As a nation, we may take pride in the fact that we are softhearted; but we cannot afford to be soft-headed.

We must always be wary of those who with sounding brass and a tinkling cymbal preach the "ism" of appeasement.

We must especially beware of that small group of selfish men who would clip the wings of the American eagle in order to feather their own nests.

I have recently pointed out how quickly the tempo of modern warfare could bring into our very midst the physical attack which we must eventually expect if the dictator nations win this war.

There is much loose talk of our immunity from immediate and direct invasion from across the seas. Obviously, as long as the British Navy retains its power, no such danger exists. Even if there were no British Navy, it is not probable that any enemy would be stupid enough to attack us by landing troops in the United States from across thousands of miles of ocean, until it had acquired strategic bases from which to operate.

But we learn much from the lessons of the past years in Europe—particularly the lesson of Norway, whose essential seaports were captured by treachery and surprise built up over a series of years.

The first phase of the invasion of this Hemisphere would not be the landing of regular troops. The necessary strategic points would be occupied by secret agents and their dupes—and great numbers of them are already here, and in Latin America.

As long as the aggressor nations maintain the offensive, they—not we—will choose the time and the place and the method of their attack.

That is why the future of all the American Republics is today in serious danger.

That is why this Annual Message to the Congress is unique in our history.

That is why every member of the Executive Branch of the Government and every member of the Congress faces great responsibility and great accountability.

The need of the moment is that our actions and our policy should be devoted primarily—almost exclusively—to meeting this foreign peril. For all our domestic problems are now a part of the great emergency.

Just as our national policy in internal affairs has been based upon a decent respect for the rights and the dignity of all our fellow men within our gates, so our national policy in foreign affairs has been based on a decent respect for the rights and dignity of all nations, large and small. And the justice of morality must and will win in the end.

Our national policy is this:

First, by an impressive expression of the public will and without regard to partisanship, we are committed to all-inclusive national defense.

Second, by an impressive expression of the public will and without regard to partisanship, we are committed to full support of all those resolute peoples, everywhere, who are resisting aggression and are thereby keeping war away from our Hemisphere. By this support, we express our determination that the democratic cause shall prevail; and we strengthen the defense and the security of our own nation.

Third, by an impressive expression of the public will and without regard to partisanship, we are committed to the proposition that principles of morality and considerations for our own security will never permit us to acquiesce in a peace dictated by aggressors and sponsored by appeasers. We know that enduring peace cannot be bought at the cost of other people's freedom.

... Today it is abundantly evident that American citizens everywhere are demanding and supporting speedy and complete action in recognition of obvious danger.

Therefore, the immediate need is a swift and driving increase in our armament production.

Leaders of industry and labor have responded to our summons. Goals of speed have been set. In some cases these goals are being reached ahead of time; in some cases we are on schedule; in other cases there are slight but not serious delays; and in some cases — and I am sorry to say very important cases — we are all concerned by the slowness of the accomplishment of our plans.

The Army and Navy, however, have made substantial progress during the past year. Actual experience is improving and speeding up our methods of production with every passing day. And today's best is not good enough for tomorrow.

I am not satisfied with the progress thus far made. The men in charge of the program represent the best in training, in ability, and in patriotism. They are not satisfied with the progress thus far made. None of us will be satisfied until the job is done. . . .

To change a whole nation from a basis of peacetime production of implements of peace to a basis of wartime production of implements of war is no small task. And the greatest difficulty comes at the beginning of the program, when new tools, new plant facilities, new assembly lines, and new ship ways must first be constructed before the actual materiel begins to flow steadily and speedily from them. . . .

New circumstances are constantly begetting new needs for our safety. I shall ask this Congress for greatly increased new appropriations and authorizations to carry on what we have begun.

I also ask this Congress for authority and for funds sufficient to manufacture additional munitions and war supplies of many kinds, to be turned over to those nations which are now in actual war with aggressor nations.

Our most useful and immediate role is to act as an arsenal for them as well as for ourselves. They do not need man power, but they do need billions of dollars worth of the weapons of defense.

The time is near when they will not be able to pay for them all in ready cash. We cannot, and we will not, tell them that they must surrender, merely because of present inability to pay for the weapons which we know they must have.

I do not recommend that we make them a loan of dollars with which to pay for these weapons — a loan to be repaid in dollars.

I recommend that we make it possible for those nations to continue to obtain war materials in the United States, fitting their orders into our own program. Nearly all their materiel would, if the time ever came, be useful for our own defense.

Taking counsel of expert military and naval authorities, considering what is best for our own security, we are free to decide how much should be kept here and how much should be sent abroad to our friends who by their determined and heroic resistance are giving us time in which to make ready our own defense.

For what we send abroad, we shall be repaid within a reasonable time following the close of hostilities, in similar materials, or, at our option, in other goods of many kinds, which they can produce and which we need.

Let us say to the democracies: "We Americans are vitally concerned in your defense of freedom. We are putting forth our energies, our resources and our organizing powers to give you the strength to regain and maintain a free world. We shall send you, in ever-increasing numbers, ships, planes, tanks, guns. This is our purpose and our pledge."

In fulfillment of this purpose we will not be intimidated by the threats of dictators that they will regard as a breach of international law or as an act of war our aid to the democracies which dare to resist their aggression. Such aid is not an act of war, even if a dictator should unilaterally proclaim it so to be.

When the dictators, if the dictators, are ready to make war upon us, they will not wait for an act of war on our part. They did not wait for Norway or Belgium or the Netherlands to commit an act of war.

Their only interest is in a new one-way international law, which lacks mutuality in its observance, and, therefore, becomes an instrument of oppression.

The happiness of future generations of Americans may well depend upon how effective and how immediate we can make our aid felt. No one can tell the exact character of the emergency situations that we may be called upon to meet. The Nation's hands must not be tied when the Nation's life is in danger.

We must all prepare to make the sacrifices that the emergency—almost as serious as war itself—demands. Whatever stands in the way of speed and efficiency in defense preparations must give way to the national need.

A free nation has the right to expect full cooperation from all groups. A free nation has the right to look to the leaders of business, of labor, and of agriculture to take the lead in stimulating effort, not among other groups but within their own groups. . . .

As men do not live by bread alone, they do not fight by armaments alone. Those who man our defenses, and those behind them who build our defenses, must have the stamina and the courage which come from unshakable belief in the manner of life which they are defending. The mighty action that we are calling for cannot be based on a disregard of all things worth fighting for.

The Nation takes great satisfaction and much strength from the things which have been done to make its people conscious of their individual stake in the preservation of democratic life in America. Those things have toughened the fibre of our people, have renewed their faith and strengthened their devotion to the institutions we make ready to protect.

Certainly this is no time for any of us to stop thinking about the social and economic problems which are the root cause of the social revolution which is today a supreme factor in the world.

For there is nothing mysterious about the foundations of a healthy and strong democracy. The basic things expected by our people of their political and economic systems are simple. They are:

Equality of opportunity for youth and for others.

Jobs for those who can work.

Security for those who need it.

The ending of special privilege for the few.

The preservation of civil liberties for all.

The enjoyment of the fruits of scientific progress in a wider and constantly rising standard of living.

These are the simple, basic things that must never be lost sight of in the turmoil and unbelievable complexity of our modern world. The inner and abiding strength of our economic and political systems is dependent upon the degree to which they fulfill these expectations.

Many subjects connected with our social economy call for immediate improvement.

As examples:

We should bring more citizens under the coverage of old-age pensions and unemployment insurance.

We should widen the opportunities for adequate medical care.

We should plan a better system by which persons deserving or needing gainful employment may obtain it.

I have called for personal sacrifice. I am assured of the willingness of almost all Americans to respond to that call.

A part of the sacrifice means the payment of more money in taxes. In my Budget Message I shall recommend that a greater portion of this great defense program be paid for from taxation than we are paying today. No person should try, or be allowed, to get rich out of this program; and the principle of tax payments in accordance with ability to pay should be constantly before our eyes to guide our legislation.

In the future days, which we seek to make secure, we look forward to a world founded upon four essential human freedoms.

The first is freedom of speech and expression—everywhere in the world.

The second is freedom of every person to worship God in his own way—everywhere in the world.

The third is freedom from want—which, translated into world terms, means economic understandings which will secure to every nation a healthy peacetime life for its inhabitants—everywhere in the world.

The fourth is freedom from fear—which, translated into world terms, means a world-wide reduction of armaments to such a point and in such a thorough fashion that no nation will be in a position to commit an act of physical aggression against any neighbor—anywhere in the world.

That is no vision of a distant millennium. It is a definite basis for a kind of world attainable in our own time and generation. That kind of world is the very antithesis of the so-called new order of tyranny which the dictators seek to create with the crash of a bomb.

To that new order we oppose the greater conception—the moral order. A good society is able to face schemes of world domination and foreign revolutions alike without fear.

Since the beginning of our American history, we have been engaged in change—in a perpetual peaceful revolution—a revolution which goes on steadily, quietly adjusting itself to changing conditions—without the concentration camp or the quick-lime in the ditch. The world order which we seek is the cooperation of free countries, working together in a friendly, civilized society.

This nation has placed its destiny in the hands and heads and hearts of its millions of free men and women; and its faith in freedom under the guidance of God. Freedom means the supremacy of human rights everywhere. Our support goes to those who struggle to gain those rights or keep them. Our strength is our unity of purpose. To that high concept there can be no end save victory.

READING AND DISCUSSION QUESTIONS

1. Examine the argument Roosevelt made to Congress regarding the threats America faced from the war in Europe. How was America's security tied to events overseas?

2. How did Roosevelt define America's interest in the war in Europe? What were the freedoms at stake that he challenged Congress and the American people to defend?

24-2 | Soldiers Describe D-Day Experience

Interviews with the Library of Congress Veterans History Project (2001, 2003)

The June 1944 Normandy invasion began the liberation of Europe from German control. Planned by General Dwight D. Eisenhower, the amphibious assault of German-occupied France, known as Operation Overlord, resulted in the landing of 160,000 soldiers along France's coastline. Nine thousand of them died there. Their comrades, including Sergeant Claud C. Woodring and Private First Class Jay S. Adams, pushed forward, with the goal of capturing Germany and ending the war. These excerpts of interviews done as part of the Library of Congress's Veterans History Project vividly evoke the soldier's experience of war.

Interview with Jay S. Adams, July 5, 2001

The order came on the sixth for us . . . to go across the channel. . . . I went across on an LCT [landing craft tank], with my crane and my dozer on there. I was a dozer operator . . . and when we got out in the channel it got pretty rough, and I had to chain my dozer down because it was sliding down the deck. I was afraid it'd punch a hole in the side and we'd sink before we got there. [M]any of the men on the boats were . . . seasick because that channel was very rough. It was a storm, really, when we was going over, and as we approached the coastline in the morning, Navy was shelling the coast, and it was just like a fog on the coast. . . . [O]n the left, our Rangers are trying to get up the cliff there with pillboxes to step on the cliff, and we was coming right into the pillboxes, and we was

The Veterans History Project at loc.gov.

supposed to have been on the second wave, and I don't know what time we got in there and dropped the ramp, and the jeep that came off, the guy got wounded, and then the fire was so heavy that the ship's Captain backed us off and we went back out into the channel. . . . [T]he guy driving the jeep, they sent him back to the States, and he had a sister that lived in Ashtabula. He wrote his sister and told his sister about me, and she got a hold of my parents and told them where I was at. They hadn't heard from me for so long and they didn't know that—then they knew that I was in the invasion in the French coast. . . .

[W]e backed off, and then we started in again, and we got stuck on a sand bar and was kind of like that, and an 88 come in under and explode it, and they pushed our boat aside just like that, and just as we done that, three 88 shells come right in where we was at and that pushed us back out, and then we tried to get in again, and the Captain of the ship, he dropped a ramp and I looked down there, and there was a .50 caliber sticking out of the water from a half track, and I told my officer, "We can't get the dozer in until we ground it out." So he said, "I'll take care of it." So he went up to see the Captain and he says, "You gotta get him in there." To this day, I'm convinced that he pulled a gun on that ship's Captain to get him in there because what they were doing, a lot of Navy guys were dropping them off in the water, and some of the quick movers going down and drowning out, and the men were drowning out. Getting drowned with the heavy packs on because it was too far out and some of the operators had flak vests on. I had a flak vest on, and I told the officer I'd take that off right here and I'd swim ashore [but]—we'll lose our equipment. He said, "We'll get her in." And so, when we finally did get in there . . . [it was] kind of gruesome to see all the dead soldiers laying on that beach. You had to zig zag around . . . to keep from running over them. One of my other buddies, that drove a dozer, he came in. I guess he got in a little ahead of me, and he heard a shell coming in, and they jumped off, and the shell came underneath his dozer and blowed the bottom out, and he . . . had a trailer behind him with TNT in there. The only thing was left was a short piece of the tongue left. Dove, Lynton Dove, had another dozer in our Company C, and he made a pass up through there. Some way or another he got through the mine field, and filled in an antitank dish, and got up over the hill so that the traffic could get going, and he received a DSC [Distinguished Service Cross] for that. . . .

And then we kind of, took us a few days to try to get organized again and get back together, and then our job was working on the beach for quite a while. We made roads in that area, and we built loading docks for the ducks that come in. . . . [W]hile we was down there, I helped clean the mine field with my dozer, and one day as I was walking down there, to get on my dozer, something grabbed—just seemed like somebody grabbed me by the shoulder and stopped me. And when I stopped and I moved my foot aside, there's a mine about an inch and a half from being stepped on, and now God was watching over us. I tell you, it's—you can't imagine it until you have something like that happen. It's just like somebody reached up, and took a hold of you, and made you stop. Just like I'm looking out at that tree, not thinking nothing about it. Walking through there, you know. Just that quick I stopped. You know, it was, and for many instances, like just a few seconds that I shifted gears or something, and a sniper shot at me one time, and I shifted a little quicker one time and a bullet went behind me, and lot of different instances went on like that. Just, moving just a little bit one way or another. A lot of our — we lost I forget how many men, but quite a few of us got through it. It's a wonder any of us made it. Within a 24-hour period there was around 5,000 men killed right there on the beach, and that's not counting the wounded. I don't know how many wounded. To this day there's probably a lot of them in the hospitals that have never come out from there. . . .

[A]fter we got done there, after they got the port open, then we moved on up . . . all the way through France, and up into Belgium, and up into Holland . . . it was getting colder weather . . . and everybody sleeping in the pup tents and everything, and there's a guy came from this village. He said, "I'd like a couple guys to come and sleep in my house where it's warm tonight." . . . They were still thankful that they'd been liberated and they was free, 'cause I don't know exactly how many years they were under German . . . control, and they couldn't do enough for the GI's going through there, and that happened through all of the towns that we went through.

Interview with Claud Woodring, January 2, 2003

I was inducted May 6th of '43. I went to Camp Perry, Ohio. Shipped from there to Camp Shelby, Mississippi, for my basic training. Basic training was to be 13 weeks. At 11 weeks, I was shipped out of Camp Shelby, Mississippi, to Fort George G. Meade, Baltimore, Maryland. I went to a staging area somewhere [in] upstate New York. I shipped out of New York on November 2, 1943. . . . We landed in Glasgow, Scotland, on November the 9th of '43. From there I went to Dorchester, Dorset, England, assigned to the First Infantry Division Company of the 18th Regiment. . . .

All of my combat training was in England. . . . I was not a good soldier when I first went into the Army. When I went to Camp Shelby, Mississippi, the first day I was taking pictures with a two-dollar Brownie camera. The company commander objected to that. We had a few words and he stomped on my camera. From then on I did not like the Army's attitude. . . . After 11 weeks, my name was posted on a shipping order. I shipped out. I did not get a three-day pass after I was inducted. I did not get a seven-day furlough after basic training. When I left home, I kissed mom goodbye, and I didn't see my mother again until after I got back after I was wounded. All of these things led up to — I developed an attitude and when I was assigned to the First Infantry Division in England I had a sergeant, Sergeant St. John, he took me aside and beat the hell out of me and convinced me I should become a soldier or I wasn't going to survive the war. He taught me to be a soldier in England. While training in England, I . . . had sniper training and demolition training. I did a lot of demolition training in anticipation of the landing. . . .

I was charged with the job of blowing up the barbed wire on the beach. That's what I trained for, specifically, along with being a foot soldier. . . . We went down to Portsmouth and we were put on LCVP, landing craft vehicle and personnel, and . . . we was on that ship all night . . . June the 5th, [the night] prior to the invasion, and when we went across the channel it was dark, of course, at night, but it was almost wall-to-wall LCVP's landing craft. Our landing craft hit a submerged mine two, three hundred yards from shore and sunk. In the process of the ship hitting the mine, one of my buddies went overboard and I let my rifle down to help ease him up. He weighed 200 pounds, I weighed 125 pounds. He won. He was in the water with two guns, so when we abandoned the ship, so to speak, I had two bangalore torpedos and inflated our life belts . . . and we swam ashore. At this point in time it was just breaking daylight. . . .

[The trip across the channel had been] terribly rough. . . . The weather was horrible, windy rough, high waves. Ships banging against each other almost. It was so bad. . . . When I got off of the ship, I swam ashore. . . . Fully clothed with all the gear on we had and no rifle and at that point I didn't need a rifle. The day and evening before the invasion the air corps had dropped thousands of little bombs on the beach to make ready-made foxholes, which were a Godsend, so I approached the barbed wire, which is strung out in coils several layers thick. You couldn't cut one strand of barbed wire. If you did, it would fly and grab you and tear you all apart and it was impossible to cut through it. It would take too much time. We had the bangalore torpedoes which screwed together with a hand grenade detonator in it and slid them under the barbed wire, pulled the pin, ducked in a foxhole and blew a hole in the barbed wire that was probably, oh, 50, 60 yards wide and all the time there's people pushing right behind you. There are thousands coming on. Probably the only reason I survived the assault on the beach was the Germans could fire into a massive crowd behind me and they weren't worried about the first person up ahead. . . .

As I remember, we were on top of the beach—on top of the sand dunes at the beach probably by two o'clock in the afternoon, maybe a little earlier than that, but at that point the beach was completely full of people and equipment and litter and the tide was coming in. . . . After we left the beaches, we got right into the hedgerow country and that was horrendous fighting, probably as difficult as the beach because of the cover they had. This hedgerow country had been there—they're little two or three acre field with hedgerows for fences. . . . Every day we ran into the enemy, whether it be Panzer or rear action—rear guard. After we got through the hedgerow country out into open country, the Germans had to travel at night because we had air supremacy. . . . As soon as it got dark, you would hear the German equipment heading towards Germany. They had a short night and can't travel very fast in the dark, consequently every day about two o'clock in the afternoon or three or noon, whatever, we would have advanced as far during the daytime as they did at night and then there would be another little war fought every day. Every day we caught the enemy and had a scrimmage. . . . The Germans that we captured, though, were conscription army, Czechs, Poles, whoever. They didn't want to fight and they [were] way—underequipped. They were still using World War I horse-drawn artillery. These people surrendered by the hundreds. One soldier could take 50 prisoners back and not have a problem. . . . The frequency and the fierceness of the fighting would decrease at that point pretty much every day because the German—hardline German soldiers were heading for Germany and they had occupation troops that were just holding us up. They were just there to irritate us. . . . The local French people were great. If there was a sniper in a tower, they told you where he was. They were informants. They were glad to see us. They helped us in any way they could.

READING AND DISCUSSION QUESTIONS

1. What perspective of war and the D-Day invasion in particular emerges from these interview transcripts? How might an account of D-Day differ if you read, for example, a report from General Dwight Eisenhower, who planned the Normandy invasion?

2. From these interviews, what can you infer about the meaning and significance of D-Day from these soldiers' perspectives? What about the invasion stands out in their memories?

24-3 | Japanese Americans in the Crosshairs of War

GORDON HIRABAYASHI, *Why I Refused to Register for Evacuation* (1942)

After Japan's 1941 attack on Pearl Harbor, President Roosevelt imposed restraints on Japanese and Japanese Americans, including curfews and eventually evacuation to internment camps. Gordon Hirabayashi, an American citizen of Japanese descent, refused to register for the forced evacuation and was convicted and sentenced to jail. His appeal to the Supreme Court ended in defeat. When the evacuation order was announced, Hirabayashi penned this note describing his reasons for resisting.

Over and above any man-made creed or law is the natural law of life—the right of human individuals to live and to creatively express themselves. No man was born with the right to limit that law. Nor, do I believe, can anyone justifiably work himself to such a position.

Down through the ages, we have had various individuals doing their bit to establish more securely these fundamental rights. They have tried to help society see the necessity of understanding those fundamental laws; some have succeeded to the extent of having these natural laws recorded. Many have suffered unnatural deaths as a result of their convictions. Yet, today, because of the efforts of some of these individuals, we have recorded in the laws of our nation certain rights for all men and certain additional rights for citizens. These fundamental moral rights and civil liberties are included in the Bill of Rights, U.S. Constitution and other legal records. They guarantee that these fundamental rights shall not be denied without due process of law.

The principles or the ideals are the things which give value to a person's life. They are the qualities which give impetus and purpose toward meaningful

Gordon K. Hirabayashi, "Why I Refused to Register for Evacuation," May 13, 1942, Ring Family Papers, Box 1, Folder 17, University of Washington, Special Collections, Seattle, Washington.

experiences. The violation of human personality is the violation of the most sacred thing which man owns.

This order for the mass evacuation of all persons of Japanese descent denies them the right to live. It forces thousands of energetic, law-abiding individuals to exist in a miserable psychological and a horrible physical atmosphere. This order limits to almost the full extent the creative expressions of those subjected. It kills the desire for a higher life. Hope for the future is exterminated. Human personalities are poisoned. The very qualities which are essential to a peaceful, creative community are being thrown out and abused. Over 60 percent are American citizens, yet they are denied on a wholesale scale without due process of law the civil liberties which are theirs.

If I were to register and cooperate under those circumstances, I would be giving helpless consent to the denial of practically all of the things which give me incentive to live. I must maintain my Christian principles. I consider it my duty to maintain the democratic standards for which this nation lives. Therefore, I must refuse this order for evacuation.

Let me add, however, that in refusing to register, I am well aware of the excellent qualities of the army and government personnel connected with the prosecution of this exclusion order. They are men of the finest type, and I sincerely appreciate their sympathetic and honest efforts. Nor do I intend to cast any shadow upon the Japanese and the other Nisei who have registered for evacuation. They have faced tragedy admirably. I am objecting to the principle of this order, which denies the rights of human beings, including citizens.

GORDON K. HIRABAYASHI
May 13, 1942

READING AND DISCUSSION QUESTIONS

1. Analyze Hirabayashi's statement to determine the argument he makes against the U.S. policy regarding Japanese internment camps. Upon what sources of authority does he base his refusal?

2. What does his form of civil disobedience reveal to you about the wartime pressures and constraints on civil liberties?

24-4 | Fighting for Democracy and Civil Rights at Home and Abroad

LULAC NEWS, *Editorial* (1945)

When the League of United Latin American Citizens (LULAC) was organized in 1929, those of Latin American descent faced racial and ethnic discrimination, exacerbated by the economic tensions of the Great Depression. Franklin Roosevelt supported a policy of repatriating many

F. Arturo Rosales, ed., *Testimonio: A Documentary History of the Mexican American Struggle for Civil Rights* (Houston: Arte Público Press, 2000), 181–182.

to Mexico in an effort to ease the economic crisis, but when wartime labor demands spiked, Mexican contract laborers were brought in to work the farms. Latin Americans also fought in the war, yet faced discrimination similar to that experienced by African American veterans upon their return home. The *LULAC News*'s 1945 editorial raises questions about the meaning of race and the hypocrisy of America's freedom rhetoric in a culture of discrimination.

"We do not serve Mexicans here." "You will have to get out as no Mexicans are allowed." "Your uniform and service ribbons mean nothing here. We still do not allow Mexicans."

These, and many other stronger-worded ones, are the embarrassing and humiliating retorts given our returning veterans of Latin American descent and their families. They may all be worded differently, and whereas some are toned with hate and loathness while others are toned with sympathy and remorse, still the implication remains that these so-called "Mexicans" are considered unworthy of equality, regardless of birthright or service. This situation is ironic indeed, in view of the fact that these same "Mexicans" have just finished helping this country to defeat countries to the east and west who would impose upon the world a superior people, a superior culture.

Why this hate, this prejudice, this tendency to discriminate against a people whose only fault seems to be that they are heirs of a culture older than any known "American Culture," to find themselves a part of a land and people they have helped to build and to defend, to find themselves a part of a minority group whose acquired passive nature keeps them from boldly demanding those rights and privileges which are rightfully theirs? Can it be the result of difference in race, nationality, language, loyalty, intelligence or ability?

There is no difference in race. Latin Americans, or so-called "Mexicans," are Caucasian or white. There are only three races: the Caucasian, the Negroid, and the Mongoloid. Racial characteristics place the Latin American among the white. Who dares contradict nature? There is no difference in nationality. These "Mexicans" were born and bred in this country and are just as American as Jones or Smith. In fact, the ancestors of these "Mexicans" were here before those of Jones or Smith decided to take up abode. Differences in language? No. These "Mexicans" speak English. Accented, perhaps, in some cases, but English all over the United States seems to be accented. That these "Mexicans" can speak Spanish is not a detriment; it is an asset. After all, there are not too many people in this country who can boast a knowledge of the most widely spoken languages of the world. Difference in loyalty? How can that be when all revere the same stars and stripes, when they don the same service uniforms for the same principles? Difference in intelligence and ability? Impossible. For every profession and category of work, from menial labor to the most scientific and technical matter, there is a qualified group of "Mexicans." All they need is the opportunity minus the discrimination and jealousy.

We could go on and on naming erroneously imagined differences to be used as a basis for this hate and find each one false. This condition is not a case of difference; it is a case of ignorance. Yes, ignorance. Odd indeed to find this banal state of mind in a country of such enlightenment and progress. But then, ignorance is like a disease that is contagious, but contagious only for those who wish to suffer from it. Ignorance, bigotry, prejudice, and intolerance all down through the centuries have tried to crush intelligence with cruelty, reason with brutality, and spirituality with madness. This quartet of banalities constitutes the curse of the world. Ignorance is the parent of the other three.

Yes, ignorance broods hate and all its resultant actions of jealousy, misunderstandings, erroneous opinions, and premeditated feelings of discord and confusion. In this particular case of unjustified failure to foment a fraternal feeling between two groups of Americans, it is an ignorance of facts that poisons the atmosphere. An ignorance of the cultural contributions of Americans of Latin American descent to the still young American Culture; an ignorance of the blood, sweat, and efforts given to this country for its betterment; an ignorance of the sufferings withstood and the lives given to preserve this country free and independent through its various periods of strife and conflict; and finally, an ignorance of a sense of appreciation for a long, profitable, and loyal association with a group of Americans whose voice cries out in desperate supplication:

"We have proved ourselves true and loyal Americans by every trial and test that has confronted us; now give us social, political, and economic equality and the opportunity to practice and enjoy that equality. We ask for it not as a favor, but as a delegated right guaranteed by our Constitution, and as a reward for faithful service."

READING AND DISCUSSION QUESTIONS

1. What conclusions can you draw from the editorial regarding the construction of race in midcentury American culture? What argument about "whiteness" did LULAC make, and why did the organization object to the term "Mexicans" as Americans used it?

2. What impact do you think the concerns raised by LULAC had on the postwar civil rights movement? How does LULAC define the source of the discrimination its members faced?

24-5 | *LIFE* Magazine Exposes the Horrors of Germany's Concentration Camps

LIFE MAGAZINE, *Atrocities* (1945)

LIFE magazine graphically captured the war's human toll in its May 7, 1945, issue featuring haunting photographs by George Rodger and Margaret Bourke-White. Titled "Atrocities," the article depicted victims of the Nazi concentration camps at Buchenwald and Bergen-Belsen. At these and other camps, Germany's campaign against Jews and others they deemed inferior resulted in millions of deaths. In one image, a boy walks along the road outside Belsen amidst rows of bodies.

"Atrocities," *LIFE* (May 7, 1945): 32–33. George Rodger/Time & Life Pictures/Getty Images.

READING AND DISCUSSION QUESTIONS

1. What impact do you think the editors at *LIFE* magazine intended the article to have on its audience? What perspective on the meaning of the war do you think they were trying to communicate?

2. How would you assess the significance of this type of photojournalism in shaping public opinion? What comparisons can you draw between the effect achieved with these images and others you may be familiar with, for instance, Jacob Riis depicting late-nineteenth-century tenements or Dorothea Lange showing Great Depression poverty?

24-6 | President Explains Use of Atomic Bomb to End War

HARRY TRUMAN, *Statement by the President Announcing the Use of the A-Bomb at Hiroshima* (1945)

Harry Truman entered the presidency in April 1945 following the death of FDR. It fell to him to oversee the end of the war in the Pacific against the Japanese. When the government of Japan ignored the Allied demand for surrender made at the Potsdam Conference in July, Truman decided to use the atomic bomb secretly developed by American scientists. Ultimately two bombs were dropped, the first on Hiroshima on August 6, followed three days later with another attack on Nagasaki. In this August 6 statement, Truman announced the bombing of Hiroshima to the American people.

Sixteen hours ago an American airplane dropped one bomb on Hiroshima, an important Japanese Army base. That bomb had more power than 20,000 tons of T.N.T. It had more than two thousand times the blast power of the British "Grand Slam" which is the largest bomb ever yet used in the history of warfare.

The Japanese began the war from the air at Pearl Harbor. They have been repaid many fold. And the end is not yet. With this bomb we have now added a new and revolutionary increase in destruction to supplement the growing power of our armed forces. In their present form these bombs are now in production and even more powerful forms are in development.

It is an atomic bomb. It is a harnessing of the basic power of the universe. The force from which the sun draws its power has been loosed against those who brought war to the Far East.

Before 1939, it was the accepted belief of scientists that it was theoretically possible to release atomic energy. But no one knew any practical method of doing it. By 1942, however, we knew that the Germans were working feverishly to find a way to add atomic energy to the other engines of war with which they hoped to enslave the world. But they failed. We may be grateful to Providence that the Germans got the V-1's and V-2's late and in limited quantities and even more grateful that they did not get the atomic bomb at all.

The battle of the laboratories held fateful risks for us as well as the battles of the air, land and sea, and we have now won the battle of the laboratories as we have won the other battles.

Beginning in 1940, before Pearl Harbor, scientific knowledge useful in war was pooled between the United States and Great Britain, and many priceless helps to our victories have come from that arrangement. Under that general policy the research on the atomic bomb was begun. With American and British scientists working together we entered the race of discovery against the Germans.

Harry S. Truman, "Statement by the President Announcing the Use of the A-Bomb at Hiroshima," August 6, 1945. Online by Gerhard Peters and John T. Woolley, *The American Presidency Project*. www.presidency.ucsb.edu/ws/?pid=12169.

The United States had available the large number of scientists of distinction in the many needed areas of knowledge. It had the tremendous industrial and financial resources necessary for the project and they could be devoted to it without undue impairment of other vital war work. In the United States the laboratory work and the production plants, on which a substantial start had already been made, would be out of reach of enemy bombing, while at that time Britain was exposed to constant air attack and was still threatened with the possibility of invasion. For these reasons Prime Minister Churchill and President Roosevelt agreed that it was wise to carry on the project here. We now have two great plants and many lesser works devoted to the production of atomic power. Employment during peak construction numbered 125,000 and over 65,000 individuals are even now engaged in operating the plants. Many have worked there for two and a half years. Few know what they have been producing. They see great quantities of material going in and they see nothing coming out of these plants, for the physical size of the explosive charge is exceedingly small. We have spent two billion dollars on the greatest scientific gamble in history—and won.

But the greatest marvel is not the size of the enterprise, its secrecy, nor its cost, but the achievement of scientific brains in putting together infinitely complex pieces of knowledge held by many men in different fields of science into a workable plan. And hardly less marvelous has been the capacity of industry to design, and of labor to operate, the machines and methods to do things never done before so that the brain child of many minds came forth in physical shape and performed as it was supposed to do. Both science and industry worked under the direction of the United States Army, which achieved a unique success in managing so diverse a problem in the advancement of knowledge in an amazingly short time. It is doubtful if such another combination could be got together in the world. What has been done is the greatest achievement of organized science in history. It was done under high pressure and without failure.

We are now prepared to obliterate more rapidly and completely every productive enterprise the Japanese have above ground in any city. We shall destroy their docks, their factories, and their communications. Let there be no mistake; we shall completely destroy Japan's power to make war.

It was to spare the Japanese people from utter destruction that the ultimatum of July 26 was issued at Potsdam. Their leaders promptly rejected that ultimatum. If they do not now accept our terms they may expect a rain of ruin from the air, the like of which has never been seen on this earth. Behind this air attack will follow sea and land forces in such numbers and power as they have not yet seen and with the fighting skill of which they are already well aware.

The Secretary of War, who has kept in personal touch with all phases of the project, will immediately make public a statement giving further details.

His statement will give facts concerning the sites at Oak Ridge near Knoxville, Tennessee, and at Richland near Pasco, Washington, and an installation near Santa Fe, New Mexico. Although the workers at the sites have been making materials to be used in producing the greatest destructive force in history they have not themselves been in danger beyond that of many other occupations, for the utmost care has been taken of their safety.

The fact that we can release atomic energy ushers in a new era in man's understanding of nature's forces. Atomic energy may in the future supplement the power that now comes from coal, oil, and falling water, but at present it cannot be produced on a basis to compete with them commercially. Before that comes there must be a long period of intensive research.

It has never been the habit of the scientists of this country or the policy of this Government to withhold from the world scientific knowledge. Normally, therefore, everything about the work with atomic energy would be made public.

But under present circumstances it is not intended to divulge the technical processes of production or all the military applications, pending further examination of possible methods of protecting us and the rest of the world from the danger of sudden destruction.

I shall recommend that the Congress of the United States consider promptly the establishment of an appropriate commission to control the production and use of atomic power within the United States. I shall give further consideration and make further recommendations to the Congress as to how atomic power can become a powerful and forceful influence towards the maintenance of world peace.

READING AND DISCUSSION QUESTIONS

1. Beyond simply announcing the dropping of the atomic bomb, what does Truman hope to accomplish with his statement to the American people? Do you think Americans were his only audience?

2. How do you assess the tone of Truman's statement? How, for instance, does he describe the work of the scientists who created the bomb?

3. Imagine yourself an advisor to Truman on August 5. What advice would you have given him concerning the use of the atomic bomb? What do you think were the common arguments for and against its use?

■ COMPARATIVE QUESTIONS ■

1. Compare Roosevelt's "Four Freedoms" speech with Woodrow Wilson's Fourteen Points (Document 21-6) to understand how the definition of America's values changed and remained consistent over time. What similarities do you see in the way they spoke about war's potential to change the world?

2. Did the experience of World War II change the way people of different races and ethnicities were treated in the United States? Consider the United States's treatment of immigrants (see Bartolomeo Vanzetti's last statement [Document 22-1]

and the Chinese Exclusion Act [Document 17-4]) and African Americans (see "New York Negroes Stage Silent Parade of Protest" [Document 19-4]) in the late nineteenth and early twentieth centuries and compare that to the evidence in Hirabayashi's statement and the LULAC editorial. What can you conclude about America's history of race and ethnic relations through the mid-twentieth century?

3. What editorial reaction can you imagine *LULAC News* having in response to Roosevelt's "Four Freedoms" speech? How might its readers have reacted to his description of American ideals?

4. How would you assess the cost of war on American society? To what extent do you see evidence of war helping or hindering the resolution of persistent social, political, and economic problems?

DOCUMENT SET

Defining American Identities in a Globalizing Age

1890–1945

While the United States entered the 1890s without significant international engagements, fifty-five years later, it had emerged as the leading power in the world. Critics of America's imperial ambitions might well have wondered what their country had become. This global expansion was driven by economic and geopolitical considerations, but many Americans maintained a centuries-old belief that they had a "rendezvous with destiny," and that their ventures overseas were selfless acts in support of democracy's onward progress. The reality at home, however, raised questions for many groups: women advocating for suffrage, immigrants and ethnic minorities defending their rights, and African Americans facing persistent racism. As each defined their identity within American society, they faced the juxtaposition of their experience with the American ideal. The theme of identity was critical to these groups as they sought to imagine their place as part of America, and as gender, class, ethnic, religious, regional, and racial factors affected the way they saw themselves and the way that others viewed them. For some, merging their identity into an American melting pot seemed best, while others saw strength in maintaining America's diversity. The tension between these perspectives fueled discussions of American identity throughout the twentieth century.

P7-1 | Lower East Side Residents Condemn Immigration Commissioner

Citizens Committee of Orchard, Rivington, and East Houston Streets, New York City to William Howard Taft (1912)

More than 600,000 immigrants passed through Ellis Island in 1912, the year residents of the Lower East Side wrote this letter to President Taft criticizing the disparaging remarks of the New York commissioner of immigration. Unlike earlier waves of immigration, increasing numbers hailed from Southern and Eastern Europe, including Jews and other groups that many Americans feared as radical and inassimilable. This anxiety led to a study published in 1911 by the Dillingham Commission recommending immigration restriction, which would later be enacted in the early 1920s. Here, a citizens' committee of the Lower East Side responds by affirming their identity as Americans.

Hon. WILLIAM H. TAFT,
President of the United States of America,
Washington, D.C.

Sir:—

The undersigned are residents of Orchard, Rivington, and East Houston Streets, in the Borough of Manhattan, City of New York. As such they respectfully call your attention to the following statement contained in the annual report for the year ending June 30, 1911, of William Williams, Esq., Commissioner of Immigration for the Port of New York:

"The new immigration, unlike that of the earlier years, proceeds in part from the poorer elements of the countries of Southern and Eastern Europe and from backward races with customs and institutions widely different from ours and without the capacity of assimilating with our people as did the early immigrants. Many of those coming from these sources have very low standards of living, possess filthy habits, and are of an ignorance which passes belief. Types of the classes referred to, representing various alien races and nationalities may be observed in some of the tenement districts of Elizabeth, Orchard and Rivington, and East Houston Streets, New York City. * * * They often herd together, forming in effect foreign colonies in which the English language is almost unknown." . . .

Although this report of Mr. Williams is supposed to relate solely to Ellis Island affairs, fully two pages are devoted to matters having no bearing whatsoever upon the affairs at Ellis Island, but are evidently interpolated for restrictionistic purposes.

Citizens Committee of Orchard, Rivington, and East Houston Streets, New York City to William Howard Taft, April 9, 1912, Records of the Immigration and Naturalization Service, Record Group 85, National Archives, ARC 3854680.

While the individual views of the Commissioner are no concern of ours, we are vitally interested in that portion of his report which undertakes to reflect upon us, as indicated in the foregoing excerpt. We deny emphatically that there is any truth in the strictures imposed by this public official upon the inhabitants of Orchard, Rivington and East Houston Streets. A large proportion of them are citizens of the United States, loyal to their country and to its institutions, seeking by their industry to add to the well-being of the community in which they reside. Those who are not citizens, intend to become such at the earliest opportunity. Although most of the residents of these streets are of foreign birth, they have come to this country for the purpose of establishing permanent homes, of rearing and educating their children as good Americans, and of enjoying the blessings of freedom, at the same time assuming and performing the obligations which residence and citizenship entail.

A survey of the district whose good name is involved in the strictures contained in Mr. Williams's report, indicating the nationalities and the moral, social and industrial activities of the population included in such district, is hereto appended. It is believed that the statistics thus presented for your consideration will demonstrate, not only that the statements made by Mr. Williams are false, but that they are libelous, and that no public official should be permitted with impunity thus to malign a large and populous section of this great city.

Remarks of this character, emanating from one occupying the official position that Mr. Williams fills, are calculated to do great injury to those who are included within them. They are particularly objectionable because they are apt to arouse unwarranted prejudices against immigrants, and especially among immigration inspectors, who are his subordinates and who, as has been pointed out by the Congressional Immigration Commission, are at present disposed "in a greater or less degree to reflect in their decisions the attitude of the commissioner," thus "tending to impair the judicial character of the board."

Under the circumstances we are impelled, not only for self-protection but because we believe it to be our duty as citizens, to protest against these wanton and unjustifiable reflections upon us; against this attempt on the part of a public official to discriminate among those who have passed through the gate at Ellis Island, and who have become absorbed in the general population of this country.

Moreover, we consider the remarks to which we have taken umbrage as a gratuitous insult, because in making them Mr. Williams did not deal with any matters which came within his jurisdiction, which is confined to Ellis Island, but has seen fit, either maliciously or without knowledge of the conditions which he seeks to describe, to animadvert upon us and those whom we represent, all of whom are striving to the utmost of their power to maintain the respect and good will of their fellow citizens.

We therefore respectfully pray, that such action may be taken in the premises as will vindicate our reputation and that of our families and neighbors, and will result in the retraction of the libelous charge of which we complain.

Dated, New York, April 9, 1912.
    Respectfully submitted,

CITIZENS COMMITTEE
of
ORCHARD, RIVINGTON AND EAST HOUSTON STREETS,
NEW YORK CITY.

READING AND DISCUSSION QUESTIONS

1. Examine the role of ethnic identity in shaping both the Commission of Immigration's characterization of Lower East Side residents and their response. To what extent did their ethnicity define them in their own minds?

2. What stereotypes about ethnic groups are these residents challenging in their letter of protest? How do they defend themselves against the commissioner's representations?

3. What can you conclude from this document about how changing patterns of migration to the United States during this period influenced the growth of racial and ethnic identities?

P7-2 | Advocating Cultural Pluralism

HORACE KALLEN, *Democracy Versus the Melting Pot* (1915)

Many "old stock" Americans assumed that the ethnic and cultural diversity of the new immigrants flooding the country's ports would quickly disappear as they merged into the "melting pot" of American society. However, evidence of their persisting ethnic identity (in foodways, language, religious practices, and customs) alarmed those Americans who questioned the immigrants' loyalties and fit. By contrast, philosopher Horace Kallen, born to Jewish parents in Germany but raised from childhood in the United States, offered an alternative to the melting pot ideal.

At the present time there is no dominant American mind. Our spirit is inarticulate, not a voice, but a chorus of many voices each singing a rather different tune. How to get order out of this cacophony is the question for all those who are concerned about those things which alone justify wealth and power, concerned about justice, the arts, literature, philosophy, science. What must, what shall this cacophony become — a unison or a harmony?

For decidedly the older America, whose voice and whose spirit was New England, is gone beyond recall. Americans still are the artists and thinkers of the

Horace Kallen, "Democracy Versus the Melting Pot," *The Nation* 100 (February 25, 1915): 217–220.

land, but they work, each for himself, without common vision or ideals. The older tradition has passed from a life into a memory, and the newer one, so far as it has an Anglo-Saxon base, is holding its own beside more formidable rivals, the expression in appropriate form of the national inheritances of the various populations concentrated in the various States of the Union, populations of whom their national self-consciousness is perhaps the chief spiritual asset. Think of the Creoles in the South and the French-Canadians in the North, clinging to French for so many generations and maintaining, however weakly, spiritual and social contacts with the mother-country; of the Germans, with their *Deutschthum*, their *Münnerchöre, Turnvereine,* and *Schutzenfeste*;[1] of the universally separate Jews; of the intensely nationalistic Irish; of the Pennsylvania Germans; of the indomitable Poles, and even more indomitable Bohemians; of the 30,000 Belgians in Wisconsin, with their "Belgian" language, a mixture of Walloon and Flemish welded by reaction to a strange social environment. Except in such cases as the town of Lead, South Dakota, the great ethnic groups of proletarians, thrown upon themselves in a new environment, generate from among themselves the other social classes which Mr. Ross[2] misses so sadly among them: their shopkeepers, their physicians, their attorneys, their journalists, and their national and political leaders, who form the links between them and the greater American society. They develop their own literature, or become conscious of that of the mother-country. As they grow more prosperous and "Americanized," as they become free from the stigma of "foreigner," they develop group self-respect: the "wop" changes into a proud Italian, the "hunky" into an intensely nationalist Slav. They learn, or they recall, the spiritual heritage of their nationality. Their cultural abjectness gives way to cultural pride and the public schools, the libraries, and the clubs become beset with demands for texts in the national language and literature. . . .

What is the cultural outcome likely to be, under these conditions? Surely not the melting pot. Rather something that has become more and more distinct in the changing State and city life of the last two decades, and which is most articulate and apparent among just those peoples whom Mr. Ross praises most—the Scandinavians, the Germans, the Irish, the Jews. . . .

Immigrants appear to pass through four phases in the course of being Americanized. In the first phase they exhibit economic eagerness, the greed of the unfed. Since external differences are a handicap in the economic struggle, they "assimilate," seeking thus to facilitate the attainment of economic independence. Once the proletarian level of such independence is reached, the process of assimilation slows down and tends to come to a stop. The immigrant group is still a national group, modified, sometimes improved, by environmental influences, but otherwise a solitary spiritual unit, which is seeking to find its way out

---

[1]*Deutschthum*: "Germanness," i.e., belonging to a German ethnic enclave; *Münnerchöre*: misspelling of *Männerchor*, or a men's chorus; *Turnvereine*: gymnastic societies or groups; *Schutzenfeste*: marksmen festivals.

[2]Sociologist Edward Alsworth Ross, author of *The Old World in the New* (1914), supported immigration restriction to preserve what he believed to be America's racial purity.

on its own social level. This search brings to light permanent group distinctions, and the immigrant, like the Anglo-Saxon American, is thrown back upon himself and his ancestry. Then a process of dissimilation begins. The arts, life, and ideals of the nationality become central and paramount; ethnic and national differences change in status from disadvantages to distinctions. All the while the immigrant has been using the English language and behaving like an American in matters economic and political, and continues to do so. The institutions of the Republic have become the liberating cause and the background for the rise of the cultural consciousness and social autonomy of the immigrant Irishman, German, Scandinavian, Jew, Pole, or Bohemian. On the whole, Americanization has not repressed nationality. Americanization has liberated nationality.

Hence, what troubles Mr. Ross and so many other Anglo-Saxon Americans is not really inequality; what troubles them is *difference*. Only things that are alike in fact and not abstractly, and only men that are alike in origin and in spirit and not abstractly, can be truly "equal" and maintain that inward unanimity of action and outlook which make a national life. The writers of the Declaration of Independence and of the Constitution were not confronted by the practical fact of ethnic dissimilarity among the whites of the country. Their descendants are confronted with it. Its existence, acceptance, and development provide one of the inevitable consequences of the democratic principle on which our theory of government is based, and the result at the present writing is to many worthies very unpleasant. Democratism and the Federal principle have worked together with economic greed and ethnic snobbishness to people the land with all the nationalities of Europe, and to convert the early American nation into the present American state. For in effect we are in the process of becoming a true federal state, such a state as men hope for as the outcome of the European war, a great republic consisting of a federation or commonwealth of nationalities. . . .

What is inalienable in the life of mankind is its intrinsic positive quality — its psychophysical inheritance. Men may change their clothes, their politics, their wives, their religions, their philosophies, to a greater or lesser extent: they cannot change their grandfathers. Jews or Poles or Anglo-Saxons, would have to cease to be. The selfhood which is inalienable in them, and for the realization of which they require "inalienable" liberty, is ancestrally determined, and the happiness which they pursue has its form implied in ancestral endowment. This is what, actually, democracy in operation assumes. There are human capacities which it is the function of the state to liberate and to protect; and the failure of the state as a government means its abolition. Government, the state, under the democratic conception, is merely an instrument, not an end. That it is often an abused instrument, that it is often seized by the powers that prey, that it makes frequent mistakes and considers only secondary ends, surface needs, which vary from moment to moment, is, of course, obvious; hence our social and political chaos. But that it is an instrument, flexibly adjustable to changing life, changing opinion, and needs, our whole electoral organization and party system declare. And as intelligence and wisdom prevail over "politics" and special interests, as the steady and continuous pressure of the inalienable qualities and purposes of human groups more and more dominate the confusion of our common life, the outlines of a possible great and truly democratic commonwealth become discernible.

Its form is that of the Federal republic; its substance a democracy of nationalities, cooperating voluntarily and autonomously in the enterprise of self-realization through the perfection of men according to their kind. The common language of the commonwealth, the language of its great political tradition, is English, but each nationality expresses its emotional and voluntary life in its own language, in its own inevitable aesthetic and intellectual forms. The common life of the commonwealth is politico-economic, and serves as the foundation and background for the realization of the distinctive individuality of each *natio* that composes it. Thus "American civilization" may come to mean the perfection of the cooperative harmonies of "European civilization," the waste, the squalor, and the distress of Europe being eliminated—a multiplicity in a unity, an orchestration of mankind. As in an orchestra, every type of instrument has its specific timbre and tonality, founded in its substance and form; as every type has its appropriate theme and melody in the whole symphony, so in society each ethnic group is the natural instrument, its spirit and culture are its theme and melody, and the harmony and dissonances and discords of them all make the symphony of civilization, with this difference: a musical symphony is written before it is played; in the symphony of civilization the playing is the writing, so that there is nothing so fixed and inevitable about its progressions as in music, so that within the limits set by nature they may vary at will, and the range and variety of the harmonies may become wider and richer and more beautiful.

But the question is, do the dominant classes in America want such a society?

READING AND DISCUSSION QUESTIONS

1. Why do you think Kallen set "democracy" against "melting pot" in his title? How does he define the relationship between these ideals?

2. What sort of society does he want America to become, and how is ethnic identity a part of his vision? What metaphor does he prefer to "melting pot"?

3. What does this document reveal about the conflicts that emerged over ethnic assimilation and distinctiveness during this time? How did Kallen and others engaged in these debates envision America's national identity differently?

P7-3 | Suffragists Bring Battle to the President

Woman Suffrage in Washington, District of Columbia (c. 1917–1918)

Gender identity was at the heart of the women's rights movement. Reformers frequently based their arguments for the vote on the notion that women's gender peculiarly fitted them to contribute to public discussions. In the years leading to the ratification of the Nineteenth Amendment, the National American Woman Suffrage Association led organizing drives, protests, and parades, rallying women as "sisters in the cause" to push for voting rights, even, as shown here, staging vigils at the White House.

READING AND DISCUSSION QUESTIONS

1. What point of view concerning women's rights does this photograph reveal? Analyze the message these women are expressing. What argument are they making?

2. Who was the audience for this photograph? To what extent do you think images like this one were created to aid in the formation of gender identity among women in support of voting rights?

"Woman Suffrage in Washington, District of Columbia," Library of Congress, Prints & Photographs Division, photograph by Harris & Ewing, LC-H261-29868.

P7-4 | Conservative Minister Defines Antimodern Identity
W. B. RILEY, *The Faith of the Fundamentalists* (1927)

In the latter nineteenth century, many Christian ministers found ways to reconcile belief with Darwin's theories regarding natural selection, but in the early twentieth century divisions emerged between those who favored a more liberal reading of scripture (which made room for Darwin) and literalists who accepted the Bible as the inerrant word of God. Conservatives mobilized, embracing metaphors of battle, waging war against "modernism" and its liberal and atheistic associations. By 1920, these religious conservatives embraced the term *fundamentalists* to describe their devotion to core Christian beliefs. Riley's 1927 essay sketched out the fundamentalist identity in an increasingly liberal culture.

Fundamentalism undertakes to reaffirm the greater Christian doctrines. Mark this phrase, "the greater Christian doctrines." It does not attempt to set forth every Christian doctrine. It has never known the elaboration that characterizes the great denominational confessions. But it did lay them side by side, and, out of their extensive statements, elect nine points upon which to rest its claims to Christian attention. They were and are as follows:

1. We believe in the Scriptures of the Old and New Testaments as verbally inspired by God, and inerrant in the original writings, and that they are of supreme and final authority in faith and life.
2. We believe in one God, eternally existing in three persons, Father, Son and Holy Spirit.
3. We believe that Jesus Christ was begotten by the Holy Spirit, and born of the Virgin Mary, and is true God and true man.
4. We believe that man was created in the image of God, that he sinned and thereby incurred not only physical death, but also that spiritual death which is separation from God; and that all human beings are born with a sinful nature, and, in the case of those who reach moral responsibility, become sinners in thought, word and deed.
5. We believe that the Lord Jesus Christ died for our sins according to the Scriptures as a representative and substitutionary sacrifice; and that all that believe in Him are justified on the ground of His shed blood.
6. We believe in the resurrection of the crucified body of our Lord, in His ascension into Heaven, and in His present life there for us, as High Priest and Advocate.
7. We believe in "that blessed hope," the personal, premillennial and imminent return of our Lord and Saviour, Jesus Christ.
8. We believe that all who receive by faith the Lord Jesus Christ are born again of the Holy Spirit and thereby become children of God.
9. We believe in the bodily resurrection of the just and the unjust, the everlasting felicity of the saved and the everlasting conscious suffering of the lost.

W. B. Riley, "The Faith of the Fundamentalists," *Church History* 24 (June 1927): 434–440.

It would seem absolutely clear, therefore, that many of the liberal writers of recent years have never taken the pains to ask for the basis of our belief. Had it been so, an Old World writer could not have said of us that we held to "a flat earth," to "an immovable world," to "the circulation of the sun, moon and stars around the same every twenty-four hours," to "a canopy or roof overhead"; and some New World textbook producers would not have been willing to assail immature student minds with similar absurd sentences. This charge of ignorance in realms of science against the leaders of Fundamentalism has about as much basis of truth as had the statement from the university professor that the author of the Tennessee anti-evolution bill had, upon learning that the Bible was not made in heaven and dropped down, expressed his regret that he ever wrote or advocated the passing of the bill. Modernism when it comes to deal with the Fundamentals movement is suddenly possessed with a strange imagination. If you want to know what the movement is *not* and who its leaders are *not*, read their descriptions of both. Certainly as to what we believe, the above declaration leaves no doubt, and only the man ignorant of the Bible or utterly indifferent to its teachings, could ever call into question that these nine points constitute the greater essentials in the New Testament doctrinal system.

Fundamentalism insists upon the plain intent of Scripture-speech. The members of this movement have no sympathy whatever for that weasel method of sucking the meaning out of words and then presenting the empty shells in an attempt to palm them off as giving the Christian faith a new and another interpretation. The absurdities to which such a spiritualizing method may lead are fully revealed in the writings of Mary Baker Eddy and modernists in general. When one is permitted to discard established and scientific definitions and to create, at will, his own glossary, language fails to be longer a vehicle of thought, and inspiration itself may mean anything or nothing, according to the preference of its employer. . . .

Fundamentalism is forever the antithesis of modernist critical theology. It is made up of another and an opposing school. Modernism submits all Scripture to the judgment of man. According to its method he may reject any portion of the Book as uninspired, unprofitable, and even undesirable, and accept another portion as from God because its sentences suit him, or its teachings inspire him. Fundamentalism, on the contrary, makes the Bible "the supreme and final authority in faith and life." Its teachings determine every question upon which they have spoken with some degree of fullness, and its mandates are only disregarded by the unbelieving, the materialistic and the immoral. Fundamentalists hold that the world is illumined and the Church is instructed and even science itself is confirmed, when true, and condemned when false, by the clear teachings of the open Book, while Liberalism, as *The Nation* once said, "pretends to preach the higher criticism by interpreting the sacred writings as esoteric fables." In other words, the two have nothing in common save church membership, and all the world wonders that they do or can remain together; and the thinking world knows that but one tie holds them, and that is the billions of dollars invested.

Nine out of ten of those dollars, if not ninety-nine out of every hundred of them, spent to construct the great denominational universities, colleges, schools of second grade, theological seminaries, great denominational mission stations, the multiplied hospitals that bear denominational names, the immense publication societies and the expensive magazines, were given by Fundamentalists and filched by modernists. It took hundreds of years to collect this money and construct these institutions. It has taken only a quarter of a century for the liberal bandits to capture them, and the only fellowship that remains to bind modernists and Fundamentalists in one body, or a score of bodies, is the Irish fellowship of a free fight—Fundamentalists fighting to retain what they have founded, and modernists fighting to keep their hold on what they have filched. It is a spectacle to grieve angels and amuse devils; but we doubt not that even the devils know where justice lies, and the angels from heaven sympathize with the fight and trust that faithful men will carry on. . . .

The future of Fundamentalism is not with claims, but with conquests. Glorious as is our past, history provides only an adequate base upon which to build. Fundamentalists will never need to apologize for the part they have played in education; they have produced it; or for their relationship to colleges and universities and theological seminaries, and all forms of social service; they have created them! . . .

But even that is not enough! Now that modernism has come in to filch from us these creations of our creed, we must either wrest them from bandit hands or begin and build again. In the last few years, in fact, since the modernist-highwaymen rose up to trouble the Church and snatch its dearest treasures, it has shown itself as virile as the promise of Christ, "The gates of hell shall not prevail against it," ever indicated. Today there are one hundred schools and colleges connected with our Fundamentalist Association, some of which have escaped the covetous clutches of modernism, but most of which have been brought into being as a protest against modernism itself. Their growth has been so phenomenal as to prove that the old tree is fruitful still, and that the finest fruit is to be found upon its newest branches, orthodox churches, Fundamentalist colleges, sound Bible training schools, evangelical publication societies, multiplied Bible conferences and stanch defenders of the faith in ever increasing numbers in each denomination. . . .

Who are my brethren? Baptists? Not necessarily, and, in thousands of instances, no! My brethren are those who believe in a personal God, in an inspired Book, and in a redeeming Christ.

READING AND DISCUSSION QUESTIONS

1. Analyze Riley's essay to see how he creates a fundamentalist identity in opposition to modernism. What definition of each emerges from his discussion?

2. To what extent does Riley see fellow fundamentalists as an oppressed group? Were fundamentalists on the defensive in the early twentieth century, and if so, did their "outsider" status help them to create and maintain a distinct religious and cultural identity?

P7-5 | African American Soldier Stands Up to Racial Discrimination

Private Charles F. Wilson to Franklin D. Roosevelt (1944)

Roosevelt's presidency was significant for the political shift it produced by luring African Americans away from their traditional Republican Party loyalties. His Executive Order 8802, issued in 1941, prohibited racially discriminatory practices in the federal government and its wartime union and private-sector contractors. The military, however, remained segregated by race. For many soldiers, their identity in the armed forces was defined almost exclusively by their race. In this letter, Private Wilson, an African American airman based in Arizona, points out the paradox to President Roosevelt, reminding him of the work remaining to be done.

33rd AAF Base Unit (CCTS(H))
Section C
DAVIS-MONTHAN FIELD
Tucson, Arizona
9 May 1944.

President Franklin Delano Roosevelt
White House
Washington, D.C.

Dear President Roosevelt:

It was with extreme pride that I, a soldier in the Armed Forces of our country, read the following affirmation of our war aims, pronounced by you at a recent press conference:

"The United Nations are fighting to make a world in which tyranny, and aggression cannot exist; a world based upon freedom, equality, and justice; a world in which all persons, regardless of race, color and creed, may live in peace, honor and dignity."

Your use of the word "world" means that we are fighting for "freedom, equality, and justice" for "all persons, regardless of race, color and creed" in our own part of the world, the United States of America, as well as all other countries where such a fight is needed to be carried through. Your use of the words "all persons, regardless of race, color and creed" means that we are fighting for "freedom, equality, and justice" for our Negro American, no less than for our white Americans, or our Jewish, Protestant and Catholic Americans, or for the subjugated peoples in Europe and China and all other lands.

And the part that our country is playing in the United Nations world struggle against "tyranny and aggression" and for "a world based upon freedom, equality

Phillip McGuire, ed., *Taps for a Jim Crow Army: Letters from Black Soldiers in World War II* (Lexington: University Press of Kentucky, 1993), 134–139.

and justice," although lacking in many respects, is certainly not one to be ashamed of.

Our driving back of the Japanese fascists in the Pacific; our driving back of the German fascists in North Africa, Sicily, and Italy, in conjunction with our British and French Allies, freeing that part of the world from "tyranny and aggression" as the prerequisite for bringing "freedom, equality and justice" to the North African and Italian peoples; the tremendous preparations and planning that we as part of the United Nations have carried out so that we now stand on the eve of the invasion, and in conjunction with our Allies, the British, Russian, French and European Underground, on the eve of freeing the subjugated peoples of Europe from the German fascist tyranny; the glorious part that we played in the decisions reached at Teheran; these are vivid records of the manner in which the war aims of the United Nations, as pronounced by you, are being fought for by us, throughout the world.

On the home front there are vivid examples also; your issuance of Executive Order 8802, which established the Fair Employment Practices Committee, to fight against the discriminatory employment practices being used against Negroes and other minority groups in the war industries; the precedent-smashing decision of the United States Supreme Court, upholding the right of Negroes to vote in the Texas Democratic Primaries; the April 10th decision of the United States Supreme Court, against peonage, which voided a Florida statute which makes it a crime to obtain a wage advance with intent to defraud an employer. The court held that the statute was a violation of the 13th Amendment and the Federal Antipeonage Act; Attorney General Biddle's clearing of the CIO Political Action Committee, against the attempts on the part of Representative Smith of Virginia to destroy it; the establishment on the part of our government of mixed housing projects like the Mother Cabrini housing Project in Chicago, where segregation because of "race, color and creed" was done away with; the cleansing of our home front of the out and out fascists . . . , who are being brought to trial by our Justice Department; the support which you have given to the fight against the flagrantly undemocratic poll tax as reported in the Afro-American of April the 8th: "President Roosevelt told his press conference last week that he feels the poll tax is undemocratic."; the production by the U.S. Army Signal Corps, as authorized by the War Department, of the film "The Negro Soldier"; these are but a few of the many examples of the fight that the democratic forces in our government, with your leadership, is carrying on in our country as part of the world struggle against "tyranny" and for a "world based upon freedom, equality, and justice; a world in which all persons, regardless of race, color and creed, may live in peace, honor and dignity."

But the picture in our country is marred by one of the strangest paradoxes in our whole fight against world fascism. The United States Armed Forces, to fight for World Democracy, is within itself undemocratic. The undemocratic policy of jim crow and segregation is practiced by our Armed Forces against its Negro members. Totally inadequate opportunities are given to the Negro members of our Armed Forces, nearly one tenth of the whole, to participate with "equality" . . .

"regardless of race and color" in the fight for our war aims. In fact it appears that the army intends to follow the very policy that the FEPC is battling against in civilian life, the pattern of assigning Negroes to the lowest types of work.

Let me give you an example of the lack of democracy in our Field, where I am now stationed. Negro soldiers are completely segregated from the white soldiers on the base. And to make doubly sure that no mistake is made about this, the barracks and other housing facilities (supply room, mess hall, etc.) of the Negro Section C are covered with black tar paper, while all other barracks and housing facilities on the base are painted white.

It is the stated policy of the Second Air Force that "every potential fighting man must be used as a fighting man. If you have such a man in a base job, you have no choice. His job must be eliminated or be filled by a limited service man, WAC, or civilian." And yet, leaving out the Negro soldiers working with the Medical Section, fully 50% of the Negro soldiers are working in base jobs, such as, for example, at the Resident Officers' Mess, Bachelor Officers' Quarters, and Officers' Club, as mess personnel, BOQ orderlies, and bar tenders. Leaving out the medical men again, based on the Section C average only 4% of this 50% would not be "potential fighting men."

It is also a fact that ". . . the employment of enlisted men as attendants at officers' clubs, whether officially designated as "Officers' Mess" or "Officers' Club" is not sanctioned by . . ." the Headquarters of the Army Air Forces.

Leaving out the medical men again, at least 50% of the members of the Negro Section C are being used for decidedly menial work, such as BOQ orderlies, janitors, permanent KP's and the like.

Let us assume as a basis for discussion that there are no civilians or limited service men to do the menial work on the base. The democratic way, based upon "equality and justice" would be to assign this work to both Negro and white. Instead the discriminatory and undemocratic method is used whereby all of this work is assigned to the Negro soldiers.

On the other hand suppose civilians were found to take over all of the base jobs and thus free the Negro soldiers for use as fighting men. They would not be given "on-the-job-training" to become members of the ground crew, such as is being done for the WAC members on the base, because there is no such program for Negroes at Davis-Monthan Field. They would not be trained to become aerial gunners, or bombardiers, or navigators, or pilots, or bombsight mechanics, or any of the many other specialists at Davis-Monthan Field, because there is no authorization in the Second Air Force for this training to be given to Negroes.

About 15% of the soldiers of Section C are in fighting jobs, and about another 5% are receiving "on-the-job-training" in Vehicle Maintenance. Thus we see that the maintenance of the ideology of "white supremacy" resulting in the undemocratic practices of jim crow and segregation of the Negro members of the Armed Forces brings about the condition on Davis-Monthan Field whereby 80% of the whole Section is removed from the fighting activities on the base.

From what I read in the Newspapers, the above example from my own experience at Davis-Monthan Field, is typical of the situation throughout the Armed Forces. There is the report in an editorial on page five of the March 25th edition of the Pittsburgh Courier which states that: "Negro combat units are being constantly broken up and transferred to service units."

How can we convince nearly one tenth of the Armed Forces, the Negro members, that your pronouncement of the war aims of the United Nations means what it says, when their experience with one of the United Nations, the United States of America, is just the opposite?

Are the Chinese people to believe that we are fighting to bring them "freedom, equality, and justice," when they can see that in our Armed Forces we are not even practicing ourselves what we are preaching?

However, we leave ourselves wide open for sowers of disunity. Nothing would suit Hitler, Tojo, and our native fascists better, than disunity. The lead editorial in the Afro-American of April the 1st entitled "Soldiers or Sissies" is a tragic example of this. The editorial after relating two cases of *tyranny* against two Negro soldiers: one in Alabama where the "civil police lynched a hand-cuffed, defenseless soldier when they were moving from one prison to another," and another case in Louisiana, where a "Bus driver shot and killed a New York [soldier] who refused to move to a rear seat," goes on to say: "This is terrorism, and the army has no answer for it. Have the soldiers themselves an answer? There are thousands of them and only a few police or bus drivers." If the advice of that editorial were followed it could only lead to disunity and civil strife. We know that isn't the answer. Disunity and civil strife would only weaken our fight against the German and Japanese fascists, or more than that result in our defeat. A victory for the German and Japanese fascists would mean a victory for our native fascists, who are at the bottom [of] this whole program of "white supremacy," race hatred, jim-crowism, and segregation. It would mean victory, not defeat for the Rankins, Bilbos, Smiths, Hearsts, McCormicks, Paglers, and Dies.[1]

Such an editorial is totally irresponsible. But decrying such an editorial will get us nowhere. The only answer is to remove the conditions which give rise to such an editorial. That means fighting for the war aims of the United Nations in our own country as well as throughout the rest of the world. That means that we must fight against the fascist shouters of "white supremacy," against the labor baiters, against segregation and jim-crowism, wherever these evils show their fangs, whether in the Armed Forces, or in the civilian population.

The Public Affairs Pamphlet "The Races of Mankind" by Ruth Benedict and Gene Weltfish, as well as many other scientific writings have exploded the antidemocratic doctrine of "race-superiority" or "white supremacy."

The achievements of heroes like Dorie Miller; the record of the 99th Pursuit Squadron in Italy; the records of the 24th Infantry and 93rd Infantry in Bougainfille,[2] disprove Secretary of War Stimson's statement in a recent letter: "Negro units . . . have been unable to master efficiently the technique of modern weapons."

---

[1]**Rankins . . . Dies**: Public figures, including members of Congress, whom Wilson singles out for what he considers their extreme conservative, anti–civil rights views.

[2]**Bougainfille**: Wilson meant Bougainville, a South Pacific island occupied during the war by Japanese forces. The all African American 93rd Infantry Division saw combat at Bougainville in March 1944.

The experience in training negro and white, on a mixed basis, in the Officers' Candidate Schools, and the Army Technical Training Schools, is proof enough, if proof is needed, that there is no justification for the present policy of jim-crow and segregation in the Armed Forces. The Navy can look to the Merchant Marine for an example of democracy in action, in which the crews are organized on a mixed basis, with Negroes and whites from North and South eating and sleeping, working and fighting together.

Just as our government in civilian life, is carrying on a fight for the full integration of the Negro and all other minority groups into the war effort, with the result that Negro men and women are producing the implements of war, in jobs from the unskilled to the most highly skilled, side by side with their white brothers and sisters, so in the Armed Forces our government must take up the same fight for the full integration of the Negro into all phases of our fighting forces from the lowest to the highest.

President Roosevelt, in the interest of the war effort you issued Executive Order 8802, which established the Fair Employment Practices Committee. Although there is still much to be done, nevertheless this committee, against heavy opposition, has played, and is playing a gallant role in fighting for democracy for the men and women behind the lines, in the industries that produce the guns, and tanks, and bombers for victory over world fascism.

With your issuance of Executive Order 8802, and the setting up of the Fair Employment Practices Committee, you established the foundation for fighting for democracy in the industrial forces of our country, in the interest of victory for the United Nations. In the interest of victory for the United Nations, another Executive Order is now needed. An Executive Order which will lay the base for fighting for democracy in the Armed Forces of our country. An Executive Order which would bring about the result here at Davis-Monthan Field whereby the Negro soldiers would be integrated into all of the Sections on the base, as fighting men, instead of in the segregated Section C as housekeepers.

Then and only then can your pronouncement of the war aims of the United Nations mean to *all* that we "are fighting to make a world in which tyranny, and aggression cannot exist; a world based upon freedom, equality and justice; a world in which all persons, regardless of race, color and creed, may live in peace, honor and dignity."

Respectfully yours,
Charles F. Wilson, 36794590
Private, Air Corps.

READING AND DISCUSSION QUESTIONS

1. To what extent did African American experiences during World War II, as described here, focus attention on public discussions regarding American national identity?

2. How does Private Wilson frame the paradox of race and democracy as he experienced it? From his perspective, how did America's involvement in international crises like World War II affect debates over national identity?

3. How important was World War II in the formation of Wilson's identity as both an American and an African American? Were these identities for him overlapping, distinct, or contradictory?

P7-6 | Labor Organizer Describes Latino Plight in America
LUISA MORENO, *Caravans of Sorrow* (1940)

The crisis of the Great Depression impacted the Latino population of the American Southwest, magnifying their economic vulnerabilities and exacerbating ethnic discrimination. In response, labor and civil rights activists rallied, creating an infrastructure of advocacy to affirm Latino rights and identity. Guatemalan immigrant Luisa Moreno emerged as a leader of these efforts, organizing the Spanish-Speaking Peoples' Congress in 1939. In her statement before the American Committee for the Protection of the Foreign Born in 1940, which came to be known as the "Caravans of Sorrow" speech, she raised awareness of the discrimination facing Spanish-speaking people and demanded equal justice for them.

One hears much today about hemisphere unity. The press sends special correspondents to Latin America, South of the Border songs are wailed by the radio, educational institutions and literary circles speak the language of cultural cooperation, and, what is more important, labor unions are seeking the road of closer ties with the Latin American working people.

The stage is set. A curtain rises. May we ask you to see behind the scenery and visualize a forgotten character in this great theater of the Americas?

Long before the "grapes of wrath" had ripened in California's vineyards a people lived on highways, under trees or tents, in shacks or railroad sections, picking crops—cotton, fruits, vegetables—cultivating sugar beets, building railroads and dams, making a barren land fertile for new crops and greater riches.

The ancestors of some of these migrant and resident workers, whose home is this Southwest, were America's first settlers in New Mexico, Texas, and California, and the greater percentage was brought from Mexico by the fruit exchanges, railroad companies, and cotton interests in great need of underpaid labor during the early postwar period. They are the Spanish-speaking workers of the Southwest, citizens and noncitizens working and living under identical conditions, facing hardships and miseries while producing and building for agriculture and industry.

Their story lies unpublicized in university libraries, files of government, welfare and social agencies—a story grimly titled the "Caravans of Sorrow."

And when in 1930 unemployment brought a still greater flood of human distress, trainloads of Mexican families with children born and raised in this country departed voluntarily or were brutally deported. As a result of the repatriation drive of 1933, thousands of American-born youths returned to their homeland,

Luisa Moreno, "Caravans of Sorrow," in *Between Two Worlds: Mexican Immigrants in the United States*, ed. David G. Gutierrez (Wilmington, DE: Scholarly Resources Inc., 1996), 120–123.

the United States, to live on streets and highways, drifting unattached fragments of humanity. Let the annals of juvenile delinquency in Los Angeles show you the consequences.

Today the Latin Americans of the United States are seriously alarmed by the "antialien" drive fostered by certain un-American elements; for them, the Palmer days[1] . . . have never ended. In recent years while deportations in general have decreased, the number of persons deported to Mexico has constantly increased. During the period of 1933 to 1937, of a total of 55,087 deported, 25,135 were deportations of Mexicans. This is 45.5 percent of the total and does not include an almost equal number of so-called voluntary departures.

Commenting on these figures, the American Committee for Protection of Foreign Born wrote to the Spanish-Speaking Peoples' Congress in 1939: "One conclusion can be drawn, and that is, where there is such a highly organized set-up as to effect deportations of so many thousands, this set-up must be surrounded with a complete system of intimidation and discrimination of that section of the population victimized by the deportation drive."

Confirming the fact of a system of extensive discrimination are university studies by . . . many other professors and social workers of the Southwest. Let me state the simple truth. The majority of the Spanish-speaking peoples of the United States are victims of a setup for discrimination, be they descendants of the first white settlers in America or noncitizens.

I will not go into the reasons for this undemocratic practice, but may we state categorically that it is the main reason for the reluctance of Mexicans and Latin Americans in general to become naturalized. For you must know, discrimination takes very definite forms in unequal wages, unequal opportunities, unequal schooling, and even through a denial of the use of public places in certain towns in Texas, California, Colorado, and other Southwestern states.

Only some 5 or 6 percent of Latin American immigrants have become naturalized. A number of years ago it was stated that in a California community with fifty thousand Mexicans only two hundred had become citizens. An average of one hundred Mexicans out of close to a million become citizens every year. These percentages have increased lately.

Another important factor concerning naturalization is the lack of documentary proof of entry, because entry was not recorded or because the immigrants were brought over en masse by large interests handling transportation from Mexico in their own peculiar way.

Arriving at logical conclusions, the Latin American noncitizens, rooted in this country, are increasingly seeing the importance and need for naturalization. But how will the thousands of migrants establish residence? What possibility have these people had, segregated in "Little Mexicos," to learn English and meet educational requirements? How can they, receiving hunger wages while

---

[1]**Palmer days**: Reference to the series of raids resulting in the deportation of foreign-born radicals conducted by Attorney General A. Mitchell Palmer from November 1919 to January 1920.

enriching the stockholders of the Great Western Sugar Company, the Bank of America, and other large interests, pay high naturalization fees? A Mexican family living on relief in Colorado would have to stop eating for two and a half months to pay for the citizenship papers of one member of the family. Is this humanly possible?

But why have "aliens" on relief while the taxpayers "bleed"? Let me ask those who would raise such a question: what would the Imperial Valley, the Rio Grande Valley, and other rich irrigated valleys in the Southwest be without the arduous, self-sacrificing labor of these noncitizen Americans? Read *Factories in the Fields*, by Carey McWilliams to obtain a picture of how important Mexican labor has been for the development of California's crop after the world war. Has anyone counted the miles of railroads built by these same noncitizens? One can hardly imagine how many bales of cotton have passed through the nimble fingers of Mexican men, women, and children. And what conditions have they had to endure to pick that cotton? Once, while holding a conference for a trade union paper in San Antonio, a cotton picker told me how necessary a Spanish paper was to inform the Spanish-speaking workers that FSA camps were to be established, for she remembered so many nights, under the trees in the rain, when she and her husband held gunny sacks over the shivering bodies of their sleeping children—young Americans. I've heard workers say that they left their shacks under heavy rains to find shelter under trees. You can well imagine in what condition those shacks were.

These people are not aliens. They have contributed their endurance, sacrifices, youth, and labor to the Southwest. Indirectly, they have paid more taxes than all the stockholders of California's industrialized agriculture, the sugar beet companies and the large cotton interests that operate or have operated with the labor of Mexican workers.

Surely the sugar beet growers have not been asked if they want to dispense with the skilled labor cultivating and harvesting their crops season after season. It is only the large interests, their stooges, and some badly misinformed people who claim that Mexicans are no longer wanted.

And let us assume that 1.4 million men, women, and children were no longer wanted, what could be done that would be different from the anti-Semitic persecutions in Europe? A people who have lived twenty and thirty years in this country, tied up by family relations with the early settlers, with American-born children, cannot be uprooted without the complete destruction of the faintest semblance of democracy and human liberties for the whole population.

Some speak of repatriation. Naturally there is interest in repatriation among thousands of Mexican families in Texas and, to a lesser degree, in other states. Organized repatriation has been going on, and the net results in one year [have] been the establishment of the Colonia "18 de Marzo" in Tamaulipas, Mexico, for two thousand families. There are 1.4 million Mexicans in the United States according to general estimates, probably including a portion of the first generation. Is it possible to move those many people at the present rate, when many of them do not want to be repatriated?

What then may the answer to this specific noncitizen problem be? The Spanish-Speaking Peoples' Congress of the United States proposes legislation that would encourage naturalization of Latin American, West Indian, and Canadian residents of the United States and that would nurture greater friendships among the peoples of the Western Hemisphere.

The question of hemispheric unity will remain an empty phrase while this problem at home remains ignored and is aggravated by the fierce "antialien" drive.

Legislation to facilitate citizenship to all natural-born citizens from the countries of the Western Hemisphere, waiving excessive fees and educational and other requirements of a technical nature, is urgently needed.

A piece of legislation embodying this provision is timely and important. Undoubtedly it would rally the support of the many friends of true hemispheric unity.

You have seen the forgotten character in the present American scene—a scene of the Americas. Let me say that, in the face of greater hardships, the "Caravans of Sorrow" are becoming the "Caravans of Hope." They are organizing in trade unions with other workers in agriculture and industry. The unity of Spanish-speaking citizens and noncitizens is being furthered through the Spanish-Speaking Peoples' Congress of the United States, an organization embracing trade unions and fraternal, civic, and cultural organizations, mainly in California. The purpose of this movement is to seek an improvement of social, economic, and cultural conditions, and for the integration of Spanish-speaking citizens and noncitizens into the American nation. The United Cannery, Agricultural, Packing, and Allied Workers of America, with thousands of Spanish-speaking workers in its membership, and Liga Obrera of New Mexico, were the initiators of the Congress.

This Congress stands with all progressive forces against the badly labeled "antialien" legislation and asks the support of this Conference for democratic legislation to facilitate and encourage naturalization. We hope that this Conference will serve to express the sentiment of the people of this country in condemnation of undemocratic discrimination practiced against any person of foreign birth and that it will rally the American people, native and foreign born, for the defeat of un-American proposals. The Spanish-speaking peoples in the United States extend their fullest support and cooperation to your efforts.

READING AND DISCUSSION QUESTIONS

1. What role did the Great Depression play in shaping public debates regarding American national identity as they related to minority groups like Latinos? How did the economic crisis focus these debates?

2. Examine how ethnicity, class, and gender intersected in the civil rights advocacy Moreno pushed for Latinos in America. How did the work of activists like Moreno help to shape or change ideas about American national identity?

■ COMPARATIVE QUESTIONS ■

1. How did Moreno's civil rights activism on behalf of Latinos compare with similar efforts promoting the interests of minority groups in America? What similarities or differences can you see?

2. Compare the suffrage photograph (Document P7-3) with Carrie Chapman Catt's 1918 statement (Document 22-2) and Mary Brown Sumner's article (Document 19-5). How do they illuminate the role that gender played in shaping women's response to their political and social marginalization?

3. What do the documents in this set reveal about the ways that American identity has been debated by various groups in the decades between the Civil War and World War II? How have these debates related to economic, social, and cultural transformations that have occurred in society?

4. How does the historian assess the significance of factors such as race, class, gender, and religion in shaping individual and group identities?

5. To what extent are issues of identity central to the American experience? How much are the debates raised in these sources continuing concerns for Americans?

25

Cold War America
1945–1963

Despite the alliance between the United States and the Soviet Union during World War II, a "cold war" of words and ideas rapidly emerged in the immediate wake of that global conflict. Beginning with the Truman administration, American policymakers increasingly viewed the Soviet Union as a hostile force committed to the worldwide expansion of its anticapitalist and atheistic, communist ideology. How best to counter Soviet aggression became the leading policy debate in the first decades of the Cold War. The urgency of addressing the Soviet menace led to the creation of the national security state, the infrastructure within the federal government created to gather information about Soviet intentions worldwide and to orchestrate the American response. Fears of communist infiltration of the federal government by spies and "fellow travelers," those sympathetic to the communist cause, resulted in a new Red Scare led by Senator Joseph McCarthy, whose investigations into alleged communist activity brought him both enormous popularity and eventual scorn and disgrace. Though the McCarthy persecutions petered out in the mid-1950s, Cold War anxieties persisted, shaping a culture shadowed by the fear of a nuclear cloud mushrooming over the liberty skies of America.

25-1 | Containing the Communist Threat

GEORGE KENNAN, *"Long Telegram" to James Byrnes* (1946)

American diplomat George Kennan was stationed in Moscow in the mid-1940s when he sent a "long telegram" to his superior in Washington, James Byrnes, President Truman's secretary of state. Subsequently published as "The Sources of Soviet Conduct" in the influential policy magazine *Foreign Affairs* under the signature X, the telegram outlined Kennan's views on the Soviet Union. To counter Soviet aggression, he called for a policy of containing the communist threat, a policy soon formulated as the Truman Doctrine, the central foreign policy strategy of the Truman administration.

We have here a political force committed fanatically to the belief that with US there can be no permanent modus vivendi,[1] that it is desirable and necessary that the internal harmony of our society be disrupted, our traditional way of life be destroyed, the international authority of our state be broken, if Soviet power is to be secure. This political force has complete power of disposition over energies of one of world's greatest peoples and resources of world's richest national territory, and is borne along by deep and powerful currents of Russian nationalism. In addition, it has an elaborate and far flung apparatus for exertion of its influence in other countries, an apparatus of amazing flexibility and versatility, managed by people whose experience and skill in underground methods are presumably without parallel in history. Finally, it is seemingly inaccessible to considerations of reality in its basic reactions. For it, the vast fund of objective fact about human society is not, as with us, the measure against which outlook is constantly being tested and re-formed, but a grab bag from which individual items are selected arbitrarily and tendenciously to bolster an outlook already preconceived. This is admittedly not a pleasant picture. Problem of how to cope with this force is undoubtedly greatest task our diplomacy has ever faced and probably greatest it will ever have to face. It should be point of departure from which our political general staff work at present juncture should proceed. It should be approached with same thoroughness and care as solution of major strategic problem in war, and if necessary, with no smaller outlay in planning effort. I cannot attempt to suggest all answers here. But I would like to record my conviction that problem is within our power to solve—and that without recourse to any general military conflict. And in support of this conviction there are certain observations of a more encouraging nature I should like to make:

(One) Soviet power, unlike that of Hitlerite Germany, is neither schematic nor adventuristic. It does not work by fixed plans. It does not take unnecessary

---

Telegram from George Kennan, *Charge d'Affaires* at United States Embassy in Moscow to the Secretary of State: The Long Telegram, February 22, 1946, Record Group 59: General Records of the Department of State, 1763-2002, ARC Identifier 2642322, National Archives.

[1]**modus vivendi**: Latin, meaning a way of living together despite differences.

risks. Impervious to logic of reason, and it is highly sensitive to logic of force. For this reason it can easily withdraw—and usually does—when strong resistance is encountered at any point. . . . Thus, if the adversary has sufficient force and makes clear his readiness to use it, he rarely has to do so. If situations are properly handled there need be no prestige engaging showdowns.

(Two) Gauged against western world as a whole, Soviets are still by far the weaker force. Thus, their success will really depend on degree of cohesion, firmness and vigor which western world can muster. And this is factor which it is within our power to influence.

(Three) Success of Soviet system, as form of internal power, is not yet finally proven. . . . In Russia, party has now become a great and—for the moment—highly successful apparatus of dictatorial administration, but it has ceased to be a source of emotional inspiration. Thus, internal soundness and permanence of movement need not yet be regarded as assured.

(Four) All Soviet propaganda beyond Soviet security sphere is basically negative and destructive. It should therefore be relatively easy to combat it by any intelligent and really constructive program.

For these reasons I think we may approach calmly and with good heart problem of how to deal with Russia. As to how this approach should be made, I only wish to advance, by way of conclusion, following comments:

(One) Our first step must be to apprehend, and recognize for what it is, the nature of the movement with which we are dealing. We must study it with same courage, detachment, objectivity, and same determination not to be emotionally provoked or unseated by it, with which doctor studies unruly and unreasonable individual.

(Two) We must see that our public is educated to realities of Russian situation. . . . I am convinced that there would be far less hysterical anti-Sovietism in our country today if realities of this situation were better understood by our people. There is nothing as dangerous or as terrifying as the unknown. It may also be argued that to reveal more information on our difficulties with Russia would reflect unfavorably on Russian American relations. I feel that if there is any real risk here involved, it is one which we should have courage to face, and sooner the better. But I cannot see what we would be risking. Our stake in this country, even coming on heels of tremendous demonstrations of our friendship for Russian people, is remarkably small. We have here no investments to guard, no actual trade to lose, virtually no citizens to protect, few cultural contacts to preserve. Our only stake lies in what we hope rather than what we have; and I am convinced we have better chance of realizing those hopes if our public is enlightened. . . .

World communism is like malignant parasite which feeds only on diseased tissue. This is point at which domestic and foreign policies meet. Every courageous and incisive measure to solve internal problems of our own society . . . is a diplomatic victory over Moscow worth a thousand diplomatic notes and joint communiques. If we cannot abandon fatalism and indifference in face of deficiencies of our own society, Moscow will profit—Moscow cannot help profiting by them in its foreign policies.

READING AND DISCUSSION QUESTIONS

1. What conclusions can you draw about Kennan's assessment of the Soviet threat to American interests around the world? What can you infer about his opinion of this larger threat, based on his description of the factors motivating Soviet aggression?

2. What advice does Kennan offer his superiors in the State Department about thwarting the Soviet threat? Why does he think his policy would be an effective counter to Soviet intentions?

3. How does Kennan's telegram help you to understand the broader context of the Cold War in the 1940s? To what extent might his telegram be seen as the start of the Cold War?

25-2 | Challenging Truman's Containment Policy

WALTER LIPPMANN, *Cold War: A Study in U.S. Foreign Policy* (1947)

Few journalists have led as influential a life as Walter Lippmann. His work was highly regarded and brought him into the personal orbit of every president from Woodrow Wilson to Lyndon Johnson. As a foreign policy intellectual, Lippmann offered a powerful counter to Truman's containment strategy by questioning Mr. X's (George Kennan) assumptions about Soviet ambitions.

[M]y criticism of the policy of containment, or the so-called Truman Doctrine, does not spring from any hope or belief that the Soviet pressure to expand can be "charmed or talked out of existence." I agree entirely with Mr. X that we must make up our minds that the Soviet power is not amenable to our arguments, but only "to contrary force" that "is felt to be too strong, and thus more rational in the logic and rhetoric of power."

My objection, then, to the policy of containment is not that it seeks to confront the Soviet power with American power, but that the policy is misconceived, and must result in a misuse of American power. For as I have sought to show, it commits this country to a struggle which has for its objective nothing more substantial than the hope that in ten or fifteen years the Soviet power will, as the result of long frustration, "break up" or "mellow." In this prolonged struggle the role of the United States is, according to Mr. X, to react "at a series of constantly shifting geographical and political points" to the encroachments of the Soviet power.

The policy, therefore, concedes to the Kremlin the strategical initiative as to when, where and under what local circumstances the issue is to be joined. It compels the United States to meet the Soviet pressure at these shifting geographical

Walter Lippmann, *The Cold War: A Study in U.S. Foreign Policy* (New York: Harper, 1947), 29–31, 35, 43–45.

and political points by using satellite states, puppet governments and agents which have been subsidized and supported, though their effectiveness is meager and their reliability uncertain. By forcing us to expend our energies and our substance upon these dubious and unnatural allies on the perimeter of the Soviet Union, the effect of the policy is to neglect our natural allies in the Atlantic community, and to alienate them.

They are alienated also by the fact that they do not wish to become, like the nations of the perimeter, the clients of the United States in whose affairs we intervene, asking as the price of our support that they take the directives of their own policy from Washington. They are alienated above all by the prospect of war, which could break out by design or accident, by miscalculation or provocation, if at any of these constantly shifting geographical and political points the Russians or Americans became so deeply engaged that no retreat or compromise was possible. In this war their lands would be the battlefield. Their peoples would be divided by civil conflict. Their cities and their fields would be the bases and the bridgeheads in a total war which, because it would merge into a general civil war, would be as indecisive as it was savage.

We may now ask why the official diagnosis of Soviet conduct, as disclosed by Mr. X's article, has led to such an unworkable policy for dealing with Russia. It is, I believe because Mr. X has neglected even to mention the fact that the Soviet Union is the successor of the Russian Empire and that Stalin is not only the heir of Marx and of Lenin but of Peter the Great, and the Czars of all the Russians.

For reasons which I do not understand, Mr. X decided not to consider the men in the Kremlin as the rulers of the Russian State and Empire, and has limited his analysis to the interaction of "two forces": "the ideology inherited by the present Soviet leaders from the movement in which they had their political origin" and the "circumstances of the power which they have now exercised for nearly three decades in Russia."

Thus he dwells on the indubitable fact that they believe in the Marxian ideology and that "they have continued to be predominantly absorbed with the struggle to secure and make absolute the power which they seized in November 1917." But with these two observations alone he cannot, and does not, explain the conduct of the Soviet government in this postwar era — that is to say its aims and claims to territory and to the sphere of influence which it dominates. The Soviet government has been run by Marxian revolutionists for thirty years; what has to be explained by a planner of American foreign policy is why in 1945 the Soviet government expanded its frontiers and its orbit, and what was the plan and pattern of its expansion. That can be done only by remembering that the Soviet government is a Russian government and that this Russian government has emerged victorious over Germany and Japan.

Having omitted from his analysis the fact that we are dealing with a victorious Russia — having become exclusively preoccupied with the Marxian ideology, and with the communist revolution — it is no wonder that the outcome of Mr. X's analysis is nothing more definite, concrete and practical than that the Soviets will encroach and expand "at a series of constantly shifting geographical and political points." Mr. X's picture of the Soviet conduct has no pattern. It is amorphous. That is why his conclusions about how we should deal with the Soviets have no pattern, and are also amorphous. . . .

I am contending that the American diplomatic effort should be concentrated on the problem created by the armistice—which is on how the continent of Europe can be evacuated by the three non-European armies which are now inside Europe. This is the problem which will have to be solved if the independence of the European nations is to be restored. Without that there is no possibility of a tolerable peace. But if these armies withdraw, there will be a very different balance of power in the world than there is today, and one which cannot easily be upset. For the nations of Europe, separately and in groups, perhaps even in unity, will then, and then only, cease to be the stakes and the pawns of the Russian-American conflict. . . .

It would be a strategic change in the balance of power. For once the Red Army had been withdrawn behind the frontiers of the Soviet Union, it could not re-enter Europe without commit[t]ing an obvious act of military aggression, which would precipitate a general war. The pressure of the Soviets upon Europe by propaganda and infiltration would continue, but that pressure would no longer be backed up by overwhelming military power throughout eastern Europe and by the threat of military intervention in western Europe. . . .

If the Kremlin really means to dominate Europe, it will not withdraw its armies which are halfway across Europe. Standing on the Elbe line in the middle of Europe and Austria, and on the vulnerable frontier of Italy, the Kremlin is in a far better position to advance farther west than it can be if it withdraws and stands on its own frontiers. The withdrawal of the army is, therefore, the acid test of Soviet conduct and purpose, incomparably clearer, more definite, more practical than whether or not they observe the Yalta Declaration in countries liberated from the Nazis but still occupied by the Red Army. . . .

Instead of seeking "to contain" the Soviet Union all over the Eurasian continent, we shall have the initiative and a definite and concrete objective; at the best we shall know the terms on which the main conflict can be settled; at the worst the Soviet Union will have shown its hand on an issue—the liberation of Europe from non-European armies—where there will be no doubt whatever that our cause is just, and that we are the champions of freedom, and that the great masses of the people of Europe will be with us because we stand for the very thing which only traitors can oppose.

We shall have written off the liabilities of the Truman Doctrine which must in practice mean inexorably an unending intervention in all the countries that are supposed to "contain" the Soviet Union. We shall be acting once more in the great American tradition which is to foster the independence of other countries, not to use other countries as the satellites of our own power, however beneficent, and as the instruments of our own policy, however well meant. Our aim will not be to organize an ideological crusade. It will not be to make Jeffersonian democrats out of the peasants of eastern Europe, the tribal chieftains, the feudal lords, the pashas, and the warlords of the Middle East and Asia, but to settle the war and to restore the independence of the nations of Europe by removing the alien armies—all of them, our own included.

We shall have a diplomatic policy that it would be exceedingly difficult for the cleverest propagandist to misrepresent. For everyone can understand such a policy. Practically everyone will wish us to succeed in it. For alien armies are hateful, however well behaved, just because they represent an alien power and are, therefore, a perpetual reminder that the people on whom they are quartered are not masters of their own destiny.

Alien armies are, however, never well behaved: invariably they become corrupted. Thus we may count confidently upon a mounting popular support if we make it our mission to emancipate the ancient and proud continent of Europe from the military control of non-European powers. We shall be drawing upon the elemental and unifying passion of patriotism in Europe which, when it is aroused, is a much stronger passion than factionalism or any ideology.

READING AND DISCUSSION QUESTIONS

1. How does Lippmann's perspective on the Soviet Union compare to Mr. X's assessment? What factors does Lippmann say Mr. X missed in his diagnosis of Soviet ambition?

2. Lippmann says "containment" was based on Mr. X's faulty assumptions; beyond that, what doesn't he like about the containment strategy? What alternative focus of American foreign policy does he advocate in its place?

25-3 | Debating the Homosexual Risk to National Security

U.S. SENATE, *Employment of Homosexuals and Other Sex Perverts in Government* (1950)

The rise of the national security state helped figures like Senator Joseph McCarthy gain traction with his accusations that the federal government was infiltrated by subversive elements who intended to undermine the nation from within. In addition to communists, whose assumed affinity for the Soviet Union made them an obvious target, homosexual men were also singled out as deviants and threats. This 1950 federal government report defines the dangers that some senators believed homosexuals posed to national security.

Those charged with the responsibility of operating the agencies of Government must insist that Government employees meet acceptable standards of personal conduct. In the opinion of this subcommittee homosexuals and other sex perverts are not proper persons to be employed in Government for two reasons; first, they are generally unsuitable, and second, they constitute security risks.

"Employment of Homosexuals and Other Sex Perverts in Government," U.S. Senate, 81st Congress, 2d sess., Document No. 241 (Washington, DC: Government Printing Office, 1950), 3–6, 19–20.

GENERAL UNSUITABILITY OF SEX PERVERTS

Overt acts of sex perversion, including acts of homosexuality, constitute a crime under our Federal, State, and municipal statutes and persons who commit such acts are law violators. Aside from the criminality and immorality involved in sex perversion such behavior is so contrary to the normal accepted standards of social behavior that persons who engage in such activity are looked upon as outcasts by society generally. The social stigma attached to sex perversion is so great that many perverts go to great lengths to conceal their perverted tendencies. This situation is evidenced by the fact that perverts are frequently victimized by blackmailers who threaten to expose their sexual deviations.

Law enforcement officers have informed the subcommittee that there are gangs of blackmailers who make a regular practice of preying upon the homosexual. The modus operandi in these homosexual blackmail cases usually follow the same general pattern. The victim, who is a homosexual, has managed to conceal his perverted activities and usually enjoys a good reputation in his community. The blackmailers, by one means or another, discover that the victim is addicted to homosexuality and under the threat of disclosure they extort money from him. . . . Many cases have come to the attention of the police where highly respected individuals have paid out substantial sums of money to blackmailers over a long period of time rather than risk the disclosure of their homosexual activities. The police believe that this type of blackmail racket is much more extensive than is generally known, because they have found that most of the victims are very hesitant to bring the matter to the attention of the authorities.

In further considering the general suitability of perverts as Government employees, it is generally believed that those who engage in overt acts of perversion lack the emotional stability of normal persons. In addition there is an abundance of evidence to sustain the conclusion that indulgence in acts of sex perversion weakens the moral fiber of an individual to a degree that he is not suitable for a position of responsibility.

Most of the authorities agree and our investigation has shown that the presence of a sex pervert in a Government agency tends to have a corrosive influence upon his fellow employees. These perverts will frequently attempt to entice normal individuals to engage in perverted practices. This is particularly true in the case of young and impressionable people who might come under the influence of a pervert. Government officials have the responsibility of keeping this type of corrosive influence out of the agencies under their control. It is particularly important that the thousands of young men and women who are brought into Federal jobs not be subjected to that type of influence while in the service of the Government. One homosexual can pollute a Government office.

Another point to be considered in determining whether a sex pervert is suitable for Government employment is his tendency to gather other perverts about him. Eminent psychiatrists have informed the subcommittee that the homosexual is likely to seek his own kind because the pressures of society are such that he feels uncomfortable unless he is with his own kind. Due to this situation the homosexual tends to surround himself with other homosexuals, not only in his social, but in his business life. Under these circumstances if a homosexual attains a position in Government where he can influence the hiring of personnel, it is almost inevitable that he will attempt to place other homosexuals in Government jobs.

SEX PERVERTS AS SECURITY RISKS

The conclusion of the subcommittee that a homosexual or other sex pervert is a security risk is not based upon mere conjecture. That conclusion is predicated upon a careful review of the opinions of those best qualified to consider matters of security in Government, namely, the intelligence agencies of the Government. Testimony on this phase of the inquiry was taken from representatives of the Federal Bureau of Investigation, the Central Intelligence Agency, and the intelligence services of the Army, Navy and Air Force. All of these agencies are in complete agreement that sex perverts in Government constitute security risks.

The lack of emotional stability which is found in most sex perverts and the weakness of their moral fiber, makes them susceptible to the blandishments of the foreign espionage agent. It is the experience of intelligence experts that perverts are vulnerable to interrogation by a skilled questioner and they seldom refuse to talk about themselves. Furthermore, most perverts tend to congregate at the same restaurants, night clubs, and bars, which places can be identified with comparative ease in any community, making it possible for a recruiting agent to develop clandestine relationships which can be used for espionage purposes. . . .

[C]ases have been brought to the attention of the subcommittee where Nazi and Communist agents have attempted to obtain information from employees of our Government by threatening to expose their abnormal sex activities. It is an accepted fact among intelligence agencies that espionage organizations the world over consider sex perverts who are in possession of or have access to confidential material to be prime targets where pressure can be exerted. In virtually every case despite protestations by the perverts that they would never succumb to blackmail, invariably they express considerable concern over the fact that their condition might become known to their friends, associates, or the public at large. The present danger of this security problem is well illustrated by the following excerpt from the testimony of D. Milton Ladd, Assistant to the Director of the Federal Bureau of Investigation, who appeared before this subcommittee in executive session:

> The Communists, without principles or scruples, have a program of seeking out weaknesses of leaders in Government and industry. In fact, the FBI has in its possession information of unquestionable reliability that orders have been issued by high Russian intelligence officials to their agents to secure details of the private lives of Government officials, their weaknesses, their associates, and in fact every bit of information regarding them, hoping to find a chink in their armor and a weakness upon which they might capitalize at the appropriate time.

The subcommittee in pointing out the unsuitability of perverts for Government employment is not unaware of the fact that there are other patterns of human behavior which also should be considered in passing upon the general suitability or security-risk status of Government employees. There is little doubt that habitual drunkards, persons who have engaged in criminal activities, and those who indulge in other types of infamous or scandalous personal conduct are also unsuitable for Government employment and constitute security risks. However, the subcommittee, in the present investigation, has properly confined itself to the problem of sex perverts. . . .

Conclusion

The subcommittee found that in the past many Government officials failed to take a realistic view of the problem of sex perversion in Government with the result that a number of sex perverts were not discovered or removed from Government jobs, and in still other instances they were quietly eased out of one department and promptly found employment in another agency. This situation undoubtedly stemmed from the fact that there was a general disinclination on the part of many Government officials to face squarely the problem of sex perversion among Federal employees and as a result they did not take the proper steps to solve the problem. The rules of the Civil Service Commission and the regulations of the agencies themselves prohibit the employment of sex perverts and those rules have been in effect for many years. Had the existing rules and regulations been enforced many of the perverts who were forced out of Government in recent months would have been long since removed from the Federal service.

It is quite apparent that as a direct result of this investigation officials throughout the Government have become much more alert to the problem of the employment of sex perverts in Government and in recent months they have removed a substantial number of these undesirables from public positions. This is evidenced by the fact that action has been taken in 382 sex perversion cases involving civilian employees of Government in the past 7 months, whereas action was taken in only 192 similar cases in the previous 3-year period from January 1, 1947 to April 1, 1950. However, it appears to the subcommittee that some Government officials are not yet fully aware of the inherent dangers involved in the employment of sex perverts. It is the considered opinion of the subcommittee that Government officials have the responsibility of exercising a high degree of diligence in the handling of the problem of sex perversion, and it is urged that they follow the recommendations of this subcommittee in that regard.

While this subcommittee is convinced that it is in the public interest to get sex perverts out of Government and keep them out, this program should be carried out in a manner consistent with the traditional American concepts of justice and fair play. In order to accomplish this end every reasonable complaint of perverted sex activities on the part of Government employees should be thoroughly investigated and dismissals should be ordered only after a complete review of the facts and in accordance with the present civil-service procedures. These procedures provide that the employee be informed of the charges against him and be given a reasonable time to answer. Furthermore, in view of the very serious consequences of dismissal from the Government on charges of sex perversion, it is believed that consideration should be given to establishing a board of review or similar appeal machinery whereby all persons who are dismissed from the Government on these charges may, if they so desire, have their cases reviewed by higher authority outside of the employing agency. No such appeal machinery exists at the present time.

READING AND DISCUSSION QUESTIONS

1. What factors do you think gave rise to the concern some senators had about the presence of homosexual men in government employment? How do they define the threats posed by these individuals?

2. What does this Senate investigation reveal to you about the extent to which concerns over national security impacted the personal lives of Americans? What evidence do you see that the senators balanced privacy and civil rights concerns with national security interests? How relevant are these issues today?

25-4 | Investigating the Communist Threat

CHARLOTTE ORAM, *Testimony Before the Senate Committee on Investigations* (1954)

Senator Joseph McCarthy (R-Wisconsin), chairman of the Senate Subcommittee on Investigations, launched a campaign to identify communist infiltration in the federal government. Thousands of Americans were affected by his allegations, many of them based on false or inaccurate evidence. His excesses eventually led to his censure by the Senate. In 1954, Charlotte Oram, a suspected member of the Communist Party, faced questions from the committee's chief counsel, Roy Cohn, about whether Annie Lee Moss, an African American woman who worked as a communications clerk in the Pentagon, was also a communist. Moss was a target because McCarthy had charged, erroneously, that she had access to the codes deciphering diplomatic messages.

MR. COHN: Could I get your full name?

MRS. ORAM: Charlotte Oram.

MR. COHN: And for the information of others present, counsel is Mr. Joseph Forer of the Washington Bar, who has been before the committee on prior occasions.

MR. FORER: That is correct.

MR. COHN: You have been before the committee on prior occasions and you know the rules?

MR. FORER: Yes, sir; I do.

Testimony of Charlotte Oram, February 23, 1954, Executive Session of the Senate Permanent Subcommittee on Investigations of the Committee on Government, Vol. 5, Eighty-Third Congress, Second Session, 1954, Made Public January 2002 (Washington, DC: Government Printing Office, 2003), 63–73.

MR. COHN: Now, Mrs. Oram, in 1944 were you a member of the northeast branch of the Communist party with a woman named Annie Lee Moss?

MRS. ORAM: I decline to answer that question on the basis of my privilege under the Fifth Amendment not to be a witness against myself.

MR. COHN: Did you hold membership card 53582 in the Communist party during those years?

MRS. ORAM: My answer to that question is on the same basis.

MR. COHN: Do you know Annie Lee Moss?

MRS. ORAM: I am sorry.

MR. COHN: Do you know Annie Lee Moss?

MRS. ORAM: That name doesn't mean anything to me.

MR. COHN: Can you name for us the members of the Communist cell to which you belonged?

MRS. ORAM: I decline to answer that question on the basis I stated previously.

MR. COHN: Are you a Communist as of today?

MRS. ORAM: I decline to answer that question on the same basis.

SENATOR JACKSON: I had a question. What is your occupation?

MRS. ORAM: I am a housewife.

SENATOR JACKSON: What is your occupation?

MRS. ORAM: I am a housewife.

SENATOR JACKSON: What does your husband do?

MRS. ORAM: He works in a drugstore.

SENATOR JACKSON: He works here in Washington, D.C.?

MRS. ORAM: Well, in Arlington County.

SENATOR JACKSON: Did you know a Mrs. Markward?[1]

MRS. ORAM: I decline to answer that question on the basis that I have stated previously.

SENATOR JACKSON: That is all.

SENATOR McCLELLAN: May I ask you a question? Are you now employed in the government in any way?

MRS. ORAM: No, I am not.

SENATOR McCLELLAN: Have you ever been?

MRS. ORAM: No, I never have been.

SENATOR McCLELLAN: You are declining to answer whether you are a Communist or have ever been a Communist? Is that correct?

MRS. ORAM: I am declining to answer that question.

SENATOR McCLELLAN: You are unwilling to cooperate with your government and its agencies to the extent of giving it any information that you may have that the government or its agencies may need in order to properly function and discharge its responsibilities in preserving our country, are you?

[The witness consulted with her counsel.]

MRS. ORAM: I decline to answer the questions for the reasons I gave.

---

[1]Mary Stalcup Markward, a member of the Communist Party, had cast suspicion on Annie Lee Moss when she claimed that Moss's name appeared on the party's membership roster.

SENATOR McCLELLAN: Are you an American citizen?

MRS. ORAM: Yes.

SENATOR McCLELLAN: Do you owe any obligations to your country as a citizen?

MRS. ORAM: Certainly.

SENATOR McCLELLAN: Do you regard an obligation to your country that protects you—

MRS. ORAM: I don't believe I understand that.

SENATOR McCLELLAN: Yes, you know what I mean. Do you regard an obligation to the country in which you have citizenship to try to serve it?

MRS. ORAM: Yes, of course.

SENATOR McCLELLAN: You do?

MRS. ORAM: Certainly.

SENATOR McCLELLAN: Do you think that you are serving your country as a good citizen and as a patriotic citizen when you refuse to give information that your government needs?

[The witness consulted with her counsel.]

MRS. ORAM: I believe it is my duty and every citizen's duty to protect and uphold the Constitution and I believe that in relying upon my constitutional rights I am certainly carrying that out.

SENATOR McCLELLAN: Is there any part of the Constitution that you hold allegiance to except the Fifth Amendment?

MRS. ORAM: I hold allegiance to every part, including the First Amendment.

SENATOR McCLELLAN: One of the parts of the Constitution is to preserve the United States, is it not?

MRS. ORAM: That is right.

SENATOR McCLELLAN: Are you going to contribute anything towards preserving your country?

MRS. ORAM: I believe I am doing that.

SENATOR McCLELLAN: If you are willing to do that, will you tell us and give us the information that has been asked as a good citizen of this country?

MRS. ORAM: I give you what information I feel I can and should give you.

SENATOR McCLELLAN: What information you feel you can and should give?

MRS. ORAM: Under the rights of the Constitution.

SENATOR McCLELLAN: Is there any information that you can, or that you are willing to give us, under the Constitution?

MRS. ORAM: That is rather a broad question.

SENATOR McCLELLAN: It is a broad question, but is there any, and I make it broad for your benefit? If you can indicate any information that you are willing to give us, to help to this fight against communism and to preserve our country. Is there any, and I make it broad to cover everything? Is there any that you are willing to give us?

MRS. ORAM: Well, of course.

SENATOR McCLELLAN: All right. Tell us. What is it? Mention one thing.

MRS. ORAM: Well, I don't know. I would have to have a specific question. I can't answer anything out of the blue.

SENATOR McCLELLAN: Are you willing to help your government fight this conspiracy of communism?

MRS. ORAM: I refuse to answer that question on the basis that I have already stated.

SENATOR McCLELLAN: You think that would incriminate you to say that you are willing to help fight a conspiracy against the United States of America?

MRS. ORAM: I think that I have to stick to my declination to answer.

SENATOR McCLELLAN: Do you think that would incriminate you? I am not asking you; I want you to state it under oath.

MRS. ORAM: It might.

SENATOR McCLELLAN: Do you think that it would incriminate you to help your government fight a conspiracy that is trying to destroy it?

[The witness consulted with her counsel.]

MRS. ORAM: I am afraid I don't understand that question, sir.

SENATOR McCLELLAN: You do understand the question and it is just as simple as it can be. Do you think that you would be incriminated if you gave information that would help your government fight a conspiracy, the conspiracy of communism that is undertaking to destroy it? You certainly understand that.

MRS. ORAM: I am afraid I don't.

SENATOR McCLELLAN: That is all, Mr. Chairman.

READING AND DISCUSSION QUESTIONS

1. From the transcript, what conclusions can you draw about the threat McClellan believed communism posed to America's national security?

2. How would you describe the strategies and tactics the committee used in attempting to understand the extent and impact of the Communist Party's influence in government?

3. Explain and evaluate how Oram's testimony reflects the broader Cold War fears concerning communism. Based on this testimony, what argument about Cold War political culture in the 1950s might a historian make?

25-5 | Secretary of State Announces Cold War Defense Policy

JOHN FOSTER DULLES, *The Evolution of Foreign Policy* (1954)

President Eisenhower's foreign policy is sometimes referred to as "brinksmanship," a term signifying his reliance on America's nuclear threat to curb Soviet aggression. Critics argued the policy automatically escalated minor crises to the brink of nuclear war. In the published version of his Council of Foreign Relations speech, Secretary of State John Foster Dulles articulated

John Foster Dulles, "The Evolution of Foreign Policy," *The Department of State Bulletin*, vol. 30 (January 25, 1954): 107–108, 110.

Eisenhower's commitment to atomic weapons as a central part of the United States's military strategy toward the Soviet Union and defended its "long time" advantages over the previous administration's approach.

We live in a world where emergencies are always possible and our survival may depend upon our capacity to meet emergencies. Let us pray that we shall always have that capacity. But, having said that, it is necessary also to say that emergency measures—however good for the emergency—do not necessarily make good permanent policies. Emergency measures are costly; they are superficial; and they imply that the enemy has the initiative. They cannot be depended on to serve our long-time interests.

This "long time" factor is of critical importance.

The Soviet Communists are planning for what they call "an entire historical era," and we should do the same. They seek, through many types of maneuvers, gradually to divide and weaken the free nations by overextending them in efforts which, as Lenin put it, are "beyond their strength, so that they come to practical bankruptcy." Then, said Lenin, "our victory is assured." Then, said Stalin, will be "the moment for the decisive blow."

In the face of this strategy, measures cannot be judged adequate merely because they ward off an immediate danger. It is essential to do this, but it is also essential to do so without exhausting ourselves.

When the Eisenhower administration applied this test, we felt that some transformations were needed.

It is not sound military strategy permanently to commit U.S. land forces to Asia to a degree that leaves us no strategic reserves.

It is not sound economics, or good foreign policy, to support permanently other countries; for in the long run, that creates as much ill will as good will.

Also, it is not sound to become permanently committed to military expenditures so vast that they lead to "practical bankruptcy."

Change was imperative to assure the stamina needed for permanent security. But it was equally imperative that change should be accompanied by understanding of our true purposes. Sudden and spectacular change had to be avoided. Otherwise, there might have been a panic among our friends and miscalculated aggression by our enemies. We can, I believe, make a good report in these respects.

We need allies and collective security. Our purpose is to make these relations more effective, less costly. This can be done by placing more reliance on deterrent power and less dependence on local defensive power.

This is accepted practice so far as local communities are concerned. We keep locks on our doors, but we do not have an armed guard in every home. We rely principally on a community security system so well equipped to punish any who break in and steal that, in fact, would-be aggressors are generally deterred. That is the modern way of getting maximum protection at a bearable cost.

What the Eisenhower administration seeks is a similar international security system. We want, for ourselves and the other free nations, a maximum deterrent at a bearable cost.

Local defense will always be important. But there is no local defense which alone will contain the mighty landpower of the Communist world. Local defenses must be reinforced by the further deterrent of massive retaliatory power. A potential aggressor must know that he cannot always prescribe battle conditions that suit him. Otherwise, for example, a potential aggressor, who is glutted with manpower, might be tempted to attack in confidence that resistance would be confined to manpower. He might be tempted to attack in places where his superiority was decisive.

The way to deter aggression is for the free community to be willing and able to respond vigorously at places and with means of its own choosing.

So long as our basic policy concepts were unclear, our military leaders could not be selective in building our military power. If an enemy could pick his time and place and method of warfare—and if our policy was to remain the traditional one of meeting aggression by direct and local opposition—then we needed to be ready to fight in the Arctic and in the Tropics; in Asia, the Near East, and in Europe; by sea, by land, and by air; with old weapons and with new weapons.

The total cost of our security efforts, at home and abroad, was over $50 billion per annum, and involved, for 1953, a projected budgetary deficit of $9 billion; and $11 billion for 1954. This was on top of taxes comparable to wartime taxes; and the dollar was depreciating in effective value. Our allies were similarly weighed down. This could not be continued for long without grave budgetary, economic, and social consequences.

But before military planning could be changed, the President and his advisers, as represented by the National Security Council, had to take some basic policy decisions. This has been done. The basic decision was to depend primarily upon a great capacity to retaliate, instantly, by means and at places of our choosing. Now the Department of Defense and the Joint Chiefs of Staff can shape our military establishment to fit what is *our* policy, instead of having to try to be ready to meet the enemy's many choices. That permits of a selection of military means instead of a multiplication of means. As a result, it is now possible to get, and share, more basic security at less cost. . . .

We do not, of course, claim to have found some magic formula that insures against all forms of Communist successes. It is normal that at some times and at some places there may be setbacks to the cause of freedom. What we do expect to insure is that any setbacks will have only temporary and local significance, because they will leave unimpaired those free world assets which in the long run will prevail.

If we can deter such aggression as would mean general war, and that is our confident resolve, then we can let time and fundamentals work for us. We do not need self-imposed policies which sap our strength.

The fundamental, on our side, is the richness—spiritual, intellectual, and material—that freedom can produce and the irresistible attraction it then sets up. That is why we do not plan ourselves to shackle freedom to preserve freedom. We intend that our conduct and example shall continue, as in the past, to show all men how good can be the fruits of freedom.

READING AND DISCUSSION QUESTIONS

1. Analyze Dulles's speech to identify the contrast he attempts to draw between the foreign policy of the Truman and Eisenhower administrations. What advantages does he note for the policy of "massive retaliation"?

2. Based on Dulles's speech, what conclusions can you draw concerning the motivations that led Eisenhower to embrace this strategy as the guiding foreign policy of the United States during this period?

25-6 | Finding Security in an Age of Anxiety

MICHIGAN OFFICE OF CIVIL DEFENSE, *The Family Fallout Shelter: Your One Defense Against Fallout* (1959)

Cold War anxiety was fueled by the threat of a nuclear war between the United States and the Soviet Union, each of which had a massive arsenal of nuclear weapons pointed at the other. The government's Office of Civil Defense (OCD), and similar state-level offices, both stoked this anxiety and helped to alleviate it by promoting readiness and preparedness campaigns to protect Americans. Do-it-yourself fallout shelters became a popular civil defense measure.

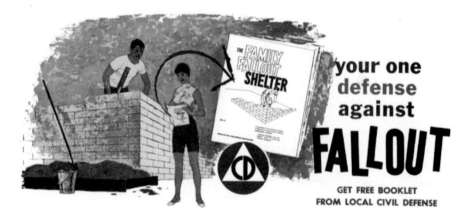

READING AND DISCUSSION QUESTIONS

1. What argument about Cold War culture can you make based on this public service announcement? Do you think promotional materials such as this heightened or allayed anxiety about nuclear war with the Soviet Union?

2. Using this poster as evidence, what argument about gender during the Cold War can you make? How are the roles of men and women depicted here? What is assumed about men's "do-it-yourself" abilities?

▪ COMPARATIVE QUESTIONS ▪

1. Consider Oram's testimony and Bartolomeo Vanzetti's last statement (Document 22-1) to compare the ways that the Red Scare manifested itself in the 1920s and 1950s. How do you account for the timing of these outbreaks, and what similarities and differences can you identify between them?

2. Synthesize the multiple perspectives from the sources in this chapter to create a persuasive argument regarding the origins of the Cold War. How did foreign policy analysts interpret the Soviet threat, and how might those interpretations have affected U.S. foreign policy?

3. Compare the Senate investigation report and the Civil Defense poster on building a fallout shelter. From these different sources, what conclusions can you make about gender stereotypes defining "normal" masculinity in this period?

4. What conclusion can you make about the role ideology has played in shaping America's foreign policy? What comparisons can you draw with the imperialism of the late-nineteenth- and early-twentieth-century era and World War II?

26

Triumph of the Middle Class
1945–1963

Following a decade and a half of economic depression and war, consumer spending burst from the constraints imposed by an era of sacrifice to power a postwar boom. The economics of the Cold War era resulted in an expanding economy and a rising standard of living that swelled the middle class. Returning veterans benefitted directly from the federal government's generous subsidies. Men who filled the growing ranks of white-collar employment were able to provide the material comforts mass media and advertising defined as indispensable to suburban living. The full-color spreads in leading magazines helped propagate an idealized image of America as a middle-class nation. The glossy images of contented housewives and happy children, however, represented only one face of Cold War America. Not all housewives were content, not all children were happy, and not all Americans could afford to live in the middle class. A small but swelling chorus of social criticism pierced the veil of apparent middle-class satisfaction. These counterpoints portrayed Cold War America not as the middle-class utopia many imagined themselves living, but as a fool's paradise, presenting a social critique that would gain traction among the generation coming of age in the Sixties.

26-1 | Congress Passes GI Bill of Rights
Servicemen's Readjustment Act (1944)

Even before the end of World War II, Congress passed the Servicemen's Readjustment Act, popularly known as the GI Bill of Rights, to provide federal benefits to veterans of the armed services. With the post–World War I recession in mind, policymakers attempted to soften the economic consequences of demobilization following World War II by providing work, education, and housing benefits. It worked. More than two million veterans used the benefits to pursue college degrees, and the legislation enabled millions of veterans' families to become home owners, pulling them into a broadening middle class.

An Act to Provide Federal Government Aid for the Readjustment in Civilian Life of Returning World War II Veterans

Be it enacted by the Senate and House of Representatives of the United States of America in Congress assembled, That this Act may be cited as the Servicemen's Readjustment Act of 1944.

Title I

Chapter I—Hospitalization, Claims, and Procedures

SEC. 100. The Veterans Administration is hereby declared to be an essential war agency and entitled, second only to the War and Navy Departments, to priorities in personnel, equipment, supplies, and material under any laws, Executive orders, and regulations pertaining to priorities, and in appointments of personnel from civil-service registers the Administrator of Veterans Affairs is hereby granted the same authority and discretion as the War and Navy Departments and the United States Public Health Service. . . .

Title II

Chapter IV—Education of Veterans

1. Any person who served in the active military or naval service on or after September 16, 1940, and prior to the termination of the present war, and who shall have been discharged or released there-from under conditions other than dishonorable, and whose education or training was impeded, delayed, interrupted, or interfered with by reason of his entrance into the service, or who desires a refresher or retraining course, and who either shall have served ninety days or more, exclusive of any period he was assigned for a course of education or training under the Army specialized training program or the Navy college training program, which course was a continuation of his civilian course and was pursued

---

An Act to Provide Federal Government Aid for the Readjustment in Civilian Life of Returning World War II Veterans, June 22, 1944; Enrolled Acts and Resolutions of Congress, 1789–1996; General Records of the United States Government; Record Group 11; National Archives.

to completion, or as a cadet or midshipman at one of the service academies, or shall have been discharged or released from active service by reason of an actual service-incurred injury or disability, shall be eligible for and entitled to receive education or training under this part. . . .

5. The Administrator shall pay to the educational or training institution, for each person enrolled in full time or part time course of education or training, the customary cost of tuition, and such laboratory, library, health, infirmary, and other similar fees as are customarily charged, and may pay for books, supplies, equipment, and other necessary expenses, exclusive of board, lodging, other living expenses, and travel, as are generally required for the successful pursuit and completion of the course by other students in the institution: Provided, That in no event shall such payments, with respect to any person, exceed $500 for an ordinary school year. . . .

6. While enrolled in and pursuing a course under this part, such person, upon application to the Administrator, shall be paid a subsistence allowance of $50 per month, if without a dependent or dependents, or $75 per month, if he has a dependent or dependents, including regular holidays and leave not exceeding thirty days in a calendar year. . . .

Title III

Loans for the Purchase or Construction of Homes, Farms, and Business Property

Chapter V—General Provisions for Loans

SEC. 501. (a) Any application made by a veteran under this title for the guaranty of a loan to be used in purchasing residential property or in constructing a dwelling on unimproved property owned by him to be occupied as his home may be approved [by] the Administrator of Veterans Affairs if he finds

(1) that the proceeds of such loans will be used for payment for such property to be purchased or constructed by the veteran;

(2) that the contemplated terms of payment required in any mortgage to be given in part payment of the purchase price or the construction cost bear a proper relation to the veteran's present and anticipated income and expenses; and that the nature and condition of the property is such as to be suitable for dwelling purposes; and

(3) that the purchase price paid or to be paid by the veteran for such property or the construction cost, including the value of the unimproved lot, does not exceed the reasonable normal value thereof as determined by proper appraisal.

Purchase of Farms and Farm Equipment

SEC. 502. Any application made under this title for the guaranty of a loan to be used in purchasing any land, buildings, livestock, equipment, machinery, or implements, or in repairing, altering, or improving any buildings or equipment, to be used in farming operations conducted by the applicant, may be approved by the Administrator of Veterans Affairs if he finds

(1) that the proceeds of such loan will be used in payment for or personal property purchased or to be purchased by the veteran, or for repairing, altering, or improving any buildings or equipment to be used in bona fide farming operations conducted by him;

(2) that such property will be useful in and reasonably necessary for efficiently conducting such operations;

(3) that the ability and experience of the veteran, and the nature of the proposed farming operations to be conducted by him, are such that there is a reasonable likelihood that such operations will be successful; and

(4) that the purchase price paid or to be paid by the veteran for such property does not exceed the reasonable normal value thereof as determined by proper appraisal.

Purchase of Business Property

Sec. 503. Any application made under this title for the guaranty of a loan to be used in purchasing any business, land, buildings, supplies, equipment, machinery, or tools, to be used by the applicant in pursuing a gainful occupation (other than farming) may be approved by the Administrator of Veterans Affairs if he finds

(1) that the proceeds of such loan will be used for payment for real or personal property purchased or to be purchased by the veteran and used by him in the bona fide pursuit of such gainful occupation;

(2) that such property will be useful in and reasonably necessary for the efficient and successful pursuit of such occupation;

(3) that the ability and experience of the veteran, and the conditions under which he proposes to pursue such occupation, are such that there is a reasonable likelihood that he will be successful in the pursuit of such occupation; and

(4) that the purchase price paid or to be paid by the veteran for such property does not exceed the reasonable normal value thereof as determined by proper appraisal. . . .

Title IV

Chapter VI—Employment of Veterans

SEC. 600. (a) In the enactment of the provisions of this title Congress declares as its intent and purpose that there shall be an effective job counseling and employment placement service for veterans . . . so as to provide for them the maximum of job opportunity in the field of gainful employment. [A] Veterans Placement Service Board . . . shall determine all matters of policy relating to the administration of the Veterans Employment Service of the United States Employment Service. . . .

SEC. 601. The United States Employment Service shall assign to each of the States a Veterans employment representative, who shall . . .

(a) be functionally responsible for the supervision of the registration of veterans in local employment offices for suitable types of employment and for placement of veterans in employment;

(b) assist in securing and maintaining current information as to the various types of available employment in public works and private industry or business;

(c) promote the interest of employers in employing veterans;

(d) maintain regular contact with employers and Veterans organizations with a view of keeping employers advised of veterans available for employment and veterans advised of opportunities for employment; and

(e) assist in every possible way in improving working conditions and the advancement of employment of veterans.

Title V

Chapter VII—Readjustment Allowances for Former Members of the Armed Forces Who Are Unemployed

SEC. 700. (a) Any person who shall have served in the active military or naval service of the United States at any time after September 16, 1940, and prior to the termination of the present war, and who shall have been discharged or released from active service under conditions other than dishonorable, after active service of ninety days or more, or by reason of an injury or disability incurred in service in line of duty, shall be entitled . . . to receive a readjustment allowance as provided herein for each week of unemployment, not to exceed a total of fifty-two weeks. . . .

READING AND DISCUSSION QUESTIONS

1. Analyze the GI Bill for evidence of policymakers' concerns regarding returning veterans. What categories of help did they assume veterans would most likely need, and how was this legislation designed to meet those needs?

2. How might a historian seeking to understand the emergence of the post–World War II middle class use the evidence from this source? What short- and long-term consequences do you think the bill's sponsors anticipated?

26-2 | Teen Culture in the Fifties

DOREEN SPOONER, *Soda Fountain* (1950)

America's adolescents carved out leisure time and space for their own activities, separate and sometimes hidden from adults' prying eyes. In addition to dances, movies, and parties, many teens met at their favorite diners or soda fountains, as shown here, which provided public spaces for a flourishing teen culture. With cars and pocket money to spend, teens both indulged and inspired a youth market that defined their lives and raised alarms among anxious parents and social critics who wondered at the liberties their children pursued.

Doreen Spooner, "Soda Fountain." Hulton Archive/Getty Images.

READING AND DISCUSSION QUESTIONS

1. What insight into postwar teen culture does this photograph reveal? What can you tell about social relationships among teens?

2. What function did places like this soda fountain play in the daily lives of young people?

3. What might this photograph suggest about the role teens played in the postwar consumer economy? How did retailers and other cultural entrepreneurs cater to this emerging market?

26-3 | Evangelical Calls America to Christ

BILLY GRAHAM, *Our Right to Require Belief* (1956)

In 1956, "In God We Trust" became the official national motto, reflecting both a Cold War culture where Americans contrasted the United States with the atheistic Soviet Union and the widespread appeal of traditional moral values embodied in the Judeo-Christian tradition. Evangelist Billy Graham emerged within this context, becoming the most significant evangelical preacher of the postwar era. His message of salvation through Christ spoke to middle-class Americans in search of some meaning in their lives.

There is a movement gathering momentum in America to take the traditional concept of God out of our national life. If this movement succeeds, IN GOD WE TRUST will be taken from our coins, the Bible will be removed from our courtrooms, future Presidents will be sworn into office with their hand on a copy of the Constitution instead of the Bible, and chaplains will be removed from the Armed Forces.

The issue of prayers in public schools is now before the Supreme Court and, if the Court decrees negatively, another victory will be gained by those forces which conspire to remove faith in God from the public conscience.

With each passing Christmas season the observing of Christmas in the school becomes a sharper issue. Many public schools, from California to New Jersey, have already ruled out the singing of carols in the classroom.

Those who are trying to remove God from our culture are rewriting history and distorting the truth. But those who advocate drastic changes in our traditional faith are only a tiny minority. Most Americans not only believe in God themselves but want their leaders to have faith in God. The Associated Press recently reported the findings of Dr. Paul Bussard, editor of the *Catholic Digest*, who learned that 99 percent of the American people believe in God; that 77 percent believe in the hereafter, and that 75 percent believe that religion is important. . . .

It is true that our forefathers meant this nation to be free from religious domination. The men who built America were primarily victims of oppression. They

Billy Graham, "Our Right to Require Belief," *The Saturday Evening Post*, vol. 235 (February 17, 1962), 8, 10.

felt that the terrors of the wilderness were as nothing to that of government oppression of religious faith. But the founding fathers in their determination to have freedom "of" religion never meant to have freedom "from" religion. Separation of church and state in no way implies separation of religion and state affairs. They are spiritually inseparable. . . .

Early American history was hallowed with a purpose greater than material wealth and a cause greater than democracy. It was forged in the fire of a burning faith in God. Many early settlers came to America with one goal in mind— namely, to advance the Kingdom of the Lord Jesus Christ.

The tremendous prosperity, power and blessing which America has enjoyed through the years came because we as a nation have honored God. It is, I believe, a direct fulfillment of the promise, "Blessed is the nation whose God is the Lord." Abraham Lincoln said during the Civil War, "I have so many evidences of God's direction that I cannot doubt His power comes from above." This was the faith of our fathers. The Great Seal of the United States is our complete acknowledgment that we are the people of His pasture and the sheep of His hand. Our national emblems testify to the fact that we are a people "under God." A Bible-reading shepherd in the desert of Mesopotamia who had never heard of the United States would say on seeing our national emblems, "Surely these are God's people."

American democracy rests on the belief in the reality of God and His respect for the individual. Ours is a freedom under law, but it is also a freedom that will evaporate if the religious foundations upon which it has been built are taken away. I'm not so sure we would continue to be free if our men in public life had no faith in God. I'm not sure that atheists and agnostics would be quite so zealous to preserve the Bill of Rights or the writ of habeas corpus or the two-party system or the right to trial by jury or the legal innocence of a man before he is proved guilty.

Castro has shown us all over again how easy it is to rationalize, to postpone elections, to justify tyranny in the name of land reform or some other benevolence. A dictator convinced that destiny lies in his own hands is bound to be proud, ruthless and ultimately destructive. . . . If a political leader fears God and believes that God is in control of the universe, that certain moral laws are operating, then his faith will be reflected in his conduct. Our beliefs make us what we are. This faith in God is the source of our liberty.

We are living in the most critical period in American history. We are faced with the possible destruction of our entire civilization. With a militant, atheistic Communism threatening to bury us, we need to rediscover national goals, to reexamine our national destiny. Whether he intends to, the American atheist administering a public office has essentially conceded the battle to Communism. By his atheism he underwrites in principle the Communist, materialistic, non-spiritual concept of life. He has surrendered spiritual, moral and rational arguments against Communism. The kind of moral conduct American life has historically demanded has grown on a religious soil which recognizes the moral laws of God. The morality of justice, the claims of honesty, the regard for and respect of the rights of others have grown on Judeo-Christian soil.

For a generation we have been emphasizing material things. We have been "living it up," reaching for that extra status symbol, milking an affluent society for all we can get. Now we are discovering, in the age of the fifty-megaton bombs, what Haggai, the prophet, wrote: "Ye have sown much, and bring in little; ye eat, but ye have not enough; ye drink, but ye are not filled with drink; ye clothe you, but there is none warm; and he that earneth wages earneth wages to put it into a bag with holes. . . . Ye looked for much, and, lo, it came to little and when ye brought it home, I did blow upon it."

When a national leader turns to God in obvious sincerity, it has a tremendous effect on the whole nation. Think how Mr. Eisenhower thrilled us when he began his first Administration with what he called his "little prayer." . . .

Dr. John A. Mackay, president emeritus of Princeton Theological Seminary, has suggested that there are several basic attitudes nations can take toward God. One is the attitude of the "secular nation," which eliminates God from its official relations and adheres to some political or philosophical idea. Another is the "demoniac nation," which manufactures a god out of the state itself. Still another is the "covenant nation," which grows out of an original loyalty and devotion to God and which continues to draw upon its origins for strength. I believe that America is such a "covenant nation" and that she will survive just as long as she remains loyal to her spiritual roots.

Yes, American political leaders owe it to our history, owe it to the people, owe it to a possible solution to the present crisis to have faith in God. I'm not advocating that faith in God is necessary merely for the holding of public office. I believe *every American* should have faith in God. This should be a deep, personal faith. Christ said, "Ye must be born again." We all must have this transforming experience if we are to enter God's kingdom and produce the type of society that our forefathers fought and prayed for. In a democracy the officeholder is only as strong as the people who support him.

Jesus continually condemned the Pharisees of His day, who served God with their lips when their hearts were far from Him. An acknowledgment of a belief in God will not turn an officeholder into a saint. There have been plenty of rascals who nodded to the Almighty. Yet there is a restraining influence in belief in God which even Kinsey acknowledged. Belief in God makes men more likely to be truthful under oath. America cannot afford to lose this kind of genuine faith.

As I travel throughout the country, I find that people are suffering from the neurosis of fear. A leading psychiatrist told me recently, "Seventy percent of the people that come to my office are afraid, and they don't know what they're afraid of." There is a jaded, banal and empty feeling on the part of millions. People are searching for a creed to believe, a song to sing and a flag to follow. In Moscow's Red Square some time ago thousands of young Russians were stamping their feet and shouting, "We're going to change the world, we're going to change the world." I could not help contrasting them with some of the young Americans we meet so often, drifting aimlessly from one pleasure spot to another, wondering what to do with themselves. Many of our young people are uncommitted. Their superficial goals do not satisfy them.

It is clearly evident that America needs a renewal of faith in God. But this renewal will have to start with the individual. The Bible teaches that "all have sinned and come short of the glory of God." We must confess our spiritual failure. There must be deep, genuine repentance. In our faith we must turn to Christ, Who died for our sins and arose again for our justification. If we are humble enough to make this deep and honest confession and commitment, God will forgive our sins and lead us to greater national heights.

Judge Luther Youngdahl has said, "A revival of the dynamic faith that sparked the Revolution is imperative." Once it was said of the Christians that they were turning the world upside down. We can do it again! What good does it do to become the wealthiest nation in the world if we are spiritually bankrupt? What would we have to offer the world?

In my travels around the world I am convinced that people everywhere are looking to America for moral leadership. Moses was able to lead a nation of slaves to freedom because he had a faith in God. We cannot survive the present crisis with anything less. Faith is not something we stumble upon by accident; it is not the way a coward flees from reality. It is the projection of reason beyond the limits of present knowledge. It is taking God at His word. It means believing, even when we don't understand all that is involved.

When John Wycliffe translated the Bible into English, he unwittingly outlined prophetically the course of history. For the Bible became not only the book of the English people of his day; it became the foundation of freedom for a nation unborn that would be called America. We inherited that priceless gift of God from the British people. Then we borrowed a tune from their national anthem and gave it new words of petition which must rise from the hearts of Americans in times of crisis. "Our fathers' God, to Thee, Author of liberty, to Thee we sing. Long may our land be bright with freedom's holy light. Protect us by Thy might, great God, our King."

READING AND DISCUSSION QUESTIONS

1. How does Graham define the crisis facing America? What solution to the crisis does he urge upon his readers?

2. What assumptions does Graham make about the relationship between democracy in America and Christianity?

26-4 | Doctor's Advice on Raising Healthy Children

BENJAMIN SPOCK, *Dr. Spock's Baby and Child Care* (1946)

The postwar domestic ideology lavished attention on the family and the healthy rearing of children. Dr. Benjamin Spock's best-selling book for parents tapped an audience of nervous mothers who sought the opinion of experts on such things as feeding habits, toilet training, and discipline. Trained as a pediatrician, Spock offered advice to mothers that contradicted the conventional wisdom practiced by earlier generations of parents.

Trust Yourself

You know more than you think you do. Soon you're going to have a baby. Maybe you have him already. You're happy and excited, but, if you haven't had much experience, you wonder whether you are going to know how to do a good job. Lately you have been listening more carefully to your friends and relatives when they talked about bringing up a child. You've begun to read articles by experts in the magazines and newspapers. After the baby is born, the doctor and nurses will begin to give you instructions, too. Sometimes it sounds like a very complicated business. You find out all the vitamins a baby needs and all the inoculations. One mother tells you you must use the black kind of nipples, another says the yellow. You hear that a baby must be handled as little as possible, and that a baby must be cuddled plenty; that spinach is the most valuable vegetable, that spinach is a worthless vegetable; that fairy tales make children nervous, and that fairy tales are a wholesome outlet.

Don't take too seriously all that the neighbors say. Don't be overawed by what the experts say. Don't be afraid to trust your own common sense. Bringing up your child won't be a complicated job if you take it easy, trust your own instincts, and follow the directions that your doctor gives you. We know for a fact that the natural loving care that kindly parents give to their children is a hundred times more valuable than their knowing how to pin a diaper on just right, or making a formula expertly. Every time you pick your baby up, even if you do it a little awkwardly at first, every time you change him, bathe him, feed him, smile at him, he's getting a feeling that he belongs to you and that you belong to him. Nobody else in the world, no matter how skillful, can give that to him.

It may surprise you to hear that the more people have studied different methods of bringing up children the more they have come to the conclusion that what good mothers and fathers instinctively feel like doing for their babies is usually best after all. Furthermore, all parents do their best job when they have a natural, easy confidence in themselves. Better to make a few mistakes from being natural than to do everything letter-perfect out of a feeling of worry. . . .

Benjamin Spock, *Dr. Spock's Baby and Child Care* (New York: Duell, Sloan and Pearce, 1946), 3–4, 16–17, 19–22.

The blue feeling. It's possible that you will find yourself feeling discouraged for a while when you first begin taking care of your baby. It's a fairly common feeling, especially with the first. You may not be able to put your finger on anything that is definitely wrong. You just weep easily. Or you may feel very badly about certain things. One woman whose baby cries quite a bit feels sure that he has a real disease; another that her husband has become strange and distant; another that she has lost all her looks.

A feeling of depression may come on a few days after the baby is born or not till several weeks later. The commonest time is when a mother comes home from the hospital, where she has been waited on hand and foot, and abruptly takes over the full care of baby and household. It isn't just the work that gets her down. She may even have someone to do all the work, for the time being. It's the feeling of being responsible for the whole household again, plus the entirely new responsibility of the baby's care and safety. Then there are all the physical and glandular changes at the time of the birth, which probably upset the spirits to some degree.

The majority of mothers don't get enough discouraged in this period to ever call it depression. You may think it is a mistake to bring up unpleasant things that may never happen. The reason I mention it is that several mothers have told me afterwards, "I'm sure I wouldn't have been so depressed or discouraged if I had known how common this feeling is. Why, I thought that my whole outlook on life had changed for good and all." You can face a thing much better if you know that a lot of other people have gone through it too, and if you know that it's just temporary.

The chance that you may feel easily discouraged is one reason for getting together all the baby's equipment and arranging the whole household for his care before he is born. It is also a reason to consider getting someone to help you in the early weeks.

If you begin to feel at all depressed, try to get some relief from the constant care of the baby in the first month or two, especially if he cries a great deal. Go to a movie, or to the beauty parlor, or to get yourself a new hat or dress. Visit a good friend occasionally. Take the baby along if you can't find anyone to stay with him. Or get your old friends to come and see you. All of these are tonics. If you are depressed, you may not feel like doing these things. But if you make yourself, you will feel a lot better. And that's important for the baby and your husband as well as yourself. (The rare mother who becomes deeply depressed should have the help of a psychiatrist without delay.)

As for a mother's feeling, when she's blue, that her husband seems different, far away, there are two sides to it. On the one hand, anyone who is depressed feels that other people are less friendly and affectionate. But on the other hand, it's natural for a father, being human, to feel "put out" when his wife and the rest of the household are completely wrapped up in the baby. So it's a sort of vicious circle. The mother (as if she didn't have enough to do already!) has to remember to pay some attention to her husband. And she should give him every chance to share the care of the baby. . . .

Enjoy Your Baby

He isn't a schemer. He needs loving. You'd think from all you hear about babies demanding attention that they come into the world determined to get their parents under their thumbs by hook or by crook. This is not true at all. Your baby is born to be a reasonable, friendly human being. If you treat him nicely, he won't take advantage of you. Don't be afraid to love him or respond to his needs. Every baby needs to be smiled at, talked to, played with, fondled—gently and lovingly—just as much as he needs vitamins and calories, and the baby who doesn't get any loving will grow up cold and unresponsive. When he cries it's for a good reason—maybe it's hunger, or wetness, or indigestion, or just because he's on edge and needs soothing. His cry is there to call you. The uneasy feeling you have when you hear him cry, the feeling that you want to comfort him, is meant to be part of your nature, too. A little gentle rocking may actually be good for him. . . .

 He doesn't have to be sternly trained. You may hear people say that you have to get your baby strictly regulated in his feeding, sleeping, bowel movements, and other habits—but don't believe this either. In the first place, you can't get a baby regulated beyond a certain point, no matter how hard you try. In the second place, you are more apt, in the long run, to make him balky and disagreeable when you go at his training too hard. Everyone wants his child to turn out to be healthy in his habits and easy to live with. But each child wants, himself, to eat at sensible hours, and later to learn good table manners. His bowels (as long as the movements don't become too hard) will move according to their own healthy pattern, which may or may not be regular; and when he is much older and wiser, you can show him where to sit to move them. He will develop his own pattern of sleep, according to his own needs. In all these habits he will fit into the family's way of doing things sooner or later without much effort on your part.

 The same thing goes, later on, for discipline, good behavior, and pleasant manners. You can't drill these into a child from the outside in a hundred years. The desire to get along with other people happily and considerately develops within him as part of the unfolding of his nature, provided he grows up with loving, self-respecting parents.

 What I am saying in different ways is that you don't have to be grimly determined, in order to bring up a healthy, agreeable, successful child. It's the parents who have a natural self-confidence in themselves and a comfortable, affectionate attitude toward their children who get the best results—and with the least effort. . . .

 He isn't frail. "I'm so afraid I'll hurt him if I don't handle him right," a mother often says about her first baby. You don't have to worry, you have a pretty tough baby. There are many ways to hold him. If his head drops backward by mistake it won't hurt him. The open spot in his skull (the fontanel) is covered by a tough membrane like canvas that isn't easily injured. The system to control his body temperature is working quite well by the time he weighs 7 pounds if he's covered halfway sensibly. He has a good resistance to most germs. During a family cold epidemic he's apt to have it the mildest of all. If he gets his head tangled in anything he has a strong instinct to struggle and yell. If he's not getting enough to eat, he will probably cry for more. If the light is too strong for his eyes, he'll blink and fuss. (You can take his picture with a flash bulb, even if it does make him jump.) He knows how much sleep he needs and takes it. He can care for himself pretty well for a person who can't say a word, can't control his arms and legs, and knows nothing about the world.

Enjoy him as he is — that's how he'll grow up best. Every baby's face is different from every other's. In the same way every baby's pattern of development is different. One may be very advanced in his general bodily strength and coordination, an early sitter, stander, walker — a sort of infant athlete. And yet he may be slow in doing careful, skillful things with his fingers, in talking. Even a baby who is an athlete in rolling over, standing, and creeping may turn out to be slow to learn to walk. A baby who's advanced in his physical activities may be very slow in his teething and vice versa. A child who turns out later to be smart in his schoolwork may have been so slow in beginning to talk that his parents were afraid for a while that he was dull; and a child who has just an ordinary amount of brains is sometimes a very early talker.

I am purposely picking out examples of children with mixed rates of development to give you an idea of what a jumble of different qualities and patterns of growth each individual person is composed.

One baby is born to be big-boned and square and chunky, while another will always be small-boned and delicate. One individual really seems to be born to be fat. If he loses weight during an illness, he gains it back promptly afterwards. The troubles that he has in the world never take away his appetite. The opposite kind of individual stays on the thin side, even when he has the most nourishing food to eat, even though life is running smoothly for him.

Love and enjoy your child for what he is, for what he looks like, for what he does, and forget about the qualities that he doesn't have. I don't give you this advice just for sentimental reasons. There's a very important practical point here. The child who is appreciated for what he is, even if he is homely, or clumsy, or slow, will grow up with confidence in himself, happy. He will have a spirit that will make the best of all the capacities that he has, and of all the opportunities that come his way. He will make light of any handicaps. But the child who has never been quite accepted by his parents, who has always felt that he was not quite right, grows up lacking confidence. He'll never be able to make full use of what brains, what skills, what physical attractiveness he has. If he starts life with a handicap, physical or mental, it will be multiplied tenfold by the time he is grown up.

Now, of course, once in a great while a baby seems to be *generally* slow in his development, doesn't hold his head up, or respond to people, or show an interest in his surroundings, at an age when other babies are doing these things. Should a parent be philosophical about this and try to forget it? That would be carrying it too far. One of these babies is just born to be that way and there's no magic way to change him; but another may have a deficiency disease which can and should be treated early. That's a reason for having a doctor check a baby regularly.

READING AND DISCUSSION QUESTIONS

1. Analyze Dr. Spock's advice to parents. What perspective on parenting does he advocate?

2. How do you account for the runaway success of his book? What factors made his advice so appealing to the middle-class audience of Cold War mothers in the 1940s and 1950s?

26-5 | National Concerns About the Corruptions of Youth

Comic Books and Juvenile Delinquency: Interim Report of the Committee on the Judiciary (1955)

The 1950s postwar affluence affirmed conventional values of middle-class morality and ideal-ized the nuclear family with a working father and stay-at-home mother. At the same time, the economic comforts provided opportunities for consumer indulgence and a relaxation of social and moral constraints. Concerns about immorality haunted the middle class as reformers began defining a problem of juvenile delinquency that they attributed to the sexual and vio-lent themes appearing in comic books, according to Democratic senator Estes Kefauver of Tennessee. The Senate investigated the link between comic books and juvenile delinquency in 1955 and determined that the mass media was a "significant factor" in the crisis of America's youth.

Juvenile delinquency in America today must be viewed in the framework of the total community-climate in which children live. Certainly, none of the children who get into trouble live in a social vacuum. One of the most significant changes of the past quarter century has been the wide diffusion of the printed word, par-ticularly in certain periodicals, plus the phenomenal growth of radio and tele-vision audiences.

The child today in the process of growing up is constantly exposed to sights and sounds of a kind and quality undreamed of in previous generations. As these sights and sounds can be a powerful force for good, so too can they be a powerful counterpoise working evil. Their very quantity makes them a factor to be reckoned with in determining the total climate encountered by today's chil-dren during their formative years.

The first phase of the subcommittee's investigation of the mass media of communication dealt with so-called comic books. . . .

It has been pointed out that the so-called crime and horror comic books of concern to the subcommittee offer short courses in murder, mayhem, robbery, rape, cannibalism, carnage, necrophilia, sex, sadism, masochism, and virtually every other form of crime, degeneracy, bestiality, and horror. These depraved

Comic Books and Juvenile Delinquency: A Part of the Investigation of Juvenile Delinquency in the United States, Interim Report of the Committee on the Judiciary, Rep. No. 62, 83rd Cong., 1st Sess., March 14, 1955.

acts are presented and explained in illustrated detail in an array of comic books being bought and read daily by thousands of children. These books evidence a common penchant for violent death in every form imaginable. Many of the books dwell in detail on various forms of insanity and stress sadistic degeneracy. Others are devoted to cannibalism with monsters in human form feasting on human bodies, usually the bodies of scantily clad women.

To point out more specifically the type of material being dealt with, a few typical examples of story content and pictures were presented at the New York hearings on April 21, 1954. From the few following examples, it will be clearly seen that the major emphasis of the material then available on America's newsstands from this segment of the comic book industry dealt with depraved violence:

Story No. 1: Bottoms Up (Story Comics)

This story has to do with a confirmed alcoholic who spends all his wife can earn on alcohol. As a result their small son is severely neglected. On the day the son is to start in the first grade in school the mother asks the father to escort him to the school building. Instead, the father goes to his favorite bootlegger and the son goes to school by himself. En route the child is struck and killed by an automobile. Informed of the accident, the mother returns home to find her husband gloating over his new supply of liquor. The last four panels show the mother as she proceeds to kill and hack her spouse to pieces with an ax. The first panel shows her swinging the ax, burying the blade in her husband's skull. Blood spurts from the open wound and the husband is shown with an expression of agony. The next panel has a montage effect: the husband is lying on the floor with blood rushing from his skull as the wife is poised over him. She holds the bloody ax, raised for more blows. The background shows an enlargement of the fear-filled eyes of the husband, as well as an enlargement of the bloody ax. To describe this scene of horror the text states that "And now the silence of the Hendrick's apartment is broken only by the soft humming of Nora as she busies herself with her 'work.'" She then cuts his body into smaller pieces and disposes of it by placing the various pieces in the bottles of liquor her husband had purchased. She then returns the liquor to the bootlegger and obtains a refund. As she leaves the bootlegger says: "HMMN, funny! I figured that rye would be inside Lou by now!" The story ends with the artist admonishing the child readers in a macabre vein with the following paragraph, "But if Westlake were to examine the remainder of the case more closely he'd see that it is Lou who is inside the liquor! Heh, Heh! Sleep well, kiddies!" We then see three of the bottles — one contains an eye, one an ear, and one a finger. . . .

It has been repeatedly affirmed that the comic book, native product of the United States, is provoking discussion in other countries. Many Americans have expressed indignation of the influence these books may have upon the children and young adults in other parts of the world.

Some hold the view that there is no way in which we could give the young people abroad a more unfavorable and distorted view of American values, aspirations, and cultural pattern [than] through crime and horror comics. The destructive potentials of the comic book must be recognized both within our domestic society and in consideration of our relationship to peoples abroad. Publishers of undesirable comic books should be made aware of the negative effects these books may exert upon the thinking and conduct of persons who read them throughout the [world] and of the deplorable impression of the United States gained through their perusal.

Several consideration[s] stem from the impact of the comic books abroad. They are:

1. Information gathered by United States Department of State personnel in many countries reveals public concern over the spread of crime and horror comic book reading. As far as can be ascertained by the subcommittee, concern has been expressed in almost every European country over the problem posed by the introduction of American comics, or comics of that pattern, since World War II.

2. Crime and horror comic books introduced to foreign cultures a lowered intellectual milieu. Detective and weird stories, American style, present a hardened version of killing, robbery, and sadism.

3. Comic books are distributed in many countries where the population is other than Caucasian. Materials depicting persons of other races as criminals may have meanings and implication[s] for persons of [other] races which were unforeseen by the publisher.

4. There is evidence that comic books are being utilized by the U.S.S.R. to undermine the morale of youth in many countries by pointing to crime and horror as portrayed in American comics as one of the end results of the most successful capitalist nation in the world. . . .

A Communist magazine, printed in East Germany and devoted to bitter criticism of the United States, appeared under the name, "USA im Wort und Bild" (USA in Word and Pictures). The publication ridicules comic books and similar American attempts to present the classics in simple form. Some of the phrases read:

> Shakespeare in Yankee dialect is the latest "cultural triumph" *** The "cultural" achievement of the publishers is expressed on the jacket of the pamphlet: "You can quote the best quotations of Shakespeare and impress your friends, without reading the play."

. . . Soviet propaganda cites the comic book in support of its favorite anti-American theme—the degeneracy of American culture. However, comic books are but one of a number of instruments used in Soviet propaganda to illustrate this theme. The attacks are usually supported with examples drawn from the less-desirable American motion pictures, television programs, literature, drama, and art.

It is represented in the Soviet propaganda that the United States crime rate, particularly the incidence of juvenile delinquency, is largely incited by the murders, robberies, and other crimes portrayed in "trash literature." The reason such reading matter is distributed, according to that propaganda, is that the "imperialists" use it to condition a generation of young automatons who will be ready to march and kill in the future wars of aggression planned by the capitalists. . . .

While not attempting to review the several findings included in this report, the subcommittee wishes to reiterate its belief that this country cannot afford the calculated risk involved in feeding its children, through comic books, a concentrated diet of crime, horror, and violence. There was substantial, although not unanimous, agreement among the experts that there may be detrimental and delinquency-producing effects upon both the emotionally disturbed child and the emotionally normal delinquent. Children of either type may gain suggestion, support, and sanction from reading crime and horror comics.

There are many who believe that the boys and girls who are the most avid and extensive consumers of such comics are those who are least able to tolerate this type of reading material. The excessive reading of this material is viewed by some observers as sometimes being symptomatic of some emotional maladjustment, that is, comic book reading may be a workable "diagnostic indicator" of an underlying pathological condition of a child.

It is during childhood that the individual's concepts of right and wrong and his reactions to society's standards are largely developed. Those responsible for the operation of every form of the mass media of communication, including comic books, which cater to the education or entertainment of children have, therefore, a responsibility to gear their products to these special considerations.

Standards for such products, whether in the form of a code or by the policies of individual producers, should not be aimed to eliminate only that which can be proved beyond doubt to demoralize youth. Rather the aim should be to eliminate all materials that potentially exert detrimental effects.

To achieve this end, it will require continuing vigilance on the part of parents, publishers and citizens' groups. The work that has been done by citizens' and parents' groups in calling attention to the problem of crime and horror comics has been far-reaching in its impact.

The subcommittee notes with some surprise that little attention has been paid by educational and welfare agencies to the potential dangers, as well as benefits, to children presented by the growth of the comic book industry. As spokesmen in behalf of children, their responsibility requires that they be concerned for the child and the whole world in which he lives. The campaign against juvenile delinquency cannot be won by anything less than an all-out attack upon all conditions contributing to the problem.

The interest of our young citizens would not be served by postponing all precautionary measures until the exact kind and degree of influence exerted by comic books upon children's behavior is fully determined through careful research. Sole responsibility for stimulating, formulating and carrying out such research cannot be assumed by parents' or citizens' groups. Rather it must also be assumed by the educational and social welfare agencies and organizations concerned.

In the meantime, the welfare of this Nation's young makes it mandatory that all concerned unite in supporting sincere efforts of the industry to raise the standards of its products and in demanding adequate standards of decency and good taste. Nor should these united efforts be relaxed in the face of monetary gains. Continuing vigilance is essential in sustaining this effort.

READING AND DISCUSSION QUESTIONS

1. From the committee's report, what inferences can you make concerning the link senators saw between the comic book industry and the problem of juvenile delinquency? What evidence from their investigations convinced them that a problem existed?

2. How does the committee define the short- and long-term effects of children's continued exposure to comic books featuring violence and crime?

3. How does this committee report reflect the broader anxieties in Cold War America?

26-6 | Social Critic Laments Emptiness of Modern Life

PAUL GOODMAN, *Growing Up Absurd* (1960)

In the 1950s, corporate America provided middle-class men with comfortable careers. For many of them, white-collar work represented the achievement of their own American Dream, providing stability and an income supporting a tidy suburban home with the creature comforts middle-class Americans expected. Yet this ideal troubled others, including social critics like Paul Goodman, whose 1960 book *Growing Up Absurd* posed searching questions about the value of the life sacrificed to the social and economic system defining success in modern America.

When the existing state of things is suddenly measured by people against far higher standards than they have been used to, it is no longer the case that there are no alternatives. People are forced by their better judgment to ask very basic questions: Is it possible, *how* is it possible, to have more meaning and honor in work? to put wealth to some real use? to have a high standard of living of whose quality we are not ashamed? to get social justice for those who have been shamefully left out? to have a use of leisure that is not a dismaying waste of a hundred million adults? The large group of independent people who have been out of the swim, with their old-fashioned virtues, suddenly have something admirable about them; one is surprised that they still exist, and their existence is relevant. And from the members of the Organized System itself come acute books criticizing the shortcomings of the Organized System.

It is my belief that we are going to have a change. And once the Americans can recover from their mesmerized condition and its astounding political apathy,

Paul Goodman, *Growing Up Absurd: Problems of Youth in the Organized Society* (New York: Random House, 1960), xiv–xv, 11–13, 30–32.

our country will be in a most fortunate situation. For the kinds of radical changes we need are those that are appropriate to a fairly general prosperity. They are practicable. They can be summed up as simply restoring, in J. K. Galbraith's phrase, the "social balance" that we have allowed to become lopsided and run-away in the present abuse of the country's wealth. For instance, since we have a vast surplus productivity, we can turn to finding jobs that will bring out a youth's capacity, and so really conserve human resources. We can find ways to restore to the worker a say in his production, and so really do something for manly inde-pendence. Since we have a problem of what to do with leisure, we can begin to think of necessary community enterprises that want doing, and that people can enthusiastically and spontaneously throw themselves into, and be proud of the results (e.g., beautifying our hideous small towns). And perhaps thereby create us a culture again. Since we have the technology, the capital, and the labor, why should we not have livable cities? . . .

[W]e see groups of boys and young men disaffected from the dominant soci-ety. The young men are Angry and Beat. The boys are Juvenile Delinquents. These groups are not small, and they will grow larger. Certainly they are suffering. Demonstrably they are not getting enough out of our wealth and civilization. They are not growing up to full capacity. They are failing to assimilate much of the culture. As was predictable, most of the authorities and all of the public spokes-men explain it by saying there has been a failure of socialization. They say that background conditions have interrupted socialization and must be improved. And, not enough effort has been made to guarantee belonging, there must be better bait or punishment.

But perhaps there has *not* been a failure of communication. Perhaps the social message has been communicated clearly to the young men and is unacceptable.

In this book I shall therefore take the opposite tack and ask, "Socialization to what? to what dominant society and available culture?" And if this question is asked, we must at once ask the other question, "Is the harmonious organization to which the young are inadequately socialized, perhaps against human nature, or not worthy of human nature, and *therefore* there is difficulty in growing up?" If this is so, the disaffection of the young is profound and it will not be finally reme-diable by better techniques of socializing. Instead, there will have to be changes in our society and its culture, so as to meet the appetites and capacities of human nature, in order to grow up.

This brings me to another proposition about growing up, and perhaps the main theme of this book. *Growth, like any ongoing junction, requires adequate objects in the environment* to meet the needs and capacities of the growing child, boy, youth, and young man, until he can better choose and make his own environ-ment. It is not a "psychological" question of poor influences and bad attitudes, but an objective question of real opportunities for worth-while experience. It makes no difference whether the growth is normal or distorted, only real objects will finish the experience. (Even in the psychotherapy of adults one finds that many a stubborn symptom vanishes if there is a real change in the vocational and sexual opportunities, so that the symptom is no longer needed.) It is here that the theory of belonging and socializing breaks down miserably. For it can be shown — I intend to show — that with all the harmonious belonging and all the tidying up of background conditions that you please, our abundant society is at present simply deficient in many of the most elementary objective opportunities and worth-while goals that could make growing up possible. It is lacking in enough man's work. It is lacking in honest public speech, and people are not taken seriously. It is lacking in the opportunity to be useful. It thwarts aptitude and creates stupidity. It corrupts ingenuous patriotism. It corrupts the fine arts. It shackles science. It dampens animal ardor. It discourages the religious convictions of Justification and Vocation and it dims the sense that there is a Creation. It has no Honor. It has no Community.

Thwarted, or starved, in the important objects proper to young capacities, the boys and young men naturally find or invent deviant objects for themselves; this is the beautiful shaping power of our human nature. Their choices and inventions are rarely charming, usually stupid, and often disastrous; we cannot expect average kids to deviate with genius. But on the other hand, the young men who conform to the dominant society become for the most part apathetic, disappointed, cynical, and wasted.

(I say the "young men and boys" rather than the "young people" because the problems I want to discuss in this book belong primarily, in our society, to the boys: how to be useful and make something of oneself. A girl does not *have* to, she is not expected to, "make something" of herself. Her career does not have to be self-justifying, for she will have children, which is absolutely self-justifying, like any other natural or creative act. With this background, it is less important, for instance, what job an average young woman works at till she is married. The quest for the glamour job is given at least a little substance by its relation to a "better" marriage. Correspondingly, our "youth troubles" are boys' troubles — female delinquency is sexual: "incorrigibility" and unmarried pregnancy. Yet as every woman knows, these problems are intensely interesting to women, for if the boys do not grow to be men, where shall the women find men? If the husband is running the rat race of the organized system, there is not much father for the children.) . . .

Our society, which is not geared to the cultivation of its young, *is* geared to a profitable expanding production, a so-called high standard of living of mediocre value, and the maintenance of nearly full employment. Politically, the chief of these is full employment. In a crisis, when profitable production is temporarily curtailed, government spending increases and jobs are manufactured. In "normalcy" — a condition of slow boom — the easy credit, installment buying, and artificially induced demand for useless goods create jobs for all and good profits for some.

Now, back in the Thirties, when the New Deal attempted by hook or crook to put people back to work and give them money to revive the shattered economy, there was an outcry of moral indignation from the conservatives that many of the jobs were "boondoggling," useless made-work. It was insisted, and rightly, that such work was demoralizing to the workers themselves. It is a question of a word, but a candid critic might certainly say that many of the jobs in our present "normal" production are useless made-work. The tail fins and built-in obsolescence might be called boondoggling. The $64,000 Question and the busy hum of Madison Avenue might certainly be called boondoggling. Certain tax-dodge Foundations are boondoggling. What of business lunches and expense accounts? fringe benefits? the comic categories of occupation in the building trades? the extra stagehands and musicians of the theater crafts? These jolly devices to put money back to work no doubt have a demoralizing effect on somebody or other (certainly on me, they make me green with envy), but where is the moral indignation from Top Management?

Suppose we would cut out the boondoggling and gear our society to a more sensible abundance, with efficient production of quality goods, distribution in a natural market, counterinflation and sober credit. At once the work week would be cut to, say, twenty hours instead of forty. (Important People have already mentioned the figure thirty.) Or alternately, half the labor force would be unemployed. Suppose too and how can we not suppose it? that the automatic machines are used generally, rather than just to get rid of badly organized unskilled labor. The unemployment will be still more drastic. . . .

Everybody knows this, nobody wants to talk about it much, for we don't know how to cope with it. The effect is that we are living a kind of lie. Long ago, labor leaders used to fight for the shorter work week, but now they don't, because they're pretty sure they don't want it. Indeed, when hours are reduced, the tendency is to get a second, part-time, job and raise the standard of living, *because* the job is meaningless and one must have something; but the standard of living is pretty meaningless, too. Nor is this strange atmosphere a new thing. For at least a generation the maximum sensible use of our productivity could have thrown a vast population out of work, or relieved everybody of a lot of useless work, depending on how you take it. (Consider with how little cutback of useful civilian production the economy produced the war goods and maintained an Army, economically unemployed.) The plain truth is that at present very many of us are useless, not needed, rationally unemployable. It is in this paradoxical atmosphere that young persons grow up. It looks busy and expansive, but it is rationally at a stalemate.

READING AND DISCUSSION QUESTIONS

1. How does Goodman define the problems he sees with the "organized system" he criticizes? What *is* the organized system, and what impact did it have on boys and men?

2. What sort of reader do you think this book attracted? How do you explain its anti-establishment appeal?

3. Consider Goodman's critique as an artifact of the Cold War era. What does the popularity of his book suggest to you about the era's cultural conflict regarding values? What values was he questioning?

■ COMPARATIVE QUESTIONS ■

1. Both Kefauver and Goodman diagnosed the problem of youth in the 1950s. How do their assessments compare? Do they define the problem in similar or dissimilar ways? How do you account for the differences you see?

2. To what extent would the teenage culture highlighted by the soda fountain photograph have confirmed Goodman's general criticism about contemporary consumer culture? What similarities do you see between Goodman and Graham in their critiques of modern America?

3. Based on your analysis and evaluation of the historical evidence presented in this chapter, what conclusion could you make about the significance of middle-class values to Cold War America?

4. Explain and evaluate the 1950s and the 1920s as two eras of cultural conservatism. To what degree do you see these periods as conservative? What apparent social norms lead you to this conclusion?

5. Compare Cold War evangelicalism with earlier periods of religious enthusiasm by identifying similarities and differences in the perspectives of Graham, Billy Sunday (Document 22-4), and W. B. Riley (Document P7-4). Did these three evangelists identify a common foe to American religiosity? If so, what was it?

27

Walking into Freedom Land: The Civil Rights Movement
1941–1973

Three years after Martin Luther King Jr. shared his dream at the Lincoln Memorial in 1963, a young civil rights activist preached: "I am black and I am beautiful! I am Somebody." Jesse Jackson's boast hinted at the extraordinary impact of the civil rights movement, which had restored a sense of self-worth to millions of people who faced discrimination. The African American civil rights movement targeted racial discrimination in its legal, social, and economic guises by embracing tactics ranging from interracial alliances to Black Power militancy. Its important victories, including the Civil Rights Act of 1964 and the Voting Rights Act of 1965, pressed forward significant changes in the lives of African Americans, who had long found themselves relegated to the margins of American society. The movement spoke to others as well, including members of many other groups who had similarly faced jeers and taunts as they struggled for political, social, and economic acceptance. The social revolution for rights mobilized America's ethnic minorities and Native Americans who saw in the struggle of African Americans some hope that the sound of their voices could also lift freedom's chorus. While the achievements of the civil rights movement were too modest for the taste of many who had long felt the oppressor's glare, they were enough to spirit others forward toward America's promised land.

27-1 | Southern Girl's Introduction to Racism
LILLIAN SMITH, *Killers of the Dream* (1949)

Lillian Smith was a minority voice in the South during the early years of the civil rights movement: a white lesbian who openly challenged the South's Jim Crow traditions. Known mostly

---

Lillian Smith, *Killers of the Dream* (New York: Norton, 1949, reissued edition 1994), 26–29.

for her novel *Strange Fruit* (1944) about an ill-fated interracial relationship set in 1920s Georgia, Smith also published *Killers of the Dream*, where she drew upon her childhood memories for a meditation on the meaning and consequences of segregation and racism.

A little white girl was found in the colored section of our town, living with a Negro family in a broken-down shack. This family had moved in only a few weeks before and little was known of them. One of the ladies in my mother's club, while driving over to her washerwoman's, saw the child swinging on a gate. The shack, as she said, was hardly more than a pigsty and this white child was living with ignorant and dirty and sick-looking colored folks. "They must have kidnapped her," she told her friends. Genuinely shocked, the clubwomen busied themselves in an attempt to do something, for the child was very white indeed. The strange Negroes were subjected to a grueling questioning and finally grew frightened and evasive and refused to talk at all. This only increased the suspicion of the white group, and the next day the clubwomen, escorted by the town marshal, took the child from her adopted family despite their tears.

She was brought to our home. I do not know why my mother consented to this plan. Perhaps because she loved children and always showed tenderness and concern for them. It was easy for one more to fit into our ample household and Janie was soon at home there. She roomed with me, sat next to me at the table; I found Bible verses for her to say at breakfast; she wore my clothes, played with my dolls and followed me around from morning to night. She was dazed by her new comforts and by the interesting activities of this big lively family; and I was as happily dazed, for her adoration was a new thing to me; and as time passed a quick, childish, and deeply felt bond grew up between us.

But a day came when a telephone message was received from a colored orphanage. There was a meeting at our home, whispers, shocked exclamations. All afternoon the ladies went in and out of our house talking to Mother in tones too low for children to hear. And as they passed us at play, most of them looked quickly at Janie and quickly looked away again, though a few stopped and stared at her as if they could not tear their eyes from her face. When my father came home in the evening Mother closed her door against our young ears and talked a long time with him. I heard him laugh, heard Mother say, "But Papa, this is no laughing matter!" And then they were back in the living room with us and my mother was pale and my father was saying, "Well, work it out, honey, as best you can. After all, now that you know, it is pretty simple."

In a little while my mother called my sister and me into her bedroom and told us that in the morning Janie would return to Colored Town. She said Janie was to have the dresses the ladies had given her and a few of my own, and the toys we had shared with her. She asked me if I would like to give Janie one of my dolls. She seemed hurried, though Janie was not to leave until next day. She said, "Why not select it now?" And in dreamlike stiffness I brought in my dolls and chose one for Janie. And then I found it possible to say, "Why? Why is she leaving? She likes us, she hardly knows them. She told me she had been with them only a month."

"Because," Mother said gently, "Janie is a little colored girl."

"But she can't be. She's white!"

"We were mistaken. She is colored."

"But she looks——"

"She is colored. Please don't argue!"

"What does it mean?" I whispered.

"It means," Mother said slowly, "that she has to live in Colored Town with colored people."

"But why? She lived here three weeks and she doesn't belong to them, she told me she didn't."

"She is a little colored girl."

"But you said yourself that she has nice manners. You said that," I persisted.

"Yes, she is a nice child. But a colored child cannot live in our home."

"Why?"

"You know, dear! You have always known that white and colored people do not live together."

"Can she come over to play?"

"No."

"I don't understand."

"I don't either," my young sister quavered.

"You're too young to understand. And don't ask me again, ever again, about this!" Mother's voice was sharp but her face was sad and there was no certainty left there. She hurried out and busied herself in the kitchen and I wandered through that room where I had been born, touching the old familiar things in it, looking at them, trying to find the answer to a question that moaned in my mind like a hurt thing. . . .

And then I went out to Janie, who was waiting, knowing things were happening that concerned her but waiting until they were spoken aloud.

I do not know quite how the words were said but I told her that she was to return in the morning to the little place where she had lived because she was colored and colored children could not live with white children.

"Are you white?" she said.

"I'm white," I replied, "and my sister is white. And you're colored. And white and colored can't live together because my mother says so."

"Why?" Janie whispered.

"Because they can't," I said. But I knew, though I said it firmly, that something was wrong. I knew my father and mother whom I passionately admired had done that which did not fit in with their teachings. I knew they had betrayed something which they held dear. And I was shamed by their failure and frightened, for I felt that they were no longer as powerful as I had thought. There was something Out There that was stronger than they and I could not bear to believe it. I could not confess that my father, who had always solved the family dilemmas easily and with laughter, could not solve this. I knew that my mother who was so good to children did not believe in her heart that she was being good to this child.

There was not a word in my mind that said it but my body knew and my glands, and I was filled with anxiety.

But I felt compelled to believe they were right. It was the only way my world could be held together. And, like a slow poison, it began to seep through me: *I was white. She was colored. We must not be together. It was bad to be together. Though you ate with your nurse when you were little, it was bad to eat with any colored person after that. It was bad just as other things were bad that your mother had told you. It was bad that she was to sleep in the room with me that night. It was bad. . . .*

READING AND DISCUSSION QUESTIONS

1. How does Smith describe the impact of her mother's reaction to the news about Janie? What effect did it have on her view of her parents?

2. What was "Out There" that so frightened her? To what degree do you think Smith believed the civil rights movement was an effort to defeat the thing "out there"?

27-2 | Southern Congressmen Issue Manifesto Against *Brown v. Board* Decision
Declaration of Constitutional Principles (1956)

In 1954, the Supreme Court ruled in *Brown v. Board of Education* that the long-standing "separate but equal" doctrine, affirmed in the 1896 case *Plessy v. Ferguson*, was unconstitutional. The *Brown* decision required the racial integration of public schools by arguing that separate institutions were "inherently" unequal. One hundred and one congressmen from southern states, outraged by the Court's decision, signed their names to the "Declaration of Constitutional Principles," often referred to as the "Southern Manifesto."

We regard the decision of the Supreme Court in the school cases as clear abuse of judicial power. It climaxes a trend in the Federal judiciary undertaking to legislate, in derogation of the authority of Congress, and to encroach upon the reserved rights of the states and the people.

The original Constitution does not mention education. Neither does the Fourteenth Amendment nor any other amendment. The debates preceding the submission of the Fourteenth Amendment clearly show that there was no intent that it should affect the systems of education maintained by the states.

The very Congress which proposed the amendment subsequently provided for segregated schools in the District of Columbia.

When the amendment was adopted in 1868, there were thirty-seven states of the Union. Every one of the twenty-six states that had any substantial racial

Congressional Record, 84th Cong., 2d Sess., vol. 102, part 4 (Washington, DC: Government Printing Office, 1956), 4460.

differences among its people either approved the operation of segregated schools already in existence or subsequently established such schools by action of the same law-making body which considered the Fourteenth Amendment.

As admitted by the Supreme Court in the public school case (Brown v. Board of Education), the doctrine of separate but equal schools "apparently originated in Roberts v. City of Boston (1849), upholding school segregation against attack as being violative of a state constitutional guarantee of equality." This constitutional doctrine began in the North—not in the South—and it was followed not only in Massachusetts but in Connecticut, New York, Illinois, Indiana, Michigan, Minnesota, New Jersey, Ohio, Pennsylvania and other northern states until they, exercising their rights as states through the constitutional processes of local self-government, changed their school systems.

In the case of Plessy v. Ferguson in 1896 the Supreme Court expressly declared that under the Fourteenth Amendment no person was denied any of his rights if the states provided separate but equal public facilities. This decision has been followed in many other cases. It is notable that the Supreme Court, speaking through Chief Justice Taft, a former President of the United States, unanimously declared in 1927 in Lum v. Rice that the "separate but equal" principle is "within the discretion of the state in regulating its public schools and does not conflict with the Fourteenth Amendment."

This interpretation, restated time and again, became a part of the life of the people of many of the states and confirmed their habits, customs, traditions and way of life. It is founded on elemental humanity and common sense, for parents should not be deprived by Government of the right to direct the lives and education of their own children.

Though there has been no constitutional amendment or act of Congress changing this established legal principle almost a century old, the Supreme Court of the United States, with no legal basis for such action, undertook to exercise their naked judicial power and substituted their personal political and social ideas for the established law of the land.

This unwarranted exercise of power by the court, contrary to the Constitution, is creating chaos and confusion in the states principally affected. It is destroying the amicable relations between the white and Negro races that have been created through ninety years of patient effort by the good people of both races. It has planted hatred and suspicion where there has been heretofore friendship and understanding.

Without regard to the consent of the governed, outside agitators are threatening immediate and revolutionary changes in our public school systems. If done, this is certain to destroy the system of public education in some of the states.

With the gravest concern for the explosive and dangerous condition created by this decision and inflamed by outside meddlers:

We reaffirm our reliance on the Constitution as the fundamental law of the land.

We decry the Supreme Court's encroachments on rights reserved to the states and to the people, contrary to established law and to the Constitution.

We commend the motives of those states which have declared the intention to resist forced integration by any lawful means.

We appeal to the states and people who are not directly affected by these decisions to consider the constitutional principles involved against the time when they too, on issues vital to them, may be the victims of judicial encroachment.

Even though we constitute a minority in the present congress, we have full faith that a majority of the American people believe in the dual system of government which has enabled us to achieve our greatness and will in time demand that the reserved rights of the states and of the people be made secure against judicial usurpation.

We pledge ourselves to use all lawful means to bring about a reversal of this decision which is contrary to the Constitution and to prevent the use of force in its implementation.

READING AND DISCUSSION QUESTIONS

1. How did the congressmen frame their opposition to the Supreme Court's decision in *Brown v. Board*? What specifically did they say they were objecting to?

2. What conclusions can you draw from the Southern Manifesto about the challenges that faced the civil rights movement in the 1950s and 1960s?

27-3 | Civil Rights Activist Challenges Racial Discrimination

FANNIE LOU HAMER, *Testimony Before the Credentials Committee of the Democratic National Convention* (1964)

The foot soldiers of the civil rights movement included women like Fannie Lou Hamer, an African American activist born in 1917 in Mississippi, where racial oppression often took violent form, as she recounts in this testimony. In 1964, Hamer's Mississippi Freedom Democratic Party (MFDP) sought delegate seats at the Democratic National Convention, but President Johnson, seeking reelection, wanted to avoid a convention split over civil rights. Johnson won, and neither Hamer nor any other MFDP delegates were seated, but her compelling story, aired on national television, brought visible attention to the movement's cause.

Mr. Chairman, and to the Credentials Committee, my name is Mrs. Fannie Lou Hamer, and I live at 626 East Lafayette Street, Ruleville, Mississippi, Sunflower County, the home of Senator James O. Eastland, and Senator Stennis.

It was the 31st of August in 1962 that eighteen of us traveled twenty-six miles to the county courthouse in Indianola to try to register to become first-class citizens. We was met in Indianola by policemen, Highway Patrolmen, and they only

The Speeches of Fannie Lou Hamer: To Tell It Like It Is, ed. Maegan Parker Brooks and Davis W. Houck (Jackson: University Press of Mississippi, 2011), 43–45.

allowed two of us in to take the literacy test at the time. After we had taken this test and started back to Ruleville, we was held up by the City Police and the State Highway Patrolmen and carried back to Indianola where the bus driver was charged that day with driving a bus the wrong color.

After we paid the fine among us, we continued on to Ruleville, and Reverend Jeff Sunny carried me four miles in the rural area where I had worked as a time-keeper and sharecropper for eighteen years. I was met there by my children, who told me the plantation owner was angry because I had gone down—tried to register.

After they told me, my husband came, and said the plantation owner was raising Cain because I had tried to register. And before he quit talking the plan-tation owner came and said, "Fannie Lou, do you know—did Pap tell you what I said?"

And I said, "Yes, sir."

He said, "Well I mean that."

Said, "If you don't go down and withdraw your registration, you will have to leave." Said, "Then if you go down and withdraw," said, "you still might have to go because we're not ready for that in Mississippi."

And I addressed him and told him and said, "I didn't try to register for you. I tried to register for myself."

I had to leave that same night.

On the 10th of September 1962, sixteen bullets was fired into the home of Mr. and Mrs. Robert Tucker for me. That same night two girls were shot in Ruleville, Mississippi. Also, Mr. Joe McDonald's house was shot in.

And June the 9th, 1963, I had attended a voter registration workshop; was returning back to Mississippi. Ten of us was traveling by the Continental Trailway bus. When we got to Winona, Mississippi, which is Montgomery County, four of the people got off to use the washroom, and two of the people—to use the restaurant—two of the people wanted to use the washroom.

The four people that had gone in to use the restaurant was ordered out. During this time I was on the bus. But when I looked through the window and saw they had rushed out I got off of the bus to see what had happened. And one of the ladies said, "It was a State Highway Patrolman and a Chief of Police ordered us out."

I got back on the bus and one of the persons had used the washroom got back on the bus, too.

As soon as I was seated on the bus, I saw when they began to get the five people in a highway patrolman's car. I stepped off of the bus to see what was happening and somebody screamed from the car that the five workers was in and said, "Get that one there." And when I went to get in the car, when the man told me I was under arrest, he kicked me.

I was carried to the county jail and put in the booking room. They left some of the people in the booking room and began to place us in cells. I was placed in a cell with a young woman called Miss Ivesta Simpson. After I was placed in the cell I began to hear sounds of licks and screams. I could hear the sounds of licks and horrible screams. And I could hear somebody say, "Can you say, 'yes, sir,' nigger? Can you say 'yes, sir'?"

And they would say other horrible names.

She would say, "Yes, I can say 'yes, sir.'"

"So, well, say it."

She said, "I don't know you well enough."

They beat her, I don't know how long. And after a while she began to pray, and asked God to have mercy on those people.

And it wasn't too long before three white men came to my cell. One of these men was a State Highway Patrolman and he asked me where I was from. And I told him Ruleville. He said, "We are going to check this." And they left my cell and it wasn't too long before they came back. He said, "You are from Ruleville all right," and he used a curse word. And he said, "We're going to make you wish you was dead."

I was carried out of that cell into another cell where they had two Negro prisoners. The State Highway Patrolmen ordered the first Negro to take the blackjack. The first Negro prisoner ordered me, by orders from the State Highway Patrolman, for me to lay down on a bunk bed on my face. And I laid on my face, the first Negro began to beat me.

And I was beat by the first Negro until he was exhausted. I was holding my hands behind me at that time on my left side, because I suffered from polio when I was six years old.

After the first Negro had beat until he was exhausted, the State Highway Patrolman ordered the second Negro to take the blackjack.

The second Negro began to beat and I began to work my feet, and the State Highway Patrolman ordered the first Negro who had beat to sit on my feet—to keep me from working my feet. I began to scream and one white man got up and began to beat me in my head and tell me to hush.

One white man—my dress had worked up high—he walked over and pulled my dress—I pulled my dress down and he pulled my dress back up.

I was in jail when Medgar Evers was murdered.

All of this is on account of we want to register, to become first-class citizens. And if the Freedom Democratic Party is not seated now, I question America. Is this America, the land of the free and the home of the brave, where we have to sleep with our telephones off of the hooks because our lives be threatened daily, because we want to live as decent human beings, in America?

READING AND DISCUSSION QUESTIONS

1. What argument about African American civil rights does Hamer make in her speech to the credentials committee? What is the nature of her appeal?

2. What evidence does her testimony provide for your understanding of the obstacles African Americans endured in seeking their civil rights? From her story, what can you infer about the peculiar vulnerabilities facing black women activists?

27-4 | Civil Rights Movement Takes a More Militant Turn

MALCOLM X, *The Ballot or the Bullet* (1964)

Martin Luther King Jr.'s nonviolent approach to civil rights frustrated some, like Malcolm X, who demanded more direct and immediate action against the system of racial oppression that faced African Americans. Malcolm X, who preached an alternative, Black Nationalist message, gave this 1964 speech to a symposium on the theme of "The Negro Revolt." His public break with the Nation of Islam precipitated his assassination in February 1965.

The question tonight, as I understand it, is "The Negro Revolt, and Where Do We Go From Here?" or "What Next?" In my little humble way of understanding it, it points toward either the ballot or the bullet. . . .

Although I'm still a Muslim, I'm not here tonight to discuss my religion. I'm not here to try and change your religion. I'm not here to argue or discuss anything that we differ about, because it's time for us to submerge our differences and realize that it is best for us to first see that we have the same problem, a common problem — a problem that will make you catch hell whether you're a Baptist, or a Methodist, or a Muslim, or a nationalist. Whether you're educated or illiterate, whether you live on the boulevard or in the alley, you're going to catch hell just like I am. We're all in the same boat and we all are going to catch the same hell from the same man. He just happens to be a white man. All of us have suffered here, in this country, political oppression at the hands of the white man, economic exploitation at the hands of the white man, and social degradation at the hands of the white man.

Now in speaking like this, it doesn't mean that we're anti-white, but it does mean we're anti-exploitation, we're anti-degradation, we're anti-oppression. And if the white man doesn't want us to be anti-him, let him stop oppressing and exploiting and degrading us. . . .

If we don't do something real soon, I think you'll have to agree that we're going to be forced either to use the ballot or the bullet. It's one or the other in 1964. It isn't that time is running out — time has run out! 1964 threatens to be the most explosive year America has ever witnessed. The most explosive year. Why? It's also a political year. It's the year when all of the white politicians will be back in the so-called Negro community jiving you and me for some votes. The year when all of the white political crooks will be right back in your and my community with their false promises, building up our hopes for a letdown, with their trickery and their treachery, with their false promises which they don't intend to keep. As they nourish these dissatisfactions, it can only lead to one thing, an explosion; and now we have the type of black man on the scene in America today — I'm sorry, Brother Lomax[1] — who just doesn't intend to turn the other cheek any longer. . . .

Malcolm X, "The Ballot or the Bullet," in *Malcolm X Speaks: Selected Speeches and Statements*, ed. George Breitman (New York: Grove Press, 1965), 24–26, 28, 30–35.

[1]**Louis Lomax**: An African American journalist and civil rights activist who spoke before Malcolm X at the 1964 symposium.

I'm not a politician, not even a student of politics; in fact, I'm not a student of much of anything. I'm not a Democrat. I'm not a Republican, and I don't even consider myself an American. If you and I were Americans, there'd be no problem. Those Hunkies that just got off the boat, they're already Americans; Polacks are already Americans; the Italian refugees are already Americans. Everything that came out of Europe, every blue-eyed thing, is already an American. And as long as you and I have been over here, we aren't Americans yet.

Well, I am one who doesn't believe in deluding myself. I'm not going to sit at your table and watch you eat, with nothing on my plate, and call myself a diner. Sitting at the table doesn't make you a diner, unless you eat some of what's on that plate. Being here in America doesn't make you an American. Being born here in America doesn't make you an American. Why, if birth made you American, you wouldn't need any legislation; you wouldn't need any amendments to the Constitution, you wouldn't be faced with civil-rights filibustering in Washington, D.C., right now. They don't have to pass civil-rights legislation to make a Polack an American.

No, I'm not an American. I'm one of the 22 million black people who are the victims of Americanism. One of the 22 million black people who are the victims of democracy, nothing but disguised hypocrisy. So, I'm not standing here speaking to you as an American, or a patriot, or a flag-saluter, or a flag-waver—no, not I. I'm speaking as a victim of this American system. And I see America through the eyes of the victim. I don't see any American dream; I see an American nightmare. . . .

So it's time in 1964 to wake up. And when you see them coming up with that kind of conspiracy, let them know your eyes are open. And let them know you—something else that's wide open too. It's got to be the ballot or the bullet. The ballot or the bullet. If you're afraid to use an expression like that, you should get on out of the country, you should get back in the cotton patch, you should get back in the alley. They get all the Negro vote, and after they get it, the Negro gets nothing in return. All they did when they got to Washington was give a few big Negroes big jobs. Those big Negroes didn't need big jobs, they already had jobs. That's camouflage, that's trickery, that's treachery, window-dressing. . . .

That's why, in 1964, it's time now for you and me to become more politically mature and realize what the ballot is for; what we're supposed to get when we cast a ballot; and that if we don't cast a ballot, it's going to end up in a situation where we're going to have to cast a bullet. It's either a ballot or a bullet. . . .

The same government that you go abroad to fight for and die for is the government that is in a conspiracy to deprive you of your voting rights, deprive you of your economic opportunities, deprive you of decent housing, deprive you of decent education. You don't need to go to the employer alone, it is the government itself, the government of America, that is responsible for the oppression and exploitation and degradation of black people in this country. And you should drop it in their lap. This government has failed the Negro. This so-called democracy has failed the Negro. And all these white liberals have definitely failed the Negro.

So, where do we go from here? First, we need some friends. We need some new allies. The entire civil-rights struggle needs a new interpretation, a broader interpretation. We need to look at this civil-rights thing from another angle—from the inside as well as from the outside. To those of us whose philosophy is black nationalism, the only way you can get involved in the civil-rights struggle is give it a new interpretation. That old interpretation excluded us. It kept us out. So, we're giving a new interpretation to the civil-rights struggle, an interpretation that will enable us to come into it, take part in it. And these handkerchief-heads who have been dillydallying and pussy footing and compromising—we don't intend to let them pussyfoot and dillydally and compromise any longer. . . .

And now you're facing a situation where the young Negro's coming up. They don't want to hear that "turn-the-other-cheek" stuff, no. In Jacksonville, those were teenagers, they were throwing Molotov cocktails. Negroes have never done that before. But it shows you there's a new deal coming in. There's new thinking coming in. There's new strategy coming in. It'll be Molotov cocktails this month, hand grenades next month, and something else next month. It'll be ballots, or it'll be bullets. It'll be liberty, or it will be death. . . .

The black nationalists, those whose philosophy is black nationalism, in bringing about this new interpretation of the entire meaning of civil rights, look upon it as meaning . . . equality of opportunity. Well, we're justified in seeking civil rights, if it means equality of opportunity, because all we're doing there is trying to collect for our investment. Our mothers and fathers invested sweat and blood. Three hundred and ten years we worked in this country without a dime in return—I mean without a dime in return. You let the white man walk around here talking about how rich this country is, but you never stop to think how it got rich so quick. It got rich because you made it rich. . . .

Whenever you're going after something that belongs to you, anyone who's depriving you of the right to have it is a criminal. Understand that. Whenever you are going after something that is yours, you are within your legal rights to lay claim to it. And anyone who puts forth any effort to deprive you of that which is yours, is breaking the law, is a criminal. And this was pointed out by the Supreme Court decision. It outlawed segregation. Which means segregation is against the law. Which means a segregationist is breaking the law. A segregationist is a criminal. You can't label him as anything other than that. And when you demonstrate against segregation, the law is on your side. The Supreme Court is on your side.

Now, who is it that opposes you in carrying out the law? The police department itself. With police dogs and clubs. Whenever you demonstrate against segregation, whether it is segregated education, segregated housing, or anything else, the law is on your side, and anyone who stands in the way is not the law any longer. They are breaking the law; they are not representatives of the law. Any time you demonstrate against segregation and a man has the audacity to put a police dog on you, kill that dog, kill him, I'm telling you, kill that dog. I say it, if they put me in jail tomorrow, kill—that—dog. Then you'll put a stop to it. Now, if these white people in here don't want to see that kind of action, get down and tell the mayor to tell the police department to pull the dogs in. That's all you have to do. If you don't do it, someone else will. . . .

If you don't take this kind of stand, your little children will grow up and look at you and think "shame." If you don't take an uncompromising stand, I don't mean go out and get violent; but at the same time you should never be nonviolent unless you run into some nonviolence. I'm nonviolent with those who are nonviolent with me. But when you drop that violence on me, then you've made me go insane, and I'm not responsible for what I do. And that's the way every Negro should get. Any time you know you're within the law, within your legal rights, within your moral rights, in accord with justice, then die for what you believe in. But don't die alone. Let your dying be reciprocal. This is what is meant by equality. What's good for the goose is good for the gander.

When we begin to get in this area, we need new friends, we need new allies. We need to expand the civil-rights struggle to a higher level—to the level of human rights. Whenever you are in a civil-rights struggle, whether you know it or not, you are confining yourself to the jurisdiction of Uncle Sam. No one from the outside world can speak out in your behalf as long as your struggle is a civil-rights struggle. Civil rights comes within the domestic affairs of this country. All of our African brothers and our Asian brothers and our Latin-American brothers cannot open their mouths and interfere in the domestic affairs of the United States. And as long as it's civil rights, this comes under the jurisdiction of Uncle Sam.

But the United Nations has what's known as the charter of human rights; it has a committee that deals in human rights. You may wonder why all of the atrocities that have been committed in Africa and in Hungary and in Asia, and in Latin America are brought before the UN, and the Negro problem is never brought before the UN. This is part of the conspiracy. This old, tricky blue eyed liberal who is supposed to be your and my friend, supposed to be in our corner, supposed to be subsidizing our struggle, and supposed to be acting in the capacity of an adviser, never tells you anything about human rights. They keep you wrapped up in civil rights. And you spend so much time barking up the civil-rights tree, you don't even know there's a human-rights tree on the same floor.

When you expand the civil-rights struggle to the level of human rights, you can then take the case of the black man in this country before the nations in the UN. You can take it before the General Assembly. You can take Uncle Sam before a world court. But the only level you can do it on is the level of human rights. Civil rights keeps you under his restrictions, under his jurisdiction. Civil rights keeps you in his pocket. Civil rights means you're asking Uncle Sam to treat you right. Human rights are something you were born with. Human rights are your God-given rights. Human rights are the rights that are recognized by all nations of this earth. And any time any one violates your human rights, you can take them to the world court. Uncle Sam's hands are dripping with blood, dripping with the blood of the black man in this country. He's the earth's number-one hypocrite. He has the audacity—yes, he has—imagine him posing as the leader of the free world. The free world! And you over here singing "We Shall Overcome." Expand the civil-rights struggle to the level of human rights. Take it into the United Nations, where our African brothers can throw their weight on our side, where our Asian brothers can throw their weight on our side, where our Latin-American brothers can throw their weight on our side, and where 800 million Chinamen are sitting there waiting to throw their weight on our side.

Let the world know how bloody his hands are. Let the world know the hypocrisy that's practiced over here. Let it be the ballot or the bullet. Let him know that it must be the ballot or the bullet.

READING AND DISCUSSION QUESTIONS

1. To what degree does Malcolm X see possibilities for interracial cooperation in the civil rights movement? Does he welcome such cooperation? Why or why not?

2. What was the nature of the choice implied in his title? Of what use to the civil rights movement were the ballot and the bullet?

27-5 | Native Americans Claim Alcatraz Island

INDIANS OF ALL TRIBES, *Proclamation: To the Great White Father and All His People* (1970)

In November 1969, a small group of Native Americans began a nineteen-month occupation of San Francisco Bay's Alcatraz Island, which had been the site of the notorious federal penitentiary until 1963. These occupiers, members of a group calling themselves Indians of All Tribes, claimed the island, citing the 1868 Treaty of Fort Laramie, wherein the federal government pledged to return abandoned land to native peoples. The occupation failed in its immediate goal of gaining ownership of the island to establish a Native American cultural and educational center and museum, but the publicity it generated forced greater accommodation of federal Indian policy.

We, the native Americans, re-claim the land known as Alcatraz Island in the name of all American Indians by right of discovery.

We wish to be fair and honorable in our dealings with the Caucasian inhabitants of this land, and hereby offer the following treaty:

We will purchase said Alcatraz Island for twenty-four dollars (24) in glass beads and red cloth, a precedent set by the white man's purchase of a similar island about 300 years ago. We know that $24 in trade goods for these 16 acres is more than was paid when Manhattan Island was sold, but we know that land values have risen over the years. Our offer of $1.24 per acre is greater than the 47 cents per acre the white men are now paying the California Indians for their land.

We will give to the inhabitants of this island a portion of the land for their own to be held in trust by the American Indian Affairs and by the bureaus of

Indians of All Tribes, "Proclamation: To the Great White Father and All His People," Museum Collections at Alcatraz Island, Golden Gate National Recreation Area, National Park Service, www.cr.nps.gov/museum/exhibits/alca/exb/Indian/documents/Goga-35158b.html.

Caucasian Affairs to hold in perpetuity — for as long as the sun shall rise and the rivers go down to the sea. We will further guide the inhabitants in the proper way of living. We will offer them our religion, our education, our life-ways, in order to help them achieve our level of civilization and thus raise them and all their white brothers up from their savage and unhappy state. We offer this treaty in good faith and wish to be fair and honorable in our dealings with all white men.

We feel that this so-called Alcatraz Island is more than suitable for an Indian reservation, as determined by the white man's own standards. By this we mean that this place resembles most Indian reservations in that:

1. It is isolated from modern facilities, and without adequate means of transportation.
2. It has no fresh running water.
3. It has inadequate sanitation facilities.
4. There are no oil or mineral rights.
5. There is no industry and so unemployment is very great.
6. There are no health care facilities.
7. The soil is rocky and non-productive; and the land does not support game.
8. There are no educational facilities.
9. The population has always exceeded the land base.
10. The population has always been held as prisoners and kept dependent upon others.

Further, it would be fitting and symbolic that ships from all over the world, entering the Golden Gate, would first see Indian land, and thus be reminded of the true history of this nation. This tiny island would be a symbol of the great lands once ruled by free and noble Indians.

What use will we make of this land?

Since the San Francisco Indian Center burned down, there is no place for Indians to assemble and carry on tribal life here in the white man's city. Therefore, we plan to develop on this island several Indian institutions:

1. A CENTER FOR NATIVE AMERICAN STUDIES will be developed which will educate them to the skills and knowledge relevant to improve the lives and spirits of all Indian peoples. Attached to this center will be traveling universities, managed by Indians, which will go to the Indian Reservations, learning those necessary and relevant materials now about.

2. AN AMERICAN INDIAN SPIRITUAL CENTER which will practice our ancient tribal religious and sacred healing ceremonies. Our cultural arts will be featured and our young people trained in music, dance, and healing rituals.

3. AN INDIAN CENTER OF ECOLOGY which will train and support our young people in scientific research and practice to restore our lands and waters to their pure and natural state. We will work to de-pollute the air and water of the Bay Area. We will seek to restore fish and animal life to the area and to revitalize sea life which has been threatened by the white man's way. We will set up facilities to desalt sea water for human benefit.

4. A GREAT INDIAN TRAINING SCHOOL will be developed to teach our people how to make a living in the world, improve our standard of living, and

to end hunger and unemployment among our people. This training school will include a center for Indian arts and crafts, and an Indian restaurant serving native foods, which will restore Indian culinary arts. This center will display Indian arts and offer Indian foods to the public, so that all may know of the beauty and spirit of the traditional INDIAN ways.

Some of the present buildings will be taken over to develop an AMERICAN INDIAN MUSEUM, which will depict our native food & other cultural contributions we have given to the world. Another part of the museum will present some of the things the white man has given to the Indians in return for the land and life he took: disease, alcohol, poverty and cultural decimation (As symbolized by old tin cans, barbed wire, rubber tires, plastic containers, etc.). Part of this museum will remain a dungeon to symbolize both those Indian captives who were incarcerated for challenging white authority, and those who were imprisoned on reservations. The museum will show the noble and the tragic events of Indian history, including the broken treaties, the documentary of the Trail of Tears, the Massacre of Wounded Knee, as well as the victory over Yellow Hair Custer and his army.

In the name of all Indians, therefore, we re-claim this island for our Indian nations, for all these reasons. We feel this claim is just and proper, and that this land should rightfully be granted to us for as long as the rivers shall run and the sun shall shine.

READING AND DISCUSSION QUESTIONS

1. How do the Indians of All Tribes define their objectives in occupying Alcatraz Island? To what extent do they link their efforts to the wider civil rights movement?

2. What rhetorical point are the occupiers making in their proclamation by offering to hold in trust a portion of the island to be administered by a "Bureau of Caucasian Affairs"? What historical references do they expect the audience to catch?

27-6 | The Poetry of Chicano Nationalism and Civil Rights
RODOLFO "CORKY" GONZALES, *I Am Joaquín* (1967)

In the 1960s, Mexican Americans were one of many groups who mobilized in the hopes of righting long-standing wrongs regarding their civil liberties. Earlier efforts had pushed a Mexican American agenda but failed to achieve lasting results. Beginning in the mid-1960s, activists launched a "homeland" campaign to force the federal government to honor nineteenth-century land claims in the American Southwest. In 1967, Rodolfo "Corky" Gonzales, who founded the Chicano civil rights organization named Crusade for Justice, wrote "I am Joaquín," a poem that became the movement's anthem. In it, he grounds Chicano identity in the Aztec past and rehearses his people's history of struggle.

Antonio Esquibel, ed., *Message to Aztlan: Selected Writings of Rodolfo "Corky" Gonzales* (Houston: Arte Publico Press, 2001), 16–29.

My land is lost
and stolen,
My culture has been raped,
I lengthen
the line at the welfare door
and fill the jails with crime.
These then
are the rewards
this society has
For sons of Chiefs
and Kings
and bloody Revolutionists.
Who
gave a foreign people
all their skills and ingenuity
to pave the way with Brains and Blood
for those hordes of Gold starved
Strangers
Who
changed our language
and plagiarized our deeds
as feats of valor
of their own.
They frowned upon our way of life
and took what they could use.
Our Art
Our literature
Our music, they ignored
so they left the real things of value
and grabbed at their own destruction
by their Greed and Avarice.
They overlooked that cleansing fountain of
nature and brotherhood
Which is Joaquín.
The art of our great señores
Diego Rivera
Siqueiros
Orozco is but
another act of revolution for
the Salvation of mankind.
Mariachi music, the
heart and soul
of the people of the earth,
the life of the child,
and the happiness of love.

The Corridos tell the tales
of life and death,
of tradition,
Legends old and new,
of Joy
of passion and sorrow
of the people . . . who I am.

I am in the eyes of woman,
sheltered beneath
her shawl of black,
deep and sorrowful eyes,
that bear the pain of sons long buried or dying,
Dead
on the battlefield or on the barbwire
of social strife.
Her rosary she prays and fingers endlessly
like the family
working down a row of beets
to turn around
and work
and work.
There is no end.
Her eyes a mirror of all the warmth
and all the love for me,
And I am her
And she is me.
We face life together in sorrow,
anger, joy, faith and wishful
thoughts.

I shed the tears of anguish
as I see my children disappear
behind the shroud of mediocrity
never to look back to remember me.
I am Joaquín.
I must fight
And win this struggle
for my sons, and they
must know from me
Who I am.
Part of the blood that runs deep in me
Could not be vanquished by the Moors.
I defeated them after five hundred years,

and I endured.
The part of blood that is mine
has labored endlessly five-hundred
years under the heel of lustful
Europeans.
I am still here!
I have endured in the rugged mountains
of our country.
I have survived the toils and slavery of the fields.
I have existed
in the barrios of the city,
in the suburbs of bigotry,
in the mines of social snobbery,
in the prisons of dejection,
in the muck of exploitation,
and
in the fierce heat of racial hatred.

And now the trumpet sounds,
The music of the people stirs the
Revolution.
Like a sleeping giant it slowly
rears its head
to the sound of
Tramping feet
Clamoring voices
Mariachi strains
Fiery tequila explosions
The smell of chile verde and
Soft brown eyes of expectation for a
better life.
And in all the fertile farmlands,
the barren plains,
the mountain villages,
smoke-smeared cities,
we start to MOVE.
La raza!
Méjicano!
Español!
Latino!
Chicano!
Or whatever I call myself,
I look the same
I feel the same

I cry
and
Sing the same.

I am the masses of my people and
I refuse to be absorbed.
I am Joaquín.
The odds are great
but my spirit is strong,
My faith unbreakable,
My blood is pure.
I am Aztec prince and Christian Christ.
I SHALL ENDURE!
I WILL ENDURE!

READING AND DISCUSSION QUESTIONS

1. Summarize the tone and perspective of Gonzales's poem. Why do you think the poem became popular among activists in the Mexican American civil rights movement?

2. Who is Joaquín? How does Gonzales use Joaquín as a character in this poem? Whom does Gonzales think Joaquín would appeal to?

▪ COMPARATIVE QUESTIONS ▪

1. Compare the civil rights philosophy of someone like Martin Luther King Jr. with the approach advocated by Fannie Lou Hamer and Malcolm X to identify similarities and differences in their approach to reform. To what extent do their differences reveal the fractures in the movement during the 1960s?

2. What continuities across time can you identify by analyzing and comparing "I Am Joaquín" with the *LULAC News* editorial (Document 24-4)? How are the approaches to Mexican American civil rights similar or different in these periods?

3. What comparison can you draw between the issues raised in the civil rights movement of the late nineteenth and early twentieth centuries and the movement during the 1960s? Compare the views of Booker T. Washington (Document 18-3) and W. E. B. Du Bois (Document 20-6) with those of Hamer and Malcolm X.

4. Analyze and evaluate the advantages and disadvantages to historical understanding of the periodization of the civil rights movement offered here. What alternatives to this periodization could you suggest and why?

28

Uncivil Wars: Liberal Crisis and Conservative Rebirth
1961–1972

Triumph and tragedy define the Sixties, two bold and conflicting themes marking a period that witnessed both man's landing on the moon and man's inhumanity to man. Americans entered this era inspired by President John Kennedy's call to serve and lifted by the dreams of a better society described by Martin Luther King Jr. and President Lyndon Johnson. This liberal current, sustained by a New Deal coalition, moved men and women to levels of political and social engagement focused on redeeming the founders' promise of liberty and equality for all. Their agenda envisioned new federal programs to right wrongs, feed and house the poor, school the children, and protect the land. The Vietnam War dashed these hopes and radicalized political and generational opposition that tore the liberal movement apart. Into this vortex moved a resurgent conservative movement that questioned the fundamentals of the liberal state. Harkening to traditional values, conservatives offered Middle America an alternative to the chaos they claimed was undermining America's strength at home and abroad. Pointing to the demonstrations, riots, and rebellions in America's streets among those demanding recognition of their rights, conservatives appealed to law and order. These liberal and conservative tensions defined the era's political mood, establishing patterns of political conflict persisting into the twenty-first century.

28-1 | President's Vision for America

LYNDON BAINES JOHNSON, *The Great Society* (1964)

Lyndon Johnson's shining moment may have come on the campus of the University of Michigan. There, in 1964, he delivered a rallying commencement address mobilizing the graduates to help him mend the fractious society over which he presided. Born in poverty, Johnson possessed determination that helped him climb the political world of Texas, becoming the Senate majority leader, then vice president, until John Kennedy's assassination brought him to the presidency exactly six months before giving this speech. Here, Johnson harnesses his rhetorical powers to define the Great Society he hoped to bequeath as his legacy.

I have come today from the turmoil of your Capital to the tranquility of your campus to speak about the future of your country.

The purpose of protecting the life of our Nation and preserving the liberty of our citizens is to pursue the happiness of our people. Our success in that pursuit is the test of our success as a Nation.

For a century we labored to settle and to subdue a continent. For half a century we called upon unbounded invention and untiring industry to create an order of plenty for all of our people.

The challenge of the next half century is whether we have the wisdom to use that wealth to enrich and elevate our national life, and to advance the quality of our American civilization.

Your imagination, your initiative, and your indignation will determine whether we build a society where progress is the servant of our needs, or a society where old values and new visions are buried under unbridled growth. For in your time we have the opportunity to move not only toward the rich society and the powerful society, but upward to the Great Society.

The Great Society rests on abundance and liberty for all. It demands an end to poverty and racial injustice, to which we are totally committed in our time. But that is just the beginning.

The Great Society is a place where every child can find knowledge to enrich his mind and to enlarge his talents. It is a place where leisure is a welcome chance to build and reflect, not a feared cause of boredom and restlessness. It is a place where the city of man serves not only the needs of the body and the demands of commerce but the desire for beauty and the hunger for community.

It is a place where man can renew contact with nature. It is a place which honors creation for its own sake and for what it adds to the understanding of the race. It is a place where men are more concerned with the quality of their goals than the quantity of their goods.

But most of all, the Great Society is not a safe harbor, a resting place, a final objective, a finished work. It is a challenge constantly renewed, beckoning us

---

Lyndon B. Johnson, "Remarks at the University of Michigan," May 22, 1964. Online by Gerhard Peters and John T. Woolley, *The American Presidency Project*. www.presidency.ucsb.edu/ws /?pid=26262.

toward a destiny where the meaning of our lives matches the marvelous products of our labor.

So I want to talk to you today about three places where we begin to build the Great Society—in our cities, in our countryside, and in our classrooms.

Many of you will live to see the day, perhaps 50 years from now, when there will be 400 million Americans—four-fifths of them in urban areas. In the remainder of this century urban population will double, city land will double, and we will have to build homes, high-ways, and facilities equal to all those built since this country was first settled. So in the next 40 years we must rebuild the entire urban United States.

Aristotle said: "Men come together in cities in order to live, but they remain together in order to live the good life." It is harder and harder to live the good life in American cities today. The catalog of ills is long: there is the decay of the centers and the despoiling of the suburbs. There is not enough housing for our people or transportation for our traffic. Open land is vanishing and old landmarks are violated.

Worst of all, expansion is eroding the precious and time honored values of community with neighbors and communion with nature. The loss of these values breeds loneliness and boredom and indifference.

Our society will never be great until our cities are great. Today the frontier of imagination and innovation is inside those cities and not beyond their borders. New experiments are already going on. It will be the task of your generation to make the American city a place where future generations will come, not only to live but to live the good life.

I understand that if I stayed here tonight I would see that Michigan students are really doing their best to live the good life.

This is the place where the Peace Corps was started. It is inspiring to see how all of you, while you are in this country, are trying so hard to live at the level of the people.

A second place where we begin to build the Great Society is in our countryside. We have always prided ourselves on being not only America the strong and America the free, but America the beautiful. Today that beauty is in danger. The water we drink, the food we eat, the very air that we breathe, are threatened with pollution. Our parks are overcrowded, our seashores overburdened. Green fields and dense forests are disappearing.

A few years ago we were greatly concerned about the "Ugly American." Today we must act to prevent an ugly America.

For once the battle is lost, once our natural splendor is destroyed, it can never be recaptured. And once man can no longer walk with beauty or wonder at nature his spirit will wither and his sustenance be wasted.

A third place to build the Great Society is in the classrooms of America. There your children's lives will be shaped. Our society will not be great until every young mind is set free to scan the farthest reaches of thought and imagination. We are still far from that goal.

Today, 8 million adult Americans, more than the entire population of Michigan, have not finished 5 years of school. Nearly 20 million have not finished 8 years of school. Nearly 54 million—more than one-quarter of all America—have not even finished high school.

Each year more than 100,000 high school graduates, with proved ability, do not enter college because they cannot afford it. And if we cannot educate today's youth, what will we do in 1970 when elementary school enrollment will be 5 million greater than 1960? And high school enrollment will rise by 5 million. College enrollment will increase by more than 3 million.

In many places, classrooms are overcrowded and curricula are outdated. Most of our qualified teachers are underpaid, and many of our paid teachers are unqualified. So we must give every child a place to sit and a teacher to learn from. Poverty must not be a bar to learning, and learning must offer an escape from poverty.

But more classrooms and more teachers are not enough. We must seek an educational system which grows in excellence as it grows in size. This means better training for our teachers. It means preparing youth to enjoy their hours of leisure as well as their hours of labor. It means exploring new techniques of teaching, to find new ways to stimulate the love of learning and the capacity for creation.

These are three of the central issues of the Great Society. While our Government has many programs directed at those issues, I do not pretend that we have the full answer to those problems.

But I do promise this: We are going to assemble the best thought and the broadest knowledge from all over the world to find those answers for America. I intend to establish working groups to prepare a series of White House conferences and meetings—on the cities, on natural beauty, on the quality of education, and on other emerging challenges. And from these meetings and from this inspiration and from these studies we will begin to set our course toward the Great Society.

The solution to these problems does not rest on a massive program in Washington, nor can it rely solely on the strained resources of local authority. They require us to create new concepts of cooperation, a creative federalism, between the National Capital and the leaders of local communities.

Woodrow Wilson once wrote: "Every man sent out from his university should be a man of his Nation as well as a man of his time."

Within your lifetime powerful forces, already loosed, will take us toward a way of life beyond the realm of our experience, almost beyond the bounds of our imagination.

For better or for worse, your generation has been appointed by history to deal with those problems and to lead America toward a new age. You have the chance never before afforded to any people in any age. You can help build a society where the demands of morality, and the needs of the spirit, can be realized in the life of the Nation.

So, will you join in the battle to give every citizen the full equality which God enjoins and the law requires, whatever his belief, or race, or the color of his skin? Will you join in the battle to give every citizen an escape from the crushing weight of poverty?

Will you join in the battle to make it possible for all nations to live in endur-ing peace — as neighbors and not as mortal enemies?

Will you join in the battle to build the Great Society, to prove that our mate-rial progress is only the foundation on which we will build a richer life of mind and spirit?

There are those timid souls who say this battle cannot be won; that we are condemned to a soulless wealth. I do not agree. We have the power to shape the civilization that we want. But we need your will, your labor, your hearts, if we are to build that kind of society.

Those who came to this land sought to build more than just a new country.

They sought a new world. So I have come here today to your campus to say that you can make their vision our reality. So let us from this moment begin our work so that in the future men will look back and say: It was then, after a long and weary way, that man turned the exploits of his genius to the full enrichment of his life.

READING AND DISCUSSION QUESTIONS

1. To what extent do you see Johnson's vision for the Great Society as something new or as a continuation of Franklin Roosevelt's New Deal efforts?

2. From his speech, what do you infer about Johnson's assessment of the challenges facing America? What obstacles stood in the way, and how were they to be overcome?

28-2 | Vietnam Vet Questions America's War in Asia

JOHN KERRY, *Testimony Before the Senate Committee on Foreign Relations* (1971)

By the time John Kerry testified before Congress as the representative of Vietnam Veterans for Peace in April 1971, the United States had been involved in that Asian conflict for more than a decade. Nothing so divided the American public as the Vietnam War, especially in its last years when protests erupted on college campuses and war weariness had set in even among those who had supported the war as an effort to turn back the spread of communism. Here, Kerry challenges those who would continue a war whose ill effects he describes in stark detail.

In 1970 at West Point Vice President Agnew said "some glamorize the criminal misfits of society while our best men die in Asian rice paddies to preserve the freedom which most of those misfits abuse," and this was used as a rallying point for our effort in Vietnam. But for us, as boys in Asia whom the country was

S. Mintz and S. McNeil (2013). John Kerry, Speech to the Senate Committee on Foreign Relations, April 22, 1971. *Digital History.* www.digitalhistory.uh.edu/learning_history/vietnam/kerry.cfm.

supposed to support, his statement is a terrible distortion from which we can only draw a very deep sense of revulsion, and hence the anger of some of the men who are here in Washington today. It is a distortion because we in no way consider ourselves the best men of this country; because those he calls misfits were standing up for us in a way that nobody else in this country dared to; because so many who have died would have returned to this country to join the misfits in their efforts to ask for an immediate withdrawal from South Vietnam; because so many of those best men have returned as quadriplegics and amputees—and they lie forgotten in Veterans Administration hospitals in this country which fly the flag which so many have chosen as their own personal symbol—and we cannot consider ourselves America's best men when we are ashamed of and hated what we were called on to do in Southeast Asia.

In our opinion, and from our experience, there is nothing in South Vietnam which could happen that realistically threatens the United States of America. And to attempt to justify the loss of one American life in Vietnam, Cambodia, or Laos by linking such loss to the preservation of freedom, which those misfits supposedly abuse, is to us the height of criminal hypocrisy. . . .

We are probably angriest about all that we were told about Vietnam and about the mystical war against communism. We found that not only was it a civil war, an effort by a people who had for years been seeking their liberation from any colonial influence whatsoever, but also we found that the Vietnamese whom we had enthusiastically molded after our own image were hard put to take up the fight against the threat we were supposedly saving them from. We found most people didn't even know the difference between communism and democracy. They only wanted to work in rice paddies without helicopters strafing them and bombs with napalm burning their villages and tearing their country apart. . . . They practiced the art of survival by siding with whichever military force was present at a particular time, be it Vietcong, North Vietnamese or American. . . .

We saw Vietnam ravaged equally by American bombs as well as by search-and-destroy missions, as well as by Vietcong terrorism, and yet we listened while this country tried to blame all of the havoc on the Vietcong. We rationalized destroying villages in order to save them. We saw America lose her sense of morality as she accepted very coolly a My Lai[1] and refused to give up the image of American soldiers who hand out chocolate bars and chewing gum. We learned the meaning of free fire zones, shooting anything that moves, and we watched while America placed a cheapness on the lives of Orientals.

We watched the United States' falsification of body counts, in fact the glorification of body counts. We listened while month after month we were told the back of the enemy was about to break. We fought [with] weapons against those people which I do not believe this country would dream of using were we

---

[1]**My Lai**: Massacre of Vietnamese civilians by U.S. Army soldiers on March 16, 1968, in the hamlet of My Lai in the central coastal region of Vietnam. Lt. William Calley was the only U.S. soldier convicted for the incident. His life sentence was commuted, and he served house arrest for three and a half years.

fighting in the European theater. We watched while men charged up hills because a general said that hill has to be taken, and after losing one platoon or two platoons, they marched away to leave the hill for reoccupation by the North Vietnamese. We watched pride allow the most unimportant battles to be blown into extravaganzas, because we couldn't lose, and we couldn't retreat, and because it didn't matter how many American bodies were lost to prove that point, and so there were Hamburger Hills and Khesahns and Hill 81's and Fire Base 6's[2] and so many others.

And now we are told that the men who fought there must watch quietly while American lives are lost so that we can exercise the incredible arrogance of Vietnamizing the Vietnamese. Each day to facilitate the process by which the United States washes her hands of Vietnam someone has to give up his life so that the United States doesn't have to admit something that the entire world already knows, so that we can't say that we have made a mistake. Someone has to die so that President Nixon won't be, and these are his words, "the first President to lose a war."

We are asking Americans to think about that because how do you ask a man to be the last man to die in Vietnam? How do you ask a man to be the last man to die for a mistake?

READING AND DISCUSSION QUESTIONS

1. Evaluate Kerry's point of view concerning the United States's policy in Vietnam. To what does he attribute the problems with American policy toward Vietnam?

2. According to Kerry, what effect was the war having on American society? On American soldiers?

3. What role does Kerry say race played in shaping America's policies in Southeast Asia? How, for instance, does he explain My Lai and the bombing campaigns?

28-3 | Radical Feminists Push for Liberation
Redstockings Manifesto (1969)

The women's movement stretched back a century and a half, but few of their predecessors achieved the radicalism of Redstockings, an outspoken feminist group organized in 1969. Embracing the direct action tactics of other civil rights movements, Redstockings edged away from the more mainstream feminism of the National Organization for Women (NOW), whose members sought equal access to opportunities within the existing system. Redstockings' feminism aimed in a different direction.

"Redstockings Manifesto," Redstockings Women's Liberation Archives, www.redstockings .org/index.php?option=com_content&view=article&id=76&Itemid=59.

[2]**Hamburger Hill . . . Fire Base 6**: Sites of battles between U.S. and North Vietnamese forces during the Vietnam War.

I. After centuries of individual and preliminary political struggle, women are uniting to achieve their final liberation from male supremacy. Redstockings is dedicated to building this unity and winning our freedom.

II. Women are an oppressed class. Our oppression is total, affecting every facet of our lives. We are exploited as sex objects, breeders, domestic servants, and cheap labor. We are considered inferior beings, whose only purpose is to enhance men's lives. Our humanity is denied. Our prescribed behavior is enforced by the threat of physical violence.

Because we have lived so intimately with our oppressors, in isolation from each other, we have been kept from seeing our personal suffering as a political condition. This creates the illusion that a woman's relationship with her man is a matter of interplay between two unique personalities, and can be worked out individually. In reality, every such relationship is a *class* relationship, and the conflicts between individual men and women are *political* conflicts that can only be solved collectively.

III. We identify the agents of our oppression as men. Male supremacy is the oldest, most basic form of domination. All other forms of exploitation and oppression (racism, capitalism, imperialism, etc.) are extensions of male supremacy: men dominate women, a few men dominate the rest. All power structures throughout history have been male-dominated and male-oriented. Men have controlled all political, economic and cultural institutions and backed up this control with physical force. They have used their power to keep women in an inferior position. *All men* receive economic, sexual, and psychological benefits from male supremacy. *All men* have oppressed women.

IV. Attempts have been made to shift the burden of responsibility from men to institutions or to women themselves. We condemn these arguments as evasions. Institutions alone do not oppress; they are merely tools of the oppressor. To blame institutions implies that men and women are equally victimized, obscures the fact that men benefit from the subordination of women, and gives men the excuse that they are forced to be oppressors. On the contrary, any man is free to renounce his superior position, provided that he is willing to be treated like a woman by other men.

We also reject the idea that women consent to or are to blame for their own oppression. Women's submission is not the result of brain-washing, stupidity or mental illness but of continual, daily pressure from men. We do not need to change ourselves, but to change men.

The most slanderous evasion of all is that women can oppress men. The basis for this illusion is the isolation of individual relationships from their political context and the tendency of men to see any legitimate challenge to their privileges as persecution.

V. We regard our personal experience, and our feelings about that experience, as the basis for an analysis of our common situation. We cannot rely on existing ideologies as they are all products of male supremacist culture. We question every generalization and accept none that are not confirmed by our experience.

Our chief task at present is to develop female class consciousness through sharing experience and publicly exposing the sexist foundation of all our institutions. Consciousness-raising is not "therapy," which implies the existence of individual solutions and falsely assumes that the male-female relationship is purely personal, but the only method by which we can ensure that our program for liberation is based on the concrete realities of our lives.

The first requirement for raising class consciousness is honesty, in private and in public, with ourselves and other women.

VI. We identify with all women. We define our best interest as that of the poorest, most brutally exploited woman.

We repudiate all economic, racial, educational or status privileges that divide us from other women. We are determined to recognize and eliminate any prejudices we may hold against other women.

We are committed to achieving internal democracy. We will do whatever is necessary to ensure that every woman in our movement has an equal chance to participate, assume responsibility, and develop her political potential.

VII. We call on all our sisters to unite with us in struggle.

We call on all men to give up their male privilege and support women's liberation in the interest of our humanity and their own.

In fighting for our liberation we will always take the side of women against their oppressors. We will not ask what is "revolutionary" or "reformist," only what is good for women.

The time for individual skirmishes has passed. This time we are going all the way.

July 7, 1969, New York City

READING AND DISCUSSION QUESTIONS

1. Was the Redstockings Manifesto a culmination of women's rights efforts or a distinct and new direction of feminist mobilization? Explain.

2. What do you think Redstockings expected to achieve with their efforts to raise "female class consciousness"? What meaning can you infer from their assertion that they intended to go "all the way"?

28-4 | Mexican American Labor Leader Seeks Peaceful Path to Worker Rights

CESAR CHAVEZ, *Letter from Delano* (1969)

Founder of the United Farm Workers union, Cesar Chavez organized nonviolent strikes and boycotts, including the famous strike against Delano, California, grape growers that lasted a remarkable five years, from 1965 to 1970. The economic impact of the long boycott led to grower concessions including recognition of farmers' collective bargaining rights. In his letter to E. L. Barr Jr., president of the consortium representing grape growers, Chavez affirms his commitment to nonviolence but veils a threat Barr could not have missed.

Dear Mr. Barr:

I am sad to hear about your accusations in the press that our union movement and table grape boycott have been successful because we have used violence and terror tactics. If what you say is true, I have been a failure and should withdraw from the struggle; but you are left with the awesome moral responsibility, before God and man, to come forward with whatever information you have so that corrective action can begin at once. If for any reason you fail to come forth to substantiate your charges, then you must be held responsible for committing violence against us, albeit violence of the tongue. I am convinced that you as a human being did not mean what you said but rather acted hastily under pressure from the public relations firm that has been hired to try to counteract the tremendous moral force of our movement. How many times we ourselves have felt the need to lash out in anger and bitterness.

Today on Good Friday 1969 we remember the life and the sacrifice of Martin Luther King, Jr., who gave himself totally to the nonviolent struggle for peace and justice. In his "Letter from Birmingham Jail" Dr. King describes better than I could our hopes for the strike and boycott: "Injustice must be exposed, with all the tensions its exposure creates, to the light of human conscience and the air of national opinion before it can be cured." For our part I admit that we have seized upon every tactic and strategy consistent with the morality of our cause to expose that injustice and thus to heighten the sensitivity of the American conscience so that farm workers will have without bloodshed their own union and the dignity of bargaining with their agribusiness employers. By lying about the nature of our movement, Mr. Barr, you are working against nonviolent social change. Unwittingly perhaps, you may unleash that other force which our union by discipline and deed, censure and education has sought to avoid, that panacea shortcut, that senseless violence which honors no color, class or neighborhood.

You must understand—I must make you understand—that our membership and the hopes and aspirations of the hundreds of thousands of the poor and dispossessed that have been raised on our account are, above all, human beings,

Cesar Chavez, "Letter from Delano," *Christian Century* 86 (April 23, 1969): 539–540.

no better and no worse than any other cross-section of human society; we are not saints because we are poor, but by the same measure neither are we immoral. We are men and women who have suffered and endured much, and not only because of our abject poverty but because we have been kept poor. The colors of our skins, the languages of our cultural and native origins, the lack of formal education, the exclusion from the democratic process, the numbers of our men slain in recent wars—all these burdens generation after generation have sought to demoralize us, to break our human spirit. But God knows that we are not beasts of burden, agricultural implements, or rented slaves; we are men. And mark this well, Mr. Barr, we are men locked in a death struggle against man's inhumanity to man in the industry that you represent. And this struggle itself gives meaning to our life and ennobles our dying.

As your industry has experienced, our strikers here in Delano and those who represent us throughout the world are well trained for this struggle. They have been under the gun, they have been kicked and beaten and herded by dogs, they have been cursed and ridiculed, they have been stripped and chained and jailed, they have been sprayed with the poisons used in the vineyards; but they have been taught not to lie down and die nor to flee in shame, but to resist with every ounce of human endurance and spirit. To resist not with retaliation in kind but to overcome with love and compassion, with ingenuity and creativity, with hard work and longer hours, with stamina and patient tenacity, with truth and public appeal, with friends and allies, with nobility and discipline, with politics and law, and with prayer and fasting. They were not trained in a month or even a year; after all, this new harvest season will mark our fourth full year of strike and even now we continue to plan and prepare for the years to come. Time accomplishes for the poor what money does for the rich.

This is not to pretend that we have everywhere been successful enough or that we have not made mistakes. And while we do not belittle or underestimate our adversaries—for they are the rich and the powerful and they possess the land—we are not afraid nor do we cringe from the confrontation. We welcome it! We have planned for it! We know that our cause is just, that history is a story of social revolution, and that the poor shall inherit the land.

Once again, I appeal to you as the representative of your industry and as a man. I ask you to recognize and bargain with our union before the economic pressure of the boycott and strike takes an irrevocable toll; but if not, I ask you to at least sit down with us to discuss the safeguards necessary to keep our historical struggle free of violence. I make this appeal because as one of the leaders of our nonviolent movement, I know and accept my responsibility for preventing, if possible, the destruction of human life and property. For these reasons, and knowing of Gandhi's admonition that fasting is the last resort in place of the sword, during a most critical time in our movement last February 1968 I undertook a 25-day fast. I repeat to you the principle enunciated to the membership at the start of the fast: if to build our union required the deliberate taking of life, either the life of a grower or his child, or the life of a farm worker or his child, then I choose not to see the union built.

Mr. Barr, let me be painfully honest with you. You must understand these things. We advocate militant nonviolence as our means for social revolution and to achieve justice for our people, but we are not blind or deaf to the desperate and moody winds of human frustration, impatience and rage that blow among us. Gandhi himself admitted that if his only choice were cowardice or violence, he would choose violence. Men are not angels, and time and tide wait for no man. Precisely because of these powerful human emotions, we have tried to involve masses of people in their own struggle. Participation and self-determination remain the best experience of freedom, and free men instinctively prefer democratic change and even protect the rights guaranteed to seek it. Only the enslaved in despair have need of violent overthrow.

This letter does not express all that is in my heart, Mr. Barr. But if it says nothing else it says that we do not hate you or rejoice to see your industry destroyed; we hate the agribusiness system that seeks to keep us enslaved, and we shall overcome and change it not by retaliation or bloodshed but by a determined nonviolent struggle carried on by those masses of farm workers who intend to be free and human.

Sincerely yours,
Cesar E. Chavez
United Farm Workers Organizing Committee, A.F.L.-C.I.O.
Delano, CA

READING AND DISCUSSION QUESTIONS

1. From Chavez's letter, what can you infer about the conditions that led to the farmworkers' strike against the grape growers in Delano, California?

2. Why do you think Chavez invoked the names of King and Gandhi? How does he draw on those individuals in his appeal to Barr? What implicit threat lies behind his letter?

3. Analyze the tone of Chavez's letter for evidence of the multiple audiences in addition to Barr that he may have had in mind. Who might they have been? What appeal does he extend to those audiences?

28-5 | Conservative Rebirth of the Republican Party

BARRY GOLDWATER, *Acceptance Speech at the Republican National Convention* (1964)

By midcentury, both Democrats and Republicans agreed on the federal government's active role in the nation's economy. By the mid-1960s, however, dissenting conservative voices rebuffed this consensus and powered their way into presidential politics. With the nomination of Arizona senator Barry Goldwater in 1964, conservatives hoped to turn back the creeping socialism they feared from the New Deal legacy. President Johnson crushed Goldwater in the November election, but conservatives scored an ideological victory, setting the stage for a conservative resurgence in the years to follow.

Now, my fellow Americans, the tide has been running against freedom. Our people have followed false prophets. We must, and we shall, return to proven ways—not because they are old, but because they are true.

We must, and we shall, set the tide running again in the cause of freedom. And this party, with its every action, every word, every breath and every heart beat, has but a single resolve, and that is freedom.

Freedom made orderly for this nation by our constitutional government. Freedom under a government limited by laws of nature and of nature's God. Freedom balanced so that order lacking liberty will not become the slavery of the prison cell; balanced so that liberty lacking order will not become the license of the mob and of the jungle.

Now, we Americans understand freedom, we have earned it; we have lived for it, and we have died for it. This nation and its people are freedom's model in a searching world. We can be freedom's missionaries in a doubting world.

But, ladies and gentlemen, first we must renew freedom's mission in our own hearts and in our own homes.

During four futile years the Administration which we shall replace has distorted and lost that faith. It has talked and talked and talked and talked the words of freedom but it has failed and failed and failed in the works of freedom.

Now failure cements the wall of shame in Berlin; failures blot the sands of shame at the Bay of Pigs; failures marked the slow death of freedom in Laos; failures infest the jungles of Vietnam; and failures haunt the houses of our once great alliances and undermine the greatest bulwark ever erected by free nations, the NATO community.

Failures proclaim lost leadership, obscure purpose, weakening wills and the risk of inciting our sworn enemies to new aggressions and to new excesses.

And because of this Administration we are tonight a world divided. We are a Nation becalmed. We have lost the brisk pace of diversity and the genius of

Barry Goldwater, "The Republican National Convention Acceptance Speech," *Vital Speeches of the Day*, vol. 30 (August 15, 1964): 642–644.

individual creativity. We are plodding at a pace set by centralized planning, red tape, rules without responsibility and regimentation without recourse.

Rather than useful jobs in our country, people have been offered bureaucratic make-work; rather than moral leadership, they have been given bread and circuses; they have been given spectacles, and, yes, they have even been given scandals.

Tonight there is violence in our streets, corruption in our highest offices, aimlessness among our youth, anxiety among our elderly, and there's a virtual despair among the many who look beyond material success toward the inner meaning of their lives. And where examples of morality should be set, the opposite is seen. Small men seeking great wealth or power have too often and too long turned even the highest levels of public service into mere personal opportunity. . . .

The growing menace in our country tonight, to personal safety, to life, to limb and property, in homes, in churches, on the playgrounds and places of business, particularly in our great cities, is the mounting concern or should be of every thoughtful citizen in the United States. Security from domestic violence, no less than from foreign aggression, is the most elementary and fundamental purpose of any government, and a government that cannot fulfill that purpose is one that cannot long command the loyalty of its citizens. . . .

Those who seek to live your lives for you, to take your liberties in return for relieving you of yours; those who elevate the state and downgrade the citizen must see ultimately a world in which earthly power can be substituted for Divine Will. And this nation was founded upon the rejection of that notion and upon the acceptance of God as the author of freedom.

Now those who seek absolute power, even though they seek it to do what they regard as good, are simply demanding the right to enforce their own version of heaven on earth, and let me remind you they are the very ones who always create the most hellish tyranny.

Absolute power does corrupt, and those who seek it must be suspect and must be opposed. Their mistaken course stems from false notions, ladies and gentlemen, of equality. Equality, rightly understood, as our founding fathers understood it, leads to liberty and to the emancipation of creative differences; wrongly understood, as it has been so tragically in our time, it leads first to conformity and then to despotism.

Fellow Republicans, it is the cause of Republicanism to resist concentrations of power, private or public, which enforce such conformity and inflict such despotism.

It is the cause of Republicanism to insure that power remains in the hands of the people. . . .

It is further the cause of Republicanism to restore a clear understanding of the tyranny of man over man in the world at large. It is our cause to dispel the foggy thinking which avoids hard decisions in the delusion that a world of conflict will somehow resolve itself into a world of harmony, if we just don't rock the boat or irritate the forces of aggression—and this is hogwash.

It is, further, the cause of Republicanism to remind ourselves, and the world, that only the strong can remain free; that only the strong can keep the peace. . . .

It has been during Democratic years that we have weakly stumbled into conflicts, timidly refusing to draw our own lines against aggression, deceitfully refusing to tell even our own people of our full participation and tragically letting our finest men die on battlefields unmarked by purpose, unmarked by pride or the prospect of victory.

Yesterday it was Korea; tonight it is Vietnam. Make no bones of this. Don't try to sweep this under the rug. We are at war in Vietnam. And yet the President, who is the Commander of Chief of our forces, refuses to say, refuses to say, mind you, whether or not the objective over there is victory, and his Secretary of Defense continues to mislead and misinform the American people, and enough of it has gone by.

And I needn't remind you, but I will, it has been during Democratic years that a billion persons were cast into communist captivity and their fate cynically sealed.

Today—today in our beloved country we have an Administration which seems eager to deal with Communism in every coin known—from gold to wheat; from consulates to confidence, and even human freedom itself.

Now the Republican cause demands that we brand Communism as a principal disturber of peace in the world today. Indeed, we should brand it as the only significant disturber of the peace. And we must make clear that until its goals of conquest are absolutely renounced, and its relations with all nations tempered, Communism and the governments it now controls are enemies of every man on earth who is or wants to be free. . . .

I believe that the Communism which boasts it will bury us will instead give way to the forces of freedom. And I can see in the distant and yet recognizable future the outlines of a world worthy of our dedication, our every risk, our every effort, our every sacrifice along the way. Yes, a world that will redeem the suffering of those who will be liberated from tyranny. . . .

My fellow Republicans, we do no man a service by hiding freedom's light under a bushel of mistaken humility.

I seek an America proud of its past, proud of its ways, proud of its dreams and determined actively to proclaim them. But our example to the world must, like charity, begin at home.

In our vision of a good and decent future, free and peaceful, there must be room, room for the liberation of the energy and the talent of the individual, otherwise our vision is blind at the outset.

We must assure a society here which while never abandoning the needy or forsaking the helpless, nurtures incentives and opportunity for the creative and the productive. . . .

During Republican years, this again will be a nation of men and women, of families proud of their role, jealous of their responsibilities, unlimited in their aspirations—a nation where all who can will be self-reliant.

We Republicans see in our constitutional form of government the great framework which assures the orderly but dynamic fulfillment of the whole man, and we see the whole man as the great reason for instituting orderly government in the first place.

We can see in private property and in economy based upon and fostering private property the one way to make government a durable ally of the whole man, rather than his determined enemy.

We see in the sanctity of private property the only durable foundation for constitutional government in a free society.

And beyond that we see and cherish diversity of ways, diversity of thoughts, of motives, and accomplishments. We don't seek to lead anyone's life for him. We only seek to secure his rights, guarantee him opportunity, guarantee him opportunity to strive with government performing only those needed and constitutionally sanctioned tasks which cannot otherwise be performed.

We, Republicans, seek a government that attends to its inherent responsibilities of maintaining a stable monetary and fiscal climate, encouraging a free and a competitive economy and enforcing law and order.

Thus do we seek inventiveness, diversity and creative difference within a stable order, for we Republicans define government's role where needed at many, many levels, preferably though the one closest to the people involved: our towns and our cities, then our counties, then our states, then our regional contacts and only then, the national government.

That, let me remind you, is the land of liberty built by decentralized power. On it also we must have balance between the branches of government at every level.

Balance, diversity, creative difference—these are the elements of Republican equation. Republicans agree, Republicans agree heartily to disagree on many, many of their applications. But we have never disagreed on the basic fundamental issues of why you and I are Republicans. . . .

[T]he task of preserving and enlarging freedom at home and safeguarding it from the forces of tyranny abroad is great enough to challenge all our resources and to require all our strength.

Anyone who joins us in all sincerity we welcome. Those who do not care for our cause, we don't expect to enter our ranks in any case. And let our Republicanism so focused and so dedicated not be made fuzzy and futile by unthinking and stupid labels.

I would remind you that extremism in the defense of liberty is no vice.

And let me remind you also that moderation in the pursuit of justice is no virtue.

READING AND DISCUSSION QUESTIONS

1. Analyze Goldwater's acceptance speech to identify the conservative themes he highlights in contrasting Republican political views with those of his Democratic opponent. What themes does he believe would best resonate with his audience of conservative Americans?

2. The most famous line of Goldwater's speech was his reminder that "extremism in the defense of liberty is no vice" and "moderation in the pursuit of justice is no virtue." Why do you think that line rallied conservatives and inflamed his liberal opponents?

▪ COMPARATIVE QUESTIONS ▪

1. Do you think Goldwater and Billy Graham (Document 26-3) appealed to the same audience of Americans? What point of view about human nature, God, and the role of government did they share? Who was excluded by their ideology?

2. What lesson about the extent of American power did Vietnam teach John Kerry? To what extent did the American experience in Southeast Asia refute Goldwater's boast that the defense of liberty at home and abroad justified "extremism"?

3. Compare the contrasting visions of American society as articulated by Johnson and Goldwater, the major party candidates for president in 1964. What choice did they present to the American people? Does Johnson's victory tell you anything about the mood of the American people?

4. Several sources refer directly to the civil rights movement. From your analysis and comparison of this chapter's documents with those by Fannie Lou Hamer (Document 27-3) and Malcolm X (Document 27-4), what conclusions can you draw about the evolution, goals, and strategies of the broadly defined civil rights movement?

5. Compare the 1920s and the 1960s as two eras of reform. Do their similarities (in goals and effects) outweigh the differences you see? Which era speaks more directly to the issues we face today?

29

The Search for Order in an Era of Limits

1973–1980

The succession of crises in the 1970s, including the ongoing war in Vietnam, antiwar protests on campuses, the Watergate scandal, and the economic recession, strained that quintessential American characteristic: optimism. It was hard for Americans to be hopeful when the indicators pointed to America's declining influence in an increasingly globalized economy. Though still the leading superpower, the United States suffered a humiliating defeat in Vietnam. The crisis between Israel and its Arab neighbors pulled America into the quagmire of the Middle East with devastating effects on oil imports that hastened the economic recession and stalled the postwar economic boom Americans had begun to take for granted. The period ended with another humiliation: Iranian revolutionaries attacked the U.S. embassy and held Americans hostage for 444 days, unmistakable proof that Henry Luce's "American Century" had ended. These international defeats occurred in the context of a political and cultural referendum on the 1960s, as conservatives tried to curb what they saw as liberalism's excesses. The polarized politics of the decade defined the electoral map for the next generation as Americans grappled with this new era of limits.

29-1 | Experiencing America's Energy Dependence

WARREN LEFFLE, *Long Lines of Cars Waiting for Fuel at a Gas Station, Maryland* (1979)

America's postwar economic boom slowed by the 1970s when the nation faced a recession as well as global political unrest. The significant oil-producing region of the Middle East further complicated America's political difficulties, as the Arab-led Organization of Petroleum Exporting Countries (OPEC) embargoed oil shipments in response to the West's support of Israel. Energy prices spiked, causing a severe recession. The oil crisis highlighted America's vulnerabilities to foreign oil, a dependency that consumers awoke to when oil shortages caused long lines at the pumps.

READING AND DISCUSSION QUESTIONS

1. What does this photograph reveal about the impact of global political and economic crises on the lives of ordinary Americans?

2. How do you think scenes like this one, experienced by Americans living during the 1970s, affected their perspective on America's role in global affairs?

"Energy Crisis Gasoline Lines," Underwood Archives/Archive Photos/Getty Images.

29-2 | Steel Town Faces Challenge of Deindustrialization

ROBERT HOWARD, *Youngstown Fights Back* (1979)

The effects of the global economy were felt across America in the 1970s as American industry faced low-wage competition from overseas, leading to an erosion of the manufacturing base. Youngstown, Ohio, long a center of steel production, lost its competitive edge to lower-priced Japanese steel and corporate buyouts. In this excerpt, *The New Republic* chronicles efforts by steelworkers to reverse the effects of deindustrialization.

Studies rate Youngstown as the most economically depressed metropolitan area in the state of Ohio (where the competition is stiff). The local economy suffers from an extreme version of the general problems affecting the entire American steel industry. Youngstown is representative of urban areas throughout the northeast—a working-class city burdened with an outmoded industrial plant and victimized by the flight of badly needed capital to more profitable climates in the south and southwest.

But there is a new big idea afloat in Youngstown today. It does not come from any of the traditional leaders in the political life of this northeastern Ohio community. . . . During the past year a group of about 200 local religious leaders calling itself the Ecumenical Coalition of the Mahoning Valley has led a sustained community effort to combat economic decline. After the closing of a major steel mill in the Youngstown area, the Mahoning Ecumenical Coalition and its supporters—an unusual mixture of church groups, veterans of the new left and local activists in the steelworkers' union—have devised a plan for a community and worker-owned corporation to purchase the mill and its operation.

In September 1977, the Youngstown Sheet and Tube company announced the closing of major portions of its Campbell Works mill. Sheet and Tube had been a locally-owned company since its establishment in 1902, but in 1969 it was swallowed up by a sunbelt conglomerate, the Lykes Corporation from New Orleans. Lykes's occupation of Sheet and Tube is a history of neglect. Lykes put in only about one-fourth of the capital investment necessary to keep the plant from deteriorating, let alone attempting to modernize it. Sheet and Tube's substantial cash-flow was diverted to other Lykes projects. Finally Lykes decided to write off the Campbell Works. The first of 4,200 workers were laid off days after the closing announcement. In the Youngstown suburb of Campbell, where most of the mill is located, 80 percent of the town's tax base disappeared from the books.

The layoffs shocked Youngstown. Industrial closings were not new to the Mahoning Valley; 10,000 jobs have been lost since 1950. But the size and suddenness of the Campbell layoffs caught everyone by surprise. Traditional business, labor and government circles were paralyzed. Local politicians could do little but point to the same villains that Lykes had cited to excuse the mill closing: foreign steel dumping, federal environmental regulations, etc. Leaders of the United

Steelworkers were equally unhelpful. In a meeting in Washington with angry Youngstown steel workers, union president Lloyd McBride urged that the lost jobs be written off, that union locals work to preserve those that still remained.

The Ecumenical Coalition led by Roman Catholic Bishop James Malone, has tried to fill the institutional vacuum with a strange blend of old-time community capitalism and 1960s participatory democracy. Two months after the layoffs, the Coalition produced a manifesto entitled "A Religious Response to the Mahoning Valley Steel Crisis," arguing that large corporations must be accountable to the individuals they employ and the communities where they are located. The Coalition statement found ready supporters among certain officials of the affected United Steelworkers' locals. Caught between the anger and disillusion of their members and the apparent indifference of the international union leadership, these union activists were the first to suggest the idea of community ownership. The Coalition then contacted experts outside the immediate community whose legacy is largely that of the new left. Economist Gar Alperovitz, director of the Washington-based National Center for Economic Alternatives, proposed that the Youngstown people risk something big—a massive project to buy the Campbell Works and to run it through a corporation owned by the workers employed at the mill, members of the Youngstown community and a minority of outside investors. . . .

Critics of the plan see it as the beginning of a permanent federal subsidy to part of the steel industry. Executives of United States Steel and Republic Steel, the two major competitors of a would-be community-owned mill in Youngstown, have condemned the proposal as "socialistic," even "communistic." Local business people express fear that big government would be invading the Mahoning Valley. William Sullivan, director of the Western Reserve Economic Development Association, a development group financed primarily by local industry, claims that the costs of modernization have been seriously underestimated and that the mill has been closed too long to retrieve its original markets.

Coalition supporters claim that the role of the federal government will be far less substantial than the feasibility study suggested. Alperovitz said, "the key issue is that of markets; it overwhelms all the subsidiary technical issues." . . . Bernt Rathaus, a steel industry consultant and former vice president of US Steel, claims that the outlook for a new small company is excellent because major steel buyers like to hedge against potential steel shortages by using a diversity of suppliers. Letters to Alperovitz's Center from the purchasing departments of American automobile manufacturers seem to confirm this judgment. Alperovitz now says guaranteed federal procurement may be unnecessary, and the only federal assistance the plant would need would be $150 to $200 million in loan guarantees.

Coalition leaders argue that their proposal is a challenge to the federal government to support a new way to confront urban problems. "Youngstown is in a situation where the other side has no answer," Alperovitz said. "We are convinced we can run the mill with a profit margin of 10 to 14 percent, but private industry wouldn't touch it unless profit approaches 18 to 22 percent. Alperovitz estimates that even doing nothing to help the Youngstown experiment would cost the public sector $60 to $70 million in tax losses and social service benefit payments during the first three years. So according to the Coalition, either the federal government can spend tax dollars on unemployment and welfare, or it can support a project that attempts to solve the central problem. "The value of the Coalition project is as a demonstration of new forms of economic organization," says Coalition lawyer Staughton Lynd. "It's not just another business. It ought to be viewed as a kind of TVA for the '70s—socially desirable for its own sake."

So far the Ecumenical Coalition's major victories have been political. With growing sophistication, it has established itself as the primary agent in any attempt to revitalize the Mahoning Valley steel industry. A year-long "Save Our Valley" organizing campaign begun shortly after the layoffs publicized Youngstown's economic problems and promoted the idea of community ownership. Local residents and unions, and church groups across the country, deposited more than four million dollars in symbolic, no-risk Save Our Valley accounts in Youngstown banks. Using its nationwide religious contacts, the Coalition had an effective national and local political network in place by the end of last summer. The public relations campaign has been so effective that those opposed to the community ownership project have found it impossible to openly criticize the religious group's work; "it's a little like coming out against apple pie and motherhood," in the words of one Youngstown business leader. Before the November election, the Ecumenical Coalition asked all Ohio candidates for public office to commit themselves for or against the community ownership plan. As a result, telegrams of support came in from all over the political spectrum. Governor James Rhodes, running hard against his liberal Democratic opponent Richard Celeste, promised to ask the state legislature for $10 million for the Youngstown project.

The real target of the Coalition's campaign has been the Carter administration. The tactic has been to appeal to the president's favorite theme of self-reliance. A full-page ad in *The Washington Post* signed by 2000 Ohio religious and community leaders announced "Mr. President, Youngstown's job crisis is a moral issue. . . . We need your help to keep self-help alive there and in the rest of Ohio."

So far the federal response has been contradictory, positive enough to suggest active interest, guarded enough to avoid any real commitment. The Youngstown project is caught in a struggle for control of federal urban policy between the Commerce Department and the Department of Housing and Urban Development. HUD officials have waxed eloquent over the project—"precisely the sort of local initiative we are looking for," HUD Secretary Patricia Harris said. An inter-agency task force under presidential aide Jack Watson is studying the proposal; it has already planned $100 million in loan guarantees to combat structural unemployment in the Mahoning Valley steel industry. But the Commerce Department, with its close ties to the business community, has opposed the plan. Also, Attorney General Griffin Bell's controversial approval of the proposed merger between Lykes and another conglomerate that owns Jones and Laughlin

Steel Corporation would create a powerful new steel company that would increase the difficulties facing a new mill in the Youngstown area.

For the moment, the Carter administration is holding off from committing itself one way or the other. Another study, a more detailed examination of potential markets was commissioned in October and is just getting underway now.

The steelworkers of the Mahoning Valley face a crisis that is not only economic but also political and cultural. The economic changes symbolized by the Campbell layoffs threaten an entire way of life. That life was shaped by the growth of the American steel industry, the labor struggles of the 1930s, and the subsequent partnership of big business and big labor forged in the Second World War.

"Since I been two or three years old, I seen that mill," one Youngstown worker said. "Then all of a sudden, you see the place dead. I worked there for years, still go by every day. 'Course you're not allowed in there now; you're out. Living here all my life I see these things, just like sand castles washed away. And I can't understand why." The same thing happened to Appalachian miners of the 1950s. "We've got guys in the mill who were run out of West Virginia and Pennsylvania when the coal mines went bust," Ed Mann said. "And now it's happening here."

These men see clearly that their needs are not being met by conventional agencies of power . . . not by government, certainly not by business, not even by labor. They make up an available constituency: disoriented, angry, increasingly willing to move toward organizations that will meet those needs—or appear to do so.

The Ecumenical Coalition has recognized this—the inadequacies of the traditional forms of political description to solving new economic problems. It has fashioned a proposal that cuts across the conventional categories. As a result, it has gained the support of a growing portion of this available constituency.

As the political system attempts to respond to citizens' distress about the economic realities of the 1970s, a social movement has developed in a direction quite opposed to America's much touted "move to the right." The Youngstown experiment may be the harbinger of a progressive movement aimed at that very group conservatives have proclaimed to be the bedrock of the silent majority, the traditional white ethnic working class.

READING AND DISCUSSION QUESTIONS

1. What conclusions can you draw about the short- and long-term effects of globalization on Youngstown, Ohio, as its steel mill closed? What happened to Youngstown's community identity?

2. How hopeful is Robert Howard that the workers' plans for community and employee ownership would reverse the ill-effects of globalization? What challenge to the existing economy is implicit in the workers' plans?

29-3 | Abortion Case Highlights Divisions
Supreme Court Decision in Roe v. Wade (1973)

The Supreme Court's decision in the controversial case of *Roe v. Wade* was both a cause and a consequence of America's cultural unrest. The decision legalized abortion, reversing state-level restrictions that had banned the procedure. Justice Harry Blackmun wrote the Court's opinion. The other excerpts are *amicus curiae* or "friend of the court" briefs. One is from Nancy Stearns on behalf of the Women's Health and Abortion Project supporting Jane Roe (the pseudonymous name of the woman bringing the appeal). The second, from the National Right to Life Committee, challenged the constitutional arguments supporting abortion rights.

Edited Decision of Justice Harry Blackmun in *Roe v. Wade*

The Constitution does not explicitly mention any right of privacy . . . however . . . the Court has recognized that a right of personal privacy, or a guarantee of certain areas or zones of privacy, does exist under the Constitution. . . .

This right of privacy, whether it be founded in the Fourteenth Amendment's concept of personal liberty and restrictions upon state action . . . or . . . in the Ninth Amendment's reservation of rights to the people, is broad enough to encompass a woman's decision whether or not to terminate her pregnancy. The detriment that the State would impose upon the pregnant woman by denying this choice altogether is apparent. Specific and direct harm medically diagnosable even in early pregnancy may be involved. Maternity, or additional offspring, may force upon the woman a distressful life and future. Psychological harm may be imminent. Mental and physical health may be taxed by child care. There is also the distress, for all concerned, associated with the unwanted child, and there is the problem of bringing a child into a family already unable, psychologically and otherwise, to care for it. In other cases, as in this one, the additional difficulties and continuing stigma of unwed motherhood may be involved. All these are factors the woman and her responsible physician necessarily will consider in consultation.

On the basis of elements such as these, appellant and some *amici* argue that the woman's right is absolute and that she is entitled to terminate her pregnancy at whatever time, in whatever way, and for whatever reason she alone chooses. With this we do not agree. At some point in pregnancy, these respective interests become sufficiently compelling to sustain regulation of the factors that govern the abortion decision. The privacy right involved, therefore, cannot be said to be absolute. . . .

We, therefore, conclude that the right of personal privacy includes the abortion decision, but that this right is not unqualified and must be considered against important state interests in regulation. . . .

Roe v. Wade 410 U.S. 113 (1973). For *amicus curiae* briefs, see Linda Greenhouse and Reva B. Siegel, *Before Roe v. Wade: Voices That Shaped the Abortion Debate Before the Supreme Court's Ruling* (New York: Kaplan Publishing, 2011), 329–337, 352–359.

Where certain "fundamental rights" are involved, the Court has held that regulation limiting these rights may be justified only by a "compelling state interest," and that legislative enactments must be narrowly drawn to express only the legitimate state interests at stake. . . .

We repeat . . . that the State does have an important and legitimate interest in preserving and protecting the health of the pregnant woman . . . and that it has still *another* important and legitimate interest in protecting the potentiality of human life. These interests are separate and distinct. Each grows in substantiality as the woman approaches term and, at a point during pregnancy, each becomes "compelling." . . .

To summarize and to repeat: A state criminal abortion statute of the current Texas type, that excepts from criminality only a *lifesaving* procedure on behalf of the mother, without regard to pregnancy state and without recognition of the other interests involved, is inviolate of the Due Process Clause of the Fourteenth Amendment. . . .

The decision leaves the State free to place increasing restrictions on abortion as the period of pregnancy lengthens, so long as those restrictions are tailored to the recognized state interests. The decision vindicates the right of the physician to administer medical treatment according to his professional judgment up to the points where important state interests provide compelling justifications for intervention. Up to those points, the abortion decision in all its aspects is inherently, and primarily, a medical decision, and basic responsibility for it must rest with the physician. If an individual practitioner abuses the privilege of exercising proper medical judgment, the usual remedies, judicial and intra-professional, are available. *It is so ordered.*

Amicus Curiae Brief in Support of Jane Roe, New Women's Lawyers; Women's Health and Abortion Project, Inc.; and National Abortion Action Coalition

Under the Fourteenth Amendment to the Constitution, no state shall ". . . deprive any person of life, liberty, or property without due process of law." The courts have not yet, however, begun to come to grips with the fact that approximately one half of our citizenry is systematically being denied those guarantees of the Fourteenth Amendment. That is exactly the effect of the abortion laws of Texas and Georgia, and nearly every other state in the United States. Amici urge this Court not to shrink from redressing the constitutional wrongs perpetrated on women. . . .

The decision by a woman of whether and when she will bear children may be the most fundamental decision of her life because of its far-reaching significance, affecting almost every aspect of her life from the earliest days of her pregnancy. . . .

Persons seeking to uphold restrictive abortion laws argue that the State has a compelling interest in protecting human life. Amici could not agree more. But, we argue that the responsibility of the State runs to persons who are living and that the State may not maintain laws which effect the most serious invasions of the constitutional rights of its citizens. . . .

[W]hile governments profess their overwhelming concern for human life, they force their female citizens into the intolerable dilemma of choosing between what in many instances would be a totally irresponsible act of bearing and casting off, or even "raising" an unwanted child or jeopardizing their life and health, both physical and mental, by obtaining an illegal abortion or attempting to self-abort. . . .

Pregnancy, from the moment of conception, severely limits a woman's liberty. In many cases of both public and private employment women are forced to temporarily or permanently leave their employment when they become pregnant. The employer has no duty to transfer a pregnant woman to a less arduous job during any stage of pregnancy (should the woman or her doctor consider this advisable); nor is there any statutory duty to rehire the woman after she gives birth. . . . [R]egardless of whether the woman wishes and/or needs to continue working, regardless of whether she is physically capable of working, she may nonetheless be required to stop working solely because of her pregnancy. In many if not most states women who are public employees are compelled to terminate their employment at some arbitrary date during pregnancy regardless of whether they are capable of continuing work. . . .

Under these circumstances, a case can well be made that the anti-abortion law, in compelling a pregnant woman to continue this condition against her wishes, is not merely a denial of liberty, but also an imposition of cruel and unusual punishment on the woman. . . .

Here we see inextricably the rights to life and liberty are mixed and even more how laws restricting abortion deny women both. . . .

For a woman perhaps the most critical aspect of liberty is the right to decide when and whether she will have a child — with all the burdens and limitations on her freedom which that entails. But that has been robbed from her by men who make the laws which govern her. . . .

Restrictive laws governing abortion such as those of Texas and Georgia are a manifestation of the fact that men are unable to see women in any role other than that of mother and wife. . . .

The statutes of Georgia, Texas and nearly every other state in the nation similarly deny to women throughout the country their most precious right to control their lives and bodies. . . .

Millions of women are now becoming truly conscious of the manifold forms of oppression and discrimination of their sex in our society. They are beginning to publicly express their outrage at what they have always known — that bearing and raising a child that they do not want is indeed cruel and unusual punishment. Such punishment involves not only an indeterminate sentence and a loss of citizenship rights as an independent person . . . great physical hardship and emotional damage disproportionate to the crime of participating equally in sexual activity with a man . . . but is punishment for her status as a woman and a potential child-bearer. . . . Abortion laws reinforce the legally legitimized indignities that women have already suffered under for too long and bear witness to the inferior position to which women are relegated. The total destruction of a woman's status in society results from compelling her to take sole responsibility for having the illegal abortion or bear the unwanted child, and suffer the physical hardship and mental anguish whichever she chooses. . . .

Men (of whom the legislature and courts are almost exclusively composed) must now learn that they may not constitutionally impose the cruel penalties of unwanted pregnancy and motherhood on women, where the penalties fall solely on them.

Amicus Curiae Brief in Support of Henry Wade, National Right to Life Committee

The National Right to Life Committee is a non-sectarian, interdisciplinary organization that is committed to informing and educating the general public on questions related to the sanctity of human life. Protecting the right to life of the unborn child is of central concern for NRLC. The Committee believes that proposals for total repeal or relaxation of present abortion laws represent a regressive approach to serious human problems. NRLC is in favor of a legal system that protects the life of the unborn child, while recognizing the dignity of the child's mother, the rights of its father, and the responsibility of society to provide support and assistance to both the mother and child. . . .

. . . NRLC sees no point in belaboring the scientifically obvious. Life begins at conception and for practical medical purposes can be scientifically verified within 14 days. . . .

Let us then address ourselves specifically to the question of balancing the two rights which may appear to be in conflict in these cases. That question must be: To what extent can the State protect the right of an unborn infant to continue its existence as a living being in the face of a claim of right of privacy on the part of a woman to decide whether or not she wishes to remain with child?

This Court has decided that the Constitution protects certain rights of privacy on the part of a woman arising from the marital relationship which cannot be unjustifiably interfered with by the State. NRLC believes that the genesis of such rights, to the extent such rights may exist, must be found among the "penumbral" personal liberties protected by the Due Process Clause of the Fifth Amendment. Yet equally unchallengeable is the proposition that an unborn child's right not to "be deprived of life," to quote the words of the Due Process Clause itself, is also a fundamental personal right or liberty protected by that same amendment and entitled to the traditional searching judicial scrutiny and review afforded when basic personal liberties are threatened by state action, whether legislative or judicial in character. Therefore, it is very clear that this case is not one, as the appellants would portray it, which involves merely the balancing of a right of personal liberty (i.e., a married woman's privacy) against some

competing, generalized state interest of lower priority or concern in an enlightened scheme of constitutional values, such as the state's police power. Here, the
Court must choose between a nebulous and undefined legal "right" of privacy
on the part of a woman with respect to the use of her body and the State's right to
prevent the destruction of a human life. That election involves the determination
as to whether the State's judgment that human life is to be preferred is a prohibited exercise of legislative power.

There would be no question of the answer, of course, if the choice were
between a woman's "right to privacy" and the destruction of an unwanted after-
born child. Yet abortion is distinguishable from infanticide only by the event of
birth. . . . Now the separate, early and independent existence of fetal life has been
conclusively proven by medical science. While it may be impossible for the State
to insist on maintaining such a life under all circumstances, can it seriously be
maintained that the Government is powerless to insist on protecting it from
intentional destruction, absent danger to the mother's life? . . .

[I]n the amicus brief filed by the American Association of University Women
and other women's organizations, the "sovereignty of the body" argument is
made in a disguised and superficially more plausible form. These amici assert a
woman's right of "reproductive autonomy." This they define as the "personal,
constitutional right of a woman to determine the number and spacing of her children, and thus to determine whether to bear a particular child. . . ." Such a right,
those amici argue, evolves inevitably from the recognition which this Court has
afforded to those human interests "which relate to marriage, sex, the family and
the raising of children." . . . Parents may have a constitutional right to plan for the
number and spacing of children. Still, that right cannot be extended to permit the
destruction of a living human being absent a threat to the life of the mother carrying the unborn baby. Family planning, including the contraceptive relationship,
is a matter between a man and a woman alone. The abortion relationship, on the
other hand, is between the parents and the unborn child. . . .

. . . NRLC disputes the assertion that a woman enjoys any right of privacy, as
yet undefined in American law, which vests in her alone the absolute authority
to terminate a pregnancy for any reason whatsoever. No precedents of this Court
have gone so far. . . .

The suggestion that abortion laws are peculiarly the product of a male-
dominated government is especially inapposite in the case of Georgia, which
enacted the abortion statute involved in this litigation in 1968. This amicus
applauds the continuing process by which illegal discriminations against women
have been removed. However, the claim that a woman should be free to destroy
a human being whom she has conceived by voluntarily having sexual intercourse can only make sense if that human being be regarded as part of herself, a
part which she may discard for her own good. However, at this point, the evolution of social doctrine favoring freedom for women collides squarely with modern scientific knowledge and with the medical and judicial recognition that the
fetus in the womb is a living person. A woman should be left free to practice
contraception; she should not be left free to commit feticide.

READING AND DISCUSSION QUESTIONS

1. What arguments does the Court rely on in making its ruling in *Roe v. Wade*? How does the Court accept or reject the arguments in the *amicus curiae* briefs?

2. What conclusions about the political culture of the early 1970s can you draw from the evidence of the Court's decision and friend of the court briefs? How do these sources reflect a range of views?

3. How do you assess the historical significance of this Court decision in the early 1970s and its legacy in the decades after? What impact did the decision have on the era's political culture?

29-4 | Conservative Response to Equal Rights Amendment

PHYLLIS SCHLAFLY, *Statement Opposing the ERA* (1977)

The proposed Equal Rights Amendment to the Constitution became a lightning rod issue during the 1970s. Feminists rallied behind the amendment claiming that its provisions barring discrimination on the basis of sex were the culmination of nearly two centuries of efforts to advance the cause of women's rights. Opponents, including the national chairman of "Stop ERA," Phyllis Schlafly, mobilized conservatives to prevent ratification. The amendment failed to win ratification before the June 1982 deadline imposed by Congress.

The Equal Rights Amendment pretends to be an advance for women, but actually it will do nothing at all for women. It will not give women equal pay for equal work or any new employment advantages, rights or benefits. There is no way it can extend the rights already guaranteed by the Equal Employment Opportunity Act of 1972. Under this act and the commission it created women have already won multi-million-dollar back-pay settlements against the largest companies in our land.

The Education Amendments of 1972 have already given women full equal rights in education at every level, from kindergarten through graduate schools. The Equal Credit Opportunity Act of 1974 has already given women equal rights and ended all discrimination in credit. There is no law that discriminates against women.

What ERA will do is to require us to "neuterize" all Federal and state laws, removing the "sexist" words such as male, female, man, woman, husband and wife, and replacing them with the sex-neutral words such as person and spouse. Every change this requires will deprive women of a right, benefit or exemption that they now enjoy.

At the federal level the most obvious result would be on the draft and military combat. ERA will take away a young girl's exemption from the draft in all

Phyllis Schlafly, "Excerpt from Statement on the ERA," *Congressional Digest* 56 (June 1977): 189, 191.

future wars and force her to register for the draft just like men. The Selective Service Act would have to read "all persons" instead of "all male citizens."

Likewise, ERA will require the military to assign women to all jobs in the armed services, including combat duty. Present federal laws that exempt women from combat duty will become unconstitutional under ERA because the U.S. Constitution is "the supreme law of the land."

Last month's newspapers featured headlines such as "Draft is Inevitable, Arms Chairman Says" and "Pentagon Urges Standby Draft." You have to be kidding to call it an advance for women to make our girls subject to military induction and combat duty in all our country's future wars!

When the laws pertaining to family support are neuterized, this will void the husband's obligation to support his wife, to provide her with a home, and to support their minor children. Those present obligations are not sex equal, and they could not survive under ERA.

When I debated the leading pro-ERA legal authority, Professor Thomas I. Emerson, he stated that ERA will change the family support law so that the financial obligation will be "reciprocal" or "mutual," and husband and wife will be obliged to support each other only if he or she is incapacitated. That would be a tremendous ripoff of the legal rights of homemakers.

The neuterization of our laws under ERA would have a great effect on the legal definition of marriage. Most people do not think a union of a person and a person is the same thing as a union of a man and a woman. No wonder Senator Sam J. Ervin, Jr., stated on Feb. 22, 1977: "I don't know but one group of people in the United States the ERA would do any good for. That's homosexuals."

Since it is the law of our land that "separate but equal is not equal" and the elimination of discrimination requires full integration, every aspect of our school system would have to be fully coed, whether our citizens want it or not. Private schools and colleges that admit only girls or only boys would be constitutionally required to go fully coed; otherwise they would be in violation of the constitutional mandate against sex discrimination.

In other words, ERA will deprive you of your freedom of choice to attend an all-girls' or all-boys' school or college. All sports, including contact sports, would have to be coed for practice and competition. If you thought the department of Health, Education and Welfare was behaving foolishly and arrogantly when it tried to outlaw mother-daughter and father-son events, that's nothing to the mischief it will do under ERA!

Probably the greatest danger in ERA is Section Two, the provision that Congress will have the power of enforcement. This means that the executive branch will administer ERA and the federal courts will adjudicate it. Section Two will transfer into the hands of the federal government the last remaining aspects of our life that the feds haven't yet got their meddling fingers into, including marriage, divorce, child custody, prison regulations, protective labor legislation, and insurance rates.

Why anyone would want to give the federal politicians, bureaucrats, and judges more power, when they can't solve the problems they have now, is difficult to understand. Yet, ERA will, in the words of former Sen. Sam J. Ervin, Jr., "virtually reduce the states of the union to meaningless zeroes on the nation's map."

While we all want equality of treatment in many aspects of life, such as freedom of speech, press, and religion, trial by jury, and due process, in other aspects, equal treatment of all our citizens would be a grievous injustice. Do you think it would be just to make everyone pay the same income tax regardless of his or her income?

Reasonable people do want differences of treatment between men and women based on their obvious factual differences, namely that women have babies (and men do not) and that women do not have the same physical strength as men. These differences vitally affect the draft, combat duty, family support, factory work, and manual labor. If ERA is permitted to deprive us of options to make the reasonable differences that reasonable men and women want, it will be the most grievous injustice ever perpetrated.

The ERA would be dead today if it were not for the unconstitutional White House pressure and illegal expenditure of Federal funds used to try to force the state legislators to ratify ERA. Article V of the U.S. Constitution gives the ratification power exclusively to state legislatures, and it is shocking the way Big Brother in the Executive Branch of the Federal Government is telling state legislators how to vote.

Nevertheless, the momentum is all going against ERA, and nine states have already defeated it this year.

READING AND DISCUSSION QUESTIONS

1. What arguments does Schlafly use to mobilize opposition to the proposed Equal Rights Amendment? What does she mean when she says the ERA will "neuterize" laws? What impact does she predict for women?

2. What does opposition to the ERA suggest about the political context of the 1970s civil rights movement?

29-5 | Diagnosing the "National Malaise"
JIMMY CARTER, *The Crisis of Confidence* (1979)

The political and economic crises of the 1970s, which included Watergate, Vietnam, and the recession and energy crisis, led Jimmy Carter to conclude that Americans suffered from a national "malaise." In a national address to Americans in the summer of 1979, Carter spoke directly to this crisis of confidence. He focused on the energy crisis to involve Americans in the effort to restore their faith in themselves while also solving the country's problems. The crisis

Jimmy Carter, "Address to the Nation on Energy and National Goals: 'The Malaise Speech,'" July 15, 1979. Online by Gerhard Peters and John T. Woolley, *The American Presidency Project.* www.presidency.ucsb.edu/ws/?pid=32596.

deepened only months later when Iranians stormed the U.S. embassy, beginning a hostage crisis that doomed his presidency.

I want to talk to you right now about a fundamental threat to American democracy.

I do not mean our political and civil liberties. They will endure. And I do not refer to the outward strength of America, a nation that is at peace tonight everywhere in the world, with unmatched economic power and military might.

The threat is nearly invisible in ordinary ways. It is a crisis of confidence. It is a crisis that strikes at the very heart and soul and spirit of our national will. We can see this crisis in the growing doubt about the meaning of our own lives and in the loss of a unity of purpose for our Nation.

The erosion of our confidence in the future is threatening to destroy the social and the political fabric of America. . . .

In a nation that was proud of hard work, strong families, close-knit communities, and our faith in God, too many of us now tend to worship self-indulgence and consumption. Human identity is no longer defined by what one does, but by what one owns. But we've discovered that owning things and consuming things does not satisfy our longing for meaning. We've learned that piling up material goods cannot fill the emptiness of lives which have no confidence or purpose. . . .

These changes did not happen overnight. They've come upon us gradually over the last generation, years that were filled with shocks and tragedy.

We were sure that ours was a nation of the ballot, not the bullet, until the murders of John Kennedy and Robert Kennedy and Martin Luther King, Jr. We were taught that our armies were always invincible and our causes were always just, only to suffer the agony of Vietnam. We respected the Presidency as a place of honor until the shock of Watergate.

We remember when the phrase "sound as a dollar" was an expression of absolute dependability, until 10 years of inflation began to shrink our dollar and our savings. We believed that our Nation's resources were limitless until 1973, when we had to face a growing dependence on foreign oil.

These wounds are still very deep. They have never been healed. . . .

What you see too often in Washington and elsewhere around the country is a system of government that seems incapable of action. You see a Congress twisted and pulled in every direction by hundreds of well-financed and powerful special interests. You see every extreme position defended to the last vote, almost to the last breath by one unyielding group or another. You often see a balanced and a fair approach that demands sacrifice, a little sacrifice from everyone, abandoned like an orphan without support and without friends.

Often you see paralysis and stagnation and drift. You don't like it, and neither do I. What can we do?

First of all, we must face the truth, and then we can change our course. We simply must have faith in each other, faith in our ability to govern ourselves, and faith in the future of this Nation. Restoring that faith and that confidence to

America is now the most important task we face. It is a true challenge of this generation of Americans. . . .

We are at a turning point in our history. There are two paths to choose. One is a path I've warned about tonight, the path that leads to fragmentation and self-interest. Down that road lies a mistaken idea of freedom, the right to grasp for ourselves some advantage over others. That path would be one of constant conflict between narrow interests ending in chaos and immobility. It is a certain route to failure.

All the traditions of our past, all the lessons of our heritage, all the promises of our future point to another path, the path of common purpose and the restoration of American values. That path leads to true freedom for our Nation and ourselves. We can take the first steps down that path as we begin to solve our energy problem.

Energy will be the immediate test of our ability to unite this Nation, and it can also be the standard around which we rally. On the battlefield of energy we can win for our Nation a new confidence, and we can seize control again of our common destiny.

In little more than two decades we've gone from a position of energy independence to one in which almost half the oil we use comes from foreign countries, at prices that are going through the roof. Our excessive dependence on OPEC has already taken a tremendous toll on our economy and our people. This is the direct cause of the long lines which have made millions of you spend aggravating hours waiting for gasoline. It's a cause of the increased inflation and unemployment that we now face. This intolerable dependence on foreign oil threatens our economic independence and the very security of our Nation.

The energy crisis is real. It is worldwide. It is a clear and present danger to our Nation. These are facts and we simply must face them:

What I have to say to you now about energy is simple and vitally important.

Point one: I am tonight setting a clear goal for the energy policy of the United States. Beginning this moment, this Nation will never use more foreign oil than we did in 1977; never. . . . The generation-long growth in our dependence on foreign oil will be stopped dead in its tracks. . . . I am tonight setting the further goal of cutting our dependence on foreign oil by one-half by the end of the next decade; a saving of over 4½ million barrels of imported oil per day.

Point two: To ensure that we meet these targets, I will use my Presidential authority to set import quotas. I'm announcing tonight that for 1979 and 1980, I will forbid the entry into this country of one drop of foreign oil more than these goals allow. These quotas will ensure a reduction in imports even below the ambitious levels we set at the recent Tokyo summit.

Point three: To give us energy security, I am asking for the most massive peacetime commitment of funds and resources in our Nation's history to develop America's own alternative sources of fuel; from coal, from oil shale, from plant products for gasohol, from unconventional gas, from the Sun.

I propose the creation of an energy security corporation to lead this effort to replace 2½ million barrels of imported oil per day by 1990. The corporation will issue up to $5 billion in energy bonds, and I especially want them to be in small denominations so that average Americans can invest directly in America's energy security.

. . . I will soon submit legislation to Congress calling for the creation of this Nation's first solar bank, which will help us achieve the crucial goal of 20 percent of our energy coming from solar power by the year 2000. . . .

Point four: I'm asking Congress to mandate, to require as a matter of law, that our Nation's utility companies cut their massive use of oil by 50 percent within the next decade and switch to other fuels, especially coal, our most abundant energy source.

Point five: . . . I will urge Congress to create an energy mobilization board which, like the War Production Board in World War II, will have the responsibility and authority to cut through the redtape, the delays, and the endless roadblocks to completing key energy projects.

We will protect our environment. But when this Nation critically needs a refinery or a pipeline, we will build it.

Point six: I'm proposing a bold conservation program to involve every State, county, and city and every average American in our energy battle. This effort will permit you to build conservation into your homes and your lives at a cost you can afford.

I ask Congress to give me authority for mandatory conservation and for standby gasoline rationing. To further conserve energy, I'm proposing tonight an extra $10 billion over the next decade to strengthen our public transportation systems. And I'm asking you for your good and for your Nation's security to take no unnecessary trips, to use carpools or public transportation whenever you can, to park your car one extra day per week, to obey the speed limit, and to set your thermostats to save fuel. Every act of energy conservation like this is more than just common sense; I tell you it is an act of patriotism.

Our Nation must be fair to the poorest among us, so we will increase aid to needy Americans to cope with rising energy prices. We often think of conservation only in terms of sacrifice. In fact, it is the most painless and immediate way of rebuilding our Nation's strength. Every gallon of oil each one of us saves is a new form of production. It gives us more freedom, more confidence, that much more control over our own lives.

So, the solution of our energy crisis can also help us to conquer the crisis of the spirit in our country. It can rekindle our sense of unity, our confidence in the future, and give our Nation and all of us individually a new sense of purpose.

You know we can do it. We have the natural resources. We have more oil in our shale alone than several Saudi Arabias. We have more coal than any nation on Earth. We have the world's highest level of technology. We have the most skilled work force, with innovative genius, and I firmly believe that we have the national will to win this war.

I do not promise you that this struggle for freedom will be easy. I do not promise a quick way out of our Nation's problems, when the truth is that the only way out is an all-out effort. What I do promise you is that I will lead our fight, and I will enforce fairness in our struggle, and I will ensure honesty. And above all, I will act.

We can manage the short-term shortages more effectively and we will, but there are no short-term solutions to our long-range problems. There is simply no way to avoid sacrifice. . . .

Little by little we can and we must rebuild our confidence. We can spend until we empty our treasuries, and we may summon all the wonders of science. But we can succeed only if we tap our greatest resources; America's people, America's values, and America's confidence.

READING AND DISCUSSION QUESTIONS

1. How does Carter account for the sense of crisis many Americans felt during the late 1970s? What factors does he cite as evidence of this crisis?

2. What solution to the nation's energy crisis does Carter recommend? How does he think these solutions would impact the crisis of confidence he describes?

3. From Carter's tone, what conclusions can you draw about the mood of the nation in the 1970s? What reaction might his speech have had on Americans?

29-6 | Evangelicals on the Rise

MARY MURPHY, *Next Billy Graham* (1978)

The 1960s cultural wars between conservatives and liberals continued into the 1970s, focused around flashpoint issues like abortion, homosexuality, and feminism. To evangelical conservatives like the Reverend Jerry Falwell, *Roe v. Wade*, gay pride, and the Equal Rights Amendment were evidence of America's unmooring from traditional values. His ministry, profiled in this *Esquire* article, responded to these moral challenges with a mix of faith and media savvy that redefined the rules of electoral politics.

". . . Come. Whatever your problems, we have trained counselors to help. . . . Praise Jesus. . . . Praise Jesus. . . . Praise Jesus. . . ." As he recites the fundamentalist mantra, the faithful make their way to the front of the church. . . . The repetition is hypnotic. . . . The organ music swells. . . .

Brother Jerry, a bootlegger's grandson who charmed and worked and prayed his way to the head of a multimillion-dollar ministry, is preparing to have enormous impact on the American public through mass communication. Already he can be heard daily on 275 radio stations and seen weekly on 310 television stations across the United States. Already he reaches approximately three million homes. Soon, he expects the number of his radio outlets to jump to 1,000 and his impact through television to increase when he moves one fourth of his

Mary Murphy, "Next Billy Graham: Jerry Falwell's Old-Time Gospel Hour," *Esquire* 90 (October 10, 1978): 25–28, 30–32.

broadcasts of the *Old-Time Gospel Hour* into prime time. By 1983, he hopes to be as powerful as any of the largest producers and packagers of commercial television. . . .

He intends to carry out this master plan to bend the world's airwaves to God's will from his hometown, Lynchburg, Virginia, where he is building a media empire on a lush 3,200-acre mountaintop. Here, construction of a $4-million radio and television studio will begin this year. Here, 2,250 students at the Liberty Baptist College, which Falwell founded in 1971, are being trained in evangelism, liberal arts, and sophisticated broadcasting techniques. Like the early apostles, the students will then be dispatched to spread the word around the world. . . .

Like country music, Bible Belt fundamentalism is moving out of the South and into the mainstream of American life. Martin Luther King led the way. He took the Baptist religion out of the churches in Montgomery, marched it into the streets, and forced it into courtrooms and legislatures, spawning a whole generation of young preacher/politicians, such as Andrew Young and Jesse Jackson. Jimmy Carter has often said that without King's efforts, he would never have been able to capture the presidency.

Carter, in fact, may have given us a clue about what is to come. His candidacy showed that Americans are prepared to respond positively to a man who professes personal spiritual regeneration, who embodies what the public takes to be the simpler moral values of simpler times. . . .

These days, religion mixes as well with business as it does with politics. The evangelical movement, or "The Electric Church," as *The Wall Street Journal* called it recently, generates thousands of jobs and brings in an annual cash flow of hundreds of millions of dollars. Evangelical-related products, such as magazines, T-shirts, bumper stickers, and religious records, represent an estimated $2-billion industry in this country and Canada. More than 5,000 evangelical bookstores are now open for business, and the number is growing. About $500 million was spent for religious broadcasting on commercial stations last year, five times the amount in 1972. And Evangelicals claim an average audience of 115 million a week on radio and another 14 million on TV. A total of twenty-five TV stations and 1,200 radio stations are entirely devoted to religious programming. And the number increases monthly. . . .

It is a typical Sunday morning at the Thomas Road Baptist Church. The parking lot is filled with tour buses and motor homes and Cadillacs. In the lobby, hundreds of visitors are lined up at the registration desk, where they are asked to fill out identification cards, which will be sent to the countinghouse and filed into a computer memory bank. Falwell's television show, the *Old-Time Gospel Hour*, will be taped this morning. While the faithful buy books and Bibles, which are on sale in the lobby, Falwell is at the barbershop having his hair washed, razor cut, blown dry, and sprayed. At 10:30 A.M., a half hour before air time, he is standing before the altar raising money.

He needs money to finance four schools. "For anyone who wants to underwrite one of our students for $100, we have free Bibles in the lobby." The Treasure

Island Summer Camp . . . The Bible Club Ministry . . . Bus Ministry . . . Media Ministry, which takes a hefty $13.5 million out of the church's total revenues . . . Youth Ministry . . . and the missionary singing groups who are traveling in Australia, Korea, and Japan. "And while you are filling out those pledge cards," Falwell says, "don't forget to ask God for $4 million for our building fund every time you pray. . . ." As the faithful reach for their pens, the lights for the broadcast go on. It is sixty seconds to air time.

In the control room, a crew of professionally trained technicians moves into action, flipping dials, adjusting headsets, scanning monitors. "We've got problems, guys," says the director. "Camera number one can't hear me, and camera number four is tearing up the picture. Before the panic sets in, let us pray." He bows his head. "Our heavenly Father, we thank You for the medium of television. We pray for the technical aspects of this program so we can produce a show worthy of Your son, Jesus Christ." He looks up, cues the technician to his left, and snaps, "Camera number two ready to pan . . . roll tape."

From the pulpit, Falwell launches an attack on abortion, homosexuality, and pornography. He calls it his Clean Up America Campaign. . . . "Homosexuality is a perversion, not an alternative life-style. . . ." "Abortion on demand is legalized murder. . . ." "Pornography, particularly in television and literature, is brainwashing the American people into accepting as normal what is abnormal."

Falwell's organization has drawn up a questionnaire asking people's opinions on abortion, homosexuality, and pornography. Fifty million ballots have been mailed to homes and have appeared as advertisements in magazines as diverse as the *National Enquirer* and *TV Guide* and in all major newspapers. By this November, they will be catalogued and computerized, and the results will be sent to the Supreme Court, Congress, legislators in all fifty states, and the mayor of every major city. Falwell plans to deliver his findings personally to Jimmy Carter. "I expect," he says, "that ninety percent of the people will vote no."

A year ago, a local paper reported that with Anita Bryant[1] at his side at the altar, Jerry Falwell called for a return to the "McCarthy era, where we register all Communists." He went even further, suggesting not only that we should register all Communists "but we should stamp it on their foreheads and send them back to Russia." He also hit hard at any attempt by the American government to normalize relations with "that murderer Castro in Cuba."

This morning he paraphrases Leviticus: "If a man also lie with a man as he lieth with a woman, both of them have surely committed an abomination, and they shall surely be put to death. Their blood shall be upon them."

At the end of the service, I asked Falwell where he draws the line between politics and morality.

"I stay totally on spiritual issues," he said. "I don't talk politics."

I asked him his definition of a political issue.

---

[1]**Anita Bryant**: A popular singer during the 1950s and 1960s, who became a vocal antigay activist in the 1970s.

"The Panama Canal," he said, "is political." "The Equal Rights Amendment is moral." So, evidently, is campaigning in Dade County with Anita Bryant, attacking Jimmy Carter on the air for his interview in *Playboy*, and planning a trip to California to help state senator John Briggs turn his antihomosexual initiative into law.

Does he think he has political influence over his followers?

"Yes." He is straightforward. "But I feel that my highest calling is spiritual, and if I'm too political it will dilute my effectiveness. For instance, I'm very much against communism, but I don't make it my main line."

Will the American people look to a religious or spiritual person as their next President?

"I think a very spiritual person could rise," Falwell says. His words are measured, his voice is soft. "Someone who would possess not only political savvy but spiritual consciousness, and I think it is what this country desperately needs."

Has Carter helped or hurt the cause?

"I didn't think Carter was the best candidate when he went in, and I think even less of him now. But I don't think Jimmy Carter has defamed Christianity in any way. His problem is that he hadn't had the opportunity to become much of a spiritual leader. The burdens of the White House are so complex. For me I think it is better to stay out of that arena to do God's will."

Do you talk to God?

"Daily."

Does he talk to you?

"Daily."

Can you hear him?

"Daily."

His voice?

"No. But I know that right now He is here with me."

The next day I went to a Roman Catholic church in Lynchburg to ask people what they thought of their home-grown prophet.

"No one is safe here anymore," said a lifelong resident of Lynchburg. "And it's all because of Jerry Falwell. He sends hundreds of student ministers out to knock on our doors to save souls. And when we turn them away, they go after our children. The kids come home all upset, crying all night because they are afraid that unless they join Jerry's church they are going to hell. His ego has gotten way out of line, and I'll tell you what I want to know: Is there anyone who can stop him?"

READING AND DISCUSSION QUESTIONS

1. To what extent did the success of Falwell's ministry depend on a sense of cultural crisis? Could his ministry have developed as rapidly as it did without the cultural wars in which he was engaged?

2. How do you assess the impact of evangelical Christians on the political culture of the 1970s? What does Falwell's ministry tell you about the intersection of faith and politics in this period?

■ COMPARATIVE QUESTIONS ■

1. From the sources in this chapter, what conclusion can you draw about the political culture of the era? How do you assess the mood of the 1970s?

2. Do you think Americans' perspective on the 1970s was shaped more by the economic crises they endured or by the cultural conflict over values? How might a historian assess the historical significance of these factors?

3. Compare Schlafly's ERA statement to the Redstockings Manifesto (Document 28-3) and Carrie Chapman Catt's 1918 statement (Document 22-2) to understand historical patterns of change and continuity on the issue of women's rights. What differences can you identify in how individuals framed the issues at different times and for different audiences?

4. To what extent is presidential rhetoric — the language presidents use in speeches — reflective of the period? Compare, for example, Carter's national address to Woodrow Wilson's Fourteen Points (Document 21-6), Franklin Roosevelt's inaugural address (Document 23-2), and Lyndon Johnson's Great Society speech (Document 28-1).

America's Economic and Military Engagement with the World

1945–1980

In a 1941 editorial in *Time* magazine, publisher Henry Luce proclaimed the dawning of what he termed the "American Century." With a missionary's optimism, Luce's expansive vision of America's role in the world included global leadership in political, military, economic, and cultural affairs. It is hard to dispute his powers of prophecy. The half century since World War II witnessed America's rise to global dominance fueled by its economic and military resources. America's foreign policy, however, was shaped by contradictory impulses. Policymakers were both confident—critics would say arrogant—from their World War II victory, but also anxious to stem the tide of communism's growing subversive influence. This marriage of confidence and anxiety led to the creation of a "national security state" with enormous and far-reaching power to defend American interests at home and abroad. Those national interests, however, were defined by policymakers wearing red-tinted glasses. They saw world events everywhere within the paradigm of the Cold War conflict between a God-fearing, capitalist, and democratic America and an atheistic, communist, authoritarian regime in the Soviet Union. Americans believed they could meet the advances of communism and feared the consequences of not doing so. So they did. Luce was right. This became the American Century, but critics wisely asked: at what cost?

P8-1 | Creating the National Security State to Fight the Cold War

NSC-68 (1950)

As President Truman's national security team was assessing the comparative strength of the United States and the Soviet Union, the latter detonated an atomic bomb. Nine months later on June 25, 1950, the North Korean military pushed across the 38th parallel, the geographical boundary separating it from South Korea, launching the Korean War. These events focused American policymakers' attention on the need to operationalize Truman's containment policy more aggressively and with greater resources than originally thought necessary. Truman's National Security Council issued its secret report (NSC-68) with recommendations for waging a global war against the communist threat.

Within the past thirty-five years the world has experienced two global wars of tremendous violence. It has witnessed two revolutions—the Russian and the Chinese—of extreme scope and intensity. It has also seen the collapse of five empires—the Ottoman, the Austro-Hungarian, German, Italian and Japanese— and the drastic decline of two major imperial systems, the British and the French. During the span of one generation, the international distribution of power has been fundamentally altered. For several centuries it has proved impossible for any one nation to gain such preponderant strength that a coalition of other nations could not in time face it with greater strength. The international scene was marked by recurring periods of violence and war, but a system of sovereign and independent states was maintained, over which no state was able to achieve hegemony.

Two complex sets of factors have now basically altered this historical distribution of power. First, the defeat of Germany and Japan and the decline of the British and French Empires have interacted with the development of the United States and the Soviet Union in such a way that power has increasingly gravitated to these two centers. Second, the Soviet Union, unlike previous aspirants to hegemony, is animated by a new fanatic faith, antithetical to our own, and seeks to impose its absolute authority over the rest of the world. Conflict has, therefore, become endemic and is waged, on the part of the Soviet Union, by violent or non-violent methods in accordance with the dictates of expediency. With the development of increasingly terrifying weapons of mass destruction, every individual faces the ever-present possibility of annihilation should the conflict enter the phase of total war.

On the one hand, the people of the world yearn for relief from the anxiety arising from the risk of atomic war. On the other hand, any substantial further extension of the area under the domination of the Kremlin would raise the

"A Report to the National Security Council by the Executive Secretary on the United States Objectives and Programs for National Security" (April 12, 1950), President's Secretary's File, Truman Papers.

possibility that no coalition adequate to confront the Kremlin with greater strength could be assembled. It is in this context that this Republic and its citizens in the ascendancy of their strength stand in their deepest peril.

The issues that face us are momentous, involving the fulfillment or destruction not only of this Republic but of civilization itself. They are issues which will not await our deliberations. With conscience and resolution this Government and the people it represents must now take new and fateful decisions. . . .

The fundamental design of those who control the Soviet Union and the international communist movement is to retain and solidify their absolute power, first in the Soviet Union and second in the areas now under their control. In the minds of the Soviet leaders, however, achievement of this design requires the dynamic extension of their authority and the ultimate elimination of any effective opposition to their authority.

The design, therefore, calls for the complete subversion or forcible destruction of the machinery of government and structure of society in the countries of the non-Soviet world and their replacement by an apparatus and structure subservient to and controlled from the Kremlin. To that end Soviet efforts are now directed toward the domination of the Eurasian land mass. The United States, as the principal center of power in the non-Soviet world and the bulwark of opposition to Soviet expansion, is the principal enemy whose integrity and vitality must be subverted or destroyed by one means or another if the Kremlin is to achieve its fundamental design. . . .

It is quite clear from Soviet theory and practice that the Kremlin seeks to bring the free world under its dominion by the methods of the cold war. The preferred technique is to subvert by infiltration and intimidation. Every institution of our society is an instrument which it is sought to stultify and turn against our purposes. Those that touch most closely our material and moral strength are obviously the prime targets, labor unions, civic enterprises, schools, churches, and all media for influencing opinion. The effort is not so much to make them serve obvious Soviet ends as to prevent them from serving our ends, and thus to make them sources of confusion in our economy, our culture and our body politic. The doubts and diversities that in terms of our values are part of the merit of a free system, the weaknesses and the problems that are peculiar to it, the rights and privileges that free men enjoy, and the disorganization and destruction left in the wake of the last attack on our freedoms, all are but opportunities for the Kremlin to do its evil work. Every advantage is taken of the fact that our means of prevention and retaliation are limited by those principles and scruples which are precisely the ones that give our freedom and democracy its meaning for us. None of our scruples deter those whose only code is, "morality is that which serves the revolution." . . .

But there are risks in making ourselves strong. A large measure of sacrifice and discipline will be demanded of the American people. They will be asked to give up some of the benefits which they have come to associate with their freedoms. Nothing could be more important than that they fully understand the reasons for this. The risks of a superficial understanding or of an inadequate appreciation of the issues are obvious and might lead to the adoption of measures which in themselves would jeopardize the integrity of our system. At any point in the process of demonstrating our will to make good our fundamental purpose, the Kremlin may decide to precipitate a general war, or in testing us, may go too far. These are risks we will invite by making ourselves strong, but they are lesser risks than those we seek to avoid. Our fundamental purpose is more likely to be defeated from lack of the will to maintain it, than from any mistakes we may make or assault we may undergo because of asserting that will. No people in history have preserved their freedom who thought that by not being strong enough to protect themselves they might prove inoffensive to their enemies. . . .

A program for rapidly building up strength and improving political and economic conditions will place heavy demands on our courage and intelligence; it will be costly; it will be dangerous. But half-measures will be more costly and more dangerous, for they will be inadequate to prevent and may actually invite war. Budgetary considerations will need to be subordinated to the stark fact that our very independence as a nation may be at stake.

A comprehensive and decisive program to win the peace and frustrate the Kremlin design should be so designed that it can be sustained for as long as necessary to achieve our national objectives. It would probably involve:

(1) The development of an adequate political and economic framework for the achievement of our long-range objectives.

(2) A substantial increase in expenditures for military purposes adequate to meet the requirements for the tasks listed in Section D-1.

(3) A substantial increase in military assistance programs designed to foster cooperative efforts, which will adequately and efficiently meet the requirements of our allies for the tasks referred to in Section D-1-e.

(4) Some increase in economic assistance programs and recognition of the need to continue these programs until their purposes have been accomplished.

(5) A concerted attack on the problem of the United States balance of payments, along the lines already approved by the President.

(6) Development of programs designed to build and maintain confidence among other peoples in our strength and resolution, and to wage overt psychological warfare calculated to encourage mass defections from Soviet allegiance and to frustrate the Kremlin design in other ways.

(7) Intensification of affirmative and timely measures and operations by covert means in the fields of economic warfare and political and psychological warfare with a view to fomenting and supporting unrest and revolt in selected strategic satellite countries.

(8) Development of internal security and civilian defense programs.

(9) Improvement and intensification of intelligence activities.

(10) Reduction of Federal expenditures for purposes other than defense and foreign assistance, if necessary by the deferment of certain desirable programs.

(11) Increased taxes. . . .

The threat to the free world involved in the development of the Soviet Union's atomic and other capabilities will rise steadily and rather rapidly. For the time being, the United States possesses a marked atomic superiority over the Soviet Union which, together with the potential capabilities of the United States and other free countries in other forces and weapons, inhibits aggressive Soviet action. This provides an opportunity for the United States, in cooperation with other free countries, to launch a build-up of strength which will support a firm policy directed to the frustration of the Kremlin design. The immediate goal of our efforts to build a successfully functioning political and economic system in the free world backed by adequate military strength is to postpone and avert the disastrous situation which, in light of the Soviet Union's probable fission bomb capability and possible thermonuclear bomb capability, might arise in 1954 on a continuation of our present programs. By acting promptly and vigorously in such a way that this date is, so to speak, pushed into the future, we would permit time for the process of accommodation, withdrawal and frustration to produce the necessary changes in the Soviet system. Time is short, however, and the risks of war attendant upon a decision to build up strength will steadily increase the longer we defer it.

READING AND DISCUSSION QUESTIONS

1. Analyze the language policymakers used in describing the Soviet Union. What does their choice of words and phrases reveal to you about their perspective on the Soviet threat?

2. To what extent did the national security state envisioned by NSC-68 establish national defense priorities for the next twenty years? What political, social, and economic impact do you think its recommendations had in shaping U.S. foreign policy goals since the mid-twentieth century?

3. How does NSC-68 help explain U.S. military and economic involvement in the latter half of the twentieth century?

P8-2 | U.S. Diplomat Defines America's Interest in Guatemala

JOHN D. PEURIFOY, *Letter to John M. Cabot, Assistant Secretary of State for Inter-American Affairs* (1953)

In 1954, a CIA covert operation ousted Guatemalan president Jacobo Arbenz in an operation codenamed PBSUCCESS. Several U.S. corporations, including the United Fruit Company, had objected to Arbenz's economic policies, which included the nationalizing of the company's unused lands for distribution to the country's poor. In a letter to John Cabot, Ambassador John Peurifoy assessed the political situation in Guatemala, emphasizing a growing communist threat to U.S. interests. President Eisenhower's secretary of state John Foster Dulles endorsed

---

"Letter from the Ambassador to Guatemala (Peurifoy) to the Assistant Secretary of State for Inter-American Affairs (Cabot)," in *Foreign Relations of the United States, 1952–1954: Guatemala,* ed. Susan K. Holly and David S. Patterson (Washington, DC: Government Printing Office, 2003), 159–161.

Peurifoy's views and heeded the appeals from America's business community, resulting in the Guatemalan coup.

Guatemala City, December 28, 1953

Dear Jack:

You will have seen my Secret Telegram No. 163 of December 23 in which I recommended certain policies which we believe would create a climate favorable for a change in the Guatemalan Government. In this supplementary letter I want to round out those recommendations by stressing the need for the U.S. Government to work actively and quickly to assure that the Guatemalan Government is taken over by elements willing and strong enough to eliminate Communist influence from the Guatemalan political scene when the time comes. When the pressures suggested in my telegram become effective here, the Communists as well as the potential opposition to the regime may be expected to seek to exploit the situation and we must then be as sure as possible that elements favorable to our objectives are in the winning position.

As a result of my conversation with President Arbenz and general evaluation of the situation since my arrival here two months ago I am fully convinced that continuance of his administration until its term expires in 1957 will result in a further and dangerous advance of Communism in this country, with all the attendant peril to our security and economic interests in this area. It might well then be too late to root it out without an internal clash of the type that occurred in Greece and elsewhere. I believe further that the internal opposition to the Arbenz regime is unlikely to act independently and that the U.S. Government must accept the risks inherent in helping to bring about a change of government here.

The principal problem now is selecting a force, which should if possible be a Guatemalan force, capable of taking control of the government with our aid and of besting the Communists in the troubled times which will almost certainly surround any change over. If a change is to be achieved in the near future, the most promising organization which meets the requirements for such a force is the Guatemalan Armed Forces, possibly acting in conjunction with such exiled military and political figures and domestic groups as will cooperate. The internal "anti-Communist" opposition now is badly divided and without a workable political program or an organization immediately available. It would, I believe, take many months of effort and failures to get the "anti-Communist" factions together behind a plan with any chance of success; there would be continual high risks of exposure, and in any case it is doubtful whether even in the event that they win they could stick together on a program which would satisfactorily reduce the chances of a Communist-influenced counter-revolution.

I would therefore recommend that the Department select the Guatemalan Armed Forces as the primary area in which any effort to stimulate anti-government action is most likely to be fruitful. Though now loyal to this government they are basically opportunistic. Efforts to win over key military personnel must be done, as I know the Department is fully aware, so as to take the minimum risk of exposing our hand, by using a judicious mixture of our clandestine channels, our influence with neighboring anti-Communist governments and our contacts with

Guatemalan exile groups together with such other contacts with the Military as we can maintain locally. It, of course, will mean expenditure and some risk of charges of intervention which could be serious if the matter is clumsily handled. But this risk must be accepted or we must be prepared to abandon this field to Communism.

The approach to subverting the Armed Forces should of course be flexible and we should attempt simultaneously to develop the other groups, such as dissatisfied and opportunistic elements within our Administration and the "anti-Communist" opposition. While our effort should be concentrated for effectiveness on one group, we must be prepared to shift quickly if our first approaches fail, and to work out combinations of forces if opportunity offers. In this connection, military personnel with government connections such as Colonel Elfego Monzon, as well as the "anti-Communist" movement, should be closely studied for any role they might usefully play.

The measures recommended in my telegram are intended to be closely coordinated with the forging of a non-Communist force to take over here, for of themselves they do not guarantee that a change favorable to us would occur. What I expect is that the program outlined in the telegram would (a) prepare hemispheric and Guatemalan opinion for a change and dull the charges of intervention which may be expected to be leveled at us, and (b) to create here a climate in which important segments of the population and especially the Armed Forces and propertied class felt their interests sufficiently threatened to be stirred from their present lethargy into a better disposition to take the risks necessary to cooperate actively in bringing a new government into power.

We must be as certain as possible, however, that a non-Communist force is prepared to step in at the proper moment. The actual application of economic sanctions would probably hit the propertied classes here harder and more quickly than it would the government, and if long-drawn-out it might well damage irreparably the propertied class and prevent it from retarding the advance of Communism. The Communists, of course, could then be expected to exploit the situation with confiscatory taxes and measures, economic sabotage laws, etc., in order to complete the ruin of the conservative segment that they have begun by their application of the Agrarian Reform Law.

What I suggest, in short, has two complementary aspects; the measures to create a climate favorable for a change recommended in my telegram, and coordinated measures to win over and support a non-Communist force capable of controlling the situation as urged in this letter. I see the risks of exposure and recognize that the program would have to be carefully worked out in Washington and here, for a misfired attempt to change the present Guatemalan Government would most probably greatly strengthen the Communists here and damage our standing everywhere if our part in a failure became generally accepted. However, as I see it, Communism is slowly strangling this country, and delay will only face us with a more difficult problem later.

Sincerely yours,
JOHN E. PEURIFOY

READING AND DISCUSSION QUESTIONS

1. Based on Peurifoy's assessment of Guatemala's internal political, social, and economic situation, what response does he urge his superiors in Washington to adopt and why?

2. Using this source as evidence, what argument might you make concerning the factors motivating American foreign policy in the Cold War era?

P8-3 | A "Peace Race" Proposal for Nuclear Disarmament

JOHN F. KENNEDY, *Address to the United Nations General Assembly* (1961)

When President Kennedy addressed the United Nations in September 1961, the prospects for peace seemed elusive and remote. An ill-fated U.S.-supported invasion at the Bay of Pigs in Cuba dealt Kennedy a humiliating foreign policy blow just three months into his term. In August, the Soviet-backed East German government erected the Berlin Wall. Shadowing these crises was a civil war in the Asian nation of Laos, which triggered American and Soviet responses, another in a series of proxy wars between the two superpowers. Kennedy's assessment of the grave threats to world peace included his bold proposal for the complete disarmament of nuclear weapons.

Today, every inhabitant of this planet must contemplate the day when this planet may no longer be habitable. Every man, woman and child lives under a nuclear sword of Damocles, hanging by the slenderest of threads, capable of being cut at any moment by accident or miscalculation or by madness. The weapons of war must be abolished before they abolish us.

Men no longer debate whether armaments are a symptom or a cause of tension. The mere existence of modern weapons—ten million times more powerful than anything the world has ever seen, and only minutes away from any target on Earth—is a source of horror, and discord and distrust. . . .

For 15 years this organization has sought the reduction and destruction of arms. Now that goal is no longer a dream—it is a practical matter of life or death. The risks inherent in disarmament pale in comparison to the risks inherent in an unlimited arms race.

It is in this spirit that the recent Belgrade Conference—recognizing that this is no longer a Soviet problem or an American problem, but a human problem—endorsed a program of "general, complete and strictly an internationally controlled disarmament." It is in this same spirit that we in the United States have labored this year, with a new urgency, and with a new, now-statutory agency fully endorsed by the Congress, to find an approach to disarmament which would be

John F. Kennedy, "Address to the United Nations General Assembly, September 25, 1961," papers of John F. Kennedy: President's Office Files, January 20, 1961 to November 22, 1963, ARC Identifier 193907, National Archives.

so far-reaching yet realistic, so mutually balanced and beneficial, that it could be accepted by every nation. And it is in this spirit that we have presented with the agreement of the Soviet Union—under the label both nations now accept of "general and complete disarmament"—a new statement of newly-agreed principles for negotiation.

But we are well aware that all issues of principle are not settled—and that principles alone are not enough. It is therefore our intention to challenge the Soviet Union, not to an arms race, but to a peace race—to advance together step by step, stage by stage, until general and complete disarmament has been achieved. We invite them now to go beyond agreement in principle to reach agreement on actual plans.

The program to be presented to this assembly—for general and complete disarmament under effective international control—moves to bridge the gap between those who insist on a gradual approach and those who talk only of the final and total achievement. It would create machinery to keep the peace as it destroys the machines of war. It would proceed through balanced and safeguarded stages designed to give no state a military advantage over another. It would place the final responsibility for verification and control where it belongs—not with the big powers alone, not with one's adversary or one's self—but in an international organization within the framework of the United Nations. It would assure that indispensable condition of disarmament—true inspection—and apply it in stages proportionate to the stage of disarmament. It would cover delivery systems as well as weapons. It would ultimately halt their production as well as their testing, their transfer as well as their possession. It would achieve, under the eye of an international disarmament organization, a steady reduction in forces, both nuclear and conventional, until it has abolished all armies and all weapons except those needed for internal order and a new United Nations Peace Force. And it starts that process now, today, even as the talks begin. . . .

Such a plan would not bring a world free from conflict or greed—but it would bring a world free from the terrors of mass destruction. It would not usher in the era of the super state—but it would usher in an era in which no state could annihilate or be annihilated by another.

In 1945, this Nation proposed the Baruch Plan to internationalize the atom before other nations even possessed the bomb or demilitarized their troops. We proposed with our allies the Disarmament Plan of 1951 while still at war in Korea. And we make our proposals today, while building up our defenses over Berlin, not because we are inconsistent or insincere or intimidated, but because we know the rights of free men will prevail—because while we are compelled against our will to rearm, we look confidently beyond Berlin to the kind of disarmed world we all prefer. . . .

The logical place to begin is a treaty assuring the end of nuclear tests of all kinds, in every environment, under workable controls. The United States and the United Kingdom have proposed such a treaty that is both reasonable, effective and ready for signature. We are still prepared to sign that treaty today.

We also proposed a mutual ban on atmospheric testing, without inspection or controls, in order to save the human race from the poison of radioactive fallout. We regret that that offer was not accepted. . . .

But to halt the spread of these terrible weapons, to halt the contamination of the air, to halt the spiraling nuclear arms race, we remain ready to seek new avenues of agreement, our new Disarmament Program thus includes the following proposals:

—First, signing the Test-Ban Treaty by all Nations. This can be done now. Test ban negotiations need not and should not await general disarmament.

—Second, stopping the production of fissionable materials for use in weapons, and preventing their transfer to any nation now lacking in nuclear weapons.

—Third, prohibiting the transfer of control over nuclear weapons to states that do not own them.

—Fourth, keeping nuclear weapons from seeding new battlegrounds in outer space.

—Fifth, gradually destroying existing nuclear weapons and converting their materials to peaceful uses; and

—Finally, halting the unlimited testing and production of strategic nuclear delivery vehicles, and gradually destroying them as well. . . .

As we extend the rule of law on earth, so must we also extend it to man's new domain: outer space.

All of us salute the brave cosmonauts of the Soviet Union. The new horizons of outer space must not be driven by the old bitter concepts of imperialism and sovereign claims. The cold reaches of the universe must not become the new arena of an even colder war.

To this end, we shall urge proposals extending the United Nations Charter to the limits of man's exploration in the Universe, reserving outer space for peaceful use, prohibiting weapons of mass destruction in space or on celestial bodies, and opening the mysteries and benefits of space to every nation. We shall further propose cooperative efforts between all nations in weather prediction and eventually in weather control. We shall propose, finally, a global system of communications satellites linking the whole world in telegraph and telephone and radio and television. The day need not be far away when such a system will televise the proceedings of this body to every corner of the world for the benefit of peace. . . .

My Country favors a world of free and equal states. We agree with those who say that colonialism is a key issue in this Assembly. . . .

But colonialism in its harshest forms is not only the exploitation of new nations by old, of dark skins by light—or the subjugation of the poor by the rich. My Nation was once a colony—and we know what colonialism means; the exploitation and subjugation of the weak by the powerful, of the many by the few, of the governed who have given no consent to be governed, whatever their continent, their class or their color.

And that is why there is no ignoring the fact that the tide of self-determination has not reached the communist empire where a population far larger than that officially termed "dependent" lives under governments installed by foreign troops instead of free institutions—under a system which knows only one party and one belief—which suppresses free debate, and free elections, and free newspapers, and free books and free trade unions—and which builds a wall to keep truth a stranger and its own citizens prisoners. Let us debate colonialism in full—and apply the principle of free choice and the practice of free plebiscites in every corner of the globe.

Finally, as President of the United States, I consider it my duty to report to this Assembly on two threats to the peace which are not on your crowded agenda, but which causes us, and most of you, the deepest concern.

The first threat on which I wish to report is widely misunderstood: the smoldering coals of war in Southeast Asia. South Vietnam is already under attack—sometimes by a single assassin, sometimes by a band of guerrillas, recently by full battalions. The peaceful borders of Burma, Cambodia and India have been repeatedly violated. And the peaceful people of Laos are in danger of losing the independence they gained not so long ago.

No one can call these "wars of liberation." For these are free countries living under governments. Nor are these aggressions any less real because men are knifed in their homes and not shot in the fields of battle.

The very simple question confronting the world community is whether measures can be devised to protect the small and weak from such tactics. For if they are successful in Laos and South Vietnam, the gates will be opened wide. . . .

Secondly, I wish to report to you on the crisis over Germany and Berlin. . . . Established international rights are being threatened with unilateral usurpation. Peaceful circulation has been interrupted by barbed wire and concrete blocks. . . .

If there is a dangerous crisis in Berlin—and there is—it is because of threats against the vital interests and the deep commitments of the Western Powers, and the freedom of West Berlin. We cannot yield these interests. We cannot fail these commitments. We cannot surrender the freedom of these people for whom we are responsible. A "peace treaty" which carried with it the provisions which destroy the peace would be a fraud. A "free city" which was not genuinely free would suffocate freedom and would be an infamy. . . .

Terror is not a new weapon. Throughout history it has been used by those who could not prevail, either by persuasion or example. But inevitably they fall—either because men are not afraid to die for a life worth living—or because the terrorists themselves came to realize that free men can not be frightened by threats, and that aggression would meet its own response. And it is in the light of that history that every nation today should know, be he friend or foe, that the United States has both the will and the weapons to join free men in standing up to their responsibilities.

But I come here today to look across this world of threats to the world of peace. In that search we cannot expect any final triumph—for new problems will always arise. We cannot expect that all nations will adopt like systems—for conformity is the jailor of freedom, and the enemy of growth. Nor can we expect to reach our goal by contrivance, by fiat or even by the wishes of all.

But however close we sometimes seem to that dark and final abyss, let no man of peace and freedom despair. For he does not stand alone. If we all can persevere—if we can in every land and office look beyond our own shores and ambitions—then surely the age will dawn in which the strong are just and the weak secure and the peace preserved.

Ladies and gentlemen of this assembly—the decision is ours. Never have the nations of the world had so much to lose—or so much to gain. Together we shall save our planet—or together we shall perish in its flames. Save it we can—and save it we must—and then shall we earn the eternal thanks of mankind and, as peace makers, the eternal blessing of God.

READING AND DISCUSSION QUESTIONS

1. How does Kennedy assess the multiple threats to peace in 1961? What role does he envision for America in the world, and what role does he hope the United Nations might play in addressing these crises?

2. What conclusion can you draw regarding Kennedy's foreign policy priorities? To what extent were his priorities in line with Cold War policies since the end of World War II?

P8-4 | Diplomatic Impasse in Vietnam

Letters Between Lyndon Johnson and Ho Chi Minh (1967)

America's involvement in Vietnam exacerbated domestic turmoil and compromised its standing in many parts of the world, especially in developing nations, which often found themselves pawns in the Cold War conflict between the United States and the Soviet Union. The United States's first steps in Vietnam began during the Truman administration but reached a crisis point during the presidencies of Johnson and Nixon. Through five presidencies, U.S. policymakers considered the defense of South Vietnam an essential element of America's strategy to defeat communist expansion. This exchange of letters between Johnson and North Vietnamese leader Ho Chi Minh reveals the conflicting perspectives on the calamity in Vietnam.

His Excellency
Ho Chi Minh
President, Democratic Republic of Vietnam

DEAR MR. PRESIDENT: I am writing to you in the hope that the conflict in Vietnam can be brought to an end. This conflict has already taken a heavy toll—in lives lost, in wounds inflicted, in property destroyed, and in simple human misery. If we fail to find a just and peaceful solution, history will judge us harshly.

"President Johnson's Proposal for Negotiations on Viet-Nam Rejected by Ho Chi Minh," *Department of State Bulletin*, vol. 56 (April 10, 1967): 595–597.

Therefore, I believe that we both have a heavy obligation to seek earnestly the path to peace. It is in response to that obligation that I am writing directly to you.

We have tried over the past several years, in a variety of ways and through a number of channels, to convey to you and your colleagues our desire to achieve a peaceful settlement. For whatever reasons, these efforts have not achieved any results.

It may be that our thoughts and yours, our attitudes and yours, have been distorted or misinterpreted as they passed through these various channels. Certainly that is always a danger in indirect communication.

There is one good way to overcome this problem and to move forward in the search for a peaceful settlement. That is for us to arrange for direct talks between trusted representatives in a secure setting and away from the glare of publicity. Such talks should not be used as a propaganda exercise but should be a serious effort to find a workable and mutually acceptable solution.

In the past two weeks, I have noted public statements by representatives of your government suggesting that you would be prepared to enter into direct bilateral talks with representatives of the U.S. Government, provided that we ceased "unconditionally" and permanently our bombing operations against your country and all military actions against it. In the last day, serious and responsible parties have assured us indirectly that this is in fact your proposal.

Let me frankly state that I see two great difficulties with this proposal. In view of your public position, such action on our part would inevitably produce worldwide speculation that discussions were under way and would impair the privacy and secrecy of these discussions. Secondly, there would inevitably be grave concern on our part whether your government would make use of such action by us to improve its military position.

With these problems in mind, I am prepared to move even further towards an ending of hostilities than your Government has proposed in either public statements or through private diplomatic channels. I am prepared to order a cessation of bombing against your country and the stopping of further augmentation of U.S. forces in South Viet-Nam as soon as I am assured that infiltration into South Viet-Nam by land and by sea has stopped. These acts of restraint on both sides would, I believe, make it possible for us to conduct serious and private discussions leading toward an early peace.

I make this proposal to you now with a specific sense of urgency arising from the imminent New Year holidays in Viet-Nam. If you are able to accept this proposal I see no reason why it could not take effect at the end of the New Year, or Tet, holidays. The proposal I have made would be greatly strengthened if your military authorities and those of the Government of South Viet-Nam could promptly negotiate an extension of the Tet truce.

As to the site of the bilateral discussions I propose, there are several possibilities. We could, for example, have our representatives meet in Moscow where contacts have already occurred. They could meet in some other country such as

Burma. You may have other arrangements or sites in mind, and I would try to meet your suggestions.

The important thing is to end a conflict that has brought burdens to both our peoples, and above all to the people of South Viet-Nam. If you have any thoughts about the actions I propose, it would be most important that I receive them as soon as possible.

Sincerely,
LYNDON B. JOHNSON

His Excellency
LYNDON B. JOHNSON
President of the United States

Excellency, on February 10, 1967, I received your message. Here is my response.

Viet-Nam is situated thousands of miles from the United States. The Vietnamese people have never done any harm to the United States. But, contrary to the commitments made by its representative at the Geneva Conference of 1954, the United States Government has constantly intervened in Viet-Nam, it has launched and intensified the war of aggression in South Viet-Nam for the purpose of prolonging the division of Viet-Nam and of transforming South Viet-Nam into an American neo-colony and an American military base. For more than two years now, the American Government, with its military aviation and its navy, has been waging war against the Democratic Republic of Viet-Nam, an independent and sovereign country.

The United States Government has committed war crimes, crimes against peace and against humanity. In South Viet-Nam a half-million American soldiers and soldiers from the satellite countries have resorted to the most inhumane arms and the most barbarous methods of warfare, such as napalm, chemicals, and poison gases in order to massacre our fellow countrymen, destroy the crops, and wipe out the villages. In North Viet-Nam thousands of American planes have rained down hundreds of thousands of tons of bombs, destroying cities, villages, mills, roads, bridges, dikes, dams and even churches, pagodas, hospitals, and schools. In your message you appear to deplore the suffering and the destruction in Viet-Nam. Permit me to ask you: Who perpetrated these monstrous crimes? It was the American soldiers and the soldiers of the satellite countries. The United States Government is entirely responsible for the extremely grave situation in Viet-Nam.

The American war of aggression against the Vietnamese people constitutes a challenge to the countries of the socialist camp, a threat to the peoples' independent movement, and a grave danger to peace in Asia and in the world.

The Vietnamese people deeply love independence, liberty, and peace. But in the face of the American aggression they have risen up as one man, without fearing the sacrifices and the privations. They are determined to continue their resistance until they have won real independence and liberty and true peace. Our just cause enjoys the approval and the powerful support of peoples throughout the world and of large segments of the American people.

The United States Government provoked the war of aggression in Viet-Nam. It must cease that aggression, it is the only road leading to the re-establishment of peace. The United States Government must halt definitely and unconditionally the bombings and all other acts of war against the Democratic Republic of Viet-Nam, withdraw from South Viet-Nam all American troops and all troops from the satellite countries, recognize the National Front of the Liberation of South Viet-Nam, and let the Vietnamese people settle their problems themselves. Such is the basic content of the four-point position of the Government of the Democratic Republic of Viet-Nam, such is the statement of the essential principles and essential arrangements of the Geneva agreements of 1954 on Viet-Nam. It is the basis for a correct political solution of the Vietnamese problem. In your message you suggested direct talks between the Democratic Republic of Viet-Nam and the United States. If the United States Government really wants talks, it must first halt unconditionally the bombings and all other acts of war against the Democratic Republic of Viet-Nam. It is only after the unconditional halting of the American bombings and of all other American acts of war against the Democratic Republic of Viet-Nam that the Democratic Republic of Viet-Nam and the United States could begin talks and discuss questions affecting the two parties.

The Vietnamese people will never give way to force, it will never accept conversation under the clear threat of bombs.

Our cause is absolutely just. It is desirable that the Government of the United States act in conformity to reason.

Sincerely,
HO CHI MINH

READING AND DISCUSSION QUESTIONS

1. What conflicting points of view regarding the Vietnam War are revealed by Johnson's letter and Ho Chi Minh's response? How does each understand the cause and significance of the war?

2. From Ho's letter, what conclusion can you draw about the effect of American foreign policy in the developing world? How did Ho assess its impact? What influence do you think Vietnam had on shaping subsequent U.S. policy?

P8-5 | Africa on America's Cold War Radar
CHARLES SANDERS, *Kissinger in Africa* (1976)

The United States's interest in Africa took a backseat to other global hotspots including Vietnam and the Middle East, but in the mid-1970s Africa became another Cold War battleground. As reported in *Ebony*, an African American magazine, Secretary of State Henry Kissinger's 1976 diplomatic tour of key African nations highlighted a renewed attention to the continent's issues, motivated by the presence of military and economic support by Soviet and Chinese communist governments. These factors within the Cold War context influenced U.S. involvement in African affairs.

Upon his arrival in Dar es Salaam, one of the first stops on his tour of Africa in the spring, U.S. Secretary of State Henry A. Kissinger stood beside his plane exchanging pleasantries with Tanzanian diplomats. Suddenly, a swarm of bees appeared above his head. They hovered for a while then flew away.

"If he had come as an enemy," said one of the African journalists at the airport, "he'd have been stung right away."

The story of the bees would be printed in The Tanzania Daily News, and mixed with the praise that Kissinger would receive for his "new program for Africa" would be a great deal of criticism and more than one comment that the bees might have made a mistake.

While in Africa, Kissinger met with six presidents—Jomo Kenyatta of Kenya, Julius Nyerere of Tanzania, Kenneth Kaunda of Zambia, Mobutu Sese Seko of Zaire, William R. Tolbert Jr. of Liberia and Léopold Sédar Senghor of Senegal. He explained details of his "new program" to African experts on international politics and economics, and held closely guarded talks with Joshua Nkomo, a leader of the African National Council, and with representatives of Mozambique, Botswana, Zambia and Tanzania, the militant "front-line" countries in the campaign to overthrow white governments in Rhodesia and South Africa.

In a long, detailed policy speech in Lusaka, Zambia, Kissinger made promises which, if implemented, will mark a radical turning point in American-African relations. He pledged U.S. support for black majority rule in Rhodesia (Zimbabwe), said that the present white regime will "face our unrelenting opposition," and warned American citizens to get out of the country because the U.S. could offer them no protection there. He said the Ford Administration would urge Congress to repeal the Byrd Amendment which permits the U.S. to import Rhodesian chromium ($43 million worth last year) in defiance of United Nations sanctions against Rhodesia. He pledged $12.5 million in aid to Mozambique, which has suffered economic hardship since closing its borders with Rhodesia in an effort to block shipment of Rhodesian products. He said the U.S. would provide a black-ruled Zimbabwe with economic, technical and educational assistance. He said that the U.S. would urge South Africa to grant independence to

South-West Africa (Namibia) and to end "institutional racism" —*apartheid*—and bring about "peaceful change" in the country's racial policies. He said the U.S. would step up its various aid projects in Africa in an effort to speed development, and would give special attention to manpower training, rural development, advanced technology and transportation problems. For the black-ruled states of southern Africa, he said he would triple financial assistance to about $85 million during the next three years.

While President Kaunda embraced Kissinger at the end of the speech and said the U.S. would find him and "my colleagues, the Presidents of Tanzania, Mozambique and Botswana, cooperative, cooperative," most other African leaders seemed to prefer a wait-and-see approach. President Nyerere, for example, responded to Kissinger's call for a "negotiated settlement" in Rhodesia by declaring: "Negotiated settlement? In Zimbabwe, the war of liberation has already begun!" Nigeria, black Africa's richest and most populous country, refused to allow Kissinger to visit it, and Ghana withdrew its invitation because of the "ill health" of the head of state, Gen. Ignatius K. Acheampong. U.S. officials blamed Nigeria and the Soviet Union for Ghana's action and said they had learned of "Soviet agitation" of students in Accra.

One of Kissinger's purposes for visiting Africa was to bolster the morale and polish the image of those heads of state—especially Mobutu of Zaire and Kaunda of Zambia—who are considered to be "friends of the United States." President Mobutu has been in serious political trouble and his country has grappled with economic crises since backing—with U.S. and South African support—the losing side in the Angolan civil war. President Mobutu's worries involve not only his political and economic problems but also the SAM-7 missiles and the estimated 350 heavy Russian tanks just across the border in the hands of his old foes. In Zambia, President Kaunda's action in closing his borders with Rhodesia caused a loss of vital revenue in the face of declining world prices for Zambian copper ore. Zambia must make decisions about whether to cast its fortunes with the U.S. and other Western powers or with the powerful Soviet bloc. Kissinger's visits to Kinshasa and Lusaka and the assurances were very well-timed.

Growing concern about Soviet influence on the African continent was one other reason for the visit. Soviet weaponry can be found in many African nations and Soviet technicians and military experts are living in Africa and lending expertise. A number of Chinese have arrived, too, especially in Tanzania, and are engaged in work ranging from teaching to building highways and railroads. Soviet and Chinese ships are the most prominent ones in the harbor at Dar es Salaam and trucks and heavy equipment built in Eastern bloc nations are seen on many roads. "For years, we begged the United States to pay some attention to us and help us, but we didn't even exist as far as the Americans were concerned," said a Tanzanian student sipping tea in the Kilimanjaro hotel. "Now that we have found friends elsewhere, Kissinger comes dashing over trying to stem the tide. Where has he been during the last 8 or 10 years?"

Kissinger was keenly aware of his Johnny-come-lately status and admitted publicly that Africa has had "low priority" in U.S. foreign policy schemes. He pleaded: "you have to remember that we've been preoccupied with a whole range of things—Vietnam, East-West relations, the Middle East, the oil crisis, our domestic problems. But my trip to Africa represents the beginning of a policy, not the end of one, so we ought to forget the mistakes of the past."

In a commentary on the Kissinger visit, the influential Kenyan magazine, The Weekly Review, reminded its readers of the lucrative trade relations the U.S. has with Rhodesia and South Africa, and of the hundreds of millions of dollars worth of U.S. investments in the two countries. This reality, coupled with that of the traditional rivalry between the U.S. and the Soviet Union, prompted this analysis by the Review: ". . . it is only by a very elastic stretch of the imagination that southern African liberation problems can be included within [U.S. foreign policy objectives] . . . it is going to take a good deal of double talking on the part of the American secretary of state to convince his African hosts with any 'ambiguous clarity,' as he puts it, that Africa means more to Washington than a mere pawn in the great global power game."

The Kissinger trip has raised a number of questions for which Africans—those whose hopes were buoyed, those whose frustrations were assuaged, those who have had no reason to believe in promises from Washington—will be waiting for answers: Is the U.S. really prepared to give meaningful help to Africa in its continuing struggle for liberation, development and eventual self-sufficiency? Has a deal been struck between the U.S. and South Africa to "sacrifice" Rhodesia in order for South Africa to "buy time" and continue *apartheid*? In the face of escalating activity by Soviet-backed guerillas against white regimes in southern Africa, would the U.S. risk war to "stop communism" and protect American investments there?

Then there is the bottom-line question: Did those bees in Dar es Salaam make a mistake?

READING AND DISCUSSION QUESTIONS

1. Examine *Ebony*'s coverage of Kissinger's trip for evidence of the magazine's perspective on U.S. policy toward Africa. What factors does the article suggest motivated changes in American policy?

2. What conclusion can you draw about Africa's strategic significance to the United States? How does Kissinger's visit reflect the challenges of Cold War diplomacy?

P8-6 | America's Crisis in Iran

Demonstrators Supporting Captors of U.S. Embassy Hostages March on the Besieged Compound (1979)

In 1953, the United States helped topple Iranian prime minister Mohammad Mossadegh, installing the pro-U.S. shah of Iran in his place. Despite his autocratic rule, the United States supported the shah for decades until he was deposed during the 1979 Iranian Revolution, which brought Ayatollah Khomeini back from exile. Relations with the United States rapidly deteriorated, culminating in the Iranian seizure of the U.S. embassy in Tehran on November 4, 1979, where fifty-two Americans were held hostage for more than a year. This image shows the embassy compound with Iranian demonstrators holding anti-American signs.

READING AND DISCUSSION QUESTIONS

1. Analyze the photograph taken one week following the seizure of the U.S. embassy in the Iranian capital of Tehran. What is the significance of the signs Iranian protesters are holding?

2. From the Iranian hostage crisis, what can you conclude about the Cold War history of America's foreign policy? How did America's economic and military

"Demonstrators Supporting Captors of U.S. Embassy Hostages March on the Besieged Compound," November 11, 1979, © Bettmann/Corbis.

involvement in the Middle East impact U.S. foreign policy goals and the country's relationship with Iran?

3. What effect do you think the hostage crisis had on domestic affairs within the United States?

■ COMPARATIVE QUESTIONS ■

1. Compare NSC-68 with George Kennan's telegram (Document 25-1) and John Foster Dulles's speech (Document 25-5) to form an argument about the point of view of American policymakers at the start of the Cold War. What did they see as the stakes involved in this global war with the Soviet Union? What strategies did they embrace in countering the Soviet threat?

2. Assess the consequences of the Cold War for the United States and the world. To what extent did the Cold War promote or hinder American interests? What effect did the Cold War have on America's domestic politics?

3. Analyze the goals of U.S. policymakers over the course of the Cold War. To what extent were their goals achieved? How did U.S. internationalism affect America's role in global affairs?

4. Was ideology or economics the driving force shaping America's foreign policy in the decades following World War II? Explain.

30

Conservative America in the Ascent
1980–1991

For many conservatives, the 1980s dawned bright with the election of Ronald Reagan, whose charismatic personality and boundless optimism became a powerful vessel for spreading their political philosophy. Following the economic and political crises of the 1970s, Reagan's unrelenting message was a well-timed antidote to the despair that had seized so many. His decisive elections in 1980 and 1984 confirmed for conservatives the power of their ideas as a repudiation of the liberal excesses of the Sixties Generation. Republicans targeted fiscal policy, cut taxes, and stripped regulations they claimed hampered free enterprise. With the support of evangelicals at his back, Reagan waged a social and cultural war to restore what conservatives described as traditional American values. Conservatives targeted pornography and drugs, supported the appointment of conservative judges to the federal bench, and opposed *Roe v. Wade*, the flashpoint case from 1973 that focused attention on abortion. Reagan's Cold War rhetoric spurred a costly arms race that his supporters claimed led to the dissolution of the Soviet Union. Despite his popularity, Reagan and the conservatives he rallied were polarizing figures, and opponents chipped away at his legacy, waiting for opportunities to turn back the conservative tide.

30-1 | Reagan Lays Out the Conservative Challenge

RONALD REAGAN, *Remarks at the Conservative Political Action Conference Dinner* (1981)

Ronald Reagan debuted as a leading conservative figure in the Republican Party when he delivered a keynote speech endorsing Barry Goldwater for president at the party's 1964 nominating convention. As governor of California, Reagan resisted Johnson's Great Society programs and condemned student protests against the Vietnam War. He quickly became a powerful voice for conservative ideas, culminating in his 1980 election as president. In this speech, just weeks after his inauguration, Reagan addresses his fellow conservatives by reminding them of the challenges and opportunities ahead.

Who can forget that July night in San Francisco when Barry Goldwater told us that we must set the tides running again in the cause of freedom, and he said, "until our cause has won the day, inspired the world, and shown the way to a tomorrow worthy of all our yesteryears"? And had there not been a Barry Goldwater willing to take that lonely walk, we wouldn't be here talking of a celebration tonight.

But our memories are not just political ones. I like to think back about a small, artfully written magazine named National Review, founded in 1955 and ridiculed by the intellectual establishment because it published an editorial that said it would stand athwart the course of history yelling, "Stop!" And then there was a spritely written newsweekly coming out of Washington named Human Events that many said would never be taken seriously, but it would become later "must reading" not only for Capitol Hill insiders but for all of those in public life.

How many of us were there who used to go home from meetings like this with no thought of giving up, but still find ourselves wondering in the dark of night whether this much-loved land might go the way of other great nations that lost a sense of mission and a passion for freedom? . . .

Our goals complement each other. We're not cutting the budget simply for the sake of sounder financial management. This is only a first step toward returning power to the States and communities, only a first step toward reordering the relationship between citizen and government. We can make government again responsive to people not only by cutting its size and scope and thereby ensuring that its legitimate functions are performed efficiently and justly.

Because ours is a consistent philosophy of government, we can be very clear: We do not have a social agenda, separate economic agenda, and a separate foreign agenda. We have one agenda. Just as surely as we seek to put our financial house in order and rebuild our nation's defenses, so too we seek to protect the unborn, to end the manipulation of schoolchildren by utopian planners, and

Ronald Reagan, "Remarks at the Conservative Political Action Conference Dinner," March 20, 1981. Online by Gerhard Peters and John T. Woolley, *The American Presidency Project*. www .presidency.ucsb.edu/ws/?pid=43580.

permit the acknowledgement of a Supreme Being in our classrooms just as we allow such acknowledgements in other public institutions. . . .

Now, during our political efforts, we were the subject of much indifference and often times intolerance, and that's why I hope our political victory will be remembered as a generous one and our time in power will be recalled for the tolerance we showed for those with whom we disagree.

But beyond this, we have to offer America and the world a larger vision. We must remove government's smothering hand from where it does harm; we must seek to revitalize the proper functions of government. But we do these things to set loose again the energy and the ingenuity of the American people. We do these things to reinvigorate those social and economic institutions which serve as a buffer and a bridge between the individual and the state—and which remain the real source of our progress as a people.

And we must hold out this exciting prospect of an orderly, compassionate, pluralistic society—an archipelago of prospering communities and divergent institutions—a place where a free and energetic people can work out their own destiny under God.

I know that some will think about the perilous world we live in and the dangerous decade before us and ask what practical effect this conservative vision can have today. When Prime Minister Thatcher[1] was here recently . . . I told [her] that everywhere we look in the world the cult of the state is dying. And I held out hope that it wouldn't be long before those of our adversaries who preach the supremacy of the state were remembered only for their role in a sad, rather bizarre chapter in human history. The largest planned economy in the world has to buy food elsewhere or its people would starve.

We've heard in our century far too much of the sounds of anguish from those who live under totalitarian rule. We've seen too many monuments made not out of marble or stone but out of barbed wire and terror. But from these terrible places have come survivors, witnesses to the triumph of the human spirit over the mystique of state power, prisoners whose spiritual values made them the rulers of their guards. With their survival, they brought us "the secret of the camps," a lesson for our time and for any age: Evil is powerless if the good are unafraid.

That's why the Marxist vision of man without God must eventually be seen as an empty and a false faith—the second oldest in the world—first proclaimed in the Garden of Eden with whispered words of temptation: "Ye shall be as gods." The crisis of the Western world, Whittaker Chambers[2] reminded us, exists to the degree in which it is indifferent to God. "The Western world does not know it," he said about our struggle, "but it already possesses the answer to this

---

[1]**Margaret Thatcher**: Conservative British prime minister from 1979 to 1990 and a strong ally of Ronald Reagan.

[2]**Whittaker Chambers**: Author of *Witness* (1952), Chambers renounced his membership in the Communist Party and became a hero among conservatives, implicating State Department official Alger Hiss in the famous espionage trial that brought notoriety to Richard Nixon, then a young member of Congress.

problem—but only provided that its faith in God and the freedom He enjoins is as great as communism's faith in man."

This is the real task before us: to reassert our commitment as a nation to a law higher than our own, to renew our spiritual strength. Only by building a wall of such spiritual resolve can we, as a free people, hope to protect our own heritage and make it someday the birthright of all men.

There is, in America, a greatness and a tremendous heritage of idealism which is a reservoir of strength and goodness. It is ours if we will but tap it. And, because of this—because that greatness is there—there is need in America today for a reaffirmation of that goodness and a reformation of our greatness.

The dialog and the deeds of the past few decades are not sufficient to the day in which we live. They cannot keep the promise of tomorrow. The encrusted bureaucracies and the engrained procedures which have developed of late respond neither to the minority or the majority. We've come to a turning point. We have a decision to make. Will we continue with yesterday's agenda and yesterday's failures, or will we reassert our ideals and our standards, will we reaffirm our faith, and renew our purpose? This is a time for choosing. . . .

I made a speech by that title in 1964. I said, "We've been told increasingly that we must choose between left or right." But we're still using those terms—left or right. And I'll repeat what I said then in '64. "There is no left or right. There's only an up or down": up to the ultimate in individual freedom, man's age old dream, the ultimate in individual freedom consistent with an orderly society—or down to the totalitarianism of the ant heap. And those today who, however good their intentions, tell us that we should trade freedom for security are on that downward path.

Those of us who call ourselves conservative have pointed out what's wrong with government policy for more than a quarter of a century. Now we have an opportunity to make policy and to change our national direction. All of us in government—in the House, in the Senate, in the executive branch—and in private life can now stand together. We can stop the drain on the economy by the public sector. We can restore our national prosperity. We can replace the overregulated society with the creative society. We can appoint to the bench distinguished judges who understand the first responsibility of any legal system is to punish the guilty and protect the innocent. We can restore to their rightful place in our national consciousness the values of family, work, neighborhood, and religion. And, finally, we can see to it that the nations of the world clearly understand America's intentions and respect for resolve.

Now we have the opportunity—yes, and the necessity—to prove that the American promise is equal to the task of redressing our grievances and equal to the challenge of inventing a great tomorrow.

This reformation, this renaissance will not be achieved or will it be served, by those who engage in political claptrap or false promises. It will not be achieved by those who set people against people, class against class, or institution against institution. So, while we celebrate our recent political victory we must understand there's much work before us: to gain control again of government, to reward personal initiative and risk-taking in the marketplace, to revitalize our system of federalism, to strengthen the private institutions that make up the independent sector of our society, and to make our own spiritual affirmation in the face of those who would deny man has a place before God. Not easy tasks perhaps. But I would remind you as I did on January 20th, they're not impossible, because, after all, we're Americans. . . .

Fellow citizens, fellow conservatives, our time is now. Our moment has arrived. We stand together shoulder to shoulder in the thickest of the fight. If we carry the day and turn the tide, we can hope that as long as men speak of freedom and those who have protected it, they will remember us, and they will say, "Here were the brave and here their place of honor."

READING AND DISCUSSION QUESTIONS

1. How does Reagan define the conservative agenda? What ideas influenced his thinking and the policy choices he supported?

2. What were Reagan and his conservative supporters reacting against? What sort of voters do you think his program appealed to and why? What can you infer from his speech about his political opponents?

30-2 | Reagan Insider Describes Supply-Side Economics

DAVID STOCKMAN, *The Triumph of Politics: Why the Reagan Revolution Failed* (1986)

Reagan's inner circle included David Stockman, who served as the director of the Office of Management and Budget and was a key player in budget negotiations with Congress. Stockman's conservative credentials included his advocacy of supply-side economics, the theory that lowering such barriers to wealth production as taxes and government regulations results in higher government revenues and cheaper goods and services. Wealth, so the theory goes, trickles down to benefit even those at the lower ends of the economic scale. Opponents challenged so-called Reaganomics and pointed out its failures by noting the snowballing federal deficit.

In December 1976, I tried to secure a seat on the House Appropriations Committee and, not surprisingly, failed. The old bulls in the GOP hierarchy take a dim view of awarding seats on such powerful committees to mere freshmen.

If I had gotten a seat on the Appropriations Committee, I might have developed a more realistic attitude toward politics. The Appropriations Committee is the cash register of the Second Republic. Sitting there, day by day, as the politicians

David Stockman, *The Triumph of Politics: Why the Reagan Revolution Failed* (New York: Harper & Row, 1986), 37–40, 42–43.

greased every squeaking wheel, might have shown me that my anti-political, anti-welfare state ideology would never succeed.

Instead, I landed on the Commerce Committee, and it reinforced my whole critique of Big Government and economic statism. In those early years of the Carter presidency, the Commerce Committee was the front line in the war between the statists and the anti-statists, between those who wanted government to dominate every aspect of American life and those who didn't.

In the spring of 1977, Carter unveiled his "moral equivalent of war" with great gravity and piousness: the National Energy Plan. It was a plan to regulate every BTU that flowed through the U.S. economy, and by marvelous coincidence its acronym, NEP, exactly matched Lenin's 1921 plan to rescue the Russian economy from the anarchy wrought by "workers' soviets."

Other plans followed: environmental regulations whereby every by-product of technological progress was to be declared carcinogenic; air bags; windfall profit taxes—innumerable ways to regulate how Americans lived and worked. Invariably these statist initiatives had been concocted by some arrogant, self-important appointee possessed of a degree in English and contempt for free enterprise. One day I listened, incredulous, as an obnoxious troll of this genre pounded the witness table and demanded that Congress delegate to him absolute, open-ended power to establish energy efficiency standards for *all* American-made appliances.

The "moral equivalent of war" and its attendant issues was really a front for state control of resources and the economy. It was a neo-Malthusian[1] ideology that held that we were running out of everything and that only the state could be trusted to hoard our diminishing supplies. We were exhausting our resources, and by using what resources we had, we were making the world unlivable. Capitalism was poisoning the earth with chemical time bombs.

Neo-Malthusianism was our term, of course; the Carter Administration preferred to speak of the "era of limits." The current glut of oil on the world market is eloquent refutation of how idiotic their position was, but at the time they were prosecuting their views with a determination befitting the smallest of their minds. The New Deal had given birth to the statist impulse; during the Great Society it had gathered momentum; with the "Era of Limits" it had become an imperative.

In the trenches of the Commerce Committee, I did battle with this monster every day, hacking away at it with a sword forged in the free market smithy of F. A. Hayek.[2] I became a militant anti-neo-Malthusian.

---

[1]**Thomas Malthus**: Author of *An Essay on the Principle of Population* (1798), Malthus argued that overpopulation led to poverty by reducing wages and by outpacing the resources to feed increased numbers of people.

[2]**F. A. Hayek**: Austrian economist and author of *The Road to Serfdom* (1944), Hayek championed free-market economics and criticized central planning by government, arguing it led to "serfdom" or the sort of managed political and economic systems he associated with socialist and communist regimes. His work became a key intellectual source for modern conservatives.

As such, I was one of the very few in the chamber of the politicians. To most of them, the false threat of depletion and environmental degradation was a boon. It kept them busy passing laws, meddling everywhere, and throwing their weight around from coast to coast.

But there was one other of my kind. I had met Congressman Jack Kemp of New York while working for John Anderson.[3] Now he was looking for allies on behalf of a new theory of economics that meshed perfectly with my own still emerging views. It was called "supply-side" economics, in stark contrast to the "demand side" that congress had so steadfastly defended. We lived in an era not of limits but of limitless possibilities. Capitalism was endlessly resourceful. If people had enough incentives, prosperity was inevitable. . . .

[T]he supply-side doctrine offered a plausible premise for idealism amidst the prevailing cynical and pessimistic ethos of the time. The latter had been perfectly captured in Carter's politically fatal "malaise" formulation. It was an epigrammatic, if unwitting, expression of all the muddled and destructive notions of scarcities, catastrophes, closing frontiers, economic limits, incurably embedded inflations, and unavoidable financial breakdowns that had by then come to enthrall his administration and most of official Washington.

The new supply-side gospel seemed at the time to be a fair bet for the monumental task of reversing this trend. As we had formulated it, the supply-side synthesis encompassed vastly more than a single nostrum—the Kemp-Roth 30 percent income tax cut. . . . [W]e viewed the supply-side doctrine as all-encompassing. It implied not merely a tax cut but a whole catalogue of policy changes, ranging from natural gas deregulation, to abolition of the minimum wage, to repeal of milk marketing orders, to elimination of federal certificates of "need" for truckers, hospitals, airlines, and anyone else desiring to commit an act of economic production. It even encompassed reform of the World Bank, and countless more. . . .

As an intellectual and moral matter, this comprehensive supply-side doctrine had a powerful appeal. It offered a rigorous standard of justice and fairness, and provided a recipe for economic growth and prosperity—the only viable way to truly eliminate poverty and social deprivation. But its elegant idealism was hostile to all the messy, expedient compromises of daily governance.

This was made dramatically evident when, toward the end of my second term, the Chrysler Corporation demanded that the federal government rescue it from its own mismanagement. The action was justified by an army of lobbyists who represented every imaginable local interest group and no discernible policy principle.

The notion that the federal government should, on demand, refinance inefficient, bankrupt private enterprises was so loathsome to me that I resolved not only to vote against it, but to take the lead in trying to stop it. So I took the floor

---

[3]**John B. Anderson**: Republican member of Congress from Illinois who ran unsuccessfully as an independent for president in 1980.

of the House to speak out against this abomination that was about to pass. I preached to the politicians my most fevered anti-statist sermon. . . .

I spoke of economic doctrine but did not manage to see a stark, dramatic truth. The Chrysler bailout passed by a margin of over one hundred votes because the impacted voters wanted it. And if the House of Representatives would go for the raw, unprincipled expediency of that measure, why should I have assumed, only a year later, that the institution, and the electorates it represented, would accept the kind of sweeping austere ideological blueprint the Reagan Revolution called for? I finally had my Grand Doctrine, but it completely overwhelmed my grasp of what the politics of American governance was all about.

READING AND DISCUSSION QUESTIONS

1. What factors shaped Stockman's political philosophy and support for supply-side economics? How does he, for example, view the New Deal's legacy?

2. What was the Reagan Revolution supposed to be, and why, according to Stockman, did it fail?

30-3 | The Eighties Culture of Greed
Wall Street (1987)

In the 1980s, Hollywood drew attention to the cultural celebration of wealth in movies like *Wall Street*, which starred actor Michael Douglas as Gordon Gekko, an investor who tries to orchestrate a hostile corporate takeover of a failing company. In the movie's iconic scene, Gekko, based loosely on real-life corporate raider Ivan Boesky, gives a speech to shareholders where he complains that modern corporate America has become a "survival of the unfittest." He tells shareholders that "you either do it right or you get eliminated." In the film's most famous line, Gekko boasts: "I am not a destroyer of companies. I am a liberator of them! The point is, ladies and gentlemen, that greed—for lack of a better word—is good. Greed is right. Greed works."

"Wall Street," The Granger Collection, New York.

READING AND DISCUSSION QUESTIONS

1. What perspective on 1980s culture emerges from the evidence of Hollywood movies like *Wall Street*? What can you conclude about the era from the evidence provided by the movie still and Gekko's speech?

2. To what extent do you think the character of Gordon Gekko, shown in this still from the movie, became an emblematic figure of the 1980s? Who do you imagine would have embraced his worldview? Who would have condemned his business and social philosophy?

3. What interpretive opportunities and challenges do movies present to historians seeking to understand the period when they were produced?

30-4 | Exposing Reagan's Latin American Policies

ROBERT J. HENLE, *The Great Deception: What We Are Told About Central America* (1986)

The Reagan administration opposed Nicaragua's leftist Sandinista regime led by Daniel Ortega on the grounds that its Marxist ideology threatened the stability of neighboring Latin American countries. Early in his term, Reagan authorized support for a group of rebels known as the Contras, aiding them in the attempt to oust Ortega's government. Congress banned such aid in 1982, but the administration secretly continued its supply of money and arms by selling weapons to Iran and diverting proceeds to the Contras. This illegal covert operation was ultimately exposed in November 1986, months after Robert Henle's article condemning Reagan's Latin American policies.

To anyone who has been following the developments in Central America, the credibility of the White House and the State Department with regard to Central America has reached absolute zero. I now believe nothing they say about Central America, unless there is clear, independent verification.

A few instances selected from many: Early on, President Reagan and then Secretary of State Alexander M. Haig jubilantly displayed photos as proof positive that the Sandinistas were committing atrocities. These photos were subsequently identified as showing Somoza's[1] National Guardsmen committing atrocities.

I was in the live audience in the Old Executive Office Building when Mr. Reagan firmly stated that he "had just received a verbal message from the Pope approving our policies in Central America." I immediately dismissed this as absurd. A few days later, the Vatican twice flatly denied the assertion.

When Nicaragua instituted a draft, President Reagan distorted this by saying, "They are forcing their [the people's] children to fight." All modern states use a draft in time of war: it is the only just means of raising a national army. It was new in Central America, since traditionally only the sons of the poor were impressed into the army. President José Napoleón Duarte has been trying to get a draft in El Salvador.

Some 150,000 families have been forced from their homes near the border by the contras. The Nicaraguan Government established camps to protect them and to provide temporary shelter until they could be relocated. President Reagan distorted this by saying, "They are putting people in concentration camps!" There are no "concentration" camps in Nicaragua.

President Reagan has consistently asserted that the Sandinistas are committing atrocities and the contras are not. While there have been some atrocities committed by Sandinistas, there is universal independent agreement (Americas

---

Robert J. Henle, "The Great Deception: What We Are Told About Central America," *America* 154 (May 24, 1986): 432–434.

[1]**Somoza**: The Somoza family ruled Nicaragua as a dictatorship from 1939 until the Sandinista National Liberation Front overthrew them in 1979.

Watch, Amnesty International, various on-the-spot documentaries, grass-roots verification, e.g., the testimony of Lisa Fitzgerald (The Washington Post, 6/18/83), various U.S. and European reporters, many personal grass-roots contacts of my own, etc.) that these very few cases pale into insignificance beside the continual, deliberate and atrocious actions of the contras. An example of the irresponsibility of the Reagan Administration concerns the coldblooded public murder of 11 civilians by the contras at Cuapa. "According to those on the scene," President Reagan said, what happened at Cuapa was "a military-to-military engagement" and "there were no civilian casualties." Americas Watch asked the State Department who "those on the scene" were. It got no answer for months, but after its report was printed, it was told by the U.S. Embassy in Nicaragua that no one from there had gone to Cuapa or otherwise investigated the incident (Anthony Lewis, The New York Times, 3/6/86). More absurdly, President Reagan, with no evidence at all, asserted that these atrocities were being committed by Sandinistas dressed in contra uniforms! Even Cardinal Miguel Obando y Bravo told a friend of mine that the Sandinistas have practically eliminated the use of torture. Massive evidence shows that the contras regularly torture their victims.

Again, President Reagan has consistently denied that the contras are Somocista National Guardsmen. His latest argument is that the average age of the contras is so low that they could not have been members of the National Guard. The argument is irrelevant. The point is that the top officers, with one or two exceptions, are all National Guardsmen. Everybody knows this; I am sure the White House knows it, too. These officers are the men who control the contra movement. It is laughable to think that they are fighting for democracy. As Edgar Chamorro, who worked with them for three years, said (Letter to the Editor, The New York Times, 1/9/86), all that these officers talk about, and plan for, is the recovery of their property and the restoration of military control in Nicaragua.

President Reagan has asserted that Nicaragua is exporting terrorism. He linked Nicaragua to terrorism in Brazil. The State Department had done this before and was forced to apologize to the Brazilian Government. With President Reagan's repetition, the Brazilian Government again demanded an explanation. The charge has no ground. President Reagan also linked Nicaragua to terrorism in Colombia. But the Colombian Government, after an investigation, completely exonerated Nicaragua. What happened in Ecuador was not terrorism. It was simply an indigenous rebellion of a dissatisfied "General." President Reagan asserted a Nicaraguan connection with the murder of four U.S. Marines in San Salvador. No evidence for this has been advanced.

Another piece of propaganda is that the Latin Americans support aid to the contras and that the neighboring countries fear a Nicaraguan invasion and an exported insurgency. Not a single Latin American leader (with the obvious exception of those in El Salvador and in the military of Guatemala) supports President Reagan. . . .

The civilian Government of Honduras has displayed increasing concern about the presence of the contras in its country. That Government is in the absurd position of officially denying that contra bases exist in its territory, since their presence violates both the laws of Honduras and international law. But the Honduran Government has opposed transport of supplies through its territory to the contras. It has even returned shipments to the United States. Information from my grass-roots contacts in Honduras indicates that the Hondurans are not worried about an invasion from Nicaragua but are afraid of the contras (who have already committed crimes, including theft and rape, against local Hondurans) and also of the Salvadoran army. The Hondurans are ambiguous about the American military subjection of their country, but the American presence brings dollars into their almost ruined economy. . . .

The Honduran Government, however, is under terrible pressure from the Reagan Administration. In fact, certain analysts doubt whether Honduras can be considered an independent sovereign state. In Latin America, Honduras is now laughingly referred to as "U.S.A. Honduras."

Finally, there is the Cecil B. De Mille vision of a red tide sweeping through Central America, overwhelming the Canal Zone and roaring up through Mexico to the Texas border. The only thing this is based on is President Reagan's imagination.

Suppose we withdrew all support from the contras and, through the United Nations, the International Red Cross and other agencies, helped relocate the contras peacefully elsewhere. (The Government of Nicaragua has often offered amnesty to the rank and file but not to the National Guardsmen in the contras.) Suppose further that the Reagan Administration gave up its hopeless goal of interfering in the internal affairs of Nicaragua and signed an honest peace treaty with Nicaragua. What would the real situation be?

From the standpoint of defense:

1. The Southern Command, which used to have control only of the Canal Zone, is now in charge of all U.S. military operations in the isthmus. In Honduras, we have spent at least $30 million constructing at least eight military bases, an unknown number of air strips capable of receiving our largest fighter planes and transport planes, and we have prepared joint port facilities. We have a U.S. military hospital in Tegucigalpa. Honduras is a huge U.S. fortification and launching pad. If Nicaragua moved to invade Honduras seriously, we could place an enormous expeditionary force in Honduras in a matter of a few days. As one Honduran general said, "They [the Nicaraguans] would never reach Tegucigalpa," let alone Mexico City or Dallas. (The Mexican Government was indignant with Mr. Reagan's idea that Nicaragua could be a threat to Mexico.) And, of course, the Rio Treaty would come into play.

2. If Nicaragua moved south, it would have to invade Costa Rica. Again, the United States would move from both Honduras and Panama. The Rio Treaty would be invoked, and all Latin America would be outraged.

President Reagan does not listen to his own military men. U.S. officers in Central America have said (The New York Times, 6/4/85) that American pilots could destroy the small Nicaraguan Air Force, radar, artillery, tanks, supply depots, and command centers and that it would take the United States two weeks to gain control of 60 percent of the Nicaraguan population. Most analysts agree that neither Russia nor Cuba would commit combat troops to Central America. Even if they did, they could not win.

3. But it is far more likely that Nicaragua would make no military moves against its neighbors. (The Nicaraguan Government is young and inexperienced. It has made many mistakes. But it does not consist of utter fools.) In this case, the Contadora peace process could go forward. Most Latin Americans believe that it is the militarism and intransigence of the Reagan Administration that is preventing progress in the Contadora diplomacy as well as stifling the initiative of the new Presidents of Guatemala (Vinicio Cerezo) and of Costa Rica (Oscar Arias Sánchez).

This tale of deception could be extended. It is, however, quite clear that, in regard to Central America, the White House and the Departments of State and Defense have been trying to deceive both the Congress and the American people.

READING AND DISCUSSION QUESTIONS

1. To what extent does Henle imply that Reagan's foreign policy was trapped in a Cold War paradigm?

2. How does Henle explain Reagan's support for the Contras and his opposition to the democratically elected Sandinista government? According to Henle, what is motivating Reagan's policies? What does he imply will be the long-term effect on America's interests in the region?

30-5 | Civil Rights Leader Urges Referendum on Reagan Years

JESSE JACKSON, *Common Ground and Common Sense* (1988)

Civil rights activist Jesse Jackson broke ground by seeking the Democratic presidential nomination as an African American in both the 1984 and 1988 elections. Though he lost both times, his strong showing surprised pundits, winning nearly seven million Democratic primary votes in 1988. His speech at the Democratic National Convention reflects Jackson's powerful oratory, his background as a Baptist minister, and his rejection of Reagan-era policies.

We meet tonight at a crossroads, a point of decision.

Shall we expand; be inclusive, find unity and power; or suffer division and impotence. . . .

Tonight there is a sense of celebration because we are moved, fundamentally moved, from racial battlegrounds by law, to economic common ground, tomorrow we will challenge to move to higher ground.

Jesse Jackson, "Common Ground and Common Sense," *Vital Speeches of the Day* 54 (August 15, 1988): 650–653.

Common ground! . . .

The good of our nation is at stake—its commitment to working men and women, to the poor and the vulnerable, to the many in the world. With so many guided missiles, and so much misguided leadership, the stakes are exceedingly high. Our choice, full participation in a Democratic government, or more abandonment and neglect. And so this night, we choose not a false sense of independence, not our capacity to survive and endure.

Tonight we choose interdependency in our capacity to act and unite for the greater good. The common good is finding commitment to new priorities, to expansion and inclusion. A commitment to expanded participation in the Democratic Party at every level. A commitment to a shared national campaign strategy and involvement at every level. A commitment to new priorities that ensure that hope will be kept alive. . . .

We find common ground at the plant gate that closes on workers without notice. We find common ground at the farm auction where a good farmer loses his or her land to bad loans or diminishing markets. Common ground at the schoolyard where teachers cannot get adequate pay, and students cannot get a scholarship and can't make a loan. Common ground, at the hospital admitting room where somebody tonight is dying because they cannot afford to go upstairs to a bed that's empty, waiting for someone with insurance to get sick. We are a better nation than that. We must do better.

Common ground. What is leadership if not present help in a time of crisis? And so I met you at the point of challenge in Jay, Maine, where paper workers were striking for fair wages; in Greenfield, Iowa, where family farmers struggle for a fair price; in Cleveland, Ohio, where working women seek comparable worth; in McFarland, Calif., where the children of Hispanic farm workers may be dying from poison land, dying in clusters with Cancer; in the AIDS hospice in Houston, Texas, where the sick support one another, 12 are rejected by their own parents and friends.

Common ground.

America's not a blanket woven from one thread, one color, one cloth. When I was a child growing up in Greenville, S.C., and grandmother could not afford a blanket, she didn't complain and we did not freeze. Instead, she took pieces of old cloth—patches, wool, silk, gabardine, crockersack on the patches—barely good enough to wipe off your shoes with.

But they didn't stay that way very long. With sturdy hands and a strong cord, she sewed them together into a quilt, a thing of beauty and power and culture.

Now, Democrats, we must build such a quilt. Farmers, you seek fair prices and you are right, but you cannot stand alone. Your patch is not big enough. Workers, you fight for fair wages. You are right. But your patch labor is not big enough. Women, you seek comparable worth and pay equity. You are right. But your patch is not big enough. Women, mothers, who seek Head Start and day care and pre-natal care on the front side of life, rather than jail care and welfare on the back side of life, you're right, but your patch is not big enough.

Students, you seek scholarships. You are right. But your patch is not big enough. Blacks and Hispanics, when we fight for civil rights; we are right, but our patch is not big enough. Gays and lesbians, when you fight against discrimination and a cure for AIDS, you are right, but your patch is not big enough. Conservatives and progressives, when you fight for what you believe, right-wing, left-wing, hawk, dove—you are right, from your point of view, but your point of view is not enough.

But don't despair. Be as wise as my grandmamma. Pool the patches and the pieces together, bound by a common thread. When we form a great quilt of unity and common ground we'll have the power to bring about health care and housing and jobs and education and hope to our nation.

. . . We believe in a government that's a tool of our democracy in service to the public, not an instrument of the aristocracy in search of private wealth.

We believe in government with the consent of the governed of, for, and by the people. We must not emerge into a new day with a new direction. Reaganomics, based on the belief that the rich had . . . too little money, and the poor had too much.

That's classic Reaganomics. . . .

So, they engaged in reverse Robin Hood—took from the poor, gave to the rich, paid for by the middle class. We cannot stand four more years of Reaganomics in any version, in any disguise.

How do I document that case? Seven years later, the richest 1 percent of our society pays 20 percent less in taxes; the poorest 10 percent pay 20 percent more. Reaganomics.

Reagan gave the rich and the powerful a multibillion-dollar party. Now, the party is over. He expects the people to pay for the damage. I take this principled position—convention, let us not raise taxes on the poor and the middle class, but those who had the party, the rich and the powerful, must pay for the party!

I just want to take common sense to high places. We're spending $150 billion a year defending Europe and Japan 43 years after the war is over. . . .

Let them share more of the burden of their own defense—use some of that money to build decent housing!

Use some of that money to educate our children!

Use some of that money for long-term health care!

Use some of that money to wipe out these slums and put America back to work!

I just want to take common sense to high places. If we can bail out Europe and Japan, if we can bail out Continental Bank and Chrysler—and Mr. Iacocca makes $8,000 an hour, we can bail out the family farmer.

I just want to make common sense. It does not make sense to close down 650,000 family farms in this country while importing food from abroad subsidized by the U.S. government.

Let's make sense. It does not make sense to be escorting oil tankers up and down the Persian Gulf paying $2.50 for every $1.00 worth of oil we bring out while oil wells are capped in Texas, Oklahoma and Louisiana. I just want to make sense. . . .

What's the fundamental challenge of our day? It is to end economic violence. Plant closing without notice, economic violence. Even the greedy do not profit long from greed. Economic violence. Most poor people are not lazy. They're not black. They're not brown. They're mostly white, and female and young.

But whether white, black or brown, the hungry baby's belly turned inside out is the same color. Call it pain. Call it hurt. Call it agony. Most poor people are not on welfare.

Some of them are illiterate and can't read the want-ad sections. And when they can, they can't find a job that matches their address. They work hard every day, I know. I live amongst them. I'm one of them.

I know they work. I'm a witness. They catch the early bus. They work every day. They raise other people's children. They work every day. They clean the streets. They work every day. They drive vans with cabs. They work every day. They change the beds you slept in these hotels last night and can't get a union contract. They work every day.

No more. They're not lazy. Someone must defend them because it's right, and they cannot speak for themselves. They work in hospitals. I know they do. They wipe the bodies of those who are sick with fever and pain. They empty their bedpans. They clean out their commode. No job is beneath them, and yet when they get sick, they cannot lie in the bed they made up every day. America, that is not right. We are a better nation than that. We are a better nation than that. . . .

Why can I challenge you this way? Jesse Jackson, you don't understand my situation. You be on television. You don't understand. I see you with the big people. You don't understand my situation. I understand. You're seeing me on TV but you don't know the me that makes me, me. They wonder why does Jesse run, because they see me running for the White House. They don't see the house I'm running from.

I have a story. I wasn't always on television. Writers were not always outside my door. When I was born late one afternoon, October 8th, in Greenville, S.C., no writers asked my mother her name. Nobody chose to write down our address. My mama was not supposed to make it. And I was not supposed to make it. You see, I was born to a teen-age mother who was born to a teen-age mother.

I understand. I know abandonment and people being mean to you, and saying you're nothing and nobody, and can never be anything. I understand. Jesse Jackson is my third name. I'm adopted. When I had no name, my grandmother gave me her name. My name was Jesse Burns until I was 12. So I wouldn't have a blank space, she gave me a name to hold me over. I understand when nobody knows your name. I understand when you have no name. I understand.

I wasn't born in a hospital. Mama didn't have insurance. I was born in the bed at home. I really do understand. Born in a three-room house, bathroom in the backyard, slop jar by the bed, no hot and cold running water. I understand. Wallpaper used for decoration? No. For a windbreaker. I understand. I'm a working person's person, that's why I understand you whether you're black or white.

I understand work. I was not born with a silver spoon in my mouth. I had a shovel programmed for my hand. My mother, a working woman. So many days she went to work early with runs in her stockings. She knew better, but she wore runs in her stockings so that my brother and I could have matching socks and not be laughed at at school. . . .

Every one of these funny labels they put on you, those of you who are watching this broadcast tonight in the projects, on the corners, I understand. Call you outcast, low down, you can't make it, you're nothing, you're from nobody, subclass, underclass—when you see Jesse Jackson, when my name goes in nomination, your name goes in nomination.

I was born in the slum, but the slum was not born in me. And it wasn't born in you, and you can make it. Wherever you are tonight you can make it. Hold your head high, stick your chest out. You can make it. It gets dark sometimes, but the morning comes. Don't you surrender. Suffering breeds character. Character breeds faith. In the end faith will not disappoint.

You must not surrender. You may or may not get there, but just know that you're qualified and you hold on and hold out. We must never surrender. America will get better and better. Keep hope alive. Keep hope alive. Keep hope alive. On tomorrow night and beyond, keep hope alive.

READING AND DISCUSSION QUESTIONS

1. How would you summarize the "common ground" Jackson seeks? What is his "common sense" message to the delegates at the convention?

2. Analyze Jackson's speech for evidence of his critique of Reagan-era policies. How does he characterize those policies, and what effect on Americans does he attribute to them?

30-6 | America Reacts to Gulf War Victory

NAJLAH FEANNY-HICKS, *Over Two Million People Watched Troops March in the Operation Welcome Home Ticker Tape Parade* (1991)

When Iraqi leader Saddam Hussein invaded neighboring Kuwait in August 1990, President George H. W. Bush rallied an international coalition to turn back the invasion, culminating in a decisive victory within days of the ground assault against Iraqi forces. Covered live on television, this quick war appeared to be a complete American victory and a psychological boost to a nation still struggling to forget its loss in Vietnam less than two decades earlier. Returning troops were welcomed home by countless celebrations, including this June 1991 parade down New York City's Broadway.

READING AND DISCUSSION QUESTIONS

1. How would you characterize the mood of Americans following the Gulf War as it is depicted in this photograph? What do you think the dog's owner was feeling while watching the parade?

2. The sign in the background says, "Let no one say America has no hero[e]s. Welcome home Troops!" What point do you think the woman holding the sign is trying to make?

3. What can you discern about the perspective of the photographer? What was she saying about America's postwar celebrations?

▪ COMPARATIVE QUESTIONS ▪

1. To what extent does Jackson draw upon a liberal tradition extending from the New Deal through the Sixties? Compare his rhetoric with the speeches of Franklin Roosevelt (Documents 23-2 and 24-1) and Lyndon Johnson (Document 28-1). What similarities do you see? Has the focus shifted at all?

2. Using the multiple perspectives gathered in this chapter, summarize both the liberal and conservative agenda during the 1980s. What was the liberal reaction to conservative policies?

3. Assess the historical significance of the Cold War and Vietnam on Reagan-era foreign policy. What evidence of earlier Cold War hysteria do you see in the 1980s?

4. Identify any changes in focus or emphasis that you see in the conservatism of Reagan in the 1980s compared to Barry Goldwater in 1964 (Document 28-5). How consistent was the conservative message?

31

Confronting Global and National Dilemmas

1989 to the Present

Called the year of revolutions, 1989 marked a transition from the Cold War to a new era of globalization and democracy. In that year, the Berlin Wall came down, Soviet-propped governments in the Eastern bloc fell, Chinese students protested in Tiananmen Square, and racial segregation began to unravel in South Africa. Pundits everywhere heralded the new era as the West's vindication of its long cold war against authoritarianism. The hoped-for peace, however, dissolved as new issues emerged. Without the simplicity of the Cold War divide between the United States (the "good guys") and the Soviet Union (the "bad guys"), Presidents George H. W. Bush and Bill Clinton struggled to articulate America's new role in the world as the only remaining superpower. Domestic politics became increasingly bitter and partisan. The devastating terrorist attacks against the United States on September 11, 2001, provided a brief bipartisan unity and refocused and centered America's foreign policy on what President George W. Bush called a "war on terror." The war continued under Barack Obama, the first African American to win the presidency. During the Obama administration, crippling partisanship stymied efforts to address national problems of war, economic crisis, and globalization.

31-1 | Protesting the World Trade Organization
ALESHA DAUGHTREY, *Interview by April Eaton* (2000)

In late November 1999, members of the World Trade Organization (WTO) convened in Seattle, Washington, to open negotiations on international trade agreements. The Clinton administration sided with Republicans and supported free-trade negotiations lowering tariffs. Opponents decried globalization's effects on labor and the environment. The Seattle meeting incited antiglobalization protests that ultimately disrupted the WTO talks. Alesha Daughtrey, a field organizer for Global Trade Watch, a division of Ralph Nader's national consumer advocacy organization, Public Citizen, describes her role in the protests.

AE: [W]hy did Global Trade Watch choose to get involved in the protest?

AD: Well, we've been fighting a lot of the more indecent parts of the WTO along the way. We are the only organization in the United States that focuses full-time on international trade and investment issues. There are lots of other organizations that do great work, but we're the only one that is entirely devoted to it. So we've been doing a lot of monitoring . . . and research into the WTO's record and . . . also just sort of keeping tabs on what the scoundrels are really up to. . . . When the Ministerial time and location was announced . . . we thought, well, nothing like this has ever happened in the United States, and it was too good an opportunity to pass up to really bring a lot of NGO and public pressure to bear on the institution, and also to try and turn the organization around in a way that we had been wanting to do, and it was finally on our turf and we could. So, we immediately jumped in and started working on the organizing and the analysis and the PR war and all that.

AE: And how would you describe or summarize the activities of Global Trade Watch at the protest?

AD: We provided . . . a lot of logistical support . . . [a]nd . . . a lot of programming and coalition building for national and international NGOs. . . . We did a lot in terms of mobilization with unions and NGOs and through getting the word out there to community groups [and] . . . to fair trade organizations on the state and local level. . . . But, for example, as soon as they announced the location, we reserved a bunch of venues in Seattle. We secured hotel rooms, we secured nearly all of the youth hostel[s] in downtown Seattle, we secured half a dozen other venues—churches and halls and things like that. Not necessarily with any particular program in mind for those, but with the idea that if we weren't going to use them, someone else would, and if we didn't get in immediately, all of these things would get snapped up by the WTO Host Committee.

AE: How did that end up? Did you end up on specifically as Global Trade Watch mobilizing those people to come to Seattle, stay in those places and participate in activities that you organized, or was it kind of a mix?

Alesha Daughtrey, interview by April Eaton, WTO History Project, University of Washington, August 17, 2000. Transcript at http://depts.washington.edu/wtohist/interviews/Daughtrey.pdf.

AD: A lot of it was coalitional. We do a lot of our field outreach and coalition building through a national fair trade coalition called the Citizens Fair Trade Campaign, which we helped to found a number of years ago. In terms of the mobilization, a lot of that was done through CTC, and the CTC partners include a number of different labor unions, mainly the major industrial unions, like the Teamsters and Steel Workers and UAW, as well as UNITE, but also the Sierra Club and Friends of the Earth, some additional consumer's organizations, National Family Farm Coalition, the Rural Coalition, some religious groups, including United Methodist Church, Board of Church and Society. So it's fairly broad-based. . . .

AE: How would you summarize the message that your organization was trying to get out during the protest? What was your sound bite? If you wanted to make one thing known, what would that be?

AD: The WTO is an undemocratic and unaccountable organization that works to promote the profit margin over the interests of the people. We feel that international trade is necessary and inevitable. But the rules by which that trade is governed need to have more to do with the interests of citizens than with the back pockets and cash wads of a couple corporate CEOs. And we want to make sure that there is a balance consideration. Obviously people are always going to be concerned with their profits—it's business, we understand that, we accept that. But we think that needs to be balanced with concern for the rights of workers, basic human rights, protecting the environment. . . . [On]e of the things that I think was really important after the NAFTA fight several years back was that was the first time, I think, that labor and environmentalists had really been able to dedicate themselves to the same project and begin to see eye to eye. But what happened in Seattle was a deepening of that. . . . I think that a lot of the union leadership was a little bit more hesitant about the direct action than say some of us were, because that wasn't something that they'd had a whole lot of exposure to and experience with, and they weren't sure how that would shake out. We weren't sure how it would shake out either, but we knew it was worth a try. So, that was somewhat of a challenge. . . .

AE: What would you describe as the biggest successes in your experience and the organization's experience in Seattle and, also, things that maybe didn't go so well? . . .

AD: I think the best part about it, frankly, was the fact that this coalition emerged. And it's sort of interesting how, for years people have been talking about the Washington consensus as something that's never going to bend, never going to break. And I think we've found the one thing that can, the Seattle coalition. And people will refer to that now, I see this in news clips, even in the mainstream press where they refer to the post-Seattle coalition, by which they mean faith-based, family farm, laborer, environmentalists, students, all of these movements converging and becoming far greater than the sum of the parts. . . . I think that it did quite a lot to sort of re-energize the left a little bit. I think it has been really hard over, especially over the last four years, but really over the last eight, because I think a lot of liberal/progressives sort of saw a Democrat in office and after the Reagan-Bush era figured that their work was done here. And they were willing to sit back, and they figured Clinton was a nice guy, and that was all there was to it. And people got really rather complacent, even though it soon became clear that not that much had changed in the White House or anywhere else. And I think having that magnitude, having a demonstration on that level was something that nobody had really seen in years, in decades actually. And I think it was a big reminder of how much power people actually had. That was good. I wasn't around for the anti-war demonstrations or for the civil rights demonstrations. And I think a lot of younger activists really sort of saw this as something that became their movement. . . . What seems to have happened was, they heard about Seattle in the news and they saw the photos from there, and they thought, there really is something wrong with this WTO thing, and there really is something wrong with the global trade and investment system, and it is very unjust, and it's not democratic, and it's not working well for the people. . . . And I think that contrary to the myth that a lot of younger people are slackers and not politically connected and disinterested in government, in the way society is headed, I think it has really done a lot to bring the student and youth movement alive in the United States, which is good, because it's been asleep for too long. . . .

AE: . . . [Ho]w much of this would have been possible without the Internet? . . .

AD: There's been a lot of cry about how great the Internet is and how it revolutionized organizing and how Seattle wouldn't have been possible without it. I think the case for the Internet has been a little overstated. I have really come to the conclusion that the numbers that were generated in Seattle would have been impossible without the Internet. Because there were so many people literally who arrived on November 30, because on November 29 they saw a live stream video of what was going on in Seattle, and they just decided they had to get in the car and drive up from Portland or San Francisco. And people literally got in the car and drove all night to get there. And it was also really good for sending around calls to action and letting people know what the mobilization points were, what the plans were. So people arrived and they already had some sense of what to expect, what was going on, who to talk to, and how the week would go. I think the level of detail and that information would not have been possible. Ride boards, housing was arranged via the Internet, all of this stuff, it made it logistically a lot easier on that level. But I think what really set the work in Seattle apart from some of the subsequent protests has been that there was a huge amount of local organizing going on and local coalition building and education and outreach. And I think, I'm not foolish enough to believe that everyone in Seattle was just thrilled to have the WTO there, much less the protest, much less the tear gas. But I think people at least had some understanding of what was going on.

They understood, even if they did not agree with the protesters' purpose and reasoning for being there and for choosing the tactics that they did. And I think it made for a much more effective message opportunity. . . .

AE: Going back to the Internet, is that a big part of facilitating your ongoing connections with partners that you have been partnered with for a long time or that you have reached that you've come into coalition with?

AD: Yeah, we operate about a half dozen list serves here. Some of them are very closed strategy lists that are just for key coalition partners that we work with around the country. Others are far more broad and include thousands of subscribers. And they include the action alerts and updates and things like that. Email on the Internet is really important for a lot of the international work that we do. We do try to have some type of conference call every six to eight weeks at least, although we're hoping to go to monthly soon. And we've tried to have physical meetings once a year. But in terms of day-to-day things, checking up on different projects that each of us has agreed to take on or whatever, it's too hard to mess with the time zones, so definitely it's good for that.

AE: Did you mention, I think you did, some pretty close relationships with labor unions. Is that long-standing, or new, more recent, Seattle centered?

AD: Fairly long-standing. We worked for a lot of unions on the NAFTA campaign, as well as on the Fast Track campaigns of '97 and '98. We are closest with the major industrials. . . .

AE: Shifting a little bit to questions about yourself and your own views, first of all, how did you get here? How did you end up doing what you're doing? . . .

AD: I spent the week before the Ministerial [conference] and the week of out there [in Seattle]. I came away with a very, very different take on all of this, because I had believed in all of these things, like I said, but it wasn't personal. And suddenly, when you're standing in the middle of the street, and you're watching somebody half a block down in a wheelchair be beaten by two police in riot gear, and when you're washing tear gas out of the eyes of an eight-year-old child, you start to realize that there is obviously something going on in that Convention Center that they're protecting. What is it that they would fight this hard to protect? And I had always had this theory, simple-minded though it was, that the police were there to serve and protect me, since they were my tax dollars at work, right? Wrong. And I just thought, okay, so what is it that's creating this? And, of course, I knew what the answer was. But for the first time, it became a very personal thing, where these were not just being visited on people via a plant closing, or things that do affect real lives in very real ways. You don't get much more real than this is in your face, than physical conflict on the streets.

READING AND DISCUSSION QUESTIONS

1. How does Daughtrey explain the importance of the issues raised by those groups protesting the WTO meeting in Seattle? What was at stake for the groups Global Trade Watch served?

2. What impact did social media have on the Seattle protests? How did the organizers use social media technology to mobilize protesters and broadcast their criticisms of globalization?

3. What evidence does the Seattle WTO protest provide for understanding changes in politics during the late twentieth century?

31-2 | Backlash Against Immigrants
California Proposition 187 (1994)

An early 1990s economic recession dogged California's economy, and many feeling the pinch began singling out scapegoats for the high unemployment and ballooning deficits they suffered. Immigrants became the easy target, especially after the 1990 federal census revealed increases in the Latino population. A state ballot initiative in 1994, Proposition 187, embraced a strategy of "deincentivizing" illegal immigration by denying public services to illegal immigrants. The ballot measure passed with nearly 60 percent of the vote, but a lawsuit resulted in a federal injunction forbidding enforcement of the measure.

Proposition 187: Text of Proposed Law

1994—California

This initiative measure is submitted to the people in accordance with the provisions of Article II, Section 8 of the Constitution.

This initiative measure adds sections to various codes; therefore, new provisions proposed to be added are printed in *italic type* to indicate that they are new.

PROPOSED LAW

SECTION 1. Findings and Declaration.

The People of California find and declare as follows:

That they have suffered and are suffering economic hardship caused by the presence of illegal aliens in this state.

That they have suffered and are suffering personal injury and damage caused by the criminal conduct of illegal aliens in this state.

That they have a right to the protection of their government from any person or persons entering this country unlawfully.

Therefore, the People of California declare their intention to provide for cooperation between their agencies of state and local government with the federal government, and to establish a system of required notification by and between such agencies to prevent illegal aliens in the United States from receiving benefits or public services in the State of California.

"Proposition 187: Text of Proposed Law," in *California Ballot Pamphlet* (Sacramento: State of California, 1994), 91–92.

SECTION 2. Manufacture, Distribution or Sale of False Citizenship or Resident Alien Documents: Crime and Punishment.

Section 113 is added to the Penal Code, to read:

113. Any person who manufactures, distributes or sells false documents to conceal the true citizenship or resident alien status of another person is guilty of a felony, and shall be punished by imprisonment in the state prison for five years or by a fine of seventy-five thousand dollars ($75,000).

SECTION 3. Use of False Citizenship or Resident Alien Documents: Crime and Punishment.

Section 114 is added to the Penal Code, to read:

114. Any person who uses false documents to conceal his or her true citizenship or resident alien status is guilty of a felony, and shall be punished by imprisonment in the state prison for five years or by a fine of twenty-five thousand dollars ($25,000).

SECTION 4. Law Enforcement Cooperation with INS.

Section 834b is added to the Penal Code, to read:

834b. (a) Every law enforcement agency in California shall fully cooperate with the United States Immigration and Naturalization Service regarding any person who is arrested if he or she is suspected of being present in the United States in violation of federal immigration laws.

(b) With respect to any such person who is arrested, and suspected of being present in the United States in violation of federal immigration laws, every law enforcement agency shall do the following:

(1) Attempt to verify the legal status of such person as a citizen of the United States, an alien lawfully admitted as a permanent resident, an alien lawfully admitted for a temporary period of time or as an alien who is present in the United States in violation of immigration laws. The verification process may include, but shall not be limited to, questioning the person regarding his or her date and place of birth, and entry into the United States, and demanding documentation to indicate his or her legal status.

(2) Notify the person of his or her apparent status as an alien who is present in the United States in violation of federal immigration laws and inform him or her that, apart from any criminal justice proceedings, he or she must either obtain legal status or leave the United States.

(3) Notify the Attorney General of California and the United States Immigration and Naturalization Service of the apparent illegal status and provide any additional information that may be requested by any other public entity.

(c) Any legislative, administrative, or other action by a city, county, or other legally authorized local governmental entity with jurisdictional boundaries, or by a law enforcement agency, to prevent or limit the cooperation required by subdivision (a) is expressly prohibited.

SECTION 5. Exclusion of Illegal Aliens from Public Social Services.

Section 10001.5 is added to the Welfare and Institutions Code, to read:

10001.5. (a) In order to carry out the intention of the People of California that only citizens of the United States and aliens lawfully admitted to the United States may receive the benefits of public social services and to ensure that all persons employed in the providing of those services shall diligently protect public funds from misuse, the provisions of this section are adopted.

(b) A person shall not receive any public social services to which he or she may be otherwise entitled until the legal status of that person has been verified as one of the following:

(1) A citizen of the United States.

(2) An alien lawfully admitted as a permanent resident.

(3) An alien lawfully admitted for a temporary period of time.

(c) If any public entity in this state to whom a person has applied for public social services determines or reasonably suspects, based upon the information provided to it, that the person is an alien in the United States in violation of federal law, the following procedures shall be followed by the public entity:

(1) The entity shall not provide the person with benefits or services.

(2) The entity shall, in writing, notify the person of his or her apparent illegal immigration status, and that the person must either obtain legal status or leave the United States.

(3) The entity shall also notify the State Director of Social Services, the Attorney General of California, and the United States Immigration and Naturalization Service of the apparent illegal status, and shall provide any additional information that may be requested by any other public entity.

SECTION 6. Exclusion of Illegal Aliens from Publicly Funded Health Care.
Chapter 1.3 (commencing with Section 130) is added to Part 1 of Division 1 of the Health and Safety Code, to read:

Chapter 1.3. Publicly-Funded Health Care Services

130. (a) In order to carry out the intention of the People of California that, excepting emergency medical care as required by federal law, only citizens of the United States and aliens lawfully admitted to the United States may receive the benefits of publicly-funded health care, and to ensure that all persons employed in the providing of those services shall diligently protect public funds from misuse, the provisions of this section are adopted.

(b) A person shall not receive any health care services from a publicly-funded health care facility, to which he or she is otherwise entitled until the legal status of that person has been verified as one of the following:

(1) A citizen of the United States.

(2) An alien lawfully admitted as a permanent resident.

(3) An alien lawfully admitted for a temporary period of time.

(c) If any publicly-funded health care facility in this state from whom a person seeks health care services, other than emergency medical care as required by federal law, determines or reasonably suspects, based upon the information provided to it, that the person is an alien in the United States in violation of federal law, the following procedures shall be followed by the facility:

(1) The facility shall not provide the person with services.

(2) The facility shall, in writing, notify the person of his or her apparent illegal immigration status, and that the person must either obtain legal status or leave the United States.

(3) The facility shall also notify the State Director of Health Services, the Attorney General of California, and the United States Immigration and Naturalization Service of the apparent illegal status, and shall provide any additional information that may be requested by any other public entity.

(d) For purposes of this section "publicly-funded health care facility" shall be defined as specified in Sections 1200 and 1250 of this code as of January 1, 1993.

SECTION 7. Exclusion of Illegal Aliens from Public Elementary and Secondary Schools.

Section 48215 is added to the Education Code, to read:

48215. (a) No public elementary or secondary school shall admit, or permit the attendance of, any child who is not a citizen of the United States, an alien lawfully admitted as a permanent resident, or a person who is otherwise authorized under federal law to be present in the United States.

(b) Commencing January 1, 1995, each school district shall verify the legal status of each child enrolling in the school district for the first time in order to ensure the enrollment or attendance only of citizens, aliens lawfully admitted as permanent residents, or persons who are otherwise authorized to be present in the United States.

(c) By January 1, 1996, each school district shall have verified the legal status of each child already enrolled and in attendance in the school district in order to ensure the enrollment or attendance only of citizens, aliens lawfully admitted as permanent residents, or persons who are otherwise authorized under federal law to be present in the United States.

(d) By January 1, 1996, each school district shall also have verified the legal status of each parent or guardian of each child referred to in subdivisions (b) and (c), to determine whether such parent or guardian is one of the following:

(1) A citizen of the United States.

(2) An alien lawfully admitted as a permanent resident.

(3) An alien admitted lawfully for a temporary period of time.

(e) Each school district shall provide information to the State Superintendent of Public Instruction, the Attorney General of California, and the United States Immigration and Naturalization Service regarding any enrollee or pupil, or parent or guardian, attending a public elementary or secondary school in the school district determined or reasonably suspected to be in violation of federal immigration laws within forty-five days after becoming aware of an apparent violation. The notice shall also be provided to the parent or legal guardian of the enrollee or pupil, and shall state that an existing pupil may not continue to attend the school after ninety calendar days from the date of the notice, unless legal status is established.

(f) For each child who cannot establish legal status in the United States, each school district shall continue to provide education for a period of ninety days from the date of the notice. Such ninety day period shall be utilized to accomplish an orderly transition to a

school in the child's country of origin. Each school district shall fully cooperate in this transition effort to ensure that the educational needs of the child are best served for that period of time.

SECTION 8. Exclusion of Illegal Aliens from Public Postsecondary Educational Institutions.
Section 66010.8 is added to the Education Code, to read:
66010.8. (a) No public institution of postsecondary education shall admit, enroll, or permit the attendance of any person who is not a citizen of the United States, an alien lawfully admitted as a permanent resident in the United States, or a person who is otherwise authorized under federal law to be present in the United States.

(b) Commencing with the first term or semester that begins after January 1, 1995, and at the commencement of each term or semester thereafter, each public postsecondary educational institution shall verify the status of each person enrolled or in attendance at that institution in order to ensure the enrollment or attendance only of United States citizens, aliens lawfully admitted as permanent residents in the United States, and persons who are otherwise authorized under federal law to be present in the United States.

(c) No later than 45 days after the admissions officer of a public postsecondary educational institution becomes aware of the application, enrollment, or attendance of a person determined to be, or who is under reasonable suspicion of being, in the United States in violation of federal immigration laws, that officer shall provide that information to the State Superintendent of Public Instruction, the Attorney General of California, and the United States Immigration and Naturalization Service. The information shall also be provided to the applicant, enrollee, or person admitted.

SECTION 9. Attorney General Cooperation with the INS.
Section 53069.65 is added to the Government Code, to read:
53069.65. Whenever the state or a city, or a county, or any other legally authorized local governmental entity with jurisdictional boundaries reports the presence of a person who is suspected of being present in the United States in violation of federal immigration laws to the Attorney General of California, that report shall be transmitted to the United States Immigration and Naturalization Service. The Attorney General shall be responsible for maintaining on-going and accurate records of such reports, and shall provide any additional information that may be requested by any other government entity.

SECTION 10. Amendment and Severability.
The statutory provisions contained in this measure may not be amended by the Legislature except to further its purposes by statute passed in each house by roll-call vote entered in the journal, two-thirds of the membership concurring, or by a statute that becomes effective only when approved by the voters.

In the event that any portion of this act or the application thereof to any person or circumstance is held invalid, that invalidity shall not affect any other provision or application of the act, which can be given effect without the invalid provision or application, and to that end the provisions of this act are severable.

READING AND DISCUSSION QUESTIONS

1. What are the problems and the solutions that supporters of Proposition 187 identify?

2. To what extent does Proposition 187 reflect broader political divisions facing Americans in the 1990s? How might you interpret California voters' significant support for this measure? What can you infer about the mood of voters?

31-3 | Cartoonist Questions the Politics of Character

DAVID HORSEY, *Character* (1996)

Bill Clinton's presidency was distracted by self-inflicted crises seized upon by his detractors as signs of moral failure. Opponents focused on Clinton's marital infidelities, particularly his intimate relations with Monica Lewinsky, a White House intern. This liaison nearly brought down his presidency when the House of Representatives passed articles of impeachment, but Clinton was acquitted by the Senate. Pulitzer Prize–winning cartoonist David Horsey comments on the character issue in a cartoon published during the 1996 presidential election, which Clinton easily won with nearly half the popular vote.

" MY *HUSBAND*, NOW *HE'S FULL* OF OPINIONS...TOO BAD HE'S AT DRUG REHAB' THIS MONTH. MY *FIRST* HUSBAND'S A KNOW-IT-ALL, TOO, BUT HE'S LIVING WITH HIS BOYFRIEND IN SAN FRANCISCO. COME BACK TOMORROW AND YOU CAN INTERVIEW MY 18-YEAR-OLD. I'M BABYSITTING HER KIDS HERE WHILE SHE DOES HER SHIFT AT THE *TOPLESS JOINT.* ...BUT, ANYWAY, IF YOU *REALLY* WANT *MY* OPINION: *NO*, THE *CHARACTER ISSUE* IS *NO BIG DEAL!*"

READING AND DISCUSSION QUESTIONS

1. What inference can you draw concerning Horsey's perspective on the character issue during the 1996 presidential election? Do you think he agrees with the view of the woman being interviewed? Explain.

2. Analyze and describe the significance of all the details of the cartoon. How does Horsey use these elements to convey his editorial perspective?

3. What can you conclude about America's social and political history during the 1990s? To what extent is the cartoonist suggesting cultural and moral issues trumped social and economic issues?

31-4 | American Ambassador Defines U.S. Interests in Post–Cold War World

MADELEINE ALBRIGHT, *Realism and Idealism in American Foreign Policy Today* (1994)

Speaking at Harvard's Kennedy School of Government commencement in 1994, U.S. ambassador to the United Nations Madeleine Albright addressed the pitfalls of developing a foreign policy in a post–Cold War world without the presence of a Soviet threat. Here she offers criteria guiding U.S. intervention overseas, a policy she would attempt to implement during Clinton's second term when she served as the first female secretary of state.

To be sustainable, American foreign policy must be guided by American interests. But in the wake of the Cold War, a whole category of conflicts has arisen in which the American stake resists precise calculation. . . .

[T]here is no perfect scale or formula for categorizing what is important to our people. Obviously, there remains an inner circle of vital interests related to the defense of our people, territory, allies, and economic well-being. Here, unilateral action, if required, is warranted and would likely have full support from Congress and the American people.

Increasingly, we also recognize an outer circle of important interests that we share with others. Global issues—such as the health of the atmosphere, stabilizing population growth, controlling international crime, and curbing AIDS—fall within this circle. Here, multilateral action is essential because national action alone is not sufficient.

But between and sometimes overlapping these two is a middle circle—a gray area of regional conflicts and potential conflicts that does not fit neatly into any national security framework but which, if left unattended, could erode the foundation of freedom and threaten world peace. Here, the destructive legacy of the Cold War is most evident and the challenge of organizing the peace most complex. Here, regional organizations and regional powers have an important

Madeleine Albright, "Realism and Idealism in American Foreign Policy Today," *U.S. Department of State Dispatch* 5, no. 26 (June 27, 1994).

role. Here, the American stake may shift dramatically with changing circumstance and must be evaluated case by case, day by day.

These regional problems do not affect us equally or in the same way. Some—such as Somalia or Rwanda—are of primarily humanitarian concern. But this afternoon, I will discuss four situations which, if not well-managed, could pose threats to the innermost circle of American concerns. Here, our interests are especially compelling and the risks especially high. . . .

North Korea

. . . A nuclear North Korea would threaten regional security in Northeast Asia and undermine the international non-proliferation regime. In so doing, it would affect alliances and interests that bear on the security of our own people. Our firm objective, which we are pursuing deliberately and consistently, is a non-nuclear Korean Peninsula.

Experience informs us that sanctions alone rarely cause even isolated regimes to reverse course. But sanctions are needed now to demonstrate international seriousness and resolve. And they are needed to provide an incentive for corrective action and a disincentive for further backsliding. . . .

Haiti

Haiti is another country where we have turned to the tool of economic sanctions. Here again, our preference is to resolve a difficult situation peacefully. Our goal is to pressure General Cedras and other military leaders to leave so that democracy may return. Both the UN and the OAS have authorized tougher sanctions and improved enforcement. . . . To further isolate the military and prepare for what may happen in the future, we will seek approval of a UN peace-keeping force to provide training and to promote calm once the military leaders have left.

Clearly, the status quo in Haiti is not tenable. The longer the current impasse continues, the greater the potential for violence, the more severe the suffering of Haiti's poor majority, and the more irreversible the environmental degradation caused by scavenging for fuel. . . .

It is a goal of this Administration, as it has been of previous ones, to help emerging democracies. We are doing so in cooperation with others in every corner of the world—from Mozambique to Cambodia to South Africa to Eastern Europe and the former Soviet Union. Obviously, we cannot insulate every new democracy from the plots of usurpers. But Haiti is in our own backyard. The Haitian people deserve to live in freedom, and we are determined to see that they do.

The Balkans

In the Balkans, we see another challenge that engages our interests and where current tragedy could grow still worse. The conflict there knows no natural boundaries. The fuse of potential violence lies like a coiled snake across the region.

A wider conflagration could threaten us strategically by undermining new democracies in Eastern Europe, dividing our NATO allies, and straining our relationship with Russia. We have a humanitarian interest in opposing the brutal violence — including acts of genocide — that has outraged the conscience and uprooted hundreds of thousands from their homes. And we have a political interest in opposing Serbia's efforts to use its Bosnian surrogates to undermine a sovereign state. . . .

To discourage aggression, we have supported tough enforcement of economic sanctions and sent peacekeepers to the former Yugoslav Republic of Macedonia. We have used NATO air power to restore a semblance of normal life in Sarajevo, to lend belated credibility to the concept of safe havens, and to maintain a humanitarian lifeline that has kept hundreds of thousands alive despite the bitter fighting.

In the name of justice, we are backing the war crimes tribunal for former Yugoslavia. . . .

And to promote peace, we have increased our diplomatic engagement. We helped broker an agreement between government and Bosnian Croat factions that has stopped the fighting in central Bosnia and improved prospects for Bosnia's survival as a multi-ethnic state. Americans have an important stake in the viability of that state, for we derive our own identity from the conviction that those of different races, creeds, and ethnic origins can live together productively, freely, and in peace.

The New Independent States

A fourth example of the challenges we face in this new era and another place where multi-ethnic states are being tested is the former Soviet Union. . . .

[W]hile the infrastructure of empire is unraveling, the infrastructure of democracy is not yet fully built. . . . U.S. policy is to buttress the sovereignty and independence of the new states, while promoting constructive relations among them and with Russia. We are using active diplomacy — economic and humanitarian aid that will amount to almost $2.5 billion this year — and a frank and open dialogue with the leaders of Russia and the other republics. . . .

Although Russia desires stability, there have been troubling aspects to its policy toward the new republics. Russian military units stationed in Georgia and Moldova have exacerbated local conflicts. Instead of cooperating fully with international bodies, Russia has often pursued a "go-it-alone" strategy toward negotiations in Nagorno-Karabakh. And Russia has occasionally used its economic clout, especially in the energy sector, to pressure its neighbors. . . .

The people of the New Independent States will bear — as they know they must — the primary burden. Our task is to work with them, not impose upon them — to help them to build their own societies and to establish relationships based on shared recognition and respect. In so doing, we validate our own values, preserve our own interests, and secure the gains of freedom for which so many — in the West and East — sacrificed so much.

U.S. Engagement: The Need and the Means

In each of the areas I have cited today—Korea, Haiti, Bosnia, and the former Soviet Union—the UN Security Council has a key part to play. The end of the superpower rivalry has made cooperation possible. So peace-keeping and sanctions—little-used previously—have moved to center stage. Each entered to high expectations; each has since received mixed reviews. The Administration's strategy has been to use these tools assertively to supplement diplomatic, political, and military initiatives we have taken on our own. We have sought, at the same time, to hone these tools—to make sanctions a more precise instrument of policy and to make UN peace-keeping more disciplined and more effective.

Although our effort to reform UN peace-keeping has bipartisan support, there are some in Congress who either would pull the plug altogether or so restrict funding as to make the management of peace-keeping impossible. Last month, an amendment was offered in the House of Representatives that . . . would have brought about the virtual collapse of UN peace-keeping. . . . It is sobering that an amendment so contrary to American interests and traditions could have been offered and only narrowly defeated. Our ability to manage the problems I have discussed today in Haiti, Bosnia, and the former Soviet Union would be seriously undermined if UN peace-keeping were no longer an option. And the chances of gaining support from other countries for our policy toward North Korea would also diminish. . . .

If we are going to meet the challenges of this new era, we will need to use every tool available—a strong defense, strong alliances, vigorous diplomacy, better UN peace-keeping, more effective multilateral sanctions, and firm support for the requirements of international law. We need to understand . . . that international peace and security depend not on a parity of power but on a preponderance of power that favors the peacekeepers over the "peace-upsetters." . . .

We have a responsibility in our time . . . to be pathfinders; not to be imprisoned by history but to shape it; to build a world not without conflict but in which conflict is effectively contained; a world, not without repression but in which the sway of freedom is enlarged; a world not without lawless behavior but in which the law-abiding are progressively more secure. . . .

READING AND DISCUSSION QUESTIONS

1. How does Albright prioritize America's foreign policy into "inner circle" and "outer circle" interests? What challenge does the United States face at the intersection of those circles of interest?

2. What responsibility does she say the United States bears as the world's only remaining superpower? How does her speech deflect critics who might object to America's active engagement in the many international crises threatening peace around the world?

31-5 | President Responds to 9/11 Attacks

GEORGE W. BUSH, *Address to Congress* (2001)

On the morning of September 11, 2001, two planes were flown into the World Trade Center Towers in New York City. Another plane was flown into the Pentagon outside the nation's capital. A fourth crashed in Pennsylvania, averting a probable attack on the White House. More than three thousand people died, including the terrorists who hijacked the planes. President George W. Bush addressed the American people before a joint session of Congress to outline the nation's response, declaring a "war on terror" sequel to the global Cold War won by his father's generation.

Tonight we are a country awakened to danger and called to defend freedom. Our grief has turned to anger and anger to resolution. Whether we bring our enemies to justice or bring justice to our enemies, justice will be done. . . .

On September 11th, enemies of freedom committed an act of war against our country. Americans have known wars, but for the past 136 years, they have been wars on foreign soil, except for one Sunday in 1941. Americans have known the casualties of war, but not at the center of a great city on a peaceful morning. Americans have known surprise attacks, but never before on thousands of civilians. All of this was brought upon us in a single day, and night fell on a different world, a world where freedom itself is under attack.

Americans have many questions tonight. Americans are asking, who attacked our country? The evidence we have gathered all points to a collection of loosely affiliated terrorist organizations known as Al Qaida. They are some of the murderers indicted for bombing American Embassies in Tanzania and Kenya and responsible for bombing the U.S.S. *Cole*. Al Qaida is to terror what the Mafia is to crime. But its goal is not making money. Its goal is remaking the world and imposing its radical beliefs on people everywhere.

The terrorists practice a fringe form of Islamic extremism that has been rejected by Muslim scholars and the vast majority of Muslim clerics, a fringe movement that perverts the peaceful teachings of Islam. The terrorists' directive commands them to kill Christians and Jews, to kill all Americans, and make no distinctions among military and civilians, including women and children.

This group and its leader, a person named Usama bin Laden, are linked to many other organizations in different countries, including the Egyptian Islamic Jihad and the Islamic Movement of Uzbekistan. There are thousands of these terrorists in more than 60 countries. They are recruited from their own nations and neighborhoods and brought to camps in places like Afghanistan, where they are trained in the tactics of terror. They are sent back to their homes or sent to hide in countries around the world to plot evil and destruction.

George W. Bush, "Address Before a Joint Session of the Congress on the United States Response to the Terrorist Attacks of September 11" (September 20, 2001). Online by Gerald Peters and John T. Woolley, *The American Presidency Project*. www.presidency.ucsb.edu/ws/?pid=64731.

The leadership of Al Qaida has great influence in Afghanistan and supports the Taliban regime in controlling most of that country. In Afghanistan, we see Al Qaida's vision for the world. Afghanistan's people have been brutalized. Many are starving, and many have fled. Women are not allowed to attend school. You can be jailed for owning a television. Religion can be practiced only as their leaders dictate. A man can be jailed in Afghanistan if his beard is not long enough.

The United States respects the people of Afghanistan—after all, we are currently its largest source of humanitarian aid—but we condemn the Taliban regime. It is not only repressing its own people; it is threatening people everywhere by sponsoring and sheltering and supplying terrorists. By aiding and abetting murder, the Taliban regime is committing murder.

And tonight the United States of America makes the following demands on the Taliban: Deliver to United States authorities all the leaders of Al Qaida who hide in your land. Release all foreign nationals, including American citizens, you have unjustly imprisoned. Protect foreign journalists, diplomats, and aid workers in your country. Close immediately and permanently every terrorist training camp in Afghanistan, and hand over every terrorist and every person in their support structure to appropriate authorities. Give the United States full access to terrorist training camps, so we can make sure they are no longer operating.

These demands are not open to negotiation or discussion. The Taliban must act and act immediately. They will hand over the terrorists, or they will share in their fate.

I also want to speak tonight directly to Muslims throughout the world. We respect your faith. It's practiced freely by many millions of Americans and by millions more in countries that America counts as friends. Its teachings are good and peaceful, and those who commit evil in the name of Allah blaspheme the name of Allah. The terrorists are traitors to their own faith, trying, in effect, to hijack Islam itself. The enemy of America is not our many Muslim friends; it is not our many Arab friends. Our enemy is a radical network of terrorists and every government that supports them.

Our war on terror begins with Al Qaida, but it does not end there. It will not end until every terrorist group of global reach has been found, stopped, and defeated.

Americans are asking, why do they hate us? They hate what we see right here in this Chamber, a democratically elected government. Their leaders are self-appointed. They hate our freedoms—our freedom of religion, our freedom of speech, our freedom to vote and assemble and disagree with each other. . . .

We have seen their kind before. They are the heirs of all the murderous ideologies of the 20th century. By sacrificing human life to serve their radical visions, by abandoning every value except the will to power, they follow in the path of fascism and nazism and totalitarianism. And they will follow that path all the way, to where it ends, in history's unmarked grave of discarded lies.

Americans are asking, how will we fight and win this war? We will direct every resource at our command—every means of diplomacy, every tool of intelligence, every instrument of law enforcement, every financial influence, and every necessary weapon of war — to the disruption and to the defeat of the global terror network. . . .

Our response involves far more than instant retaliation and isolated strikes. Americans should not expect one battle but a lengthy campaign, unlike any other we have ever seen. It may include dramatic strikes, visible on TV, and covert operations, secret even in success. We will starve terrorists of funding, turn them one against another, drive them from place to place, until there is no refuge or no rest. And we will pursue nations that provide aid or safe haven to terrorism. Every nation, in every region, now has a decision to make: Either you are with us, or you are with the terrorists. From this day forward, any nation that continues to harbor or support terrorism will be regarded by the United States as a hostile regime.

Our Nation has been put on notice: We are not immune from attack. We will take defensive measures against terrorism to protect Americans. Today dozens of Federal departments and agencies, as well as State and local governments, have responsibilities affecting homeland security. These efforts must be coordinated at the highest level.

So tonight I announce the creation of a Cabinet-level position reporting directly to me, the Office of Homeland Security. . . .

These measures are essential. But the only way to defeat terrorism as a threat to our way of life is to stop it, eliminate it, and destroy it where it grows. . . .

This is not, however, just America's fight, and what is at stake is not just America's freedom. This is the world's fight. This is civilization's fight. This is the fight of all who believe in progress and pluralism, tolerance and freedom.

We ask every nation to join us. We will ask, and we will need, the help of police forces, intelligence services, and banking systems around the world. The United States is grateful that many nations and many international organizations have already responded with sympathy and with support, nations from Latin America to Asia, to Africa, to Europe, to the Islamic world. Perhaps the NATO Charter reflects best the attitude of the world: An attack on one is an attack on all. . . .

Americans are asking, what is expected of us? I ask you to live your lives and hug your children. I know many citizens have fears tonight, and I ask you to be calm and resolute, even in the face of a continuing threat.

I ask you to uphold the values of America and remember why so many have come here. We are in a fight for our principles, and our first responsibility is to live by them. No one should be singled out for unfair treatment or unkind words because of their ethnic background or religious faith. . . .

The thousands of FBI agents who are now at work in this investigation may need your cooperation, and I ask you to give it.

I ask for your patience with the delays and inconveniences that may accompany tighter security and for your patience in what will be a long struggle.

I ask your continued participation and confidence in the American economy. Terrorists attacked a symbol of American prosperity. They did not touch its source. America is successful because of the hard work and creativity and enterprise of our people. These were the true strengths of our economy before September 11th, and they are our strengths today.

And finally, please continue praying for the victims of terror and their families, for those in uniform, and for our great country. Prayer has comforted us in sorrow and will help strengthen us for the journey ahead. . . .

Tonight we face new and sudden national challenges. We will come together to improve air safety, to dramatically expand the number of air marshals on domestic flights and take new measures to prevent hijacking. We will come together to promote stability and keep our airlines flying, with direct assistance during this emergency.

We will come together to give law enforcement the additional tools it needs to track down terror here at home. We will come together to strengthen our intelligence capabilities, to know the plans of terrorists before they act and find them before they strike. We will come together to take active steps that strengthen America's economy and put our people back to work. . . .

Fellow citizens, we'll meet violence with patient justice, assured of the rightness of our cause and confident of the victories to come. In all that lies before us, may God grant us wisdom, and may He watch over the United States of America.

READING AND DISCUSSION QUESTIONS

1. How does President Bush explain the cause of the September 11 attacks to the American people? What motives did he attribute to the Al Qaeda terrorist organizations that perpetrated these attacks?

2. What role does Bush see the federal government playing in prosecuting a war on terror? In speaking to other nations and to the American people, what role does he expect them to play?

31-6 | Democratic Presidential Candidate Confronts the Issue of Race

BARACK OBAMA, *A More Perfect Union* (2008)

Barack Obama's historic campaign for president in 2008 was nearly derailed when video clips of his former Chicago pastor, the Reverend Jeremiah Wright, surfaced in which Wright implied that the nation's foreign policies had invited the 9/11 terrorist attacks. In another widely circulated sermon, Wright's litany of America's failings—including its treatment of minority citizens— culminated with: "God Bless America. No . . . not God Bless America. God damn America." Obama's widely praised speech in Philadelphia defanged the issue and rescued his campaign, leading to his fall victory over his rival, Senator John McCain.

Barack Obama, "A More Perfect Union" (March 18, 2008). Online by Gerald Peters and John T. Woolley, *The American Presidency Project*. www.presidency.ucsb.edu/ws/?pid=76710.

[I]t has only been in the last couple of weeks that the discussion of race in this campaign has taken a particularly divisive turn.

On one end of the spectrum, we've heard the implication that my candidacy is somehow an exercise in affirmative action; that it's based solely on the desire of wide-eyed liberals to purchase racial reconciliation on the cheap. On the other end, we've heard my former pastor, Reverend Jeremiah Wright, use incendiary language to express views that have the potential not only to widen the racial divide, but views that denigrate both the greatness and the goodness of our nation; that rightly offend white and black alike.

I have already condemned, in unequivocal terms, the statements of Reverend Wright that have caused such controversy. For some, nagging questions remain. Did I know him to be an occasionally fierce critic of American domestic and foreign policy? Of course. Did I ever hear him make remarks that could be considered controversial while I sat in church? Yes. Did I strongly disagree with many of his political views? Absolutely—just as I'm sure many of you have heard remarks from your pastors, priests, or rabbis with which you strongly disagreed.

But the remarks that have caused this recent firestorm weren't simply controversial. They weren't simply a religious leader's effort to speak out against perceived injustice. Instead, they expressed a profoundly distorted view of this country—a view that sees white racism as endemic, and that elevates what is wrong with America above all that we know is right with America; a view that sees the conflicts in the Middle East as rooted primarily in the actions of stalwart allies like Israel, instead of emanating from the perverse and hateful ideologies of radical Islam.

As such, Reverend Wright's comments were not only wrong but divisive, divisive at a time when we need unity; racially charged at a time when we need to come together to solve a set of monumental problems—two wars, a terrorist threat, a falling economy, a chronic health care crisis and potentially devastating climate change; problems that are neither black or white or Latino or Asian, but rather problems that confront us all.

Given my background, my politics, and my professed values and ideals, there will no doubt be those for whom my statements of condemnation are not enough. Why associate myself with Reverend Wright in the first place, they may ask? Why not join another church? And I confess that if all that I knew of Reverend Wright were the snippets of those sermons that have run in an endless loop on the television and YouTube, or if Trinity United Church of Christ conformed to the caricatures being peddled by some commentators, there is no doubt that I would react in much the same way.

But the truth is, that isn't all that I know of the man. The man I met more than twenty years ago is a man who helped introduce me to my Christian faith, a man who spoke to me about our obligations to love one another; to care for the sick and lift up the poor. . . .

As imperfect as he may be, he has been like family to me. He strengthened my faith, officiated my wedding, and baptized my children. Not once in my conversations with him have I heard him talk about any ethnic group in derogatory terms, or treat whites with whom he interacted with anything but courtesy and respect. He contains within him the contradictions—the good and the bad—of the community that he has served diligently for so many years.

I can no more disown him than I can disown the black community. I can no more disown him than I can my white grandmother—a woman who helped raise me, a woman who sacrificed again and again for me, a woman who loves me as much as she loves anything in this world, but a woman who once confessed her fear of black men who passed by her on the street, and who on more than one occasion has uttered racial or ethnic stereotypes that made me cringe.

These people are a part of me. And they are a part of America, this country that I love. . . .

But race is an issue that I believe this nation cannot afford to ignore right now. We would be making the same mistake that Reverend Wright made in his offending sermons about America—to simplify and stereotype and amplify the negative to the point that it distorts reality.

The fact is that the comments that have been made and the issues that have surfaced over the last few weeks reflect the complexities of race in this country that we've never really worked through—a part of our union that we have yet to perfect. . . .

We do not need to recite here the history of racial injustice in this country. But we do need to remind ourselves that so many of the disparities that exist in the African-American community today can be directly traced to inequalities passed on from an earlier generation that suffered under the brutal legacy of slavery and Jim Crow.

Segregated schools were, and are, inferior schools; we still haven't fixed them, fifty years after Brown v. Board of Education, and the inferior education they provided, then and now, helps explain the pervasive achievement gap between today's black and white students.

Legalized discrimination—where blacks were prevented, often through violence, from owning property, or loans were not granted to African-American business owners, or black homeowners could not access FHA mortgages, or blacks were excluded from unions, or the police force, or fire departments . . . helps explain the wealth and income gap between black and white, and the concentrated pockets of poverty that persists in so many of today's urban and rural communities.

A lack of economic opportunity among black men, and the shame and frustration that came from not being able to provide for one's family, contributed to the erosion of black families—a problem that welfare policies for many years may have worsened. And the lack of basic services in so many urban black neighborhoods—parks for kids to play in, police walking the beat, regular garbage pick-up and building code enforcement—all helped create a cycle of violence, blight and neglect that continue to haunt us.

This is the reality in which Reverend Wright and other African-Americans of his generation grew up. They came of age in the late fifties and early sixties, a time when segregation was still the law of the land and opportunity was systematically constricted. What's remarkable is not how many failed in the face of discrimination, but rather how many men and women overcame the odds; how many were able to make a way out of no way for those like me who would come after them.

But for all those who scratched and clawed their way to get a piece of the American Dream, there were many who didn't make it—those who were ultimately defeated, in one way or another, by discrimination. That legacy of defeat was passed on to future generations—those young men and increasingly young women who we see standing on street corners or languishing in our prisons, without hope or prospects for the future. . . .

For the men and women of Reverend Wright's generation, the memories of humiliation and doubt and fear have not gone away; nor has the anger and the bitterness of those years. That anger may not get expressed in public, in front of white co-workers or white friends. But it does find voice in the barbershop or around the kitchen table. . . .

And occasionally it finds voice in the church on Sunday morning, in the pulpit and in the pews. The fact that so many people are surprised to hear that anger in some of Reverend Wright's sermons simply reminds us of the old truism that the most segregated hour in American life occurs on Sunday morning. That anger is not always productive; indeed, all too often it distracts attention from solving real problems; it keeps us from squarely facing our own complicity in our condition, and prevents the African-American community from forging the alliances it needs to bring about real change. But the anger is real; it is powerful; and to simply wish it away, to condemn it without understanding its roots, only serves to widen the chasm of misunderstanding that exists between the races.

In fact, a similar anger exists within segments of the white community. Most working- and middle-class white Americans don't feel that they have been particularly privileged by their race. . . . They've worked hard all their lives, many times only to see their jobs shipped overseas or their pension dumped after a lifetime of labor. They are anxious about their futures, and feel their dreams slipping away; in an era of stagnant wages and global competition, opportunity comes to be seen as a zero sum game, in which your dreams come at my expense. So when they are told to bus their children to a school across town; when they hear that an African American is getting an advantage in landing a good job or a spot in a good college because of an injustice that they themselves never committed; when they're told that their fears about crime in urban neighborhoods are somehow prejudiced, resentment builds over time. . . .

But I have asserted a firm conviction—a conviction rooted in my faith in God and my faith in the American people—that working together we can move beyond some of our old racial wounds, and that in fact we have no choice if we are to continue on the path of a more perfect union.

For the African-American community, that path means embracing the burdens of our past without becoming victims of our past. It means continuing to insist on a full measure of justice in every aspect of American life. But it also means binding our particular grievances—for better health care, and better schools, and better jobs — to the larger aspirations of all Americans — the white woman struggling to break the glass ceiling, the white man who's been laid off, the immigrant trying to feed his family. . . .

In the end, then, what is called for is nothing more, and nothing less, than what all the world's great religions demand — that we do unto others as we would have them do unto us. Let us be our brother's keeper, Scripture tells us. Let us be our sister's keeper. Let us find that common stake we all have in one another, and let our politics reflect that spirit as well.

For we have a choice in this country. We can accept a politics that breeds division, and conflict, and cynicism. . . . But if we do, I can tell you that in the next election, we'll be talking about some other distraction. And then another one. And then another one. And nothing will change.

That is one option. Or, at this moment, in this election, we can come together and say, "Not this time." This time we want to talk about the crumbling schools that are stealing the future of black children and white children and Asian children and Hispanic children and Native American children. This time we want to reject the cynicism that tells us that these kids can't learn; that those kids who don't look like us are somebody else's problem. The children of America are not those kids, they are our kids, and we will not let them fall behind in a 21st century economy. Not this time.

This time we want to talk about how the lines in the Emergency Room are filled with whites and blacks and Hispanics who do not have health care; who don't have the power on their own to overcome the special interests in Washington, but who can take them on if we do it together.

This time we want to talk about the shuttered mills that once provided a decent life for men and women of every race, and the homes for sale that once belonged to Americans from every religion, every region, every walk of life. This time we want to talk about the fact that the real problem is not that someone who doesn't look like you might take your job; it's that the corporation you work for will ship it overseas for nothing more than a profit.

This time we want to talk about the men and women of every color and creed who serve together, and fight together, and bleed together under the same proud flag. We want to talk about how to bring them home from a war that never should've been authorized and never should've been waged, and we want to talk about how we'll show our patriotism by caring for them, and their families, and giving them the benefits they have earned.

I would not be running for President if I didn't believe with all my heart that this is what the vast majority of Americans want for this country. This union may never be perfect, but generation after generation has shown that it can always be perfected. And today, whenever I find myself feeling doubtful or cynical about this possibility, what gives me the most hope is the next generation — the young people whose attitudes and beliefs and openness to change have already made history in this election.

READING AND DISCUSSION QUESTIONS

1. How does Obama explain the historical context of Reverend Wright's comments? Though he distanced himself from Wright's more inflammatory language, how does Obama explain to Americans the source and significance of Wright's anger?

2. To what extent do you think historians will interpret Obama's speech as a turning point in the history of America's race relations? How would you assess its short-term effect on the 2008 campaign and its longer-term effect on Americans' discussion of race?

■ COMPARATIVE QUESTIONS ■

1. Compare Albright's speech with the foreign policy views expressed by John Foster Dulles (Document 25-5). How do their views differ, and what factors account for those differences? Analyze the historical context of the 1950s and 1990s for clues.

2. What evidence does the Seattle WTO protest provide for understanding changes in social protest politics during the late twentieth century? Compare strategies at Seattle with the Indians of All Tribes proclamation (Document 27-5). What comparison could a historian make between the WTO protest and the civil rights movement?

3. What historical patterns can you identify in the experience of racial and ethnic minorities in America by comparing the evidence from Proposition 187 to the Citizen Committee letter (Document P7-1), the World War II African American soldier's letter (Document P7-5), Luisa Moreno's speech (Document P7-6), and Cesar Chavez's letter from Delano (Document 28-4)? How were the challenges similar or different in these different periods?

4. What challenges face the historian attempting to write the history of contemporary America? How might personal opinion and memory interfere with the analysis of the last chapter's documents more than previous chapters' sources?

DOCUMENT SET

Work, Exchange, and Technology in America's Global Economy

1980 to the Present

The last quarter of the twentieth century revealed the promise and peril of the new era of globalization. Changes in technology and America's economic integration into world markets developed new opportunities for growth on a scale unimaginable to policymakers in the post–World War II era. However, unforeseen side effects demonstrated America's economic and political vulnerabilities. Global markets inspired profit fantasies for corporate America, but blue-collar workers in the traditional manufacturing industries were seized with anxiety as they saw their jobs exported to lower-wage countries. A period of deindustrialization coincided with the rise of a new labor market in service-sector jobs. The erosion of working-class manufacturing jobs and the rise of sophisticated financial markets widened the income gap, resulting in social and political consequences. Technology pushed globalization by opening a worldwide web of information and commercial exchange, but it too came with costs. These seismic changes in work and global exchange created a new economy for the twenty-first century, but they also inspired an ongoing debate over economic values and the role of government that continues to affect America's political culture.

P9-1 | Free-Market Fundamentalism Defines Conservative Movement

IRVING KRISTOL, *Two Cheers for Capitalism* (1978)

The modern conservative movement traces its origins to the free-market ideology that developed in opposition to Franklin Roosevelt's New Deal, which critics sometimes decried as evidence of creeping socialism. These critics worried that excessive government interference with the economy would strangle free enterprise and lead inevitably to constraints on individual liberty, and this ideology captured the Republican Party, informing Reagan-era "supply-side economics." Here, the intellectual hero of neoconservatism, Irving Kristol, discusses the effect of government regulation on the national economy.

In all of the recent discussion of our economic condition, there has been controversy over whether tax cuts are really necessary and, if so, what kind would be most beneficial. To the best of my knowledge, no one—not even John Kenneth Galbraith[1]—has dreamed of proposing *a tax increase*. Yet that is what we keep on getting—specifically an increased tax on corporate income—only no one seems to notice.

It is not really as surprising as one might think that our economists, our accountants, even our business executives should be oblivious to the steady increase in corporate taxation that has been taking place. Habitual modes of perception and conventional modes of reckoning are likely to impose themselves on a changing reality rather than go through a painful process of adaptation. And the learned economist or alert executive can fail to observe an important feature of a situation because he wasn't looking for it.

Here is an example of what I mean. Corporation X, in order to meet water pollution standards set by the Environmental Protection Agency, has to install new filtering equipment that costs $2 million. How is this expenditure to be accounted for? Well, at present, it is counted as a "capital investment" and is carried on the books as an "asset" of the corporation. But does that make any sense?

After all, a "capital investment" is supposed to promise an increase in production or productivity, or both. An "asset," similarly, is supposed to represent earning power, actual or potential. But that new filtering equipment may do none of these things. Indeed, it may actually decrease productive capacity and productivity. In short, the $2 million ought properly to be counted as a government-imposed cost—in effect a surtax or effluent tax—and the company's stated after-tax income should be reduced accordingly.

Instead of imposing an actual tax and using the proceeds to purchase and install the equipment, the government mandates that the firm do so. The end result, however, is the same.

Irving Kristol, *Two Cheers for Capitalism* (New York: Basic Books, 1978), 50–53, 54.

[1]**John Kenneth Galbraith**: Liberal economist and author of several best-selling books, including *The Affluent Society* (1958).

I am not saying that the new filtering equipment is just money down the drain. It does buy cleaner water, after all. But that cleaner water is a free "social good" and a "social asset" to the population in the neighborhood (and for the fish, too); it represents no economic gain to the corporation, which has only economic assets and knows nothing of "social assets." It also buys governmental "good will," but so do bribes to foreign officials, and I am not aware that anyone has yet thought to capitalize them. On the other hand, the new equipment is unquestionably an *economic cost* to the corporation and, of course, to the economy as a whole.

As things now stand, we render those economic costs invisible. That is both silly and undesirable. Silly, because they are real costs. Undesirable, because we shall never persuade the American people to take the problem of regulation seriously until they appreciate, in the clearest possible way, what it is costing them as stockholders, consumers, and employees.

The costs we are talking about are by no means small, and their impact by no means marginal. In fact, they are far, far larger and more serious than most people realize. Unfortunately, there are no comprehensive, precise estimates available. But one can get a sense of the magnitude of such costs from the following bits and pieces of information.

- In 1977 U.S. Steel signed a seven-year agreement with federal, state, and local environmental agencies that will require it to spend $600 million over that period to eliminate air pollution from its Clairton Coke Works in Pittsburgh.
- The steel industry as a whole will be spending well over $1 billion annually on pollution controls—and that is a conservative estimate. This expenditure amounts to over one quarter of the industry's total annual capital investments.
- Meeting EPA's 1983 waste pollution standards will cost all of American industry, over the next seven years, about $60 billion for capital equipment and another $12 billion annually in operating and maintenance costs.
- Meeting noise pollution standards, as mandated by Congress and enforced by the Occupational Safety and Health Administration (OSHA), will involve expenditures of over $15 billion in capital costs and $2 billion to $3 billion in operating costs in the years immediately ahead. If these noise standards are raised to the level recommended by the U.S. National Institute for Occupational Safety and Health—a recommendation endorsed by the EPA—the capital costs will climb over $30 billion.
- According to the *Wall Street Journal*, new health regulations in the cotton industry will, in the period from 1977 through 1983, cost some $3 billion. It has been estimated by Professor Murray Weidenbaum that American industry's cost to meet OSHA safety standards in 1977 alone were over $4 billion.
- The EPA is on record—for what that is worth—as calculating that industry's total capital investment requirements for all kinds of pollution control equipment will, in the decade 1972–81, add up to $112 billion.

None of the above figures is particularly reliable, and they may not even be entirely consistent with one another. But they do suffice to give a pretty fair indication of what is going on. Even so, important costs are omitted—those, for example, which involved product redesign or the design of the work place. Thus, the increased cost of housing over these past years results, to a significant degree, from various environmental regulations. And Ewan Clague, former U.S. Commissioner of Labor Statistics, points out that productivity in bituminous mining has decreased 30 percent since 1970, largely as a result of the passage in that year of the Coal Mine Health and Safety Act. These indirect costs are not capitalized, of course, and technically are not "hidden." On the other hand, who would claim that the public appreciates their dimensions?

As one contemplates those numbers, various inferences suggest themselves. One is that a clear distinction ought to be made between "capital spending" and "capital investment." We were told, for instance, that capital investment in 1976 amounted to $121 billion, and economists were somewhat disappointed that this represented only a 7.5 percent increase over 1975. But if, as seems likely, as much as 10 percent of that figure should not have been counted as "capital investment" at all—since it consisted of economically unproductive *expenditures*—where does that leave us? It leaves us, I would suggest, with a net reduction in true capital investment in 1976, the economic effects of which will be with us for years ahead. One such probable effect, a decline in the rate of growth of the American worker's productivity, has already been noticed, though never accounted for.

It may be argued that these economically unproductive expenditures do, after all, create jobs (temporarily) and do contribute to the Gross National Product. But so would the corporate construction of beautiful pyramids, at government behest. That would create jobs (temporarily), inflate the GNP, and provide us with a "social good" (a great spectacle). But it would be a cost to the economy, and if our conventional statistics are incapable of showing it as such, then those statistics need revision.

It is also true that, in many cases, corporations are able to maintain their profit margins by passing on their increased costs directly to the consumer and indirectly to their stockholders (by holding down dividends) or to their employees (by granting lower wages than they otherwise might). But that is what usually happens to corporate taxes; they get passed on to *someone* since the corporation itself is only an economic mechanism, not an economic person (except, fictitiously, in law). In the world market of today, however, not all corporations can pass on those costs. In those instances, we get declining businesses, declining industries, and a sagging economy. In any case, those costs—passed on or not—should be visible, instead of hidden as they now are. The Federal Reserve's index of plant capacity, for example, apparently makes no effort to distinguish between capital expenditures and capital investments, and to that degree is misleading.

It is true, too, that firms can depreciate their uneconomic, mandated capital expenditures. But that equipment will have to be replaced as it depreciates with age; we are not talking about a one-time expense.

The situation we have gotten ourselves into would be ridiculous if it were not so serious. We have been much exercised—and quite rightly—by the fact that the OPEC monopoly has cost this country well over $30 billion in increased oil prices since 1972. But in that time we have inflicted upon ourselves much larger economic costs through environmental and other regulations and will continue to do so, perhaps at an increasing rate.

Yes, these economic costs do buy real "social goods." But may the prices not be too high? Is the resulting inflation of prices, constriction of productive capacity, and increase in unemployment worth it? Would it not be appropriate for us to ask ourselves this question openly, instead of going along with the environmentalists' pretense—so pleasing to our politicians—that our "social goods" cost us nothing at all? Isn't it time that business stopped bleating in a general way about those costs and showed us what they really mean, all the way down to the bottom line?

READING AND DISCUSSION QUESTIONS

1. How would you summarize the neoconservative contribution to the debates over the value of market capitalism? What was the historical significance of Kristol's economic ideas during the last quarter of the twentieth century?

2. Why does Kristol focus his attention on environmentalists? What does he say has been their impact on the national economy?

P9-2 | Steelworker Explains Industry's Collapse

LEROY McCLELLAND SR., *Interview with Bill Barry* (2006)

The Sparrows Point plant of Bethlehem Steel outside Baltimore, Maryland, typified the effects of twentieth-century globalization. During the 1950s, the steel plant was the industry's largest, employing more than thirty thousand men and women and selling steel domestically and around the world. The United Steelworkers union negotiated contracts that helped pull these workers into middle-class comfort. But factors such as technology enhancements and global competition changed everything for the workers, who consequently witnessed their industry collapse. In 2001, Bethlehem Steel sought bankruptcy protection and eliminated its pension liabilities, destroying retirement security for many workers. Here LeRoy McClelland Sr., who worked at "the Point" for forty-two years, describes his experiences and the factors that caused the industry's decline.

MR. McCLELLAND: Well, now you enter into another part of the change, and that's technology. When we looked at the safety aspect of it we knew that there were certain procedures that could protect certain things from happening, but with that protection in mind it took technology to put it in place, so that meant a job was no longer necessary. So when you are looking for one issue

Interview with LeRoy McClelland, Sr., by Bill Barry, May 1, 2006. Transcript at www .sparrowspointsteelworkers.com/interviews/LeRoy_McClelland_Sr.html.

to resolve another, sometimes you've got to take the outcome of it, too. And in our case with technology being advanced and computers and what have you, we've had operations that would never ever operate unless you had a person there. Now, that's not necessary. In fact, it can have a crew—it used to be six people on a mill reduced to three. Why? Computer, and then it advances further on down the road for technology. When that happened, too, you've got to understand that the idea of the union was to protect jobs, create jobs, not eliminate jobs. Well, I had the unfortunate experience of being the zone committeeman at the time when a lot of this technology was starting to really grow.

MR. BARRY: When was this?

MR. McCLELLAND: Well, it really started in 1975, from '75 on, '80, '90s, biggest part being in the '80s really, the advanced technology. But when these other things started to take place, guys and gals sort of looked at this change coming down, felt hey, that's a God send, not realizing that when that takes place you ain't going to be there to see it because your job is going to be gone. So we would have meetings, I would have department meetings up here trying to make that message as clear as I could I guess to soften the idea that hey, we're going to be losing jobs. That protection that used to be there is not going to be dependable anymore. You can't defend something that's no longer necessary, so we had to take these strong measures, and in my case you could find my name on every bathroom shit house wall in Sparrows Point, because I was wanting these guys to—saw the road coming real fast at me and realized technology is going to replace jobs, and if nothing else, gain something from it. So I was sort of accused of selling people for jobs and jobs for job classes, and all that sort of gets caught up in the big mess in itself, but it's nothing you can do. I mean reality is technology is the future and competitiveness is strong. If you can't deal with competitiveness, if you don't have tons per hour and manpower per hour was the way it was, and that's what had to happen. . . .

MR. BARRY: How difficult was it for you to learn how to use a computer?

MR. McCLELLAND: Well, it was a bit of a challenge because everything we did before was pencil and paper, and it was a challenge, and in fact, I didn't think I would like it, I really didn't. My wife is the one who really got started on it, and she got it basically for games and then it advanced into other things. I happened to go down the cellar here and we've got two computers down there, which I bought one for me, one for her, and I didn't want to tell her I didn't know, so I was trying to just ease my way across to get her to show me what these—God, I can use a typewriter, always can use a typewriter, but the keys are—they do different things and you can screw up very easy if you hit the wrong key or be something on the websites, you can really create a problem. So I got down there a couple times, just watched what she was doing. She said, "Well, do you want to learn this?" I said, "I don't want to learn nothing, just go ahead and do what you are doing," but I watched her, and one night I went down there by myself and I got on the web and I was so overwhelmed by things that I could get on the web, the web addresses, the e-mail addresses that you can get and the information. I got more information about our politicians, I got more information about what is going on in Annapolis, I got more information on what's going on in the Senate and the Congress right there firsthand. I don't have to wait for the newspaper the next day, it's right there. I can get into every newspaper in this country and get what's going on and whatever is happening in that country that very day. It just engulfs you, and then the fear of the computer doesn't exist anymore. And even at work when the transition of computerization took place, we used to take our scrap buckets, big buckets, big bins I should say, and haul them down there and weigh them. We used to have a scale man there. To show you how advanced that got with technology, they eliminated the scale person and they put a scale there, and all you had to do was hit certain buttons, boom, boom, boom, and it would weigh it, it would give you a card in return of what the weight was and you put the box there and the scrap crane come down and dumped it. You put it back to your place and turned in the weight, and it was all computerized, and they simplified it because they had a red key—a monkey could have done it. That's what they were dealing with, the transition, and with technology also a lot of guys did leave the mill because they were embarrassed, they couldn't make the mental change from using the keyboard to using the hands on.

MR. BARRY: These were people who were eligible to retire and the technology in effect drove them out?

MR. McCLELLAND: Yes, absolutely did. And change is tough for anybody. With me, I'm lucky to be able to experience what I did. . . . [Y]ou and I may not be on this earth, but the generation that does exist, jobs itself, availability, is not going to be here because everything we have done in this country has been an outsourcing and we are outsourcing every day of the week. I mean we're talking about—here, my daughter who worked 12 years at Hecht's, it's no longer a[t] Hecht's, they bought her out. They give her a buyout or she can go to Macy's, but I think it's Macy they are now, she can go there but not where she was originally working at in Whitemarsh. She would be somewhere where they needed her. She is raising a five-year-old. She just can't jump and go. So that change is brought on. Places like Wal-Mart, Sam's, Dollar Stores, I mean people don't realize this is why the economy in this country is going down the tube because we are not exporting anything, we are importing, we are importing more, and when you import, the jobs necessary to make the product isn't needed here because it's done outside. Our own steel industry, our steel industry Mitel, now here is a global giant of steel. He has got operations all around the world. Before it's over with, this person, this family is going to end up absolutely controlling the price of steel, and here America sits when defending this country is going to depend on getting steel from other sorts of the world or other parts of the world. What a challenge that's going to be. Right now Mitel has shut down operations here. Why? Because he has places around the world. Weirton Steel, they shut down the steel side completely. No way down the road are they going to open, reactivate it. It is over. So that's one section. And when that character came here, he made it clear that if productivity becomes a problem, then that place is gone, and he ain't just saying that to threaten them. He said it and meant it, and it's happening. What I see going to come down here again, and this is just me, this isn't standing—this is me, my wave length, my tunnel—sometimes tunnel vision, but it turns out that Weirton Steel produces a better tin plate than Sparrows Point. I say—and my son who works there right now, he's an operator on the halogen lines, I said, "John, don't be surprised if some of your operations here starts shutting down permanently. Do not be surprised." Lo and behold there's no more chrome line down there. Where is it? Weirton. Well, it's just a matter of time before some of the other operations that used to depend on the tin mill to supply them will not be operating there.

READING AND DISCUSSION QUESTIONS

1. How does McClelland explain the effect of changes in technology and the global integration of the steel industry on both the Bethlehem Steel Company and its workers?

2. What can you infer from McClelland's interview about the role of the union in the lives of steelworkers as the company faced the effects of globalization?

P9-3 | President Champions Promise of Free Trade

BILL CLINTON, *Remarks on Signing the North American Free Trade Agreement Implementation Act* (1993)

The North American Free Trade Agreement (NAFTA) eliminated trade barriers between Canada, Mexico, and the United States. Signed into law by President Bill Clinton, the initial agreements were negotiated under Republican president George H. W. Bush, a sign of the legislation's bipartisan support. Opponents, however, predicted job losses, lowered wages, and the erosion of environmental protections. In his public remarks, President Clinton defended NAFTA from critics' charges.

This whole issue turned out to be a defining moment for our Nation. I spoke with one of the folks who was in the reception just a few moments ago who told me that he was in China watching the vote on international television when it was taken. And he said you would have had to be there to understand how important this was to the rest of the world, not because of the terms of NAFTA, which basically is a trade agreement between the United States, Mexico, and Canada, but

William J. Clinton, "Remarks on Signing the North American Free Trade Agreement Implementation Act," December 8, 1993. Online by Gerhard Peters and John T. Woolley, *The American Presidency Project*. www.presidency.ucsb.edu/ws/?pid=46216.

because it became a symbolic struggle for the spirit of our country and for how we would approach this very difficult and rapidly changing world dealing with our own considerable challenges here at home.

I believe we have made a decision now that will permit us to create an economic order in the world that will promote more growth, more equality, better preservation of the environment, and a greater possibility of world peace. We are on the verge of a global economic expansion that is sparked by the fact that the United States at this critical moment decided that we would compete, not retreat.

In a few moments, I will sign the North American free trade act into law. NAFTA will tear down trade barriers between our three nations. It will create the world's largest trade zone and create 200,000 jobs in this country by 1995 alone. The environmental and labor side agreements negotiated by our administration will make this agreement a force for social progress as well as economic growth. Already the confidence we've displayed by ratifying NAFTA has begun to bear fruit. We are now making real progress toward a worldwide trade agreement so significant that it could make the material gains of NAFTA for our country look small by comparison.

Today we have the chance to do what our parents did before us. We have the opportunity to remake the world. For this new era, our national security we now know will be determined as much by our ability to pull down foreign trade barriers as by our ability to breach distant ramparts. Once again, we are leading. And in so doing, we are rediscovering a fundamental truth about ourselves: When we lead, we build security, we build prosperity for our own people.

We've learned this lesson the hard way. Twice before in this century, we have been forced to define our role in the world. After World War I we turned inward, building walls of protectionism around our Nation. The result was a Great Depression and ultimately another horrible World War. After the Second World War, we took a different course: We reached outward. Gifted leaders of both political parties built a new order based on collective security and expanded trade. They created a foundation of stability and created in the process the conditions which led to the explosion of the great American middle class, one of the true economic miracles in the whole history of civilization. Their statecraft stands to this day: the IMF and the World Bank, GATT, and NATO.

In this very auditorium in 1949, President Harry Truman signed one of the charter documents of this golden era of American leadership, the North Atlantic Treaty that created NATO. "In this pact we hope to create a shield against aggression and the fear of aggression," Truman told his audience, "a bulwark which will permit us to get on with the real business of Government and society, the business of achieving a fuller and happier life for our citizens."

Now, the institutions built by Truman and Acheson, by Marshall and Vandenberg, have accomplished their task. The cold war is over. The grim certitude of the contest with communism has been replaced by the exuberant uncertainty of international economic competition. And the great question of this day is how to ensure security for our people at a time when change is the only constant.

Make no mistake, the global economy with all of its promise and perils is now the central fact of life for hard-working Americans. It has enriched the lives of millions of Americans. But for too many those same winds of change have worn away at the basis of their security. For two decades, most people have worked harder for less. Seemingly secure jobs have been lost. And while America once again is the most productive nation on Earth, this productivity itself holds the seeds of further insecurity. After all, productivity means the same people can produce more or, very often, that fewer people can produce more. This is the world we face.

We cannot stop global change. We cannot repeal the international economic competition that is everywhere. We can only harness the energy to our benefit. Now we must recognize that the only way for a wealthy nation to grow richer is to export, to simply find new customers for the products and services it makes. That, my fellow Americans, is the decision the Congress made when they voted to ratify NAFTA.

I am gratified with the work that Congress has done this year, bringing the deficit down and keeping interest rates down, getting housing starts and new jobs going upward. But we know that over the long run, our ability to have our internal economic policies work for the benefit of our people requires us to have external economic policies that permit productivity to find expression not simply in higher incomes for our businesses but in more jobs and higher incomes for our people. That means more customers. There is no other way, not for the United States or for Europe or for Japan or for any other wealthy nation in the world.

That is why I am gratified that we had such a good meeting after the NAFTA vote in the House with the Asian-Pacific leaders in Washington. I am gratified that, as Vice President Gore and Chief of Staff Mack McLarty announced 2 weeks ago when they met with President Salinas, next year the nations of this hemisphere will gather in an economic summit that will plan how to extend the benefits of trade to the emerging market democracies of all the Americas.

And now I am pleased that we have the opportunity to secure the biggest breakthrough of all. Negotiators from 112 nations are seeking to conclude negotiations on a new round of the General Agreement on Tariffs and Trade; a historic worldwide trade pact, one that would spur a global economic boon, is now within our grasp. Let me be clear. We cannot, nor should we, settle for a bad GATT agreement. But we will not flag in our efforts to secure a good one in these closing days. We are prepared to make our contributions to the success of this negotiation, but we insist that other nations do their part as well. We must not squander this opportunity. I call on all the nations of the world to seize this moment and close the deal on a strong GATT agreement within the next week. . . .

My fellow Americans, bit by bit all these things are creating the conditions of a sustained global expansion. As significant as they are, our goals must be more ambitious. The United States must seek nothing less than a new trading system that benefits all nations through robust commerce but that protects our middle class and gives other nations a chance to grow one, that lifts workers and the environment up without dragging people down, that seeks to ensure that our policies reflect our values.

Our agenda must, therefore, be far reaching. We are determining that dynamic trade cannot lead to environmental despoliation. We will seek new institutional arrangements to ensure that trade leaves the world cleaner than before. We will press for workers in all countries to secure rights that we now take for granted, to organize and earn a decent living. We will insist that expanded trade be fair to our businesses and to our regions. No country should use cartels, subsidies, or rules of entry to keep our products off its shelves. And we must see to it that our citizens have the personal security to confidently participate in this new era. Every worker must receive the education and training he or she needs to reap the rewards of international competition rather than to bear its burdens.

Next year, our administration will propose comprehensive legislation to transform our unemployment system into a reemployment and job retraining system for the 21st century. And above all, I say to you we must seek to reconstruct the broad-based political coalition for expanded trade. For decades, working men and women and their representatives supported policies that brought us prosperity and security. That was because we recognized that expanded trade benefited all of us but that we have an obligation to protect those workers who do bear the brunt of competition by giving them a chance to be retrained and to go on to a new and different and, ultimately, more secure and more rewarding way of work. In recent years, this social contract has been sundered. It cannot continue.

When I affix my signature to the NAFTA legislation a few moments from now, I do so with this pledge: To the men and women of our country who were afraid of these changes and found in their opposition to NAFTA an expression of that fear — what I thought was a wrong expression and what I know was a wrong expression but nonetheless represented legitimate fears — the gains from this agreement will be your gains, too.

I ask those who opposed NAFTA to work with us to guarantee that the labor and side agreements are enforced, and I call on all of us who believe in NAFTA to join with me to urge the Congress to create the world's best worker training and retraining system. We owe it to the business community as well as to the working men and women of this country. It means greater productivity, lower unemployment, greater worker efficiency, and higher wages and greater security for our people. We have to do that.

We seek a new and more open global trading system not for its own sake but for our own sake. Good jobs, rewarding careers, broadened horizons for the middle class Americans can only be secured by expanding exports and global growth. For too long our step has been unsteady as the ground has shifted beneath our feet. Today, as I sign the North American Free Trade Agreement into law and call for further progress on GATT, I believe we have found our footing. And I ask all of you to be steady, to recognize that there is no turning back from the world of today and tomorrow. We must face the challenges, embrace them with confidence, deal with the problems honestly and openly, and make this world work for all of us. America is where it should be, in the lead, setting the pace, showing the confidence that all of us need to face tomorrow. We are ready to compete, and we can win.

READING AND DISCUSSION QUESTIONS

1. How does Clinton describe the advantages of the North American Free Trade Agreement to skeptics? What impact on the American economy does he predict?

2. Analyze Clinton's remarks concerning NAFTA for evidence of the increased importance of globalization in the 1990s. What perspective toward globalization does Clinton embrace?

P9-4 | Retail Giant Dominates Global Marketplace
CHARLES FISHMAN, *The Wal-Mart You Don't Know* (2003)

Wal-Mart's success is indicative of the late-twentieth-century shift in the American economy from an industrial and manufacturing base to a growing service economy. As Charles Fishman describes in this profile of the company, Wal-Mart's global supply chains managed by cutting-edge technology revolutionized all aspects of the retail industry, leading supporters to praise the company's innovations and causing opponents to lament the economic and social fallout from its relentless quest to shave cents off the price of everyday consumer goods.

A gallon-sized jar of whole pickles is something to behold. The jar is the size of a small aquarium. The fat green pickles, floating in swampy juice, look reptilian, their shapes exaggerated by the glass. It weighs 12 pounds, too big to carry with one hand. The gallon jar of pickles is a display of abundance and excess; it is entrancing, and also vaguely unsettling. This is the product that Wal-Mart fell in love with: Vlasic's gallon jar of pickles.

Wal-Mart priced it at $2.97—a year's supply of pickles for less than $3! "They were using it as a 'statement' item," says Pat Hunn, who calls himself the "mad scientist" of Vlasic's gallon jar. "Wal-Mart was putting it before consumers, saying, This represents what Wal-Mart's about. You can buy a stinkin' gallon of pickles for $2.97. And it's the nation's number-one brand."

Therein lies the basic conundrum of doing business with the world's largest retailer. By selling a gallon of kosher dills for less than most grocers sell a quart, Wal-Mart may have provided a service for its customers. But what did it do for Vlasic? The pickle maker had spent decades convincing customers that they should pay a premium for its brand. Now Wal-Mart was practically giving them away. And the fevered buying spree that resulted distorted every aspect of Vlasic's operations, from farm field to factory to financial statement.

Charles Fishman, "The Wal-Mart You Don't Know," *Fast Company* 77 (December 2003): 68–76.

Indeed, as Vlasic discovered, the real story of Wal-Mart, the story that never gets told, is the story of the pressure the biggest retailer relentlessly applies to its suppliers in the name of bringing us "everyday low prices." It's the story of what that pressure does to the companies Wal-Mart does business with, to U.S. manufacturing, and to the economy as a whole. That story can be found floating in a gallon jar of pickles at Wal-Mart. . . .

Wal-Mart wields its power for just one purpose: to bring the lowest possible prices to its customers. At Wal-Mart, that goal is never reached. The retailer has a clear policy for suppliers: On basic products that don't change, the price Wal-Mart will pay, and will charge shoppers, must drop year after year. But what almost no one outside the world of Wal-Mart and its 21,000 suppliers knows is the high cost of those low prices. Wal-Mart has the power to squeeze profit-killing concessions from vendors. To survive in the face of its pricing demands, makers of everything from bras to bicycles to blue jeans have had to lay off employees and close U.S. plants in favor of outsourcing products from overseas.

Of course, U.S. companies have been moving jobs offshore for decades, long before Wal-Mart was a retailing power. But there is no question that the chain is helping accelerate the loss of American jobs to low-wage countries such as China. Wal-Mart, which in the late 1980s and early 1990s trumpeted its claim to "Buy American," has doubled its imports from China in the past five years alone, buying some $12 billion in merchandise in 2002. That's nearly 10% of all Chinese exports to the United States.

One way to think of Wal-Mart is as a vast pipeline that gives non-U.S. companies direct access to the American market. "One of the things that limits or slows the growth of imports is the cost of establishing connections and networks," says Paul Krugman, the Princeton University economist. "Wal-Mart is so big and so centralized that it can all at once hook Chinese and other suppliers into its digital system. So—wham!—you have a large switch to overseas sourcing in a period quicker than under the old rules of retailing."

Steve Dobbins has been bearing the brunt of that switch. He's president and CEO of Carolina Mills, a 75-year-old North Carolina company that supplies thread, yarn, and textile finishing to apparel makers—half of which supply Wal-Mart. Carolina Mills grew steadily until 2000. But in the past three years, as its customers have gone either overseas or out of business, it has shrunk from 17 factories to 7, and from 2,600 employees to 1,200. Dobbins's customers have begun to face imported clothing sold so cheaply to Wal-Mart that they could not compete even if they paid their workers nothing.

"People ask, 'How can it be bad for things to come into the U.S. cheaply? How can it be bad to have a bargain at Wal-Mart?' Sure, it's held inflation down, and it's great to have bargains," says Dobbins. "But you can't buy anything if you're not employed. We are shopping ourselves out of jobs."

There is no question that Wal-Mart's relentless drive to squeeze out costs has benefited consumers. The giant retailer is at least partly responsible for the low rate of U.S. inflation, and a McKinsey & Co. study concluded that about 12% of the economy's productivity gains in the second half of the 1990s could be traced to Wal-Mart alone.

There is also no question that doing business with Wal-Mart can give a supplier a fast, heady jolt of sales and market share. But that fix can come with long-term consequences for the health of a brand and a business. Vlasic, for example, wasn't looking to build its brand on a gallon of whole pickles. Pickle companies make money on "the cut," slicing cucumbers into spears and hamburger chips. "Cucumbers in the jar, you don't make a whole lot of money there," says Steve Young, a former vice president of grocery marketing for pickles at Vlasic, who has since left the company.

At some point in the late 1990s, a Wal-Mart buyer saw Vlasic's gallon jar and started talking to Pat Hunn about it. Hunn, who has also since left Vlasic, was then head of Vlasic's Wal-Mart sales team, based in Dallas. The gallon intrigued the buyer. In sales tests, priced somewhere over $3, "the gallon sold like crazy," says Hunn, "surprising us all." The Wal-Mart buyer had a brainstorm: What would happen to the gallon if they offered it nationwide and got it below $3? Hunn was skeptical, but his job was to look for ways to sell pickles at Wal-Mart. Why not?

And so Vlasic's gallon jar of pickles went into every Wal-Mart, some 3,000 stores, at $2.97, a price so low that Vlasic and Wal-Mart were making only a penny or two on a jar, if that. It was showcased on big pallets near the front of stores. It was an abundance of abundance. "It was selling 80 jars a week, on average, in every store," says Young. Doesn't sound like much, until you do the math: That's 240,000 gallons of pickles, just in gallon jars, just at Wal-Mart, every week. Whole fields of cucumbers were heading out the door.

For Vlasic, the gallon jar of pickles became what might be called a devastating success. "Quickly, it started cannibalizing our non-Wal-Mart business," says Young. "We saw consumers who used to buy the spears and the chips in supermarkets buying the Wal-Mart gallons. They'd eat a quarter of a jar and throw the thing away when they got moldy. A family can't eat them fast enough."

The gallon jar reshaped Vlasic's pickle business: It chewed up the profit margin of the business with Wal-Mart, and of pickles generally. Procurement had to scramble to find enough pickles to fill the gallons, but the volume gave Vlasic strong sales numbers, strong growth numbers, and a powerful place in the world of pickles at Wal-Mart. Which accounted for 30% of Vlasic's business. But the company's profits from pickles had shriveled 25% or more, Young says—millions of dollars.

The gallon was hoisting Vlasic and hurting it at the same time.

Young remembers begging Wal-Mart for relief. "They said, 'No way,'" says Young. "We said we'll increase the price"—even $3.49 would have helped tremendously—"and they said, 'If you do that, all the other products of yours we buy, we'll stop buying.' It was a clear threat." Hunn recalls things a little differently, if just as ominously: "They said, 'We want the $2.97 gallon of pickles. If you don't do it, we'll see if someone else might.' I knew our competitors were saying to Wal-Mart, 'We'll do the $2.97 gallons if you give us your other business.'" Wal-Mart's business was so indispensable to Vlasic, and the gallon so central to the Wal-Mart relationship, that decisions about the future of the gallon were made at the CEO level.

Finally, Wal-Mart let Vlasic up for air. "The Wal-Mart guy's response was classic," Young recalls. "He said, 'Well, we've done to pickles what we did to orange juice. We've killed it. We can back off.'" Vlasic got to take it down to just over half a gallon of pickles, for $2.79. Not long after that, in January 2001, Vlasic filed for bankruptcy—although the gallon jar of pickles, everyone agrees, wasn't a critical factor. . . .

In the end, of course, it is we as shoppers who have the power, and who have given that power to Wal-Mart. Part of Wal-Mart's dominance, part of its insight, and part of its arrogance, is that it presumes to speak for American shoppers.

If Wal-Mart doesn't like the pricing on something, says Andrew Whitman, who helped service Wal-Mart for years when he worked at General Foods and Kraft, they simply say, "At that price we no longer think it's a good value to our shopper. Therefore, we don't think we should carry it."

Wal-Mart has also lulled shoppers into ignoring the difference between the price of something and the cost. Its unending focus on price underscores something that Americans are only starting to realize about globalization: Ever-cheaper prices have consequences. Says Steve Dobbins, president of thread maker Carolina Mills: "We want clean air, clear water, good living conditions, the best health care in the world—yet we aren't willing to pay for anything manufactured under those restrictions."

Randall Larrimore, a former CEO of MasterBrand Industries, the parent company of Master Lock, understands that contradiction too well. For years, he says, as manufacturing costs in the United States rose, Master Lock was able to pass them along. But at some point in the 1990s, Asian manufacturers started producing locks for much less. "When the difference is $1, retailers like Wal-Mart would prefer to have the brand-name padlock or faucet or hammer," Larrimore says. "But as the spread becomes greater, when our padlock was $9, and the import was $6, then they can offer the consumer a real discount by carrying two lines. Ultimately, they may only carry one line."

In January 1997, Master Lock announced that, after 75 years making locks in Milwaukee, it would begin importing more products from Asia. Not too long after, Master Lock opened a factory of its own in Nogales, Mexico. Today, it makes just 10% to 15% of its locks in Milwaukee—its 300 employees there mostly make parts that are sent to Nogales, where there are now 800 factory workers.

Larrimore did the first manufacturing layoffs at Master Lock. He negotiated with Master Lock's unions himself. He went to Bentonville. "I loved dealing with Wal-Mart, with Home Depot," he says. "They are all very rational people. There wasn't a whole lot of room for negotiation. And they had a good point. Everyone was willing to pay more for a Master Lock. But how much more can they justify? If they can buy a lock that has arguably similar quality, at a cheaper price, well, they can get their consumers a deal."

It's Wal-Mart in the role of Adam Smith's invisible hand. And the Milwaukee employees of Master Lock who shopped at Wal-Mart to save money helped that hand shove their own jobs right to Nogales. Not consciously, not directly, but inevitably. "Do we as consumers appreciate what we're doing?" Larrimore asks. "I don't think so. But even if we do, I think we say, Here's a Master Lock for $9, here's another lock for $6—let the other guy pay $9."

READING AND DISCUSSION QUESTIONS

1. What factors does Fishman cite as the leading causes of Wal-Mart's unrivaled success? To what extent do those factors illuminate broader economic trends in America during the early twenty-first century?

2. How does Fishman describe the effects of Wal-Mart's business model on America's labor market? What impact does Wal-Mart have on its workers and the communities in which they live?

P9-5 | Globalization's Middle-Class Squeeze
KEVIN CLARKE, *Outsourcing Around* (2004)

The economic growing pains induced by globalization had destabilized American manufacturing since the 1970s, but its pain reached the middle class later as white-collar jobs also began to be outsourced to less expensive workers in other countries. Here, Kevin Clarke, an editor at *U.S. Catholic* magazine, urges compassion in responding to the ill-effects of the global economy.

Most of us have already had the experience once or twice: Dialing a tech support number for our latest gadget or cellular provider delivers us into a fiber optic wonderland where we could be chatting with a service rep just as likely to be seated at a desk in Bangalore, Manila, or Limerick as in Anytown, U.S.A.

The surprise international calling plan used to provoke a head scratching, gee-whiz-what-will-they-think-of-next amazement, but these days the promise of a transglobal service industry has been transformed into the political "problem" of white-collar outsourcing. Democrats have been making political hay out of the telecommuting of jobs outside of the United States while exasperated Bush administration policy wonks try to explain to us thick-headed Americans why losing our jobs is actually a *good* thing. Gosh, when *will* we understand economics?

New technology, better education in the developing world, and last but certainly not least, profit optimization bring a new generation of U.S. workers into globalization's crosshairs. White-collar workers who shrugged off the suffering of their blue-collar brothers and sisters over the last two decades now have a much different perspective on all that union grousing.

Kevin Clarke, "Outsourcing Around: A New Round of Job Losses Reaches White-Collar Workers. Could Whiny Columnists Be Next," *U.S. Catholic* 69 (May 2004): 33.

During the Reagan years, Americans were told not to worry about the blood-letting within our industrial labor base and the by now almost complete eradication of the nation's manufacturing infrastructure as a new morning of service industry predominance was dawning in America. How globalized time flies. Now even those jobs within economic sectors purported to replace manufacturing don't appear safe.

Previous rounds of outsourcing did not provoke the heated cries for intervention we hear today now that demographic samples among computer engineers and mid-management are exploring the dark side of globalization. I mean, it was one thing when some line workers at an assembly plant lost their jobs to teenagers in Mexico and China, but some of these guys have BMWs to pay off, for God's sake. When will it end?

The short answer is that it never will. Capitalism is a force of incessant "creative destruction," economist Joseph Schumpeter wrote in 1942, capable of provoking rapid and violent change in economic sectors and by extension among the lives of us mere mortals who inhabit them. This is actually good news, Schumpeter argues, since it means that, while many suffer, new opportunity and improved wages await those who survive economic restructuring. The problem is that while creative destruction can appear bloodless and rational from an academic distance, looking at the process through the filter of your last pay stub—something guys like Schumpeter are never forced to do themselves—the phenomenon is a lot more gory and unpleasant.

Fortunately, capitalism's relentless creativity can be matched by some of our culture's other relentless forces: Christian mercy and human empathy. It may be essentially beyond our power to stop economic "progress," but that doesn't mean we can't shape it into something a little more humane as we experience it. That's something America essentially failed to do when creative destruction swept through the ranks of its manufacturing workers.

Ultimately, no one can lay a geographically exclusive claim to a job or a standard of living. If workers in other countries are capable and qualified in our economically integrated world, then jobs will flow to places where they are frequently desperately needed. It is unclear if this kind of economic equilibrium-seeking could—or should—be interrupted.

What we can do, however, is try to imagine societal structures that mitigate the impact of job loss while preparing a new generation of U.S. workers with better educations and an improved industrial infrastructure. While economic upheavals continue, we can respond with strategies that protect human dignity, acknowledging that no one deserves to be abandoned on the other side of a cycle of creative destruction.

At the same time, we should build in protections against worker exploitation in the developing world. There's no reason to reconstruct the 19th century in emerging economies as our globalization-empowered and -assailed world steps into, with some trepidation and no little tumult, the 21st.

READING AND DISCUSSION QUESTIONS

1. How does Clarke assess changes in the response to the outsourcing of jobs over the past generation? What is different about the public debate over outsourcing in the early years of the twenty-first century?

2. What is Clarke's attitude toward the "creative destruction" inherent in capitalism? How does he urge readers to mitigate its effects?

3. To what extent does his perspective on globalization reflect the political debate over issues such as free trade?

■ COMPARATIVE QUESTIONS ■

1. Compare how Kristol and McClelland each would have explained the demise of the steel industry. Which factors would each single out as leading causes? How might you account for the differences you see?

2. Assess the role of organized labor in debates about America's economic policy during the twentieth century by comparing McClelland's observations with those of John Lewis (Document 23-5) and Cesar Chavez (Document 28-4). What similarities or differences can you identify in their assessments of the problems facing workers?

3. To what extent do you see Wal-Mart as a culmination of trends begun during the late-nineteenth-century industrial and managerial revolution? Did Wal-Mart build on those earlier transformations, or does Wal-Mart represent a new phase in global economics?

4. What conclusions can you draw about capitalism as an economic and social force by comparing Kristol with William Graham Sumner (Document P6-1), Herbert Hoover (Document 23-1), and Huey Long (Document 23-3)? What changes over time can you identify in their respective assessments of the value of America's market-based economy?

Acknowledgments *(continued from p. ii)*

Chapter 16

16-3 "Buffalo Days" (1933). From J. Wright Mooar, "The Killing of the White Buffalo." In *Buffalo Days: Stories from J. Wright Mooar As Told to James Winford Hunt*, edited by Robert F. Pace, pp. 76–81. Copyright © 2005 by State House Press. Buffalo Days provided by State House Press.

16-5 "A Salishan Autobiography" (1990). Reprinted from *Mourning Dove: A Salishan Autobiography* edited by Jay Miller by permission of the University of Nebraska Press. Copyright 1990 by the University of Nebraska Press.

Chapter 18

18-4 "Black and White Sat Down Together: The Reminiscences of an NAACP Founder" (1932–1933). Mary White Ovington, excerpts from "National Association of Colored Women" from *Black and White Sat Down Together: The Reminiscences of an NAACP Founder*, edited by Ralph E. Luker. Copyright © 1995 by The Feminist Press. Reprinted with the permission of The Permissions Company, Inc., on behalf of The Feminist Press, www.feministpress.org.

Part 6

P6-4 "The Mind of Primitive Man" (1911). Reprinted with the permission of Scribner Publishing group from *The Mind of Primitive Man, Revised Edition* by Franz Boas. Copyright © 1938 by The Macmillan Company, copyright renewed 1966 by Franziska Boas Michelson. All rights reserved.

Chapter 22

22-5 "Negro Artist and the Racial Mountain" (1926). Langston Hughes, "Negro Artist and the Racial Mountain," by Langston Hughes. Reprinted by permission of Harold Ober Associates Incorporated. From *The Nation*, June 23, 1926. Copyright 1926 by Langston Hughes.

Chapter 23

23-5 "The Battle for Industrial Democracy" (1936). From "The Battle for Industrial Democracy," by John L. Lewis in *Vital Speeches of the Day*, Volume 2 (August 1, 1936), pp. 675–678. Courtesy of UMWA Archives.

Chapter 24

24-2 "Interviews with the Library of Congress Veterans History Project" (2001, 2003). Interview with Claud Woodring, January 2, 2003, from Veterans History Project, American Folklife Center, Library of Congress. Courtesy of Claud Woodring. Interview with Jay S. Adams, July 5, 2001, from Veterans History Project, American Folklife Center, Library of Congress. Courtesy of Bonnie Walker.

24-4 "Editorial" (1945). From *LULAC News*, Volume 12 (October 1945), pp. 5–6 as it appears in *Testimonio: A Documentary History of the Mexican American Struggle for Civil Rights*, edited by F. Arturo Rosales. Copyright © 2000 by F. Arturo Rosales. Used by permission of LULAC News.

Part 7

P7-4 "The Faith of the Fundamentalists" (1927). From "The Faith of the Fundamentalists," by W. B. Riley, *Church History* 24 (June 1927), pp. 434–440. Reprinted with permission from *Current History* magazine (June 1927). © 2013 Current History, Inc.

P7-6 "Caravans of Sorrow" (1940). Address delivered at the panel of Deportation and Right of Asylum of the 4th Conference of the American Committee for Protection of the Foreign Born, Washington D.C. March 3, 1940. Box 1, Folder 1, Carey McWilliams Collection, University Research Library, Department of Special Collections UCLA. Published by permission of Nancy McWilliams, PhD.

Chapter 25

25-2 "Cold War: A Study in U.S. Foreign Policy" (1947). Excerpts from pp. 29–31, 35, 43–45 [1750 words] from *The Cold War: A Study in U.S. Foreign Policy by Walter Lippmann.* Copyright 1947 by Walter Lippmann. Copyright renewed © 1975 by Walter Lippmann. Reprinted by permission of HarperCollins Publishers.

Chapter 26

26-3 "Our Right to Require Belief" (1956). From "Our Right to Require Belief," by Billy Graham, *The Saturday Evening Post,* Volume 235 (February 17, 1962), pp. 8, 10. "Our Right to Require Belief" article by Billy Graham © SEPS licensed by Curtis Licensing Indianapolis, IN. All rights reserved.

26-4 "Dr. Spock's Baby and Child Care" (1946). Reprinted with the permission of Gallery Publishing Group from the Pocket Books edition of *Dr. Spock's Baby and Child Care* 9/e by Benjamin Spock, M.D. Updated and Revised by Robert Needlman, M.D. Copyright 1945, 1946, © 1957, 1968, 1976, 1985, 1992 Benjamin Spock, M.D.; copyright renewed © 1973, 1974, 1985, 1996 Benjamin Spock, M.D. Revised and updated material copyright © 1998, 2004, 2011 The Benjamin Spock Trust.

26-2 "Growing Up Absurd" (1960). From *Growing Up Absurd: Problems of Youth in the Organized Society,* by Paul Goodman. Published by New York Review of Books. Copyright © 1956, 1957, 1958, 1959, 1960 by Paul Goodman.

Chapter 27

27-1 "Killers of the Dream" (1949). From *Killers of the Dream,* by Lillian Smith, pp. 26–29. Copyright 1949, © 1961 by Lillian Smith. Used by permission of W. W. Norton & Company, Inc.

27-3 "Testimony Before the Credentials Committee of the Democratic National Convention" (1964). Fannie Lou Hamer Speech before DNC, August 22, 1964. Used by permission of Vergie Hamer Faulkner.

27-4 "The Ballot or the Bullet" (1964). From "The Ballot or the Bullet" in *Malcolm X Speaks: Selected Speeches and Statements,* by Malcolm X, edited by George Breitman, pp. 24–26, 28, 30–35. Copyright © 1965, 1989 by Betty Shabazz and Pathfinder Press. Reprinted by permission.

27-6 "I Am Joaquin" (1967). From *Message to Aztlan: Selected Writings of Rodolfo "Corky" Gonzales,* edited by Antonio Esquibel, pp. 25–29. 149 lines from "I am Joaquin" is reprinted with permission from the publisher of "Message to Aztlan" by Rodolfo "Corky" Gonzales (© Arte Público Press—University of Houston).

Chapter 28

28-3 "Redstockings Manifesto" (1969). "Redstockings Manifesto," Redstockings Women's Liberation Archives. The Redstockings Manifesto was issued in New York City on July 7, 1969. It first appeared as a mimeographed flyer designed for distribution at women's liberation events. Further information about the Manifesto and other materials from the 1960s rebirth years of feminism is available from the Redstockings Women's Liberation Archives for Action at www.redstockings.org or P.O. Box 744, Stuyvesant Station, NY, NY 10009.

28-4 "Letter from Delano" (1969). Cesar Chavez, "Letter from Delano," by Cesar Chavez, in *Christian Century* 86 (April 23, 1969), pp. 539–540. TM/© the Cesar Chavez Foundation www.chavezfoundation.org. Used by permission of the Cesar Chavez Foundation.

Chapter 29

29-2 "Youngstown Fights Back" (1979). From "Youngstown Fights Back," by Robert Howard, in *The New Republic* 180 (January 6, 1979), pp. 19–21. © Robert Howard. Used by permission of the author.

29-4 "Statement Opposing the ERA" (1977). From "Statement on the ERA, by Phyllis Schlafly, in *Congressional Digest* 56 (June–July 1977), pp. 189, 191. Used by permission of Phyllis Schlafly.

29-6 "Next Billy Graham" (1978). From "Next Billy Graham: Jerry Falwell's Old Time Gospel Hour," by Mary Murphy in *Esquire* 90 (October 10, 1978), pp. 27–28, 30–32. Used by permission of the author.

Part 8

P8-5 "Kissinger in Africa" (1976). From "Kissinger in Africa," by Charles Sanders in EBONY® Magazine August 1976 article, pp. 52–54, 56, 58. Courtesy Johnson Publishing Company, LLC. All rights reserved.

Chapter 30

30-2 "The Triumph of Politics: Why the Reagan Revolution Failed" (1986). From *The Triumph of Politics: Why the Reagan Revolution Failed*, by David Stockman, pp. 37–40, 42–43. Copyright © 1986 by David Stockman. Used by permission of the author.

30-4 "The Great Deception: What We Are Told About Central America" (1986). From "The Great Deception: What We are Told About Central America," by Robert J. Henle, in *America* 154 (May 24, 1986), pp. 432–434. Reprinted from *America* May 24, 1986, with Permission of America Press, Inc. 2013. All rights reserved. For subscription information, call 1-800-627-9533 or visit www.americamagazine.org.

30-5 "Common Ground and Common Sense" (1988). "Common Ground and Common Sense," by Jesse Jackson in *Vital Speeches of the Day* 54 (August 15, 1988), pp. 650–653. Used by permission of Rev. Jesse Jackson Sr.

Chapter 31

31-1 "Interview by April Eaton" (2000). From Alesha Daughtrey, interview by April Eaton, WTO History Project, University of Washington, August 17, 2000. Transcript at http://depts.washington.edu/wtohist/interviews/Daughtrey.pdf. Used by permission.

31-2 "California Proposition 187" (1994). "Proposition 187: Text of Proposed Law," in *California Ballot Pamphlet* (Sacramento: State of California, 1994), pp. 91–92. Courtesy of the Office of the California Secretary of State.

Part 9

P9-1 "Two Cheers for Capitalism" (1978). From "The Hidden Costs of Regulation" by Irving Kristol, originally published in the *Wall Street Journal*, January 12, 1977, as it appears in *Two Cheers for Capitalism*, by Irving Kristol, pp. 50–53, 54. Used by permission of Gertrude Kristol.

P9-2 "Interview with Bill Barry" (2006). Interview with LeRoy McClelland Sr. by Bill Barry, May 1, 2006. www.sparrowspointsteelworkers.com/interviews/LeRoy_McClelland_Sr.html. Used by permission of Bill Barry, Director of Labor Studies, Community College of Baltimore County/Dundalk.

P9-4 "The Wal-Mart You Don't Know" (2003). "The Wal-Mart You Don't Know," by Charles Fishman, *Fast Company* 77 (December 2003), pp. 68–76. FAST COMPANY by FAST COMPANY, INC. Reproduced with permission of FAST COMPANY, INC. in the format Republish in a book via Copyright Clearance Center.

P9-5 "Outsourcing Around" (2004). From Kevin Clarke, "Outsourcing Around: A New Round of Job Losses Reaches White-Collar Workers. Could Whiny Columnists Be Next," by Kevin Clarke, *U.S. Catholic* 69 (May 2004), p. 33. Copyright 2004 U.S. Catholic. Reproduced by permission from the May 2004 issue of *U.S. Catholic*.